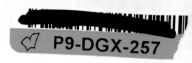

Advanced Social Psychology

Advanced Social Psychology

Abraham Tesser
University of Georgia–Athens

Boston, Massachusetts   Burr Ridge, Illinois   Dubuque, Iowa
Madison, Wisconsin   New York, New York   San Francisco, California   St. Louis, Missouri

McGraw-Hill

A Division of The McGraw·Hill Companies

This book was set in Palatino by Ruttle, Shaw & Wetherill, Inc.
The editors were Jane Vaicunas, Laura Lynch, and Scott Amerman;
the production supervisor was Richard A. Ausburn.
The cover was designed by John Hite.

Cover Painting
Chagall, Marc.
I and the Village, 1911.
Oil on canvas, 6'3 5/8" × 59 5/8".
The Museum of Modern Art, New York. Mrs. Simon Guggenheim Fund.
Photograph © 1995 The Museum of Modern Art, New York.

ADVANCED SOCIAL PSYCHOLOGY

14 15 16 17 18 19   BKM BKM   0 9 8 7 6

ISBN-13: 978-0-07-063392-6
ISBN-10: 0-07-063392-4

Library of Congress Cataloging-in-Publication Data

Advanced social psychology / [compiled by] Abraham Tesser.
    p.   cm.
Includes bibliographical references and index.
ISBN 0-07-063392-4
1. Social psychology.   I. Tesser, Abraham.
HM251.A32   1995
302—dc20   94-30982

http://www.mhhe.com

About the Author

ABRAHAM TESSER grew up in Brooklyn, New York. He completed his Ph.D. in social psychology at Purdue University in 1967. From there, he took a faculty position at the University of Georgia where he is currently research professor of psychology and the director of the university's interdisciplinary Institute for Behavioral Research. In the intervening years he has been a visiting Fellow at Yale University, Princeton University, and the Center for Advanced Study in the Behavioral Sciences. His research has been on interpersonal communication, attitudes, and self-evaluation maintenance processes. He has served the discipline as an associate editor of *Personality and Social Psychology Bulletin* and as editor of the attitudes and social cognition section of the *Journal of Personality and Social Psychology*.

*To My Children, Louis and Rachel
and to Carmen,
My Inspiration and Support*

Contents

Preface

For the last 25 years or so, social psychology has been both a vocation and an avocation. (Indeed, I am always a little astonished and feel a little guilty to find that I am being paid to pursue the things that interest me so much.) The questions that social psychologists address are the questions that individuals and societies have asked for all of recorded time. How do we know what another person is like? What makes people favor one policy over another? What is the most effective way to influence someone's behavior? What makes one person more attractive than another? Is there something special about successful intimate relationships? Does altruism exist? Why is aggression so ubiquitous? What sustains prejudice? How does group behavior differ from individual behavior? Imagine. I am paid to think about, read about, and write about these questions.

But it is not merely the content of social psychology that keeps me intrigued. It is that these questions can be addressed scientifically. It is possible to generate hypotheses and theories about each of these issues. It is also possible to make systematic observations that bear on them. Sometimes, it is even possible to do full-fledged experiments. In particular, it is the creativity associated with the formulation of the hypotheses and the ingenuity associated with testing these hypotheses that have sustained my interest all these years.

I regularly teach a graduate survey course in social psychology. In addition to covering "the field," what I hope to do in that course is to acquaint students with the excitement associated with making social psychology, i.e., formulating hypotheses, testing theories, collecting data, rethinking ideas, and so on. I typically use one of the standard social psychology texts available and then develop a series of readings in each of these areas. The readings are selected to give students a feel for what is happening on the cutting edge and to expose them to the original thinking of the scientists who are making our discipline. So it went for 20-odd years. And in all this time I never had so much as an urge to produce a textbook. Then, while planning this course for winter 1992, I had a stroke of good fortune.

The University of Georgia made some money available to me. Quite frankly, as strange as it seems, I had no productive use for this money, which had to be spent by the end of the fiscal year. One day, I mentioned to my wife, Carmen, who knew that I was planning the social psychology course, that I wasn't sure what to do with the money. Carmen, who is a well-respected academic and a celebrated teacher, suggested, "Why not bring in the best people in each area and expose your students to them? If this could be videotaped, then students here and elsewhere from now until interest waned could also be exposed to these people. Each could talk about the area of social psychology in which they have made a major contribution." That idea immediately seemed right. I thought about it for a couple of days and drew up my dream list of participants. Within another week or two each of the contributors was scheduled to give a lecture and prepare a chapter for this volume. The speed with which this could be done amazed me. The value of having the videotape and the lecture from people who are actively shaping each area was immediately apparent to each of the participants, and they were willing to take time from their busy schedules to become actively involved.

What you have before you is the actualization of the desire to bring to beginning graduate students and advanced undergraduates the approach, thoughts, and style of the people who are actively shaping the content of social psychology. The chapters are not encyclopedic in coverage. They are intended as jumping-off points for additional reading. The videos are intended to provide an overview to each of the areas and to give the student a more personal and human idea of who it is that is constructing the discipline.

ACKNOWLEDGMENTS

There is a long list of people to be thanked for their help in putting this work together. To my wife, Carmen, who provided the initial idea and enthusiastically continued to support the project through all its ups and downs, I owe my greatest debt. At the University of Georgia, I am grateful to William Prokasy, vice president for Academic Affairs, Ron Simpson, director of the Office of Instructional Development, and Roger Thomas, head of the Department of Psychology for providing resources and encouragement to make this project a reality.

Pat Frye of the University of Georgia's Office of Instructional Development was the actual hands-on director and technical producer of the videos. Thank you Pat for your expertise, patience, and cooperativeness. The job of editing two hours of lecture down to about 30 to 35 minutes was extremely difficult. It required expert knowledge of social psychology and a creative eye and ear. I am grateful to my colleague, Bill McIntosch of Georgia Southern University, for doing the bulk of that editing.

More than a nod of thanks is due to the graduate students who participated in the course that served as the backbone of this book. They made the almost weekly trek to the TV studio with patience and good cheer. To my colleagues in this social psychology program—Mike Kernis, Lenny Martin, Dave Shaffer, and Gail Williamson—I owe a debt of appreciation for helping to make each of our visitors to the university feel welcome. Thanks go to the graduate students in the social psychology program who hosted each of our visitors. I would also like to recognize Gilda Ivory of the Institute for Behavioral Research, who co-ordinated all the visits and typed much of the correspondence.

Thanks go to Chris Rogers, McGraw-Hill's editor for most of the project. His advice and encouragement are most appreciated. I also appreciate the help of Jane Vaicunas and Laura Lynch, who helped us complete the project, and Scott Amerman, who supervised the various editing tasks. Part of the time I spent on this book was in the beautiful Bay Area of California at the Center for Advanced Study in the Behavioral Sciences. I am grateful to the center and to the John D. and Catherine T. MacArthur Foundation (#8900078) for their support during that time.

McGraw-Hill and I would like to thank the following reviewers for their many helpful comments and suggestions: Ronnie Janoff-Bulman, University of Massachusetts, Amherst; Michael R. Leippe, Adelphi University; David G. Myers, Hope College; Delia S. Saenz, Arizona State University; and Mark R. Zanna, University of Waterloo.

I am most grateful, however, to each of the authors of the individual chapters. I thank them for coming to Athens and making the video. I thank them for systematically presenting an area of social psychology to which their research contributes. Finally, I thank them and the giants on whose shoulders we stand, for pushing the edge of social psychology forward through their research and keeping the discipline such a vibrant and exciting enterprise.

Abraham Tesser

Advanced Social Psychology

Abraham Tesser is Research Professor of Psychology and Director of the Institute for Behavioral Research at the University of Georgia. He received his Ph.D. degree in psychology from Purdue University. He is a former editor of the Journal of Personality and Social Psychology: Attitudes and Social Cognition *and is a Fellow of the American Psychological Association and of the American Psychological Society. He has been a visiting Fellow at Yale University, Princeton University, and the Center for Advanced Studies in the Behavioral Sciences. Tesser's research has touched on interpersonal communication, attitudes, social cognition, and self-evaluation maintenance. He is the author of several research monographs and numerous publications in journals, and he recently coedited (with L. Martin) the volume* The Construction of Social Judgments. *Tesser has been awarded a number of research grants and contracts and is a winner of the William A. Owens Award for creative research from the University of Georgia. In addition to social psychology, he enjoys woodworking, bird watching, movies, and walking (very slowly).*

CHAPTER 1

Introduction

Abraham Tesser
University of Georgia–Athens

CHAPTER OUTLINE

The purpose of psychology is to give us a completely different idea of the things we know best.

—PAUL VALERY, *Tel Quel*, 1943

Social psychology is a young and exciting discipline. The ancient philosophers had important things to say that inform social psychology (as they did for almost every "-ology"). However, social psychology as an empirical discipline emerged much more recently. The first social psychological experiment is usually attributed to Triplett (1898). He had children wind fishing reels as fast as they could. They did this either alone or in the company of other children also winding fishing reels. Triplett found that children wound their reels faster in the company of others than when they were alone. Since then, social psychologists have (e.g., Zajonc, 1965) and continue to make great strides in understanding social facilitation or what Triplett called the dynamogenic effect of others.

In the 1930s Sherif (1936) did groundbreaking experimental work on the psychology of norms. His creative procedure for studying norms exploited a visual illusion called the autokinetic effect: a stationary point of light in a totally dark room appears to move. Since the light is actually stationary and the room is dark and provides no visual frame of reference, how much the light moves is a very ambiguous judgment. Sherif found that individuals in this situation developed personal norms, i.e., regularities in judgments. Interestingly, the judgments of individuals placed into groups converged onto a group norm, which then regulated judgments even when the individuals were outside of the group. Moreover, the participants in this research reported no awareness of the group's influence. Research on social influence continues to be a mainstay of social psychology.

The decade of the 1930s also saw the publication of Bartlett's (1932) *Remembering*. In some of his studies he asked people to remember a story from a different culture, or to repeat a story to another, who would repeat it to another, and so on. He found that memory and this kind of serial transmission was strongly influenced by one's own cultural ways of thinking or *schemata*. A concern with underlying cognitive processes is currently found in almost all areas of social psychological inquiry.

Although important contributions to the science of social psychology began accumulating before, the real impetus to the growth of social psychology in the United States came during World War II. It came out of efforts to handle morale problems in the Army (Stouffer, Suchman, DeVinney, Star, & Williams, 1949), to understand attitudes and attitude change for purposes of training and propaganda (Hovland, Lumsdaine, & Sheffield, 1949), and even to get its citizenry to eat culturally unusual cuts of organ meat such as sweetbreads (Lewin, 1947).

Today social psychology is a thriving discipline. There is at least one social psychologist in almost all psychology departments, and there are several, large, vigorous professional societies devoted to it in this country (Berscheid, 1992). Social psychology is also becoming an important intellectual force in Europe as well. This textbook and its accompanying video are intended to acquaint students with the content and methods of social psychology. In this project, some of the people who are actively advancing social psychology have taken the responsibility for introducing you to their own area of expertise. The essays that follow are representative of some of the major subfields written by experts.

The Content of Social Psychology

Social psychology's subject matter deals, in part, with the questions of philosophers and warriors, of lovers and hucksters. For example, can we deceive ourselves (Chapter 3)? What are the circumstances under which we are likely to be most aggressive (Chapter 10)? Will the passionate attraction I now feel last

(Chapter 8)? Will a movie star's endorsement or a list of benefits lead to a more favorable attitude toward Acme widgets (Chapter 6)?

Answers to these questions clearly have practical benefits. One can sell more widgets, enjoy a better sex life, or put combatants into a more aggressive frame of mind. Social psychologists also address questions of when people will help one another (Chapter 9) or be responsive to charitable requests (Chapter 7) and even of what underlies prejudice and stereotyping (Chapter 12). Interpersonal processes like these and the working of groups (Chapter 11) are implied by the word *social* in social psychology. But much of contemporary social psychology is concerned with mental mechanics, better known as cognition.

Have you ever wondered why someone expressed a particular opinion? Chapter 4 addresses the general question of how we analyze the influence of internal, personal forces and external, environmental forces in understanding another's behavior. Have you ever noticed that you seem to know more about people than they actually revealed? Chapter 5 examines the role of preconceived ideas (schemas), memory, mental shortcuts (heuristics), and the confusing buzz of "on-line" experience in constructing an understanding of our social world.

Some social psychologists are motivated by practical concerns like how can I sell more widgets. An even greater number are motivated by the enormous potential social good inherent in the social psychological knowledge they produce. Still others are not trying to sell anything or wanting to change the world but are simply interested in the domain of social psychology and are getting paid to pursue that interest! Regardless of whether they are working out of selfish interest, social interest, or self-interest, the best social psychologists are pursuing these questions in a way that leads to a deeper understanding of the phenomenon they study.

To these people, the answer "Passion does not last" to one of our earlier questions is not enough. They want to know, what it is that generated the passion in the first place? How is romantic passion the same; how is it different from other emotional states? What is the typical time course? What makes it wax and wane? What other changes in interpersonal feelings accompany changes in passion? And, most important, are the answers to one question related to the answers to the other questions in a way that helps us understand the causes of passion and romantic relationships? In short, like scientists in any other discipline, the best social psychologists are groping toward theory through the methods of empirical psychological research.

All of us are consumers of information. A laundry list of facts is not nearly as interesting as a story with a plot. In a story the facts emerge as a result of the behavior of characters with motives that make them act in particular ways. A story lets us know *why* the facts are as they are. A scientific theory serves the same function. It provides one account of how variables interact with one another to produce the facts that we observe. Each of the chapter authors has made important integrative connections, and each of the chapters is organized and unfolds with a great appreciation for the importance of understanding as opposed to simply listing the facts.

The Methods of Social Psychology

We have barely scratched the surface of the domain of social psychology. The importance of theory cannot be underestimated, but the approach of social psychology to its subject matter is scientific, and the studies themselves are often lively and capture much of what is interesting and noteworthy in social behavior. Social psychology is a data-driven enterprise. Its "facts" are based on systematic observations, and its generalizations are subject to falsification through systematic observations. Chapter 2 deals with some of the issues concerning the methods of social psychology. Using this as a touchstone, the student will be able to develop an appreciation for the methods of social psychology all through the book.

The goals of social psychologists are quite serious, and the methods they use to answer the questions they pose are as rigorous and objective as the methods of any scientific discipline. But at the same time the experiments we review are inherently interesting and captivating on their own. For example, it is difficult to think of a popular TV show in any country built on the methods of chemistry, but a number of TV shows incorporate some of the methods of social psychology, such as the survey and the face-to-face interview. Call-in and interview shows are currently particularly popular, for example. Naturally, these shows are intended to maximize entertainment value, and they do so often at the cost of scientific utility, i.e., theoretical relevance and sound methodology such as representative sampling. However, they do illustrate various survey technologies borne out of social psychology.

As you read this book, you will also become acquainted with the laboratory experiment. Sometimes the experiments are very much like one's stereotype of what happens in the lab. For example, when social psychologists measure things like response time or physiological changes, the subject interacts with complicated equipment designed to take precise data. The environment is relatively sterile, and the experimenter might even be in a white lab coat. On the other hand, since Lewin, Lippitt, and White's (1939) groundbreaking studies on the effects of leadership, laboratory studies in social psychology often involve the staging of relatively elaborate social scenarios more like *Candid Camera* than *Mr. Wizard.* In Lewin's work, boys joined clubs that "turned out to be" run by an autocratic leader, a democratic leader, or a laissez-faire leader. Actually each club had the same group leader who was trained to act out different leadership styles. Over a number of sessions, the investigators were able to observe the boys' productivity with the group (highest under the authoritarian leader) and satisfaction (highest with the democratic leader). The laboratory studies in social psychology are often ingenious in their design and, over the years, have productively addressed questions associated with each chapter of this book.

WHAT'S IN THE BOOK

Each of the chapters has been written to stand alone. That is to say that they can be approached in any order, and the instructor can proceed with any order that makes most sense to him or to her. On the other hand, the order is not entirely arbitrary. Since all the other chapters are based on research findings, the chapter on methodological issues is first.

For a long time, Robert Rosenthal's work has had an impact on the way social psychologists do research. For example, he was a major force in raising our consciousness about the notion that an experimenter's expectancy about the outcome of a study can subtly influence that outcome (e.g., Rosenthal, 1966). In his clearly written chapter for this book he focuses on issues that are fundamental, such as error, bias, and reliability. He discusses causal inference and when drawing such inferences is inappropriate. He also deals with a variety of issues that he is currently helping to shape. For example, Rosenthal argues for the utility of focused comparisons. The idea here is that data can be made to yield more powerful conclusions if we restrict our attention to theoretically relevant comparisons instead of all comparisons or a set of comparisons dictated by tradition. He also argues for the use of meta-analysis, a systematic and quantitative way of reviewing the scientific literature regarding a particular hypothesis.

Intrapersonal Social Psychology

As noted above, in spite of its name, some of the most interesting work being done in social psychology is on cognition, i.e., mental mechanics. Social psychology was concerned with cognitive processes even before the so-called cognitive revolution overtook psychology in general during the 1980s. For the social psychologist, the cognitive mechanisms are either triggered by or have as their focus social stimuli. I call it *intra*personal social psychology because the cognitive mechanisms, for the most part, unfold unseen within the individual.

Roy Baumeister provides an unusually lucid and comprehensive portrait of the self. Although the self occupied a central place in William James' (1890/1952) social psychology, it is only in the last decade or two that social psychology has rediscovered the self as an important organizing concept. Now the self is one of the most popular areas of study in the discipline. Baumeister puts these concepts into historical and cultural context. He describes how the self functions and how self-knowledge forms. He also tackles important questions concerning self-esteem, self-defense, and self-presentation, areas to which he has made important contributions through primary research. One premise of the chapter that will be explored is that persons with low self-esteem tend toward floccinaucinihilipilification. (Look that up in your Funk & Wagnall's*!)

---

*I actually found it in the *Oxford English Dictionary* (1989). It means "the action or habit of estimating as worthless" (p. 1073).

On the other side of self-knowledge, for the social psychologist, is knowl-edge of other people. If there was one topic that captured social psychology in the '70s and early '80s it was what we call *attribution theory.* This theory is concerned with how we come to understand behavior as caused by something internal, reflecting something about the person, or as caused by something external, reflecting environmental pressures which would cause anybody to behave in exactly the same way. Daniel Gilbert was a high school dropout and science fiction writer before being seduced by social psychology. And it shows, at least the science fiction writer part does. Using the famous Patty Hearst kidnapping case as a vehicle, Gilbert makes the principles underlying attribution and his own substantial recent contributions to that literature come vividly to life.

Science meanders. Sometimes it focuses on one aspect of a phenomenon; sometimes, on another. For a long time psychology focused on behavior. Anything unobservable like thinking, for example, was suspect as a topic of scientific study. In the 1970s, the mainstream of social psychology moved toward a focus on cognition. Now concern with cognitive processes is central throughout psychology. Issues of attention, information processing, memory and the constructive processes associated with it, and mental shortcuts used in making judgments appear in each subdiscipline. And for the subdiscipline of social psychology, Susan Fiske literally wrote the book (Fiske & Taylor, 1991). Her chapter for this volume is a particularly clear introduction to the area. She uses examples from her own personal life and her own research to illustrate the concepts and processes of social cognition.

If there is a single concept that social psychologists find indispensable, it is that of attitude (Allport, 1935). It is represented in some of the field's earliest literature (e.g., Thomas & Znaniecki, 1918–1920). There is at least one chapter (and often two or three) devoted to it in every textbook I have ever seen; there are probably as many theories for attitude formation and change as there are for any other concept in social psychology. Attitude has always been a popular topic for research, but after a slight dip in interest (when the work on attributions exploded), it is currently enjoying a renaissance. Richard Petty's chapter covers the high points of this area. His thoughtful introduction deals with definitional issues, the relationship between attitude and behavior, and the dynamics of attitude change, including a review of his own influential model concerning the antecedents and consequences of attitude change based on thoughtful vs. superficial information processing.

Interpersonal Social Psychology

The next group of chapters go beyond the intrapersonal. Any division is to some extent arbitrary. In the next four chapters, the focus is decidedly more *in-terpersonal.* Here the focus is on behavior that requires two or more people. Face-to-face social influence, interpersonal attraction, helping and harming another (aggression) require the presence of at least two people.

Robert Cialdini had a good job in academia and was one of the most highly respected social psychologists in the world when he left academe to sell encyclopedias . . . and used cars, and to telemarket family photos. He was interested in social influence processes and decided to learn from the social influence professionals such as used car salesmen and solicitors for charities. He returned to academe a year later and distilled and analyzed what he learned from all those experiences. In his chapter on social influence he summarizes six principles of influence. The summary shows clearly how lay knowledge (i.e., the knowledge of influence professionals) can be made to advance the cause of scientific knowledge when shaped by a gifted scientist.

The approach taken to interpersonal attraction by Margaret Clark and Sherri Pataki is unique. It is a wonderful illustration of the way in which science works. Any empirical science is concerned with observations and the explanation of those observations. For example, if you watch closely, you will observe that the sun comes up in the morning and goes down in the evening. (You don't even have to watch very closely.) Now that we have an observation, how do we explain it? Ptolemy interpreted these observations to mean that the sun must be revolving around the earth. Copernicus, working with the same data, interpreted it to mean that it is the earth that is rotating.

Clark and Pataki illustrate this same scientific process in the area of interpersonal relationships. They start with observations or empirical regularities. For example, a number of social psychologists have observed that people are attracted to others who hold similar attitudes. Clark and Pataki then introduce different theoretical approaches to interpersonal relationships. After being described, each theory is made to confront the observations; e.g., how well can it explain the observation that attitude similarity is associated with attraction? The reader can't help but develop an appreciation for the way theory makes observations understandable and how the same observations can be understood from multiple points of view.

Some social psychologists are trying to understand when we will and when we won't be helpful to another human being. Sometimes that understanding is difficult to come by. We are puzzled when we read about someone being beaten or even killed in front of witnesses and yet the witnesses do nothing, not even call the police. It was an attempt to understand what looked like bystander apathy that started social psychology's systematic inquiry into when people will or will not help others. This early work by Latané and Darley (e.g., 1968) showed that it was possible to study and understand phenomena like "bystander apathy" with laboratory experiments. It turns out that witnesses to emergencies are not apathetic, they often care very deeply about what is happening. However, the situation often leads them to conclude that there is no emergency or that someone else should take responsibility.

Emergencies are not the only context for helping, and apparent bystander apathy is not the only question that intrigues social psychologists about helping. Dan Batson is interested in the general question of why people help one another. When A helps B, is there always an expectation of a reward of some sort or the avoidance of some cost like guilt for not helping? Or is it possible that at least on some occasions, A is acting altruistically, without anything but the benefit of B in mind? Dan Batson argues that altruism can be demonstrated. In his chapter he reviews some of the literature on helping and focuses on why it is important to examine the motivation for helping and how it is possible to recognize motives for helping.

No area in this book has greater social significance than the area of aggression. Why will one individual set out to harm another? What are the factors that facilitate or inhibit aggression? These questions have been pondered by ethologists, philosophers, writers, and politicians. They are also questions that have been addressed by social psychologists. Not surprisingly, there are many important factors ranging from internal states of the individual like frustration or pain, to social influences like the presence of aggressive models, to calculations of rewards and costs, to subtle cognitive factors associated with environmental cues. Russell Geen has made important contributions to this literature and recently completed a book (Geen, 1990) on it. In this chapter he reviews much of this work and provides a useful model that integrates many of the important factors contributing to aggressive behavior.

Collective Social Psychology

The final two chapters deal with social entities of more than two persons. In the 1950s, the heart of social psychology was in "group dynamics." For example, there were studies that varied the extent to which a communication structure in a group was centralized (i.e., all information had to go through a central person) or decentralized (i.e., any group member could communicate with any other group member) to see how that would affect the efficiency of communication, the quality of group problem solving, and group morale. Other studies examined the interrelationships among cohesiveness or attraction to the group, status in the group such as leader/nonleader, and deviance and conformity. While research continues on each of these important variables, the work is typically reported in the context of social influence or attitude change rather than small group processes. Why small group research had become less popular has been the subject of analysis (Steiner, 1974) but is not entirely clear.

But growing interest in this area appears to be reemerging. Much of the impetus for this renaissance comes from our European colleagues. Although American social psychologists are concerned with self-identity, the English psychologists Tajfel (1981) and Turner (1987) remind us that our identity is tied up in the groups to which we belong. And French psychologist Serge Moscovici (1985) argues that all social influence is not the same. The influence of the majority on group members is direct and not internalized. If the majority of a group says that Acme widgets are better than Bolt widgets, group members are likely to go along with that evaluation without giving the matter much thought. This is qualitatively different from the influence of the minority, which is likely to be indirect and the result of information processing. If a consistent, persistent minority says that Acme widgets are better, there may be little influence on widget buying behavior, but group members will have thought about the issue and might be more likely to buy Acme whizzbangs. John Levine and Richard Moreland review this work and the classic work on groups in their chapter on group processes. Moreover, they focus on the ecology of small groups, including their own model of group development.

It remains crystal clear that much of humanity's suffering is a result of prejudice and stereotypes. Prejudice is a social phenomenon. Stereotypes are shared "pictures in our heads" about other groups. We've learned quite a bit about these pictures since Lippmann (1922), a newspaper columnist, coined the term *stereotype*. On the one hand, recent work has shown that the mere categorization of people as belonging to groups other than our own leads to a negative shift in the way we evaluate them, behave toward them, and even the language we use to describe them. Fortunately, surveys over the last few decades have shown that when asked, people in this country respond with increasingly more tolerant attitudes. This suggests that prejudice is on the decline. However, covert and indirect assessments of racial attitudes suggest that race continues to be an important determinant of behavior. This suggests that prejudice hasn't declined but merely gone "underground." Patricia Devine's masterful chapter on prejudice reviews this burgeoning literature clearly and, utilizing her own research, shows how even "automatic" components of stereotyping and prejudice can be controlled.

MORE ABOUT THIS BOOK

The Authors

In this book aspects of social psychology are introduced by persons who are currently pushing back the frontier. All of the authors are accomplished social scientists; each has made noteworthy research contributions to the domain of social psychology on which he or she writes; each remains fascinated with what he/she is doing, and each has tried to convey that fascination.

But that is about all the authors have in common. They differ with respect to age and gender. Moreover there are big differences in the way they were socialized into the discipline, in what they think are more or less important or interesting questions, and in their approaches to understanding social psychological phenomenon. And they are idiosyncratic in the way they describe their areas.

Daniel Gilbert wields a broad brush and seeks a general intuitive understanding of attributional phenomena; Russell Geen paints a detailed picture of a model intended to encompass much of what we know about aggressive behavior. Roy Baumeister puts the self into its cultural and historical frame and gives us well-researched answers to the most important questions concerning the self. Margaret Clark and Sherri Pataki show how it is possible to understand the very same facts about interpersonal relationships and understand them from a variety of theoretical frameworks. Daniel Batson finds that he can't understand prosocial behavior without raising broader, more general questions about motivation.

If you are looking for uniformity in these chapters, you will be disappointed. They are written by different people with different points of view. They reflect different philosophies of science, different foci, different writing styles, and even different ways of knowing. But that is true of the discipline and of science, generally. If it is frustrating, hang on; you are learning something from that too.

The Video

Each of the contributors to this volume has made important contributions to social psychology. If you continue to take courses in this area, you will undoubtedly be exposed to other things they have written. When I was a student and, later, a young faculty member, I often wondered what the "famous" people were really like. How do they think? How do they interact with students? What do they look like? In order to give the student some feel for the answers to these questions each of the authors gave a lecture on his/her selected topic to one of my graduate introductory social psychology classes. Each of the lectures was taped, and an edited version of each of these lectures is available to you.

The lectures provide a useful overview of each of the chapters. More than that, they will bring you a step closer to understanding the human side of the enterprise. Perhaps you will be surprised to find that these people who are burning up the academic journals with their complicated ideas and even more complicated statistics really do have a sense of humor or are younger than you would guess from their accomplishments. Perhaps you will be less surprised that they can make complicated ideas comprehensible and exciting. The course in which these people lectured was one of the best I have ever been exposed to!

The Open-Ended Concept

This book is designed to capture the excitement and vitality of an ongoing, open-ended enterprise. It is intended to be used by graduate students or undergraduates who are advanced enough to understand that any single text can capture only a fragment of what is a dynamic, changing body of knowledge.

Like any scientific discipline, social psychology is not one thing. Each person who is contributing to its knowledge base or teaching it has a different idea of what should and should not be included. This book is intended to be a scaffold on which you and your instructor can build and shape the course to conform to your own view. The number and length of the chapters have been kept relatively short so that there is time for a good bit of auxiliary reading. Each of the chapters includes an annotated bibliography of suggested readings. The student is encouraged to pursue any of the areas presented here in greater depth or to pursue other aspects of the discipline.

Social psychology has kept me interested and enthusiastic about its prospects over many years. Here is a version of it. Enjoy!

References

ALLPORT, G. W. (1935). Attitudes. In C. Murchison (Ed.), *Handbook of social psychology* (pp. 798–844). Worcester, MA: Clark University Press.

BARTLETT, F. C. (1932). *Remembering.* Cambridge: Cambridge University Press.

BERSCHEID, E. (1992). A glance back at a quarter century of social psychology. *Journal of Personality and Social Psychology, 63,* 525–633.

FISKE, S. E., & TAYLOR, S. E. (1991). *Social cognition.* New York: McGraw-Hill.

GEEN, R. G. (1990). *Human aggression.* Pacific Grove, CA.: Brooks-Cole.

HOVLAND, C. I., LUMSDAINE, A. A., & SHEFFIELD, F. D. (1949). *Experiments on mass communication.* Princeton: Princeton University Press.

JAMES, W. (1950). *The principles of psychology.* Chicago: Encyclopaedia Britannica. (Original work published in 1890.)

LATANÉ, B., & DARLEY, J. M. (1968). Group inhibition of bystander intervention in emergencies. *Journal of Personality and Social Psychology, 10,* 215–221.

LEWIN, K. (1947). Group decision and social change. In T. M. Newcomb & E. L. Hartley (Eds.), *Readings in social psychology.* New York: Henry Holt.

LEWIN, K., LIPPITT, R., & WHITE, R. K. (1939). Patterns of aggressive behavior in experimentally created "social climates." *Journal of Social Psychology, 10,* 271–299.

LIPPMANN, W. (1922). *Public opinion.* New York: Macmillan.

MOSCOVICI, S. (1985). Social influence and conformity. In G. Lindzey & E. Aronson (Eds.), *The handbook of social psychology* (Vol. 2, pp. 347–412). New York: Random House.

OXFORD ENGLISH DICTIONARY (2nd ed.), Vol. 5 (1989). Oxford: Clarendon Press.

ROSENTHAL, R. (1966). *Experimenter effects in behavioral research.* New York: Appleton-Century-Crofts.

SHERIF, M. (1936). *The psychology of social norms.* New York: Harper Bros.

STEINER, I. D. (1974). Whatever happened to the group in social psychology? *Journal of Experimental Social Psychology, 10,* 94–108.

STOUFFER, S. A., SUCHMAN, E. A., DEVINNEY, S. A., STAR, S. A., WILLIAMS, JR., R. M. (Eds.) (1949). *The American soldier: Adjustment during army life.* Princeton: Princeton University Press.

TAJFEL, H. (1981). *Human groups and social categories: Studies in social psychology.* London: Cambridge University Press.

THOMAS, W. I., & ZNANIECKI, F. (1918–1920). *The Polish peasant in Europe and America* (5 vols.). Boston: Badger.

TRIPLETT, N. (1898). The dynamogenic factors in pacemaking and competition. *American Journal of Psychology, 9,* 507–533.

TURNER, J. C. (1987). *Rediscovering the social group: A self-categorization theory.* Oxford: Basil Blackwell.

ZAJONC, R. B. (1965). Social facilitation. *Science, 149,* 269–274.

Further Readings

LINDZEY, G., & ARONSON, E. (Eds.) (1985). *The handbook of social psychology* (Vols. I & II) (3rd ed.). New York: Random House.

   Although a bit dated (the new edition is in preparation), this set of volumes provides a comprehensive review of the field by experts in each area. It includes history, methodology, theory, topical reviews of the literature, and applications of social psychology.

ARON, A., & ARON, E. N. (1986). *The heart of social psychology.* Lexington, Mass.: D. C. Heath.

A review of some of the major areas of social psychology with something extra. The authors interviewed many of the researchers. Included are personal stories about the strategies, philosophies, and feelings of the researchers as their work unfolded.

ARONSON, E. (1992). *The social animal* (6th ed.). New York: W. H. Freeman.

A beautifully written, easily understood introduction to the field by one of its most sensitive practitioners.

Major Serials in Social Psychology

BERKOWITZ, L. (Ed.) (1964–1989). *Advances in experimental social psychology* (Vols. 1–22). New York: Academic Press.

ZANNA, M. (Ed.) (1990–   ). *Advances in experimental social psychology* (Vols. 23–   ). San Diego: Academic Press.

A volume of the *Advances* is published at the rate of about one per year. Each volume contains monograph-type reports of individual research programs. It is a great place to see how a research *program* comes together, and how an individual investigator or research team knits theory and data into a fabric of understanding. It is one of social psychology's richest archives.

Journal of Personality and Social Psychology (American Psychological Association).

Personality and Social Psychology Bulletin (Sage Periodicals Press for the Society for Personality and Social Psychology).

Journal of Experimental Social Psychology (Academic Press).

Social Psychology Quarterly (American Sociological Association).

These are major broad-brush journals devoted to social psychology. Each of them publishes original empirical research. The *Journal of Personality and Social Psychology* (JPSP) is the oldest of the social psychology journals and the most frequently cited. *Personality and Social Psychology Bulletin* (PSPB) sometimes publishes reviews of the literature, whole issues concerned with a particular theme, and "symposia," i.e., groups of papers on a particular topic within an issue. *Social Psychology Quarterly* is the only one of the group that is published and edited by sociologists who are social psychologists.

Some Additional Serials in Social Psychology

European Journal of Social Psychology (New York: Chichester).

Journal of Social Psychology (Washington, DC: Heldref Publications).

Review of Personality and Social Psychology (Beverly Hills, CA: Sage Periodicals Press for the Society for Personality and Social Psychology).

The Ontario Symposium on Personality and Social Psychology (Hillsdale, NJ: Lawrence Erlbaum Associates).

Some Specialty Journals of Interest to Social Psychologists

Basic and Applied Social Psychology (Hillsdale, NJ: Lawrence Erlbaum Associates).

Journal of Applied Social Psychology (Washington, DC: V. H. Winston).

Journal of Personality (Durham, NC: Duke University Press).

Journal of Research in Personality. (New York: Academic Press).

Journal of Social and Clinical Psychology (New York: Guilford Press).

Journal of Social and Personal Relationships (London: Sage Publications).

Motivation and Emotion (New York: Plenum Press).

Public Opinion Quarterly (New York: Elsevier North-Holland).
Social Cognition (New York: Guilford Press).

Some General Psychology Serials of Interest to Social Psychologists

American Psychologist (Washington, DC: American Psychological Association).
Annual Review of Psychology (Palo Alto, CA: Annual Reviews).
Nebraska Symposium on Motivation (Lincoln, NE: University of Nebraska Press).
Psychological Bulletin (Washington, DC: American Psychological Association).
Psychological Review (Washington, DC: American Psychological Association).
Psychological Inquiry. (Hillsdale, NJ: Lawrence Erlbaum Associates).

Robert Rosenthal received his Ph.D. in psychology from UCLA and is a Diplomate in clinical psychology. He is currently Chair of the Department of Psychology at Harvard University where he has been since 1962. Professor Rosenthal's research has centered on the role of the self-fulfilling prophecy in everyday life and in laboratory situations. He also has a lasting interest in nonverbal communication, in quantitative procedures, and in sources of artifact in behavioral research. Professor Rosenthal is a Fellow of the American Association for the Advancement of Science and the American Psychological Society. He has been a Fellow at the Center for Advanced Study in the Behavioral Sciences and has held both Guggenheim and Fulbright Fellowships. Among other research awards, he has received the AAAS Prize for behavioral science research twice, in 1960 and in 1993. He is the author or coauthor of over 300 articles and is an editor, coeditor, author, or coauthor of more than 20 books. He plays squash frequently, gracelessly, and enthusiastically.

CHAPTER 2

Methodology

Robert Rosenthal
Harvard University

CHAPTER OUTLINE

Prepared for a text in advanced social psychology edited by Abraham Tesser.

Scientists are like sailors who must rebuild their boat, plank by plank, not in drydock, but at sea. The process is never finished, but the ship is getting better all the time.

—BASED ON AN ANALOGY BY OTTO NEURATH

This chapter is an *informal introduction* to *some* methodological issues in understanding and conducting social and behavioral science research. It is *informal* to fit in with the video-text idea conceived by Abraham Tesser to put students into contact with active researchers. It is an *introduction* in the sense that one chapter can do little more than raise questions and sensibilities about research. It deals with *some* issues because that is all there is space to address.[1] The material of this chapter is drawn from three different courses I teach at Harvard University: an introductory course in research methods, an intermediate course in data analysis, and an advanced course in research methods and data analysis. The first of those courses is for undergraduates, the second is for both graduate and undergraduate students, and the third is for graduate students only. The textbooks and other readings for these courses are listed at the end of this chapter.

OBSERVATION, RANDOMIZATION, CONTROL, AND CAUSIST LANGUAGE

Three Levels of Observation

We begin with the fundamental idea that observation is the cornerstone of science and that it is useful for us to distinguish three types or levels of observation: the descriptive, the relational, and the experimental.

We begin with the descriptive, drawing our examples from a research area that is close to my heart—research on teachers' expectations and pupils' intellectual performance (Rosenthal, 1991b; Rosenthal & Jacobson, 1968; 1992). To operate at the descriptive level we choose one variable at a time, say pupil intellectual performance, and show the distribution of pupils' performance scores, giving various measures of central tendency, spread, and the like. We might, in addition, ask teachers about their expectations for the intellectual performance of their students. We might have each teacher rate each of their students on a scale of 1 to 9 where 1 means very low expectation and 9 means very high expectation. For each teacher, then, we could describe their distribution of the ratings of their students. In addition, we could describe the distribution of mean ratings assigned by the different teachers. From all these descriptions we could learn that students differed in their intellectual performance, that they differed in the expectations that their teachers held for them, that some teachers typically held higher expectations for their students than other teachers held for *their* students, and that teachers differed from one another in the average intellectual performance of their students. All this is at the descriptive level.

At the relational level, we consider at least two variables at the same time, for example, teachers' expectations and pupils' intellectual performance. Suppose we measure, for many teachers and their students, the students' performance and their teachers' expectations for that performance. We then compute a correlation coefficient between teachers' expectations and pupils' intellectual performance. That correlation, let's say, is .50. Aha, we say, teachers' expectations cause pupils' intellectual development.

How justified would that conclusion be? How would we know, for example, whether that correlation comes about because the teachers' expectation has led to the intellectual performance of the students or whether the intellectual performance of the students, in the eyes of the sophisticated teacher, translates into an accurate diagnosis. In other words, at the relational level we are very hard put to draw any kind of causal inference. It is of course possible that the teachers' expectations do have an effect on the students. It is also possible that the students' actual performance affects the teachers' judgment and vice versa so that each can be partially causing the other variable, or there might not be any causal relationship at all. The sad truth is that we will never know. The problem with relational research generally is that without experimental manipulation, causal inference is extremely difficult to come by. Now, people have from time to time made sterling efforts to try to get a little bit more leverage on causal inference than you can possibly get from one-time measurement. Time is the independent variable that is often brought in to give us more leverage.

An early example of this comes from the field of sociology where Paul Lazarsfeld (1978) was interested in trying to learn whether party affiliation caused preference for a candidate or whether candidate preference caused party affiliation. Lazarsfeld developed an ingenious procedure of table analysis in which he used time as a variable to get some leverage for drawing causal inference from observational, correlational data. And although most psychologists don't know about the Lazarsfeld table analysis procedure, there is a more modern form of it that many of you are familiar with, the so called cross-lagged panel design.

We have two variables, teachers' expectations and pupils' performance, and they show a Pearson r of .50. We have talked about that correlation coefficient and how hard put we are to try to draw causal inference from it. But now we are going to extend this over time. So let's say after a semester of contact between teachers and students we again measure the correlation between teacher expectation and pupil performance, and let's assume it's still .50. So far, we haven't learned too much except that the correlation seems to hold up over time. Other correlations are possible, however. For example, the Time 1 to Time 2 correlation between teacher expectations can be measured. And we would call that the reliability, consistency, or stability of measurement of teacher expectation. Now let's pretend that the correlation is .60. We can do the same for pupils' performance. We can measure pupil performance at Time 1 and at Time 2 and correlate them, and let's say that that's also a .60. It's the stability or consistency or reliability of the pupil performance measure. So far, there isn't anything dramatic that we've gained by having time as a dimension. But here is the Lazarsfeld idea as developed later by Donald Campbell (1963) and his students, in particular David Kenny (1979). They would look at the cross correlations, that is, the correlation between teacher expectations at Time 1 and pupil performance at Time 2, and the correlation between pupil performance at Time 1 and teacher expectancy at Time 2. For example, if there were a .20 correlation between pupil performance at one time and teacher expectation at a later time, but there were a .40 correlation between teacher expectation at Time 1 and pupil performance at Time 2, then one might speak of this data array as suggesting a preponderance of causal influence from teacher expectation to pupil performance over pupil performance to teacher expectation (see Figure 2.1). This is merely an example of an imaginative and creative way to try to use all that you have available to make some very good educated guesses about causal inference. But let's make no mistake about it, there is no royal road to causal inference in the absence of a designed experiment.

What do we mean by an experiment? There must be an intervention by the experimenter and random assignment. The intervention cannot be an act of nature in which there has been no random assignment. If we have not randomly assigned our subjects to the experimental and control conditions, we do not have a true experiment and causal inference is extremely difficult. A nonexperimental analysis can often be useful, but we should emphasize that it can't tell the tale no matter how fancy it gets.[2]

There is no royal road to causal inference other than random assignment of subjects, the only way known to remove bias. Sometimes, of course, we cannot do random assignment of subjects for ethical reasons. Then we're stuck with the best that we can do, and in fact, that's what science is all about—doing the best we can. One view of science that I like very much (by Otto Neurath and serving as the headnote to this chapter) is that doing science is like rebuilding a wooden boat while at sea, one plank at a time. When some time has gone by, we have replaced the boat but there is always something wrong with it; still, it is always getting better, and that is how doing science goes.

In the area of teacher expectations, for example, if we were going to do an experiment, rather than simply measuring at Time 1 and Time 2 we'd introduce an intervention or manipulation, and that's what we did quite a few years ago (Rosenthal & Jacobson, 1968; 1992). Lenore Jacobson and I went into a school and, for each of the teachers in the school, told the teacher that certain of the students in her class or his class had shown, on the basis of a special computer software package, that they were going to show unexpected, unpredicted intellectual development. So our experimental intervention was manipulating the teacher's expectation for the pupils' intellectual development. We measured the students' IQ at the beginning of the school year and again at the end of the school year. Then we compared the gains of the "ordinary" children in the

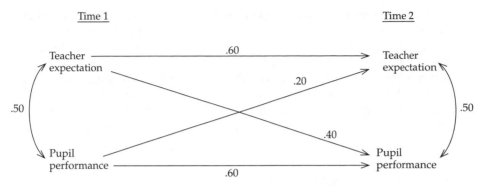

FIGURE 2.1. Hypothetical results of a cross-lagged panel analysis.

school with the children in the school whose teachers had been told that the children would bloom intellectually. We found that if the teachers had been led to expect an improvement in intellectual performance, then, in fact, teachers got that kind of improved performance. An experimental manipulation was really the only way to nail down that it was the teachers' expectation that was a causal variable. Procedures like the cross-lagged panel analysis can get you some additional mileage over simple correlational data and can be very valuable in an exploratory and suggestive sense. But they cannot directly nail down questions of causality.

Randomization

Why is randomization so important? Suppose we thought instead of using a table of random numbers: we'd just assign everybody whose name begins with the letters A–L to the experimental group and everybody whose name begins with the letters M–Z to the control group. This is not a very good way to design an experiment. Why? Well, because there may be ethnic differences. That is, certain cultures have names beginning with later letters, so we might get a cultural difference between the experimental and control groups. The cultural difference would be a plausible rival hypothesis to the hypothesis of the independent variable, the variable that we think is having the causal impact. Suppose we decided that because the experimental procedure took longer than the control procedure we would assign those who arrive earlier to the experimental and those who arrive later to the control conditions. That won't work very well either because we know that people who arrive early for psychological experiments differ in personality variables from those who arrive later for some psychological experiments (on need for social approval, for example) (Rosenthal & Rosnow, 1975).

How about an experimental design in which every other person was in the experimental and in the control conditions? But imagine in a thought experiment that we are psychological-zoological investigators doing research on all the animals coming in two-by-two to Noah's ark. So we have everybody coming up the gangplank and we say everybody on the left will be in the experimental and everybody on the right will be in the control condition. And since those were the days before we knew about sexism, it turned out that the ladies were always on the right. So, what we thought was the experimental vs. the control condition just turned out to be the sex effect because we were comparing the females to the males. This won't work. The only safe way to get random assignment to conditions is to use random numbers. Either tables in the back of a statistics book or computer-generated tables will do (Rosenthal & Rosnow, 1991).

Constructing Control Groups

We have talked about experimental vs. control comparisons. A word more needs to be said about constructing a suitable control group. A statistician or methodologist cannot tell a substantive or content expert in the field what the right control group is. One has to know the field to be able to develop an appropriate group. For example, in the area of psychopharmacology we may be developing drugs to improve mood, or lift depression, or affect any other psychological states. Nowadays, if we did a randomized experiment in which we assigned half the patients to the drug and the other half to no drug, we'd never be able to publish that paper in a selective journal.

Why? Nowadays we know so much about the placebo effect that it would be regarded as the height of naiveté for anybody to have compared a drug against the absence of it. At the very least we would have to have a placebo control group. So half the patients would get the drug and the other half would get something that looked, tasted, and smelled like the drug except that it didn't have the presumed active ingredients. A placebo control makes sense today where 50 or 100 years ago the drug/nothing comparison would have made sense. As we've learned more about the field, we've learned more about how to set up a control group (Rosenthal, 1985). But we never finish in our search for the right control group, because that, in a way, captures the history of the research area.

Suppose that we want to investigate the effects of psychotherapy or any other kind of social intervention. We can make a list of all the things that we think are involved in psychotherapy, e.g., *exclusive* time spent with the patient if this is individual psychotherapy, spending a certain *amount* of time, spending time with a person who is presumably *better adjusted than the patient* so that we can model behavior, and so on through all the many characteristics of psychotherapy. Now, if all this is psychotherapy, to what do we want to compare psychotherapy? Much of the psychotherapy research literature compares people getting psychotherapy to people not getting psychotherapy. For the purpose of finding out whether it pays to have psychotherapy that may be a very useful thing (Smith, Glass, & Miller, 1980). Suppose, on the other hand, we want to test certain theories about the "effective ingredients" of psychotherapy, for example, the use of the transference relationship, or the working through of the patient's resistance. Then, the appropriate control group is psychotherapy without those "effective ingredients." Therefore, if we want to know whether psychoanalytic therapy works, it would make sense to compare it to, let's say, a waiting list control group, randomly assigned. But if we want to know specifically whether it is certain features of the psychotherapy—e.g., the psychoanalytic features such as transference and resistance—that make it work, then we want a control condition that has everything except the critical elements of treatment.

Table 2.1 shows a list of ingredients found in psychoanalytic psychotherapy. Control group A could be used to learn whether the treatment works, but control group D allows us to learn whether the specifically psychoanalytic features are effective or not. Control groups B and C control for being in any kind of helping relationship (B) and being in any kind of psychotherapy (C), respec-

TABLE 2.1. Testing the Effectiveness of Psychoanalytic Treatment

	Psycho-analytic Treatment (T)	No Treatment Control (A)†	Helping Control (B)‡	Psycho-therapy Control (C)§	Insight Psycho-therapy Control (D)¶
1. Features common to all interactions	*		*	*	*
2. Features common to all hierarchical interactions	*		*	*	*
3. Features common to all helping relationships	*		*	*	*
4. Features common to all psychotherapy	*			*	*
5. Features common to all insight psychotherapy	*				*
6. Features common to all psychoanalytic psychotherapy	*				

†Differences between the treatment and this control could be due to the operation of features 1, 2, 3, 4, 5, and 6.
‡Differences between the treatment and this control could be due to the operation of features 4, 5, and 6.
§Differences between the treatment and this control could be due to the operation of features 5, and 6.
¶Differences between the treatment and this control could be due to the operation of feature 6.

tively. In short, the definition, selection, or construction of the control group depends on the precise question it is that we want to address.

Procedural Control

Control group formation is one important sense of the term *control*. There is another sense of control that has to do with the idea of control of the situation in which the data are being collected. This is control in the sense of precision of measurement. So, for example, we usually have greater experimental control when we have a laboratory situation where it is possible to treat every subject in as nearly identical a way as we can. Laboratory analog psychotherapy research often has greater experimental control than does field psychotherapeutic research, which has more hurly-burly in it and a lot more random variation among the ways in which different practitioners practice the psychotherapy, even a specific form of psychotherapeutic intervention. Basically, the control group sense of control is what allows us to draw causal inference. The control of the conditions kind of control tends to increase the precision of our experiment. That is, it allows us to pick up a signal more easily from a background of noise.

Causist Language

We'll have a little more to say about signal and noise very shortly. But before we leave the topic of causal inference and how hard valid causal inferences are to come by, we should mention the problem of causist language. We are often causist without knowing it. To be causist means using terms like the *effect* of variable *a* on *b* or the *impact* of *a* on *b*. It is valuable for us to read the literature very carefully for that kind of language. When authors have used words like *impact* or *effect*, we should go back and see whether there has been a randomized experiment. Often there will not have been. What there may have been is a multiple regression equation which shows that we can predict some dependent variable from one or more predictor variables, and the language in which the results are discussed is often causist language. People speak of the *effect* of the independent variables, but that's not what they mean at all, or it's not what they should be meaning at all. What they should be saying is that variables *a, b, c,* and *d* can be used to predict variable *y*, or that these variables are associated with *y*. But being able to predict, or having variables associated with, another variable is not at all the same thing as knowing that variables *a, b, c,* and *d* have contributed causally to the outcome *y*.

ERROR, BIAS, AND PRECISION

A bit now more on signal and noise and on precision and bias. Bias has to do with systematic error in observation. Precision has to do with random error. For example, if you step on a scale ten times and each time it says 152, then that scale is said to be precise. That is, it does not vary. It's consistent in its measurement. But we don't know whether it's correct. We have to somehow calibrate that scale. It may be that the scale has a 2-pound bias, that the person being weighed ten times really weighs 150 pounds. A perfect scale would yield ten readings of 150. Instead, the scale described gave ten readings of 152. In real-life situations there's very often a trade-off between these two features of measurement—a trade-off between bias and precision.

Table 2.2 gives an example in which nine different scales are each tested by having a person known to weigh 150 pounds weigh themselves five times.

For Scale A we have a range of 20 pounds with an average reading of 150, an example of no bias. On the average, it gives the correct weight. Scale C shows high bias. We have the same range, the same standard deviation of weighings, but we're 10 pounds off. There's a 10-pound bias. Now compare these scales to Scale G, which yields five readings of 150, and Scale I, which yields five readings of 160. Scale G is unbiased, but Scale I shows a 10-pound bias. There is very high precision in Scale I but very low precision in Scale C, or B, or A. The high precision means there's very little variation in the readings. And low precision means there's a lot of variability. If we knew that we could only weigh ourselves one time, even though there's no bias in Scale A, we'd be in big trouble if we owned this scale. We'd have only a one in five chance of getting the right reading.

On the other hand, high bias with high precision can sometimes be a pretty good trade-off. That is, if we knew the bias of Scale I, we'd be better off to have

TABLE 2.2. Bias and Inconsistency in Nine Scales, Each Tested Five Times

Levels of Inconsistency	*Levels of Bias*		
	0 Bias	1-Pound Bias	10-Pound Bias
20-pound spread	160	161	170
(S = 7.9)	155	156	165
	150 A	151 B	160 C
	145	146	155
	140	141	150
4-pound spread	152	153	162
(S = 1.6)	151	152	161
	150 D	151 E	160 F
	149	150	159
	148	149	158
0-pound spread	150	151	160
(S = 0.0)	150	151	160
	150 G	151 H	160 I
	150	151	160
	150	151	160

Scale I than to have Scale A. We'd rather have the scale that always reads the same because it's not that hard to subtract 10 pounds. Having a scale that is unbiased in the sense that, on the average, it gives the right reading is not all that wonderful. Do we really want to weigh ourselves five or ten times every morning and take the average? No.

One of the newer developments in statistical thinking is the idea that bias may not be the terrible thing that we've always been led to believe. The main thing we want to do about bias is to assess it, to measure it. We want to know how big it is. Then, sometimes a very useful trade-off can be effected between bias and precision. We may be willing to suffer some known bias in exchange for greater precision.

RELIABILITY

Precision and Blocking

Ideas of precision lead us very naturally to ideas of reliability, a further discussion of signal and noise. Noise in data is best represented by variability. Lots of noise means low precision, i.e., lots of variability among the observations. Back in 1980 Lewis Branscomb, the famous physicist, was heard to say: "God loves the noise as much as the signal." We might add that God might love it more because she made so much more of it.

One of the things that scientists are challenged to do is to convert noise to signal. And that's something that we do with clever experimental design. Suppose we're interested in an experimental manipulation to reduce anxiety, and the subjects are females and males who are in mental hospitals, schools for the retarded, universities, parent-teachers organizations, and church groups. Then we compute a t test comparing all experimentals to all controls. There's nothing wrong with that in terms of bias, but the noise may be considerable. So good experimental designers try to reduce the noise by blocking.

Blocking is the subdividing or stratifying of an overall experiment into smaller subgroups. If we block on sex so that now we have treatment and control conditions for females and males separately, the variation within each group will be much smaller, and that variation is the variation that is used for our test of significance. If we further subdivide the females and subdivide the males into the different levels of pathology or background or educational level or whatever, that decrease in noise will continue.

Being able to block, subdivide, or stratify our subjects into smaller and smaller subgroups, each of which is more homogeneous, reflects how much we understand substantively about a particular field of research. Nowadays it would be regarded as very inexpert, very amateurish, to do certain kinds of experiments without blocking on variables like sex, age, education, or degree of pathology.

Reliability of Measurement

Reliability of measurement is a concept that is very much tied to the idea of precision. When we have perfect precision, we have perfect reliability. Yet, precision is not quite the same as reliability. More on that will follow later, but first, a bit of context. I have a friend who's a crackerjack statistician and highly sophisticated mathematically. He has an interesting reaction when anyone raises the question of reliability. For example, someone will say: "You used such and such a test, but I understand the reliability of that test is not very high." My friend is likely to respond: "Why do you want to know the reliability anyhow?" They usually reply: "Because the reliability has to be .90 or .80" or whatever they have read somewhere that's required.

Particularly high reliability is not required at all. If a measure predicts something of consequence, or correlates with something of consequence—i.e., *shows validity*—there's no need whatever to demonstrate reliability.[3] It is important to know about reliability for the following reason: Low reliability is one reason that we get low validity. Our measure may not correlate well with things that our theory says it ought to correlate with because of low reliability.

Two Levels of Reliability

It's important to think about reliability at two levels: the reliability of the element (e.g., an item, a subtest, or a rater) and the reliability of the composite (e.g., the mean or sum of the items, subtests, or raters). Suppose a social psychologist or a personality psychologist is going to be using the Wechsler Adult Intelligence Scale. There is a reliability for the full scale; there is a reliability for the verbal part and for the performance part. There is a reliability for each of the 11 subtests and so on. It's possible to talk about the reliability of any of those, even about the reliability of individual items.

In another context, one that we use a lot in our own research, we employ observers to make ratings of social interactions—teachers interacting with students, experimenters interacting with research subjects, or psychotherapists interacting with their patients. We rate the psychotherapists' behavior, for example, on variables like warmth, dominance, task orientation, empathy, and so on. We are interested in knowing the degree of reliability that our raters have with each other. We are able to use the average rating of the raters to predict things like the outcome of the interaction. We can tell how effective a classroom teacher is from observing 30 seconds of silent videotape, for example, and having undergraduate observers make ratings of variables like warm, supportive, friendly, and so on (Ambady & Rosenthal, 1992). Let's take an example of examining the reliability of *individual* raters *and* the reliability of the mean of the set of raters. Suppose we are rating a group of five people on a variable like "warm"; maybe these are therapists, and there are three raters making ratings as shown in Table 2.3.

One way to get the reliability is to compute the correlation between each of the three pairs of judges. If we did that for these data, we get an average corre-

TABLE 2.3. Reliability of Three Raters

	Raters		
	A	B	C
Person 1	5	6	7
Person 2	3	6	4
Person 3	3	4	6
Person 4	2	2	3
Person 5	1	4	4

CORRELATIONS (*r*) BETWEEN RATERS

A & B	.645
A & C	.800
B & C	.582
Mean *r*	.676

SPEARMAN-BROWN RELIABILITY OF A COMPOSITE VARIABLE (*R*)

$$R = \frac{nr}{1+(n-1)r} = \frac{(3)(.676)}{1+(3-1)(.676)} = .862$$

Note: n is the number of judges, raters, items, or subtests; r is the mean correlation among individual judges, raters, items, or subtests.

lation of about .68. That's the reliability of the element, each element being a judge or rater. The estimation procedure would be exactly the same if these were three subtests of an overall test of ability or three items of a three-item questionnaire thought to measure self-esteem, for example. But if we're going to use the mean or sum of those three ratings to characterize the therapists' warmth, the reliability of that variable is not .68; it is .86.

The reliability of the sum or mean is higher than the average reliability of the elements. Whether we use as our index the .68 or the .86 depends really on what it is we're trying to do. When we publish our paper about this particular measuring scheme, it's important to give both values for the following reason: If we use the mean of the three raters to predict the outcome of psychotherapy from the psychotherapists' warmth, the .86 is actually the reliability of the instrument we used because the instrument we used was the sum or the mean of all three judges. However, if we don't mention the .68 and just say our reliability was .86, somebody reading the article might think that's the reliability between two judges and might conclude: "Oh well, if the reliability is that high, I just need one judge or one rater."

To estimate reliability we usually compute all the intercorrelations among the individual items or subtests or raters or judges, and get the average intercorrelation. The Spearman-Brown correlation correction gives us the reliability of the mean (or composite) item or rater as shown in Table 2.3. The Spearman-Brown equation is a formal statement of the basic idea that adding more items or raters of the same degree of correlation with the other items or raters leads to increased reliability of the mean, sum, or composite of the items or raters. There are analogous procedures for doing this through analysis of variance approaches (Guilford, 1954; Rosenthal, 1987; Rosenthal & Rosnow, 1991). Table 2.4 shows the analysis of variance of the data at the top of Table 2.3. The ingredients of the analysis (i.e., the mean squares) can then be used to estimate the reliability of the individual *or* mean item or rater.

So far in this chapter we have discussed some basic ideas about causal inference and how hard it is to draw, some ideas about measurement in the sense of bias and precision, and we have touched on some of the major ideas underlying careful consideration of the concept of reliability. We have not been able to do full justice in this space to any of those topics, but our intent was only to make a good beginning.

EFFECT SIZE AND SIGNIFICANCE TESTS

In the rest of this chapter we will discuss some basic ideas of data analysis, some ways of thinking about the results of research.

We begin with a fundamental equation of all data analysis, one that should be emblazoned upon our minds. In prose, the equation reads:

Test of significance = effect size × size of study

Social scientists often write as though the goal of the scientific enterprise were to come up with a significance test. But if we look carefully at this equation, we'll see that the significance test depends on two ingredients. The magnitude

TABLE 2.4. Analysis of Variance Approach to Reliability for the Example Given in Table 2.3

Source	SS	df	MS
Person (P)	24.0	4	6.00
Rater (R)	11.2	2	5.60
Person × Rater (P × R)	6.8	8	0.85

RELIABILITY OF SINGLE, TYPICAL JUDGE (INTRACLASS r OR r_{ic})

$$r_{ic} = \frac{MS_P - MS_{P \times R}}{MS_P + (n-1) MS_{P \times R}} = \frac{6.00 - 0.85}{6.00 + (3-1)(0.85)} = .669$$

RELIABILITY OF THE COMPOSITE OF ALL JUDGES (R_c)

$$R_c = \frac{MS_P - MS_{P \times R}}{MS_P} = \frac{6.00 - 0.85}{6.00} = .858$$

Note: n is the number of judges, raters, items, or subtests; MS_P is the mean square for persons; and $MS_{P \times R}$ is the mean square for the person × rater interaction.

of the effect or the relationship (the effect size) and the size of the study. There is an important implication—namely, that any effect size that is not zero, given a large enough study, is going to yield significant results. So significant results tell you as much about the size of the study as about the size of the relationship. It behooves us to keep this very clearly in mind.

Now, to get concrete examples of this relationship, let us examine some statistical tests and effect sizes that we know very well. First a friendly χ^2 on one degree of freedom, the kind we'd get from a 2×2 table of counts of Republicans and Democrats voting for a Republican or a Democratic candidate, for example. This χ^2 is the product of a ϕ^2 (a squared correlation coefficient between an independent and a dependent variable) times the number of cases in the study:

$$\chi^2(1) = \phi^2 \times N \tag{1}$$

Given $\chi^2(1)$ and the size of a study, ϕ^2, an index of the magnitude of the relationship, can be obtained by dividing $\chi^2(1)$ by N. Should we prefer a Z test [a Z is the square root of the $\chi^2(1)$], we can employ equation 2 instead of equation 1:

$$Z = \phi \times \sqrt{N} \tag{2}$$

Often we want to use t tests, as when we're comparing two groups, e.g., experimental vs. control, or any other two groups. The difference between the group means divided by the common standard deviation (computed separately within the two groups) is one index of the size of the effect. Table 2.5 shows that it yields t when multiplied by the quantity shown in the last column of Table 2.5 for equations 3 or 4, where n_1 and n_2 are the sample sizes of the experimental and control groups. So the larger the n's are, the larger the t will be. And, of course, the larger the difference between the means relative to the standard deviation, the larger t will be.

If we wanted to employ F tests, we just take the variance of the means around the grand mean (S^2_{means}), divide that by s^2, the within-group variance, and multiply that effect size index by n, the number of observations in each of the groups, for the moment assuming equal sample sizes in the groups. So F is large when the means are far apart, i.e., very variable relative to the noise within the system. We can think of how far apart the means are as a kind of signal and the s^2 of the variation within the groups as a kind of noise, and that signal to noise ratio is multiplied by n, the size of each group, to yield the significance test F (see equation 8 of Table 2.5).

Many other indices are available; for example, we can think of t in terms of $r/\sqrt{1-r^2} \times \sqrt{df}$ where r is just the correlation between the independent variable (that is, being in the experimental or the control group coded 1 or 0) and the dependent variable. So the larger r is, the larger t will be; the larger the degrees of freedom, basically the sample size, the larger t will be (see equation 7 of Table 2.5). There are dozens of possible effect size estimates, and a very common one to use is the difference between the means divided by the standard deviation collected from both conditions (g). But there are variations of this index as well. Gene Glass and his colleagues, for example, like to use the quantity g computed using the standard deviation only from the control group rather than

TABLE 2.5. Examples of the Relationship between Tests of Significance, Effect Size, and Size of Study for $\chi^2(1)$, Z, t, and F

Equation	Test of Significance	=	Size of Effect	×	Size of Study
1.	$\chi^2(1)$	=	ϕ^2	×	N
2.	Z	=	ϕ	×	$\sqrt{N}$
3.	t	=	$\left(\dfrac{M_1 - M_2}{S}\right)^{\dagger}$	×	$\dfrac{1}{\sqrt{\dfrac{1}{n_1} + \dfrac{1}{n_2}}}$
4.	t	=	g	×	$\sqrt{\dfrac{n_1 n_2}{n_1 + n_2}}$
5.	t	=	$\dfrac{M_1 - M_2}{\sigma}^{\ddagger}$	×	$\left[\dfrac{\sqrt{(n_1 n_2)}}{(n_1 + n_2)} \times \sqrt{df}\right]$
6.	t	=	d	×	$\dfrac{\sqrt{df}}{2}$
7.	t	=	$\dfrac{r}{\sqrt{1-r^2}}$	×	$\sqrt{df}$
8.	F	=	$\dfrac{S^2_{\text{mean}}}{s^2}$	×	n

$\dagger$ Also called g (Hedges, 1981).
$\ddagger$ Also called d (Cohen, 1969, 1988).

from both the control group and the experimental group (Glass, McGaw, & Smith, 1981). Their reason for doing so is that sometimes the effect of the experimental manipulation is to increase or decrease the variance of the experimental group. When that happens, it's a perfectly reasonable thing to collect the s just from the control group. If we're interested in effect size estimation for the purposes of meta-analysis, the quantitative summary of a research domain, we often don't really have that choice, however. As meta-analysts, we usually will not have access to the data that allows us to compute the s separately for the control group. We'll often be stuck with just looking at an analysis of variance type table, and we'll have to use a pooled estimate of s2. But with our own data we can do it either way, and there are pros and cons for both of those indices.

Jack Cohen, a very fine methodologist at New York University, prefers to divide the difference between the means by the standard deviation (σ) rather than the square root of the unbiased estimate of the population variance (S)

(Cohen, 1969; 1988). So instead of s we would use σ for the sample. But that's not very different from s unless the samples are very tiny. In short, there are many alternative ways of indexing effect sizes, and the strongest take-home message about effect size estimates is that it doesn't matter all that much which one we use.

We should never publish a paper in which we don't give any such estimate. The most important result we have in any study is the effect size estimate. If we also want to give a significance test or, better still, a confidence interval around the effect size, that's okay too. But we should always give the effect size estimate.

Incidentally, my personal favorite effect size estimate is r, simply because it always works. That is, it can be used in a two-group situation because then r is just a point biserial correlation, i.e., a product-moment correlation coefficient (r) between the independent variable coded 1 or 0 (that is, experimental or control) and the dependent variable. So, r works just as well as Hedges' g or Cohen's d for the two-group situation. But for other kinds of situations—for contrasts, for example—these latter indices don't make any sense at all. To illustrate, suppose we were developmental psychologists and our prediction was that as children get older—going through ages 10, 11, 12, 13, 14, and 15—their cognitive performance improves. We compute a linear contrast (predicting equal increments of performance over the six age levels), an associated significance test for that contrast, and an effect size estimate for it. Well, it doesn't make an awful lot of sense to compute a quantity like the difference between *two* means divided by the standard deviation if the prediction is about a linear increase in *six* means with age. On the other hand, r is the perfectly natural thing to use. So we can always use r, and it will always be sensible. But we can't always use some of the other indices.

THE INTERPRETATION OF EFFECT SIZES

With such an emphasis on effect size estimates, more should be said about their interpretation. Perhaps the most commonly used effect size indices have been those having to do with the squared indices: e.g., r^2, a proportion of variance accounted for; Omega squared; and Epsilon squared. Let me argue against their use for most practical purposes, i.e., on most occasions on which we are testing a specific hypothesis such as this treatment will be better than that treatment, or this group will score higher than that group, or an ordering of means of a certain sort will be found. For most such situations we're going to miss the point completely if we get too much into the business of r^2. Here is an example.

The Physicians' Aspirin Study

There's a very famous study conducted over a period of a few years that was recently discontinued. There were 22,071 doctors who were the subjects of that experiment, and a random half took an aspirin every other day and the random other half took a placebo (Steering Committee of the Physicians Health Study Research Group, 1988). This study went on for a while and was then discontinued on ethical grounds because preliminary analyses showed that there was such a reduction in heart attacks for those who were on the aspirin, compared to those who were on the placebo, that it was regarded as unethical to continue the experiment. Well, that's a pretty dramatic thing, to interrupt a clinical trial like that for ethical reasons so that lives won't be lost, so that heart attacks won't be suffered.

So what must have been the magnitude of the effect to lead to such a dramatic termination of the experiment? Surely the r must have been .90 or .80 or .70 or .60, i.e., with r^2 of .81 or .64 or whatever. No, that's not what happened at all. The r^2 was .00! If we added a few more decimal places, we'd get some nonzero values. What was the r? The r was actually less than .04, an r^2 of .0016.

Now surely an r of .04 is like a fish so small you want to throw it back because it isn't worth the trouble. But if it weren't worth the trouble, why would they discontinue the experiment? Let's look at a device called a *binomial effect size display*, which is a procedure for displaying the practical consequences of a particular effect size estimate, r (Rosenthal & Rubin, 1982).

The Binomial Effect Size Display

In a binomial effect size display for research on some possibly lifesaving intervention like aspirin, you might have an experimental and a control condition as the independent variable, and a dependent variable might be some nice simple dichotomous outcome variable that we can all understand like being alive or being dead. A binomial effect size display is set up in such a way that even though we may not have had equal sample sizes in our experimental and control conditions, even though we may not have had equal outcome rates for the two kinds of outcome, the display procedure, the binomial effect size display is always set up as though it were. That's only to make the tables standard so that we can compare the different experimental results by referring to a common 1.00 all around the table.

If 52 out of 100 experimental patients lived compared to only 48 out of 100 control patients, that means there are fewer deaths per 100 (see Table 2.6, Part A). That is an enormous benefit, saving 4 lives out of 100. Most people would not regard that as an effect too small to keep, an effect so small it should be thrown back. What we're looking at in Table 2.6, Part A, is a correlation of .04. We're also looking at an r^2 of .0016. If we computed the correlation between the independent variable coded 1 and 0 and a dependent variable coded 1 and 0, we would find an r of .04.

The binomial effect size display always starts with the assumption of the zero r, which is an entry of .50 in each cell (Table 2.6, Part B). In order to refer whatever result we have to a binomial effect size display all we do is add half the correlation coefficient to one condition and subtract half from the other. So if the correlation is .04, take half of that (.02), add it to the .50 of Cell A to make .52, and subtract it from the .50 of Cell C to make .48. Now we find the differ-

TABLE 2.6. The Binomial Effect Size Display for the Physicians' Aspirin Study, for an *r* of .00, and for the Effects of Psychotherapy

A. ASPIRIN EFFECT[†]

	No Heart Attack	Heart Attack	Σ
Aspirin	.52	.48	1.00
Placebo	.48	.52	1.00
Σ	1.00	1.00	2.00

B. *r* = .00

	Benefit	No Benefit	Σ
Treatment	.50A	.50B	1.00
Control	.50C	.50D	1.00
Σ	1.00	1.00	2.00

C. PSYCHOTHERAPY EFFECT

	Benefit	No Benefit	Σ
Psychotherapy	.66	.34	1.00
Control	.34	.66	1.00
Σ	1.00	1.00	2.00

[†]Rounded from *r* = .034 to *r* = .04.

ence between the rate .52 and .48, or .52 − .48. The difference between the success rates is equal to *r*. That's a very useful way to think about *r*. The correlation (*r*) is simply the difference between success rates. If we had an *r* of .10, it would be equivalent to 55 percent vs. 45 percent surviving. If we had an *r* of .20, it would be equivalent to 60 percent vs. 40 percent surviving. That *r* of .20, with 60 percent surviving instead of only 40 percent, when we square it, is an r^2 of "only" .04.

Now let's get a feel for some of the big results in psychology and in other fields. The aspirin effect was matched by another drug—propranolol—a drug given to people who have had heart attacks. That *r* was virtually the same as the aspirin *r*, .04. We've heard a lot about Vietnam veterans having a lot of alcohol and drug addiction problems, and they do. But most workers are surprised to learn the correlation between having been a Vietnam veteran and having alcohol problems. That correlation is .07; the r^2 is .0049. I recently took an informal poll of about a half-dozen physicians: I asked them to tell me what the really big medical breakthrough of recent times might be, something that really made a big difference. They all agreed on what it was. They said it was the introduction of a drug called cyclosporine, a drug given to patients who are going to have organ transplants. It reduces the likelihood that they will reject the new organ. Cyclosporine was positively associated with survival. That is, those who got the drug compared to the control were more likely to survive their transplant. But what was the magnitude of this really breakthrough result? The r was .15; the r^2 was .0225, i.e., 2 percent of the variance. Of all the effects that I've looked at recently, the most dramatic and the largest effect was actually the effect of psychotherapy, which showed an effect size correlation of about .32 (see Table 2.6, Part C). For a correlation of .32, r^2 is about .10; and one critic of the Smith, Glass, and Miller (1980) meta-analytic work on psychotherapy said that if $r = .32$, or 10 percent of the variance is all we can account for with psychotherapy, we'd better throw in the towel. But a correlation of .32 is doubling the rate of improvement from 34 to 66 percent. There's nothing very small about that effect!

The purpose of my emphasis on the binomial effect size display is to make us all more keenly aware of what the practical import is of the particular effect size that we get. These effect sizes are especially important if they are based either on very large studies like the physicians' aspirin study or on meta-analytic results, that is, the systematic, quantitative summary of a whole set of experiments (a topic to be discussed later in this chapter). These effect sizes have the same meaning even in an individual study that we might conduct, but the particular effect size estimate that we come up with is very likely to be different in the next study that we conduct. If we have a meta-analysis of many studies and have computed the average effect size as in the psychotherapy research domain where there were hundreds of experiments, conducting 10, 20, 30, or 40 more psychotherapy outcome studies is not going to change that average effect size estimate very much. But if we conduct an experiment that is the first of the series and we get an effect size estimate say of $r = .22$, then we shouldn't expect the next study also to give us an r of .22. It might be a .30; it might be only .08. In short, the effect size estimate that is better nailed down is more conclusive in terms of what it's likely to mean practically, but we give the same interpretation to an effect size no matter how many studies it comes from.

Correlation and Percent Agreement

While we're discussing correlations, my favorite effect size estimate, let me interject a quick note that relates to ideas of reliability that psychologists have been exposed to, especially if they're using raters or judges to make ratings. For example, a developmental psychologist may be observing children on the playground and asking two judges to code aggressive behavior with an eye to learning the degree of agreement between the two judges' ratings. Let me enter a cautionary note about the use of a particular way of computing reliability called *percent agreement*. Suppose we have two playground observers, judge A and judge B, and they're coding 100 children on the playground for being high or not high on aggressiveness. We find, let's say, that we have 98 percent agreement, as shown in Part I of Table 2.7. Most psychologists are surprised to learn

TABLE 2.7. Two Examples of 98 Percent Agreement

I. LOW CORRELATION ($r = -.01$)

	Judge A	
Judge B	Aggressive Behavior	Nonaggressive Behavior
Aggressive behavior	98	1
Nonaggressive behavior	1	0

II. HIGH CORRELATION ($r = .96$)

	Judge A	
Judge B	Aggressive Behavior	Nonaggressive Behavior
Aggressive behavior	49	1
Nonaggressive behavior	1	49

that the Pearson product moment correlation between judge A's and judge B's rating of aggressiveness is actually negative: $-.01$! The reason is that there is so little variance in these results. If we had a very well balanced table—that is, with equal margins all around, as in part II of Table 2.7—then percent agreement would come very close to giving us the same kind of meaning that we would get out of the product moment correlation coefficient. In most cases it does not do that, and it can be extremely misleading as in the example of Table 2.7, Part I. In any type of research in which we are to code behavior, percent agreement is a very high risk method of indexing reliability. The product moment correlation takes the difference in variabilities into account, whereas the method of percentage agreement does not.

CONTRASTS

Preanalysis of an Experiment

Both in meta-analytic work and in the analysis of our own research, one of the most important things that we can do is to get as clear in our own mind as we can exactly what it is we're trying to get the data to tell us about. We can think of it as "learning what our theory is." Here is a practical suggestion on how we can learn what our theory is.

Suppose we had some sort of experimental plan where we're going to have either an experimental treatment or a control treatment applied to females and males at three age levels, yielding a $2 \times 2 \times 3$ factorial design. Before we do the first bit of data collection, we think hard about each cell of that design. In a $2 \times 2 \times 3$ design we have 12 cells. We take a number between 0 and 10 (or 0 and

100). The 0 means the smallest possible score we could get, and 10 (or 100) is the largest possible score we could get. In each one of the 12 cells we put the number we expect to get if our theory is correct. Then, we do an analysis of variance on those predicted numbers of our 2 × 2 × 3. We won't get an error term, and we won't get a significance test, but we don't need those. What we want to learn is what our prediction is in terms of the three main effects, the three two-way interactions, and the three-way interaction. It may turn out to be the case, for example, that the worst thing we could possibly do is to analyze our data as a 2 × 2 × 3 factorial analysis of variance. Here is an example.

Suppose the following hypothesis: Female and male patients are assigned to a psychological intervention, experimental or control, and at the same time to a pharmacological intervention, experimental or control. Let's say that our theory says that the particular disorder for which we're offering this combination of treatments is one in which both the psychological and the pharmacological intervention must be applied for there to be any benefits. Furthermore, because of the testosterone factor we only expect benefits for females. Ordinarily, we might just go ahead and compute a 2 × 2 × 2 factorial analysis of variance with factors of sex, psychological intervention, and pharmacological intervention. This analysis would result in three main effects, three two-way and one three-way interaction. But our prediction is that just one cell will be different from all the others and that the others will not be different from each other (see Table 2.8). It would be very unwise for us to compute a 2 × 2 × 2 factorial analysis in this situation. This 2 × 2 × 2 analysis of the predictions we

TABLE 2.8. Preanalysis of an Experiment: Predicted Results and Their Analysis of Variance

Psychological Intervention	Pharmacological Intervention			
	Treatment		Control	
	Female	Male	Female	Male
Treatment	8 (+7)[†]	0 (−1)	0 (−1)	0 (−1)
Control	0 (−1)	0 (−1)	0 (−1)	0 (−1)

Source	SS	df	MS	$F_{(1,72)}$[‡]	p	r
Psychological	8	1	8	1.00	.32	.12
Pharmacological	8	1	8	1.00	.32	.12
Sex of patient	8	1	8	1.00	.32	.12
Psy. × pharm.	8	1	8	1.00	.32	.12
Psy. × sex	8	1	8	1.00	.32	.12
Pharm. × sex	8	1	8	1.00	.32	.12
Psy. × pharm. × sex	8	1	8	1.00	.32	.12
Planned contrast	56	1	56	7.00	.01	.30

[†]Appropriate contrast weights for these predicted results are given in parentheses.
[‡]Assuming $n = 10$ per cell and $MS_{error} = 8.00$.

made is shown in the bottom of Table 2.8. All the variance among the eight conditions was divided equally into three main effects, three two-way interactions, and one three-way interaction. It could easily happen that none of these effects would be significant even if the specific prediction we had made were very significant. In short, our question was a question of comparing a single group against seven others. It was not a question addressed by the $2 \times 2 \times 2$ factorial. We were not interested in the average effect of sex. We were not interested in the average effect of drugs. We were not interested in the average effect of psychological intervention. Our specific interest was in comparing one group against all others. That's a contrast. And the contrast coding, which means the assigning of weights to the contrast, would proceed as follows.

Contrast Coding

We use any numbers we like for our contrast weights as long as these numbers accurately reflect our prediction about what will happen and the contrast weights add up to zero (Rosenthal & Rosnow, 1985; 1991). In our present example of Table 2.8 we predicted 1 score of 8 and 7 scores of 0. The mean of these 8 predictions is +1. When we subtract that mean from all 8 of our conditions, we end up with 1 prediction of +7 and 7 predictions of −1, giving us contrast weights that do add up to 0. Virtually all scientific questions we put to our data should be addressed by the specific contrasts that we construct as predictions for our research results. That is not to say that we should not do factorial analyses of variance. However, we shouldn't do them because we know how to do them, or because our software allows us to do them. We should address the questions that we really care about. When we employ contrasts to address these questions, we will be rewarded with greater conceptual clarity and with more significant results because we will have put our power where our questions are. Indeed, in the example shown in Table 2.8, where each of the effects associated with the standard analysis of variance yield an F of 1.00, the effect associated with the planned contrast is 7.00, a seven-fold increase in the test of significance.

META-ANALYSIS

It is a common criticism of the behavioral sciences that they cumulate poorly. Psychology, for example, does not seem to show the orderly progress and development shown by the physical sciences. The newer work of these "harder" sciences is seen to build directly on the earlier work of these sciences. Psychology, on the other hand, in particular social psychology, seems nearly to be starting anew with each succeeding volume of our journals. While it appears that the physical sciences have problems of their own when it comes to successful cumulation (Collins, 1985; Hedges, 1987), there is no denying that in the matter of cumulating evidence we have much to be modest about.

Poor cumulation does not seem to be primarily due to lack of replication or to failure to recognize the need for replication. Indeed, the clarion calls for further research with which we so frequently end our articles are carried wherever social psychological journals are read. It seems, rather, that we have been better at issuing such calls than at knowing what to do with the answers. There are many areas of social psychology for which we do have available the results of two, ten, or many more studies all addressing essentially the same question. Our summaries of the results of these sets of studies, however, have not been nearly as informative as they might have been, either with respect to summarized significance levels or with respect to summarized effect sizes. Even the best reviews of research by the most sophisticated workers have rarely told us more about each study in a set of studies than the direction of the relationship between the variables investigated and whether or not a given p level was attained. This state of affairs is beginning to change with psychology's increasing use of the procedures of meta-analysis.

Our purpose in this section is to provide a general framework for conceptualizing meta-analysis and to illustrate some of the quantitative procedures within this framework so that they can be applied by the reader and/or understood more clearly when applied by others.

If we were to trace briefly the development of the movement to quantify runs of studies, we might well begin with Fisher (1938), for his thinking about the combination of the significance levels of independent studies. We would then move through Mosteller and Bush (1954), for their broadening of the Fisher perspective both in (1) introducing several new methods of combining independent probability levels to social and behavioral scientists in general and to social psychologists in particular, and in (2) showing that effect sizes as well as significance levels could be usefully combined. We would end in the present day with an expanding number of investigators whose work has been summarized elsewhere, e.g., Cooper, 1989; Glass, McGaw, and Smith, 1981; Hedges and Olkin, 1985; Hunter and Schmidt, 1990; Light and Pillemer, 1984; and Rosenthal, 1991a.

A Framework for Meta-Analytic Procedures

Table 2.9 provides a general summary of six types of meta-analytic procedures. When studies are compared as to their significance levels (Cell A) or their effect sizes (Cell B) by diffuse tests, we learn whether they differ significantly among themselves with respect to significance levels or effect sizes, respectively, but we do not learn how they differ or whether they differ according to any systematic basis. When studies are compared as to their significance levels (Cell C) or their effect sizes (Cell D) by focused tests, or contrasts, we learn whether the studies differ significantly among themselves in a theoretically predictable or meaningful way. Thus, important tests of hypotheses can be made by the use of focused tests. Cells E and F of Table 2.9 represent procedures used to estimate overall level of significance and average size of the effect, respectively.

TABLE 2.9. Six Types of Meta-Analytic Procedures

Analytic Process	Results Defined in Terms of:	
	Significance Testing	Effect Size Estimation
Comparing studies: diffuse tests[†]	A	B
Comparing studies: focused tests	C	D
Combining studies	E	F

[†]Applicable for three or more results.

Comparing Studies: Diffuse Tests

Significance Testing. Diffuse tests are employed only when we have three or more p levels to compare. We begin by finding the standard normal deviate, Z, corresponding to each p level. All p levels must be one-tailed, and the corresponding Z's will have the same sign if all studies show effects in the same direction, but different signs if the results are not all in the same direction. The statistical significance of the heterogeneity of the Z's can be obtained from a χ^2 computed as follows:

$$\Sigma(Z_i - \overline{Z})^2 = \chi^2 \quad \text{with} \quad K-1 \, df \tag{3}$$

In this equation Z_j is the Z for any one study, Z is the mean of all the Z_j's obtained, and K is the number of studies being combined.

Example 1. Studies A, B, C, and D yield one-tailed p values of .15, .05, .01, and .001, respectively. Study C, however, shows results opposite in direction from those of studies A, B, and D. From a normal table we find the Z's corresponding to the four p levels to be 1.04, 1.64, 1 −2.33, and 3.09. (Note the negative sign for the Z associated with the result in the opposite direction.) Then, from the preceding equation we have

$$\Sigma(Z_j - \overline{Z})^2 = [(1.04)-(0.86)]^2 + [(1.64)-(0.86)]^2$$

$$+ [(-2.33)-(0.86)]^2 + [(3.09)-(0.86)]^2$$

$$= 15.79$$

as our χ^2 value, which for $K-1 = 4-1 = 3 \, df$ is significant at $p = .0013$. The four p values we compared, then, are clearly significantly heterogeneous.

Effect Size Estimation. Here we want to assess the statistical heterogeneity of three or more effect size estimates. We again restrict our discussion to r as the effect size estimator, though analogous procedures are available for comparing such other effect size estimators as Cohen's d, Hedges' g, or differences between proportions (Rosenthal, 1991a).

For each of the three or more studies to be compared we compute the effect size r, its associated Fisher z, and $N-3$, where N is the number of sampling units on which each r is based. Then the statistical significance of the heterogeneity of the r's can be obtained from a χ^2 computed as follows (Snedecor & Cochran, 1989):

$$\Sigma(N_j-3)(z_j-\bar{z})^2 = \chi^2 \qquad \text{with} \qquad K-1 \qquad (4)$$

In this equation z_j is the Fisher z corresponding to any r, and $\bar{z}$ is the weighted mean z, i.e.,

$$\bar{z} = \frac{\Sigma(N_j-3)z_j}{\Sigma(N_j-3)} \qquad (5)$$

Example 2. Studies A, B, C, and D yield effect sizes of $r = .70$ $(N = 30)$, $r = .45$ $(N = 45)$, $r = .10$ $(N = 20)$, and $r = -.15$ $(N = 25)$, respectively. The Fisher z's corresponding to these r's are found from tables of Fisher z to be .87, .48, .10, and $-.15$, respectively. The weighted mean z is found from the equation just above to be

$$[27(.87)+42(.48)+17(.10)+22(-.15)]/(27+42+17+22) = 42.05/108 = .39$$

Then, from the equation for χ^2 above (equation 4), we have

$$\Sigma(N_j-3)(z_j-\bar{z})^2 = 27(.87-.39)^2 + 42(.48-.39)^2$$

$$+17(.10-.39)^2 + 22(-.15-.39)^2$$

$$= 14.41$$

as our χ^2 value, which for $K - 1 = 3$ df is significant at $p = .0024$. The four effect sizes we compared, then, are clearly significantly heterogeneous.

Comparing Studies: Focused Tests (Contrasts)

Significance Testing. Although we know how to answer the diffuse question of the significance of the differences among a collection of significance levels, we are often able to ask a more focused and more useful question. For example, given a set of p levels for studies of teacher expectancy effects, we might want to know whether results from younger children show greater degrees of statistical significance than do results from older children. (Normally we would have greater scientific interest in focused questions relevant to effect sizes than to significance levels.)

As was the case for diffuse tests, we begin by finding the standard normal deviate, Z, corresponding to each p level. All p levels must be one-tailed, and the corresponding Z's will have the same sign if all studies show effects in the same direction, but different signs if the results are not all in the same direction. The statistical significance of the contrast testing any specific hypothesis about the set of p levels can be obtained from a Z computed as follows:

$$\frac{\Sigma \lambda_j Z_j}{\sqrt{\Sigma \lambda_j^2}} = Z \tag{6}$$

In this equation λ_j is the theoretically derived prediction or contrast weight for any one study, chosen such that the sum of the λ_j's will be zero, and Z_j is the Z for any one study.

Example 3. Studies A, B, C, and D yield one-tailed p values of $1/10^7$, .0001, .21, and .007, respectively, all with results in the same direction. From a normal table we find the Z's corresponding to the four p levels to be 5.20, 3.72, .81, and 2.45. Suppose that studies A, B, C, and D had involved differing amounts of therapist contact such that studies A, B, C, and D had involved 8, 6, 4, and 2 hours of contact per month, respectively. We might, therefore, ask whether there was a linear relationship between number of hours of contact and statistical significance of the result favoring the intervention. The weights of a linear contrast involving four studies are 3, 1, −1, and −3. (These are obtained from a table of orthogonal polynomials, e.g., Rosenthal & Rosnow, 1985; 1991.) Therefore, from the preceding equation we have

$$\frac{\Sigma \lambda_j z_j}{\sqrt{\Sigma \lambda_j^2}} = \frac{(3)5.20 + (1)3.72 + (-1).81 + (-3)2.45}{\sqrt{(3)^2 + (1)^2 + (-1)^2 + (-3)^2}}$$

$$= \frac{11.16}{\sqrt{20}} = 2.50$$

as our Z value, which is significant at $p = .006$, one-tailed. The four p values, then, tend to grow linearly more significant as the number of hours of contact time increases.

Effect Size Estimation. Here we want to ask a more focused question of a set of effect sizes. For example, given a set of effect sizes for studies of therapy intervention, we might want to know whether these effects are increasing or decreasing linearly with the number of hours of contact per month. We again restrict our discussion to r as the effect size estimator, though analogous procedures are available for comparing other effect size estimators (Rosenthal, 1991a).

As was the case for diffuse tests, we begin by computing the effect size r, its associated Fisher z, and $N-3$, where N is the number of sampling units on which each r is based. The statistical significance of the contrast, testing any specific hypothesis about the set of effect sizes, can be obtained from a Z computed as follows:

$$\frac{\Sigma\lambda_j z_j}{\sqrt{\Sigma(\lambda_j^2 / w_j)}} = Z \tag{7}$$

In this equation λ_j is the contrast weight determined from some theory for any one study, chosen such that the sum of the λ_j's will be zero. The z_j is the Fisher z for any one study, and w_j is the inverse of the variance of the effect size for each study. For Fisher z transformations of the effect size r, the variance is $1/(N_j - 3)$, so $w_j = N_j - 3$.

Example 4. Studies A, B, C, and D yield effect sizes of $r = .89, .76, .23,$ and .59, respectively, all with $N = 12$. The Fisher z's corresponding to these r's are found from tables of Fisher z to be 1.42, 1.00, .23, and .68, respectively. Suppose that studies A, B, C, and D had involved differing amounts of therapist contact such that studies A, B, C, and D had involved 8, 6, 4, and 2 hours of contact per month, respectively. We might, therefore, ask whether there was a linear relationship between number of hours of contact and size of effect favoring the intervention. As in example 3, the appropriate weights, or λ's, are 3, 1, −1, and −3. Therefore, from the preceding equation we have

$$\frac{\Sigma\lambda_j z_j}{\sqrt{\Sigma(\lambda_j^2 / w_j)}} = \frac{(3)1.42 + (1)1.00 + (-1).23 + (-3).68}{\sqrt{(3)^2/9 + (1)^2/9 + (-1)^2/9 + (-3)^2/9}}$$

$$= \frac{2.99}{\sqrt{2.222}} = 2.01$$

as our Z value, which is significant at $p = .022$, one-tailed. The four effect sizes, therefore, tend to grow linearly larger as the number of hours of contact time increases. Interpretation of this relationship must be very cautious. After all, studies were not assigned at random to the four conditions of contact hours. It is generally the case that variables moderating the magnitude of effects found should not be interpreted as giving strong evidence for any causal relationships. Moderator relationships can, however, be very valuable in suggesting the possibility of causal relationships, possibilities that can then be studied experimentally or as nearly experimentally as possible.

Before leaving the topic of focused tests it should be noted that their use is more efficient than the more common procedure of counting each effect size or significance level as a single observation. In that procedure we might, for example, compute a correlation between the Fisher z values and the λ's of example 4 to test the hypothesis of greater effect size being associated with greater contact time. Although that r is substantial (.77), it does not even approach significance because of the small number of df upon which the r is based. The procedures employing focused tests, or contrasts, use much more of the information available and, therefore, are less likely to lead to p values that are too high.

Combining Studies

Significance Testing. After comparing the results of any set of studies it is an easy matter also to combine the p levels of the set of studies to get an overall estimate of the probability that the set of p levels might have been obtained if the null hypothesis of no relationship between X and Y were true. Of the various methods available and described elsewhere in detail (Rosenthal, 1991a) we present here only the simplest and most generally useful.

This method requires only that we obtain a one-tailed Z for each of our p levels. Z's disagreeing in direction from the bulk of the findings are given negative signs. Then, the sum of the Z's divided by the square root of the number (K) of studies yields a new statistic distributed as Z. Recapping,

$$\Sigma Z_i / \sqrt{K} = Z \tag{8}$$

Should we want to do so, we could weight each of the Z's by its df, its estimated quality, or any other desired weights so long as they are assigned prior to inspection of the results (Mosteller & Bush, 1954; Rosenthal, 1991a).

Example 5. Studies A, B, C, and D yield one-tailed p values of .15, .05, .01, and .001, respectively. Study C, however, shows results opposite in direction from the results of the remaining studies. The four Z's associated with these four p's, then, are 1.04, 1.64, −2.33, and 3.09. From the preceding equation we have

$$\Sigma Z_j / \sqrt{K} = \frac{(1.04)+(1.64)+(-2.33)+(3.09)}{\sqrt{4}} = 1.72$$

as our new Z value, which has an associated p value of .043 one-tailed, or .086 two-tailed. This combined p supports the results of the majority of the individual studies. However, even if these p values (.043 and .086) were more significant, we would want to be very cautious about drawing any simple overall conclusion because of the very great heterogeneity of the four p values we were combining. Example 1, which employed the same p values, showed that this heterogeneity was significant at $p = .0013$. It should be emphasized, however, that this great heterogeneity of p values could be due to heterogeneity of effect sizes, heterogeneity of sample sizes, or both. To find out about the sources of heterogeneity, we would have to look carefully at the effect sizes and sample sizes of each of the studies involved.

Effect Size Estimation. When we combine the results of several studies, we are as interested in the combined estimate of the effect size as we are in the combined probability. We follow here our earlier procedure of considering r as our effect size estimator while recognizing that many other estimates are possible. For each of the three or more studies to be combined we compute r and the associated Fisher z and have

$$\Sigma z / K = \bar{z} \tag{9}$$

as the Fisher z corresponding to our mean r (where K refers to the number of studies combined). We use a table of Fisher z to find the r associated with our mean z. Should we want to give greater weight to larger studies, we could weight each z by its $df (N - 3)$ (Snedecor & Cochran, 1989), or by any other desired weights.

Example 6. Studies A, B, C, and D yield effect sizes of $r = .70, .45, .10,$ and $-.15$, respectively. The Fisher z values corresponding to these r's are $.87, .48, .10,$ and $-.15$, respectively. Then, from the preceding equation we have

$$\Sigma z_j / K = \frac{(.87)+(.48)+(.10)+(-.15)}{4} = .32$$

as our mean Fisher z. From a table of Fisher z values we find a z of .32 to correspond to an r of .31. Just as in the previous example of combined p levels, however, we would want to be very cautious in our interpretation of this combined effect size. If the r's we have just averaged were based on substantial sample sizes, as was the case in example 2, they would be significantly heterogeneous. Therefore, averaging without special thought and comment would be inappropriate.

Comparing and Combining Results That Are Not Independent

In all the meta-analytic procedures we have discussed so far it has been assumed that the studies being compared or combined were separate, independent studies. That is, we have assumed that different subjects (or other sampling units) were found in the studies being compared or summarized. Sometimes, however, the same subjects (or other sampling units) contribute data to two or more studies or to two or more dependent variables within the same study. In such cases the results of the two or more studies or the results based on two or more dependent variables are not independent, and the meta-analytic procedures we have described so far cannot be applied without adjustment.

Two common methods for summarizing the results of a single study with multiple effect sizes have been simply to compute the mean and/or median of the effect sizes. Both of these procedures are quite conservative in practice, however. More accurate and more useful procedures for comparing and combining nonindependent results have been described elsewhere by Strube (1985) for the case of significance levels and by Rosenthal and Rubin (1986) for the case of effect sizes.

CONCLUSION

Our purpose has been to raise some questions and some sensibilities about research methodology. We have dealt with a number of issues and ideas: issues of causal inference, of measurement in the sense of bias and precision, of the reliability of psychological measurement. We have also emphasized the relationship between effect size estimates and significance testing with special emphasis on the interpretation of effect sizes. Finally, we tried to make a brief case for the routine employment of contrasts in our analyses of our data. Our brief chapter could cover no topic in sufficient detail, but the hope is that readers will be stimulated to want to learn more details in the suggested readings that follow.

Notes

Development of some of the ideas presented here benefited from the support of the Spencer Foundation; the content of the chapter is solely the responsibility of the author.

[1]One important issue that could not be addressed was the problem of artifacts in behavioral research, especially the artifacts deriving from the social nature of behavioral research including such issues as suspiciousness of experimenter intent (McGuire, 1969), pretest sensitization (Lana, 1969), demand characteristics (Orne, 1969), evaluation apprehension (Rosenberg, 1969), the volunteer subject (Rosenthal & Rosnow, 1975), the effects of the experimenter's expectations (Rosenthal, 1966, 1976), and others (Rosenthal & Rosnow, 1969).

Another issue that could not be addressed was that of ethical issues in behavioral research including, specifically, the role of deception and some newer views of cost-benefit analyses (Rosenthal, 1994; Rosenthal & Blanck, 1993; Rosenthal & Rosnow, 1991).

[2]Some of you are familiar with some very fancy formats—path analysis, or structural equation modeling; in particular some of the software developed by very talented people like Jöreskog (1973). These are sophisticated procedures that are best thought of as exploratory. They are in the spirit of John Tukey's (1977) exploratory data analysis. And if we think of complex structural equation modeling, or even simpler path analyses as exploratory, as being suggestive rather than as nailing things down, then probably we will not get into a lot of trouble. If we think of these procedures as giving us royal access to truth about causal effects, we are likely to be misled.

[3]An example that surprises many psychologists is that a test made up of 100 items, each of which correlates zero with the other 99 items (zero reliability), can show a correlation of 1.00 with a criterion variable (perfect validity) if each item shows a correlation with the criterion of $r = .10$ (Guilford, 1954, p. 407).

References

AMBADY, N., & ROSENTHAL, R. (1992). Thin slices of expressive behavior as predictors of interpersonal consequences: A meta-analysis. *Psychological Bulletin, 111,* 256–274.

CAMPBELL, D. T. (1963). From description to experimentation: Interpreting trends as quasi-experiments. In C. W. Harris (Ed.), *Problems in measuring change.* Madison: University of Wisconsin Press.

COHEN, J. (1969). *Statistical power analysis for the behavioral sciences.* New York: Academic Press.

COHEN, J. (1988). *Statistical power analysis for the behavioral sciences* (2nd ed.). Hillsdale, NJ: Erlbaum.

COLLINS, H. M. (1985). *Changing order: Replication and induction in scientific practice.* Beverly Hills, CA: Sage.

COOPER, H. M. (1989). *Integrating research: A guide for literature reviews* (2nd ed.). Newbury Park, CA: Sage.

FISHER, R. A. (1938). *Statistical methods for research workers* (7th ed.). London: Oliver & Boyd.

GLASS, G. V, McGAW, B., & SMITH, M. L. (1981). *Meta-analysis in social research.* Beverly Hills, CA: Sage.

GUILFORD, J. P. (1954). *Psychometric methods* (2nd ed.). New York: McGraw-Hill.

HEDGES, L. V. (1981). Distribution theory for Glass's estimator of effect size and related estimators. *Journal of Educational Statistics, 6,* 107–128.

HEDGES, L. V. (1987). How hard is hard science, how soft is soft science? *American Psychologist, 42,* 443–455.

HEDGES, L. V., & OLKIN, I. (1985). *Statistical methods for meta-analysis.* New York: Academic Press.

HUNTER, J. E., & SCHMIDT, F. L. (1990). *Methods of meta-analysis: Correcting error and bias in research findings.* Newbury Park, CA: Sage.

JÖRESKOG, K. G. (1973). A general method for estimating a linear structural equation system. In A. S. Goldberger & O. D. Duncan (Eds.), *Structural equation models in the social sciences* (pp. 85–112). New York: Seminar Press.

KENNY, D. A. (1979). *Correlation and causality.* New York: Wiley.

LANA, R. E. (1969). Pretest sensitization. In R. Rosenthal & R. L. Rosnow (Eds.), *Artifact in behavioral research* (pp. 119–141). New York: Academic Press.

LAZARSFELD, P. F. (1978). Some episodes in the history of panel analysis. In D. B. Kandel (Ed.), *Longitudinal research for drug abuse.* New York: Hemisphere Press.

LIGHT, R. J., & PILLEMER, D. B. (1984). *Summing up: The science of reviewing research.* Cambridge, MA: Harvard University Press.

McGUIRE, W. J. (1969). Suspiciousness of experimenter's intent. In R. Rosenthal & R. L. Rosnow (Eds.), *Artifact in behavioral research* (pp. 13–57). New York: Academic Press.

MOSTELLER, F. M., & BUSH, R. R. (1954). Selected quantitative techniques. In G. Lindzey (Ed.), *Handbook of social psychology. Volume 1: Theory and method* (pp. 289–334). Cambridge, MA: Addison-Wesley.

ORNE, M. T. (1969). Demand characteristics and the concept of quasi-controls. In R. Rosenthal & R. L. Rosnow (Eds.), *Artifact in behavioral research* (pp. 143–179). New York: Academic Press.

ROSENBERG, M. J. (1969). The conditions and consequences of evaluation apprehension. In R. Rosenthal & R. L. Rosnow (Eds.), *Artifact in behavioral research* (pp. 279–349). New York: Academic Press.

ROSENTHAL, R. (1966). *Experimenter effects in behavioral research.* New York: Appleton-Century-Crofts. (Enlarged edition, Irvington, 1976.)

ROSENTHAL, R. (1985). Designing, analyzing, interpreting and summarizing placebo studies. In L. White, B. Tursky, & G. E. Schwartz (Eds.), *Placebo: Theory, research, and mechanisms* (pp. 110–136). New York: Guilford Press.

ROSENTHAL, R. (1987). *Judgment studies: Design, analysis, and meta-analysis.* Cambridge, Eng.: Cambridge University Press.

ROSENTHAL, R. (1991a). *Meta-analytic procedures for social research* (rev. ed.). Newbury Park, CA: Sage.

ROSENTHAL, R. (1991b). Teacher expectancy effects: A brief update 25 years after the Pygmalion experiment. *Journal of Research in Education, 1,* 3–12.

ROSENTHAL, R. (1994). Science and ethics in conducting, analyzing, and reporting psychological research. *Psychological Science, 5,* 127–134.

ROSENTHAL, R., & BLANCK, P. D. (1993). Science and ethics in conducting, analyzing, and reporting social science research: Implications for social scientists, judges, and lawyers. *Indiana Law Journal, 68,* 1209–1228.

ROSENTHAL, R., & JACOBSON, L. (1968). *Pygmalion in the classroom.* New York: Holt.

ROSENTHAL, R., & JACOBSON, L. (1992). *Pygmalion in the classroom* (expanded ed.). New York: Irvington.

ROSENTHAL, R., & ROSNOW, R. L. (1969), *Artifact in behavioral research.* New York: Academic Press.

ROSENTHAL, R., & ROSNOW, R. L. (1975). *The volunteer subject.* New York: Wiley-Interscience.

ROSENTHAL, R., & ROSNOW, R. L. (1985). *Contrast analysis: Focused comparisons in the analysis of variance.* New York: Cambridge University Press.

ROSENTHAL, R., & ROSNOW, R. L. (1991). *Essentials of behavioral research: Methods and data analysis* (2nd ed.). New York: McGraw-Hill.

ROSENTHAL, R., & RUBIN, D. B. (1982). A simple, general purpose display of magnitude of experimental effect. *Journal of Educational Psychology, 74,* 166–169.

ROSENTHAL, R., & RUBIN, D. B. (1986). Meta-analytic procedures for combining studies with multiple effect sizes. *Psychological Bulletin, 99,* 400–406.

SMITH, M. L., GLASS, G. V, & MILLER, T. I. (1980). *The benefits of psychotherapy.* Baltimore: Johns Hopkins University Press.

SNEDECOR, G. W., & COCHRAN, W. G. (1989). *Statistical methods* (8th ed.). Ames: Iowa State University Press.

STEERING COMMITTEE OF THE PHYSICIANS HEALTH STUDY RESEARCH GROUP (1988). Preliminary report: Findings from the aspirin component of the ongoing physicians' health study. *The New England Journal of Medicine, 318,* 262–264.

STRUBE, M. J. (1985). Combining and comparing significance levels from nonindependent hypothesis tests. *Psychological Bulletin, 97,* 334–341.

TUKEY, J. W. (1977). *Exploratory data analysis.* Reading, MA: Addison-Wesley.

Further Readings

ROSENTHAL, R. (1987). *Judgment studies: Design, analysis, and meta-analysis.* Cambridge, Eng.: Cambridge University Press.

Summarizes issues in the design, analysis, and meta-analysis of studies involving judges' ratings of any type of stimulus object.

ROSENTHAL, R. (1991). *Meta-analytic procedures for social research* (rev. ed.). Newbury Park, CA: Sage.

Basic textbook on meta-analytic procedures.

ROSENTHAL, R., & ROSNOW, R. L. (1985). *Contrast analysis: Focused comparisons in the analysis of variance.* New York: Cambridge University Press.

Brief, fairly comprehensive introduction to the logic and computations of contrasts in behavioral research.

ROSENTHAL, R., & ROSNOW, R. L. (1991). *Essentials of behavioral research: Methods and data analysis* (2nd ed.). New York: McGraw-Hill.

Overview of issues in the design and analysis of studies in the social and behavioral sciences.

Roy F. Baumeister is the E. B. Smith Professor in the Liberal Arts at Case Western Reserve University. He received his Ph.D. in social psychology from Princeton in 1978. His fundamental interest is in the human condition, and several of his books have attempted to address basic philosophical questions using social science methods. He also does mainstream experimental research in social psychology on topics that include the self, performance under pressure, the interpersonal nature of motivation and emotion, and defense mechanisms. His books include Meanings of Life *(1991),* Escaping the Self *(1991),* Breaking Hearts *(1992),* Self-Esteem *(1993), and* Losing Control *(1995). He lives on the shores of the Great Lakes with his beloved wife, his two dogs, three computers, and his well-worn windsurfer.*

CHAPTER 3

Self and Identity: An Introduction

Roy F. Baumeister
Case Western Reserve University

CHAPTER OUTLINE

Self is the great Anti-Christ and Anti-God in the World.
                    —*Oxford English Dictionary*, 1680 (sample usage)

Respect to self and its ultimate good pertains to the very nobility of man's nature.
                    —*Oxford English Dictionary*, 1870 (sample usage)

The nature of self and identity is one of the great enduring questions in the study of human beings. It has exerted a continuing fascination on both the lay public and professional social scientists. Social psychology, in particular, has kept returning to the study of the self with new and different approaches, methods, assumptions, and theories. This chapter will offer a survey of social psychology's contribution to the study of the self.

Because *the self* is used as a familiar term to describe a research area, and because unity is part of the essential nature of selfhood, people expect research on the self to fit together into a coherent whole. In fact, however, the diversity of approaches, methods, and ideas is linked to a multiplicity of topics and issues, and so there is no coherent psychology of self. This chapter will survey a loose amalgam of research findings rather than a tightly integrated body of work. That loose diversity has probably been a key reason for the continued vitality of the study of the self, but it also increases the room for subjective bias as to what to include. Undoubtedly another researcher would differ somewhat as to which topics to include, which to emphasize, and which to downplay. A further complication is that the research community's focus of interest shifts to different topics. A decade ago, self-schema structure and self-presentation would undoubtedly have been listed among the hottest topics of study in the area of self research, but now both of those fields have diminished in frequency of new findings, while the topics of self-deception and self-regulation are attracting much more attention now than a decade ago.

Definitions

Everyone knows what the self is, and probably everyone uses the term *self* (at least as a part word) many times every day. Yet it is surprisingly difficult to define. The difficulties are compounded by common tendencies to use *self* to refer to the *self-concept*. Thus, for example, some people define the self as a cognitive structure, but how can a cognitive structure initiate action or own things? Meanwhile, people in many other cultures, and most children in our own culture, use the term *self* in a predominantly physical manner, to refer to the body.

A full understanding of the nature of self must encompass several things. First, it includes the body. Second, it includes the social identity, which can be understood as a cluster of meaningful definitions that become attached to the body, including a name, social roles, membership in various groups, and various other attributes. (Baumeister, 1986a, defined identity as composed of interpersonal roles and traits, a particular conception of potentiality, and a structure of values and priorities.) Third, self is the active agent involved in making decisions.

Some theorists have been influenced by this multiplicity of aspects of the self to begin speaking as if each person had multiple selves. This, however, is misleading and leads to severe conceptual confusion. It is undoubtedly true, as Markus and Nurius (1986) and others have argued, that one person can conceptualize himself or herself in many possible future roles and circumstances and thus even as having different attributes. Still, it is important to realize that it is essentially the same self in all of those. To imagine yourself being a dentist is different than imagining someone else as being a dentist. These multiple versions of self are all, in the final analysis, referring to the same self. Unity and continuity (despite possible change) are thus essential to the definition of self.

The multiplicity of self-conceptions is theoretically important, however. Markus and Nurius have argued that people are guided and influenced by these various conceptions of how they might possibly become. They are disturbed and are motivated to diet by the imagination of the overweight, unloved self, just as they may be inspired, elated, and galvanized by the thought of the professionally successful, rich, and famous self. Ogilvie (1987) has proposed that people have an "undesired self" that forms a powerful source of motivation, as people try to avoid turning into this undesired self or developing these disliked aspects of self. In fact, happiness in life may depend more on the undesired self than on the ideal self. When Ogilvie measured the distance between real (i.e., perceived) self and ideal self, and between real and undesired self, the real-undesired discrepancy had the stronger correlation with life satisfaction.

Higgins (1987) has suggested that people have various *self-guides* consisting of how they ideally would like to be and how they think they ought to be, according to either their own or other people's standards and expectations. Furthermore, Higgins says that many emotions arise from comparing oneself to these self-guides. If you think you are falling short of your *ought-self* (i.e., the way you think you ought to be), you will tend to feel unpleasant, high-arousal emotions such as guilt, anxiety, and anger. On the other hand, if you think you are falling short of your *ideal-self* (i.e., the way you would ideally like to be), you will tend to experience unpleasant but low-arousal emotions such as sadness, depression, and disappointment.

The notion that people are motivated to reach their ideals and become the person they have envisioned has been proposed by a broad variety of personality theorists. In social psychology, the most extensive empirical work on it has been contributed by Wicklund and Gollwitzer (1982), using the term *self-completion*. In a series of studies, they have shown that people who are made to feel "incomplete" (i.e., made to believe that they are not reaching their ideals) will engage in a variety of strategies to acquire symbols and engage in symbolic activities that will support their claim to the desired identity. Thus, if someone wants to be an accomplished guitarist but then experiences something that makes him feel he is not reaching this goal, he is more likely than others to say he would want to be active as a guitar teacher or to dress like a guitarist.

Functions of Selfhood

To put the individual findings about the self in perspective, it is useful to keep in mind the functions that the self serves. A first function is that the self is an interpersonal tool (see Baumeister, 1986; Baumeister & Tice, 1990; Sullivan, 1953). Having some kind of identity is a prerequisite for social life and human interaction. Thus, to carry on a conversation requires some understanding of "you" and "I," and to sustain a relationship over time requires that the identities of the people involved will remain stable over time (otherwise it would be no different from a series of brief interactions with strangers). Moreover, people shape their selves so as to attract and maintain relationships they want. People try to be attractive, competent, honest and trustworthy, intelligent, friendly, witty, and so forth—all traits that will support interpersonal relationships. People are strongly and fundamentally concerned with how their selves are perceived by other people, and this concern may well be rooted in the need to form and maintain interpersonal ties.

A second function is to make choices. Having a well-defined self helps the person to make the many large and small decisions that fill everyday life, and to make them in a systematic, consistent, and organized fashion. The self typically comes to have a collection of values, preferences, and priorities that can be invoked whenever necessary to make a decision. The ideal-self, the ought-self, and other goals of selfhood are also extremely useful in structuring the person's choices across time, because they enable small, daily decisions to be understood in the context of progress toward one's goals. A small decision about whether to spend an afternoon reading a book or playing tennis, for example, might be seen as fairly inconsequential on its own terms, but if placed in the context of a long-term goal to become a writer or athlete, that decision takes on additional meaning that enables the person to decide which will be more helpful.

Interacting with others and making decisions are probably the two most important functions of selfhood, but it is also necessary to point out that the self needs to devote part of its time and energy to managing itself. The self, after all, is a diverse and complex entity and has to be kept in some sort of order. Moreover, any given individual is likely to have a broad assortment of values and preferences, some of which may come into conflict at any given time. (Thus, the person may desire to play tennis while also thinking that reading the book will be more useful in the long run, and so it is necessary to decide between two of the self's own impulses.) *Self-regulation* thus becomes an important function of the self. One has to take care of one's own body and its functions; one must manage one's interpersonal relationships; one must keep one's work activities in order; and so forth. Information relevant to these potential tasks must be organized in order that one may draw on this information in the future as necessary. Emotional states must be kept from going out of control in ways that will impair one's relationships or task performances, and indeed managing emotion may be desirable as an end in itself in order that one will feel good. During task performance, people must sometimes struggle to maintain concentration and persistence rather than, say, yielding to an impulse to take a nap. Thus, managing the self is another behind-the-scenes function of the self.

Given all these functions, the self becomes a vitally important entity for the storing and organizing of information. To fulfill all its functions effectively, the self has to process and have access to an immense amount of information, and not surprisingly many researchers have been fascinated simply by the cognitive structure of self-knowledge. The role of self in information processing has been well documented in what has become known as the *self-reference effect* (Rogers, Kuiper, & Kirker, 1977; see also Markus, 1977). This effect entails simply that information that has any bearing on the self will be processed more thoroughly and remembered better than otherwise similar information that lacks reference to the self. In one study, Rogers and associates asked subjects to make one of several judgments about a stimulus word. If they were asked to judge whether the word described them, they remembered it better (even if their answer was "no"!) than if they had made any other judgment. Simply thinking about things in relation to the self apparently left a stronger memory trace than thinking about the same things in another context.

Culture, History, and the Self

The self begins with the body, and people everywhere have bodies, but beyond that basic fact selves begin to vary. Identity is very much a product of culture and society. The self will therefore have a different nature as a function of the social context in which it evolves.

Social psychologists are slowly beginning to find ways to understand how culture shapes the self. Triandis (1989) developed several of the key concepts. First, he distinguished between public, private, and collective aspects of self. The private self is, obviously, how the person understands himself or herself, including introspection, private decision making, self-esteem, and self-perception. The public self refers to how one is perceived (as an individual) by other people, and it includes one's reputation, impressions made on specific others, and so on. Lastly, the collective self refers to one's memberships in social groups, such as ethnic identity and family ties.

Next, Triandis explained how cultures vary in the emphasis they place on these different aspects of the self. *Collectivistic* societies raise children to conform to the group, as opposed to individualistic societies that support diversity and self-expression. As a result, collectivistic societies emphasize the public and collective aspects of self at the expense of the private self, whereas individualistic societies emphasize the private self. By the same token, *"tight"* societies— in which there are strong demands that people conform to in-group norms, role definitions, and values—tend to produce people with well-developed public and collective selves but less attention to the private self. In highly *complex* cultures, people can belong to many different groups, and so there is less pressure to stay on good terms with any one of them. For that reason, the collective self may be weaker, but the public self is quite important (because it is something one carries through all one's relationships and interactions), and people can afford to focus on their private selves too. Empirical research suggests, however, that complex cultures apparently foster identity problems and confusion. Thus, for example, Katakis (1976, 1978, 1984) showed that children growing up in fishing villages said quite clearly that when they grew up, they would be fishermen, whereas children growing up in large cities responded to questions about their future identities by saying things like "I will find myself."

To illustrate some of these differences, Triandis (1989) suggested several comparisons between American and Japanese societies. Japan is much tighter than the United States, resulting in much greater pressures to conform to group norms extending even to things like clothing and food preferences. Although the public self matters in both societies, Japanese society also emphasizes the collective self, whereas the private self is much more important in the United States. The cultural differences extend to relations among the three aspects of self. Thus, Americans place a premium on sincerity, which entails congruency between public and private selves. In Japan, on the other hand, the important thing is to behave properly, regardless of what one privately thinks (see also Doi, 1986). Triandis cited research by Iwao (1988), who asked Japanese and American citizens to evaluate various possible responses to hypothetical scenarios. For example, the subject was supposed to imagine having his or her daughter bring home someone from a different race, and one of the possible responses was to privately think that one would never allow the marriage but to tell the daughter and the young man that one was in favor of their marriage. Fully half the American subjects said that this was the worst of all the possible responses, and only 2 percent of them said it was the best response, but the Japanese subjects saw the matter quite differently. In fact, 44 percent of the Japanese subjects said that that was the best possible response.

Markus and Kitayama (1991) focused on one dimension of cultural variation in selfhood, namely, interdependence versus independence. They noted that American and Western European views of selfhood have emphasized autonomy and separateness, whereas Japanese and other Asian and African cultures have understood the self as fundamentally and essentially interconnected with other people and interdependent with them. Markus and Kitayama illustrated the difference by quoting contrasting proverbs. In America, "the squeaky wheel gets the grease" is repeated to indicate the value of asserting oneself individually, whereas Japanese say "the nail that stands out gets pounded down" to emphasize the desirability of blending in with the group.

Social psychology has been dominated by the Western view of the self as an independent structure, and it is helpful to realize that people from other cultures may not share the assumptions that underlie the research conducted and published in American journals. Furthermore, the impact of self-knowledge and the related motivations on behavior may be quite different in cultures for whom the self is seen as blending in with others and defined and fulfilled through interpersonal relationships, as compared to the Western view of self as standing alone.

The cultural relativity of selfhood can also be seen in the historical changes of selfhood within our own culture. Although these have been extensive and complex (see Baumeister, 1986a, 1987), some main themes can be summarized briefly. First, the identity part of the self has become increasingly elaborate over the past several centuries. Whereas our ancestors defined themselves in simple, constant terms, people today have many more facets and aspects to their identities and change these more often. Second, the self has become a much more frequent source of problem, conflict, and uncertainty than it once was. Identity crisis, a need to find oneself, an uncertainty about who one is—such problems of selfhood were largely unknown in the Middle Ages but are a familiar part of modern discourse about self. As we have increased the importance and complexity of the self, as well as raising the pressures on the individual self, we have generated an increasing rate of problems in defining and maintaining the self.

Part of the reason for the increase in problems of the self is that modern selves are based much more on changing, unstable matters than were the identities of our ancestors. Consider, for example, a stereotypical medieval life. The identity was defined by one's extended family and their social position (i.e., social class), which did not change during life. In many cases one spent one's entire life living in the same place and not traveling very much. Marriage was often arranged by the parents and family and was usually maintained until death, because divorce was impossible and premarital romance was minimized. Most people were farmers, and the rest were usually well set in their career path before they became teenagers. Thus, for these people, identity was firmly grounded in unchanging features. In contrast, the modern individual is not seriously constrained by the extended family, is free to choose relationships and jobs according to inclination, and can abandon them at will if they become unsatisfactory. Hardly anyone remains in the same locale for an entire life, it seems, and even those who stay put find that their neighbors and friends keep changing. It is possible to rise to wealth, status, and power from obscurity, and it is also possible to sink into poverty.

Thus, because the modern self is not tied to unchangeable attributes, it is constantly subject to renegotiation. People must create and define who they are, rather than having this all done for them (or done to them, depending on one's point of view) by society. Centuries ago, for example, one's worth as a person was a direct consequence of one's social class and rank and was thus a fixed quantity, subject only to small variations based on moral behavior and martial valor. In modern America, however, we have rejected the notion that some people are innately superior to others, and that presumption of equality means that each person is required to negotiate and prove his or her worth over and over.

A particularly important change in the conception of selfhood is the expansion of the conception of an inner self (Baumeister, 1986a, 1987). Our ancestors did not have much of a notion of an inner or hidden self beyond the metaphysical concept of a soul. Starting around Shakespeare's time, however, people began to think increasingly in terms of an inner self that might differ in important ways from the surface impression and overt behavior (see Trilling, 1971). Initially the inner-outer distinction focused on issues like honesty, deception, hypocrisy, and sincerity, but over time the notion of inner self was expanded to encompass a broad variety of things, including the basis for creativity, "true" personality traits (i.e., not the ones displayed in behavior and interpersonal relations), the basis for personal values and moral choices, a personal destiny or mission, and more. Modern conceptions of the self—both in psychological theories and in the assumptions of the average person—are built on the postulate of an inner self and an outer self, but the nature of this postulate is historically relative. In examining psychological theories it is useful to keep in mind that the distinction between inner and outer selves is, in the final analysis, a metaphor constructed and shaped by our culture (see also Markus & Kitayama, 1991; Triandis, 1989).

A full understanding of the modern obsession with selfhood requires at least one more perspective, however. In a recent effort to understand how people find meaning in life (Baumeister, 1991b), I came to the conclusion that the most acute problem of meaning in modern life concerns value; that is, people in modern society find it difficult to find firm, unshakable, seemingly objective bases for making moral decisions and justifying their actions (see also Bellah, Madsen, Sullivan, Swidler, & Tipton, 1985). This value gap has prompted society to experiment with an assortment of new values over the last couple centuries, including the work ethic, the family, and motherhood. One of the most powerful new values, however, is the individual self. Instead of regarding the self as the enemy of virtue and value, modern individuals focus on the self's entitlements. People consider it a right and even a duty to try to know themselves, to cultivate their true inner natures, to accept and express themselves, and so forth. Obligations toward others have gradually receded into a secondary position such that obligations to the self take priority. Thus, for example, if a marriage is seen as stifling one's growth and self-expression, our grandparents would probably have assumed that the marriage should take priority, but today many people would think that the self should take priority (Zube, 1972). The modern fascination with the self goes beyond the mere difficulty of self-knowledge; people rely increasingly on the self to give meaning and value to life. Hence its sudden importance.

SELF-KNOWLEDGE

Conceptions of Self

It is clear that people have a great deal of knowledge, or perhaps more accurately *beliefs* (not implying correctness), about themselves. This large amount of information would of course amount to chaos if not stored in some systematic, organized fashion. Social psychologists have been interested in both the various particular beliefs about the self, called *self-schemas,* and the total organized body of information that any given person has about himself or herself (called the *self-concept*). Thus, the self-concept consists of a large number of self-schemas, organized or integrated in some coherent, usable fashion.

For decades psychologists often found it useful to refer to "the self-concept," because responses to so many events depended on how people thought about themselves and on what implications those events had regarding the self. When researchers began collecting thorough and detailed information about self-conceptions, however, the notion of a single "self-concept" began to seem inadequate. People have a great deal of information about themselves, and they keep track of this information in some organized fashion, but the result is more similar to a loose network than a single conception. Accordingly, over the last 15 years there has been a growing tendency for psychologists to discuss particular self-schemas instead of referring to the overall self-concept.

It is important not to overstate the degree of organization in the self-concept. True, it is necessary to have some organization to deal with such a large mass of information, but this does not have to be perfect. It is possible, for example, for people to hold somewhat contradictory beliefs about themselves. Inconsistencies can cause problems, and there is some effort to resolve these contradictions when they are discovered, but many inconsistencies may exist in a given self-concept for a long time without being discovered.

Thus, if we begin to probe someone's self-knowledge, we are more likely to find a great deal of loosely interrelated information than to find a single, unified, articulated self-concept. Roles, traits, values, relationships, and past experiences may all be mixed together into a large mass of information without being fully blended or integrated. Suppose, for example, that Mary tells us that she is friendly and optimistic, an obedient daughter, a tax accountant, a former high school tennis champion, a mother of two, a lapsed Catholic, a good wife except for occasional episodes of hostility, sometimes cynical but mostly idealistic, a graduate of Duke University, an extravert, prone to ear infection, moderate in self-esteem, a believer in racial equality, a romantic, and a brunette. She has given us a large mass of information about herself, yet certainly this information does not exhaust her stock of self-knowledge, nor does all this information fit together in any obvious way into what might be called a single concept (i.e., a unified and coherent structure). Beyond the fact that all those attributes pertain to Mary, many of them seem to have little or no relation to each other. Many researchers have therefore given up trying to understand people in terms of having "a" self-concept and chosen to focus instead on all the individual self-schemas that people have. The notion of a self-concept is now understood much more as a loosely organized collection of self-schemas instead of as a single concept.

Because people have so much information about themselves, it is impossible to think of it all at once. Only a small part of the entire self-concept can be present in awareness at any one time. This part is called the *phenomenal self* (Jones & Gerard, 1967), the *spontaneous self-concept* (McGuire, McGuire, Child, & Fujioka, 1978; McGuire, McGuire, & Winton, 1979), or the *working self-concept* (Markus & Kunda, 1986). It is sometimes helpful to think of conscious attention as a spotlight that can move around the large structure of the self-concept, illuminating various parts of it one after the other. The phenomenal self is the illuminated part. Thus, when people reflect on their self-concepts, they actually bring only a small part of the self-concept to mind. Even the parts of the self-concept that seem to be global because they pull together many specific, small bits of information are themselves only bits of information. For example, one may reflect on one's global self-esteem without bringing to mind all the particular virtues, abilities, and successes on which that self-esteem is based.

The operation of the phenomenal self may help prevent certain inconsistencies in self-knowledge from being discovered. Only certain parts of the large stock of self-knowledge are loaded into awareness at any given time, and these parts might be internally consistent without being consistent with each other. For example, Roger might act one way with his colleagues at work, a different way with his wife and children, and yet a different way with his drinking buddies, without ever really concluding that he is inconsistent, simply because he never compares these different views of himself.

Where does the self-concept come from? Our culture likes to imagine that there is a true inner self with definite, stable traits and qualities that one can gradually discover and learn. This true inner self is almost certainly a myth, however. (By *myth*, I mean an appealing idea with heuristic or didactic value but, in the final analysis, a falsehood.) The self, after all, can change rapidly or gradually; behavior is often a response to situational pressures rather than an expression of fixed inner traits; traits are only crude generalizations about behavior; and a great deal of self-knowledge is acquired socially, through interactions with other people. The only approach to something like a true inner self that currently seems viable is the one pursued by Deci and Ryan (1987; Ryan, 1991), in which patterns of thought, feeling, and action that grow and flourish independently of external pressures are seen as reflecting a kind of true inner self. Autonomy, growth, and intrinsic motivation may well offer a new and useful basis for conceptualizing a true inner nature of selfhood, but the old basis—a kind of predetermined identity—must first be discarded.

The importance of other people's reflected appraisals was made dramatically in a study by Rosenberg (1979). He asked children of various ages a series of questions about themselves. These included the question, "Who knows best what kind of person you really are, deep down inside?" Even up to age 11, over half the children said that their parents knew them better than they knew themselves.

Symbolic interactionists (e.g., Mead, 1934) took to extremes the argument that self-knowledge is gleaned from the reflected appraisals of others. In their view, the self-concept was heavily or even entirely based on such communications; to put it simply, you are whatever other people tell you you are. This view gradually became one of the most influential theories in the social sciences and shaped a great deal of research. In 1979, Shrauger and Schoeneman published a work that sought to sum up all the evidence pertaining to the symbolic interactionist views of self-knowledge. At first glance, their conclusion seemed to strike a severe blow to symbolic interactionist theory. They found that the correlations between self-appraisals and others' appraisals were generally quite weak. That is, people's self-conceptions agree only very slightly with how others perceive them. If self-knowledge were based entirely on how one is perceived by others, the correlations should have been strong and clear, but they were not.

Shrauger and Schoeneman's further findings were, however, supportive of some symbolic interactionist assertions, at least in a revised form. Shrauger and Schoeneman found that people's self-appraisals did have fairly strong correlations with their *perceptions* of how others appraised them. The big inconsistency is not between self-knowledge and feedback received by others; instead, the problem is apparently an inconsistency between the feedback one receives from others and what those others actually believe to be true. Thus, Ann's self-concept may not agree with what Harry thinks of her, but her self-conception is similar to what she *believes* Harry thinks of her. Social interaction and communication does therefore seem to play a potentially important role in shaping self-concepts. The problem is simply that such communication is not terribly accurate. In short, although a great deal of self-knowledge may indeed be gained from other people, that information is heavily filtered and biased by the time the individual is ready to incorporate it into his or her self-concept. This brings up the issue of the accuracy of self-knowledge.

Accuracy of Self-Knowledge

Do people have accurate knowledge of themselves? Most adults believe strongly that they know more about themselves than anyone else possibly could. A major reason for this advantage is what is often called *privileged access*—that is, the notion that people can know things directly about their inner states that others can only gain indirect knowledge about. People also have an epistemological advantage over others because of memory; that is, memory allows one to draw on a great deal more information about the self than is available to other people. No one remembers as much about your life as you do.

But quantity and accuracy are not the same thing. In the previous section, I suggested that although people do rely on feedback from others to learn about themselves, they also filter and distort this information in various ways. One may have more information about oneself than anyone else has, but one also has more reason to distort and bias this information than anyone else has. After all, if you are inept at mathematics, or insensitive, or prone to fall apart under pressure, most people in the world will not be affected at all, and among those who might be affected, it will be most helpful for them to know these things about you. You, on the other hand, may experience anxiety and fear and loss of self-esteem if you accept these facts. You are thus the person with the most reason to refuse to see these facts.

When the sixteenth-century essayist Montaigne wrote his autobiography, he included a preface to justify his work, because it had long been considered sinfully egotistical to want to write about oneself. His justification was that, although his topic might not be as important as the topics chosen by other authors, he at least could claim that he knew his topic better than any other author, because he was writing about himself. The underlying assumption was that self-knowledge is the most complete and perfect form of knowledge avail-

able. Today, however, such a claim would sound ludicrous, because we have become accustomed to thinking of self-knowledge as biased and distorted.
Indeed, earlier in this century the viewpoint of psychoanalysis was widely influential, and psychoanalysis was perhaps the all-time low point in the epistemological status of self-knowledge. According to the psychoanalysts, people
could only learn to know themselves after spending thousands of dollars and
countless hours with a trained specialist, and even then they could only claim
to have made progress rather than to have attained a full self-understanding.

Thus, the epistemological advantage that the self enjoys is at least partly
nullified by the biasing tendencies arising from one's desire to think well of
oneself. For this reason, the accuracy of self-knowledge is very much an open
question. It is one that has preoccupied social psychologists for years. At the
center of it is the issue of self-deception: Do people fool themselves into believing that they are different, and in particular better, than they are?

A first contribution by social psychology was to challenge the notion of
privileged access and, indeed, to suggest that introspection is not nearly as effective as people may think. Nisbett and Wilson (1977) proposed that people do
not have access to their own mental processes; they may consciously know their
feelings and conclusions, but they are often unable to know how those
emerged. Moreover, people believe they do know, and so they will give explanations and accounts that may be seriously inaccurate. Nisbett and Wilson's experiments showed clear effects of causal factors that were completely missing
from people's introspective accounts. In one study, for example, preferences
among nylon stockings showed a strong serial position effect, but people's explanations for their preferences never mentioned serial position. Nisbett and
Wilson concluded that when people explain why they did something, they
often simply resort to standard theories about why people do things and use
those theories in place of genuine introspection—because genuine introspection is severely limited in its capacity.

Several subsequent papers have argued that Nisbett and Wilson's work
should not be interpreted to mean that introspection is never accurate (Sabini &
Silver, 1981; Smith & Miller, 1978). People are able to know their own subjective
states and to recognize the influence of some factors. Still, it is clear that there
are many operations within one's mind that one is not able to know. And people are often unaware of their lack of self-knowledge. Since people do not realize how much they do not know, they tend to fill in the blanks (so to speak)
without realizing that that is what they are doing. The result is a false sem-
blance of introspection. You may ask someone why she did something, and she
may give you a sincere but completely wrong answer.

In fact, such efforts at introspection can even be counterproductive, leading
one away from the truth. Wilson, Dunn, Bybee, Hyman, and Rotondo (1984)
asked half a sample of dating couples to analyze why their relationship was
going as it was. Control subjects performed an irrelevant filler task, and then all
subjects were asked to rate their overall satisfaction with the relationship. Eight
months later, the couples were contacted to see whether they were still going together or not. Among control subjects, there was a significant correlation be-

tween their satisfaction ratings and their subsequent tendency to break up or stay together: The more satisfied they were, the more likely they were to still be together many months later. Among the subjects who had first analyzed the reasons behind their relationship, however, there was no correlation. Apparently the exercise of analyzing the relationship had actually misled subjects and distorted their perception of their overall satisfaction, leading to unreliable ratings. One might of course have predicted the opposite finding, that people's ratings would be more meaningful and reliable following a careful analysis of how things were going, but instead these efforts at analysis and introspection threw people off the track. Wilson and associates suggested that the underlying process may have to do with how introspection focuses attention on certain aspects, such as those that are easiest to verbalize or that sound appropriate or that stand out in memory without necessarily being typical. As the person focuses on these aspects, they assume disproportionate weight in the subsequent global evaluation, which is thereby distorted.

The next landmark attack on self-knowledge was written by Greenwald (1980). He compared the self to a totalitarian regime in its propensity to rewrite history and distort facts in order to support preordained conclusions. People reinterpret events so as to increase their own apparent good qualities, such as benevolence and efficacy, and they place themselves at the center of events as they remember them. Greenwald's analysis portrayed the self as actively twisting information in the service of maintaining a particular, favorable set of beliefs about the self.

Greenwald's analysis was particularly timely because the concept of self-deception was coming under question and attack in other arenas. Gur and Sackeim (1979) labeled it "a concept in search of a phenomenon," noting that empirical demonstrations had repeatedly fallen short of satisfying the defining criteria of self-deception, namely, that the person should both know and not know some particular information. In their analysis, self-deception requires that the same person play both the role of knowledgeable deceiver and unwitting dupe. Not surprisingly, such demonstrations have continued to elude researchers, but Greenwald's analysis pointed to a new direction for understanding self-deception. Instead of casting the phenomenon in black and white terms, Greenwald portrayed it as a matter of shades of gray. Subtle biases, distortions, embellishments, and omissions can operate together to create a pleasant yet false view of events.

A later paper by Greenwald (1988) suggested one possible mechanism for self-deception, using the analogy to junk mail. The philosophical paradox of self-deception is the seeming impossibility of simultaneously knowing and not knowing the same fact (e.g., Sartre, 1953), and psychologically this can take the form of needing to watch out for precisely the threatening event that one is trying not to notice. Greenwald observed, however, that one handles junk mail precisely that way: One cannot fully prevent oneself from knowing that one has received junk mail, but one can toss the envelope into the trash unopened and hence minimize the amount of time and mental exertion devoted to it. In the same way, one can detect advance indications that some information may pose a threat to one's self-concept and can turn one's attention away from it, thereby minimizing its impact.

Do people use this strategy? In one study, subjects took a personality test and were randomly assigned to receive either flattering or unfavorable feedback, administered by a computer. The experimenters secretly timed how long people spent reading the feedback they received. Sure enough, when the feedback was unfavorable, people spent significantly less time reading it (and recalled less of it later) than when it was generally positive (Baumeister & Cairns, 1992). Apparently people tuned out when the feedback started off being bad, with the result that they even failed to register the occasional compliment embedded in the flattery—which normally should have stood out as contrasting and highly welcome information.

Taylor and Brown (1988) amassed broad support for three systematic patterns of *positive illusions.* First, people consistently overestimate their good qualities, achievements, successes, and abilities. Second, people overestimate how much control they have. Third, people tend to be more optimistic than is warranted by objective circumstances. The majority of normal, well-adjusted people appear to exhibit all three of those illusions most of the time, whereas the absence of these patterns is linked to depression and other forms of dysfunction, unhappiness, and maladjustment. To go around thinking "I'm a great person, my fate is in my hands, and things will turn out fine" is apparently a hallmark of the happy, well-adjusted person. Seeing the world in an accurate, realistic fashion is not as beneficial as one might assume, and indeed Taylor and Brown's work suggests that it may not be helpful to approach psychotherapy as a means of helping people gain an accurate perception of reality. The noted clinical researcher C. R. Snyder said that one of his patients once observed, "What's so great about reality, anyway?" Taking a highly positive view of self and world is, if less realistic, much more pleasant and adaptive.

Subsequent work has suggested that Taylor and Brown's conclusions should not be taken to the extreme of assuming that the more egotistical and conceited a person is, the better, with no limits. Taylor (1989) noted that there may be important elements of cultural relativity, for although modern Americans generally support confidence and optimism, other cultures sometimes have strong values in favor of modesty and humility. Baumeister (1989) suggested also that there can be dangers of overconfidence, as one sees in major historical catastrophes such as Napoleon's and Hitler's invasions of Russia, the Children's Crusade, medieval millennial movements, America's misfortune in Vietnam, and so forth. The implication is that there is an "optimal margin of illusion" that entails seeing self and world as *slightly* better than they are. With small distortions, one can enjoy the emotional benefits of confidence and optimism without suffering from the potentially disastrous effects of distorted judgment.

Still, careful experimental work has generally tended to support Taylor and Brown's conclusions about the value of positive illusions, and exceptions or limits seem to be relatively few. Pelham and Taylor (1991) found that people with high self-esteem are more likely than others to ride a motorcycle without wearing a helmet, which in the long run is likely to lead to life-threatening injuries. Baumeister, Heatherton, and Tice (1993) found that people with high self-esteem were more prone than others to overcommit themselves by setting excessive goals, thereby setting themselves up for costly failure. At present, these costs of high self-esteem appear to be isolated findings, while the majority of work continues to support the view that the better one regards oneself, the better off one is.

Perhaps the most elegant (and startling) elaboration of Taylor and Brown's (1988) work was provided by Gollwitzer and Kinney (1989). These authors reasoned that high levels of confidence can be helpful when one is engaged in performance (because of self-fulfilling prophecy effects) but become costly or dangerous when one is making decisions (because of the tendency to overcommit oneself). Their experiment showed that people seem able to turn their illusions on and off as appropriate to the situation. When people are making a decision, they enter into a frame of mind that is fairly accurate and realistic. When they begin to carry out their decisions and perform the tasks they have decided on, they return to a state of mind marked by self-serving distortions and other positive illusions. The implication is that people can control the degree of realism versus illusion in their state of mind. Gollwitzer and Kinney's work comes closest to satisfying the strict criteria of self-deception, namely, knowing and not knowing the same information, because it suggests that people can choose to believe or not believe some particular view depending on the demands of their immediate situation.

Thus, it appears that people do know a great deal of information about themselves, but this information is not entirely accurate. There are systematic limits and distortions in what people know about themselves. Still, these appear to be mostly confined to a moderate size, and so self-knowledge is not wildly inaccurate. Montaigne's suggestion that the autobiographer knows his topic better than any other author may yet prove to be true, although if it is, that is a somewhat sad commentary on authorship in general!

Identity Crisis

When Erik Erikson coined the term *identity crisis* during the early 1940s, he did not anticipate that it would become a household word for decades thereafter. He had in mind a particular developmental task faced by everyone in the normal course of growing up, which Erikson understood within the psychoanalytic framework in which he worked. But the term soon became widely used to refer to a broad range of concerns and uncertainties about the self. Clearly, the culture had developed a host of problems and concerns for which no name was apparent, and so it quickly adopted Erikson's term, regardless of the fact that his definition was not entirely consistent with many of the term's later usages (see Erikson, 1968, for his views).

Identity crisis is an important topic to cover in any psychology of the self, because it is a fundamental and far-reaching problem of selfhood. Identity crises begin and end with difficulties of defining the self. To learn how people manage these problems is a valuable lesson in how self-knowledge is structured and what it can and cannot do.

The most influential approach to assessing and studying identity crises was that of Marcia and his colleagues (e.g., Marcia, 1966, 1967, 1976). Empirical observations soon contradicted Erikson's hypothesis that everyone has identity crises, and so Marcia undertook to classify people based on whether they had ever had an identity crisis or not, and whether they had formed a committed identity or not. (Later Marcia became disenchanted with the melodramatic term *crisis* and substituted the term *exploration*.) The resulting four categories can be summarized as follows. People who show signs of both having had an identity crisis and having formed a committed identity are classified as *identity achieved,* and they are generally recognized as the most mature and well-adjusted individuals. Crisis without commitment generally means that the identity crisis is still in progress, and Marcia used Erikson's term *moratorium* to define them. Their efforts to redefine identity are often marked by fascinating explorations, as well as by emotional ups and downs, confusion, and frequent changes. Commitment without crisis generally indicates that the person has simply accepted the identity that was predetermined or assigned by his or her parents, which Erikson called a *foreclosed identity.* The stereotype of them as rigid, inflexible, and somewhat shallow appears to be true for males but not females. Lastly, people with neither crisis nor commitment are said to suffer from *identity diffusion,* and people in this category appear to suffer from confusion, aimlessness, unhappiness, and sometimes chronic immaturity. These are people who don't know who they are but don't care; some of them seek to remain indefinitely in a transitional or uncommitted state, becoming akin to perpetual adolescents.

Research on identity crises has led to several broad conclusions (see Baumeister, Shapiro, & Tice, 1985; Bourne, 1978 for reviews). It appears that there are not one but two major kinds of identity crisis. *Identity deficit* is the sort of crisis commonly (but not exclusively) linked to male adolescence and midlife transitions, marked by not having a sufficiently well defined identity to enable one to make the important decisions facing one. *Identity conflict,* in contrast, arises when the multiple definitions of self come into conflict and dictate competing, incompatible courses of action. Identity conflicts seem to occur at any time and in either sex. Whereas identity deficit crises are marked by an emotional roller-coaster and an often exciting exploratory search for new definitions of self, identity conflicts produce passivity, guilt, and feelings of being a traitor.

Much of the difference can be understood on the basis of what is needed to resolve the two kinds of identity crisis. Identity deficit is a need for more definition of self. When an adolescent male rejects everything his parents taught or believed in, he may find himself adrift and lacking a basis for making major decisions about his life. To resolve such a crisis, he needs to expand his concept of self to encompass some new values and commitments. In contrast, identity conflict requires contraction rather than expansion of self. When people find that their parental obligations conflict with their chosen career path, or find that their marital plans are incompatible with their family's religious belief, they must effectively sacrifice part of themselves. At best, one may compartmentalize or compromise in some fashion that minimizes the loss of self.

The operation of identity conflict suggests that inconsistency within the self is not necessarily a problem. Rather, potential inconsistencies may exist in someone's identity for years and only become troublesome when external circumstances change. For example, in their study of the identity conflicts of female medical students, Roeske and Lake (1977) observed that the intentions of being a physician and being a mother had coexisted in these women for many years but only became problematic when the person realized she would not have enough time and energy to discharge both sets of responsibilities effectively. Unlike cognitive dissonance theory, which proposed that inconsistency per se needs to be resolved, the literature on identity crisis suggests that inconsistency can be tolerated until one encounters a situation that makes it impossible to sustain both definitions of self (see also Tetlock, 1986). Thus, the problem of consistency is not located inside the self but rather at the interface between the person and the social environment.

In recent years, identity crisis has ceased to be a thriving area of research. Several possible reasons could be suggested for this. Possibly researchers became discouraged by cumbersome measures, conflicting findings, and slippery, ill-defined concepts and phenomena. Possibly the key points have already been studied and established, so that researchers do not see exciting questions or issues to address. Demographic trends may also be suggested as a factor. It may be no coincidence that research on identity crisis peaked when the baby boom was struggling through adolescence (a time of many identity crises); as the baby boom moves through middle age, public and professional interest has shifted to issues of maintaining intimate relationships, maximizing physical health, making sound decisions, and other middle-aged concerns. Whatever the explanation, however, the current lapse in research on identity crisis should not prevent researchers from learning from the body of work that was built up in the preceding decades.

Self-Concept Change

Thus far I have portrayed self-knowledge as if it were a matter of discovering facts (or creating fantasies) about enduring features of the self. Yet it is also apparent that self-concepts do change. For example, longitudinal research by Harter (1993) on a sample of older children and adolescents found that in a single year, between one-third and one-half of the subjects changed their level of self-esteem significantly. Research has just begun to understand the processes of self-concept change.

To be sure, powerful forces appear to oppose self-concept change. Sullivan (1953), for example, articulated what he called the "theorem of escape," which held that once any part of the self-system is formed, it tends to remain stable. Self-concepts probably change and fluctuate the most in childhood, and as one gets older and various aspects of the self begin to crystallize, less and less change will occur. Swann and Hill (1982) showed that people can sometimes be changed by external feedback and other manipulations, but if they are given the opportunity to assert their own views about themselves, they tend to thwart such changes and maintain stable self-concepts.

One important mechanism for changing self-concepts is *internalization*. That is, people appear to internalize the implications of their behavior, and so acting in a certain way can lead to thinking of oneself in that way. Jones, Rhodewalt, Berglas, and Skelton (1981) provided an early and highly influential demonstration of self-concept change. Subjects were induced to present themselves either very favorably or very unfavorably, and their subsequent, confidential self-ratings showed that they had internalized these views of themselves to some extent. Internalization was most apparent when people had voluntarily expressed their willingness to perform the task (as opposed to being passively assigned to play the role) and when they had devised their answers based on their own lives rather than merely following a script.

Jones and colleagues (1981) proposed that self-concept change occurs by a mechanism they called *biased scanning*. This mechanism invokes the concept of the phenomenal self. The full stock of information about the self may be large, unwieldy, and potentially inconsistent. If events cause the person to focus on a certain portion of his or her knowledge, that information will seem to gain in salience and become a powerful factor in how the person subsequently sees himself or herself. In other words, situational forces cause people to scan their personal memories and self-concepts in a biased fashion, looking for information that supports a certain view of self. The results of the biased search will then exert a disproportionate effect on subsequent judgments about the self.

Further evidence consistent with a biased scanning view emerged from studies using a "loaded questions" paradigm (Fazio, Effrein, & Fallender, 1981). In one condition, subjects were asked questions that pulled for introverted behavior, such as "What annoys you most about loud, crowded parties?" In another condition, the questions pulled for extraverted behavior. Subjects had to search their memory for information that portrayed them in the desired fashion, and as a result they started to think about themselves in that way—that is, answering introverted questions made people think of themselves as introverts. Moreover, when later seated in a waiting room, subjects who had been asked the introvert questions were less likely to approach another person or initiate a conversation than were people who had been asked the extravert questions.

These early studies provided useful techniques for studying self-concept change as well as some initial findings about how the change occurs. The theory they developed was based on self-perception; scanning one's memory in a certain way alters how one regards oneself. Recent work has however begun to indicate that interpersonal factors are extremely important in self-concept change. Apparently it is not just the intrapsychic process but also the social context that guides people to revise their views of themselves.

The importance of interpersonal factors was strongly indicated by Tice's (1992) work. She noted that although the studies by Jones and colleagues (1981) and Fazio and associates (1981) had used theories based on intrapsychic processes, their empirical procedures had been interpersonal, such as having subjects misrepresent themselves to another person. Tice induced subjects to answer loaded questions in either a public, interpersonal setting or in a confidential, anonymous setting (such as speaking their answers into a tape recorder, anonymously, while no one else was present). Although subjects gave roughly the same answers in both conditions, they only internalized their answers when given in a face-to-face contact with another person, and not when given anonymously. In principle, similar intrapsychic processes (such as biased scanning for relevant memories) should have occurred regardless of whether others were present, but Tice found internalization only in the public condition. In another study, she found that people were less likely to internalize their answers if they had spoken them to someone they did not expect to meet again, and this result also attests to the importance of an ongoing interpersonal context or relationship for producing internalization.

Further evidence was provided by Schlenker, Dlugolecki, and Doherty (1994). Like Tice, they found that internalization occurred only if the behavior was publicly identified in an interpersonal context. They went on to challenge the biased scanning hypothesis. In one study, they followed the loaded questions with instructions telling subjects to search their memory for times when they behaved in a relevant fashion. Thus, for example, a subject might be asked a series of questions designed to pull for extraversion and then be instructed to recall incidents in which he or she had acted in an introverted fashion. Based on biased scanning theory, Schlenker and his colleagues worried initially that memory search manipulation would be so powerful that it would wipe out any effects of the loaded questions, but that did not happen. Instead, people seemed to internalize their public behavior regardless of how they were told to scan their memories. Meanwhile, another group of subjects was told to prepare answers to the loaded questions for an interview, but at the last minute the interview was ostensibly canceled. Because these subjects had already engaged in biased scanning, they should have shown self-concept change even despite the cancellation, but they did not. Schlenker and his associates concluded that the mechanism responsible for internalization must invoke some interpersonal process (such as public commitment, or seeing oneself through another's eyes) rather than simple biased scanning.

Thus, research on self-concept change appears to be gaining momentum as researchers have developed better methodologies and refined their ideas. The importance of the topic is beyond dispute, and as researchers develop better tools for studying self-concept change, it seems reasonable to anticipate significant advances and contributions in the coming decade.

MOTIVATIONS

We turn now from cognition to motivation. Although recent work has increasingly depicted the self as a cognitive structure, it would be reckless to overlook the motivational aspects of the self. That is, the self may be a knower, but it is also a wanter. Two main motivations have gained wide recognition as driving many self-processes and underlying a broad variety of cognitive, emotional, and behavioral responses. These are the drive for favorability and the drive for consistency. There is little doubt but that people want to find some positive basis for self-esteem, to think well of themselves, and to have others think well of them too. Likewise, it is clear that people strive to maintain stable, consistent views of themselves. These two motives often operate in harmony, but there is a potential for conflict, and in such cases researchers are divided as to which is more important and powerful.

As already described, people generally tend to hold positive, somewhat inflated opinions of themselves, and so in most cases the consistency and favorability motives operate together. People will seek out opportunities to make a good impression, will avoid events that threaten them with a loss of esteem, and will present themselves to others in a positive, favorable light. As Schlenker (e.g., 1980, 1986) has repeatedly emphasized, people try to make not the best *possible* but rather the best *plausible* impression. Implausible, excessively favorable claims will tend to be discredited, and experiences of that sort can be painfully humiliating, such as when a person brags about how well he or she will perform and then makes a poor showing. At the end of the regular 1990 baseball season, several members of the triumphant Oakland A's speculated publicly that they were among the greatest baseball teams of all time, but these boasts came back to haunt them when they lost the World Series to an underdog Cincinnati team. The tension between the pressures of plausible consistency and the desire for favorability provides the context in which the individual self-concept is constructed and maintained. Let us examine each of them in turn.

Considerable work has documented the many ways in which people seek to support a favorable view of self. Steele and his colleagues (see Steele, 1988; and Spencer, Josephs, and Steele, 1993, for reviews) have conducted an extensive program of research on *self-affirmation* processes. In their view, people need to find something positive to affirm about themselves. They do not need to succeed at everything, but they do need to succeed at something. When one dimension of the self is threatened, such as by a failure in one realm, people will be motivated to compensate for it by succeeding in some other area. Thus, in one study, subjects were insulted by being called bad drivers, and these subjects were consequently much more likely to comply with a request for help than were control subjects or praised subjects (Steele, 1975). The key point for understanding threats to self is that people want to maintain a generally positive view of themselves, which does not necessarily require doing well at everything. In Steele's (1988, p. 268) words, ". . . after an important self-concept is threatened, an individual's primary self-defensive goal is to affirm the general integrity of the self, not to resolve the particular threat."

Likewise, allowing people to affirm themselves in a positive light appears sufficient to remove the effects of many potential threats to self. Although in most cases people who suffer a loss of control over their situation report a variety of negative reactions (see Pittman & Pittman, 1980), this effect can be eliminated by self-affirmation. If subjects are allowed to express their personal values regarding various important issues, a subsequent experience of control deprivation loses much of its impact (Liu & Steele, 1986). Even cognitive dissonance effects can be reduced or eliminated by allowing subjects to make an irrelevant self-affirmation first (see Steele, 1988).

One of the most elegant models regarding the maintenance of a favorable self-concept was furnished by Tesser (e.g., Tesser, 1988). In his model, two processes and three major variables determine the impact of events on self-esteem, and people use and respond to these processes so as to maximize their esteem. Tesser's model is heavily interpersonal and thus once again replaces a strictly intrapsychic analysis with a more social (i.e., interpersonal) approach to the self.

The first process is one of self-reflection, in which one benefits from the achievements and good qualities of others with whom one is linked. For example, if one's alma mater wins the national basketball championship, or one's spouse receives a major award, one enjoys "reflected glory" (see Cialdini et al., 1976; Cialdini & Richardson, 1980) that brings a boost in esteem. The second process is one of comparison (see Festinger, 1954; also Wills, 1981) and is based on gaining esteem by doing better than someone else. Thus, your own performance may initially seem mediocre but can start to seem pretty good if several other people do significantly worse.

These two processes are guided by the variables of closeness, relevance, and performance. *Performance* is, obviously, how well the other person does, including success or failure and possibly how it compares with your own success or failure in that area. *Closeness* refers to the degree of linkage between yourself and the other person involved. Thus, you may gain more reflected glory if your husband wins the award than if your second cousin wins it. *Relevance* refers to the importance of the other's performance to your own self-concept. If your sister wins an award for something that you have never tried to succeed at, you may feel proud and brag about her achievement, but if she wins an award that you were competing for and hoping to get, her success may be a blow rather than a boost to your self-esteem.

In short, another person's performance can have radically different effects on your self-esteem depending on closeness, relevance, and level of performance. Having close ties to others who succeed on irrelevant dimensions will boost your self-esteem, as will having close ties to others who fail on dimensions highly relevant to your esteem. If someone has to succeed at a dimension that is highly relevant to your self-concept, you would probably rather that it be someone who is not close to you.

An extensive program of research by Tesser, his colleagues, and others has shown how these self-evaluation maintenance (SEM) processes operate (see Tesser, 1988, for review). People apparently prefer to see strangers succeed rather than friends when a dimension relevant to their own self-concept is involved, and they will actually do more to help strangers than friends under such circumstances (Tesser & Smith, 1980). By the same token, subjects will distance themselves from others who perform too well on highly relevant dimensions (Pleban & Tesser, 1981). Lastly, they will downplay the relevance of a dimension on which someone close to them does well (Tesser & Paulhus, 1983).

A great deal of interpersonal behavior may be influenced by these processes. We boost esteem by emphasizing close ties to people who are terrific on dimensions irrelevant to our own self-concept, and by emphasizing ties to people who are not as good as we are on dimensions that are highly relevant. People want to interact more with others who are good at irrelevant things, but they avoid people who outperform them on their own main strengths. Tesser's work sheds light on the question of whether it is lonely at the top (i.e., whether success fosters social isolation): The successful person may be avoided by colleagues and by defeated competitors, but he or she is likely to be very popular with people in other lines of work, because their self-esteem is not threatened by one's success. The self-evaluation maintenance processes also shed light on some potential sources of conflict and problems in intimate relationships (see Beach, 1992): A spouse or lover who is highly successful will be cherished as long as that success is irrelevant to one's own strivings, but if the spouse or lover succeeds in an area that is too relevant to one's own self-concept, the reaction may be negative and intimacy may be harmed.

Thus, the desire for a favorable view of self is well established. Its many forms, widespread manifestations, and apparent universality even across cultural boundaries has suggested the conclusion that a need for some sense of self-worth is one of the pillars of finding a meaningful life (Baumeister, 1991b). Even people who are depressed, downtrodden, or victims of severely low self-esteem seem driven to find some strongly positive thing on which to base a positive self-worth (e.g., Pelham, 1993).

The drive to maintain a stable, consistent self-concept has also been supported by a wide variety of evidence. In particular, Swann has devoted most of his career to exploring self-consistency motives, which he labels *self-verification* (see Swann, 1985, 1987). One approach is to examine how people with very negative views of themselves respond to positive, flattering feedback such as praise or success. If consistency is the overriding motive, they should react negatively to such good news, because it may threaten to change their self-conceptions in a positive direction. Although it is often necessary to use stringent   criteria for selecting such individuals, such as people with extremely low self- esteem scores and additional ratings of being highly committed to these negative views, it does appear that these people will indeed react negatively to success (Swann, 1987). Swann concludes that people would rather have their   unflattering views about themselves confirmed than receive praise, success, or social approval.

Many find it intuitively implausible that people would actually desire failure, rejection, or criticism, and recent work by Swann and his colleagues has sought to establish some understanding of how the favorability and consistency motives interact. One integration invokes the distinction between cognitive and emotional reactions. A literature review by Shrauger (1975) reached the conclusion that consistency effects were found primarily with cognitive measures (such as belief and perceived plausibility) whereas favorability effects were found with affective measures (such as feeling happy). Subsequent work has continued to support this view (e.g., McFarlin & Blascovich, 1981). Swann, Griffin, Predmore, and Gaines (1987) formulated this in terms of a "cognitive-affective crossfire" experienced by people who receive excessively positive feedback. Affectively, people like to receive strongly positive feedback, but cognitively they are skeptical and distrustful of it. They are more inclined to believe feedback that confirms their views of themselves, even though emotionally they feel best after highly positive feedback.

Sedikides (1993) recently undertook to assess the relative strength of these two motives and a third, namely, the desire to gain an accurate understanding of oneself. In six experiments, he examined people's preferences for feedback about certain vs. uncertain and positive vs. negative aspects of their self-concepts. In all six experiments, self-enhancement emerged as the strongest motive. Self-verification, although not as strong as self-enhancement, was also a strong motive and consistently overpowered the third (self-assessment) motive. Thus, perhaps ironically, the desire to reduce uncertainty and gain new information about the self was not found to be an influential motive, at least not when pitted against the desire for favorable feedback or the desire for self- confirming feedback.

Thus, it appears that people's actions and reactions are guided by two main motives, namely, favorability and consistency, with favorability being perhaps the most powerful of all. In many situations, these two motives agree; in particular, both motives impel people to avoid any threat of losing self-esteem. When it comes to revising one's self-concept toward a more favorable view, however, the two motives diverge, and people appear to have mixed and complex reactions. In any case, these two basic motivations appear to be well established. The challenge for the coming decade is to identify and explore any additional motivations associated with the self, beyond the "big two" of consistency and favorability.

SELF-PRESENTATION

While the self may be regarded as a grammatical reflex and/or as a cognitive construct, it is also an interpersonal tool. Without an established, stable identity, it would be all but impossible to interact with other people and maintain social relationships. Moreover, if the self is an interpersonal tool, then the better one's tool, the better one's interpersonal relationships. Hence people will become extremely concerned with managing the impressions they make on others and fashioning a self that will bring them social approval and acceptance.

The basic goal of making a good impression has long been familiar. Jones and Wortman (1973) confirmed that a carefully managed self-presentation is one of the most common strategies of ingratiation. In one of the classic papers on self-presentation, Schlenker (1975) sought to determine whether people present themselves accurately (i.e., consistently with what they knew about themselves) or in a highly positive fashion. Subjects in his study were given feedback about their abilities and led to believe that this feedback would accurately predict how well they would perform on an upcoming test. Before the test, subjects were given an opportunity to describe themselves to other members of their group, thereby giving them a chance to be either suitably modest or recklessly self-aggrandizing. Schlenker found that responses seemed to conform to a trade-off between plausibility and favorability. If the upcoming test was to be public, subjects presented themselves in a fairly accurate fashion, presumably because one looks especially bad to fail after bragging (as in the preceding section's example of the Oakland baseball team). On the other hand, if the upcoming test was to be confidential, subjects went ahead and portrayed themselves in highly positive terms. Apparently they felt they could get away with presenting themselves favorably if no one would be able to ascertain that their actual performance would fall short of their exaggerated claims.

The goal of making a good impression is not quite so simple as it may first appear, however, particularly if the self-presenter and the audience disagree about the nature of "good." Evidence has accumulated that there are two basic patterns of self-presentation (see Baumeister, 1982, 1986b). In one, people seek simply to portray themselves in whatever fashion the audience will like best (see also Jones & Wortman, 1973). In the other, however, they are guided by their own values, using self-presentation to claim and validate the identity they desire (see also Gollwitzer, 1986; Wicklund & Gollwitzer, 1982). The latter motive, which can be called *self-construction* (Baumeister, 1982) or *self-completion* (Wicklund & Gollwitzer, 1982), explains why people may sometimes reveal aspects of themselves that those present may not like, such as when one stands up for political views that contradict those held by other people present. To be the person you want to be, it is necessary to establish some social recognition for that identity; after all, it is difficult to regard yourself as a great artist or popular socialite or promising genius if no one else shares that view of you. Self- presentation is thus more than a way of getting along with others; it is a means of building one's identity.

The topic of self-presentation was introduced to social psychology by Goffman (1959), and for a long time it remained associated with that work and, perhaps unfortunately, with the observational, impressionistic methodology that Goffman employed. This began to change with Tedeschi, Schlenker, and Bonoma's (1971) article suggesting that the extensive findings on cognitive dissonance reflected subjects' attempts to make a good impression rather than any inner need for consistency. The sophisticated laboratory techniques of dissonance research were adapted to testing self-presentational hypotheses, which helped bring self-presentation into the mainstream of empirical work in social psychology. Efforts to distinguish intrapsychic processes versus interpersonal ones both built up self-presentation methods and extended dissonance theory (in particular, see Croyle & Cooper, 1983; Gaes, Kalle, & Tedeschi, 1978; Zanna & Cooper, 1974). Ultimately, a compromise was reached, suggesting that there are multiple dissonance processes, some driven by interpersonal concerns with self-presentation, others sparked by intrapsychic factors such as choice and self-perceived responsibility (Baumeister & Tice, 1984; Paulhus, 1982).

The emergence of self-presentation research into social psychology's mainstream prompted many researchers to reconsider their theoretical assumptions and models. Many phenomena that had been interpreted in largely intrapsychic terms were now found to depend on self-presentational motives, indicating the need to add an interpersonal dimension to the theories. Baumeister (1982) reviewed this work and noted that self-presentation had been shown to have a significant impact on helping and receiving help, conformity, influence, reactance, attitude change, responses to evaluations, aggression, attributions, task performance, and other variables. Leary and Kowalski (1990) updated this work to add a distinction between the motivation to make an impression, which may vary greatly in strength, and the actual construction of the impression, which may or may not happen regardless of the motivation.

Perhaps the most significant development in recent years has been the awakening interest in the cognitive processes associated with self-presentation. To put this development into perspective, it is necessary to recall that the first large wave of empirical self-presentation studies was designed to show that many seemingly intrapsychic responses actually had a strong interpersonal dimension (such as cognitive dissonance, as described above). The standard research design therefore tended to pit purely intrapsychic processes against interpersonal ones, by looking for whether responses differed in public versus private circumstances. In a widely cited paper, Tetlock and Manstead (1985) critiqued this approach as unsatisfactory and doomed. Noting that the supposedly "critical experiments" would usually fail to convince the strong adherents of the opposing view, Tetlock and Manstead suggested that the approach of pitting self-presentational versus intrapsychic explanations was a misguided effort based on false dichotomy. Tetlock and Manstead's work was interpreted by some as a call to abandon self-presentation research, but this is a misinterpretation based on a superficial reading, and the authors themselves have deplored such a reading of their work (Manstead, personal communication, 1991).

Instead, the most important call made by Tetlock and Manstead was for an integration of interpersonal and intrapsychic processes. After all, a great deal of cognitive processing is necessary to do an effective job of managing the impression one makes on other people: One must form a sense of their values and expectations, anticipate how one's own behavior will look to others, select behaviors that will produce the desired inferences, and so forth. Moreover, people think most about things that are most important to them, and if self-presentational concerns are really as powerful as many researchers have asserted, then people would certainly spend a great deal of time and effort thinking about them.

Devine, Sedikides, and Fuhrman (1989) provided evidence that self-presentation stimulates cognitive processing. These authors presented subjects with information about target persons, some of whom they expected to meet. People spent more time and effort thinking about the people they expected to meet than about other people. Although the expectation of future interaction invokes several motives, one of the leading ones is self-presentation. In a related vein, Baumeister and Cairns (1992) found that people responded more thoughtfully to evaluations if these evaluations were to be shown to future interaction partners. The earlier section of this chapter concerned with self-deception covered that study's finding that people avoided bad feedback but spent longer times studying positive, flattering feedback. That pattern was reversed, however, if the evaluative feedback was public; people spent the longest time thinking about bad feedback that would be seen by others. The additional time was largely devoted to worrying about the other person's incipient bad impression and thinking up ways to counteract it. Apparently, considerable cognitive work is involved in responding to self-presentational predicaments.

In order to fully understand the cognitive processes involved in self-presentation, it would be necessary to examine live interactions and determine what people notice, infer, and remember. An initial study of this type was conducted by Baumeister, Hutton, and Tice (1989). They found that presenting oneself in a modest, unfavorable fashion apparently requires more thought and mental effort than presenting oneself favorably, because subjects who were instructed to present themselves modestly showed impaired memory for the interaction. The more you think about the impression you are trying to make on the other person, the less you remember about the other person (and the less you remember about what you said too). Furthermore, people failed to correct their impressions of their interaction for the effects of their own self-presentations. That is, it was found that if the first subject bragged, the second one tended to follow suit and brag too. The first one, however, failed to realize that his own bragging had stimulated the other's bragging and concluded, instead, that the second partner must simply be conceited (see also Gilbert & Jones, 1986, on failure to adjust for one's effects on the interaction partner).

Further evidence that modesty takes extra mental effort was provided in an intriguing study by Paulhus and Levitt (1987). Normally, subjects can respond to questions about themselves by providing fairly balanced, neutral self-appraisals. However, when subjects in this study were distracted by emotionally laden cues (i.e., words like *death, penis, blood, coffin, slut, torture*), they responded to these questions in much more positive terms. Paulhus and Levitt suggested that people respond to threat with "automatic egotism," that is, an immediate and efficient response that portrays themselves in strongly positive terms. When they can think calmly about what they are doing, people can provide modest and balanced self-appraisals, but when aroused and distracted they fall back on the pattern of simply depicting themselves in a positive light.

Thus, self-presentation is well established as an important source of motivations and concerns. Research has just begun to understand the intrapsychic dynamics that accompany and shape self-presentation, and those dynamics may be the major focus of the next generation of self-presentation research.

SELF-ESTEEM

Self-esteem has been an enduring focus of research. The term is widely used in research, although this frequency of usage may conceal the fact that there are two quite different sources of interest in it. One is the broad, general desire for self-esteem, as discussed earlier in this chapter (the favorability motive). The other source is personality differences in self-esteem. These two do not readily map into each other; low self-esteem is not some simple absence of the desire to think well of oneself.

Importance of Self-Esteem

Interest in self-esteem has recently been stimulated by popular interest and discussion, the most dramatic instance of which was probably the California Task Force to Promote Self-Esteem and Personal and Social Responsibility. This committee's report concluded that self-esteem might function as a "social vaccine" which would inoculate individuals and society "against the lures of crime, violence, substance abuse, teen pregnancy, child abuse, chronic welfare dependency, and educational failure," because in the Task Force's view, "the lack of self-esteem is central to most personal and social ills plaguing our state and nation" (1990, p. 4). In my view, these hopes are excessive and to some extent misplaced. It may be true that low self-esteem is linked to welfare dependency, school failure, drug addiction, and so forth, but in many cases the low self- esteem may be a result, not a cause. Still, there is no denying the fact that self-esteem has become a topic in which there is considerable interest, both within and outside of professional psychology.

Current fads of popular interest aside, why is self-esteem so important? After all, there is no obvious reason why high self-esteem should be beneficial. Thinking well of oneself may feel good, but it does not have any apparent practical or material advantage, and many people dislike and resent others whom they perceive as conceited or egotistical. Indeed, high self-esteem could be compared to addictive patterns, laziness, or selfishness, in that it brings pleasure to the self while constituting a burdensome strain on others close to one.

One answer to the question of the desirability of self-esteem has been provided by Solomon, Greenberg, and Pyszczynski (1991; also Greenberg, Pyszczynski, & Solomon, 1986). Building on the theories of Becker (1973), they propose that human activity and culture is fundamentally driven by fear of death, and so self-esteem becomes important as a vital buffer against death anxiety. By regarding oneself as a valued participant in a culturally meaningful activity, the person can presumably ward off the threat of meaninglessness that arises from knowing one's mortality. Elevating self-esteem is thus a strategy of "terror management," that is, of coping with the terror of knowing that one will eventually die.

There is indeed considerable evidence in support of the view that self- esteem is inversely related to anxiety, suggesting that self-esteem is indeed an anxiety buffer (see Solomon, Greenberg, & Pyszczynski, 1991, for review). Moreover, experimental studies by those authors have confirmed that reminding people of their mortality causes them to bolster their self-esteem in apparent defense, and that if self-esteem is bolstered first, then subjects do not show an increase in anxiety in response to death-related stimuli. Thus, there do seem to be links among self-esteem, anxiety, and death.

At present, the main objection to the terror management view is the notion that death is not a common or pervasive enough threat to be behind all the anxiety and all the concern with self-esteem. Although reminding subjects of death may indeed cause anxiety, it may be that everyday sources of anxiety are not linked to mortality. My own view is that the more common roots of anxiety lie in concerns about belongingness and social exclusion. Nearly all threats to social belongingness—such as romantic rejection, loss of employment, and bereavement—cause anxiety (see Baumeister & Tice, 1990, for review). The desire for close interpersonal attachments appears very early in life, well before knowledge of death, and may be a powerful source of motivation and emotion without being linked to mortality (see Baumeister & Leary, 1994, for review). In this perspective, self-esteem is comforting because it signifies that one has the traits that will make one attractive to others. High self-esteem is typically a perception of oneself as likable, physically attractive, competent, and morally good, and that is precisely the person whom others are likely to include in their social groups. Thus, aloneness, rather than death, may be the most common source of anxiety that drives people to erect high self-esteem to prevent.

Still, there is no reason to assume that all anxieties or all concerns with self-esteem have one and the same basis. The most likely answer is that the twin threats of death and loneliness are both involved in creating anxiety and that people seek to raise their own self-esteem as a way of protecting themselves against both threats. Further research may establish additional threats as well.

Self-Esteem as Trait and State

Self-esteem may be considered one of the core features of the self-concept. Its importance was empirically confirmed by Greenwald, Bellezza, and Banaji (1988). Their article was entitled "Is self-esteem a central ingredient of the self-concept?" and their work answered the question with an emphatic yes.

Self-esteem appears to have two main roots (e.g., Harter, 1993). The first is direct experiences of competence and efficacy, which convince people that they have valuable abilities and are able to function effectively in the world. The second is social feedback, particularly the reflected appraisals of significant other people. Anyone who manages to perform an assortment of important tasks effectively and who is surrounded by people who give him or her positive, supportive evaluations is unlikely to have low self-esteem. To be sure, different people may place different emphasis on these two criteria. Josephs, Markus, and Tafarodi (1992) suggested that men's self-esteem tends to be based on individualistic criteria, especially achievements, whereas women's self-esteem tends to be based on interpersonal connectedness.

Popular intuitions about self-esteem suggest that it frequently changes, and this intuition has been a concern of researchers because anything that fluctuates widely cannot be called a trait. Fortunately, it appears that self-esteem is actually quite stable. In one recent study, for example, a large sample of students filled out a self-esteem measure on two occasions separated by two weeks, and the correlation (retest reliability) of their scores was .904 (Baumeister, 1991c), suggesting extreme consistency.

On the other hand, there are undoubtedly some fluctuations. Heatherton and Polivy (1991) have recently developed a state measure of self-esteem that can be used to measure how people's momentary self-evaluations fluctuate in response to short-term events. Heatherton and Polivy showed that the state measure correlates strongly with the trait measure but does respond to situations and events. The implication is that self-esteem changes somewhat after each flattering or degrading event but then returns to a stable baseline.

Kernis and his colleagues have concluded the most ambitious program concerned with state fluctuations in self-esteem (see Kernis, 1993, for review). Their approach has been based on assessing how stable a person's self-esteem is; that is, some people's self-esteem is the same every time it is measured, whereas other people show wider fluctuations. Attending to the stability of self-esteem adds significant information over simply measuring the level of esteem. For example, Kernis, Granneman, and Mathis (1991) showed that the familiar correlation between self-esteem and depression pertains only among people who show stable levels of self-esteem. People with *unstable* low self-esteem do not show elevated levels of depression.

Perhaps the most interesting finding to emerge from Kernis' program concerns aggression. Kernis, Granneman, and Barclay (1989) found that the highest levels of hostility and anger are found among people with high but unstable self-esteem. This finding offers valuable insight into the psychology of the bully. Aggressive and hostile actions may often arise from the combination of egotism and insecurity. People who have *stable* high self-esteem do not become aggressive, presumably because events do not easily threaten them. In contrast, people who have high opinions of themselves but feel that these are in danger of being deflated are ready to lash out at other people if events threaten to lower their self-esteem. As noted previously in this chapter, people are extremely reluctant to lose self-esteem (because both the favorability and the consistency motives are strongly opposed to suffering any such loss), and people with unstable high self-esteem are the ones who are most in danger of suffering such a loss. They are therefore the most violently defensive.

The Puzzle of Low Self-Esteem

A particular focus of recent research has been to understand people with low self-esteem. People with high self-esteem are relatively easy to understand: They think well of themselves, want and expect to succeed, and want and expect others to admire, like, and love them. In contrast, people with low self-esteem have been the focus of a series of conflicting hypotheses, suggesting that they hate and despise themselves, desire to prove their worthlessness, are desperate to try any means to gain success and approval, seek out failure and rejection, want success but expect failure, and so forth. It is fundamentally puzzling to researchers to understand why people would portray themselves in highly unfavorable terms, and hence the assortment of conflicting theories. A coherent picture has only recently begun to emerge.

A first task is to clarify just how badly people with low self-esteem think of themselves. The standard research approach has been to give a self-esteem measure—typically composed of a questionnaire with many questions about self-evaluation, confidence, and insecurity—and divide the stack of question-naires in the middle, defining those above the median as high in self-esteem and those below the median as low. A review of published articles and statistics using this method found, however, that in practice the median was usually rather high. If the range of possible self-esteem scores ran from 0 to 100, for ex-ample, a typical distribution of scores might run from 40 to 80, with 60 as the median. Thus, most people labeled as low in self-esteem are only relatively low; in an absolute sense, they are intermediate (Baumeister, Tice, & Hutton, 1989).

Several recent works have shed light on the nature of people with low self-esteem. One vital contribution concerns self-knowledge: Apparently people with low self-esteem have self-concepts that are confused, self-contradictory, inconsistent, incomplete, and ill-defined (Campbell, 1990; see also Baum- gard-ner, 1990; Campbell & Lavallee, 1993). This may help explain their neutral and intermediate responses to self-esteem questions, because they simply do not know enough about themselves to make strong or articulate statements. The self-knowledge problem may well underlie a great many of the consequences and correlates of low self-esteem, because people who do not understand them-selves well cannot manage their affairs as effectively, keep relationships on an even keel, seek out an environment that will enable them to flourish, and so forth.

Another useful insight comes from research on threats and stressful events (see Spencer, Josephs, & Steele, 1993). Self-esteem can be understood as a re-source that helps one cope with life and be happy, and people with low self-es-teem simply have less of this resource than others. When threats to self-esteem arise, people affirm their self-worth by shifting the focus to another dimension where their standing is secure. For people with low self-esteem, however, that strategy is hampered by the fact that their positive self-worth does not have a great many firm foundations. Hence they may be more vulnerable than other people to stresses and threats.

The greater vulnerability of people with low self-esteem probably under-lies another key point about them, which is their broad orientation in interper-sonal and achievement domains. Unlike people with high self-esteem, who seem generally oriented toward self-enhancement, people with low self-esteem are guided by an overriding motive of self-protection (Baumeister, Tice, & Hutton, 1989; Tice, 1993). People with high self-esteem can take chances and gamble on success because they are confident that they will succeed, but peo-ple with low self-esteem avoid such risks because of the danger of failure or re-jection.

Other insights continue to emerge and shed light on low self-esteem. It ap-pears that such individuals have a tendency toward floccinaucinihilipilifica-tion; they are not just negative about themselves but are negative toward every-one (see Brown, 1986; Crocker & Schwartz, 1985). To maintain their self-esteem, they are reluctant to adopt the obvious tactic of boasting and bragging, perhaps because such excessive claims leave them vulnerable to humiliating disconfir-mation (see Blaine & Crocker, 1993; Tice, 1993). Instead, they adopt various in-direct strategies, such as derogating rivals so as to feel good by comparison

(Pelham, 1993; Spencer, Josephs, & Steele, 1993), or using "indirect self-   en-hancement" such as speaking favorably about a group to which they belong (Brown, 1993; Brown, Collins, & Schmidt, 1988).

Ultimately, it is clear that people with low self-esteem want to think well of themselves, but they feel unable to satisfy that wish for various reasons. Low self-esteem is generally not the presence of firmly held views that the self is bad; rather, it is the absence of reasons for believing that the self is good. This absence is presumably linked to the deficiency in self-knowledge, the shortage of coping resources, and the self-protective orientation.

SELF-AWARENESS

In 1971, Wicklund and Duval published a seminal set of experiments in which subjects were seated in front of a mirror or exposed to a tape recording of their own voice in order to create a state of "objective self-awareness." These manipulations altered several behavioral responses, including effortful task performance and attitude change. Self-awareness has proved to be one of the most durable and fertile topics for study, slowly expanding its range of applications and implications and continuing to yield new findings after two decades of steady work.

Basic Theory of Self-Awareness

Like most productive theories, self-awareness theory has evolved and adapted under the influence of accumulating data, and the original formulation by Duval and Wicklund (1972) is today regarded more as the starting point than as the final word (see also Wicklund, 1975). Still, several key points have remained constant. One is the distinction between subjective states; at any given moment, attention is either focused on the self, or it is not. Another is the importance of *standards*, that is, evaluative criteria against which the self is compared. After all, a glance in the mirror is not simply a dispassionate noticing of a human image; instead, one compares the image against various standards of attractiveness, stylish clothing, thinness, condition of hair, and so on, sometimes even comparing oneself against romantic rivals or movie stars.

Initially, Duval and Wicklund conceptualized self-awareness as an aversive state. They noted that people's standards are usually above realities and concluded, quite reasonably, that comparing oneself against high standards would make one notice one's shortcomings and hence feel bad. Subsequent work has suggested, however, that people do often find more agreeably low standards against which to compare themselves (see especially Wills, 1981) and can enjoy the state of self-awareness simply by reflecting on how they are above average (Carver & Scheier, 1981). It is however still quite true that self-awareness often produces a discouraging recognition of how far short of one's ideals one is.

Self-awareness theory was extended by Carver and Scheier (1981), who described a feedback loop process. They suggested that when one recognizes a discrepancy between oneself and one's standards, this initiates a process designed to reduce the discrepancy. Like a thermostat checking the temperature, self-awareness continues to verify one's progress toward reaching the goal or standard and signals when to cease one's efforts because one has met the standard—or because one realizes that the standard is impossible to meet. Carver and Scheier (1981, 1982) also proposed a hierarchy of levels of self-awareness, with high levels furnishing the standards that guide low levels. People can be aware of themselves in broad, abstract, far-reaching terms (e.g., as someone who is succeeding in life) or in narrow, specific, short-term, and concrete terms (e.g., as someone who is unable to get the mayonnaise jar open). When one falls short of a high-level goal, self-awareness shifts to a lower level, as if to find the specific problem and resolve it.

It has also become apparent that more than attention is involved in self-awareness, even though *self-attention* continues to be one of the terms used to refer to that state. In addition to noticing themselves, self-aware people are defined by thinking about themselves, reflecting on their own traits or accomplishments (or lack thereof), and elaborating implications of recent events in relation to the self (see also Hull & Levy, 1979). Attention, strictly defined, is merely the first step in information processing, but self-awareness theory has expanded to encompass a full range of cognitive processes as well as behavioral responses.

State and Trait

Although the initial studies of self-awareness treated it exclusively as a state that a person may move into and out of at varying intervals, later work soon began to suggest trait differences. Fenigstein, Scheier, and Buss (1975) published a trait measure that has been a powerful tool for researchers interested in self-awareness. Some people seem to focus attention on themselves frequently, others only rarely, and these differences are related to many behavioral patterns (see Carver & Scheier, 1981, for review).

The scale furnished by Fenigstein and associates (1975) has three subscales, concerned with private self-consciousness, public self-consciousness, and social anxiety, respectively. Researchers disagree about the meaning, value, and utility of these distinctions (e.g., Carver & Scheier, 1987; Fenigstein, 1987; Gollwitzer & Wicklund, 1987; Wicklund & Gollwitzer, 1987). Private self-consciousness refers to introspective tendencies, ruminating about oneself and one's goals or values, and other thoughts about the self. Public self-consciousness, in contrast, means attending to how one is perceived by others. Social anxiety is concern over being disliked or rejected, corresponding to the more colloquial use of the term *self-conscious.*

Despite the controversy about the validity of these distinctions, empirical work has amply confirmed that public and private self-consciousness have different behavioral correlates. Thus, for example, alcohol use is most strongly linked to private self-consciousness (e.g., Hull, Young, & Jouriles, 1986), whereas bulimia is linked to public self-consciousness (Heatherton & Baumeister, 1991). In other words, alcohol use seems driven by an urge to cease introspecting and stop reflecting on how one falls short of one's own goals and standards, whereas bulimia is based on an excessive concern with how one is regarded by others.

Effects of Self-Awareness

The essence of self-awareness is comparing oneself against meaningful, relevant standards, and these comparisons affect behavior in multiple ways. For example, they motivate people to try harder in order to meet performance goals (Wicklund, 1975; Wicklund & Duval, 1971).

Self-awareness appears to support inhibitions and foster virtuous, honest, proper behavior, presumably because the state makes people examine their potential actions in light of moral standards. Diener and Wallbom (1976), for example, found that people who were made self-aware (through exposing them to a mirror and a tape recording of their own voice) were much less likely to cheat on a test than were control subjects. Beaman, Klentz, Diener, and Svanum (1979) found that children who were made self-aware were less likely than others to steal candy. Gibbons (1978) found that self-awareness strengthened sexual inhibitions: People with high levels of sexual guilt and shame rated erotic stimuli more negatively when self-aware. Scheier, Fenigstein, and Buss (1974) showed that self-awareness intensified men's inhibitions about behaving aggressively toward women. When aggression is presented as proper and desirable, however, self-awareness increases it, which is particularly compelling evidence that these effects of self-awareness depend on the activation of relevant standards.

Not all the effects of self-awareness depend on standards, however. Some effects may derive simply from salience. Some evidence suggests that self-awareness makes people more likely to attribute responsibility to themselves, perhaps especially for positive outcomes (Hull & Levy, 1979; Ross & Sicoly, 1979). Scheier and Carver (1977) found that various emotional states are intensified by self-awareness. Attention to self can also make certain of the self's attitudes and beliefs more salient and accessible, and so self-reports furnished may increase in accuracy. Pryor, Gibbons, Wicklund, Fazio, and Hood (1977) showed that attitude ratings furnished while in a state of high self-awareness predicted subsequent behavior more accurately and consistently than ratings furnished without a self-awareness manipulation.

Although self-awareness may improve performance by increasing effort, it may also impair performance. Baumeister (1984) proposed that when events are particularly important, people pay extra attention to what they are doing, but that extra attention may disrupt the smooth execution of automatic or overlearned tasks (i.e., skills). A series of studies confirmed self-awareness as a crucial factor in causing people to *choke under pressure,* that is, to perform badly just when it is most important to do well. Even such events as interpersonal praise may affect performance through the mediation of self-awareness. Thus, praise increases effort but disrupts skills, and so the effects of praise on performance depend on whether effortful or skilled processes are involved (Baumeister, Hutton, & Cairns, 1990).

One of the most important of the harmful effects of self-awareness concerns depression. Greenberg and Pyszczynski (1986) identified a "depressive self-focusing style" that is to remain self-aware for a long time after failure. By thus dwelling on one's shortcomings and failures, particularly the ones that cannot be rectified, people put themselves into enduring states of unpleasant affect. Self-awareness may thus help depression become self-perpetuating.

Escaping Self-Awareness

Although most research has examined the consequences of being in a self-aware state having a trait level of self-awareness, it is apparent that people do try to regulate their level of self-awareness. In particular, there are certain circumstances under which people find self-awareness to be aversive or to be an impediment, and in those circumstances people actively try to escape from self-awareness.

Several studies demonstrated the motivation to escape self-awareness by measuring people's efforts to avoid cues (such as mirrors) that would remind them of themselves. Following receipt of a bad evaluation (Duval & Wicklund, 1972), or after receiving an interpersonal rejection or putdown (Gibbons & Wicklund, 1976), people were quick to leave a room filled with mirrors, suggesting that such events made self-awareness aversive so that people wanted to avoid that state. Carver and Scheier's (1981) view of self-awareness as a feedback loop received early support from a study by Steenbarger and Aderman (1979). In that work, all subjects received feedback that they possessed some undesirable personality attributes. Subjects who were told these character flaws could be remedied were much more willing to remain in a self-aware state (i.e., stayed longer in a room lined with mirrors) than subjects who were told that their bad traits were permanent and immutable.

Greenberg and Musham (1981) studied both avoiding or seeking self-awareness, by measuring whether subjects chose to sit facing a wall of mirrors or facing away from that wall. Subjects who had affirmed their own attitudes and acted consistently were quite willing to sit facing mirrors, but subjects who had spoken statements that contradicted their personal beliefs preferred to face away from the mirrors. Thus, self-awareness can be aversive when one's recent actions violate one's personal standards and invalidate one's beliefs.

Avoidance of mirrors is one way to minimize self-awareness, but in everyday life people who wish to escape from self-awareness must find other strong and effective means. It may be logically impossible to avoid self-awareness by sheer mental effort, because in order to monitor one's success one has to attend to oneself, thereby undermining what one is trying to accomplish. Apparently, therefore, the most common approach to escaping self-awareness is to restrict one's attention to an extremely narrow focus on the here and now, thereby reducing self to a mere body, experience to mere sensation, and action to mere muscle movement (Baumeister, 1991a; see also Vallacher & Wegner, 1985, 1987). Escape thus becomes escape from meaning, and the meaningful definitions of self are forgotten even as one focuses on the relatively meaningless, concrete, physical self.

Efforts to escape self-awareness appear to underlie a broad variety of activities. Hull (1981) proposed that one of the major effects of alcohol consumption is a reduction of self-awareness, and people often drink in order to achieve precisely that escape (see also Hull, Levenson, Young, & Sher, 1983; Hull & Young, 1983; Hull, Young, Jouriles, 1986; Steele & Josephs, 1990). Sexual masochism is apparently a set of techniques designed to blot out the meaningful identity (such as by removing control and responsibility, and systematically undermining self-esteem) while focusing attention on here-and-now stimuli including sensations of pain (Baumeister, 1988, 1989). Binge eating, which spans a broad range from broken diets to severe bulimia, also appears to be marked by strong patterns of escape from self-awareness (Heatherton & Baumeister, 1991). At the extreme, suicide attempts are often the result of strong desires to escape from self-awareness, typically because recent personal calamities have rendered self-awareness intolerable (Baumeister, 1990, 1991a).

Not all forms of escaping the self are pathological or self-destructive. Contrary to stereotypes, sexual masochism appears to be relatively harmless and is not linked to maladjustment or mental illness, and alcohol can be used in an innocuous fashion over long periods of time. Some consequences of escaping self-awareness may even be beneficial (see Baumeister, 1991a). Meditation and other religious or spiritual exercises are often considered to be among the highest forms of human striving, and many of them contain systematic steps for eliminating self-awareness, because self-focus and self-concern is widely regarded as an impediment to spiritual progress and salvation. At a less exalted level, sexual dysfunction often arises from excessive self-awareness, such as when people fail to enjoy sex because they are constantly worrying about whether they are doing it right and having the appropriate responses, and so sex therapists find it helpful to minimize self-awareness (Masters & Johnson, 1970). In general, many of life's happiest moments and best experiences are marked by a subjective state called *flow,* one characteristic of which is a loss of self-awareness (Csikszentmihalyi, 1982, 1990).

DEFEAT AND DESTRUCTION

Self-defeating behavior is one of the most intriguing and exasperating paradoxes in the research area concerned with the self. The essence of rationality is the pursuit of enlightened self-interest, so self-defeating behavior is quintessentially irrational. This very irrationality has made researchers especially interested in noting and documenting self-destructive behavior patterns, and a broad assortment of these has been demonstrated by social psychologists. (Note: The terms *self-defeating* and *self-destructive* are here used interchangeably.)

To understand why people defeat themselves, it is necessary to grasp the motivation that drives them. Several levels of intentionality can be distinguished. At one extreme, *deliberate self-destruction* involves behavior that is undertaken for the sake of the harmful consequences to the self—consequences that are foreseen and desired. At the other extreme, people may unwittingly defeat themselves by adopting *counterproductive* or *backfiring strategies,* in which their efforts are directed toward positive, desirable goals but their methods are ill-chosen and produce the opposite result. In that case, the self-defeating outcomes are neither foreseen nor desired. In between are *trade-offs*, in which harm to self is potentially foreseen but not desired. Trade-offs involve pursuing positive, desirable goals and receiving certain costs or risks of harm to the self as unwanted by-products.

A recent review of the literature on self-defeating behavior found evidence for only two of the three levels of self-destructive intentions (Baumeister & Scher, 1988). No evidence was found to support the hypothesis of deliberate self-destruction, contrary to the Freudian hypotheses of death wishes and self-destructive urges. Both trade-offs and backfiring strategies were found, however.

Trade-offs are widely familiar from everyday life. Alcohol and substance abuse can often be self-destructive, for example, but people do not engage in those forms of abuse in order to harm themselves. Rather, they seek the pleasure or relief or other benefits that accompany the intoxicated state, and the long-term costs are an unwanted side effect. Likewise, people show remarkably high levels of apparent disregard for physicians' instructions, such as in failing to take their medicine or complete a regimen of prescribed treatment. Evidence indicates that these failures are guided by a wish to avoid unpleasant medical procedures and perhaps an unwillingness to acknowledge that one is ill. Thus, once again, short-term hedonic benefits are pursued despite the long-term risks and costs of harm.

A similar trade-off appears to lie at the heart of the dilemma of shyness. Shy people are acutely, painfully sensitive to how others might regard them (Schlenker & Leary, 1982), and the fear of making a bad impression and being socially rejected causes them to withdraw from social interaction, adopting a protective self-presentational style (Arkin, 1981) and refusing to open up to others (Leary, Knight, & Johnson, 1987). Possibly as a result of this social reticence, they fail to develop social skills that might enable them to win friends, thereby making their social isolation self-perpetuating (e.g., Maroldo, 1982).

Self-handicapping is one of the best known self-defeating trade-offs in social psychology. Self-handicapping involves creating obstacles in the way of one's own performance, with the result that future anticipated failure will be blamed on the obstacle rather than on any lack of ability, and success will receive extra recognition (Higgins, Snyder, & Berglas, 1990; Jones & Berglas, 1978). Studies have shown that people will engage in self-handicapping in response to noncontingent success experiences that breed insecurity about being able to live up to inflated expectations (Berglas & Jones, 1978). Self-presentational motives appear to play an important role in producing self-handicapping (Kolditz & Arkin, 1982; Tice & Baumeister, 1990). People with low self-esteem self-handicap to protect themselves against possible failure, whereas people with high self-esteem self-handicap in order to enhance their credit for future success (Tice, 1991).

Counterproductive strategies, like trade-offs, have been well documented as an authentic feature of normal human behavior. People persist in losing endeavors, thereby enmeshing themselves ever deeper into costly predicaments (e.g., Rubin & Brockner, 1975; Staw, 1976). They adopt bargaining strategies that lead to loss, ruin, or stalemate (e.g., Bazerman, 1986; Pruitt, 1981; Pruitt & Rubin, 1984). They follow techniques of ingratiation that not only fail to increase liking but, in some cases, actually produce a negative reaction (Jones & Wortman, 1973).

Learned helplessness may be another important pattern of self-defeat. The essence of learned helplessness is that failure or experiences of control deprivation teach people that there is nothing they can do, and as a result they subsequently fail to learn or exert control even when the situation would allow them opportunities to take charge and control their fate (Seligman, 1975). To be sure, some have questioned whether learned helplessness actually occurs among human beings (e.g., Boyd, 1982; Frankel & Snyder, 1978). Still, it is quite apparent that various demoralizing and traumatic experiences do leave people unwilling or unable to respond adaptively to new, subsequently encountered challenges.

In general, it appears that counterproductive strategies are adopted following misjudgments about self and world. When people overestimate or underestimate what they can accomplish, they are vulnerable to making decisions and commitments that can lead to frustration, failure, and misfortune. Research has by now well established that normal, healthy people are prone to engage in a variety of self-defeating actions, and the challenge for researchers in this area is to shed further light on the mechanisms that mediate self-destruction. Thus, for example, preliminary evidence suggests that states of negative affect and high self-awareness are particularly prone to produce self-destructive responses (Baumeister & Scher, 1988). If researchers can succeed at illuminating these mechanisms, self-defeating behavior may cease to be as paradoxical as it once seemed.

CONCLUSION

Although many researchers identify themselves as involved in the study of "the self," it should be apparent by now that this is not a single area of research so much as it is a broad umbrella under which a great many topics, which are at best very loosely related, are studied. This heterogeneity is probably responsible for the continued interest in the self, because when one "self" topic begins to lose its interest or vitality, other topics emerge as the focus of new findings and ideas. For the most part, research on the self has managed to avoid developing large sets of conflicting, contradictory, incoherent findings, which often prove frustrating and discouraging to researchers attempting to make sense out of an interesting topic. The main reason that "self" subtopics seem to cease stimulating new findings is that key points and principles are gradually established and burning questions are answered. Researchers, after all, can be compared to miners, who will work in an area until it begins to run dry. Career pressures impel social scientists to produce new findings, and as soon as one set of questions has been answered, it is often time to move on to a new set of questions.

Over two thousand years ago, the Greek thinker Solon articulated the maxim "Know thyself." Although he probably had something quite different in mind from how modern individuals respond to that phrase, the maxim still serves as a valuable and useful guide. In social psychology, thousands of researchers have labored to approach Solon's injunction with scientific and systematic methods rather than relying on intuition, introspection, and superstition. The result of these efforts is a large and growing body of information. If Solon could return from the dead, he would no doubt be pleased to find that the self is better known today than at any previous time in history.

References

ARKIN, R. M. (1981). Self-presentation styles. In J. T. Tedeschi (Ed.), *Impression management theory in social psychological research* (pp. 311–333). New York: Academic Press.

BAUMEISTER, R. F. (1982). A self-presentational view of social phenomena. *Psychological Bulletin, 91,* 3–26.

BAUMEISTER, R. F. (1984). Choking under pressure: Self-consciousness and paradoxical effects of incentives on skillful performance. *Journal of Personality and Social Psychology, 46,* 610–620.

BAUMEISTER, R. F. (1986a). *Identity: Cultural change and the struggle for self.* New York: Oxford University Press.

BAUMEISTER, R. F. (1986b) (Ed.). *Public self and private self.* New York: Springer-Verlag.

BAUMEISTER, R. F. (1987). How the self became a problem: A psychological review of historical research. *Journal of Personality and Social Psychology, 52,* 163–176.

BAUMEISTER, R. F. (1988). Masochism as escape from self. *Journal of Sex Research, 25,* 28–59.

BAUMEISTER, R. F. (1989a). *Masochism and the self.* Hillsdale, NJ: Erlbaum.

BAUMEISTER, R. F. (1989b). The optimal margin of illusion. *Journal of Social and Clinical Psychology, 8,* 176–189.

BAUMEISTER, R. F. (1990). Suicide as escape from self. *Psychological Review, 97,* 90–113.

BAUMEISTER, R. F. (1991a). *Escaping the self: Alcoholism, spirituality, masochism, and other flights from the burden of selfhood.* New York: Basic Books.

BAUMEISTER, R. F. (1991b). *Meanings of life.* New York: Guilford Press.

BAUMEISTER, R. F. (1991c). On the stability of variability: Retest reliability of metatraits. *Personality and Social Psychology Bulletin, 17,* 633–639.

BAUMEISTER, R. F., & CAIRNS, K. J. (1992). Repression and self-presentation: When audiences interfere with self-deceptive strategies. *Journal of Personality and Social Psychology, 62,* 851–862.

BAUMEISTER, R. F., HEATHERTON, T. F., & TICE, D. M. (1993). When ego threats lead to self-regulation failure: Negative consequences of high self-esteem. *Journal of Personality and Social Psychology, 64,* 141–156.

BAUMEISTER, R. F., HUTTON, D. G., & CAIRNS, K. J. (1990). Negative effects of praise on skilled performance. *Basic and Applied Social Psychology, 11,* 131–148.

BAUMEISTER, R. F., HUTTON, D. G., & TICE, D. M. (1989). Cognitive processes during deliberate self-presentation: How self-presenters alter and misinterpret the behavior of their interaction partners. *Journal of Experimental Social Psychology, 25,* 59–78.

BAUMEISTER, R. F., & LEARY, M. R. (1994). The need to belong: Desire for interpersonal attachments as a fundamental human motivation. Manuscript submitted for publication.

BAUMEISTER, R. F., & SCHER, S. J. (1988). Self-defeating behavior patterns among normal individuals: Review and analysis of common self-destructive tendencies. *Psychological Bulletin, 104,* 3–22.

BAUMEISTER, R. F., SHAPIRO, J. J., & TICE, D. M. (1985). Two kinds of identity crisis. *Journal of Personality, 53,* 407–424.

BAUMEISTER, R. F., & TICE, D. M. (1984). Role of self-presentation and choice in cognitive dissonance under forced compliance: Necessary or sufficient causes? *Journal of Personality and Social Psychology, 46,* 5–13.

BAUMEISTER, R. F., & TICE, D. M. (1990). Anxiety and social exclusion. *Journal of Social and Clinical Psychology, 9,* 165–195.

BAUMEISTER, R. F., TICE, D. M., & HUTTON, D. G. (1989). Self-presentational motivations and personality differences in self-esteem. *Journal of Personality, 57,* 547–579.

BAUMGARDNER, A. H. (1990). To know oneself is to like oneself: Self-certainty and self- affect. *Journal of Personality and Social Psychology, 58,* 1062–1072.

BAZERMAN, M. H. (1986a). *Human judgment in managerial decision making.* New York: John Wiley & Sons.

BAZERMAN, M. H. (1986b). Why negotiations go wrong. *Psychology Today, 20,* 54–58.

BEACH, S. R. H. (1992: May). Self-evaluation maintenance and marital functioning. Presented at the conference of the Midwestern Psychological Association, Chicago IL.

BEAMAN, A. L., KLENTZ, B., DIENER, E., & SVANUM, S. (1979). Self-awareness and transgression in children: Two field studies. *Journal of Personality and Social Psychology, 37,* 1835–1846.

BECKER, E. (1973). *The denial of death.* New York: Free Press.

BELLAH, R. N., MADSEN, R., SULLIVAN, W. M., SWIDLER, A., & TIPTON, S. M. (1985). *Habits of the heart: Individualism and commitment in American life.* Berkeley, CA: University of California Press.

BERGLAS, S., & JONES, E. E. (1978). Drug choice as a self-handicapping strategy in response to noncontingent success. *Journal of Personality and Social Psychology, 36,* 405–417.

BLAINE, B., & CROCKER, J. (1993). Self-esteem and self-serving biases in reactions to positive and negative events: An integrative review. In R. Baumeister (Ed.), *Self-esteem: The puzzle of low self-regard* (pp. 55–85). New York: Plenum.

BOURNE, E. (1978). The state of research on ego identity: A review and appraisal. Part II. *Journal of Youth and Adolescence, 7,* 371–392.

BOYD, T. L. (1982). Learned helplessness in humans: A frustration-produced response pattern. *Journal of Personality and Social Psychology, 42,* 738–752.

BROWN, J. D. (1986). Evaluations of self and others: Self-enhancement biases in social judgments. *Social Cognition, 4,* 353–376.

BROWN, J. D. (1993). Motivational conflict and the self: The double-bind of low self- esteem. In R. Baumeister (Ed.), *Self-esteem: The puzzle of low self-regard* (pp. 117–145). New York: Plenum.

BROWN, J. D., COLLINS, R. L., & SCHMIDT, G. W. (1988). Self-esteem and direct versus indirect forms of self-enhancement. *Journal of Personality and Social Psychology, 55,* 445–453.

CALIFORNIA TASK FORCE TO PROMOTE SELF-ESTEEM AND PERSONAL AND SOCIAL RESPONSIBILITY (1990). *Toward a state of self-esteem.* Sacramento, CA: California State Department of Education.

CAMPBELL, J. D. (1990). Self-esteem and clarity of the self-concept. *Journal of Personality and Social Psychology, 59,* 538–549.

CAMPBELL, J. D., & LAVALLEE, L. F. (1993). Who am I? The role of self-concept confusion in understanding the behavior of people with low self-esteem. In R. Baumeister (Ed.), *Self-esteem: The puzzle of low self-regard* (pp. 3–20). New York: Plenum.

CARVER, C. S., & SCHEIER, M. F. (1981). *Attention and self-regulation: A control theory approach to human behavior.* New York: Springer-Verlag.

CARVER, C. S., & SCHEIER, M. F. (1982). Control theory: A useful conceptual framework for personality-social, clinical and health psychology. *Psychological Bulletin, 92,* 111–135.

CARVER, C. S., & SCHEIER, M. F. (1987). The blind men and the elephant: Selective examination of the public-private literature gives rise to a faulty perception. *Journal of Personality, 55,* 525–541.

CIALDINI, R. B., BORDEN, R. J., THORNE, A., WALKER, M. R., FREEMAN, S., & SLOAN, L. R. (1976). Basking in reflected glory: Three (football) field studies. *Journal of Personality and Social Psychology, 34,* 366–375.

CIALDINI, R. B., & RICHARDSON, K. D. (1980). Two indirect tactics of image management: Basking and blasting. *Journal of Personality and Social Psychology, 39,* 406–415.

CROCKER, J., & SCHWARTZ, I. (1985). Prejudice and ingroup favoritism in a minimal intergroup situation: Effects of self-esteem. *Personality and Social Psychology Bulletin, 11,* 379–386.

CROYLE, R. T., & COOPER, J. (1983). Dissonance arousal: Physiological evidence. *Journal of Personality and Social Psychology, 45,* 782–791.

CSIKSZENTMIHALYI, M. (1982). Toward a psychology of optimal experience. In L. Wheeler (Ed.), *Review of personality and social psychology* (Vol. 2, pp. 13–36). Beverly Hills, CA: Sage.

CSIKSZENTMIHALYI, M. (1990). *Flow: The psychology of optimal experience.* New York: Harper & Row.

DECI, E. L., & RYAN, R. M. (1987). The support of autonomy and the control of behavior. *Journal of Personality and Social Psychology, 53,* 1024–1037.

DEVINE, P. G., SEDIKIDES, C., & FUHRMAN, R. W. (1989). Goals in social information processing: The case of anticipated interaction. *Journal of Personality and Social Psychology, 56,* 680–690.

DIENER, E., & WALLBOM, M. (1976). Effects of self-awareness on antinormative behavior. *Journal of Research in Personality, 10,* 107–111.

DOI, T. (1986). *The anatomy of conformity: The individual versus society.* Tokyo, Japan: Kodansha.

DUVAL, S., & WICKLUND, R. A. (1972). *A theory of objective self-awareness.* New York: Academic Press.

ERIKSON, E. H. (1968). *Identity: Youth and crisis.* New York: Norton.

FAZIO, R. H., EFFREIN, E. A., & FALENDER, V. J. (1981). Self-perceptions following social interactions. *Journal of Personality and Social Psychology, 41,* 232–242.

FENIGSTEIN, A. (1987). On the nature of public and private self-consciousness. *Journal of Personality, 55,* 543–554.

FENIGSTEIN, A., SCHEIER, M. F., & BUSS, A. H. (1975). Public and private self-consciousness: Assessment and theory. *Journal of Consulting and Clinical Psychology, 43,* 522–527.

FESTINGER, L. (1954). A theory of social comparison processes. *Human Relations, 7,* 117–140.

FRANKEL, A., & SNYDER, M. L. (1978). Poor performance following unsolvable problems: Learned helplessness or egotism? *Journal of Personality and Social Psychology, 36,* 1415–1423.

GAES, G. G., KALLE, R. J., & TEDESCHI, J. T. (1978). Impression management in the forced compliance situation: Two studies using the bogus pipeline. *Journal of Experimental Social Psychology, 14,* 493–510.

GIBBONS, F. X. (1978). Sexual standards and reactions to pornography: Enhancing behavioral consistency through self-focused attention. *Journal of Personality and Social Psychology, 36,* 976–987.

GIBBONS, F. X., & WICKLUND, R. A. (1976). Selective exposure to self. *Journal of Research in Personality, 10,* 98–106.

GILBERT, D. T., & JONES, E. E. (1986) Perceiver-induced constraint: Interpretations of self-generated reality. *Journal of Personality and Social Psychology, 50,* 269–280.

GOFFMAN, E. (1959). *The presentation of self in everyday life.* New York: Anchor Books.

GOLLWITZER, P. M. (1986). Striving for specific identities: The social reality of self-symbolizing. In R. Baumeister (Ed.), *Public self and private self* (pp. 143–159). New York: Springer-Verlag.

GOLLWITZER, P. M., & KINNEY, R. F. (1989). Effects of deliberative and implemental mind-sets on illusion of control. *Journal of Personality and Social Psychology, 56,* 531–542.

GOLLWITZER, P. M., & WICKLUND, R. A. (1987). Fusing apples and oranges: A rejoinder to Carver & Scheier and to Fenigstein. *Journal of Personality, 55,* 555–561.

GREENBERG, J., & MUSHAM, C. (1981). Avoiding and seeking self-focused attention. *Journal of Research in Personality, 15,* 191–200.

GREENBERG, J., PYSZCZYNSKI, T., & SOLOMON, S. (1986). The causes and consequences of self-esteem: A terror management theory. In R. Baumeister (Ed.), *Public self and private self.* New York: Springer-Verlag.

GREENWALD, A. G. (1980). The totalitarian ego: Fabrication and revision of personal history. *American Psychologist, 35,* 603–618.

GREENWALD, A. G. (1988). Self-knowledge and self-deception. In J. B. Lockard & D. Paulhus (Eds.), *Self-deception: An adaptive mechanism* (pp. 113–131)? Englewood Cliffs, NJ: Prentice-Hall.

GREENWALD, A. G., BELLEZZA, F. S., & BANAJI, M. R. (1988). Is self-esteem a central ingredient of the self-concept? *Personality and Social Psychology Bulletin, 14,* 34–45.

GUR, R. C., & SACKEIM, H. A. (1979). Self-deception: A concept in search of phenomenon. *Journal of Personality and Social Psychology, 37,* 147–169.

HARTER, S. (1993). Causes and consequences of low self-esteem in children and adolescents. In R. Baumeister (Ed.), *Self-esteem: The puzzle of low self-regard* (pp. 87–116). New York: Plenum.

HEATHERTON, T. F., & BAUMEISTER, R. F. (1991). Binge eating as escape from self-awareness. *Psychological Bulletin, 110,* 86–108.

HEATHERTON, T. F., & POLIVY, J. (1991). Development and validation of a scale for measuring state self-esteem. *Journal of Personality and social Psychology, 60,* 895–910.

HIGGINS, E. T. (1987). Self-discrepancy: A theory relating self and affect. *Psychological Review, 94,* 319–340.

HIGGINS, R. L., SNYDER, C. R., & BERGLAS, S. (1990). *Self-handicapping: The paradox that isn't.* New York: Plenum.

HULL, J. G. (1981). A self-awareness model of the causes and effects of alcohol consumption. *Journal of Abnormal Psychology, 90,* 586–600.

HULL, J. G., LEVENSON, R. W., YOUNG, R. D., & SHER, K. J. (1983). Self-awareness-reducing effects of alcohol consumption. *Journal of Personality and Social Psychology, 44,* 461–473.

HULL, J. G., & LEVY, A. S. (1979). The organizational functions of the self: An alternative to the Duval and Wicklund model of self-awareness. *Journal of Personality and Social Psychology, 37,* 756–768.

HULL, J. G., & YOUNG, R. D. (1983). Self-consciousness, self-esteem, and success-failure as determinants of alcohol consumption in male social drinkers. *Journal of Personality and Social Psychology, 44,* 1097–1109.

HULL, J. G., YOUNG, R. D., & JOURILES, E. (1986). Applications of the self-awareness model of alcohol and consumption: Predicting patterns of use and abuse. *Journal of Personality and Social Psychology, 51,* 790–796.

IWAO, S. (1988, August). Social psychology's models of man: Isn't it time for East to meet West? Presented to the International Congress of Scientific Psychology, Sydney, Australia.

JONES, E. E., & BERGLAS, S. C. (1978). Control of attributions about the self through self-handicapping strategies: The appeal of alcohol and the role of underachievement. *Personality and Social Psychology Bulletin, 4,* 200–206.

JONES, E. E., & GERARD, H. B. (1967). *Foundations of social psychology.* New York: Wiley.

JONES, E. E., RHODEWALT, F., BERGLAS, S. C., & SKELTON, A. (1981). Effects of strategic self-presentation on subsequent self-esteem. *Journal of Personality and Social Psychology, 41,* 407–421.

JONES, E. E., & WORTMAN, C. (1973). *Ingratiation: An attributional approach.* Morristown, NJ: General Learning Press.

JOSEPHS, R. A., MARKUS, H. R., & TAFARODI, R. W. (1992). Gender and self-esteem. *Journal of Personality and Social Psychology, 63,* 391–402.

KATAKIS, C. D. (1976). An exploratory multilevel attempt to investigate interpersonal and intrapersonal patterns of 20 Athenian families. *Mental Health and Society, 3,* 1–9.

KATAKIS, C. D. (1978). On the transaction of social change processes and the perception of self in relation to others. *Mental Health and Society, 5,* 275–283.

KATAKIS, C. D. (1984). *The three identities of the Greek family.* Athens, Greece: Kedros.

KERNIS, M. H. (1993). The roles of stability and level of self-esteem in psychological functioning. In R. Baumeister (Ed.), *Self-esteem: The puzzle of low self-regard* (pp. 167–182). New York: Plenum.

KERNIS, M. H., GRANNEMAN, B. D., & BARCLAY, L. C. (1989). Stability and level of self-esteem as predictors of anger arousal and hostility. *Journal of Personality and Social Psychology, 56,* 1013–1022.

KERNIS, M. H., GRANNEMAN, B. D., & MATHIS, L. C. (1991). Stability of self-esteem as a moderator of the relation between level of self-esteem and depression. *Journal of Personality and Social Psychology, 61,* 80–84.

KOLDITZ, T. A., & ARKIN, R. M. (1982). An impression management intepretation of the self-handicapping strategy. *Journal of Personality and Social Psychology, 43,* 492–502.

LEARY, M. R., KNIGHT, P. D., & JOHNSON, K. A. (1987). Social anxiety and dyadic conversation: a verbal response analysis. *Journal of Social and Clinical Psychology, 5,* 34–50.

LEARY, M. R., & KOWALSKI, R. M. (1990). Impression management: A literature review and two-component model. *Psychological Bulletin, 107,* 34–47.

LIU, T. J., & STEELE, C. M. (1986). Attribution as self-affirmation. *Journal of Personality and Social Psychology, 51,* 351–360.

MARCIA, J. E. (1966). Development and validation of ego-identity status. *Journal of Personality and Social Psychology, 3,* 551–558.

MARCIA, J. E. (1967). Ego identity status: Relationship to change in self-esteem, "general maladjustment," and authoritarianism. *Journal of Personality, 35,* 118–133.

MARCIA, J. E. (1976). Studies in ego identity. Unpublished manuscript, Simon Fraser University.

MARKUS, H. (1977). Self-schemata and processing information about the self. *Journal of Personality and Social Psychology, 35,* 63–78.

MARKUS, H. R., & KITAYAMA, S. (1991). Culture and the self: Implications for cognition, emotion, and motivation. *Psychological Review, 98,* 224–253.

MARKUS, H., & KUNDA, Z. (1986). Stability and malleability of the self-concept. *Journal of Personality and Social Psychology, 51,* 858–866.

MARKUS, H., & NURIUS, P. S. (1986). Possible selves. *American Psychologist, 41,* 954–969.

MAROLDO, G. K. (1982). Shyness and love on the college campus. *Perceptual and Motor Skills, 55,* 819–824.

MASTERS, W. H., & JOHNSON, V. E. (1970). *Human sexual inadequacy.* Boston, MA: Little, Brown & Co.

MCFARLIN, D. B., & BLASCOVICH, J. (1981). Effects of self-esteem and performance feedback on future affective preferences and cognitive expectations. *Journal of Personality and Social Psychology, 40,* 521–531.

MCGUIRE, W. J., MCGUIRE, C. V., CHILD, P., & FUJIOKA, T. (1978). Salience of ethnicity in the spontaneous self-concept as a function of one's ethnic distinctiveness in the social environment. *Journal of Personality and Social Psychology, 36,* 511–520.

MCGUIRE, W. J., MCGUIRE, C. V., & WINTON, W. (1979). Effects of household sex composition on the salience of one's gender in the spontaneous self-concept. *Journal of Experimental Social Psychology, 15,* 77–90.

MEAD, G. H. (1934). *Mind, self, and society.* Chicago, IL: University of Chicago Press.

NISBETT, R., & WILSON, T. D. (1977). Telling more than we can know: Verbal reports on mental processes. *Psychological Review, 84,* 231–259.

OGILVIE, D. M. (1987). The undesired self: A neglected variable in personality research. *Journal of Personality and Social Psychology, 52,* 379–385.

PAULHUS, D. L. (1982). Individual differences, self-presentation, and cognitive dissonance: Their concurrent operation in forced compliance. *Journal of Personality and Social Psychology, 43,* 838–852.

PAULHUS, D. L., & LEVITT, K. (1987). Desirable responding triggered by affect: Automatic egotism? *Journal of Personality and Social Psychology, 52,* 245–259.

PELHAM, B. W. (1993). On the highly positive thoughts of the highly depressed. In R. Baumeister (Ed.), *Self-esteem: The puzzle of low self-regard* (pp. 183–199). New York: Plenum.

PELHAM, B. W., & TAYLOR, S. E. (1991). On the limits of illusions: Exploring the costs and hazards of high self-regard. Unpublished manuscript, University of California at Los Angeles.

PITTMAN, T. S., & PITTMAN, N. L. (1980). Deprivation of control and the attribution process. *Journal of Personality and Social Psychology, 39,* 377–389.

PLEBAN, R., & TESSER, A. (1981). The effects of relevance and quality of another's performance on interpersonal closeness. *Social Psychology Quarterly, 44,* 278–285.

PRUITT, D. G. (1981). *Negotiation behavior.* New York: Academic Press.

PRUITT, D. G., & RUBIN, J. Z. (1984). *Social conflict: Escalation, stalemate, and settlement.* New York: Random House.

PRYOR, J. B., GIBBONS, F. X., WICKLUND, R. A., FAZIO, R. H., & HOOD, R. (1977). Self-focused attention and self-report validity. *Journal of Personality, 45,* 514–527.

ROESKE, N. A., & LAKE, K. (1977). Role models for women medical students. *Journal of Medical Education, 52,* 459–466.

ROGERS, T. B., KUIPER, N. A., & KIRKER, W. S. (1977). Self-reference and the encoding of personal information. *Journal of Personality and Social Psychology, 35,* 677–688.

ROSENBERG, M. (1979). *Conceiving the self.* New York: Basic Books.

ROSS, M., & SICOLY, F. (1979). Egocentric biases in availability and attribution. *Journal of Personality and Social Psychology, 48,* 322–336.

RUBIN, J. Z., & BROCKNER, J. (1975). Factors affecting entrapment in waiting situations: The Rosencrantz and Guildenstern effect. *Journal of Personality and Social Psychology, 31,* 1054–1063.

RYAN, R. M. (1991). The nature of the self in autonomy and relatedness. In J. Strauss & G. R. Goethals (Eds.), *The self: Interdisciplinary approaches* (pp. 208–238). New York: Springer-Verlag.

SABINI, J., & SILVER, M. (1981). Introspection and causal accounts. *Journal of Personality and Social Psychology, 40,* 171–179.

SARTRE, J.-P. (1953). *The existential psychoanalysis* (H. E. Barnes, trans.). New York: Philosophical Library.

SCHEIER, M. F., & CARVER, C. S. (1977). Self-focused attention and the experience of emotion: Attraction, repulsion, elation, and depression. *Journal of Personality and Social Psychology, 35,* 625–636.

SCHEIER, M. F., FENIGSTEIN, A., & BUSS, A. H. (1974). Self-awareness and physical aggression. *Journal of Experimental Social Psychology, 10,* 264–273.

SCHLENKER, B. R. (1975). Self-presentation: Managing the impression of consistency when reality interferes with self-enhancement. *Journal of Personality and Social Psychology. 32,* 1030–1037.

SCHLENKER, B. R. (1980). *Impression management: The self-concept, social identity, and interpersonal relations.* Monterey, CA: Brooks/Cole.

SCHLENKER, B. R. (1986). Self-identification: Toward an integration of the private and public self. In R. Baumeister (Ed.), *Public self and private self* (pp. 21–62). New York: Springer-Verlag.

SCHLENKER, B. R., DLUGOLECKI, D. W., & DOHERTY, K. (1994). The impact of self-presentations on self-appraisals and behavior: The roles of commitment and biased scanning. *Personality and Social Psychology Bulletin, 20,* 20–33.

SCHLENKER, B. R., & LEARY, M. R. (1982). Social anxiety and self-presentation: A conceptualization and model. *Psychological Bulletin, 92,* 641–669.

SEDIKIDES, C. (1993). Assessment, enhancement, and verification determinants of the self-evaluation process. *Journal of Personality and Social Psychology, 65,* 317–338.

SELIGMAN, M. E. P. (1975). *Helplessness: On depression, development, and death.* San Francisco, CA: Freeman.

SHRAUGER, J. S. (1975). Responses to evaluation as a function of initial self-perceptions. *Psychological Bulletin, 82,* 581–596.

SHRAUGER, J. S., & SCHOENEMAN, T. J. (1979). Symbolic interactionist view of self-concept: Through the looking glass darkly. *Psychological Bulletin, 86,* 549–573.

SMITH, E. R., & MILLER, F. D. (1978). Limits on perception of cognitive processes: A reply to Nisbett and Wilson. *Psychological Review, 85,* 355–362.

SOLOMON, S., GREENBERG, J., & PYSZCZYNSKI, T. (1991). A terror management theory of social behavior: The psychological functions of self-esteem and cultural world-views. In M. P. Zanna (Ed.), *Advances in experimental social psychology* (Vol. 24, pp. 93–159). San Diego, CA: Academic Press.

SPENCER, S. J., JOSEPHS, R. A., & STEELE, C. M. (1993). Low self-esteem: The uphill struggle for self-integrity. In R. Baumeister (Ed.), *Self-esteem: The puzzle of low self-regard* (pp. 21–36). New York: Plenum.

STAW, B. M. (1976). Knee-deep in the big muddy: A study of escalating commitment to a chosen course of action. *Organizational Behavior and Human Performance, 16,* 27–44.

STEELE, C. M. (1975). Name calling and compliance. *Journal of Personality and Social Psychology, 31,* 361–369.

STEELE, C. M. (1988). The psychology of self-affirmation: Sustaining the integrity of the self. In L. Berkowitz (Ed.), *Advances in experimental social psychology* (Vol. 21, pp. 261–302). New York: Academic Press.

STEELE, C. M., & JOSEPHS, R. A. (1990). Alcohol myopia: Its prized and dangerous effects. *American Psychologist, 45,* 921–933.

STEENBARGER, B. N., & ADERMAN, D. (1979). Objective self-awareness as a nonaversive state: Effect of anticipating discrepancy reduction. *Journal of Personality, 47,* 330–339.

SULLIVAN, H. S. (1953). *The interpersonal theory of psychiatry.* New York: Norton.

SWANN, W. B. (1985). The self as architect of social reality. In B. R. Schlenker (Ed.), *The self and social life* (pp. 100–125). New York: McGraw-Hill.

SWANN, W. B. (1987). Identity negotiation: Where two roads meet. *Journal of Personality and Social Psychology, 53*, 1038–1051.

SWANN, W. B., GRIFFIN, J. J., PREDMORE, S. C., & GAINES, B. (1987). The cognitive-affective crossfire: When self-consistency confronts self-enhancement. *Journal of Personality and Social Psychology. 52*, 881–889.

SWANN, W. B., & HILL, C. A. (1982). When our identities are mistaken: Reaffirming self-conceptions through social interaction. *Journal of Personality and Social Psychology, 43*, 59–66.

TAYLOR, S. E. (1989). *Positive illusions: Creative self-deception and the healthy mind.* New York: Basic Books.

TAYLOR, S. E., & BROWN, J. D. (1988). Illusion and well-being: A social psychological perspective on mental health. *Psychological Bulletin, 103*, 193–210.

TEDESCHI, J. T., SCHLENKER, B. R., & BONOMA, T. V. (1971). Cognitive dissonance: Private ratiocination or public spectacle? *American Psychologist, 26*, 685–695.

TESSER, A. (1988). Toward a self-evaluation maintenance model of social behavior. In L. Berkowitz (Ed.), *Advances in experimental social psychology* (Vol. 21, pp. 181–227). San Diego, CA: Academic Press.

TESSER, A., & PAULHUS, D. (1983). The definition of self: Private and public self-evaluation management strategies. *Journal of Personality and Social Psychology, 44*, 672–682.

TESSER, A., & SMITH, J. (1980). Some effects of friendship and task relevance on helping: You don't always help the one you like. *Journal of Experimental Social Psychology, 16*, 582–590.

TETLOCK, P. E. (1986). A value pluralism model of ideological reasoning. *Journal of Personality and Social Psychology, 50*, 819–827.

TETLOCK, P. E., & MANSTEAD, A. S. (1985). Impression management versus intrapsychic explanations in social psychology: A useful dichotomy? *Psychological Review, 92*, 59–77.

TICE, D. M. (1992). Self-presentation and self-concept change: The looking glass self as magnifying glass. *Journal of Personality and Social Psychology, 63*, 435–451.

TICE, D. M. (1993). The social motivations of people with low self-esteem. In R. Baumeister (Ed.), *Self-esteem: The puzzle of low self-regard* (pp. 37–53). New York: Plenum.

TICE, D. M. (1991). Esteem protection or enhancement? Self-handicapping motives and attributions differ by trait self-esteem. *Journal of Personality and Social Psychology, 60*, 711–725.

TICE, D. M., & BAUMEISTER, R. F. (1990). Self-esteem, self-handicapping, and self-presentation: The strategy of inadequate practice. *Journal of Personality, 58*, 443–464.

TRIANDIS, H. C. (1989). The self and social behavior in differing cultural contexts. *Psychological Review, 96*, 506–520.

TRILLING, L. (1971). *Sincerity and authenticity.* Cambridge, MA: Harvard University Press.

VALLACHER, R. R., & WEGNER, D. M. (1985). *A theory of action identification.* Hillsdale, NJ: Erlbaum.

VALLACHER, R. R., & WEGNER, D. M. (1987). What do people think they're doing: Action identification and human behavior. *Psychological Review, 94*, 3–15.

WICKLUND, R. A. (1975). Objective self-awareness. In L. Berkowitz (Ed.), *Advances in experimental social psychology* (Vol. 8, pp. 233–275). New York: Academic Press.

WICKLUND, R. A., & DUVAL, S. (1971). Opinion change and performance facilitation as a result of objective self-awareness. *Journal of Experimental Social Psychology, 7*, 319–342.

WICKLUND, R. A., & GOLLWITZER, P. M. (1982). *Symbolic self-completion*. Hillsdale, NJ: Erlbaum.

WICKLUND, R. A., & GOLLWITZER, P. M. (1987). The fallacy of the private-public self-focus distinction. *Journal of Personality, 55,* 491–523.

WILLS, T. A. (1981). Downward comparison principles in social psychology. *Psychological Bulletin, 90,* 245–271.

WILSON, T. D., DUNN, D. S., BYBEE, J. A., HYMAN, D. B., & ROTONDO, J. A. (1984). Effects of analyzing reasons on attitude-behavior consistency. *Journal of Personality and Social Psychology, 44,* 5–16.

ZANNA, M. P., & COOPER, J. (1974). Dissonance and the pill: An attribution approach to studying the arousal properties of dissonance. *Journal of Personality and Social Psychology, 29,* 703–709.

ZUBE, M. J. (1972). Changing concepts of morality: 1948–1969. *Social Forces, 50,* 385–393.

Further Readings

It is almost inevitably absurd and arbitrary to choose a short list from the many publications on the self. I have made this list by focusing on review articles and integrative papers or books.

Self-Knowledge

GREENWALD, A. G. (1980). The totalitarian ego: Fabrication and revision of personal history. *American Psychologist, 35,* 603–618.
A seminal examination of how the personal construction of self-knowledge can produce distortion.

SHRAUGER, J. S., & SCHOENEMAN, T. J. (1979). Symbolic interactionist view of self-concept: Through the looking glass darkly. *Psychological Bulletin, 86,* 549–573.
An authoritative examination of the social roots of self-knowledge.

SWANN, W. B. (1987). Identity negotiation: Where two roads meet. *Journal of Personality and Social Psychology, 53,* 1038–1051.
A forceful statement of how the author's work on consistency of self-concept integrates with the motivation to think well of oneself.

TAYLOR, S. E., & BROWN, J. D. (1988). Illusion and well-being: A social psychological perspective on mental health. *Psychological Bulletin, 103,* 193–210.
A highly influential review of evidence about how normal people end up with overly favorable views of themselves and their prospects.

Cultural and Historical Context

BAUMEISTER, R. F. (1987). How the self became a problem: A psychological review of historical research. *Journal of Personality and Social Psychology, 52,* 163–176.
An examination of how the current Western view of self evolved.

TRIANDIS, H. C. (1989). The self and social behavior in differing cultural contexts. *Psychological Review, 96,* 506–520.
A seminal exploration of how cultural differences can produce differences in the way the self is constructed.

Interpersonal Aspects

BAUMEISTER, R. F. (1982). A self-presentational view of social phenomena. *Psychological Bulletin, 91,* 3–26.

An integrative effort to show how a broad range of social behaviors is affected by basic concerns with how the person is regarded by others.

SCHLENKER, B. R. (1980). *Impression management: The self-concept, social identity, and interpersonal relations.* Monterey, CA: Brooks/Cole.
An integrative statement on how people manage the public aspect of identity.

TESSER, A. (1988). Toward a self-evaluation maintenance model of social behavior. In L. Berkowitz (Ed.), *Advances in experimental social psychology* (Vol. 21, pp. 181–227). San Diego, CA: Academic Press.
An overview of research on how social relations with others are affected by concern with a well-articulated group of self-evaluation processes.

Emotion and Motivation

HIGGINS, E. T. (1987). Self-discrepancy: A theory relating self and affect. *Psychological Review, 94,* 319–340.
An influential theory about how emotional reactions follow from self-appraisals.

MARKUS, H., & NURIUS, P. S. (1986). Possible selves. *American Psychologist, 41,* 954–969.
A thoughtful articulation of how possible rather than actual self-conceptions may motivate behavior and influence emotion.

SCHLENKER, B. R., & LEARY, M. R. (1982). Social anxiety and self-presentation: A conceptualization and model. *Psychological Bulletin, 92,* 641–669.
A thoughtful review and theory about how self-presentational motivations determine the interpersonal structure of shyness and anxiety.

STEELE, C. M. (1988). The psychology of self-affirmation: Sustaining the integrity of the self. In L. Berkowitz (Ed.), *Advances in experimental social psychology* (Vol. 21, pp. 261–302). New York: Academic Press.
An integrative overview of research concerned with a fundamental need to affirm a positive view of self.

WICKLUND, R. A., & GOLLWITZER, P. M. (1982). *Symbolic self-completion.* Hillsdale, NJ: Erlbaum.
A research program that presents the self in goal-directed terms.

Special Topics

BAUMEISTER, R. F. (1993) (Ed.). *Self-esteem: The puzzle of low self-regard.* New York: Plenum.
A compilation of chapters in which most major self-esteem researchers summarize their research programs.

BAUMEISTER, R. F., & SCHER, S. J. (1988). Self-defeating behavior patterns among normal individuals: Review and analysis of common self-destructive tendencies. *Psychological Bulletin, 104,* 3–22.
An integrative overview of these paradoxical patterns of behavior.

CARVER, C. S., & SCHEIER, M. F. (1981). *Attention and self-regulation: A Control theory approach to human behavior.* New York: Springer-Verlag.
An eloquent and influential version of self-awareness theory and the research associated with it.

Daniel Gilbert is an Associate Professor of Psychology at the University of Texas at Austin and Chair of the Program in Social and Personality Psychology. His research focuses primarily on understanding the processes by which ordinary people understand each other. As well, he has studied and written about the philosophical and psychological aspects of belief. He is the winner of the American Psychological Association's Distinguished Scientific Award for an Early Career Contribution. He has also published a half dozen works of science fiction. His hobbies include collecting, composing, and playing music.

CHAPTER 4

Attribution and Interpersonal Perception*

Daniel T. Gilbert
University of Texas –Austin

CHAPTER OUTLINE

The stellar universe is not so difficult of comprehension as the real actions of other people.

—MARCEL PROUST (1923/1949, p. 253)

At about 9 P.M. on February 4, 1974, a young college student and her fiancé sat down to study at the dining room table in their apartment on Benvenue Street

*This chapter was written while the author was a Fellow at the Center for Advanced Study in the Behavioral Sciences. That fellowship was made possible by the John D. and Catherine T. MacArthur Foundation and by a Research Scientist Development Award from the National Institute of Mental Health (1-KO2-MH00939-01). The generous support of these institutions is gratefully acknowledged. An earlier version of this chapter benefited from the comments of David Meyers, Robert Sekuler, and several anonymous reviewers.

in Berkeley. The doorbell rang, and when Steven Weed answered, two men and a woman armed with M-1 carbines forced their way into the apartment. They beat Steven Weed into unconsciousness, bound, gagged, and blindfolded Patty Hearst, and dragged her to a waiting car. Eight days later, a tape was delivered to radio station KPFA. The kidnappers were members of a militant leftist organization that called itself the Symbionese Liberation Army (SLA) and they demanded that Patty's father, a wealthy publisher, distribute millions of dollars in food to the poor in exchange for his daughter's life. Ten days later, Randolph Hearst complied with that demand, but his daughter was not returned. Rather, a series of new demands, negotiations, and more food giveaways ensued. Finally, on April 2, a small newspaper, *The Phoenix*, published a letter from the SLA promising Patty's release within seventy-two hours.

Her family's joy was short-lived. The very next day, radio station KSAN received a tape in which Patty Hearst made an announcement that shocked the nation:

> I would like to begin this statement by informing the public that I wrote what I am about to say. It's what I feel. I have never been forced to say anything on any tape. Nor have I been brainwashed, drugged, tortured, hypnotized, or in any way confused. . . . I have been given the choice of (1) being released in a safe area or (2) joining the forces of the Symbionese Liberation Army and fighting for my freedom and the freedom of all oppressed people. I have chosen to stay and fight (Hearst, 1982, pp. 118–119).

Patty explained that in the months of her incarceration she had come to see the moral imperative of the SLA's mission as well as the meaninglessness of her former life. As such, she had renounced her past and adopted the name of the Bolivian guerrilla fighter, Tania Burke. She ended her speech this way: "It is in the spirit of Tania that I say *Patria o Muerte, venceremos,*" which means "Fatherland or death, we shall be victorious."

And victorious they were. Twelve days later, a security camera at the Hibernia Bank in San Francisco photographed Tania Hearst as she and her comrades withdrew slightly more than $10,000—not with an automatic teller card but with automatic weapons. As others gathered the money, Tania trained her carbine on the customers, who had been ordered to lie on the floor, and announced, "This is Tania . . . Patricia Hearst." As they fled the bank, Donald DeFreeze, the leader of the SLA, fired his carbine through the plate glass window and killed two elderly passersby. The SLA's attempt at bank robbery, like its attempt at kidnapping, was completely successful; by the time the FBI found their hideout just a few miles away, the SLA was long gone. But a year and a half later, on September 18, 1975, several members of the SLA were arrested following a holdup at Mel's Sporting Goods Store. Among those arrested was Patricia Campbell Hearst, who was charged with the robbery of the Hibernia Bank.

The jury faced a difficult dilemma. In many cases, a jury must decide whether a person entered a bank, wielded a weapon, and absconded with money. In this case there was no doubt: The robbery had certainly been committed by Patty Hearst—at least, it had been committed by that physical assemblage of eyes and ears and fingerprints that had once answered to the name of Patty. There was no question about *who* robbed the bank. As Patty's own attorney, F. Lee Bailey, told the jury, "She did rob the bank. You are not here to answer that question. We could answer that question without you. The question you are here to answer is why?" (Hearst, 1976, p. 590)

The defense argued that Patty Hearst had merely reacted as a 19-year-old girl might be expected to react to terror. Combat veterans who become prisoners of war often "identify with the aggressor" as a way of surviving the psychological pain of imprisonment, and Patty was just a teenage POW who could not even rely on the protection of the Geneva Convention. Patty Hearst was not a felon: She was a child who had been savagely abducted from her home and kept bound and blindfolded in a closet for 57 days. During those weeks in the closet she had been repeatedly threatened with death, repeatedly raped, and repeatedly indoctrinated with leftist ideology. "Never had I felt so degraded, so much in the power of others, so vulnerable," she wrote many years later (Hearst, 1982, p. 40). After weeks of physical and psychological abuse, she weighed little more than 85 pounds and could barely stand. After a while "there was no point in objecting to anything anymore, not even in my thoughts" (Hearst, 1982, p. 90). When DeFreeze finally asked if she would prefer to join the SLA or be released, "I knew that the *real* choice was . . . to join them or be executed. They would never release me . . . I knew too much about them. He was testing me and I must pass the test or die" (Hearst, 1982, p. 96). Patty Hearst had been in the bank during the robbery, but she surely did not deserve to be punished for having endured a nightmare of 17 months.

The prosecution admitted that Patty was a victim—at first. But the SLA had not forced her to rob a bank. In fact, they offered to let her go weeks before the robbery occurred. No, even before the kidnapping Patty had been "a rebel looking for a cause." The SLA's amateur crusade for social justice gave voice to Patty's adolescent rebellion against her wealthy father, whom Tania had compared to Hitler and publicly called "the Hearst pig." As with any draftee there had been an involuntary conscription, but Patty quickly became a willing "soldier in the people's army," and she actively thwarted the FBI's attempts to find her. She had fallen in love with another SLA member, passed up numerous opportunities to escape, and reveled in the romantic image of herself as a swashbuckling commando—a cultural icon who appeared on as many posters and T-shirts as Jimi Hendrix. When she was finally arrested, she gave the photographers a closed-fist salute and then listed her occupation as "Urban Guerrilla" on her arrest forms. Tania was Patty Hearst's chance to be more than just another nondescript, overprivileged, rich girl. There were photographs, films, signed notes, taped statements—all of which showed Tania acting with what appeared to be complete freedom of will. "Rarely has so much evidence of apparent intent been available to a jury," said the prosecutor, James Browning (Hearst, 1976, p. 581).

ATTRIBUTION

Poor jury. Trying to determine the cause of Patty Hearst's actions is a bit like viewing one of those optical illusions in which one sees a certain image (perhaps an old woman, or a chalice, or an upright box) and then suddenly it "flips" and one sees an entirely different image (a young woman, two profiles, a sideways box). No one can see both images at the same time, but everyone knows that both are perfectly valid ways of interpreting the drawing. Why did Patty Hearst do what she did? As with the illusion, jurors must certainly have felt torn between two viable interpretations: A *situational* interpretation (she robbed the bank because of the hellish situation she had been forced to endure) and a *dispositional* interpretation (she robbed the bank because of the kind of person she had been and had become). Even now, both of these interpretations seem true to some degree: We feel confident that Patty Hearst would not have robbed a bank had she never been kidnapped by the SLA, but we feel equally confident that a different person—one with stronger character or deeper values—would not have joined her captors so quickly and with such enthusiasm. The situational and dispositional interpretations of Patty Hearst's behavior may both be right *to some degree,* but the degree to which each is right makes a tremendous difference. The jury had to decide whether Patty Hearst's behavior was *primarily* a function of the situation she was in or *primarily* a product of her own personal dispositions.

If you find it difficult to make up your own mind, then the epigram that opened this chapter should remind you that you are in distinguished company. (And if you prefer less difficult problems, then you might want to take Proust's advice and switch from psychology to physics.) But just because this problem is unusually vexing does not mean it is unusual. Indeed, the dilemma of the jury in the Patty Hearst case is very much the dilemma of ordinary life. Every day we are called on to make decisions about the people with whom we interact: Is the new secretary competent? Does that attractive person like me? Will the professor in this course be interesting? Answers to these questions are based largely on what the respective persons say and do—but not *merely* on what they say and do. Thoughtful people are not concerned with *what* happens so much as with *why* it happens. Two receptionists may be equally congenial during a job interview, but we want to hire the one who is truly affable and not the one who merely smiles in our presence. Two classmates may be equally brusque with us, but we want to be friends with the one who was temporarily upset by news of a failing grade and not the one who is just plain nasty.

Indeed, this fundamental distinction between situational and dispositional causes of behavior is the heart and soul of virtually all *attribution theories* (Heider, 1958; Hilton & Slugoski, 1986; Jones & Davis, 1965; Kelley, 1967; Medcof, 1990; Reeder & Brewer, 1979; cf. Kruglanski, 1975; Zuckerman & Feldman, 1984). It would be nice if attribution theories could tell us why people behave as they do, but that is not their function; no one can provide a scientific answer to such a question, which is why 12 honest men and women had to scratch their heads and do their best when judging Patty Hearst. Rather, attribution theories attempt to describe the psychological operations that lead people to embrace situational or dispositional interpretations of other people's behavior. Attribution theories cannot tell us why Patty Hearst robbed a bank, but they *can* tell us why the jury came to the conclusion that it did. Attribution theories describe how people think about each other, and as we will see, an attribution theorist could have predicted the jury's verdict quite well.

The Logic of Attribution

Well then. How *do* people think about each other? How *do* people decide whether another person's behavior was primarily caused by situational or dispositional forces? If you reflect on your own thinking as you weighed the different stories of Patty Hearst's life, you can probably identify a few of the most basic principles you used in making your own decision. If you felt she was innocent, you probably had thoughts such as "I would have done *anything* to get out of a closet after 57 days" or "It wasn't her fault she got kidnapped in the first place." On the other hand, if you felt she was guilty, you probably thought something like "It was a terrible situation, but she didn't have to go quite as far as she did" or "She could have escaped if she'd really wanted to." Can we articulate in a precise way the logic that these sorts of thoughts draw upon? Indeed we can:

$$B = S + D$$

The *attributional equation* or the *Lewinian equation* (named after the father of modern social psychology, Kurt Lewin, who first suggested its importance) acknowledges the fact that a person's behavior (B) is thought to be a joint function of the situation the person is in (S) and the person's unique predispositions to act (D). Virtually no one believes that human behavior is *entirely* the product of situational forces (otherwise, two people who are in the same situation would necessarily behave identically), and virtually no one believes that it is *entirely* the product of dispositions (otherwise, behavior would not be affected by the kind of situation the person was in). Just as the motion of a tennis ball is a joint product of its mass and the forces acting on it (the racquet), so the Lewinian equation suggests that inner and outer forces combine to produce human behavior. Thus, if we want to answer the question "Did Patty Hearst have a disposition to rob the bank?" we merely rearrange the equation and solve for D.

$$D = B - S$$

The new equation suggests that if we want to know whether a person has a disposition to behave in a certain way, we should observe their behavior and then try to "subtract out" the effect of the situation in which the behavior took place. That is, we should try to figure out how much of the behavior can be explained by the situation; if anything is left unexplained after we have performed this subtraction, then we can safely conclude that the person has a disposition to behave as they did. Imagine, for example, a measuring scale that runs from zero to ten, where ten means "extremely criminal" and zero means "not at all criminal." If we can tolerate a bit of linguistic sloppiness, we can use this scale to measure all three of the *attributional elements*. How "criminal" were Patty's actions? Robbing a bank is fairly serious business, so let's say that B equals 8. How "criminal" was the situation? That is, how much criminality should being kidnapped induce in a normal person? If we suspect that the situation was powerful enough to induce serious criminality, then perhaps we should let S equal 8 also. In this case D must equal 0. In other words, we conclude that Patty did not have a criminal disposition because *her behavior was exactly what the situation demanded.* If, on the other hand, we were to judge the situation as powerful enough to induce a normal person to engage in *some* criminal behavior (e.g., jaywalking), but not powerful enough to induce that person to rob a bank, then we might assign a lower value to S, for example, 5. In that case, D must equal 3, and we would conclude that Patty did have a mildly criminal disposition because *her behavior was more extreme than the situation demanded.*

No one is claiming that jurors or bosses or classmates or lovers actually do math when they think about each other; God knows that most of us would be lost in computation for the better part of our lives. Rather, the Lewinian equation is merely meant to illustrate the dynamic relation between the three attributional elements. These relations constitute the core logic of all attribution theories. There are many attribution theories that differ in important ways, but the logic of the Lewinian equation unites them. Indeed, if there is one "decision rule" that is common to all attribution theories it is this:

> An observer should *not* conclude that a person has a unique predisposition to behave when the person does exactly what the situation demands.

In other words, an observer should not assume that D is positive or negative when S and B are equal. This statement is so important in attributional logic that it has a special name, the *discounting principle.* The principle suggests that when we try to estimate a person's dispositions, the person's behavior should be "discounted," or ignored, when it is precisely the sort of behavior that the situation demands. Such behavior is said to be *nondiagnostic;* that is, it tells us nothing about the person's unique and enduring tendencies to behave. Polite nodding during a job interview does not tell us that a person is dispositionally cheerful and attentive, just as a rude remark after the receipt of bad news does not tell us that a person is dispositionally mean. In both cases, the behavior is nondiagnostic and should be discounted because it is precisely what one would expect of normal folks who are being interviewed or flunked. If a tennis ball travels exactly as fast as it should given the power of the serve, then one should not conclude that the tennis ball has a "disposition" to move. One should not conclude that it is actually a superball, that it is lighter than normal, or that it has a flock of miniature geese inside it. The ball is only doing what external forces made it do, and thus its behavior tells us nothing very interesting about its composition. It is just a normal tennis ball.

The Correspondence Bias

The discounting principle is a simple rule that tells us how we can estimate the dispositions of others by watching their behavior. But the world is filled with rules that people don't follow. We have reasonable prescriptions for health ("Eat light"), wisdom ("Read books"), and happiness ("Laugh hard"), and yet we see illness, idiocy, and sorrow all around us. Do people obey the discounting principle any more than they obey the speed limit? Thirty years of research gives us a clear answer: *Sort of.*

In 1967, Jones and Harris tested people's use of the discounting principle. Subjects were shown essays that either supported Fidel Castro (the Communist president of Cuba) or opposed him. Some subjects were told that the essayist had been free to determine the content of the essay; that is, he had been asked to write an essay reflecting what he believed. Other subjects were shown the same essays but were told a different story. These subjects were told that the essayist was a member of a debate team, and that he had been assigned to defend this position by his debate coach. As everyone knows, debaters (like lawyers and teenagers) argue for the sake of arguing; they do not necessarily endorse the positions they defend. All subjects were asked to read an essay and then to estimate the essayist's true, *personal* opinion about Castro. As Figure 4.1 shows, some of the results of this experiment were quite surprising.

The leftmost bars show that when the essayist was free to write whatever he pleased, subjects took his essay as direct evidence of his opinion; that is, they used the essay (behavior) to estimate the essayist's attitude (disposition). This is precisely what the Lewinian equation suggests they should do, because when S equals zero, then B equals D (i.e., when there is no situational force, then a person's behavior is a perfect measure of his or her dispositions). But the rightmost bars defy the logic of the Lewinian equation. Those bars show that even when the essayist was merely following the instructions of an authority, subjects still attributed to him a disposition that corresponded to his behavior. A pro-Castro essayist who chose his own topic was judged to have a more favorable opinion of Castro than was a pro-Castro essayist who was merely following orders; *but* a pro-Castro essayist who was merely following orders was judged to have a more favorable opinion of Castro than was an anti-Castro essayist who was merely following orders. This moderate but significant difference between the two rightmost bars in Figure 4.1 is known as the *correspondence bias,* which is *the tendency to conclude that a person has a disposition that corresponds to his or her behavior even when that behavior is attributable to the situation.*

You can probably think of times when a waitress took your order impatiently and you thought "What a jerk" without pausing to consider that she might have had a particularly rough day, times when you heard a dynamic political candidate and thought "She's really smart" without pausing to consider that someone else had written her speech, times when you read about a convicted drug dealer and thought "What a lowlife" without pausing to consider just what poverty can drive a person to do. In each of these instances you made

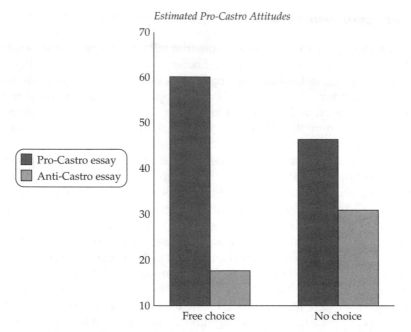

FIGURE 4.1. Estimates of the true attitudes toward Castro of essayists who were free or not free to choose the content of their essays.
Adapted from Jones, E. E., & Harris, V. A. (1967). The attribution of attitudes. Journal of Experimental Social Psychology, 3, 1–24.

an inference about a person's character or ability even though their behavior might well have been explained in terms of the situations in which they found themselves. If you have had such experiences, you are not alone. In the history of social psychology, few experimental phenomena have proved as stubborn as the correspondence bias. In study after study, people who observe behavior seem prone to attribute corresponding dispositions to the people who behaved. In study after study, observers do not use the discounting principle quite as well or quite as often as the Lewinian equation suggests they should. In study after study, observers claim that others "are the way they act," and they make such claims even when compelling circumstances can explain the observed behavior quite adequately. Scores of experiments show the correspondence bias to be one of the most reliable and robust findings in the annals of research on human attribution—so basic and pervasive that it is often called the *fundamental attribution error* (Ross, 1977). Regardless of what we call it, the fact is plain: People attribute behavior to dispositions even when there is every reason not to do so.

Oh. By the way. Patty Hearst was sentenced to 25 years in prison for robbing the Hibernia Bank. Who would have guessed?

The Causes of Correspondence Bias

Within seconds of hearing about the Jones and Harris experiment, most people's brains generate at least nine different responses, all of which begin with the phrase "But maybe . . ." But maybe the subjects didn't realize that debaters argue for positions they don't hold. But maybe the essays were incredibly slick and persuasive. But maybe the subjects felt funny about ignoring an essay that was handed to them by the experimenter. But maybe subjects thought the debater would refuse to write an essay he was really against. But maybe, but maybe. These sorts of considerations are of two kinds: the damning and the interesting. The damning objections suggest that some funny quirk of the experimental setting caused subjects to make judgments that they would not normally make, and that the results therefore tell us more about the particulars of social psychology experiments than about the way people make attributions. You will be comforted to know that in dozens of follow-ups to this study, virtually every damn objection has been ruled out (see Jones, 1979). The second class of objections is actually quite interesting because they suggest general psychological mechanisms that might cause people to make dispositional attributions when they should not. Social psychologists have given a great deal of attention to these sorts of objections and, after many years of work, have assembled a list of four factors that they believe cause the correspondence bias (see Gilbert & Malone, in press). An exploration of these factors not only sheds light on the nature of correspondence bias but also traces the evolution of attribution theory over the last three decades.

Wanting Dispositions

Samuel Johnson (1756/1751, p. 259) observed with some amusement that "no estimate is more in danger of erroneous calculations than those by which a man computes the force of his own genius." Indeed, poets, pundits, psychologists, and grandmothers have long realized that human beings tend to see the world as they wish to see it. Reality keeps us from straying too far from the facts (e.g., I would believe that I am Mel Gibson's better-looking brother if the mirror would stop getting in the way), but even beliefs that are firmly grounded in reality can be lightly shifted in the direction of desire. We overestimate how long we will live, how well we can drive, how smart we are, and how much others like us (Taylor & Brown, 1988; Weinstein, 1980), so it should be no surprise that we are capable of making rose-colored attributions as well (Miller & Ross, 1975; Mullen & Riordan, 1988; Ross & Sicoly, 1979). One reason why people may show the correspondence bias is that they prefer to make dispositional attributions. But why should they have such a preference? The answer, it seems, is that dispositional attributions give us a sense of control, and they do this in two ways.

Let's face it. The world is a scary place. Disaster, disease, homelessness, heartbreak: In some ways, life is a run through a mine field that nobody survives. Some of us last a while, some of us fall early on, but no matter how artfully we tumble and roll, each of us is ultimately claimed by that cold, invisible enemy. Think about the people you saw today at the library, the bus stop, the Kmart. It is virtually certain that one of those people will die of inoperable cancer before the year is out. He did not know it when you saw him today, but soon he and his family will receive the worst news they can imagine. One of the people whose air you shared in the elevator this morning will encounter a drunk driver on a rain-soaked highway and will not live to watch her own children grow up. Think about them. Remember their faces. They have plans, worries, people who cherish them. They are just like you. But one of the men you saw will be murdered with a gun, one of the women will be beaten and raped, and one of the children will be abandoned on the street to beg strangers for food. Perhaps the novelist Philip Dick (1982, p. 7), was right: "I think I know why we are here on this Earth; it's to find out that what you love the most will be taken away from you, probably due to an error in high places rather than by design."

If you are like most people, the preceding paragraph made you feel a bit depressed. Indeed, if we dwell on the capriciousness of life, the unfairness and arbitrariness of the tragedies that befall those around us, we cannot help but be depressed. Now, can you imagine walking around all day feeling this way? If you truly believed that people were entirely at the mercy of the situations in which they found themselves, then the preceding paragraph would be a fairly good rendition of your chronic emotional state. Who could function in that much darkness? Very few of us indeed, and thus we have developed a *dispositionist worldview* to chase away the gloom. A dispositionist worldview is not a well-articulated philosophy of human behavior but, rather, a general sense that people do what they do because of the kinds of people they are, and that as such, whatever happens to them is pretty much their own doing. Sure, there are vivid exceptions, but by and large, we get what we work for, get what we ask for, and get what we deserve (Janoff-Bulman, Timko, & Carli, 1985; Lerner, 1980). This worldview is instilled in us in subtle ways by a culture that has hundreds of words to describe the different dispositions of people and virtually none to describe the causal power of situations (Brown & Fish, 1983). From language to economics to social policy, our culture reflects the emphasis on individuality that it inherited from the Greeks (Aristotle believed that even *objects* behaved as they did because of their dispositions), and this emphasis is part of the dispositionist worldview that encourages the correspondence bias. Indeed, there is some evidence to suggest that correspondence bias may actually be less pervasive in collectivist cultures that do not share this worldview (Miller, 1984; Newman, 1991). All of this is simply to say that the belief that people are the authors of their own behavior, and that their lives are therefore controllable, serves an important emotional function for citizens on this side of the globe in the twentieth century. As such, we should not be surprised to see people "err on the side of dispositions" from time to time.

There is a second way in which dispositional attributions may serve our psychological needs, and therefore a second reason why people may prefer them. If behavior is a product of inner forces, then not only can people control their own lives but, moreover, they can predict the ways in which others will do so. As every scientist knows, the ability to predict the behavior of an entity—whether a planet or a pebble—allows one to control the effects of the entity upon oneself. If we can foresee the coming rainstorm, the fluctuations in the stock market, or the outcome of the World Series, we can use these predictions to guide our own behavior and improve the quality of our existence (e.g., we can carry an umbrella, buy Microsoft, and bet against the Cubs). But to predict something correctly and routinely, one must have a decent *theory* about it: Astronomers can predict eclipses with pinpoint accuracy only because they have such precise theories about how planets wander through space. Similarly, if we want to predict the behavior of a teacher or a spouse or a friend, we need to have a theory about what kind of entity that person is.

In a sense, dispositions serve some of the same functions that scientific theories do. They give us a simple way of thinking about a multitude of past observations, and they allow us to predict what we will observe in the future. When one wants to predict Fred's behavior, one need not recall that he said hello to the bank teller on Thursday, that he offered to let Alan use his car on Friday, and that he shoveled his elderly neighbor's walk on Saturday. Rather, if we have concluded that Fred is a friendly fellow, then this trait ascription allows us to predict what he will do on National Secretary's Day. Indeed, careful research has shown that when people are asked to predict the behavior of others about whom they have made dispositional attributions, they can do so without ever consulting their specific memories of the person's past behavior (Carlston, 1992; Carlston & Skowronski, 1986; Dreben, Fiske, & Hastie, 1979; Klein & Loftus, 1993). Dispositional attributions, then, give us a "handle" on others; they afford us a sense of *predictive control.*

If this line of reasoning is correct, then we would expect people to be particularly likely to make dispositional attributions when they have a strong need to predict another's behavior. Miller, Norman, and Wright (1978) examined just this hypothesis. In their study, subjects (called *observers* because that's what they did) watched a person (called the *target* because he was the target or object of the observers' judgments) as he played a game called Prisoner's Dilemma. This well-known game of strategy can be played in either a competitive style (one attempts to attain large rewards by causing one's opponent to lose them) or a cooperative style (one attempts to attain modest rewards by teaming up with one's opponent and splitting the loot). Observers watched either a cooperative or a competitive target (actually a *confederate,* or a person who pretends to be a subject but who is actually playing a role at the behest of the experimenter) under one of four conditions: *Players* played the game with the target, *normal observers* simply watched the player and the target as they played the game, and *expectant observers* watched the game with the belief that they would play against the target on the second round. Finally, *postexpectant* observers watched the game without expecting to play it but, when the first round was over, were suddenly told that they would play the target in the second round. Ultimately, all of these observers were asked a number of questions that measured how much "person information" they thought they had received (e.g., "How well do you think you could describe the target's personality to a person who had never met him?"). In essence, these sorts of questions measure the "dispositionalness" of the observer's attribution.

Figure 4.2 shows the kinds of attributions that subjects in each of these conditions made about the target. Although all subjects viewed the same competitive or cooperative behavior, both expectant observers and players clearly made more dispositional attributions than did normal observers—which is pre-

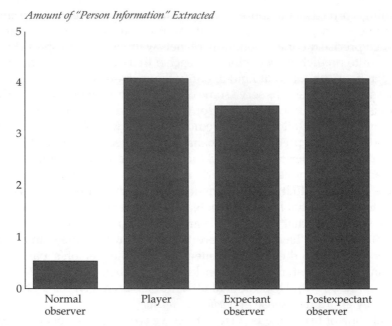

FIGURE 4.2. "Dispositionality" of attributions made about a partner by normal observers, players, expectant observers, and preexpectant observers. (Raw data are transformed for presentation.)

Adapted from Miller, D. T., Norman, S. A., & Wright, E. (1978). Distortion in person perception as a consequence of the need for effective control. Journal of Personality and Social Psychology, 36, 598–607.

cisely what the predictive control hypothesis suggests they should do. Playing (or expecting to play) a game with a person should increase one's desire to predict that person's behavior; after all, behavior is much more important when it affects us personally than when it doesn't (Jones & Davis, 1965). As such, playing (or expecting to play) should encourage one to attribute the other person's playing style to his or her personal dispositions.

But perhaps players and normal observers did *not* make different attributions about the same behavior. Perhaps players actually *perceived* the target's behavior differently than did normal observers; for example, maybe they noticed the many competitive moves the target made but failed to notice his few cooperative moves. The attributions of the postexpectant observers make such an explanation unlikely. Recall that postexpectant observers and normal observers watched the game under identical psychological conditions; neither believed they would ever play against the target. Only after watching the game (but before making their ratings of the target) were the postexpectant observers led to believe that they would play in the next round, and thus their need to predict the target's behavior should have been piqued only after they made their observations. As the figure shows, postexpectant observers made dispositional attributions for the target person's behavior—just like players and expectant observers (but not normal observers) did.

It seems, then, that both our general dispositionist worldview and our need to predict a specific person's actions can cause us to lean toward dispositional explanations of behavior (see also Berscheid, Graziano, Monson, & Dermer, 1976; Erber & Fiske, 1983; Monson, Keel, Stephens, & Genung, 1982; Pittman & D'Agostino, 1985). Would it not make us, as jurors, vaguely uneasy to admit that Patty Hearst could have been "anyone's daughter" (Alexander, 1979)— that her actions were largely caused by a situation over which she had no control? Is it not more reassuring to believe that something unique in Patty's constitution led her to rob the Hibernia Bank? As long as we can attribute her criminal behavior to a corresponding disposition, then we can feel confident that a similar fate could not befall those of us who are free of such hideous character defects. How much more pleasant to believe that bank robbers—like beggars, bums, and Nazis—are born and not made.

Misunderstanding Situations

So far, the story is a bit like the lecture that Mr. Spock gave Dr. McCoy in the last three minutes of virtually every episode of *Star Trek*: "Desires and passions pervert human judgment, and thus people make errors to which more logical life-forms are not prone." The Vulcan science officer was right in one sense: Our ambitions and fears, our hopes and our hungers, can indeed impair our ability to draw accurate inferences about others. But in another sense he was wrong: Even without these throbbing needs, there are plenty of ways for attributional analysis to be derailed. As Bones might say, even a "pointy-eared, green-blooded, infernal computer" can show correspondence bias.

The second cause of correspondence bias is the tendency for people to underestimate the power of situations. The Lewinian equation requires us to subtract the situation's "causal power" (i.e., its ability to induce certain kinds of behavior in a normal person) from the observed behavior in order to assess the level of the target's disposition. That sounds fine in theory, but assigning values to these variables in real life is no easy task. Just how much criminal behavior should 57 days in a closet induce? Just what sort of essay should a debate coach's instructions engender? Unfortunately, *Britannica* does not publish a Yearly Table of Situational Forces that we can look to for an authoritative answer, and thus we have to use what we know and make a guess. As you would expect, people's estimates of situational power are not always accurate, and research suggests that the inaccuracies tend to be of a particular sort, namely, *under*estimations rather than *over*estimations of situational power. Why should people consistently underestimate the strength of situations? There are two reasons.

The first problem, it seems, is that situations are often invisible. Behavior can be seen, heard, touched, smelled, and occasionally tasted. Situations almost never can. When a father tells his daughter that he will disinherit her if she gets her nose pierced, most of us would agree that the father's threat constitutes a fairly potent situational force. Yet, when we see the young woman walk past a booth at the mall that advertises "Free Nose Piercing While-U-Wait," we only see walking. The father's threat is nowhere to be seen. It has no physical presence, no depth, no mass. It leaves no telltale stains or odors. It is most certainly a strong situational force, but at this moment it is a force that exists only in the memory of the walking woman. It is not surprising that observers will assign a value of zero to S when S is an unseeable phantom. In plain language, correspondence bias occurs because people often don't realize that there *is* a constraining situation to be considered.

This phenomenon was particularly well illustrated in an experiment by Ross, Amabile, and Steinmetz (1977). In this experiment, subjects were randomly assigned to play the role of either quizmaster, contestant, or observer.[2] Quizmasters were asked to compose 10 "challenging but not impossible" questions that would test the contestants' general knowledge (e.g., "What is the capital of New Mexico?"), and they were encouraged to draw from their own idiosyncratic areas of expertise when doing so. (Quizmasters, of course, had to know the correct answer to the questions they asked so that they could tell the contestant whether he or she was right or wrong.) So quizmasters asked their questions, contestants tried to answer them, and observers monitored the game. At the end of the game, all three subjects were asked to estimate the dispositional knowledgeability of both the quizmaster and the contestant. Nice and simple. Nothing unusual here.

Ah, but there is. If you think about the structure of this game for a moment, you will realize that it is heavily rigged against the contestant. Virtually *anyone* can think of 10 questions that another person of equal intelligence could not answer. You could turn to a friend right now and ask "Who said 'The stellar universe is not so difficult of comprehension as the real actions of other people?' " or "What are the three attributional elements in the Lewinian equation?" and your friend would probably say something terribly clever like "Huh?" You just happen to know the answers to these questions because you've been reading about them, and the fact that you can say "Marcel Proust" and "S, D, and B" only means that you have a moderately reliable memory and *not* that you are well versed in French literature and the behavioral sciences. It does not mean that you are especially bright, and it *certainly* does not mean that you are brighter than your friend, who could probably look up from his or her physics book and ask you to answer equally perplexing questions about the origin of the azimuthal number in quantum theory and the precise value of Planck's constant. Although subjects were randomly assigned to the roles of contestant or quizmaster (and therefore must have been equally knowledgeable on the average), contestants could only answer an average of 40 percent of the questions that quizmasters generated; quizmasters, of course, could answer 100 percent of their own questions. Clearly, being assigned to play the role of quizmaster gives anyone a *role-conferred advantage* in the game. Playing the quizmaster allows you to say smarter stuff than playing the contestant does.

This point may seem obvious to you now, but it was not obvious to the Stanford students who participated as subjects in this experiment. Figure 4.3 shows how they rated the quizmaster and the contestant. As the leftmost bars indicate, observers considered the quizmaster to be more knowledgeable than the contestant; as the rightmost bars show, quizmasters and contestants rated themselves in just the same way. In other words, everyone showed the corre-

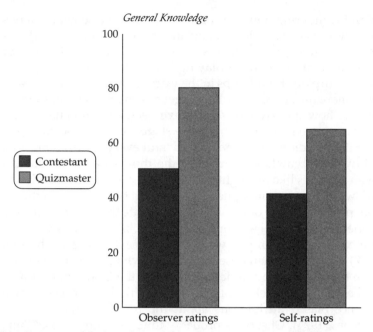

FIGURE 4.3. Estimates of the knowledgeability of contestants and quizmasters by observers and by themselves. (Data from separate experiments are collapsed for presentation.)
Adapted from Ross, L., Amabile, T. M., & Steinmetz, J. L. (1977). Social roles, social control, and biases in social-perception processes. Journal of Personality and Social Psychology, 35, 485–494.

spondence bias. But why would perfectly reasonable college students assume that a subject who was arbitrarily given an advantage was actually smarter than a subject who was arbitrarily given a handicap? The answer should be clear: The role-conferred advantage is an idea that we can discuss, ponder, and spell—but it is not a thing that can be seen or weighed or made to cast a shadow. When observers look out on the game being played, they see subjects doing. One is doing well, and one isn't. But they don't see role-conferred advantages hanging from the ceiling or streaking in and out of the room, and thus they simply do not realize that such advantages exist. If we were to point it out to them, they would probably say "Yeah, now that you mention it, I guess the game *is* rigged against the contestant," but without our help, this thought just does not occur to the average observer.

The second problem is related to the first. When people do not recognize the presence of situational forces, they cannot be expected to subtract them out of their behavioral observations. But even when people recognize the *presence* of such forces, they still may underestimate the *capacity* of those forces to alter behavior. The reason for this is not so hard to understand. How many times has someone dismissed your viewpoint by saying, "Until you've gone through it, you just can't understand what it's like" or "You just had to be there"? Such claims can be annoying, but oftentimes they're right. For instance, many of us have had the experience of watching one of those midmorning game shows on television and wondering how the contestants could be so exquisitely stupid. ("No, I'm sorry, Lassie was a dog, not an ancient Sumerian beer goddess.") We think, "I ought to go on one of those shows. I knew more of the answers than any of those dimwits who were playing." Yes, it is true: As we sit in our bathrobes and slurp our Fruit Loops in the warm glow of the Zenith, we can indeed answer more questions than the widget salesman from Pasadena. But we might consider how quickly we would have been able to generate those answers with cameramen moving around the stage, hot lights beaming down on our heads, $17,000 riding on our next word, and everyone from our mother to our dental hygienist gawking at us from the third row. Under such circumstances, even geniuses like us might momentarily confuse Lassie with Ninkasi.

Indeed, when we try to imagine what it would be like to be in the situation that another person is in, we don't always appreciate the nuances and subtleties of the experience. (If we did, we could experience life vicariously without ever leaving the couch.) For example, we know from extensions of the Jones and Harris (1967) study that when observers are shown pro-Castro essays that are said to have been written by undergraduates at the instruction of an experimenter (rather than at the behest of a debate coach), these observers will make correspondence biased attributions about the undergraduate essay writers (Snyder & Jones, 1974). Observers probably think to themselves, "Well, if the writer of this essay was anti-Castro, then she would have refused to write it. After all, her life wasn't threatened. She was merely *asked* to do it. The situation wasn't *that* coercive. I mean, *I* wouldn't have done it." But are such thoughts correct? How much pressure does an undergraduate feel when a well-dressed graduate student requests that she write an essay at odds with her own personal beliefs? A lot? A little? Three iotas and half a smidgen?

When Sherman (1980) asked students to predict whether they would write an essay arguing against co-ed dormitory visits if an experimenter asked them to do so, about 70 percent said they would not. But when another group of students was actually asked to write that essay, only about 30 percent refused. In other words, at least 40 percent of the people mispredicted their own behavior! Why is there a disparity between what we think we would do and what we actually do in such a situation? Because when we are asked how we would behave in a certain situation, our *psychological construal* (or mental picture) of that situation does not usually include all its intricate details (Ross & Nisbett, 1991; see also Gilovich, 1987). When Sherman asked people to predict their own responses, they probably did not consider the puppy dog look on the experimenter's face, the aura of authority that his crisp white lab coat created, or that awkward, funny feeling that accompanies looking anyone in the eye and saying no. Unless one takes great pains to imagine the situation in all its vivid and glorious detail, one will probably underestimate its power. And underestimation of situational power is, of course, the royal road to correspondence bias.

James Browning, the attorney who prosecuted Patty Hearst, capitalized on this psychological phenomenon. He told the jury:

> Mr. Bailey [the defense attorney] pointed out that victims often do what they're told to do when they're told to do it, and so would I or he, he says. Well, would

we, ladies and gentlemen? I think most of us want to protect our lives when threatened with death, but I also think it's very unlikely that we would pick up an automatic weapon and spray an area with machine gun fire which is peopled by innocent persons, and run the risk of killing or injuring them in order to protect ourselves (Hearst, 1982, p. 594).

The prosecutor argued that the situation was just not powerful enough to have been the primary cause of Patty Hearst's actions, and he invited the jury to imagine the situation themselves and decide whether he was right. The jury sat back, thought about it, and decided that he was. But ask yourself this question: Would you spray machine gun fire and risk the lives of innocent people in order to save your own? Perhaps you would. Perhaps you would not. Or perhaps until you've spent 57 days in a closet, until you've been raped a few times and threatened with execution, until you've stood in the marble lobby of the Hibernia Bank and felt the steel and smelled the sweat, you just can't be sure.

Misperceiving Behavior

The Lewinian equation requires that we assign values to S and B if we want to find a value for D. As we have seen, situational forces are often invisible, and thus we do not always know they exist; when we do know, we often imagine them incompletely and therefore underestimate their power to shape behavior. In other words, estimating S is tricky business. Behavior, on the other hand, has an "in your face" quality. It is palpable and dynamic, bombarding our senses with its noises and colors and aromas. It is tangible, conspicuous, and concrete. So although it is generally difficult to estimate S, you would expect that it is generally easy to estimate B. In fact, when we see someone do something, we feel like we *know* what B is; we don't feel like we *estimate* it.

If you remember only one piece of psychological wisdom, remember this: Things ain't always how they feel (see Nisbett & Wilson, 1977). Although it feels like we can simply *see* what behavior is, such *seeing* is actually a complex inferential process. For example, none of us has ever *seen* a nurse help a patient or a used-car dealer cheat a customer. What we have seen is a series of physical movements: Thigh muscles contracting and releasing, bodies going boldly where none have gone before, heads rotating on their stalks, lips flapping, and all that. But nowhere in this constellation of physical motions will we find *helping* and *cheating*, because *helping* and *cheating* are not actions but *action identifications,* or inferences we draw about the meaning of the physical changes that constitute behavior (see Vallacher & Wegner, 1985). Estimating B is not always an easy task because action identification, like any other form of inference, can go wrong.

What factors determine the accuracy of our action identifications? There are, of course, many, but our prior knowledge or our *expectations* exert a particularly strong influence on what we perceive others to do. For example, our beliefs and expectations about a nurse's job enable us to see that he is "helping" those into whose flesh he jams needles, just as our expectations about a used-car dealer's tactics enable us to see that she is "cheating" those to whom she sells overpriced sedans. These expectations need not be conscious to have their effects. For example, when you read the previous sentence about the nurse and the car dealer you probably slowed or stopped in the middle, and perhaps even reread a word or two, because the genders of the pronouns were not what you expected. Most nurses are women and most used-car dealers are men, and thus you expected to read that *she* was helping and *he* was cheating. When your expectations were violated, you did a sudden, brief double take—"Huh? What? Oh, a male nurse"—and then went on. Even though you had not consciously been thinking "Nurses are usually women" when you read the sentence, your expectation about the gender of nurses was still having a strong, unconscious influence on what and how you thought. Oftentimes we don't even know we *have* expectations until they are violated and we find our train of thought curiously derailed.

Rosenhan (1973) demonstrated the power of expectations to influence our identifications of another's behavior. Rosenhan recruited eight perfectly normal people (a few psychologists, a physician, a painter, a housewife, and so on) to go to San Francisco area mental hospitals and check themselves in under fictitious names. These "pseudopatients" were instructed to behave normally and to answer all questions honestly, with one exception: Upon admission, they were to report having heard a nonexistent voice say the words *hollow, empty,* and *thud.* Everything else that they told the psychiatrists about themselves was true. The object of the game was to see if the psychiatrists would admit them, and if so, how many hours it would take before they realized that the pseudopatient was not in the least crazy. As it turned out, every pseudopatient was hospitalized, and they were kept for an average of 19 days. What's more, seven of the eight were diagnosed as schizophrenic and, on their eventual release, were labeled as "schizophrenic in remission." None of the pseudopatients was ever found out by the psychiatrists (though about a third of their fellow mental patients accused them of faking).

What does this demonstration tell us? None of the pseudopatients was actually schizophrenic, and thus the demonstration must lead us to wonder how several smart and well-meaning psychiatrists could have diagnosed them as such. One psychiatrist's notes may provide a clue. When the pseudopatient explained (truthfully) that he and his wife had a few ups and downs, that he rarely spanked his children, and that he and his father had not gotten along as well when he was young as they did now, the psychiatrist noted:

> This 39 year old white male . . . manifests a long history of considerable ambivalence in close relationships, which begins in early childhood. . . . Affective stability is absent. His attempts to control emotionality with his wife and children are punctuated by angry outbursts and, in the case of the children, spankings. And while he says he has several good friends, one senses considerable ambivalence embedded in those relationships (Rosenhan, 1973, p. 253).

Okay, sure. Having ups and downs is, in some sense, "considerable ambivalence," and liking your dad more over time is literally a lack of "affective stability." But both of these characteristics are particularly common among schizophrenics, which suggests that once the diagnosis of schizophrenia was made, the psychiatrist proceeded to identify the pseudopatient's actions (which were, by definition, normal) as confirming that diagnosis. That is, the psychiatrist "read in" to the behavior what he expected to see there—a phenomenon known as *perceptual assimilation* (Bruner, 1957; Higgins, Rholes, & Jones, 1977; Taylor & Crocker, 1981). Generations of psychology students have had a good laugh at the psychiatrist's expense, but do not for a moment think that this psychiatrist was lazy, stupid, or in any other way different from you or me. "I'm having a friend for dinner" means one thing when said by a chef and quite another when said by a cannibal, and knowing the hobby of the speaker is necessary for the correct interpretation of the utterance. Similarly, "We're having some ups and downs in our relationship" means one thing when said by a normal housewife and possibly quite another when said by a schizophrenic (who may be talking only about himself). The psychiatrist who read this comment as a sign of "considerable ambivalence" was experiencing perceptual assimilation; but that experience led to a mistaken diagnosis only because the psychiatrist was misinformed in the first place (i.e., hollow, empty, thud).

It is the nature of perception, then, that we often see things (such as behavior) as conforming more to our expectations than they actually do. Interestingly, this fact can pave the way for correspondence bias. Trope's (1986) *two-stage model* of attribution (see Figure 4.4) reminds us that action identification precedes attributional inference; in other words, before we can ask *why* a person behaved in a certain way, we must first know *what* the person is doing (see also Brewer, 1989; Fiske & Neuberg, 1990). This might be a rather tame theoretical point were it not for one very important fact: Just as having information about the situational constraints on a target can *increase* the accuracy of our attributions (by preventing us from underestimating S), it can also *decrease* the accuracy of our identifications (by causing us to overestimate B). As such, we can end up making reasonable attributions about something the target didn't really do! Trope (1986) has shown just how this can happen.

Trope showed subjects photographs of people with different facial expressions. Some of the faces were clearly and unambiguously calm, whereas other faces had a somewhat ambiguous expression that might or might not be reasonably interpreted as fearful. Trope told some subjects to imagine that the targets had been in scary situations when the photographs were taken (e.g., a swarm of bees had just flown into the room) and told other subjects to imagine

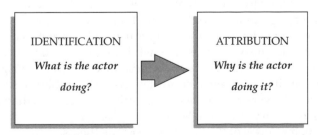

FIGURE 4.4. A two-stage model of attribution.

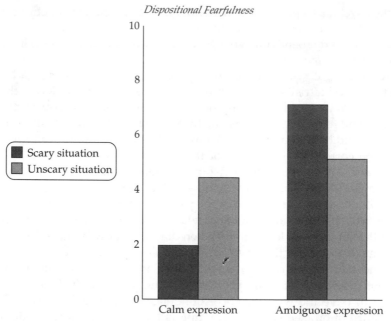

FIGURE 4.5. Estimates of the dispositional fearfulness of people who displayed calm and ambiguous facial expressions in scary and nonscary situations.
Adapted from Trope, Y. (1986). Identification and inferential processes in dispositional attribution. Psychological Review, 93, 239–257.

that the targets had been in nonscary situations (e.g., they had just won some money on a television quiz show). Subjects estimated both the extremity of the targets' emotional expressions (e.g., "How fearful does the target look in this picture?") and the targets' dispositions (e.g., "How fearfully does the target behave in her day to day life?").

Consider first the attributions made about targets who had unambiguously calm expressions. The logic of the Lewinian equation suggests that targets who look clearly relaxed in a scary situation (the bee attack) are not as dispositionally fearful as are targets who look relaxed in a nonscary situation (winning money). This conclusion about the value of D for the two targets follows when we subtract S (a large value for the target who suffered a bee attack and a smaller value for the target who won money) from B (the same value for both targets). Subjects apparently applied this logic and, as the leftmost bars of Figure 4.5 show, considered the unambiguously calm target to be less dispositionally fearful when he or she was calm while being chased by bees than when he or she was calm when awarded a bundle of cash. But the rightmost bars show that this finding was reversed for targets with ambiguous facial expressions. These targets were seen as *more* dispositionally fearful when they were in a scary than a nonscary situation. Why?

Subjects' perceptions of the facial expressions themselves (shown in Figure 4.6) give us the answer. When the target's expression was unambiguously calm,

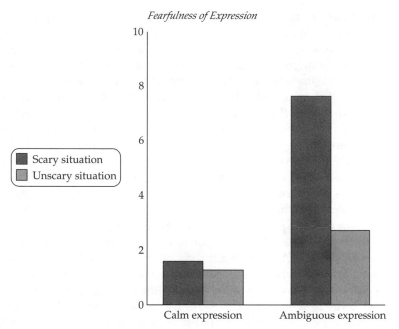

FIGURE 4.6. Estimates of the fearfulness of the facial expressions of people who displayed calm and ambiguous expressions in scary and nonscary situations.
Adapted from Trope, Y. (1986). Identification and inferential processes in dispositional attribution. Psychological Review, 93, 239–257.

the situation that the target was in had little impact on subjects' perceptions of those expressions: An unquestionably calm expression looks unquestionably calm under any circumstances. But when the target's facial expression was ambiguous, something very different happened: When subjects knew that a target was in a scary situation, they interpreted the ambiguous expression as extremely fearful. That is, the situation caused them to expect to see fear in the target's face, and because of perceptual assimilation, that's just what they saw. Once they overestimated the fearfulness of the target's expression, it did them little good to proceed through the Lewinian equation and subtract out the value of the situational constraint. Subtracting S did not give them the right answer because they had overestimated B in the first place! Ironically, the very information that allowed them to discount the behavior (i.e., information about the bee attack) also caused them to misperceive it. In the previous section you might have begun to think that people would not display correspondence bias if only they had good, solid information about the power of the situation. But as the two-stage model predicts, good, solid information can have negative as well as positive consequences; it can promote, as well as prevent, correspondence bias.

During Patty Hearst's trial, much fuss was made about the way in which she held her gun during the Hibernia Bank robbery. The defense argued that she was merely holding it at a slight downward angle and that it moved a bit, back and forth, as her body turned. The prosecution argued that she was actively waving her weapon to frighten the customers whom she was guarding, and that this sort of aggressive display of force was far beyond the demands of the situation. Was it mere holding or flagrant brandishing? No one can say for sure, and because Patty's behavior in this instance was ambiguous, the jurors had to decide *what* she was doing before they could decide *why* she had done it.

The jurors knew that Patty Hearst had, to some extent, been coerced to take part in the bank robbery; indeed, they could see in the films and photographs that as Patty pointed her weapon at the customers, other members of the SLA were pointing *their* weapons at Patty! One might think that such clear and direct evidence of situational constraint (a literal "gun to the head") would have caused the jurors to discount Patty's tenuous gun waving that day. And perhaps the jurors *did* know how powerful the situation was and *did* take that fact into account. But it is also possible that by the time the jurors were ready to subtract out the effects of the situational constraint, they had already undergone perceptual assimilation. A juror might reasonably expect a bit of gun waving from a young woman who was ordered to wave and who was now in the crosshairs of the person who gave the orders. But this very expectation might have caused jurors to see *a bit of gun waving* as *the wanton and reckless flourishing of a deadly weapon,* just as the psychiatrist saw mere "ups and downs" as "considerable ambivalence." Once a juror has misidentified mild gun waving as wild gun waving, then subtracting out the effects of being in the crosshairs does little good. In short, the effect of a situation may be subtracted out during attribution, but the two-stage model shows that this effect can sneak in during identification.

Failing to Use Information

By all rights, that should conclude *The Saga of the Correspondence Bias,* and we should be ready to roll the credits. After all, the Lewinian equation has only three elements, and one of them (D) is the one whose value we are trying to find. That leaves only two others to play with (S and B), and we have already seen how underestimating S or overestimating B can lead to correspondence bias. With only two elements to estimate, how could a person make more than two kinds of mistakes? How can there be another way to go wrong?

When we talk about estimating B and estimating S, we are talking metaphorically about what people know. But we haven't said anything about how they *use* what they know. Having and using information are not the same thing, and as it turns out, people can estimate S and B quite splendidly and *still* fall prey to the correspondence bias—simply because they cannot always *use* the estimates they have made. If you glance back at Figure 4.4, you will notice that the two-stage model contains a big box labeled *attribution.* Modern psychology relies on a method of analysis that philosophers call *homuncular functionalism* (Lycan, 1981), which essentially means that psychologists make theoretical progress by breaking big boxes into littler ones. The attribution box certainly qualifies as big, so just what goes on inside it? It turns out that the attribution box can be broken down into two smaller boxes, but before we can understand what happens in those two subboxes (and how what happens can lead to correspondence bias), we must briefly explore the notion of *automaticity* (Bargh 1989; Hasher & Zacks, 1979; Schneider & Shiffrin, 1977).

Many of us have had the somewhat unnerving experience of driving a car along a familiar route only to find on our arrival that we have no recollection of where we've been. Perhaps you drove from your home to school and then a friend asked, "Did you notice the new restaurant on Highway 101?" and you thought, "Notice the restaurant? Woah. I didn't even notice the highway." From the psychologist's point of view there is something very interesting about this remark: How can a person execute a set of behaviors so intricate and complex that even the most sophisticated computer cannot imitate them, and yet have no recollection of having performed those behaviors? How can we negotiate intersections, obey traffic signals, and avoid pedestrians without even thinking about it? The answer is clear: There are a whole host of things people can do without thinking about what they are doing, and these behaviors are, for obvious reasons, called *automatic*. Automatic behaviors are those that require little or no conscious deliberation, little or no thought or attention, little or no mental effort. Usually these behaviors are either very simple (e.g., shutting your eye when a foreign object approaches too quickly) or complex but extremely practiced (e.g., driving, typing, or playing the harmonica; see Smith, 1989; Smith & Lerner, 1986).

One way to tell whether a behavior is automatic or *effortful* is to see how easily it breaks. Take driving, for instance. If you were driving along when suddenly your passenger said, "Recite the alphabet backwards," you could probably do so without causing an accident. Reciting the alphabet backwards would certainly require your attention, but that would be okay, because driving does not require your attention and thus your attention is available to be spent on the alphabet task. While you paid attention to the recitation, your driving could proceed "on its own," so to speak, and the fact that your driving was not impaired by your recitation can be taken as evidence that your driving is done automatically. By similar logic, if you were driving a nine-speed car with the steering wheel on the right and the brake pedal to the left of the clutch, then driving would probably require your utmost attention. If you tried to indulge your passenger's request in *this* case, you would soon find yourself tangled in the shrubbery. Why? Because alphabet recitation is an attention-consuming task whose concurrent performance impairs driving an unfamiliar car. Indeed, the fact that you crashed can be taken as evidence for the effortfulness of such driving. Effortful processes, but not automatic processes, are impaired when the person's attention is otherwise occupied.

End of detour. Back now to attribution.

Thus far we have thought of dispositional and situational attributions as though they were two sides of a coin, two options from which an observer may choose. But Quattrone (1982) suggested another way to think about them, namely, as sequential operations. Quattrone suggested that people *first* make dispositional inferences and *then* change those inferences into situational ones. For example, rather than concluding that "Roger is a mean fellow" (a dispositional attribution) or concluding that "Roger is a normal fellow who was provoked into behaving meanly" (a situational attribution), perhaps people always begin by thinking "Roger is a mean fellow" and then occasionally change their minds ("But given how Wanda provoked him, I guess he really isn't such a mean fellow after all"). We might imagine a sliding scale (like the volume control on a cheap stereo), one end of which is marked *dispositional* and the other end of which is marked *situational*. According to Quattrone, making attributions is like sliding the knob up and down the scale. When people make attributions, they almost always begin with the knob up at the dispositional end; then, if they have good, solid information about situational constraints on the target's behavior, they slide the knob down the scale as far as it should go. When people make any kind of judgment by this sliding scale method, they are said to be using the *anchoring heuristic* (Tversky & Kahneman, 1974).

If we combine Quattrone's conception of attribution as a series of sequential operations with what we know about automaticity, a new theory of attribution emerges (see Figure 4.7). Gilbert, Pelham, and Krull (1988) suggested that the first of the sequential operations (i.e., making a dispositional inference) might be a relatively automatic operation, whereas the second (changing or *correcting* that inference) might be more effortful.[3] In other words, when people see a behavior, they automatically make a dispositional inference about the target—*regardless* of what they may or may not know about the situation (see also Kassin & Baron, 1985; Newman & Uleman, 1989; Uleman, 1987). Then, if they (a) have good, solid information about the situation and (b) are not too busy reciting the alphabet backwards, they can make an effortful correction to that dispositional inference. The attribution box, then, really contains two little boxes: *automatic dispositional inference* followed by *effortful situational correction.* The first step is a cinch, and the second one is a doozy. Because that second step is impaired by other attention-consuming tasks, people who are busy doing other things (e.g., thinking about themselves, trying to make a good impression, worrying about the future, trying to persuade their partner, and so on) should be particularly susceptible to correspondence bias. Such *cognitively busy* perceivers should automatically generate dispositional inferences about the persons whose behavior they observe, but should be too busy to correct those inferences—even when they *have* all the information required to do so.

Gilbert, Pelham, and Krull (1988) used the divided attention technique to test this *three-stage model.* Subjects were shown a videotape of a woman who was having a discussion with a stranger (who was off camera). Subjects were told that this woman had been a participant in an earlier experiment (in fact, she was an experimental confederate), and that the experimenter had given her several topics to discuss with the stranger. The subject's job was simply to watch the videotape and decide how dispositionally anxious the woman was. But there was a catch. The videotape would be shown without any sound (ostensibly to protect the woman's privacy), and thus the subject would not be able to tell what topic was being discussed at any given time. To compensate for this problem, the experimenter explained that he had inserted one- or two-word subtitles on the videotape. These subtitles did not describe what the woman

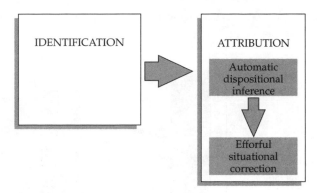

FIGURE 4.7. A three-stage model of attribution.

was saying; rather, they described which of the experimenter-assigned topics she was presently discussing. So, for example, the phrase *ideal vacations* indicated that at that particular moment the woman was (per the experimenter's instructions) discussing her notion of an ideal vacation. Some subjects saw a videotape in which the subtitles were entirely mundane: ideal vacations, fashion trends, world travel, and so on. Other subjects saw *precisely the same videotape*, but with anxiety-provoking subtitles instead of mundane ones: sexual fantasies, public humiliation, personal failures, hidden secrets, and the like. During most of the film, the woman appeared unambiguously anxious: She pulled at her hair, shifted in her seat, and tapped her fingers when she wasn't biting them.

Subjects in these two conditions had everything they needed to solve the Lewinian equation. In one condition of the experiment the situation (that is, the current discussion topic) was very anxiety-provoking (S had a high value), and in one condition it was not (S had a lower value). In both cases the situation was vivid and clear: In fact, it was written on the screen in big block letters! The behavior was identical in both conditions, and in both conditions it was unambiguous: That woman was behaving anxiously, and there were no two ways about it. So subjects knew S, and subjects knew B. As such, they should have been more likely to attribute the woman's behavioral anxiety to her anxious disposition when the situation was mundane rather than anxiety-provoking. Surely, a person who freaks out when asked to describe her ideal vacation *is* more dispositionally anxious than the one who freaks out when asked to describe her sexual fantasies to a stranger, and this is what the Lewinian equation should have led subjects to conclude.

This is, in fact, what subjects who were allowed to watch the videotape under normal conditions concluded. But this is *not* what a second set of subjects, who were asked to memorize a list of words while they watched the videotape, concluded. When people try to memorize a list, they usually say the words over and over to themselves in their minds. If you've ever repeated a phone number to yourself while you scrambled to find a pad of paper or a pen, you know how it feels to do this. You also know that if you are busy repeating

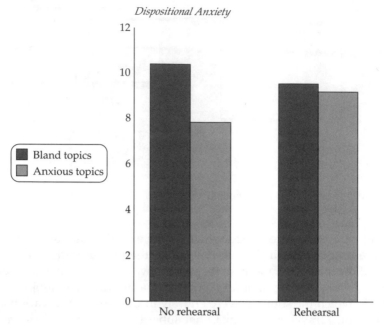

FIGURE 4.8. Estimates of the dispositional anxiety of a person who was discussing bland or anxious topics by subjects who rehearsed or did not rehearse.
Adapted from Gilbert, D. T., Pelham, B. W., & Krull, D. S. (1988). On cognitive busyness: When person perceivers meet persons perceived. Journal of Personality and Social Psychology, 54, 733–740.

a phone number, you cannot devote your attention to another difficult task at the same time. As Figure 4.8 shows, the memory task affected subjects' attributions precisely as the three-stage model predicted it would: Subjects who rehearsed the word list considered the woman to be dispositionally anxious whether she was discussing mundane or anxiety-provoking topics. In short, cognitively busy subjects did not take into account the topics that the woman was discussing. They never got around to subtracting *S* from *B*.

But wait a minute. How do we know that cognitively busy subjects failed to subtract *S* from *B*? Maybe they simply underestimated *S*. Maybe all that rehearsal made them so distracted that they never bothered to read the subtitles on the screen, and thus never realized what kind of topics the woman was discussing (which is to say, maybe they did do the subtraction but assigned *S* a value of zero). This is a good hypothesis, but a wrong one. In fact, the word list that the cognitively busy subjects were rehearsing was a very special list: It was the list of the topics themselves! In other words, subjects were made cognitively busy by being asked to memorize the topics that the woman was discussing as they appeared on the screen. One might think that asking subjects to pay extra attention to the situational constraints on the woman's behavior would *eliminate* the correspondence bias, but as the three-stage model predicted, it did exactly the opposite. At the end of the experiment all subjects were asked to name the topics that the woman had been discussing, and cognitively busy subjects had *better* memory for these topics than did normal subjects. But even though they had superior knowledge—more good, solid information about the situation than did their normal counterparts—the busy subject's state of mind was such that she could not use her knowledge. The rehearsal task did not prevent busy subjects from making dispositional inferences (which is done automatically), but it did prevent them from correcting those inferences (which is done effortfully).

All of this is rather complicated but makes a rather simple point: If one wants to use the Lewinian equation to make careful attributions, one must devote a moment of thought to the process. But people do not always have a moment for thought. In the course of the most routine interaction, countless thoughts compete for our attention ("Does she like me? That calculus final was dreadful. I think that shirt is from Sears. What's that funny smell? Did I leave my lights on this morning? Her earrings look like Christmas tree ornaments. I hope I passed that calculus final. What do I say next?"), and we find ourselves distracted, making attributions on the fly. Frankly, it is probably rarer for us to sit and deliberate about the causes of another's behavior than to make a snap judgment and get on to other things. One might hope that jurors, at least, would focus all their attention on making accurate attributions, but this is a lot to ask of anyone. The transcript of Patty Hearst's trial is 732 pages of *really tiny* print, and that does not even include the various exhibits, supporting documents, films, photographs, tape transcriptions, affidavits, and whatnot. Jurors are vastly overloaded with complicated information, and yet are prohibited from taking notes. It would be a bit of a leap to suggest that Patty Hearst's fate would have been different had the jurors been able to devote more attention to what she did and less attention to 60 billion other details of the trial. A bit of a leap, but perhaps not a gold-medal jump.

Section Summary

Attribution theories describe the logical rules that ordinary people use to determine whether another person's behavior was caused by the person's dispositions or by the situation the person was in. The most fundamental of these rules is the discounting principle, which suggests that behaviors that conform to the demands of a situation should not be attributed to dispositions. Sometimes people follow the logic of the discounting principle, but other times they attribute conforming behavior to dispositions, even though the discounting principle says they should not. This tendency is known as the correspondence bias, and it has four discrete causes. First, dispositonal attribution gives people a sense of control over their fate and the feeling that they can predict the behavior of those around them. As such, people *like* to make dispositional attributions when they can. Second, people often do not have reliable or complete information about the situations that may have caused another person's behavior because such information is inherently difficult to come by. Without this information, people make dispositional attributions out of ignorance of other options. Third, people's expectations can lead them to have a distorted picture of the other person's behavior, which may appear to be stronger than it really is. Even when people use the discounting principle, this distorted view of the behavior itself can lead them to make unwarranted dispositional attributions. Finally, dispositional attributions may be easier to make than situational attributions, and because people do not always have the mental energy necessary for lengthy contemplation, they may not move beyond the easiest conclusion.

INTERPERSONAL PERCEPTION

B. F. Skinner believed that psychologists should explain behavior without reference to unobservable mental events. But even committed behaviorists found this an extraordinary challenge, and within a few years some began to reintroduce the vocabulary of the mental into their psychological work. Edward Tolman, for instance, described the "cognitive maps" that enabled his rats to negotiate a maze, which led his hard-line colleagues to suggest (only half in jest) that a rat in Tolman's laboratory would starve to death because, rather than chasing cheese, it would just sit in the maze "perpetually lost in thought." As it turned out, Tolman, and not his critics, won the day: Most modern psychologists are intimately concerned with judgments, thoughts, inferences, ideas, beliefs, attitudes, attributions—the entire menagerie of unobservable beasts that frolicked in Skinner's nightmares. But even though they lost the fight, Tolman's critics had a very good point: Studying thought can take us only so far. If we really want to understand people, we have to understand what they *do* with what they think.

Everyone knows that, to some extent, what we think determines how we act. But how we act also affects what others think, which affects what others do, which affects what we think about them. This last, awful, murky, run-on sentence describes one of social psychology's most profound insights about people, and is worth the work it takes to understand it. Let's begin by extracting the sentence from the text, carving it up with parentheses as though it were an algebraic expression, and changing the pronouns to make clear who's who:

> (What I think) affects (how I behave) which affects (what you think) which affects (how you behave) which affects (what I think).

This statement describes how any mental event (an attribution, for instance) can change the world and then be affected by the world it changed. Indeed, once we replace those pallid parenthetical phrases with fleshy examples, the statement might even sound familiar. Imagine, for example, that you are a new graduate student, I am a professor, and you are taking my graduate seminar. Imagine that, for whichever of the four reasons, I have made an unwarranted dispositional attribution about you; for example, I have decided that you are an anxious person when you are not. This attribution will certainly affect how I behave toward you. For instance, I will invite the other students (but not you) to come to my office to see my pet boa constrictor, Ned, who lives on top of my file cabinet. Because I think you are an uptight, high-strung individual, I will keep you and Ned as far apart as possible. Moreover, I will never ask you to join me for a beer at the local pub as I do with some of the other students because, frankly, I just don't like anxious people around when I'm trying to relax with my foam. I may even feel so uncomfortable around you that I will unconsciously attempt to put some distance between us by addressing you as "Ms. Smith" or "Mr. Jones." How will my cold and stilted behavior affect you? Well, when your professor calls you by your surname and never invites you to see his snake, you should start to suspect that something's wrong. *Maybe,* you think, *I offended him by calling him Dan the first day. I mean, maybe new graduate students are supposed to act stuffy with their professors.*

So you conclude that the role of new graduate student calls for more formality than you realized, and you begin to address me as "Doctor" and "Professor Sir" and occasionally "Your Highness." You type letters on embossed stationery, seal them with wax, and mail them to me instead of just slipping a note under my door. You ask for "the honor of an appointment" instead of "a minute of your time." And all this just makes matters worse because I *hate* being called Professor, I *hate* pretentious people, and I really have to wonder what kind of neurotically anxious person would mail letters from across the hall. I find myself avoiding you whenever possible. You notice this, of course, and you feel terribly self-conscious and awkward in my presence. You bite your nails when we are finally forced to meet and discuss your term paper (which we have to do in the hallway, because I don't want you to upset Ned). You stammer, you stutter, you sweat from glands you didn't even know you had. In short, you begin to behave precisely like the anxious person I mistakenly thought you were in the first place. Is it any wonder that I come away from our interactions convinced that I was right about you all along?

As this example illustrates, a small error in thought can have big consequences in reality. Attributional errors (such as correspondence biased judgments of others) may seem like relatively harmless mistakes when viewed in the context of a laboratory experiment, and sometimes they are. But this example shows how such errors can perpetuate themselves—how they can gather momentum, so to speak, in the behavioral stream. Attributional errors can grow out of control in much the same way that a melon-sized snowball can roll down a hill and become a truck-sized snowball by the time it reaches the bottom. (Okay. That only happens in Roadrunner cartoons. But you get the idea.) As such, we can refer to this phenomenon as the *snowball effect*. Snowball effects are important in many areas of physical and social science. Indeed, whenever the final nature of an event (e.g., the formation of a cell, a cloud pattern, or an opinion) is strongly influenced by minor changes in its antecedent conditions, scientists say that the event exhibits *sensitive dependence on initial conditions* (see Gleick, 1987). As we shall see, people's final judgments about each other are, like the flow of a river and the shape of a snowflake, very sensitive to small changes in the initial impressions from which they grow. In general, there are three mechanisms by which a somewhat mistaken attribution can be snow-balled into a full-blown error, and although all three of these mechanisms are usually working simultaneously, we can disentangle them for discussion.

Matching Reactions

You may have noticed during your journey through life that a punch in the nose is rarely reciprocated with a kiss and that the question "How are you?" is al-most never answered with the phrase "Tuna fish nuggets." In social life, be-haviors play "call and answer," and everyone knows just which kinds of offers warrant just which kinds of responses. If a person is cold and hostile toward us, then we will probably act coolly in return; if a person is lively and interested, we will feel flattered and repay their warmth with our own. Punches ask for punches, kisses ask for kisses, and "How are you?" absolutely begs for "I'm fine." In short, much of our behavior is simply a *matched reaction* to the behav-ior of another.

Snyder, Tanke, and Berscheid (1977) showed how matched reactions can cause a minor misconception to snowball into a major misunderstanding. Snyder and associates invited male and female undergraduates to have a con-versation in their laboratory. The men and women arrived at and remained in separate rooms and thus never saw each other. These rooms were connected by an intercom system, and the subjects were instructed to spend 10 minutes chat-ting and getting acquainted. But before the conversation began, the men were given two pieces of information about the woman with whom they would be chatting. First, they were given a brief biographical sketch of their partner, which included only mundane facts such as her college major, the name of her high school, and so on. In addition, each man was given a Polaroid snapshot of a woman. The men were *told* that this was a snapshot of their female partner and that it had been taken just a few moments before, but in fact, the snapshot was actually a picture of an experimental confederate. Some of the men were given a snapshot of a very attractive female confederate, and other men were given a snapshot of a relatively unattractive female confederate. The men, then, were falsely led to expect to interact with either a beautiful or a homely woman. After the men read the brief biography and looked at the snapshot, they began the conversation.

At the end of the conversation, the men rated their female partners on a number of dimensions (e.g., sociable, poised, humorous, and so on). The logic of perceptual assimilation suggests that men who *thought* they were talking to an attractive woman would rate her more positively than would men who *thought* they were talking to an unattractive woman. Just as the label "schizo-phrenic" caused psychiatrists in the Rosenthal (1973) study to expect signs of mental illness and thus to see those signs in the pseudopatient's behavior, so the snapshot should have caused men to expect their conversation partner to be ei-ther sociable and poised or introverted and uneasy, and thus to *see* evidence of such attributes in the female partner's behavior. (As you probably know, there is a pervasive belief in our culture that attractive people have superior personal qualities.) And this it did: Men did indeed rate the "thought-to-be-pretty" woman more positively than the "thought-to-be-ugly" woman—despite the fact that, in reality, the women were equally attractive people, equally sociable people, and equally poised people.

But this is not the end of the story; in fact, it is just the beginning, because the experimenters recorded the conversation between the male and female subject. After the subjects left the laboratory, the experimenters edited the tapes so that only the woman's part of the conversation could be heard (i.e., they erased the man's voice). They then played these edited tapes to a new set of judges who did *not* see the fake photographs and who did *not* read the woman's biography. These new judges merely listened to what the woman actually said and then rated her on several dimensions. These ratings revealed a remarkable fact: Judges *also* rated the thought-to-be-pretty women more highly than the thought-to-be-ugly women. Now think about that. The judges had no expectations; unlike the male conversation partners, judges did *not* expect the women to be pretty or ugly. Because the judges had no expectations about the two kinds of women, we cannot explain their different ratings of the two kinds of women as an instance of perceptual assimilation. So why *did* they rate some women more positively than others? Only one explanation seems plausible: The women whose male partners mistakenly thought they were attractive actually *behaved* more sociably, more poised, and so on, than did women whose male partners thought they were unattractive.

It is not difficult to see how this could happen. Imagine the scenario. Scott comes to a psychology experiment and is told that all he has to do is chat with a young woman named Joanne. *Good deal,* he thinks, *and I even get credit for it!* Now he sees her picture. *Oh no! She looks like Jack Nicholson. With a mustache. Major disappointment. This is going to be painful. This woman looks really boring. She's probably dumb too. Why didn't I sign up for that study with the parakeets and the electric shock?* And with that happy thought, the conversation begins.

"Hi. I'm Joanne. But I guess you know that from my biography, huh? Well, this is a little strange. I mean I've never been in a psychology experiment before and . . . well, it's just a little strange, don't you think?"

Not as strange as a woman who looks like Jack Nicholson with a mustache, thinks Scott. *Even her voice sounds stupid. Kind of like Elmer Fudd.* "Yeah," he mumbles.

"So. I guess we're supposed to get to know each other. I'm an English major. My mom and dad want me to go to law school, but I'm actually not sure I want to."

Great. Another brain-dead lawyer. Just what the world needs. "Hmm," says Scott.

"How about you? What's your major?"

Now there's a novel question, Scott thinks. *What's next? Is she going to ask me my zip code?* "Marine biology."

"Oh," says Joanne. She suddenly realizes that this is the first word of more than one syllable that Scott has spoken so far. *Something's wrong,* she thinks. *He must not have liked my biography. Or my voice. Or maybe it's me. Well, who cares what he thinks anyway? I'm just trying to be nice here and he's grunting at me like a pig. Do*

I need this kind of abuse? Who does this little twerp think he is anyway? "So you study goldfish or something?"

Wow. Not only stupid, but a nasty streak too. Probably one of those liberal arts types who envies anyone who can count without moving his lips. "No, actually I study computer models of aquatic ecosystems, but it involves some pretty complicated mathematics that I don't think you'd really want me to bore you with."

He ends his sentence with a preposition and thinks that I'm too stupid to understand math? What an ego! I hate these more-scientific-than-thou types. "Hmm. Well, I don't know about the complicated part, but I'm sure you're right about the boring part." And the conversation goes on in this vein for another seven minutes until both Scott and Joanne leave by separate doors, head to the registrar's office, and beg to drop their psychology class.

What was a disastrous experience for Joanne and Scott can be an illuminating experience for us. Look closely at what happened in the first few moments of this imaginary conversation. Scott begins with a mistaken impression of Joanne and gets the ball rolling in the wrong direction with his monosyllabic grunts. Joanne quickly senses Scott's disdain and displays a matched reaction: She becomes righteously indignant and makes a flip remark about biology majors. Scott naturally takes offense at that comment and matches it with a nasty remark about the mathematical ineptitude of English majors. But Joanne turns that one to her own advantage and . . . well, the entire conversation just dissolves into a bickering contest, all because of Scott's initially mistaken belief that Joanne is an unattractive, stupid person. Too bad for Scott. What he doesn't know is that Joanne models for *Vogue*, she once had a small part in a movie filmed on location in Nepal, her grandfather rode behind John F. Kennedy's car on the day he was assassinated, she speaks mandarin and cooks Hunan . . . The list goes on. Joanne is fabulously interesting and bright, but Scott's initial brusqueness invoked her wrath, which invoked his, which eventually triggered a most idiotic conversation.

Our mistaken impressions, then, can cause us to behave in ways that elicit matched reactions from those with whom we interact. But what is so insidious about this snowball effect is that a perceiver can confirm his or her badly mistaken impression *without* distorting the facts of behavior. As noted at the outset, sane and healthy people can have distorted perceptions of the world, but those distortions cannot be too severe without qualifying as delusions and hallucinations. But Scott's mistaken beliefs about Joanne required no distortion or delusion at all: Joanne really *did* behave unpleasantly, and Scott was *not* just seeing it that way. It is true that Joanne's unpleasant behavior was provoked by Scott's unpleasant behavior (which was itself based on his misimpression), and that such snootiness was not typical of Joanne, who is usually quite charming. But even though her behavior was unusual, it was perfectly *real*. Joanne provided true, tangible, objective *behavioral confirmation* of Scott's initial suspicion. That suspicion was a *self-fulfilling prophecy,* or an expectation that causes the expected event to happen (see Darley & Fazio, 1980; Harris & Rosenthal, 1985; Miller & Turnbull, 1986; Snyder, 1984). Just as an expectation about the imminent stock market crash can cause a real collapse, so an expectation about a person's behavior can bring that behavior about. One way that our thoughts affect the behavior of others, then, is by evoking matched reactions (see also Word, Zanna, & Cooper, 1974; Zanna & Pack, 1975).

Providing Opportunities

In 1964, two Harvard psychologists visited Oak Elementary School. The psychologists explained to the teachers that "all children show hills, plateaus, and valleys in their scholastic progress," and that the Harvard Test of Inflected Acquisition (or the Harvard TIA) had been developed in order to identify those children who were about to "show an inflection point or 'spurt' in the near future" (Rosenthal & Jacobson, 1968, p. 66). The psychologists administered the Harvard TIA along with a well-established test of general ability known as the Test of General Abilities (TOGA). After the psychologists scored the Harvard TIA, they gave each teacher a list of names of the children in his or her class who had scored highest on the test. These few children, the psychologists explained, were about to experience a dramatic leap forward in their general learning abilities—a sort of "intellectual growth spurt."

When the psychologists returned in 1966, they readministered the TOGA and compared each child's new TOGA score with his or her score from 1964. As the Harvard TIA had predicted, those children who had been identified as "spurters" had gained an average of 12.22 points in general learning ability during the previous year, whereas children who were identified as "non-spurters" had gained an average of only 8.42 points. In other words, the Harvard TIA was successful in identifying a group of children who would show almost 50 percent more intellectual growth than their peers. There was just one small catch: The Harvard TIA was not a real test. It was, in fact, a completely fabricated, totally fictitious, thoroughly ersatz, pseudo-psychological quiz that had all the validity and reliability of an astrological forecast. What had actually happened was this: Rosenthal and Jacobson made up a bogus story about intellectual growth spurts, *randomly* picked 20 percent of the children from a list of names, and then told the children's teachers to expect significant intellectual growth. Given what we know about perceptual assimilation, it is little wonder that after a year and a half teachers rated these so-called spurters as happier and more intellectually curious than their peers and awarded them higher grades in reading. But as the change in TOGA scores shows, the teachers' expectations also had a dramatic impact on the *actual performance* of the spurters. Somehow, mysteriously, children who were expected to "get smart" really did.

After almost 30 years of follow-up studies, the mechanisms that caused the spurters to spurt are no longer so mysterious (see Harris & Rosenthal, 1985). Surely there are many ways for a teacher's expectations to influence a child's performance, but one is particularly easy to imagine. Penny and Nancy are classmates in Ms. Waters fourth grade. Although Penny and Nancy have about the same level of general ability, Ms. Waters has been led to believe that Penny is a spurter and that Nancy is not.

"Who knows the capital of Illinois?" Ms. Waters asks. Penny and Nancy both raise their hands. *That's a tricky question,* thinks Ms. Waters. *I better not let Nancy take it. She'll get it wrong and be embarrassed in front of the class.* "Penny?"

"Chicago!" says Penny.

"No, dear, it's Springfield, but that's the right state. And Chicago probably *should* be the capital," says Ms. Waters. Nancy thinks, *Gee, I knew it was Springfield. Why didn't she call on me?* "Okay, what is the capital of the United States?" Ms. Waters asks next. Again, both hands shoot into the air. *I suppose I'll have to call on her sometime,* thinks Ms. Waters. *And she can probably handle this one.* "Nancy?"

"Washington," says Nancy.

"Very good," Ms. Waters says unenthusiastically. *She does alright with the easier questions.* "Now, who was the famous president who came from Illinois?" Penny and Nancy have studied together, and they both know the answer. "Penny?"

"Lincoln," says Penny.

"That's right, Penny, it *is* Lincoln!" cries Ms. Waters and thinks, *This is remarkable. Those Harvard psychologists were right. Usually Penny and Nancy work at about the same level, but I think I can see Penny starting to spurt right here before my eyes.*

Anybody could have guessed Lincoln, thinks Nancy, who feels increasingly frustrated that she is not being called on to answer any of the good questions. *But Ronald Reagan came from Dixon, Illinois, so it could have been him, too. Why won't she call on me?*

"And while we're on the topic, do you know any other presidents from Illinois?" Ms. Waters says to Penny.

"Reagan," says Penny.

"Right!" says Ms. Waters. *Oh, this is so exciting. I am a gardener; she is a flower. Spurt, spurt, spurt!* "One last question, Penny. Can you name the only president never to be elected to his office?"

Ford! Ford! Ford!, thinks Nancy. *Why won't she ask me? I can even name his vice president! I can name his wife! I can name his dog for godsakes!* "Ford?" says Penny.

"Terrific!" says Ms. Waters. *This child is transforming. It is amazing. Three right answers in a row. I think I'm having a religious experience.*

"Ms. Waters?" says Nancy, "I didn't get to answer another question."

"Oh yes, sorry." *Better give the poor girl something she can handle.* "Which is bigger, a nation or a city?"

"A nation," says Nancy, and thinks, *That's the simplest question I ever heard.*

"Very good," says Ms. Waters, and thinks, *That's the simplest question I ever asked.*

Clearly a number of things are going on in Ms. Waters' classroom, the least of which is American history. But the one thing to notice is how Ms. Waters provides different *opportunities* for the two students to express what they know. If anything, Penny is less skilled than Nancy. But Ms. Waters suspects that Penny is especially smart, and so she asks her challenging questions that provide ample opportunity for Penny to confirm that suspicion. If Penny happens to know that Gerald Ford was never elected to office, then she seems like a genius;

and if she doesn't, well, who can expect such things from a fourth-grader? Similarly, Ms. Waters suspects that Nancy is a bit dim, and thus she tries to be kind to Nancy, but ends up giving her few opportunities to disconfirm that suspicion. If Nancy states that a nation is larger than a city, Ms. Waters thinks, *Any moron should know that.* If Nancy says that a city is larger than a nation, Ms. Waters thinks, *Only a moron would say such a thing.* In either case, Nancy can't win. There is virtually nothing she can do to disconfirm the teacher's mistaken impression. After a while, of course, Nancy is bound to give up. Why bother studying when the teacher never calls on you? Why tackle the difficult issues when all she ever asks is your name and shoe size? Penny, on the other hand, basks in the glow of her teacher's attention. It is not surprising that she begins to study harder, takes new books out of the library, and watches *National Geographic* specials on public television.

The point here is that our beliefs about people, right or wrong, determine our behavior toward them—specifically, they determine the sorts of opportunities we provide for others to corroborate or rectify our first impressions. Opportunity provision is by no means limited to the classroom. If we suspect that an employee is dishonest, we may never leave her alone with the cash register and thus never get a chance to see that our suspicion was unfounded. If we believe that a roommate is a coward, we will probably ask someone else to kill the 3-pound spider in the bath tub and thereby demonstrate his machismo. If we are convinced that a student is dull-witted, we may not challenge her with the sorts of problems that allow her to display creativity and imagination (see also Rothbart & Park, 1986).

Not only do we fail to provide opportunities for others to repudiate our suspicions, but we also *create* special opportunities for them to confirm what we suspect. Snyder and Swann (1978), for instance, showed that when a person has the slightest suspicion that another person may be extroverted (e.g., when the experimenter tells the person to "test the hypothesis that the guy next door is extroverted"), she will choose to ask questions that elicit evidence of extroversion (e.g., "Okay guy-next-door, what would you do to liven up a dull party?"). This question may seem innocent on the face of it, but in fact it is a *leading question*. Leading questions are those that have hidden premises (in this case, that the guy-next-door goes to parties) and thereby encourage answers that confirm those premises. Even an introvert can say what he *might* do to liven up a dull party (e.g., "I guess I'd wear a lampshade on my head and yell 'Yabba dabba do' "), but in so saying he gives the false impression that he actually *goes* to parties. The tendency to ask questions that encourage responses that confirm our suspicions is known as the *hypothesis-confirming bias* (Klayman & Ha, 1987; Snyder & Swann, 1978; Swann, Giuliano, & Wegner, 1982; Wason & Johnson-Laird, 1972). The introvert's response could lead the questioner to conclude that her initial suspicions were correct when, in fact, the introverted guy-next-door was merely repeating something he once saw in a *Flintstones* cartoon. Which he watches every Friday night. At home. Alone.

Why do people ask hypothesis-confirming questions? Why didn't the questioners in Snyder and Swann's (1978) experiment ask the guy-next-door a more neutral question, such as "Do you tend to go to parties or stay home alone and watch the *Flintstones*?" Imagine this. You are a writer for *Rolling Stone* magazine. One day the phone rings, and the caller identifies himself as Mick Jagger. Would you begin your interview by asking "Which do you prefer more, classical or rock music?" Probably not. Your knowledge of Mick Jagger's long career as a rock musician suggests that this is a pointless question that will only cause him to wonder how much you really know about your job. Rather, since you already *know* that Mick favors rock, you should ask something like "Which group do you prefer more, The Black Crowes or Nine Inch Nails?" Now, *if* you were right about Mick's preference for rock music, then this latter question is a good one because it cuts right to the chase. It doesn't waste time noodling around with the obvious.

Unfortunately, you misunderstood the caller. He didn't say "This is Mick Jagger calling." He said "This is Dick Haggard calling." Dick, it turns out, is a viola player in the local symphony who was answering your ad about the used Volkswagen. Dick would be willing to trade vital organs for an original manuscript version of Bartóks sixth string quartet, but you didn't ask him about that. You asked him whether he liked The Black Crowes or Nine Inch Nails, and that question has a hidden premise, namely, that *Dick likes rock music.* Being a good fellow who wants to answer your question and then get on to negotiating about the Volkswagen, Dick tries to remember some of that junk his teenage son is always blasting. *Oh yes,* he thinks, *Crowes were melodic, not too offensive. Nails, on the other hand . . . just industrial noise,* and so he says "Black Crowes." And you conclude that he is a Crowes fan extraordinaire!

Now, this merry madcap mixup does make a point: Questions that have hidden premises are the right ones to ask *when the premise is correct.* When the premise is correct, we call them informed, thoughtful, penetrating, incisive questions. If it had actually been Mick Jagger on the phone, then the "Crowes versus Nails" question would have been a perceptive one. If Penny truly *was* brilliant and Nancy truly *was* feebleminded, then the sophisticated and simple questions that they were respectively asked would have been perfectly appropriate. But when a question's hidden premise is incorrect, the question has the unhappy consequence of constraining the respondent's answer. It provides ample opportunity for the respondent to confirm the hidden premise, but little opportunity for him or her to refute it.

There are, of course, circumstances under which questioners do not ask hypothesis-confirming questions (e.g., Trope & Bassock, 1982), just as there are circumstances under which respondents will stand up and challenge the hidden premises of such questions (Swann & Ely, 1984). But by and large, people don't ask about what they already know, and this means that they often don't get to find out what they already know is wrong (Grice, 1975). A second way that our thoughts affect the behavior of others, then, is by providing and limiting their opportunities to act.

Setting Norms

In one of his most famous fairy tales, Hans Christian Andersen described a pair of swindlers who convinced an emperor that they had developed a beautiful new cloth that "had the strange quality of being invisible to anyone who was unfit for his office or unforgivably stupid" (1974/1874, p. 77). The emperor invited the swindlers to sew him some royal clothes. Sometime later, the emperor, his councilor, and his prime minister went to check on the swindlers' progress.

> "Isn't it a marvelous piece of material?" asked one of the swindlers. . . . "I think it is the most charming piece of material I have ever seen," declared the councilor to the emperor. . . . "Isn't it *magnifique*?" asked the prime minister. "Your Majesty, look at the colors and the patterns," said the councilor. . . . "What!" thought the emperor. "I can't see a thing! Why, this is a disaster! Am I stupid? Am I unfit to be emperor? Oh, it is too horrible!" Aloud he said, "It is very lovely. It has my approval," while he nodded his head and looked at the empty loom (p. 79).

As you probably recall, because the emperor refused to admit that he could not see the cloth, he was ultimately forced to parade around the kingdom clad in nothing but stretch marks. Although the emperor could plainly see that there was no cloth in the loom, the swindlers, the councilor, and the prime minister all said that *they* could see it, and thus the emperor (so to speak) followed suit.

The emperor's behavior exemplifies a very basic tenet of social psychology: People often determine "the right thing" to do by watching how others behave. That is, other people's behavior tells us what is normal in new or ambiguous situations. When we find ourselves at a fancy dinner with seven spoons and sixteen forks, we watch the host's choice of silverware and pray for a clue. When we join a new organization, we sit in the back row at the first meeting and observe the established members whose behavior tells us whether one is supposed to question the leader or simply accept her authority. When we enter a crowded restaurant, we let the behavior of other patrons tell us whether we should elbow our way to the bar or wait politely in line. In a multitude of situations, other people's actions tell us what is expected, what is appropriate, and what is proper (Cialdini, 1985; Darley & Latane, 1968; Walden, 1993). A detailed discussion of this phenomenon can be found in Chapters 7 and 11.

The tendency to use the behavior of others as a guide to social norms, and the power of these norms to shape our behaviors, can together cause a third kind of snowball effect. Baumeister, Hutton, and Tice (1989) invited two subjects to help evaluate the usefulness of group interviews. The experimenter explained that an interviewer would ask a question (e.g., "Describe your prospects for fulfillment and success in your chosen career"), and that each of the subjects would then take a turn answering the question. Before the interview began, however, one of the subjects (whom we will call the self-presenter) was taken aside and given a special instruction. In one condition, the self-presenter was told to boast and brag during the interview, and in another condition the self-presenter was told to be modest and self-effacing during the interview. The other subject (whom we will call the naive subject) knew nothing of these special instructions. So the interview was conducted and, by no coincidence, the interviewer always asked the self-presenter to respond first. When the interview was over, the self-presenter made a judgment about the naive subject's level of self-esteem.

A number of fascinating things happened in this study, but for our purposes, only one counts: Self-presenters who were instructed to boast thought that their naive partners had higher self-esteem than did self-presenters who were instructed to be humble. Why should this have happened? Think about how the naive subject who has been assigned a boastful partner must have felt. Bernard and Todd are thrust into a new and unusual situation: the group interview. The interviewer asks them about their career prospects. How should Bernard respond? Should he treat the situation like a real job interview in which people try desperately to impress the interviewer with their talent and charm, or should he treat it like a psychology experiment in which people usually lay back, say a few indulgent words, but generally avoid tooting their own horns at high volume. Happily, Bernard finds that his problem is solved because Todd has been asked to respond first. Todd says, "I expect to become the president of Yale University and sit on the board of directors of three different Fortune 500 companies." *Woah!* thinks Bernard, *this dude is going all out! Clearly, this must be the kind of situation where everybody is supposed to make grandiose claims, and anyone who doesn't will seem like a total loser.* So Bernard opens his mouth and is almost surprised to hear himself say, "I expect to be the president of *Harvard* University, sit on *five* Fortune 500 boards, and break Hank Aaron's home run record." Go Bernie!

Although Bernard's and Todd's claims are somewhat extravagant, they do illustrate the point: When the self-presenter boasted, he set a norm for self-aggrandizement, but when he was humble, he set a norm for humility. Indeed, objective ratings of the naive subject's behavior during the interview showed that naive subjects with boasting partners were much more likely to boast themselves than were naive subjects with humble partners. Just as opportunity provision was powerful enough to alter the behavior of a partner, so was norm setting. In the experiment of Baumeister and colleagues, Todd bragged because he was instructed to do so. But the story would have unfolded in just the same way if Todd had not been instructed but instead had a "sneaking suspicion" that Bernard was a notorious self-promoter and so assumed that he'd better get the jump on Bernard by bragging first. An initial misimpression can, like an experimenter's instruction, cause us to behave in ways that set norms for our partner's behavior.

Perceiver-Induced Constraints

Snowball effects occur when (1) my feelings about you or the situation (2) determine my actions, (3) which determine how you feel about me or how you define the situation, (4) which determines how you act, (5) which determines how I feel about you. We have seen that response matching, opportunity provision, and norm setting are ways in which the first four of these steps may be accomplished—methods for turning my thoughts into your behaviors, so to speak. But there is something decidedly odd about the fifth step. It is perfectly clear why one person's thoughts and actions might alter the subsequent thoughts and actions of another, but why on earth doesn't the first person take this fact into account? Scott provoked Joanne's petulant remark about biologists; shouldn't he have been aware of this fact and taken it into account when trying to decide how nice Joanne was in general? Ms. Waters provided the opportunity for Penny's excellent answers; shouldn't she have been aware of this fact and taken it into account when trying to decide how smart Penny was? Todd laid the groundwork for Bernard's remark about Hank Aaron's home run record; shouldn't he have been aware of this fact and taken it into account when trying to decide how well Bernard really thought of himself? As we have seen, *should* and *do* are different verbs, and what people should do is not always what they do do. If you consider the studies on snowball effects, you will see that we have come full circle. If we want to understand the behavior of people in the snowball studies, we must ultimately ask the question with which we began: Why do people make dispositional inferences about others when the other's behavior was caused by the situation? What is new here is that in each of the cases we are now considering, the situations that constrained the target's behavior were situations created by the perceiver herself. They were *perceiver-induced constraints*.

Snowball effects occur when perceivers make dispositional attributions about those who are operating under the influence of perceiver-induced constraints—in other words, when I cause you to act in certain ways and then conclude that you are predisposed to those actions. Gilbert and Jones (1986) showed that this phenomenon can happen even under the least likely conditions. In their study, subjects constrained the behavior of a target by pushing buttons that were wired to a set of colored lights; the color of the light instructed the target to make either a liberal or a conservative statement. The rules of this "signaling game" were such that the target *had* to comply with the instruction signal; that is, he had to make a liberal statement when the green light came on in his room and a conservative statement when the red light came on. Even though the subjects had pushed the buttons and therefore issued the instructions themselves, they took the target's compliant responses as evidence of the target's liberal or conservative dispositions. Even though these *inducers* (i.e., perceivers who constrain the behavior of a target) should have been especially aware that their button pressing was causing the target's liberal or conservative behavior, their judgments were no more accurate than were the judgments of uninvolved observers. As with other sorts of situational forces, people do not seem particularly adept at discounting behavior under conditions of perceiver-induced constraint.

Perceiver-induced constraints are not theoretically different than any other kind of situational constraints, and the four causes of correspondence bias that we have reviewed can explain why people make dispositional attributions about those whose behavior they have shaped. Nonetheless, two interesting problems are uniquely associated with perceiver-induced constraints; that is, there are two special reasons why we are unlikely to take the effect of our own behavior into account when we make judgments of others. The first is the *co-variation problem*. One of the early attribution theorists, Gustav Ichheiser (1949), asked us to consider what would happen if we were to enter a white room, day after day, by a door that automatically switched on a green light when it was opened. Ichheiser predicted that we would believe the room was green. Because we would never see the room in any other light, we would be unaware that our entrance by this special door had simply made the room appear green (just as a child believes that the light in the refrigerator stays on when the door is closed). In statistical language, we would have no information about the *covariation* of our presence and the room's color. In order to know that our presence in the room caused it to appear green, we would need to observe the room in both our presence and our absence—a most difficult task. Covariation is a conventional rule of scientific methodology: We know that cigarettes cause cancer because we can see that there is more cancer in the presence than the absence of cigarettes. If gravity caused cancer, we would never discover it.

The fact that we can rarely gather information about how people behave in our absence is the crux of the covariation problem (as well as the reason for the high value of information obtained by eavesdropping). You will recall that the prisoner's dilemma is a game that can be played either cooperatively or competitively. Kelley and Stahelski (1970) found that when a person who wanted to cooperate and a person who wanted to compete were left to play the game, the competitor quickly caused the cooperator to compete. The cooperator started out by making kinder and gentler moves, but the competitor blasted him, and soon the cooperator realized that it was either blast or be blasted. Interestingly, when competitors were later asked what they thought of their partners, they rated them as competitive! The competitors did not realize that it was their own behavior that had led the cooperators to compete—something the competitors surely would have realized had they been given the opportunity to watch their partners play the game with another cooperative person.

Such ironies are a familiar part of everyday life: A mother cannot believe that the teacher thinks her little angel is a spoiled brat, because the mother has never seen the angel when mummy isn't giving him everything his heart desires. A bombastic husband is surprised to learn that mutual friends consider his wife a witty conversationalist because he has never seen how articulate she can be when he is not busy dominating the discussion. A therapist is amazed to find that her depressed client is actually a paragon of good cheer when no one is asking him how he feels about his job, his sex life, and his mother. A college professor is taken aback to see that his anxious graduate student (who was so uptight that she actually *mailed* her requests for an appointment) is actually calm and self-confident when she plays Lady Macbeth before an audience of hundreds. In each of these cases, a person is surprised to find that another person behaves differently than he has always known the person to behave. We do not realize how much our presence influences the behaviors we observe because it is so difficult to observe behavior in our absence.

The second unique problem associated with perceiver-induced constraints is the *self-regulation problem*. The terms *observer* and *perceiver* may evoke a science-fictional image of a disembodied brain floating in a vat of pink jelly, watching the world through a pair of tethered eyeballs. But people are not disembodied brains. Not only do they perceive each other, but they are perceived back and they know it. In even the most familiar interaction, a person may make an attribution about her partner ("He's a very interesting man"), but she will also realize that her partner is simultaneously making attributions about her. As such, she will probably take active steps to shape the attributions that her partner draws. She will *regulate* her own behavior, smiling and nodding when appropriate (DePaulo, 1992), taking care to say the right things ("Tell me about your job") and to avoid the wrong ones ("Tell me about your ex-wife"; see Jones, 1964; Snyder, 1979; Tedeschi & Riess, 1981). If she feels tired while the evening is still young, she may mention that she has a cold or that she recently received some bad news and hope that her partner uses this information to discount her early exit (Baumgardner, Lake, & Arkin, 1985; Snyder & Smith, 1982). What she does and what she says will be, to some degree, in the service of *impression management* (Schlenker, 1980) or *strategic self-presentation* (Goffman, 1959; Jones & Pittman, 1982). At virtually any moment, some of her energy will be devoted to making her partner think that she is smart, interesting, worthy, competent, and fun.

These self-regulatory efforts have their price. As we have seen, people only have so much conscious attention to devote to information-processing tasks at a given time. If we spend our energy selecting, choosing, and planning our own behavior, then we may have less energy with which to think about the behavior of others. We saw earlier how a shortage of conscious attention can impair the correction stage of the attribution process and thereby cause people to display correspondence bias. The self-regulation problem is a problem because our attempts to regulate our own behavior during an interaction may impair our attempts to make attributions about the person with whom we are interacting. Gilbert, Krull, and Pelham (1988) showed how this can occur. Female subjects were asked either to interview a male confederate about his political beliefs or to watch the confederate being interviewed. Both the female interviewer and the female observer understood that the male confederate had been instructed to give only conservative responses to each question. The female interviewer was asked to do two things during the interview: (a) to determine the male confederate's true political attitudes (the attribution task), and (b) to regulate her own behavior such that the male confederate would truly like her (the self-regulation task).

This self-regulation task was not as easy as it sounds—at least, not for some of the female interviewers. Prior to the start of the experiment, the experimenter arranged for both the female interviewer and the female observer to be left alone with the male confederate. In some cases he behaved in a thoughtful and polite manner toward the two females, but in other cases he was blatantly rude and obnoxious. Regardless of his behavior, the female interviewer was instructed to be very cordial during the interview. This meant that some female interviewers (those who had met a polite confederate) had an easy self-regulation task: They merely needed to smile and nod at someone of whom they were genuinely fond. But other female interviewers had a very difficult self-regulation task: They needed to smile and nod at someone whom they thoroughly despised. Fawning over pond scum requires a great deal of mental effort: One

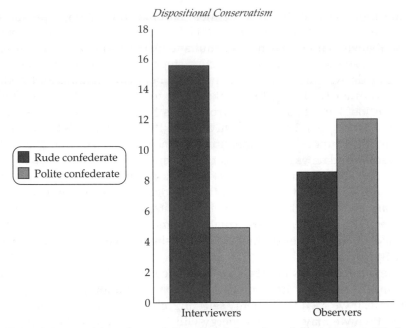

FIGURE 4.9. Estimates of the polite confederate's and the rude confederate's true political conservatism by ingratiating interviewers and by observers.
Adapted from Gilbert, D. T., Krull, D. S., & Pelham, B. W. (1988). Of thoughts unspoken: Social inference and the self-regulation of behavior. Journal of Personality and Social Psychology, 55, 685–694.

must actively suppress an urge to snarl and scowl; and one must constantly remind oneself to smile, lean forward, and "be nice." As such, female interviewers who performed the difficult self-regulation task were expected to make dispositional attributions about the confederate; that is, they were expected to conclude that he really *was* conservative (as his answers to the interview questions implied). As Figure 4.9 shows, this is just what happened. The rightmost bars show that mere observers (who, you should recall, were also treated well or badly by the male confederate in the waiting room) thought the polite confederate and the rude confederate were equally conservative. (The slight difference between the two bars is not statistically significant.) But as the leftmost bars show, real, live, self-regulating interviewers thought the rude confederate was much more conservative than the polite one. Apparently, self-regulation can impair attribution.

It seems, then, that there are two reasons why we may fail to take into account the effects of our own behavior on others: (a) We often have little or no information about how others behave in our absence, and (b) we may be too busy regulating our own behavior to think deeply about the causes of the other's behavior. Once again, it is important to emphasize that the problems associated with perceiver-induced constraints are special forms of phenomena that we have already dealt with. The covariation problem is a matter of not *having* information about perceiver-induced constraints—a phenomenon we earlier referred to as *misunderstanding situations*. The self-regulation problem is a matter of not *using* information about perceiver-induced constraints—a phenomenon we earlier referred to as *failing to use information*. But while the covariation and self-regulation problems do not add anything new to our theoretical understanding of correspondence bias itself, they do highlight a fundamental paradox of social life: The fact that we are living, breathing, interacting participants in the very dramas we seek to understand means that we are often especially poorly positioned to understand them. Unlike immersion in a vat of pink jelly, immersion in the world of people may make it particularly difficult to know why those people act as they do.

Section Summary

Snowball effects occur when a person's initial impression of another influences the dynamics of an interaction such that the interaction verifies that initial impression. Our initial impressions influence our interactions in three ways. First, they cause us to evoke matched reactions from our partners; second, they cause us to provide opportunities for our partner to confirm our impressions and limit opportunities for our partner to disconfirm them; and third, they cause us to behave in ways that our partner may see as defining what is normative and appropriate in the situation. Although our impressions of a person can clearly affect the person's behavior, we may not realize the extent to which we have induced (rather than simply observed) that behavior, and we may therefore draw a dispositional inference about our partner. Social interaction fosters such dispositional inferences by depriving us of information about how our partner behaves in our absence and by placing a premium on how we behave in his presence. In a wide variety of ways, then, our beliefs about a person can structure the behaviors to which the person must respond, and thereby influence the other person's behavior.

CHAPTER SUMMARY

As Marcel Proust suggested at the start of this chapter, it may well be easier to comprehend a planet and its orbit than a person and her actions. Two thousand years of conflict, carnage, prejudice, and oppression suggest that understanding why others act as they do is a most difficult and most pressing matter. To know a person by their behavior is to determine the extent to which that behavior reflects the person's unique and enduring predispositions rather than common social pressures. This determination is never easy to make, and thus people sometimes err. A host of cultural, motivational, and cognitive factors seem to push people toward dispositional rather than situational explanations of others' actions. Accurate attributions require a perceiver to seek, possess, and use a significant amount of complex information, and the failure to do any one of these will result in misunderstanding. In addition, people cannot separate themselves from the social worlds they hope to know. Just as Heisenberg found that an observer changes an electron's location or velocity when he attempts to measure it, so human beings change the behavior of those whom they attempt to analyze. A perceiver's initial impression can alter her partner's behavior such that the behavior provides artificial evidence for the initial impression. Once this has happened, the perceiver may not be in a position to realize that she has herself evoked the behavior, and she may attribute the behavior to the disposition of the person who performed it.

Attribution theory is modern social psychology's attempt to bring order to a set of issues that have always been and will always be at the very center of human curiosity. And although much progress has been made in 30 years, it is not at all clear that these issues will ever be completely resolved. The Hebrew aphorism urges us to ponder: "Is not a flower a mystery no flower can explain?" Perhaps. Perhaps not. But even if we cannot fully solve the problems raised in this chapter, we seem compelled by our nature to try to make a dent in them. The ancient philosopher, the modern scientist, and the poet of the next century are bound together across their epochs when each asks that most human of questions: "Who are you, and how can I know?" Indeed, it does not seem too bold to suggest that when all this vast universe is finally understood, when all the stars are charted and all their mysteries explained, each of us will still have the pleasure of trying to solve the riddle that is the other.

Notes

[1] Technically, the discounting principle states that "the role of a given cause in producing a given effect is discounted if other plausible causes are also present" (Kelley, 1972, p. 8). For our purposes, though, this formal definition is equivalent to our simpler one.

[2] In this and several other instances I have "collapsed" data across experiments; that is, I will occasionally describe the data and procedures from two or three different experiments that were published together as if they had also been performed together as a single experiment. This practice will not distort the findings of any study and will spare us a great deal of irrelevant detail.

[3] It is a custom in scientific writing to refer to oneself in the third person when describing one's own research. This enables scientists to refer to their own work as "pioneering," "brilliant," and "seminal" without looking altogether foolish. Now, of course, is not the time to break with tradition.

References

ALEXANDER, S. (1979). *Anyone's daughter*. New York: Viking.

ANDERSEN, H. C. (1974). *The complete fairy tales and stories* (E. C. Haugaard, Trans.). New York: Doubleday. (Original work published in 1874.)

ASCH, S. E. (1955). Opinions and social pressure. *Scientific American, 193*, 31–35.

BARGH, J. A. (1989). Conditional automaticity: Varieties of automatic influence in social perception and cognition. In J. S. Uleman & J. A. Bargh (Eds.), *Unintended thought* (pp. 3–51). New York: Guilford.

BAUMEISTER, R. F., HUTTON, D. G., & TICE, D. M. (1989). Cognitive processes during deliberate self-presentation: How self-presenters alter and misinterpret the behavior of their interaction partners. *Journal of Experimental Social Psychology, 25,* 59–78.

BAUMGARDNER, A., LAKE, E. A., & ARKIN, R. M. (1985). Claiming mood as a self-handicap: The influence of spoiled and unspoiled public identities. *Personality and Social Psychology Bulletin, 11,* 349–357.

BERSCHEID, E., GRAZIANO, W., MONSON, T., & DERMER, M. (1976). Outcome dependency: Attention, attribution, and attraction. *Journal of Personality and Social Psychology, 34,* 978–989.

BREWER, M. B. (1989). A dual process model of impression formation. In R. S. Wyer & T. K. Srull (Eds.), *Advances is social cognition* (Vol. 1, pp. 1–36). Hillsdale, NJ: Erlbaum.

BROWN, R., & FISH, D. (1983). The psychological causality implicit in language. *Cognition, 14,* 237–273.

BRUNER, J. S. (1957). On perceptual readiness, *Psychological Review, 64,* 123–152.

CARLSTON, D. E. (1992). Impression formation and the modular mind: The associated systems theory. In L. Martin & A. Tesser (Eds.), *Construction of social judgment.* Hillsdale, NJ: Erlbaum.

CARLSTON, D. E., & SKOWRONSKI, J. J. (1986). Trait memory and behavior memory: The effects of alternative pathways on impression judgment response times. *Journal of Personality and Social Psychology, 50,* 5–13.

CIALDINI, R. B. (1985). *Influence: Science and practice.* Glenview, IL: Scott, Foresman, & Company.

DARLEY, J. M., & FAZIO, R. H. (1980). Expectancy confirmation processes arising in the social interaction sequence. *American Psychologist, 35,* 867–881.

DARLEY, J. M., & LATANE, B. (1968). Bystander intervention in emergencies: Diffusion of responsibility. *Journal of Personality and Social Psychology, 8,* 377–383.

DEPAULO, B. M. (1992). Nonverbal behavior and self-presentation. *Psychological Bulletin, 111,* 203–243.

DICK, P. K. (1982). *The transmigration of Timothy Archer.* New York: Timescape.

DREBEN, E. K., FISKE, S. T., & HASTIE, R. (1979). The independence of evaluative and item information: Impression and recall order effects in behavior-based impression formation. *Journal of Personality and Social Psychology, 37,* 1758–1768.

ERBER, R., & FISKE, S. T. (1983). Outcome dependency and attention to inconsistent information. *Journal of Personality and Social Psychology, 47,* 709–726.

FISKE, S. T., & NEUBERG, S. L. (1990). A continuum model of impression formation, from category-based to individuating processes: Influences of information and motivation on attention and interpretation. In M. P. Zanna (Ed.), *Advances in experimental social psychology* (Vol. 23, pp. 1–74). New York: Academic Press.

GILBERT, D. T., & JONES, E. E. (1986). Perceiver-induced constraint: Interpretations of self-generated reality. *Journal of Personality and Social Psychology, 50,* 269–280.

GILBERT, D. T., KRULL, D. S., & PELHAM, B. W. (1988). Of thoughts unspoken: Social inference and the self-regulation of behavior. *Journal of Personality and Social Psychology, 55,* 685–694.

GILBERT, D. T., & MALONE, P. S. (in press). The correspondence bias. *Psychological Bulletin.*

GILBERT, D. T., PELHAM, B. W., & KRULL, D. S. (1988). On cognitive business: When person perceivers meet persons perceived. *Journal of Personality and Social Psychology, 54,* 733–740.

GILOVICH, T. (1987). Secondhand information and social judgment. *Journal of Experimental Social Psychology, 23* 59–74.

GLEICK, J. (1987). *Chaos: Making a new science.* New York: Viking.

GOFFMAN, E. (1959). *The presentation of self in everyday life.* New York: Doubleday Anchor.

GRICE, H. P. (1975). Logic and conversation. In P. Cole & J. L. Morgan (Eds.), *Syntax and semantics, Vol. 3: Speech acts* (pp. 41–58). New York: Seminar Press.

HARRIS, M. J., & ROSENTHAL, R. (1985). Mediation of interpersonal expectancy effects: 31 meta-analyses. *Psychological Bulletin, 97,* 363–386.

HASHER, L., & ZACKS, R. T. (1979). Automatic and effortful processes in memory. *Journal of Experimental Psychology: General, 108,* 356–388.

HEARST, P. (1976). *The trial of Patty Hearst.* San Francisco: Great Fidelity Press.

HEARST, P. (1982). *Every secret thing* (with A. Moscow). Garden City, NY: Doubleday.

HEIDER, F. (1958). *The psychology of interpersonal relations.* New York: Wiley.

HIGGINS, E. T., RHOLES, W. S., & JONES, C. R. (1977). Category accessibility and impression formation. *Journal of Experimental Social Psychology, 13,* 141–154.

HILTON, D. J., & SLUGOSKI, B. R. (1986). Knowledge-based causal attribution: The abnormal conditions focus model. *Psychological Review, 93,* 75–88.

ICHHEISER, G. (1949). Misunderstandings in human relations: A study in false social perception. *The American Journal of Sociology, 55,* Part 2.

JANOFF-BULMAN, R., TIMKO, C., & CARLI, L. L. (1985). Cognitive biases in blaming the victim. *Journal of Experimental Psychology, 21,* 161–177.

JOHNSON (1756). *The rambler* (4th ed.). London: Hodges, Rivington, Baldwin, & Collins. (Original work published in 1751.)

JONES, E. E. (1964). *Ingratiation.* New York: Appleton-Century-Crofts.

JONES, E. E. (1979). The rocky road from acts to dispositions. *American Psychologist, 34,* 107–117.

JONES, E. E., & DAVIS, K. E. (1965). From acts to dispositions: The attribution process in person perception. In L. Berkowitz (Ed.), *Advances in experimental social psychology* (Vol. 2, pp. 219–266). New York: Academic Press.

JONES, E. E., & HARRIS, V. A. (1967). The attribution of attitudes. *Journal of Experimental Social Psychology, 3,* 1–24.

JONES, E. E., & PITTMAN, T. S. (1982). Toward a general theory of strategic self-presentation. In J. Suls (Ed.), *Psychological perspectives on the self* (Vol. 1, pp. 231–260). Hillsdale, NJ: Erlbaum.

KASSIN, S. M., & BARON, R. M. (1985). Basic determinants of attribution and social perception. In J. Harvey & G. Weary (Eds.), *Attribution: Basic issues and applications* (pp. 37–64). New York: Academic Press.

KELLEY, H. H. (1967). Attribution theory in social psychology. In D. Levine (Ed.), *Nebraska Symposium on Motivation* (Vol. 15, pp. 192–238). Lincoln: University of Nebraska Press.

KELLEY, H. H. (1972). Attribution in social interaction. In E. E. Jones, D. E. Kanouse, H. H. Kelley, R. E. Nisbett, S. Valins, & B. Weiner (Eds.), *Attribution: Perceiving the causes of behavior* (pp. 1–26). Morristown, NJ: General Learning Press.

KELLEY, H. H., & STAHELSKI, A. J. (1970). The social interaction basis of cooperators' and competitors' beliefs about others. *Journal of Personality and Social Psychology, 16,* 66–91.

KLAYMAN, J., & HA, Y. W. (1987). Confirmation, disconfirmation, and information in hypothesis-testing. *Psychological Review, 94,* 211–228.

KLEIN, S. B., & LOFTUS, J. (1993). The mental representation of trait and autobiographical knowledge about the self. In T. K. Srull & R. S. Wyer (Eds.), *Advances in social cognition* (Vol. 5, pp. 1–50). Hillsdale, NJ: Erlbaum.

KRUGLANSKI, A. W. (1975). The endogenous-exogenous partition in attribution theory. *Psychological Review, 82,* 387–406.

LERNER, M. J. (1980). *The belief in a just world: A fundamental delusion.* New York: Plenum.

LYCAN, W. G. (1981). Form, function, and feel. *Journal of Philosophy, 72,* 24–50.

MEDCOF, J. W. (1990). PEAT: An integrative model of attribution processes. In M. P. Zanna (Ed.), *Advances in Experimental Social Psychology, 23,* 111–209.

MILLER, D. T., NORMAN, S. A., & WRIGHT, E. (1978). Distortion in person perception as a consequence of the need for effective control. *Journal of Personality and Social Psychology, 36,* 598–607.

MILLER, D. T., & ROSS, M. (1975). Self-serving biases in attribution of causality: Fact or fiction? *Psychological Bulletin, 82,* 213–225.

MILLER, D. T., & TURNBULL, W. (1986). Expectancies and interpersonal processes. In M. R. Rozenzweig & L. W. Porter (Eds.), *Annual review of psychology, vol. 37* (pp. 233–256).

MILLER, J. G. (1984). Culture and the development of everyday social explanation. *Journal of Personality and Social Psychology, 46,* 961–978.

MONSON, T. C., KEEL, R., STEPHENS, D., & GENUNG, V. (1982). Trait attributions: Relative validity, covariation with behavior, and prospect of future interaction. *Journal of Personality and Social Psychology, 42,* 1014–1024.

MULLEN, B., & RIORDAN, C. A. (1988). Self-serving attributions for performance in naturalistic settings: A meta-analytic review. *Journal of Applied Social Psychology, 18,* 3–22.

NEWMAN, L. S. (1991). Why are traits inferred spontaneously? A developmental approach. *Social Cognition, 9,* 221–253.

NEWMAN, L. S., & ULEMAN, J. S. (1989). Spontaneous trait inference. In J. S. Uleman & J. A. Bargh (Eds.), *Unintended thought* (pp. 155–188). New York: Guilford.

NISBETT, R. E., & WILSON, T. D. (1977). Telling more than we can know: Verbal reports on mental processes. *Psychological Review, 84,* 231–259.

PITTMAN, T. S., & D'AGOSTINO, P. R. (1985). Motivation and attribution: The effects of control deprivation on subsequent information-processing. In J. Harvey & G. Weary (Eds.), *Attribution: Basic issues and applications.* New York: Academic Press.

PROUST, M. (1949). *Remembrance of things past: The captive* (C. K. S. Moncrieff, Trans.). London: Chatto and Windus. (Original work published in 1923.)

QUATTRONE, G. A. (1982). Overattribution and unit formation: When behavior engulfs the person. *Journal of Personality and Social Psychology, 42,* 593–607.

REEDER, G. D., & BREWER, M. B. (1979). A schematic model of dispositional attribution in interpersonal perception. *Psychological Review, 86,* 61–79.

ROSENHAN, D. L. (1973). On being sane in insane places. *Science, 179,* 250–258

ROSENTHAL, R., & JACOBSON, L. F. (1968). *Pygmalion in the classroom.* New York: Holt, Rinehart, & Winston.

ROSS, L. (1977). The intuitive psychologist and his shortcomings. In L. Berkowtiz (Ed.), *Advances in experimental social psychology* (Vol. 10, pp. 173–220). New York: Academic Press.

ROSS, L., AMABILE, T. M., & STEINMETZ, J. L. (1977). Social Roles, social control, and biases in social-perception processes. *Journal of Personality and Social Psychology, 35,* 485–494.

ROSS, L., & NISBETT, R. (1991). *The person in the situation.* New York: McGraw Hill.

ROSS, M., & SICOLY, F. (1979). Egocentric biases in availability and attribution. *Journal of Personality and Social Psychology, 37,* 322–336.

ROTHBART, M., & PARK, B. (1986). On the confirmability and disconfirmability of trait concepts. *Journal of Personality and Social Psychology, 50,* 131–142.

SCHLENKER, B. R. (1980). *Impression management: The self-concept, social identity, and interpersonal relations.* Monterey, CA: Brooks Cole.

SCHNEIDER, W., & SHIFFRIN, R. M. (1977). Controlled and automatic human information processing: Detection, search, and attention. *Psychological Review, 84,* 1–66.

SHERMAN, S. J. (1980). On the self-erasing nature of errors of prediction. *Journal of Personality and Social Psychology, 39,* 211–221.

SMITH, E. R. (1989). Procedural efficiency and on-line social judgments. In J. Bassili (Ed.), *On-line cognition in person perception* (pp. 19–38). Hillsdale, NJ: Erlbaum.

SMITH, E. R., & LERNER, M. (1986). Development of automatism of social judgments. *Journal of Personality and Social Psychology, 50,* 246–259.

SNYDER, C. R., & SMITH, T. W. (1982). Symptoms as self-handicapping strategies: The virtues of old wine in a new bottle. In G. Weary & H. Mirels (Eds.), *Integrations of clinical and social psychology* (pp. 104–127). New York: Oxford University Press.

SNYDER, M. (1979). Self-monitoring processes. In L. Berkowitz (Ed.), *Advances in experimental social psychology* (Vol. 12, pp. 86–131). New York: Academic Press.

SNYDER, M. (1984). When belief creates reality. In L. Berkowitz (Ed.), *Advances in experimental social psychology* (Vol. 18, pp. 248–306). New York: Academic Press.

SNYDER, M., & SWANN, W. B., JR. (1978). Hypothesis testing processes in social interaction. *Journal of Personality and Social Psychology, 10,* 1202–1212.

SNYDER, M., TANKE, E. D., & BERSCHEID, E. (1977). Social perception and interpersonal behavior: On the self-fulfilling nature of social stereotypes. *Journal of Personality and Social Psychology, 35,* 656–666.

SNYDER, M. L., & JONES, E. E. (1974). Attitude attribution when behavior is constrained. *Journal of Experimental Social Psychology, 10,* 585–600.

SWANN, W. B., JR., & ELY, R. M. (1984). The battle of wills: Self-verification versus behavioral confirmation. *Journal of Personality and Social Psychology, 46,* 1287–1302.

SWANN, W. B., JR., GIULIANO, T., & WEGNER, D. M. (1982). Where leading questions can lead: The power of conjecture in social interaction. *Journal of Personality and Social Psychology, 42,* 1025–1035.

TAYLOR, S. E., & BROWN, J. D. (1988). Illusion and well-being: A social-psychological perspective on mental health. *Psychological Bulletin, 103,* 193–210.

TAYLOR, S. E., & CROCKER, J. (1981). Schematic bases of social information processing. In E. T. Higgins, C. P. Herman, & M. P. Zanna (Eds.), *Social Cognition: The Ontario Symposium* (Vol. 1, pp. 89–134). Hillsdale, NJ: Erlbaum.

TEDESCHI, J. T., & RIESS, M. (1981). Verbal strategies in impression formation. In C. Antaki (Ed.), *The psychology of ordinary explanations of social behaviour* (pp. 271–309). London: Academic Press.

TROPE, Y. (1986). Identification and inferential processes in dispositional attribution. *Psychological Review, 93,* 239–257.

TROPE, Y., & BASSOCK, M. (1982). Confirmatory and diagnosing strategies in social information gathering. *Journal of Personality and Social Psychology, 43,* 22–34.

TVERSKY, A., & KAHNEMAN, D. (1974). Judgments under uncertainty: Heuristics and biases. *Science, 185,* 1124–1131.

ULEMAN, J. S. (1987). Consciousness and control: The case of spontaneous trait inferences. *Personality and Social Psychology Bulletin, 13,* 337–354.

VALLACHER, R. R., & WEGNER, D. M. (1985). *A theory of action identification.* Hillsdale, NJ: Erlbaum.

WALDEN, T. A. (1993). Communicating the meaning of events through social referencing. In A. Kaiser and D. Gray (Eds.), *Enhancing children's communication: Research foundations for intervention* (pp. 187–199). Baltimore, MD: Paul H. Brooks Publishing Co.

WASON, P. C., & JOHNSON-LAIRD, P. N. (1972). *The psychology of reasoning.* Cambridge, MA: Harvard University Press.

WEINSTEIN, N. D. (1980). Unrealistic optimism about future life events. *Journal of Personality and Social Psychology, 39,* 806–820.

WORD, C. O., ZANNA, M. P., & COOPER, J. (1974). The nonverbal mediation of self-fulfill-ing prophecies in interracial interaction. *Journal of Experimental Social Psychology, 10,* 109–120.

ZANNA, M. P., & PACK, S. J. (1975). On the self-fulfilling nature of apparent sex differences in behavior. *Journal of Experimental Social Psychology, 11,* 583–591.

ZUCKERMAN, M., & FELDMAN, L. S. (1984). Actions and occurrences in attribution theory. *Journal of Personality and Social Psychology, 46,* 541–550.

Further Readings

BEM, D. J. (1972). Self-perception theory. In L. Berkowitz (Ed.), *Advances in experimental social psychology* (Vol. 6, pp. 1–61). New York: Academic Press.
A theory that uses attributional logic to explain how people come to know them-selves.

DEPAULO, B. M. (1992). Nonverbal behavior and self-presentation. *Psychological Bulletin, 111,* 203–243.
A thorough review of work on the self-presentation and attribution of nonverbal be-havior.

GILBERT, D. T. (1991). How mental systems believe. *American Psychologist, 46,* 107–119.
An exploration of the roots of correspondence bias and human credulity.

ICHHEISER, G. (1949). Misunderstandings in human relations: A study in false social per-ception. *The American Journal of Sociology, 55,* Part 2.
An early, prescient essay on attributional error.

JONES, E. E., & NISBETT, R. E. (1971). The actor and the observer: Divergent perceptions of the causes of behavior. In E. E. Jones, D. E. Kanouse, H. H. Kelley, R. E. Nisbett, S. Valins, & B. Weiner (Eds.), *Attribution: Perceiving the causes of behavior* (pp. 79–94). Morristown, NJ: General Learning Press.
A discussion of the differences between attributions for self and other.

JONES, E. E. (1990). *Interpersonal perception.* New York: Macmillan.
A personal account of attribution theory by one of its founders. Also contains an ex-cellent chapter on strategic self-presentation.

MILLER, D. T., & TURNBULL, W. (1986). Expectancies and interpersonal processes. In M. R. Rozenzweig & L. W. Porter (Eds.), *Annual review of psychology, Vol. 37* (pp. 233–256).
A thorough review of research on snowball effects.

ROSS, L. & NISBETT, R. (1991). *The person in the situation.* New York: McGraw Hill.
A meditation on the power of situations to explain human behavior.

SWANN, W. B., JR. (1984). Quest for accuracy in person perception: A matter of pragmat-ics. *Psychological Review, 91,* 457–477.
A discussion of attributional accuracy and error.

Susan T. Fiske is Distinguished University Professor of Psychology at the University of Massachusetts at Amherst. She received both her B.A. in social relations and her Ph.D. in social psychology from Harvard University. Her federally funded social cognition research focuses on how cooperation, competition, and power can motivate or discourage stereotyping. Her expert testimony on these issues was cited by the U.S. Supreme Court in a landmark gender discrimination case. The broader context was set by Fiske's book Social Cognition, *authored with Shelley E. Taylor (1984; 2d ed., 1991). Fiske won the 1991 American Psychological Association Award for Distinguished Contributions to Psychology in the Public Interest, Early Career; was elected the 1994 President of the Society for Personality and Social Psychology; and is editor, with Daniel Gilbert and Gardner Lindzey, of the forthcoming fourth edition of the* Handbook of Social Psychology. *In the rest of her life, she advocates for diversity, travels to Europe as often as possible, tells stories with daughter Lydia, and discovers their meaning together with her psychoanalyst husband.*

CHAPTER 5

Social Cognition

Susan T. Fiske
University of Massachusetts–Amherst

CHAPTER OUTLINE

*I would like to thank Jennifer Canfield for her patient and skilled help with the preparation of this manuscript and its references. For their helpful comments, I would also like to thank Jennifer Canfield, Julia Fishstein, Jeff Olson, Sara Pollak, and some anonymous reviewers.

Understanding, n. A cerebral secretion that enables one having it to know a house from a horse by the roof on the house. Its nature and laws have been exhaustively expounded by Locke, who rode a house, and Kant, who lived in a horse.

—BIERCE, 1911, p. 356

PRELUDE

A number of years ago, in Cambridge, Massachusetts, I was sitting on a bench in a shopping complex with a friend of mine. The two of us were talking casually, classical music drifting through the air, when all of a sudden, we heard behind us the sound of running feet. Just as we turned around, we saw tearing past us two black men followed by a white man in a security guard's uniform. My friend, who has an active civic conscience, jumped up, too late to catch the first guy, but tackled the second guy. They both went sprawling to the floor, my friend broke his glasses, and the security guard nearly landed on the two of them, my friend and the second black guy. The first guy got away. It turned out that the guy my friend had tackled was the owner of the store that had just been robbed. So, the real thief, who was the first African-American fellow, escaped, thanks to my friend. For everyone involved, it was truly maddening and humiliating.

This story illustrates understanding processes in a social context. It shows what one might call, in a sort of grandiose way, the miracle of social cognition. But it also shows the debacle of social cognition, the ways in which it can go really wrong, very quickly. In the few seconds that it took for my friend to size up the situation, he (a) noticed the races of all three people running, (b) grouped the first two into one category, (c) made an assumption (this is all in microseconds) that the two people who were the same race were together, (d) made an assumption that somebody in a certain uniform was a security guard, (e) made the complex assumption that, if the security guard was chasing these other two people (particularly a white man running after a couple of black men), the latter had probably done something wrong, and finally (f) decided to intervene on behalf of the security guard and help the security guard capture these people. Unfortunately, of course, he read the situation all wrong.

This illustrates a couple of things: One is how quickly people make sense of other people. That is the miracle part. It is amazing how rapidly people take in complex information about other people; there were so many cues in that situation, and it was within split seconds that he constructed the situation, made a decision, and reacted. At the same time, the story illustrates the debacle of social cognition, how tragically wrong one can be and how expectations can bias one's perceptions of what is going on. If he had looked a little closer, he might have noticed that fellow number two was somewhat older and better dressed, and that fellow number one was younger and not as well dressed. So, he might not have made the same decision, given more time to think about it. Whether he was right or wrong to do what he did is not really relevant here. Social cognition researchers are concerned with the phenomenon that occurred: the process of making those split-second decisions about people and how people understand what is going on in a social situation.

The striking paradox is how quickly people can make sense of other people, yet how complicated people are as objects of perception. And that is what social cognition researchers study. *Social cognition* is the process by which people think about and make sense of people. People are so complicated that it is miraculous that we can make sense of each other at all, and particularly so quickly. I would like to argue that most of the time we do not do such a bad job, although researchers often argue that we make a lot of costly errors. The opening example clearly depicts someone who did a bad job, as it happens. If he had been an off-duty police officer carrying a gun, the consequences might have been far worse. Do you think his error was preventable? Toward the end of the chapter, we will come back to this issue.

Overview

This chapter will start out by talking about the field of social cognition generally: what it is, why it is interesting, how people think about people as opposed to things. It will then give a little background about where this line of work started. Then, the next section takes up the building blocks of social cognition, schemas (what are they anyway? what kinds are there? and what do they do?). This section addresses the content of our understanding, whereas the last parts of the chapter discuss processes of our understanding. The basic social cognition processes will be covered in what could be seen as a sequential fashion: attention, memory, and inference. Each of these has important implications, as applied to social situations. For instance, in the opening example, processes of attention and immediate inference turned out to be crucial.

Social Cognition: Understanding People

To start out, what is social cognition? Although we had a capsule definition a moment ago, let's think about it both conceptually and operationally. From the point of view of a conceptual (dictionary) definition, social cognition is simply thinking about people. How do people think about other people and make sense of them? How do people think about themselves in social situations? The conceptual definition implies, first, an interest in thinking strategies and, as a corollary, not so much interest in affect (i.e., feelings, evaluations, and emotions). Nor has the field focused so much on actual, overt behavior (for reviews, see Fiske, 1993b; Fiske & Taylor, 1991; Higgins & Bargh, 1987; Markus & Zajonc, 1985; Sherman, Judd, & Park, 1989). While social cognition researchers have been figuring out the thinking, they have not always gotten around to its links to affect and behavior, but they will. For social psychologists, affect and behavior are rarely far behind. In particular, as this chapter will show, current research trends favor a growing appreciation of hot (as opposed to cold) cognition, as well as being aware that thinking is, after all, for doing.

Thinking about people is central to all of us. People are the single most important parts of our worlds. The Pentagon once developed a neutron bomb that would destroy people but not buildings, vehicles, bridges, and the like. Would you rather live in a postwar zone hit by a neutron bomb or one where all the physical structures had been destroyed but all the people had been saved by hiding in an underground shelter?

Even under less dramatic circumstances, consider how much time you spend thinking about your parents, your roommate, your lover, your professors. How does that compare to the effort you expend understanding your bathroom sink? Even the effort you expend on your car? People are extraordinarily important to us; as someone in psychology, you probably appreciate this more than most people. Because so much of our lives depends on other people, we have developed many strategies for thinking about them. Social cognition research explores these strategies. People often make sense of other people very quickly, in a matter of a few seconds, as described in the opening example. But people also ruminate about other people, thinking about their complexities over time. Which strategies people use, and when, are matters of some interest, and social cognition research recently has portrayed the social thinker as a "*motivated tactician*" (Fiske & Taylor, 1991), someone who thinks about people for specific reasons and chooses relevant strategies accordingly. The view of social thinkers as pragmatic dates back to America's first psychologist, William James (1890/1983), who said, "My thinking is first and last and always for the sake of my doing, and I can only do one thing at a time" (p. 960). As this chapter will indicate, people think about each other in a rather selective fashion, as needed for their current social and personal purposes. At the same time, these selective strategies, depending as they do upon goals, seem to work well enough for most practical purposes. In this sense, the social thinker is pragmatic.

How do the abstract definitions play out in the workaday world of research? What does social cognition mean operationally? What do social cognition researchers concretely do? How are the theories specifically tested? From an operational point of view, the field of social cognition is defined by people borrowing and adapting cognitive methods and theories for application to social psychology. This was a radical idea because, originally, studying cognition was a subversive enterprise.

The cognitive revolution, in the 1960s, marked the time at which American psychology remembered that people can think. For the prior two or three decades, American psychology in general had been dominated by behaviorist perspectives that did not consider how people think (Boring, 1950). Cognition was considered irrelevant at best (Skinner, 1963), a superstition at worst (Watson, 1930). Psychologists were more interested in how external factors would lead to overt behavior of various kinds, and the thought processes that went on between stimulus and response were considered to be epiphenomena, things really not worth studying in and of themselves. In his last public remarks, B. F. Skinner called studying cognition "the creationism of psychology" (Skinner, 1990), an anathema to true science.

Then came the turning point. Several events encouraged the subversive movement called cognitive psychology (J. R. Anderson, 1990; Holyoak & Gordon, 1984). First, behaviorist psychology was bumping into the limits of explaining complex, especially verbal, behavior in behaviorist terms (Chomsky, 1959). Second, there emerged a new metaphor for the mind: information processing (Broadbent, 1958). Computers came along, and suddenly they seemed like a great metaphor for the human mind (in Freud's time it had been the steam engine, giving rise to the hydraulic model of the psyche). The information-processing metaphor portrayed people as comparatively dumb computers: people taking in information from the outside world, encoding it in some fashion, and storing it away for later retrieval and use. The metaphor heralded a coup. Cognitive psychology came into power and replaced a lot of the behaviorist work in most psychology departments.

From a social psychologist's perspective, it was less a revolution than a change in party control. Social psychology had always harbored the resistance; certain kinds of cognition had long had a home in the study of attitudes, stereotyping, and person perception (Manis, 1977; Zajonc, 1980). So social psychology always was a hotbed of thinking about thinking. One of the grandparents of social psychology, Kurt Lewin (e.g., 1951), had insisted that some of the primary determinants of social behavior were people's perceptions of their situations. Similarly, Allport (1954a) defined social psychology as studying the influences of the actual, imagined, or implied presence of others. Two of these factors, the "imagined" and "implied," are clearly cognitive, and the third, the "actual," is *mediated* by (i.e., operates via) cognitive representation of the reality of the other person. In these and other respects, social psychology has always been cognitive (as well as motivational) in orientation, but the revolution next door in experimental psychology allowed a new infusion of theories and methods that revitalized the field (Devine, Hamilton, & Ostrom, 1994).

Now, this brief history may seem a little dry, but what fascinates social cognition researchers is how simple little quirks of information processing can determine really important social phenomenon, the everyday interactions that form the core of our personal and professional lives, as well as the larger world beyond. Cognition both determines and is determined by how we live our lives. And I hope to convince you of that in this chapter.

Thinking about Objects versus People: Similarities

In some significant ways, social and nonsocial perceptions resemble each other. Most important, the basic, fundamental processes have to be the same. You manage information about another person in some ways that are fundamentally similar to how you manage information about an object.

This principle, drawing on the ways that social cognition resembles nonsocial cognition, creates some core principles that set social cognition apart from other kinds of social psychology. And one of those principles is the principle of people as *cognitive misers*. This is a term that Shelley Taylor and Susan Fiske thought up once in a Nashville hotel room the night before one had to use it for a talk. ("There must be some way to describe this! You know, people don't like to think. They don't like to think in complicated ways. They like to hoard their scarce mental resources. What can we call it?" And then we came up with "cognitive miser.") The basic idea is that people do not like to take a lot of trouble thinking if they do not have to. Not that people are not capable of thinking hard, but the world is so complicated, and especially the world of other people is so complicated, that we cannot think carefully all the time. So, we take a lot of shortcuts, and we create a lot of approximations; the remainder of this chapter has a lot to do with these shortcuts and approximations. People use them both in thinking about people and in thinking about nonsocial things.

The next principle here concerns what one might call *unabashed mentalism;* this term goes back to the erstwhile dominance of behaviorism in American psychology. That is, social cognition researchers are neither too intimidated nor too ashamed to study and analyze thinking. It is as simple as that. This may seem like old news, but, coming on the heels of a behaviorist ideology that refused respectability to anyone studying anything that went on between people's ears, this was a daring enterprise. To be unafraid of studying people's mental processes means of course that one is trying to guess the contents of the black box one cannot open. One assumes that its contents create certain overt manifestations.

Another principle concerns a *process orientation.* Because of the information-processing metaphor—because of the idea that people, like computers, take in information, encode it in some fashion, store it away for later retrieval, inference, and use—cognitive psychology generally and social cognitive psychology specifically tend to look at things in stages. Researchers analyze social thinking in terms of flowcharts, depicting a series of processes: A leads to B leads to C leads to D. Suppose, for example, that you are interested in how people form impressions of presidential candidates; it matters whether they gather information from a variety of sources, store it away, and then make a judgment at the last minute (attention $\rightarrow$ memory $\rightarrow$ judgment) or whether they gather information, updating their judgment each time, and incidentally remember some of the information (attention $\rightarrow$ judgment and, separately, attention $\rightarrow$ memory). This has practical implications. In one case, a presidential campaign would want to create (favorable) media events as memorable as possible, but in the other case, they would not have to be particularly memorable, just as favorable as possible (Hastie & Park, 1986; Lodge, McGraw, & Stroh, 1989). In every type of person perception and social cognition, there are stages and steps along the way. Researchers break down phenomena into fine-grained processes to understand them better. Along with the cognitive miser perspective and unabashed mentalism, a process orientation characterizes the study of social as well as nonsocial cognition.

Thinking about Objects versus People: Differences

But let's back up for a moment. We just said that social and nonsocial cognition resemble each other in fundamental ways. Earlier, we said that social cognition is defined by how people think about other people, and operationally it has to do with borrowing from cognitive psychology. If we are borrowing from cognitive psychology, that immediately raises the issue: How can you study how people think about other people in the same way that you study how people think about nonsense syllables, opossums, or lawn ornaments? Surely, thinking about people is not the same thing as thinking about a lawn ornament. Indeed, it is not, and it is worth making some distinctions between how people and objects differ as targets of perception (Fiske & Taylor, 1991; Heider, 1958; Higgins, Kuiper, & Olson, 1981; Krauss, 1981; Schneider, Hastorf, & Ellsworth, 1979; Tagiuri 1958).

One important difference between people and objects is that people do things intentionally. People are *causal agents*. People are driven internally toward their actions. So, when you think about a lawn ornament, an opossum, or even a car, none of these are causal agents in and of themselves. So, that makes people much more interesting, because people have internal agendas. Of course, you may *feel* that your car has an internal agenda when it refuses to start the morning of the final exam, but of course you know better once you are safely on the bus.

Another thing that makes people more complicated than objects is that people perceive you back. Consider your first encounter with a new professor. Not only are you busy making sense of the professor, but the professor is busy making sense of you at the same time. Clearly, you are busy trying to figure out, "Well, what's this one like? Let's see, she's from California," and what are your thoughts about people from California. But at the same time she is looking back at you, and you want to make an impression on her, maybe as a serious student, paying attention, taking notes, laughing at her jokes. But the point is that social cognition is *mutual perception*, a two-way street. With an object, if you are forming an impression of a new lawn ornament, you do not try to look earnest because you are not worried about what the lawn ornament thinks of you.

One of the things that follows from mutual perception is that perceiving another person *implicates the self* in a way that perceiving an object does not. That is, you may look at another person to decide whether you are appropriately dressed, to decide whether the person is paying attention to you, to decide whether you are interesting that day, to decide whether you are similar to that person, whether you might like the person and want to spend time together, to determine what are the appropriate norms in the situation, how to behave. Other people have important implications for your self in a way that objects simply do not. You look at a lawn ornament, whether a Kmart reflector ball or an antique imported from Italy, but it does not have implications for your self-image the way a person would. Alternatively, suppose you arrive for a new graduate class, wearing standard-issue blue jeans, but everybody else is wearing suits. Think how you would feel under those circumstances. ("They're so professional; they're all going to get jobs; I'm washed up and this is only day 2.") Now consider how you would react if they were all wearing clown costumes. ("Oops. Whose joke is this? A bunch of Bozos. Not so funny. I'm clearly the only true scholar here.") In either case, your perception of other people has important implications for your sense of yourself.

Implicit in all of this is the idea that perceiving people involves perceiving something that is concerned with its own *self-presentation.* People adjust themselves when they know they are being looked at. There are probably a lot of things that you do when the elevator door closes, leaving you momentarily alone, things that you would not do if you had happened to notice the recently installed video security camera. Self-presentation is universal, and as perceivers we know that people are engaging in self-presentation when we are trying to make sense of them (see Baumeister, Chapter 3). The point is simply that we know that people may be manipulating how they appear because they are concerned about how they might come across. So, that is different because a lawn ornament does not do that; even a dog does not really do that. Animals constitute an interesting intermediate area, but we are mainly contrasting people versus objects.

A concern with self-presentation implies that people have *nonobservable traits* and characteristics that are important to us. If you are trying to decide if a lawn ornament is fragile, for example, you could, in theory, find out very easily. Throw it to the ground, and see whether it breaks. How about a person? How do you decide if a person is fragile or not? And would you really want to conduct your test? It is much harder to decide if a person is fragile or not. Such nonobservable traits are important because they have implications for what the person's intentions will be, how the person will decide to behave as a causal agent, how the person will perceive you back, how the person might be relevant to yourself, how the person might be engaging in self-presentation. So, these hidden characteristics of people are very important to us, and attribution theory in social psychology concerns precisely the processes by which we decide whether or not certain traits and motives have caused a particular behavior (see Gilbert, Chapter 4).

Nonobservable traits are much harder to verify for people than they are for objects. In trying to decide how fragile George is, perhaps you talk to a mutual friend and say, "So, what do you think? Do you think George is fragile?" "Well, no, I never thought of him as fragile." "Well, I was just thinking of the time he fell apart when someone joked about his haircut." In conversations about a third party, it is often hard to agree on whether the person is truly fragile, generous, intelligent, friendly, etc. Oftentimes there is some consensus, but just as often, there is some disagreement. (This is an interesting, understudied phenomenon—the social negotiation of someone else's identity—but see Levine, Resnick, & Higgins, 1993; Resnick, Levine, & Teasley, 1992; Ruscher & Hammer, 1994.) The same problems with a lack of consensus hold true within psychology. Psychologists cannot even agree on how to measure whether someone is a certain way or not. There is some consensus, but it is shaky. Different researchers come to different conclusions. This is essentially the *accuracy problem:* It is harder to verify what people are really like than what objects are really like. One of the big problems in personality research, it is also a classic problem in person perception—how accurate is one person's perception of another person (for discussions, see Funder, 1987; Kenny, 1991; Kruglanski, 1989b; Swann, 1984).

People are, on the average, more *variable* than objects. Moment to moment, year to year, the lawn ornament just sits there being itself; but your roommate, your sister, your neighbor each change a lot over time, and also in the short-term. People have moods. People change their minds. People evolve.

So how does this all add up? People are *unavoidably complex* as objects of perception. Trying to make sense of another person is a very difficult enterprise, to put it bluntly. This means that when one studies how people make sense of another person, one has to simplify things somewhat, or else one cannot study the phenomenon; the problem would be intractable, too hard. But, at the same time, as soon as one begins to simplify the person, one is already doing some violence to people's essence, because people are inherently complicated. That is always the trade-off: How simple do we have to make it so we can study it, but how complicated do we have to keep it so it is real? How can we study this so that what people are looking at is a person, not a thing?

Finally, it is, after all, *social* cognition, with an emphasis on the "social." Some people in the field put more emphasis on the "social" and some more on the "cognition." I personally subscribe to the point of view that it is very important to put a lot of emphasis on the "social." If thinking is for doing, as James pointed out, what people are doing with their social thoughts is interacting with other people, planning to interact, or rehashing interactions. The *pragmatic social context* of thinking about others means that social cognition is both a cause and an effect of social interaction. The link to social interaction means that (a) people are generally accurate enough for everyday purposes; (b) they construct meaning based on the most useful (convenient and coherent) traits, stereotypes, and stories; and (c) their goals determine how they think (Fiske, 1993). The importance of people's pragmatic orientation to their everyday thinking about other people led to the term *motivated tactician* (noted earlier) as a way to describe social thinkers' ability to choose among multiple strategies depending on their purposes (Fiske & Taylor, 1991, Chap. 1).

Such a pragmatic, social emphasis also puts a premium on social realism in research. The studies need to create highly involving social situations that resemble life outside the laboratory. Another corollary of this idea is that social cognition figures importantly in real-world issues such as health, economics, prejudice, conflict, the environment, and more. Social cognitive processes, in short, are important, and all of this research will not be worth a hoot unless it has some bearing on how people live their lives.

Where Do These Ideas Come From?

The quotation from *The Devil's Dictionary* that opened this chapter held that understanding enables one to know a horse from a house, and then it referenced Locke and Kant. These references are not facetious. Psychology has its origins in philosophy, and there one finds the beginning of two quite different descriptions of thinking. According to Locke (1690/1979), thinking operates like mental chemistry, in which discrete basic elements form associations that create more and more complex "compounds." His *elemental approach* maintains that the basic elements remain unchanged regardless of the other elements with which they are associated. Hence, mental compounds resemble salt and pepper, in which each component retains its identity within their association.

Kant (1781/1969) disagreed with the elemental approach, emphasizing more the interpretative and constructive activity of the mind in perception. His more holistic ideas led to the *Gestalt approach* (Koffka, 1935; Kohler, 1938/1976). In contrast to the salt-and-pepper elemental view, it took more of a coffee-with-cream approach, in which the components were altered by being combined, losing their original identities.

These two contrasting views of understanding carried over to early person perception research. Consider the following thought experiment: What kind of person is *intelligent, skillful, industrious, cold, determined, practical,* and *cautious*? Think about this person for a moment; form an impression.

Now, consider how you would feel about competing with this person. How would the person behave—play fair? not play fair? "No, I'm not sure this person would be fair. I would not like competing with him," one person responds. You would perhaps keep your eyes open about this person. You read that this person was intelligent. Can you think of some synonyms for how this person is intelligent? What particular kind of intelligence? "Calculating," perhaps? When a person is intelligent and cold, it comes across as calculating and sly, and not too trustworthy.

Now consider a different person. Without looking back at the other list, this person is (read carefully): *intelligent, skillful, industrious, warm, determined, practical,* and *cautious*. What kind of person is this? Would this person play fair in a competition? "Probably fair but very competitive," one person responds. Would this person be intelligent like a spy, like a grandmother, or like a friend? "Bright and creative," one might respond. This person does not seem calculating. If a person is intelligent and warm, the person might be a nice mentor, might be a nice creative, friendly person, somebody you would definitely want on your team; you would not have to watch behind your back about this person.

Why does the meaning of intelligence seem to differ in the two different lists? There were seven words, and there was only one word that differed between the two lists. The only difference was *warm* and *cold*. So, the point here is that this simple word pair has a big impact on the rest of the words in the list, and on the meaning of those words in context. So, the impression of the person that you form from these words is a unified whole or Gestalt; it hangs together, it coheres together, as an impression. The mind makes the pieces fit together. It is not so hard to make *skillful* and *industrious* fit together, or *practical* and *cautious* fit together, but it does change the meaning of the words slightly as you are putting them together.

This experiment is not original; it was first conducted in 1946 by Solomon Asch. He did this experiment originally to support what he called a configural model, or a Gestalt model of how people form an impression. He was arguing that impressions are a configuration; they fit together as a pattern; they are unified and integrated. People try to make all the pieces go together, and people "go beyond the information given," in Bruner's (1957) phrase. So when I ask you, "What would this person be like as a competitor?" and you say that this person might or might not play by the rules and be fair, you are making some inferences about the person. Of course even before I asked you the question, the meanings of the terms, such as *intelligent*, were shaped by the other terms that were in the impression.

The basic point that Asch was making in this particular set of studies was that impressions are a single Gestalt, a unified whole. And, specifically, there are *central traits* that particularly shape the unified whole. "Warm" and "cold" are central traits; not just any trait would have the same kind of influence. For example, "polite" and "blunt" would not have quite the same impact as "warm" and "cold." "Warm" and "cold" are important features of making sense of people. Asch asked two different groups of students what they thought of each of these people, and he asked them to describe the people in an open-ended way. They said that the warm person was also good-looking, honest, happy, and strong. Obviously, they were going well beyond the information that was given to them; they were making inferences about the person because they were constructing some meaning in their understanding of the person. They constructed an impression. That is not a bad thing; people have to do that in order to function. One cannot take everything as a literal copy of the world out there. One actively constructs meaning based on prior knowledge of what people are like: what warm people are like, what cold people are like. What are the different ways to be intelligent? It is an active process on the part of the perceiver.

How can one evaluate the Gestalt model of person perception? Presented with a theory or a model, it is always good to ask, "Compared to what? What is the alternative?" In this case, Asch himself gave an alternative. The paper that he wrote was a classic, in which he laid out two potential ways that people could make sense of other people. One is the unified, configural Gestalt approach, which he favored, and then there was an alternative which he did not favor, but which other people have subsequently taken up and supported as well.

The alternative one might call an elemental (as stated earlier), or *algebraic*, kind of model, and the most famous proponent of this in person perception is Norman Anderson (e.g., 1981). The elemental or algebraic model basically says that people take the components of the impression and extract from them the evaluations, the likability of each individual component. So going back to the previous lists, one might say, "Intelligence. That's seven on a ten-point scale. Skillful, that's six. Industrious, that's five." And one basically takes all these and averages them up. Note that intelligence has the same value, regardless of whether it is paired with "cold" or "warm," in this viewpoint. This elemental approach does not have the sense of a Gestalt, a holistic, integrated unit, because it takes components in a piecemeal fashion, separately.

This kind of model has become rather sophisticated, the argument being that an impression is actually an algebraic, weighted average of the components. And there is a lot of evidence for this. (Here is where we get technical.) In the elemental, algebraic view, an impression is simply the sum of *weights* (w_i) multiplied by some *scale values* (s_i).

impression = $\Sigma w_i s_i$

A weight is simply the importance of a particular trait, and the scale value is the individual person's evaluation of it. These are the intuitively important aspects of an impression. It might matter quite a lot whether someone is warm or cold, so "warm" or "cold" could have a lot of weight in an impression, whereas it really does not matter much how practical the person is. The weights are constrained to add up to one, making them all relative weights, as if each is worth so much of the proportion of the impression. On the other hand, the scale value (evaluation) of the traits determines just how likable a particular trait is in a person. The model is simple and elegant: It asks, "How likable is that trait?" and then, "How important is it?" Something can be very likable but not very important, or it can be very likable and rather important indeed; the same is true of dislikable characteristics.

To work through a concrete example, one could decide that intelligence has a scale value of, say, eight on a one-to-ten scale; it is really a good thing. Being mean has a scale value of one; it is really bad. So the scale values of those two things are, respectively, eight and one. But in terms of picking a friend, the weight of intelligence is not so great; maybe it is a quarter of the whole impression, but if the person is mean, that counts perhaps three-quarters of the impression. (Why befriend someone mean?) So the weight and the scale value are more or less independent of each other. What Anderson and others would argue is that you would multiply the weight of being intelligent times its scale value, and add it to the weight of being mean times its scale value, and you come up with an impression: 2.75 on a nine-point scale.

This kind of model, as noted, is called a weighted-average model. There are similar kinds of models called expectancy-value models (see them in Chapter 6 on attitudes). If you have ever taken an economics or political science course, this kind of general, linear model should look familiar to you. This is how economists say people make decisions. They take the value of the attributes of the thing that they are evaluating. For example, take a possible car and look at what kind of gas mileage it gets, how safe it is, how attractive. Then weight these factors, and come up with an evaluation of the car. Same process. So this kind of decision-making model is a very basic model within the social sciences. There is a lot of evidence that it is highly predictive of how people make their decisions.

But. But, you really cannot be sitting there calculating, "Well let's see. 'Intelligent'—that's pretty good; 'mean'—that's not so good. Let's see—one-fourth times eight plus three-fourths times one . . . " Whatever else is going on, this seems an unlikely train of thought the minute one meets somebody. Perhaps, the models' supporters would argue, people merely approximate the algebraic processes by some type of processing outside of awareness (Lopes, 1982). This has yet to be demonstrated, and one still wonders what could be the psychological process by which algebraic impressions are created. So we have a paradox, which is that these models are highly predictive under certain circumstances, but at the same time, they do not seem psychologically real. So this is an unresolved problem for future research. At the end of the chapter, we will come back to this and hope to provide some closure.

For now, the basic point is that Asch (1946) proposed two competing models, both of which have some plausibility. One is the configural, Gestalt, holistic model; and the other is the elemental, algebraic, piecemeal type of model. The two sides subsequently warred with each other for a while (Hamilton & Zanna, 1974; Schumer, 1973; Wyer, 1974; Wyer & Watson, 1969; Zanna & Hamilton, 1972, 1977; versus Anderson, 1966; Anderson & Lampel, 1965; Kaplan, 1971, 1975), and then finally Ostrom (1977) said that this could not be resolved with the theoretical and methodological tools then available. Nevertheless, the configural, Gestalt, or holistic model set the stage for a major area of research within subsequent social cognition research, namely, work on what we call schemas.[1]

SCHEMAS

What Are Schemas?

A *schema* is a "cognitive structure that represents knowledge about a concept or type of stimulus, including its attributes and the relations among those attributes" (Fiske & Taylor, 1991, p. 98). Schemas are basically preconceptions or theories, in this case about the social world. So, presumably you have a concept of a warm person: What are warm people like? What do warm people do? "They are friendly." What else? "Thoughtful." "Helpful." Do they say "Hi" to you in the hallway? "Yes." You have some preconceptions about what a warm person is like. So, the term *schema* is just a fancy way of saying that. There are a lot of elements to this preconception, but the elements are connected to each other in some fashion, and they influence each other's meaning. They form a theory about what warm people are like.

What Kinds Are There?

Different types of schemas have been studied (Taylor & Crocker, 1981). We just described what might be called a *person schema*, that is, a schema for warm people. People have schemas for all kinds of personality traits, such as what it means to be irritable, outgoing, or conventional (Cantor & Mischel, 1979). People also have schemas for social goals, such as ingratiation, revenge, and helpfulness (R. C. Anderson & Pichert, 1978; Owens, Bower, & Black, 1979; Zadny & Gerard, 1974; see Pervin, 1989, for a collection of related work). Person schemas also include people in situations, such as a shy person at a party or a practical person at a meeting (Cantor, Mischel, & Schwartz, 1982).

Self-schemas form the core of our self-concept; people have schemas for themselves. For example, do you consider yourself independent or dependent? Why? If one has a well-developed self-concept on a dimension, one is *schematic* on that dimension (Markus, 1977; Markus & Wurf, 1987). People's schemas for themselves are much more complicated than their schemas for other people, as you might imagine (Linville, 1982a; Lord, 1980). That has some interesting implications, such as increasing one's ability to remember information considered self-relevant (for a review, see Kihlstrom, Cantor, Albright, Chew, Klein, & Niedenthal, 1988). People also differ in the *chronic accessibility* of different traits. That is, for certain people, certain traits are easily activated and readily applied to self and others (Higgins, King, & Mavin, 1982; Higgins, 1989).

Role schemas contain our understanding of the behaviors and attributes expected of people in particular social positions. For example, you may have learned what the role of graduate student means, how that is different from being an undergraduate. Which one routinely calls professors by their first names? And for which one does Saturday night become a night when you can get a lot of work done? And graduate students are the only people who spend more money on books than on food. Graduate students are people undergoing an initiation to become part of the community of scholars. If you saw a graduate student coming to class in a new fur coat and a BMW, you'd wonder what was going on with this person. The point is that one has some conceptions about what graduate students are like. One important distinction is between *achieved roles*, such as graduate student, chain gang member, or zookeeper (sometimes "graduate student" seems to include the other two); achieved roles are those we acquire through some activity. In contrast, *ascribed roles* are those given to us automatically (e.g., age, race, gender). Schemas for roles are equivalent to *stereotypes*, people's expectations about people who fall into particular social categories. Allport (1954b) described them as the "nouns that cut slices." Of course, there are many different explanations for stereotypes besides schemas, but role schemas are one way to think about stereotypes.

Finally, we have schemas for certain kinds of events. To imagine an event without a schema, consider the following:

> The procedure is actually quite simple. First, you arrange things into different groups. Of course, one pile may be sufficient depending on how much there is to do . . . It is important not to overdo things. That is, it is better to do too few things at once than too many. In the short run this may not seem important, but complications can easily arise. A mistake can be expensive as well. At first, the whole procedure will seem complicated. Soon, however, it will become just another facet of life (Bransford & Johnson, 1972, p. 722).

Reading this event sequence without the proper script makes it all seem rather disconnected and mysterious. Doubtless, it would be difficult to remember the whole passage a few minutes from now. *Event schemas* contain appropriate sequences of events in social situations. What happens when one goes to a restaurant: get seated, look at a menu, order something, eat, pay, and leave. It is a predictable sequence, almost a *script* (Abelson, 1981; Schank & Abelson, 1977). Recently, the understanding of event sequences has been applied to phenomena as varied as theft, defecting from one's country, underdogs winning, stressful life events, and jury decision making. By the way, the mystery procedure described earlier was washing clothes. Now does it seem a more familiar and memorable script?

Organized prior knowledge or preconceptions—schemas of all types—smooth our information management and social experiences. The point is that people seek simplicity and good-enough accuracy, good-enough understanding of the world around them, and schemas are guides. Having these preconceptions helps one to understand things with relative efficiency and accuracy.

What Do Schemas Do?

> Pat woke up feeling sick again and wondered if she really was pregnant. How would she tell the professor she had been seeing? And the money was another problem. . . . Pat went into the kitchen, took the pot out of the cabinet, put in some mix, made some coffee, looked at the coffee, and decided to add some milk and sugar. After that, Pat got dressed and went to the doctor. After arriving at the office, Pat checked in with the receptionist, and then saw the nurse, who went through the usual procedures. Pat stepped on the scale, and the nurse recorded Pat's weight. The doctor entered the room and examined the results of the procedures, smiled, and said, "Well, it seems that all my expectations have been confirmed." Then Pat left the office. Pat arrived at the lecture hall and decided to sit in the front row. Pat walked down the aisle, sat down. The professor went to the podium and began the lecture right away. All through the lecture, Pat just could not seem to concentrate on what was being said. The lecture seemed really long. But, finally, it ended. The professor was surrounded by people after class, so Pat quickly left. Later that afternoon, Pat went to a department cocktail party and looked around the room to see who was there. Pat went over to the professor, wanting to talk to him, but feeling kind of nervous about what to say. A group of people began to play some games. Pat went over and had some refreshments. The hors d'oeuvres were good, but Pat did not feel very interested in talking to some of the other people at the party. After awhile, Pat decided to leave (after Owens, Bower, & Black, 1979).

Suppose Pat and the professor had had a chance to have a conversation. How do you suppose that Pat would have been feeling under those circumstances? What are some emotions that come to mind? "Anxious." "Uncomfortable." Do you think Pat and the professor might have made arrangements to meet to talk later, or would they have been able to take care of what they had to talk about right there at the party? "Definitely later." Is Pat glad when Pat discovers that the scale has gone up recently? "Hardly."

Now consider the same story with a different lead-in replacing the first sentences up through the ellipses (. . . .): "Pat woke up wondering how much weight he had gained so far. His football coach had told him he could start in the game Saturday only if he gained enough weight and passed the chemistry test. The pressure was intense. . . ." Now reread the rest of the original story after the ellipses.

The meaning changes rather dramatically, doesn't it? How is football Pat feeling about the professor? What are his goals for talking to the professor at the party? How does this Pat feel about the scales? When we have two different Pats, it becomes rather a different story, doesn't it? This experiment, conducted by Gordon Bower and his colleagues (Owens, Bower, & Black, 1979), presented versions of essentially this story to undergraduates, with a third receiving the pregnant lead-in for a character named Nancy, a third receiving the football lead-in for a character named Jack, and a third receiving no lead-in. Half an hour later, they asked subjects to recall the action sequences, as close to verbatim as possible. Subjects given a lead-in problem remembered more episodes, more often in correct order, and displayed many more intrusions of recall than did control subjects. The memory intrusions included thematic interpretations of ambiguous statements (for Nancy, the nurse's "usual procedures" became "pregnancy tests"), as well as inferences about motives and feelings (at the party, Nancy "was feeling miserable"). This research pointed out that we have schemas for would-be athletes and for unwanted pregnancies, and they shape how we encode, remember, and judge the information that follows.

Schemas Direct Attention and Guide the Encoding of Schema-Relevant Information. What did you notice in the first story? Given the pregnant Pat schema, one is particularly likely to notice that the doctor goes through the "usual procedures," which one may encode as a gynecological examination. For would-be athlete Pat, that interpretation is unlikely. Indeed, the "usual procedures" is not a relevant phrase and probably rather meaningless in that context. It is not something that one would notice. But would-be athlete Pat getting on the scale is something noteworthy, because this poor person is trying to gain some weight. Pat's dealing with food is probably significant in both cases but in different ways. Pat's noticing whether there are a lot of other people around the professor takes on a different significance in the two cases. So, what one notices and how one interprets what one does notice are both affected by the schema applied to the particular situation.

People's encoding processes balance the schema against the data, neither completely relying on the schema and completely ignoring the data nor completely allowing the data to speak for themselves without any influence of the schema. On the other hand, schemas do have a major impact, in several respects: Schemas often are cued by visually prominent physical features (e.g., age, race, gender, dress indicating social class) or immediately provided labels (e.g., occupation). From the earliest moments of perception, schemas affect how quickly people notice, what people notice, and how people interpret what they notice. For example, racial labels automatically can cue stereotypic associations within milliseconds (Devine, 1989). Schemas, because they stem from categorization processes, tend to minimize differences among instances of the same schema ("They all look alike") and maximize differences between groups (for a review, see Mullen & Hu, 1989). Schemas provide simple concepts of outgroup members (e.g., Linville, 1982b). And schemas encourage stereotypic interpretations of behavior (e.g., Darley & Gross, 1983). When people do not attend to inconsistency (information that may dispute their schemas), their subsequent processing is biased toward the schema (Hilton, Klein, & von Hippel, 1991; White & Carlston, 1983).

On the other hand, people sometimes do pay close attention to schema-inconsistent evidence (e.g., Brewer, Dull, & Lui, 1981). When people do attend to inconsistency, their processing is more idiosyncratic and (for some people) more responsive to the individual confronting them (Fiske, 1992, 1993b). People do balance schema-based processes, i.e., prior theories, against the data they encounter (for reviews, see Fiske & Neuberg, 1990; Higgins & Bargh, 1987). In the next section, we will consider the circumstances under which people do and do not remember the inconsistent information they notice.

Schemas Also Guide Memory. Think back to pregnant Pat. Some story items were more related to pregnancy, and some were more related to football. Afterward, without benefit of knowing the alternative opening to the story, people who get the pregnancy lead-in remember more of the pregnancy items, and people who get the football lead-in remember more of those (Owens, Bower, & Black, 1979). In general, when people have very well developed schemas, they remember things that are consistent with the schema (Fiske & Neuberg, 1990; Higgins & Bargh, 1987; Ruble & Stangor, 1986). In contrast, if people are just beginning to develop a theory or an impression of a particular person, then people notice both the consistent and the inconsistent information. People may then remember the inconsistent information, as a consequence of the effort to integrate it into a developing impression (Hastie & Kumar, 1979; Srull, 1981; Srull & Wyer, 1989). Without a strong prior theory, people remember the inconsistencies, but with strong prior theories, they do not recall as much inconsistent information (for other conditions of the inconsistency advantage, see Stangor & McMillan, 1992). In any case, people remember schema-relevant information (both consistent and inconsistent) better than irrelevant information.

Schemas Influence Judgment. People sometimes make judgments based on what they can remember, particularly if the judgment is unanticipated (Hastie & Park, 1986). However, many judgments are made *on-line*, as the information is received (Bassili, 1989). For example, people have immediate evaluative responses to other people they meet; they know rapidly whom they like and dislike, as the initial encounter unfolds. When we meet someone who reminds us of someone else we once knew, the new person elicits the same emotional response as the old one; this might be called schema-triggered affect or, in psychoanalytic terms, transference (Andersen & Cole, 1990; Fiske, 1982; Westen, 1988). Sometimes the newly met person does not remind us of anyone in particular but instead comes from a category (occupational, ethnic, or otherwise), to which we have attached a strong *affective tag* (Dijker, 1987; Fiske, 1982; Fiske & Pavelchak, 1986; see Devine, Chapter 12). The most powerful type of category is "us" versus "them," a primitive intergroup divide that precipitates in-group favoritism (Brewer, 1979; Mullen, Brown, & Smith, 1992). Schemas can allow simplified, polarized judgments and evaluations (Linville, 1982a, b; but also see Judd & Park, 1988, Marques, Yzerbyt, & Leyens, 1988; Millar & Tesser, 1986). In short, schemas shape judgments in various and important ways.

Schemas versus Evidence. Schemas have far-reaching effects on attention, memory, and judgment, no doubt about it. But data themselves also influence people's thinking. People's use of schemas versus evidence depends on, for example, the fit between the schema and the relevant data (Fiske, Neuberg, Beattie, & Milberg, 1987) and the perceived diagnosticity of the data (Hilton & Fein, 1989; Leyens, Yzerbyt, & Schadron, 1992).

People's trade-off between schemas and data also depends on motivation, as described by several current theories (Brewer, 1988; Fiske & Neuberg, 1990; Gollwitzer, 1990; Hilton & Darley, 1991; Kruglanski, 1989a; Ruble, 1994; Snyder, 1992; Stangor & Ford, 1992). Under some conditions, people conserve mental resources and rely on a prior schema or expectancy, namely, when they are oriented toward efficiency, speed, action, or interaction, or when they are distracted, anxious, or defensive. Such conditions all promote *category-based processes.* When people are overloaded, they are more likely to form superficial judgments. Under other conditions, people are concerned with accuracy and examine the data more carefully, namely, when they are outcome-dependent, subordinate, stigmatized, accountable, depressed, or instructed to be accurate; these conditions promote *data-driven* or *piecemeal processes* (for reviews, see Fiske & Taylor, 1991, Chap. 5; Fiske, 1992, 1993a, 1993b).

This resolution—when people use schemas and when they use data—did not come easily. Indeed, it has been a recurring problem in social perception. Initially, as discussed earlier (see "Where Do These Ideas Come From?"), person perception researchers faced the apparent contradiction between the psychological plausibility of schema-like Gestalt models and the predictive value of algebraic models that seem to emphasize data. Later, as another example of theory-driven versus data-driven processes, social cognition researchers faced apparent contradictions between people's use of stereotypes and their neglect of population base rates (see below; Locksley, Hepburn, & Ortiz, 1982). Researchers wondered, so how can that be? How can both kinds of models be right? Is one wrong, and the other one's right, or what is going on?[2]

Basically, the bottom line is that both approaches are right; it just depends on the circumstances. One way to think about it is that there is a continuum between the two. On the one end are schema-based or categorical kinds of impressions that are the more holistic, integrated impressions that we form about people. And on the other end are more individuating and attribute-oriented impressions, elemental kinds of impressions, piecemeal kinds of impressions. So, we have a continuum between the schematic kinds of impressions and the elemental, algebraic kinds of impressions. In between are some intermediate kinds of processes, including subtyping and self-reference (for more detail, see Fiske & Pavelchak, 1986; Fiske & Neuberg, 1990).

Basically, I would argue, the normal, default option is to go with the schema, the category, the preconception, the theory. That is what my friend did in the shopping mall. In the first nanoseconds, the automatic reaction was to go with the schema (see Devine, Chapter 12). People's immediate reaction is to go with the category unless they have more time, attention, and motivation to be more careful. Then, in that case, they may move down the continuum toward the more individuated, personalized, piecemeal kinds of responses where they take in each piece of information about the person and think hard about it as an individual piece of information. So what this means is that the more motivated one is, the more attention that one can pay to a person, the less schema-based is one's impression, all else being equal. You can think of this as "How do you overcome stereotypes?" How do you get people to go beyond their initial schemas and stereotypes, moving into a more individuated impression of somebody else? The answer is: attention and motivation. It takes more time to form a fully attribute-oriented, elemental kind of impression of somebody. That is why, when you buy a car, you may in fact buy a car by saying, "What kind of mileage? What does it look like?" and so on, because that is a very involving and highly motivated kind of decision. Suppose you are trying to pick somebody to advise your dissertation: That also might be a more considered pros and cons kind of decision. So, when it is really important to people, they can make those kinds of decisions. But most of the time it is the initial, knee-jerk reaction, which is to go with our schemas, to go with our prior categories.

Conclusion

I hope this section has convinced you that people use schemas for good-enough, very rapid understanding. Schemas can have a big impact, yet people also can engage in more individually tailored understanding of other people. There are a couple of different processes, and both of them operate, depending on information and motivation.

The schema section has discussed what might be called one of the major elements of social cognition. Are the basic elements the individual items of the impression, or are they somehow the whole schema or configuration? What are the building blocks? What are some of the elements of making sense of other people? Schemas are clearly one. I would also argue that attributions are another element in making sense of other people. People are causal agents (think back to differences between perceiving people and perceiving objects), so it is important for us to figure out why they do what they do and to predict what they will do in the future. And that is why attribution theory has become such an important part of social cognition research, because causal explanation is so important in perceiving people and not so important in perceiving nonsocial objects (see Gilbert, Chapter 4). When attributions are made to personal dispositions, we then have available all the information stored in the relevant trait schema.

Schemas and attributions are fundamental building blocks of social cognition. As suggested earlier, one can consider causal attributions and schemas as some of the elements of social cognition. In effect, these are the contents on which we operate when we form impressions. Next, we consider three major processes that operate on schemas and attributions. What are the processes by which we make sense of other people? The chapter next turns to these information processes: attention, memory, and inference. They are ordered as if they make a sequence, but we will rapidly see that there is a constant interplay among them.

ATTENTION

This section discusses some basics of what attracts attention in social situations and, then, why does it matter. An important aspect of attention is the salience of objects and people in the environment. What effects does salience have on people's perceptions of other people? Attention turns out to influence fundamentally the contents (attributions and schemas) that make up people's impressions of each other.

Attention: Conceptually and Operationally

So let's start by paying attention to attention. What do we mean by attention here, and why is it important? *Attention* simply involves two different kinds of processes, at least the way it has been studied most commonly (Fiske & Taylor, 1991, Chap. 7; Kahneman, 1973). It has to do, first, with an *encoding* process whereby people take information that is outside of them and represent it inside their heads. So somehow people make sense of certain configurations of images that impinge on their retinas and eardrums, and then represent them internally in some kind of code that enables thinking. The exact nature of these processes is more the concern of perceptual and cognitive psychology than of social psychology, but it has implications for social cognition as well. This kind of attention is studied under the rubric of environmental salience effects, as we will see.

A second process of attention that has been studied a lot is *consciousness*, the experience of awareness itself. One can be awake in a silent, dark room, and yet one is still thinking and paying attention to something. Cognitions inside the head are being brought into consciousness. This kind of attention relies more heavily on memory and is studied under the rubric of priming the accessibility of mental constructs; we will discuss these phenomena in the section on memory.

Social cognition researchers have talked about both encoding and consciousness as attention. Regardless of which is meant, the most important feature of attention is that it is limited. People are limited-capacity information processors, and our ability to attend is very constrained. In particular, attention is *selective* in direction. Think about, for example, visual attention. One's eyes can only be looking in a particular place at a particular time. Why is this important to social psychology? Think about how complicated people are, and how complicated any given social situation is; given that inherent complexity, the nature of attention is going to determine a lot of what happens between people. One can only deal with or react to whatever captures one's attention within a situation. If you think about a crowd of people at a party, what captures your attention is going to be what then determines how you interact with people. So, your eye lights on a particular person whom you know, and you walk over to that person, ignoring someone else whom you know equally well but who happened to be standing in a dark spot at the party. Presumably, you could even miss meeting the person of your dreams at this party because the person happened to be dressed in dark colors that night. So attention, even though it seems as though it might be a rather nitty-gritty topic, has important social implications.

Determinants of Salience

Attention is very much determined by context. *Salience,* which is another way of talking about what external objects capture attention, is a property of a stimulus in a particular context (McArthur, 1981; Taylor & Fiske, 1978). So, for example, someone who is six foot six would tend to stand out a bit in social psychology class. But think about a person who is six foot six on a basketball team; that person does not stand out at all. So, it is not a property of the person per se being six foot six; it is a property of that person in a given context. And that is what captures attention. It is how that person or that stimulus, more generally, fits into a particular context. Let's elaborate on that a bit.

Salience can be determined by *immediate context,* so a person can be novel or figural in a particular situation. Have you ever walked into a nursing home where you are the youngest person by 40 or 50 years? People turn to see this novelty; you look different from the other people. Not only are you a newcomer, but you are also considerably younger than everyone else. You are clearly a novelty in an otherwise drab environment. Or have you ever been the only person of your gender in a room? People all orient to you; they want to know "What is this man doing in a group of women?" or "What is this woman doing in a group of men?" The same is true of race. If you are the only person of your particular ethnicity, then that tends to capture people's attention. Or in the same way, if you happen to have the misfortune to wear a Hawaiian shirt in a room full of people wearing gray suits, people are going to look at you. Not just because you are wearing a Hawaiian shirt and you look funny in that context, but because it is bright. It's noticeable. So it can be determined by the immediate context and by things as important as somebody's ethnicity or gender, or by something as trivial as what color shirt you are wearing that day. Or even seating arrangement. Think about the typical seminar that is conducted around a rectangular table. Where do you sit if you have not done the reading that day? If the professor is sitting at one end, do you sit at the opposite end facing the professor? "No way." Where do you sit? You hide along the sides, preferably in some corner, not directly next to the professor but some place where the professor's line of sight will not exactly fall on you. Why is that? Because you know that you will capture the person's attention if you sit directly opposite. And as a faculty member, I have noticed that if somebody has a confrontational point to make, or has a habit of arguing with me (which may be good or bad), the person often sits directly opposite me at a rectangular table. (I think of it as the devil's advocate seat.) Salience, thus, can be determined by all kinds of features of the physical context, some of them quite apparently trivial, but they can have a big impact on people's interactions. The next section will describe some experiments that follow these principles of salience.

Something can also capture attention because of one's schema or *prior knowledge.* That is, when somebody does something that is unusual or surprising, that captures attention. So, if your social psychology professor one day shows up in a clown suit, that would capture your attention because, chances are, the particular professor is not the kind of person to do that; moreover, all the professors that you have had so far have never done that, and in fact most people do not wear clown suits. So, it could be unusual for the specific person. It could be unusual for the role that the person occupies. Or it could just be unusual for people in general; not too many people walk around in clown suits. In effect, there are three levels of prior knowledge or schemas that are important. One is the person, one is the role, and one is people in general. This should bring back echoes of our schema discussion (schema inconsistency attracts attention). And this should echo back some of the attribution chapter, namely, what might be informative when making attributions (Jones & Davis, 1965).

Besides the immediate context and one's prior schemas, there is finally the *current task*. Attention is determined by what a person is up to at any given time. What is one's goal in a given situation? Goals determine people's attention. People direct attention depending on what they are trying to accomplish, their task. For example, Ellen Berscheid and her colleagues (Berscheid, Graziano, Monson, & Dermer, 1976) did a scenario in which the subjects could volunteer for a dating study. They then watched a videotape of three opposite-sex people talking and were told that one of these three people was going to be their date. The three people appeared on three separate tapes, recorded in parallel. To simulate attention, the researchers arranged a switching mechanism that allowed subjects to choose which one of the three people they wanted to watch at any given time. Berscheid and her associates measured how long the subjects looked at each person, and not surprisingly, people were pretty curious about this person with whom they were expecting to share an evening, so naturally they watched that person more than the others. Below, we will note some consequences of their increased attention to this psychologically salient prospective date. More generally, interdependence (having one's outcomes depend on another person) focuses one's attention on that person (Erber & Fiske, 1984; Neuberg & Fiske, 1987; Ruscher & Fiske, 1990; see also Fiske, 1993a).

Consequences of Salience

We have seen that attention is determined by a number of different factors: context, prior knowledge, and current goals. What difference does such environmental salience make to social interaction? One of its major effects is that it exaggerates people's causal attributions. Whatever attracts people's attention then seems larger than life: It seems more important, causal, influential. We are not yet certain precisely why this exaggeration occurs; it could be a matter of perceivers having the sense that they know a lot about someone who has been salient, precisely because they have gathered more information about that person. Regardless of the mechanism, a particular person who just happens to capture your attention in a given situation gets credited with having more influence than other people.

Now think about that for a minute. If you are wearing a Hawaiian shirt in a room full of people in gray shirts, people will think that you had more impact on that group simply because you are wearing that shirt. Now transfer it to gender or race. If you are the only person of your gender or race in a particular group, people will think that you had a lot of impact on that group, simply because they are watching you more. In a series of experiments, researchers held people's behavior absolutely constant by using videotapes and other technology. For example, in a tape-recorded discussion accompanied by slides of each speaker, one could manipulate the apparent racial composition of the group without altering the interaction itself (Taylor, 1981). Subjects thought they were watching a brainstorming session for a publicity campaign for a student play. The experimenters held people's behavior constant and just manipulated whether the person was a solo, the only one of a particular race or gender, and found that other people perceive the solo person as having a lot of impact on the group, being highly influential, simply because they looked at the solo more. Similar effects occur when one person is salient by virtue of lighting, motion, or pattern complexity (McArthur & Post, 1977). So attention exaggerates people's causal attributions.

Attention also exaggerates people's evaluations of the person who captures attention. If one likes the person, one likes the same person even more when salient. If one dislikes the person, one dislikes the same person even more when salient. The evaluations are *polarized*. Now think about this from the point of view of the solo. If you are doing a good job, you may be perceived as doing a better job than you were, and that can be dangerous because maybe you will be pushed into a situation prematurely. Also, people may be disappointed if they see that you are actually doing the kind of job that you were doing; they may say "But you were so great initially!" when in fact they just perceived you that way because they were paying a lot of attention to you and it exaggerated their impressions. Admiration that is not fully deserved can be awkward.

But polarization can also go the other way. That is, as a solo, if you fall down or make a mistake, it looms larger than when other people make mistakes. So if you make a joke and it falls flat and everybody looks at you, and there is this horrible silence, it lasts longer than if you are a member of a group in a situation. If you make a terrible presentation, it falls harder than if a member of the majority had done the same thing. So polarizing of the evaluations can cut both ways (see Fiske & Taylor, 1991, for a review). It could perhaps be seen as leading to a sort of warped advantage, but it could also be profoundly to one's disadvantage. This occurs not only in solo situations but also in other situations where people focus their attention on somebody else, for example, when someone stands out by virtue of mere physical arrangements. A colleague once pointed out that office placement can create undeservedly extreme evaluations, when someone is "in your face," for better or worse. The same is true, of course, for neighbors at home. And in the dating study too, people's evaluations of their dates were much more extreme than their evaluations of people that they were not watching so much.

Finally, sometimes salience helps people's memory; sometimes paying attention to another person helps you to remember more, sometimes not (for a review, see Taylor & Fiske, 1978). The unreliable correlation between attention and memory is not surprising if one assumes that memorability depends on the specific processes occurring during attention. One could assimilate information rapidly and remember it, or one could mull over information for a long time but alter it so much that the original data are unrecognizable on a memory test. The next section addresses memory processes; it will become clearer how attention is by no means the main determinant of memory.

Before leaving attention, however, the most important point is that whomever you happen to heed—whether attention is determined by seating arrangement, distinctive clothing, or solo status in a group—can really change how you judge a person and how interactions proceed. Attention is important also because so much of what we do in making sense of people happens on-line, as we are receiving the information. We are very skilled at this, at making sense of people as we get the information. Thus, the arbitrary fact (to what or to whom are you paying attention at a given moment) shapes what gets encoded as an impression of another person, and it stays there. All of these processes are happening on-line and in an astonishingly rapid way (see Gilbert, Chapter 4). Given all the action at this early stage, it is rather surprising that social psychologists have not paid more attention to attention. The work so far indicates much promise for future work.

PERSON MEMORY

Now we turn to what people remember about other people, and how. Once people have attended to someone else, the possibility exists that they will remember something about that person. In particular, the first section will cover the effects of sets or goals on how people organize and remember new information. The second will talk about the processing of old information, how it gets brought to mind, known as the priming of old information.

Sets or Goals Related to Learning New Information

Okay, it's experiment time again; I would like you to memorize the following words: *reckless, conceited, aloof, stubborn*. Take a minute to look up from the page and memorize the words. Seriously. I will test you on them in a few pages, so give it a try.

What kind of strategy did you use to memorize the words? "Repeat over and over." Rehearsal is one of the predominant strategies for memorizing things. What else might you have done? "Use the first letters." Okay, use the first letters and try to make up some acronym or something. Good for test taking, right? If you can remember the acronym. What else? "Imagine the typical person." Well, that's very interesting. Clearly, there is a range of ways to remember trait adjectives, or anything else. Your explicit goal here was to memorize the word list, and the strategies people report depend on what they think will be the most effective way to memorize the words.

It turns out that the goal, the strategy, or the set that people have when learning information about another person has a big impact on how much they remember. And this is, in some ways, one of the bigger contributions of social cognition research to the understanding of memory, going back to cognitive psychology. Person memory research discovered that when people are memorizing information about a person, the *set* or goal that they have, which determines the strategy they use, seems to make a crucial difference. The importance of set is far more apparent in social memory than in nonsocial memory. So, for example, if one is memorizing a series of nonsense syllables, one could repeat them over and over to oneself, or one could try to look at the first letters, but one certainly could not form an impression of a group of nonsense syllables, in the same way that one could form an impression of a person described by a series of trait adjectives.

The moral of the story is that sets or goals influence memory for new information (e.g., Devine, Sedikides, & Fuhrman, 1989; Hamilton, 1981; Hamilton, Katz, & Leirer, 1980; Srull, 1983). Should it be easier to remember a list of personality trait adjectives, if you are trying to remember them or if you are trying to form an impression? It is kind of counterintuitive, but if you are specifically trying to memorize personality information, you are not going to do as good a job as if you were just trying to form a casual impression. At the beginning of this section, I tried to give you a *memory set* (to memorize the words). If you are trying to remember information about another person (such as a list of trait adjectives), it turns out that a memory set—which tends to make people use strategies such as rehearsal or mnemonics (make a word of the first letters)—is the worst possible set to have. So, I was setting you up, basically.

A better goal is to have an *impression set* (imagine the person described by those adjectives), a strategy that people sometimes discover for themselves. Why would it be easier to remember information about another person if you are trying to form an impression? Integrating it helps you remember. You have to make links among the traits. And making links among the items increases your odds of finding them again. The more links they have to each other, the more likely they are to cue each other (e.g., Srull & Wyer, 1989). And so if you are trying to make sense of a person, you have to figure out how the person could be (going back to our opening example) "reckless" and "stubborn" at the same time; the traits become linked in your mind, and they are easier to remember.

It turns out there are even better ways of memorizing person information. The principle seems to be that the more engaged you are and the more self-relevant the set is, the better your memory. So an *empathy set* is an even better way to remember information about another person. Empathy involves trying to put yourself in that person's shoes, trying to figure out how that person feels about things, how the person would react to things. Think about it in terms of a roommate. You have a new roommate, and you are trying to learn that person's morning routine so that you can have a shower when the bathroom is free. So, you are trying to memorize what the person does first, what next, and so on. If you just try to memorize it, it is not going to work so well. If you try to integrate that information into your general impression of that person, it is going to work a little better. For example, "This is somebody who is very compulsive and immediately has a shower, and only after that has breakfast, but then goes back and brushes teeth for 15 minutes, etc." But if you empathize with that person, put yourself in that person's shoes, imagine what it is like to be that person waking up in the morning, how the person feels upon getting up, dreading the day or feeling good about it, you can remember the routine even better. This would be even more true with personality trait adjectives.

Self-reference (referring it to yourself) is an even better way. In thinking about each trait adjective in terms of whether or not it applies to you, this set improves memory even more (e.g., Klein & Loftus, 1988; Kuiper & Rogers, 1979; Reeder, McCormick, & Esselman, 1987). It is probably true also that *anticipated interaction* (expecting to meet the person and talk to the person and deal with the person in some meaningful way) improves memory the most (Devine, Sedikides, & Fuhrman, 1989; Srull & Brand, 1983). Imagine the interaction strategies you might consider if you were going to spend a day hiking alone with the person whose traits you memorized at the beginning of this section. (What were those traits again?)

So far, the more involving the set, the better people's memory. The final ironic twist is that *actual interaction,* apparently the most involving set of all, may not be the best way to remember information about a person. Think about what happens in an actual interaction. You are trying to decide what to say at the same time as you are forming an impression of the other person, so you are very busy (in Gilbert's, 1989, sense, perhaps). So it is not clear that that is actually a very good way to learn information about another person, if you are busy trying to monitor your own thoughts and feelings, as well as participate in the interaction.

The basic message here is that memory for new information about people is better, the more structure you have. The more involving the set, the more you can link together different pieces of information because you are trying to make sense of them in a more psychologically complicated and meaningful way.

Priming of Old Information

Let's have another story:

Donald spent a great deal of time in search of what he liked to call excitement. He had already climbed Mt. McKinley, shot the Colorado Rapids in a kayak, driven in a demolition derby, and piloted a jet-powered boat without knowing very much about boats. He had risked injury and even death a number of times. Now he was in search of new excitement. He was thinking, perhaps, that maybe he would do some skydiving, or maybe cross the Atlantic in a sailboat. By the way he acted, one could really guess that Donald was well aware of his ability to do many things well. Other than business engagements, Donald's contacts with other people were rather limited. He felt that he did not need to rely on anyone. Once Donald made up his mind to do something, it was as good as done, no matter how long it might take or how difficult the going might be. Only rarely did he change his mind, even when it might have been better if he had.

Do you have a generally positive impression of this guy? Negative? If you are like many people, you do not have a very positive impression of this guy. Crossing the Atlantic in a saiboat sounds a bit foolhardy. His limited contacts with other people make him sound like a bit of a loner. His persistence comes across as perhaps a bit bullheaded. Does he seem just a bit reckless, conceited, aloof, and stubborn? (Where have you recently seen those terms before?) Do you think those interpretations of his behavior are intrinsic in Donald's behavior, or is it possible to see his behavior in a more positive light? Suppose you had initially memorized an alternative set of words, such as *adventurous, self-confident, independent,* and *persistent*. Do you think your impression of Donald would have differed?

This is exactly what Higgins, Rholes, and Jones (1977) did in their study. In an apparently separate experiment, some of the subjects were exposed to one set of positive, applicable words and others to the other set of negative but equally applicable words. What do you see about the words in the two sets: adventurous and reckless, self-confident and conceited, independent and aloof, persistent and stubborn? "They are portraying the same trait." Exactly. So the first ones are positive ways of portraying a trait, and the others are negative ways of portraying the same trait. The "Donald" paragraph is written to be relatively ambiguous about whether he is a good person, or not. The point is that the "Donald" paragraph is essentially ambiguous, and the people's behavior is essentially ambiguous. You can interpret the same behavior as adventurous or reckless, as self-confident or conceited. Behavior is open to interpretation. Different people will interpret the same behavior in different ways, and in this instance, it may depend on what else has been in one's head lately.

We have changed gears here to talk about another phenomenon of memory, and that is priming. Given that you have a set of ambiguous information about another person, you are trying to make sense out of another person, what will determine how you interpret that information? People have a lot of schemas: Which schema are you going to use? Any given person can be interpreted on the basis of a number of different schemas. What determines which one? An important determinant of schema use is what schemas have been *primed*, what constructs are accessible. What is at the top of the mental heap, in effect. The words you memorized at the beginning of the section made negative constructs accessible for interpreting Donald's behavior.

Not just any negative or positive words will do; they have to be relevant to the behavior, *applicable* to the particular stimulus. In the original experiment, for half the people the words were negative, for the other half the words were positive, and then, in addition, they were split as to whether or not they were relevant, applicable, to the Donald paragraph. So, if you had to memorize *obedient, neat, satirical,* and *grateful,* those are more or less positive terms, but they are not related to the Donald paragraph, so they would not make as much difference. Or, if I told you to memorize *disrespectful, listless, clumsy,* and *sly,* those are negative terms, but they also are not so relevant to the Donald paragraph. Thus, the prediction is that primed concepts have much more impact if they are relevant, if they are applicable. Not just any old thing at the top of your head, not just anything that is accessible, will have an impact; it is things that are accessible and relevant to the new information that you are getting. And that is indeed what Higgins and colleagues found. They found that the positivity of people's impressions was determined by what was accessible, what was primed. That is, they measured Donald's perceived desirability (on rating scales) and subjects' recall for his behavior. After a 10- to 14-day delay, the positivity of impressions depended on whether the prime was positive or negative and whether it was applicable or not. Subsequent work has supported and extended these results (e.g., Bargh, Bond, Lombardi, & Tota, 1986; Higgins, Bargh, & Lombardi, 1985; Sherman, Mackie, & Driscoll, 1990; Srull & Wyer, 1979, 1980). One interesting finding has been that people differ in what is *chronically accessible,* so that temporary accessibility and individual differences in chronic accessibility operate in much the same way (e.g., Bargh, Bond, Lombardi, & Tota, 1986).

In this section on memory, we have discussed two important topics, first, how goals influence the organization of new information in memory, which influences its subsequent memorability. Second, we discussed how accessibility in memory then influences the interpretation of new information. Other memory phenomena include the conditions under which schema-consistent and inconsistent information each are better remembered, a topic that was discussed earlier. (For overviews of research on social memory, see Hastie, Ostrom, Ebbesen, Wyer, Hamilton, & Carlston, 1980; Srull & Wyer, 1989; Wyer & Srull, 1984.)

Before we turn to the final social cognition process to be covered, namely, inference, let's consider the relationship between memory and inferences. You might think that people make judgments and inferences on the basis of what they can remember about other people. This is, however, only sometimes the case. When people are making unexpected judgments or inferences, they have to go back and rely on memory as their basis. In that case, memory and judgment are of course correlated with each other. Much of the time, however, people are making spontaneous inferences or judgments, at the time they are receiving information about another person. For example, deciding how much you like someone is probably a fairly automatic process. In that case, the judgment is made *on-line.* The judgment is then independent of whether you remember the information on which it was based (Hastie & Park, 1986). If memory and judgment are so often independent processes, it behooves us to study judgment processes for their own sake, a task to which we now turn.

HUMAN INFERENCE

In describing social cognitive processes, so far we have touched on attention and memory. At the beginning of the chapter, we noted that social cognition researchers tend to analyze thinking in stages. The first stage is attention: You have got to take in the information. The second stage is remembering things—putting it into long-term memory, being able to retrieve it. What is accessible in memory determines how you encode it, so there is some feedback between these stages. In the same way, as just noted, one might assume that people make inferences based on what they can remember, but as we said, inferences and judgments often occur on-line, during attention and encoding. (It is sort of a fiction that these all are separate stages, actually, but it is convenient sometimes to think that way.)

In any case, let's close by looking at inference. What do you do with all the information once it is in your head? How do you make inferences to go beyond present information? The basic question that gets asked about making inferences is, "How good are we at it?" (Hastie, 1983; Hastie & Rasinski, 1988; Kahneman, Slovic, & Tversky, 1982; Nisbett & Ross, 1980). Essentially it is asking what is called a *normative* question: Compared to some norm or standard, how good are people at making judgments? It is apparent why the normative question comes up in studying human inference. It does not come up so much in other areas. With attention, for example, it is not so clear what the normative question would be. How good are people at attending to things? It is not so sensible. But with decision making and inference, there is a very strong normative thread running through this work, which assumes there are better and worse ways of making a decision. Frankly, it concludes that people are not too good at making decisions when one compares them to computers, for example, or to certain kinds of models, such as the expectancy-value models, the algebraic models described earlier. But even so, we do muddle along, apparently well enough, I will argue later.

In describing human inference, how human beings make inferences as compared to how computers make inferences, we will discuss the stages of inference and some examples of some heuristics, or shortcuts, that people use when they are making inferences.

Errors and Biases at Different Stages

Let's take an example of this. Again, we will look at different stages to break down the errors, to take apart how good are people at what stages. Suppose I asked you to evaluate the burning psychological question of whether or not blondes have more fun. Now this is an important research question; you have been hired by a hair-dye company, and they could make a lot of money depending on whether or not you can prove that blondes do, in fact, have more fun.

How would you go about it? Whom would you study? How would you study them? "Okay, well let me think about the blondes I know, and are they fun or not." That is the obvious direction to take. But what about all the fun brunettes you know? Are they relevant to this question? Yes. Why? You need a comparison group: fun brunettes, fun blondes. Suppose you know a lot of fun blondes but even more fun brunettes. Or maybe you can think of a lot of fun blondes and no fun brunettes. Have you answered your question? No. What about all those boring blondes? The nonfun blondes. You need to know relative proportions of fun and unfun blondes, as well as fun and unfun brunettes. It is really more complicated than thinking about all the fun blondes you know. The fun blondes are the hypothesis-confirming $(+ +)$ case. Most people who are trying to decide questions of *co-variation* (e.g., are blondness and fun correlated?) tend to look at just that double positive (i.e., blonde and fun, or $+ +$) of the four combinations $(+ -, - +, - -)$ (Crocker, 1981; Fiske & Taylor, 1991, Chap. 9; Nisbett & Ross, 1980).

Once convinced that there are four kinds of people you have to look at, you could go out and interview all your friends. "Are you having a good time? What color is your hair?" Although you yourself might never get invited to another party again, theoretically, you could gather these data. What would be wrong with talking to your friends? Most are graduate students, certainly a biased sample. People appear to be insensitive to *sample bias* in several respects. For example, sampling one's friends means one is likely to oversample people who are fun because people who are fun have more friends, and people who are not fun have fewer friends. Probably the proportion of fun people who have friends is higher. So a sample of friends is a poor idea for this reason. Nevertheless, laypeople tend to use whatever convenience sample is available, such as their friends or whatever comes to mind.

People also tend not to draw a large enough sample. People are willing to make inferences based on very few cases, which violates the *law of large numbers*. Larger random samples are more reliable than smaller random samples, but people do not act as if they know this (Kunda & Nisbett, 1986; Nisbett & Ross, 1980; Tversky & Kahneman, 1974, 1980). Moreover, people do not attend to information concerning the *representativeness of the sample* (Hamill, Wilson, & Nisbett, 1980). A large representative sample, as statistics teaches us, gives a superior estimate of the population parameters.

Another problem is that people are likely to ignore *base rates* (e.g., Hamill, Wilson, & Nisbett, 1980; Kahneman & Tversky, 1973; Nisbett & Borgida, 1975). That is, people have a tendency to ignore the population statistics in favor of (not necessarily representative) vivid case studies. You can demonstrate this phenomenon even among psychology students. Nisbett and Borgida (1975) described the base-rate responses of subjects in a bystander helping study (most people don't help promptly, if at all) and in a study of shock tolerance (most people let themselves be shocked severely). Subjects then saw vivid case studies (either videotapes or physical descriptions) of target individuals, containing no information that would be diagnostic with regard to predicting help or shock tolerance. Control subjects never saw the base-rate information. The case-study subjects then ignored the more useful base-rate information and predicted that the targets would behave just as predicted by control subjects (i.e., helping promptly and not tolerating much shock). Hence, subjects receiving the individuating case studies made inferences as if they had never even seen the base-rates (population statistics). Potentially misleading case studies are more compelling than statistics. To go back to our earlier example, it may be totally convincing to know one person who dyed his hair blonde and suddenly developed an amazing social life. In comparison, dreary statistics about the proportions of extroverts in the population, cross-categorized by hair color, may be less convincing to the layperson.

People also tend to rely on their expectations, schemas, or theories. *Theory-driven* processes bias data gathering and labeling. People are affected by their expectations, and so people are likely to overrely on the fun blondes in the sample in drawing their conclusions. Theory-driven inferences may be accurate under some circumstances, but if the theory is faulty, if one believes one is unaffected by the theory, or if the theory dominates the data, then using the theory is normatively problematic (Nisbett & Ross, 1980). If people gather information under the influence of their theories, inferences are likely to be biased.

There is a more subtle version of theory-driven data gathering, at the stage of interpreting the information. One may categorize people wrong. So a friend who has light brown hair and is amusing may be considered a blonde. People *miscategorize* in the service of their theories.

Ironically, although people's theories can bias their judgments without people's intent or awareness, people also abandon their theories prematurely when provided irrelevant *nondiagnostic* information. A person who fits one's theory, according to diagnostic criteria (i.e., truly informative cues), should be judged according to that theory. Normatively, the addition of a few bits of irrelevant information should not make any difference. However, the *dilution effect* indicates that people will neglect diagnostic cues when they are diluted by nondiagnostic ones (e.g., Nisbett, Zukier, & Lemley, 1981). For example, someone with a rotten childhood and deviant sexual fantasies seems more likely to be a child molester than someone with a rotten childhood, a liking for pizza, deviant sexual fantasies, and a job managing a hardware store.

Once the information is categorized into all the different cells of an imaginary data table, whether it is wrong or not, one has to combine it in some fashion. People are not so good at combining information either. One way in which they are bad at combining information is called the *conjunction error* (Abelson & Gross, 1987; Tversky & Kahneman, 1983). Suppose people estimate the proportion of the population who are fun and the proportion of the population who are blonde. Then separately ask the people to estimate the proportion of the population who are fun blondes; typically, you will find that people overestimate the proportion who have both these two specific characteristics, compared to their estimates of the characteristics in isolation from each other. This is a logical error. If there are particular proportions of people who are blonde and particular proportions of people who are fun, there have to be fewer people who are both fun and blonde because it is a conjunction, so it has to be more rare than either characteristic alone. But because it fits people's theory, they overestimate the number of people in the population with both characteristics.

Another way people are bad at combining information is termed *illusory correlation*. That is, people tend to be guided by their theories, so in their daily lives they especially notice people who fit. They notice the depressed brunette and the fun blonde. Hamilton and Rose (1980) demonstrated this phenomenon by giving people descriptions of people from particular occupations (e.g., accountant or librarian, salesman or waitress); on separate index cards, the people were described by eight adjectives, a couple of which fit common stereotypes about the occupations (e.g., accountants as perfectionist and timid). Afterward, subjects overestimated the frequency of theory-consistent (i.e., stereotypic) pairings. Illusory correlations are also particularly affected by extreme cases. So somebody who is, say, towhead and the life of the party is very noticeable. Likewise, somebody who has raven hair and gloomy perspectives is especially noticed; both are extreme cases. An illusion develops that hair color and fun are correlated when in fact they might not be, simply because the extreme cases stand out. On a more serious note, violent crime and minority status create paired distinctiveness, leading to the illusion that the two are correlated.

Knowing all these pitfalls of everyday inference, what is the safest course to follow, as a lay decision maker? Drawing inferences from a small, unrepresentative, unreliable sample, one's best bet is to stay close to the population mean if available. In any case, one should not fall prey to drawing extreme inferences from a limited sample, for future events will probably *regress toward the mean* (Jennings, Amabile, & Ross, 1982; Kahneman & Tversky, 1973). That is, extreme cases tend to be outliers created by chance, so they are unlikely to be as extreme in a second sample or test. The center of a normal distribution contains most of the cases, so moderation is the best prediction.

In general, when people are compared to statistical normative standards, we do not fare well. People fall prey to all kinds of errors, as this section has indicated. And even when people elucidate the *decision rules* they do use, people do not use them consistently, so they do not perform as well as a computer programmed to do what they claim they do (e.g., Dawes, 1976, 1980). Everyday judgment is routinely trusted but not well validated.

Heuristics

One final set of ideas about inference concerns the seat-of-the-pants rules that people use. If people are not very good at going through all the normative stages of making an inference, what do people do instead? *Heuristics* are essentially shortcuts, first described by Tversky and Kahneman (1974), who have my personal nomination for a Nobel prize in economics. (You read it here first.) Basically, a lot of their ideas fly in the face of traditional economic theory and in the face of similar models in psychology that follow an expectancy-value framework (described here earlier).

All the work on heuristics involves judgments under uncertainty, and many pertain to probability judgments. To illustrate, suppose I flip a coin, a fair coin, eight times. Which is the most likely pattern to get in terms of heads and tails: HHTHTTHT or HHHHTTTT? Most people answer, "The first one." It looks more random, according to lay theories of randomness. If you were flipping a coin to randomly assign subjects to experimental conditions, you would probably feel kind of funny about obtaining the second sequence. But in fact the probabilities of the two patterns are equal. The misperception of what looks truly random is due to the *representativeness* heuristic (Kahneman & Tversky,

1973; Tversky & Kahneman, 1982). People have a stereotype of what is random, and some phenomenon that fits or seems representative of that stereotype seems, to them, more probable. So, in the case of randomness, the disordered sequence seems more random than the ordered one, despite the fact that they have equal numbers of heads and tails and are objectively equally likely to occur.

The representativeness heuristic also works with judgments about people. Consider Steve, who "is very shy and withdrawn, invariably helpful, with little interest in people, or the world of reality. A meek and tidy soul, he has a need for order and structure and a passion for detail" (Tversky & Kahneman, 1974). Now, guess: Is he a trapeze artist, a farmer, or a librarian? Sounds a lot like a librarian, doesn't he? Most subjects answer this way. But consider the probabilities from a logical point of view. There are many more farmers than librarians, so there are bound to be more neat and tidy farmers than there are librarians, let alone neat and tidy ones. Again, it is the recurring problem of using a stereotype. He seems more similar to a librarian than he does to a farmer, so people guess librarian, despite the population base rates. People overestimate the probability of a representative occurrence because it fits their theories.

Let's turn to another heuristic people use for estimating frequency. What do you think is the frequency of words that would fit here: ——n-? Are they rare or frequent? What about the frequency of words that would fit here: ——ing? Are the second set more frequent or more rare? To most people, the second type seems more frequent. It is easier to think of words ending in *ing* than it is to think of seven-letter words where the next to the last letter is *n*. So when people estimate the frequency of words ending in *ing* versus words ending in -n-, the former seems more frequent because they are easier to generate. The heuristic people use here is the *availability* heuristic, which is the ease of remembering examples. People often estimate frequencies by the ease of remembering examples. To illustrate, what is the divorce rate among people in your age group? How would you go about giving a quick answer? Most people think of couples they know who have gotten divorced, and depending on the availability of examples, they estimate the rate to be high or low. If it is easy to remember examples, people would tend to overestimate.

A third kind of heuristic is the *simulation* heuristic, which is defined by the ease of mentally undoing an outcome. Let me give you an example. "Mr. Crane and Mr. Tees were scheduled to leave the airport on different flights at the same time. They traveled from town in the same limousine, were caught in a traffic jam, and arrived at the airport thirty minutes after the scheduled departure of their flights. Mr. Crane is told his flight left on time. Mr. Tees is told that his flight was delayed and just left five minutes ago" (Kahneman & Tversky, 1982). Who is more upset? "The guy whose flight just left." Right. Why? Because it seems easier to undo the bad outcome. That is, it is easier to imagine how things could have turned out so that they could have made the plane they missed by minutes, but harder to imagine how they could have made the plane that was missed by a wide margin. So people mentally simulate the event. If it seems easier to undo, then it is more frustrating: It has more impact (also see Kahneman

& Miller, 1986). Counterfactual thinking (imagining what might have been) affects our reactions to what actually was.

The final heuristic to mention here is called *anchoring and adjustment*. If you wanted to estimate the number of car radio thefts per month in Los Angeles and New York, it might be helpful to know that there are 5 per month in Atlanta, so what would you estimate for LA and New York? "Eight or ten." Now assume that I had started this out by explaining that the number of car radio thefts per month in Boston is 115, which is the top in the country. Then, what do you estimate it is in New York? "At least 100." You probably would not say 8 or 10. So the point is that the initial starting value has a big impact. It is an anchor, if you will, and people make estimates by adjusting up or down from the anchor. However, people adjust insufficiently, so it counts as a shortcut.

The point of these heuristics is that they demonstrably can lead people astray. However, they are designed to work, much of the time. In this sense, they are handy rules people use to estimate probabilities of things occurring in the real world. They doubtless developed in situations in which they originally worked, but people apply them indiscriminately, with sometimes disastrous results.

Can We Improve?

In this section, we have seen that people make a mess of each stage of the inference process: sampling the population, gathering information, combining it, and making a judgment. People use all kinds of heuristics for decision making, and much of the time they seem downright illogical. Essentially, a lot of the work on inference, and also some of the work on memory and attention, seems to conclude that people are not very good at social cognition. If you compare us to computers, we are not very skilled at making sense of other people. Recall that we wondered at the beginning of the chapter whether people can learn to anticipate and monitor their own social cognitive errors.

Richard Nisbett and his colleagues (Cheng, Holyoak, Nisbett, & Oliver, 1986; Fong, Krantz, & Nisbett, 1986; Nisbett, Krantz, Jepson, & Fong, 1982; see also Einhorn, 1980) have investigated whether or not one can ameliorate our biased judgment processes, whether or not one can train people to become better everyday thinkers. To some extent, one can. It also turns out that going to graduate school in psychology or medicine is one way to make people more careful everyday thinkers, as compared to going to graduate school in chemistry or law, because training in statistics helps people think more carefully about these kinds of issues (Lehman, Lempert, & Nisbett, 1988).

Pragmatics: Thinking Is for Doing

The work on human inference takes a dim view of the everyday perceiver. But many have criticized the research for in effect setting people up to perform badly (for an overview, see Fiske & Taylor, 1991, Chap. 9). In contrast to the bleak errors-and-biases view, I would argue that the way we think about other people is good enough. It develops over time, we have a lot of practice at it, most of the time our schemas work well enough, most of the time the heuristics and shortcuts that we use are good enough, and most of the time the rules that we use for remembering and attending are good enough. The experiments tend to overemphasize the ways that people are stupid and wrong because it is interesting, but in fact, people muddle along pretty well. And social situations tend to be somewhat self-correcting; people help each other out (Levine, Resnick, & Higgins, 1993; Resnick, Levine, & Teasley, 1991).

So, the bottom line is that it is a miracle that we make sense out of each other, and we do pretty well at it. One can argue that, within the context of their everyday goals, people are surprisingly accurate perceivers, and they should not be held to statistical normative models (e.g., Ambady & Rosenthal, 1992; Fiske, 1992; Funder, 1987; Kenny & Albright, 1987; Kruglanski, 1989b; Swann, 1984; Zebrowitz, 1990). Social cognition both determines our lives and is determined by them, so it is a matter of some considerable significance.

CHAPTER SUMMARY

The chapter started out by describing what social cognition is, what social cognition researchers study, what sets it apart from other topics, how people and things compare as objects of perception, and why it is an interesting topic to study in the first place (in part, because people are so incredibly complicated, it is hard to believe that we can make sense of them so fast). Then we saw two different approaches to study how people think about other people. One is the holistic, configural approach that Asch favored, and that really gave rise to the schema approach. The major alternative, a highly predictive approach, is the algebraic, elemental, piecemeal approach.

Then we examined schemas, namely, what they are, what kinds there are (person, self, role, and script), and what they do in guiding attention, memory, and inference. The section closed with a consideration of schemas versus evidence, concluding that it depends on information configurations (what fits, what is diagnostic) and on motivation (people can be motivated to reach a decision quickly or accurately).

Turning to the processes of social cognition, attention is determined by context, prior theories, and goals. It exaggerates causal attributions and polarizes judgments. Memory strategies are influenced by sets or goals related to new information, and information recently or frequently primed in memory influences the encoding of new information into memory. Human inference is fraught with errors and biases, at each stage of the process. People use quick and dirty heuristics, such as representativeness, availability, simulation, as well as anchoring and adjustment. Against a normative standard, we may not fare well, but people seem to muddle along in everyday life. After all, our thinking is for our doing, and we survive well enough.

Notes

[1]There is not a lot of agreement on whether one properly says *schemas* or *schemata*, so if writers jump back and forth, you will know why. If you are writing, schemata is a more formal way to make the plural, but beware; even graduate students sometimes say, "A schemata is . . .," which is like saying, "A schemas is . . .," and so it is really probably better to stay with the *s* for plural. But anyway. This is just a little note from the Better Use of Language League.

[2]My own professional development was tangled up in this particular paradox, because I did my dissertation on Norman Anderson's piecemeal algebraic model (Fiske, 1980), and at the same time I was studying stereotyping and schemas, the more configural approach. I went to give my first colloquium as a fresh assistant professor, and at the end of my colloquium (on the dissertation) a graduate student raised a hand and said, "How can you study this algebraic stuff and that schema stuff at the same time? They aren't compatible." I said to myself, "Wow, you're right." Out loud, I think I said something more dignified or perhaps, to create a diversion, spilled my water over the microphone. I did not have a good answer for the person. I went home, and I have been thinking about it ever since.

References

ABELSON, R. P. (1981). The psychological status of the script concept. *American Psychologist, 36,* 715–729.

ABELSON, R. P., & GROSS, P. H. (1987). The strength of conjunctive explanations. *Personality and Social Psychology Bulletin, 13,* 141–155.

ALLPORT, G. W. (1954a). The historical background of modern social psychology. In G. Lindzey (Ed.), *The handbook of social psychology* (Vol. 1, pp. 1–80). Reading, MA: Addison-Wesley.

ALLPORT, G. W. (1954b). *The nature of prejudice.* Reading, MA: Addison-Wesley.

AMBADY, N., & ROSENTHAL, R. (1992). Thin slices of expressive behavior as predictors of interpersonal consequences: A meta-analysis. *Psychological Bulletin, 111,* 256–274.

ANDERSEN, S. M., & COLE, S. W. (1990). "Do I know you?": The role of significant others in general social perception. *Journal of Personality and Social Psychology, 59,* 384–399.

ANDERSON, J. R. (1990). *Cognitive psychology and its implications* (3rd ed.). New York: Freeman.

ANDERSON, N. H. (1966). Component ratings in impression formation. *Psychonomic Science, 6,* 179–180.

ANDERSON, N. H. (1981). *Foundations of information integration theory.* New York: Academic Press.

ANDERSON, N. H., & LAMPEL, A. K. (1965). Effect of context on ratings of personality traits. *Psychonomic Science, 3,* 433–434.

ANDERSON, R. C., & PICHERT, J. W. (1978). Recall of previously unrecallable information following a shift in perspective. *Journal of Verbal Learning and Verbal Behavior, 17,* 1–12.

ASCH, S. E. (1946). Forming impressions of personality. *Journal of Abnormal and Social Psychology, 41,* 1230–1240.

BARGH, J. A., BOND, R. N., LOMBARDI, W. L., & TOTA, M. E. (1986). The additive nature of chronic and temporary sources of construct accessibility. *Journal of Personality and Social Psychology, 50,* 869–879.

BASSILI, J. N. (Ed.). (1989). *On-line cognition in person perception.* Hillsdale, NJ: Erlbaum.

BERSCHEID, E., GRAZIANO, W., MONSON, T., & DERMER, M. (1976). Outcome dependency: Attention, attribution, and attraction. *Journal of Personality and Social Psychology, 34,* 978–989.

BIERCE, A. (1911). *The devil's dictionary.* Cleveland, OH: The World Publishing Company.

BORING, E. G. (1950). *A history of experimental psychology.* Englewood Cliffs, NJ: Prentice-Hall.

BRANSFORD, J. D., & JOHNSON, M. K. (1972). Contextual prerequisites for understanding: Some investigations of comprehension and recall. *Journal of Verbal Learning and Verbal Behavior, 11,* 717–726.

BREWER, M. B. (1979). In-group bias in the minimal intergroup situation: A cognitive-motivational analysis. *Psychological Bulletin, 86,* 307–324.

BREWER, M. B. (1988). A dual process model of impression. In T. K. Srull & R. S. Wyer, Jr. (Eds.), *Advances in social cognition* (Vol. 1, pp. 1–36). Hillsdale, NJ: Erlbaum.

BREWER, M. B., DULL, V., & LUI, L. (1981). Perceptions of the elderly: Stereotypes as prototypes. *Journal of Personality and Social Psychology, 41,* 656–670.

BROADBENT, D. E. (1958). *Perception and communication.* London: Pergamon Press.

BRUNER, J. S. (1957). Going beyond the information given. In H. Gruber, K. R. Hammond, & R. Jesser (Eds.), *Contemporary approaches to cognition.* Cambridge, MA: Harvard University Press.

CANTOR, N., & MISCHEL, W. (1979). Prototypes in person perception. In L. Berkowitz (Ed.), *Advances in experimental social psychology* (Vol. 12, pp. 3–52). New York: Academic Press.

CANTOR, N., MISCHEL, W., & SCHWARTZ, J. (1982). A prototype analysis of psychological situations. *Cognitive Psychology, 14,* 45–77.

CHENG, P. W., HOLYOAK, K. J., NISBETT, R. E., & OLIVER, L. M. (1986). Pragmatic versus syntactic approaches to training deductive reasoning. *Cognitive Psychology, 18,* 293–328.

CHOMSKY, N. (1959). Verbal behavior. [Review of Skinner's book.] *Language, 35,* 26–58.

CROCKER, J. (1981). Judgment of covariation by social perceivers. *Psychology Bulletin, 90,* 272–292.

DARLEY, J. M., & GROSS, P. H. (1983). A hypothesis-confirming bias in labeling effects. *Journal of Personality and Social Psychology, 44,* 20–33.

DAWES, R. M. (1976). Shallow psychology. In J. Carroll & J. Payne (Eds.), *Cognition and social behavior* (pp. 3–12). Hillsdale, NJ: Erlbaum.

DAWES, R. M. (1980). You can't systematize human judgment: Dyslexia. In R. A. Shweder (Ed.), *New directions for methodology of social and behavioral science* (Vol. 4, pp. 64–78). San Francisco: Jossey-Bass.

DEVINE, P. G. (1989). Stereotypes and prejudice: Their automatic and controlled components. *Journal of Personality and Social Psychology, 56,* 5–18.

DEVINE, P. G., HAMILTON, D., & OSTROM, T., (Eds.). (1994). *Social cognition: Impact on social psychology.* San Diego: Academic Press.

DEVINE, P. G., SEDIKIDES, C., & FUHRMAN, R. W. (1989). Goals in social information processing: The case of anticipated interaction. *Journal of Personality and Social Psychology, 56,* 680–690.

DIJKER, A. J. M. (1987). Emotional reactions to ethnic minorities. *European Journal of Social Psychology, 17,* 305–325.

Einhorn, H. J. (1980). Overconfidence in judgment. In R. A. Shweder (Ed.), *New directions for methodology of social and behavioral science* (Vol. 4, pp. 1–16). San Francisco, CA: Jossey-Bass.

Erber, R., & Fiske, S. T. (1984). Outcome dependency and attention to inconsistent information. *Journal of Personality and Social Psychology, 47,* 709–726.

Fiske, S. T. (1980). Attention and weight in person perception: The impact of negative and extreme behavior. *Journal of Personality and Social Psychology, 38,* 889–906.

Fiske, S. T. (1982). Schema-triggered affect: Applications to social perception. In M. S. Clark & S. T. Fiske (Eds.), *Affect and cognition: The 17th Annual Carnegie Symposium on Cognition* (pp. 55–78). Hillsdale, NJ: Erlbaum.

Fiske, S. T. (1992). Thinking is for doing: Portraits of social cognition from daguerreotype to laserphoto. *Journal of Personality and Social Psychology, 63,* 877–889.

Fiske, S. T. (1993a). Controlling other people: The impact of power on stereotyping. *American Psychologist, 48,* 621–628.

Fiske, S. T. (1993b). Social cognition and social perception. In M. R. Rosenzweig & L. W. Porter (Eds.), *Annual review of psychology* (Vol. 44, pp. 155–194). Palo Alto, CA: Annual Reviews Inc.

Fiske, S. T., & Neuberg, S. L. (1990). A continuum of impression formation, from category-based to individuating processes: Influences of information and motivation on attention and interpretation. In M. P. Zanna (Ed.), *Advances in experimental social psychology* (Vol. 23, pp. 1–74). New York: Academic Press.

Fiske, S. T., Neuberg, S. L., Beattie, A. E., & Milberg, S. J. (1987). Category-based and attribute-based reactions to others: Some informational conditions of stereotyping and individuating processes. *Journal of Experimental Social Psychology, 23,* 399–427.

Fiske, S. T., & Pavelchak, M. A. (1986). Category-based versus piecemeal-based affective responses: Developments in schema-triggered affect. In R. M. Sorrentino & E. T. Higgins (Eds.), *Handbook of motivation and cognition: Foundations of social behavior* (pp. 167–203). New York: Guilford.

Fiske, S. T., & Taylor, S. E. (1991). *Social cognition* (2nd ed.). New York: McGraw-Hill.

Fong, G. T., Krantz, D. H., & Nisbett, R. E. (1986). The effects of statistical training on thinking about everyday problems. *Cognitive Psychology, 18,* 253–292.

Funder, D. C. (1987). Errors and mistakes: Evaluating the accuracy of social judgment. *Psychological Bulletin, 101,* 75–90.

Gilbert, D. T. (1989). Thinking lightly about others: Automatic components of the social inference process. In J. S. Uleman & J. A. Bargh (Eds.), *Unintended thought* (pp. 189–211). New York: Guilford.

Gollwitzer, P. M. (1990). Action phases and mind-sets. In E. T. Higgins & R. M. Sorrentino (Eds.), *Handbook of motivation and cognition: Foundations of social behavior* (Vol. 2, pp. 53–92). New York: Guilford.

Hamill, R., Wilson, T. D., & Nisbett, R. E. (1980). Insensitivity to sample bias: Generalizing from atypical cases. *Journal of Personality and Social Psychology, 39,* 578–589.

Hamilton, D. L. (1981). Organizational processes in impression formation. In E. T. Higgins, C. P. Herman, & M. P. Zanna (Eds.), *Social cognition: The Ontario Symposium* (Vol. 1, pp. 135–160). Hillsdale, NJ: Erlbaum.

Hamilton, D. L, Katz, L. B., & Leirer, V. O. (1980). Cognitive representation of personality impressions: Organizational processes in first impression formation. *Journal of Personality and Social Psychology, 39,* 1050–1063.

HAMILTON, D. L., & ROSE, T. L. (1980). Illusory correlation and the maintenance of stereotypic beliefs. *Journal of Personality and Social Psychology, 39,* 832–845.

HAMILTON, D. L., & ZANNA, M. P. (1974). Context effects in impression formation: Changes in connotative meaning. *Journal of Personality and Social Psychology, 29,* 649–654.

HASTIE, R. (1983). Social inference. In M. R. Rosenzweig & L. W. Porter (Eds.), *Annual review of psychology* (Vol. 34, pp. 511–542). Palo Alto, CA: Annual Reviews Inc.

HASTIE, R., & KUMAR, P. A. (1979). Person memory: Personality traits as organizing principles in memory for behavior. *Journal of Personality and Social Psychology, 37,* 25–88.

HASTIE, R., OSTROM, T. M., EBBESEN, E. B., WYER, R. S., HAMILTON, D. L., & CARLSTON, D. E. (Eds.). (1980). *Person memory: The cognitive basis of social perception.* Hillsdale, NJ: Erlbaum.

HASTIE, R., & PARK, B. (1986). The relationship between memory and judgment depends on whether the judgment task is memory-based or on-line. *Psychological Review, 93,* 258–268.

HASTIE, R., & RASINSKI, K. A. (1988). The concept of accuracy in social judgment. In D. Bar-Tal & A. W. Kruglanski (Eds.), *The social psychology of knowledge* (pp. 193–208). Cambridge, England: Cambridge University Press.

HEIDER, F. (1958). *The psychology of interpersonal relations.* New York: Wiley.

HIGGINS, E. T. (1989). Knowledge accessibility and activation: Subjectivity and suffering from unconscious sources. In J. S. Uleman & J. A. Bargh (Eds.), *Unintended thought* (pp. 75–123). New York: Guilford.

HIGGINS, E. T., & BARGH, J. A. (1987). Social cognition and social perception. In M. R. Rosenzweig & L. W. Porter (Eds.), *Annual review of psychology* (Vol. 38, pp. 369–425). Palo Alto, CA: Annual Reviews Inc.

HIGGINS, E. T., BARGH, J. A., & LOMBARDI, W. (1985). The nature of priming effects on categorization. *Journal of Experimental Psychology: Learning, Memory, and Cognition, 11,* 59–69.

HIGGINS, E. T., KING, G. A., & MAVIN, G. H. (1982). Individual construct accessibility and subjective impressions and recall. *Journal of Personality and Social Psychology, 43,* 35–47.

HIGGINS, E. T., KUIPER, N. A., & OLSON, J. M. (1981). Social cognition: A need to get personal. In E. T. Higgins, C. P. Herman, & M. P. Zanna (Eds.), *Social cognition: The Ontario Symposium* (Vol. 1, pp. 395–420). Hillsdale, NJ: Erlbaum.

HIGGINS, E. T., RHOLES, W. S., & JONES, C. R. (1977). Category accessibility and impression formation. *Journal of Experimental Social Psychology, 13,* 141–154.

HILTON, J. L., & DARLEY, J. M. (1991). The effects of interaction goals on person perception. In M. P. Zanna (Ed.), *Advances in experimental social psychology* (Vol. 24, pp. 235–267). New York: Academic Press.

HILTON, J. L., & FEIN, S. (1989). The role of typical diagnosticity in stereotype-based judgments. *Journal of Personality and Social Psychology, 57,* 201–211.

HILTON, J. L., KLEIN, J. G., & VON HIPPEL, W. (1991). Attention allocation and impression formation. *Personality and Social Psychology Bulletin, 17,* 548–559.

HOLYOAK, K. J., & GORDON, P. C. (1984). Information processing and social cognition. In R. S. Wyer, Jr., & T. K. Srull (Eds.), *Handbook of social cognition* (Vol. 1, pp. 39–70). Hillsdale, NJ: Erlbaum.

JAMES, W. (1983). *The principles of psychology.* Cambridge, MA: Harvard University Press. (Originally published in 1890.)

Jennings, D., Amabile, T. M., & Ross, L. (1982). Informal covariation assessment: Data-based vs. theory-based judgments. In A. Tversky, D. Kahneman, & P. Slovic (Eds.), *Judgment under uncertainty: Heuristics and biases* (pp. 211–230). New York: Cambridge University Press.

Jones, E. E., & Davis, K. E. (1965). From acts to dispositions: The attribution process in person perception. In L. Berkowitz (Ed.), *Advances in experimental psychology* (Vol. 2, pp. 220–266). New York: Academic Press.

Judd, C. M., & Park, B. (1988). Out-group homogeneity: Judgments of variability at the individual and group levels. *Journal of Personality and Social Psychology, 54,* 778–788.

Kahneman, D. (1973). *Attention and effort.* Englewood Cliffs, NJ: Prentice-Hall.

Kahneman, D., & Miller, D. T. (1986). Norm theory: Comparing reality to its alternatives. *Psychological Review, 80,* 136–153.

Kahneman, D., Slovic, P., Tversky, A. (Eds.). (1982). *Judgment under uncertainty: Heuristics and biases.* New York: Cambridge University Press.

Kahneman, D., & Tversky, A. (1973). On the psychology of prediction. *Psychological Review, 80,* 237–251.

Kahneman, D., & Tversky, A. (1982). The simulation heuristic. In D. Kahneman, P. Slovic, & A. Tversky (Eds.), *Judgment under uncertainty: Heuristics and biases* (pp. 201–208). New York: Cambridge University Press.

Kant, I. (1969). *Critique of pure reason.* New York: St. Martin's Press. (Originally published in 1781.)

Kaplan, M. F. (1971). Contextual effects in impression formation: The weighted average versus the meaning-change formulation. *Journal of Personality and Social Psychology, 19,* 92–99.

Kaplan, M. F. (1975). Evaluative judgments are based on evaluative information: The weighted average versus the meaning-change formulation. *Memory and Cognition, 3,* 375–380.

Kenny, D. A. (1991). A general model of consensus and accuracy in interpersonal perception. *Psychological Review, 98,* 155–163.

Kenny, D. A., & Albright, L. (1987). Accuracy in interpersonal perception: A social relations analysis. *Psychological Bulletin, 102,* 390–402.

Kihlstrom, J. F., Cantor, N., Albright, J. S., Chew, B. R., Klein, S. B., & Niedenthal, P. M. (1988). Information processing and the study of the self. In L. Berkowitz (Ed.), *Advances in experimental social psychology* (Vol. 21, pp. 145–180). New York: Academic Press.

Klein, S. B., & Loftus, J. (1988). The nature of self-referent encoding: The contributions of elaborative and organizational processes. *Journal of Personality and Social Psychology, 55,* 5–11.

Koffka, K. (1935). *Principles of Gestalt psychology.* New York: Harcourt, Brace, & World.

Kohler, W. (1976). *The place of value in a world of facts.* New York: Liveright. (Originally published in 1938.)

Krauss, R. M. (1981). Impression formation, impression management, and nonverbal behaviors. In E. T. Higgins, C. P. Herman, & M. P. Zanna (Eds.), *Social cognition: The Ontario Symposium* (Vol. 1, pp. 323–341). Hillsdale, NJ: Erlbaum.

Kruglanski, A. W. (1989a). *Lay epistemics and human knowledge.* New York: Plenum.

Kruglanski, A. W. (1989b). The psychology of being "right": On the problem of accuracy in social perception and cognition. *Psychological Bulletin, 106,* 395–409.

Kuiper, N. A., & Rogers, T. B. (1979). Encoding of personal information: Self-other differences. *Journal of Personality and Social Psychology, 37,* 499–514.

KUNDA, Z., & NISBETT, R. E. (1986). Prediction and the partial understanding of the law of large numbers. *Journal of Experimental Social Psychology, 22,* 339–354.

LEHMAN, D. R., LEMPERT, R. O., & NISBETT, R. E. (1988). The effects of graduate training on reasoning: Formal discipline and thinking about everyday-life events. *American Psychologist, 43,* 431–442.

LEVINE, J. M., RESNICK, L. B., & HIGGINS, E. T. (1993). Social foundations of cognition. In L. M. PORTER & M. R. ROSENZWEIG (Eds.), *Annual review of psychology* (Vol. 44, pp. 585–612). Palo Alto, CA: Annual Reviews Inc.

LEWIN, K. (1951). *Field theory in social science.* New York: Harper.

LEYENS, J. PH., YZERBYT, V. Y., & SCHADRON, G. (1992). The social judgeability approach to stereotypes. *European Review of Social Psychology* (Vol. 3, pp. 91–120). New York: Wiley.

LINVILLE, P. W. (1982a). Affective consequences of complexity regarding the self and others. In M. S. Clark & S. T. Fiske (Eds.), *Affect and cognition: The 17th Annual Carnegie Symposium on Cognition* (pp. 79–109). Hillsdale, NJ: Erlbaum.

LINVILLE, P. W. (1982b). The complexity-extremity effect and age-based stereotyping. *Journal of Personality and Social Psychology, 42,* 193–211.

LOCKE, J. (1979). *Essay concerning human understanding.* New York: Oxford University Press. (Originally published in 1690.)

LOCKSLEY, A., HEPBURN, C., & ORTIZ, V. (1982). Social stereotypes and judgments of individuals: An instance of the base rate fallacy. *Journal of Experimental Social Psychology, 18,* 23–42.

LODGE, M., MCGRAW, K. M., & STROH, P. (1989). An impression-driven model of candidate evaluation. *American Political Science Review, 83,* 399–419.

LOPES, L. L. (1982). Towards a procedural theory of judgment (Tech. Rep. No. 17, pp. 1–49). Information Processing Program, University of Wisconsin, Madison, WI.

LORD, C. G. (1980). Schemas and images as memory aids: Two modes of processing social information. *Journal of Personality and Social Psychology, 38,* 257–269.

MANIS, M. (1977). Cognitive social psychology. *Personality and Social Psychology Bulletin, 3,* 550–566.

MARKUS, H. (1977). Self-schemata and processing information about the self. *Journal of Personality and Social Psychology, 35,* 63–78.

MARKUS, H., & WURF, E. (1987). The dynamic self-concept: A social psychological perspective. In M. R. Rosenzweig & L. W. Porter (Eds.), *Annual review of psychology* (Vol. 38, pp. 299–337). Palo Alto, CA: Annual Reviews Inc.

MARKUS, H., & ZAJONC, R. B. (1985). The cognitive perspective in social psychology. In G. Lindzey & E. Aronson (Eds.), *The handbook of social psychology* (3rd ed.) (Vol. 1, pp. 137–230). New York: Random House.

MARQUES, J. M., YZERBYT, V. Y., & LEYENS, J. PH. (1988). The "black sheep effect": Extremity of judgments towards ingroup members as a function of group identification. *European Journal of Social Psychology, 18,* 1–16.

MCARTHUR, L. Z. (1981). What grabs you? The role of attention in impression formation and causal attribution. In E. T. Higgins, C. P. Herman, & M. P. Zanna (Eds.), *Social cognition: The Ontario Symposium* (Vol. 1, pp. 201–246). Hillsdale, NJ: Erlbaum.

MCARTHUR, L. Z., & POST, D. L. (1977). Figural emphasis and person perception. *Journal of Experimental Social Psychology, 13,* 520–535.

MILLAR, M. G., & TESSER, A. (1986). Thought-induced attitude change: The effects of schema structure and commitment. *Journal of Personality and Social Psychology, 51,* 259–269.

MULLEN, B., BROWN, R., & SMITH, C. (1992). Ingroup bias as a function of salience, relevance, and status: An integration. *European Journal of Social Psychology, 22,* 103–122.

MULLEN, B., & HU, L. (1989). Perceptions of ingroup and outgroup variability: A meta-analytic integration. *Basic and Applied Social Psychology, 10,* 233–252.

NEUBERG, S. L., & FISKE, S. T. (1987). Motivational influences on impression formation: Outcome dependency, accuracy-driven attention, and individuating processes. *Journal of Personality and Social Psychology, 53,* 431–444.

NISBETT, R. E., & BORGIDA, E. (1975). Attribution and the psychology of prediction. *Journal of Personality and Social Psychology, 32,* 932–943.

NISBETT, R. E., KRANTZ, D. H., JEPSON, C., & FONG, G. T. (1982). Improving inductive inference. In D. Kahneman, P. Slovic, & A. Tversky (Eds.), *Judgment under uncertainty: Heuristics and biases* (pp. 445–462). New York: Cambridge University Press.

NISBETT, R. E., & ROSS, L. (1980). *Human inference: Strategies and shortcomings of social judgment.* Englewood Cliffs, NJ: Prentice-Hall.

NISBETT, R. E., ZUKIER, H., & LEMLEY, R. E. (1981). The dilution effect: Non-diagnostic information weakens the implications of diagnostic information. *Cognitive Psychology, 13,* 248–277.

OSTROM, T. M. (1977). Between-theory and within-theory conflict in explaining context effects in impression formation. *Journal of Experimental Social Psychology, 13,* 492–503.

OWENS, J., BOWER, G. H., & BLACK, J. B. (1979). The "soap-opera" effect in story recall. *Memory and Cognition, 7,* 185–191.

PERVIN, L. (Ed.). (1989). *Goal concepts in personality and social psychology.* Hillsdale, NJ: Erlbaum.

REEDER, G. C., MCCORMICK, C. B., & ESSELMAN, E. D. (1987). Self-referent processing and recall of prose. *Journal of Educational Psychology, 79,* 243–248.

RESNICK, L. B., LEVINE, J. M., & TEASLEY, S. D. (Eds.). (1991). *Perspectives on socially shared cognition.* Washington, DC: American Psychological Association.

RUBLE, D. N. (1994). A phase model of transitions: Cognitive and motivational consequences. In M. P. Zanna (Ed.), *Advances in experimental social psychology* (Vol. 26, pp. 163–214). San Diego: Academic Press.

RUBLE, D. N., & STANGOR, C. (1986). Stalking the elusive schema: Insights from developmental and social-psychological analyses of gender schemas. *Social Cognition, 4,* 227–261.

RUSCHER, J. B., & FISKE, S. T. (1990). Interpersonal competition can cause individuating impression formation. *Journal of Personality and Social Psychology, 58,* 832–842.

RUSCHER, J. B., & HAMMER, E. D. (1994). Revising disrupted impressions through conversation. *Journal of Personality and Social Psychology, 66,* 530–541.

SCHANK, R. C., & ABELSON, R. P. (1977). *Scripts, plans, goals, and understanding: An inquiry into human knowledge structures.* Hillsdale, NJ: Erlbaum.

SCHNEIDER, D. J., HASTORF, A. H., & ELLSWORTH, P. C. (1979). *Person perception.* Reading, MA: Addison-Wesley.

SCHUMER, R. (1973). Context effects in impression formation as a function of the ambiguity of test traits. *European Journal of Social Psychology, 3,* 333–338.

SHERMAN, S. J., JUDD, C. M., & PARK, B. (1989). Social cognition. In M. R. Rosenzweig & L. W. Porter (Eds.), *Annual review of psychology* (Vol. 40, pp. 281–326). Palo Alto, CA: Annual Reviews.

SHERMAN, S. J., MACKIE, D. M., & DRISCOLL, D. M. (1990). Priming and the differential use of dimensions in evaluation. *Personality and Social Psychology Bulletin, 16,* 405–418.

SKINNER, B. F. (1963). Operant behavior. *American Psychologist, 18,* 503–515.

SKINNER, B. F. (1990). The place of an experimental analysis of behavior in psychology. Keynote address to the 98th Annual Convention of the American Psychological Association, Boston, MA.

SNYDER, M. (1992). Motivational foundations of behavioral confirmation. In M. P. Zanna (Ed.), *Advances in experimental social psychology* (Vol. 25, pp. 67–114). New York: Academic.

SRULL, T. K. (1981). Person memory: Some tests of associative storage and retrieval models. *Journal of Experimental Psychology: Human Learning and Memory, 7*, 440–462.

SRULL, T. K. (1983). Organizational and retreival processes in person memory: An examination of processing objectives, presentation format, and the possible role of self-generated retrieval cues. *Journal of Personality and Social Psychology, 4*, 1157–1170.

SRULL, T. K., & BRAND, J. F. (1983). Memory for information about persons: The effect of encoding operations on subsequent retrieval. *Journal of Verbal Learning and Verbal Behavior, 22*, 219–230.

SRULL, T. K., & WYER, R. S., JR. (1979). The role of category accessibility in the interpretation of information about persons: Some determinants and implications. *Journal of Personality and Social Psychology, 37*, 1660–1672.

SRULL, T. K., & WYER, R. S., JR. (1980). Category accessibility and social perception: Some implications for the study of person memory and interpersonal judgments. *Journal of Personality and Social Psychology, 38*, 841–856.

SRULL, T. K., & WYER, R. S., JR. (1989). Person memory and judgment. *Psychological Review, 96*, 58–83.

STANGOR, C., & FORD, T. E. (1992). Accuracy and expectancy-confirming processing orientations and the development of stereotypes and prejudice. *European Review of Social Psychology* (Vol. 3, pp. 57–90).

STANGOR, C., & MCMILLAN, D. (1992). Memory for expectancy-congruent and expectancy-incongruent information: A review of the social and social developmental literatures. *Psychological Bulletin, 111*, 42–61.

SWANN, W. B., JR. (1984). Quest for accuracy in person perception: A matter of pragmatics. *Psychological Review, 91*, 457–477.

TAGIURI, R. (1958). Introduction. In R. Tagiuri & L. Petrullo (Eds.), *Person perception and interpersonal behavior* (pp. ix–xvii). Palo Alto, CA: Stanford University Press.

TAYLOR, S. E. (1981). A categorization approach to stereotyping. In D. L. Hamilton (Ed.), *Cognitive processes in stereotyping and intergroup behavior* (pp. 88–114). Hillsdale, NJ: Erlbaum.

TAYLOR, S. E., & CROCKER, J. (1981). Schematic bases of social information processing. In E. T. Higgins, C. P. Herman, & M. P. Zanna (Eds.), *Social cognition: The Ontario Symposium* (Vol. 1, pp. 89–134). Hillsdale, NJ: Erlbaum.

TAYLOR, S. E., & FISKE, S. T. (1978). Salience, attention, and attribution: Top of the head phenomena. In L. Berkowitz (Ed.), *Advances in experimental social psychology* (Vol. 11, pp. 249–288). New York: Academic Press.

TVERSKY, A., & KAHNEMAN, D. (1974). Judgment under uncertainty: Heuristics and biases. *Science, 185*, 1124–1131.

TVERSKY, A., & KAHNEMAN, D. (1980). Causal schemata in judgments under uncertainty. In M. Fishbein (Ed.), *Progress in social psychology* (pp. 49–72). Hillsdale, NJ: Erlbaum.

TVERSKY, A., & KAHNEMAN, D. (1982). Judgments of and by representativeness. In D. Kahneman, P. Slovic, & A. Tversky (Eds.), *Judgment under uncertainty: Heuristics and biases* (pp. 84–100). New York: Cambridge University Press.

TVERSKY, A., & KAHNEMAN, D. (1983). Extensional versus intuitive reasoning: The conjunction fallacy in probability judgment. *Psychological Review, 90*, 293–315.

WATSON, J. (1930). *Behaviorism.* New York: Norton.

WESTEN, D. (1988). Transference and information processing. *Clinical Psychology Review, 8,* 161–179.

WHITE, J. D., & CARLSTON, D. E. (1983). Consequences of schemata for attention, impressions, and recall in complex social interactions. *Journal of Personality and Social Psychology, 45,* 538–549.

WYER, R. S., JR. (1974). Changes in meaning and halo effects in personality impression formation. *Journal of Personality and Social Psychology, 29,* 829–835.

WYER, R. S., JR., & SRULL, T. K. (Eds.). (1984). *Handbook of social cognition* (Vols. 1–3). Hillsdale, NJ: Erlbaum.

WYER, R. S., & WATSON, S. F. (1969). Context effects in impression formation. *Journal of Personality and Social Psychology, 12,* 22–33.

ZADNY, J., & GERARD, H. B. (1974). Attributed intentions and informational selectivity. *Journal of Experimental Social Psychology, 10,* 34–52.

ZAJONC, R. B. (1980). Cognition and social cognition: A historical perspective. In L. Festinger (Ed.), *Retrospections on social psychology* (pp. 180–204). New York: Oxford University Press.

ZANNA, M. P., & HAMILTON, D. L. (1972). Attribute dimensions and patterns of trait inferences. *Psychonomic Science, 27,* 353–354.

ZANNA, M. P., & HAMILTON, D. L. (1977). Further evidence for meaning change in impression formation. *Journal of Experimental Social Psychology, 13,* 224–238.

ZEBROWITZ, L. A. (1990). *Social perception.* Pacific Grove, CA: Brooks-Cole.

Further Readings

DEVINE, P. G., OSTROM, T., & HAMILTON, D. (Eds.). (1992). *Social cognition: Contributions to classical issues in social psychology.* New York: Springer-Verlag.

A collection of chapters by experts, evaluating the progress in basic social psychological problems brought about by social cognition approaches.

FISKE, S. T. (1993). Social cognition and social perception. In M. R. Rosenzweig & L. W. Porter (Eds.), *Annual review of psychology* (Vol. 44, pp. 155–194). Palo Alto, CA: Annual Reviews Inc.

A dense but readable overview of social cognition research, 1989–1991, arguing for the pragmatic perspective on social thinkers.

FISKE, S. T., & TAYLOR, S. E. (1991). *Social cognition* (2nd ed.). New York: McGraw-Hill.

A broad and deep overview of the field, designed to be scholarly and entertaining, organized similarly to this chapter but a few hundred pages longer.

HIGGINS, E. T., & BARGH, J. A. (1987). Social cognition and social perception. In M. R. Rosenzweig & L. W. Porter (Eds.), *Annual review of psychology* (Vol. 38, pp. 369–425). Palo Alto, CA: Annual Reviews Inc.

An original, innovative, and provocative look at controversies in social cognition, with an intensive review of the literature from the mid-1980s.

MARKUS, H., & ZAJONC, R. B. (1985). The cognitive perspective in social psychology. In G. Lindzey & E. Aronson (Eds.), *The handbook of social psychology* (3rd ed.) (Vol. 1, pp. 137–230). New York: Random House.

A scholarly overview and evaluation from two of the field's leading experts, designed for graduate students.

WYER, R. S., JR., & SRULL, T. K. (Eds.). (1984). *Handbook of social cognition* (Vols. 1–3). Hillsdale, NJ: Erlbaum.

A central, heavily cognitive collection of chapters on core topics and processes.

ZEBROWITZ, L. A. (1990). *Social perception.* Pacific Grove, CA: Brooks-Cole.

A readable overview of traditional person perception research, as described from an anticognitive perspective.

Richard E. Petty received his Ph.D. in social psychology from Ohio State University after majoring in political science at the University of Virginia. In 1987, he left his position as Middlebush Professor of Psychology at the University of Missouri to return to Ohio State as Professor and Director of the social psychology doctoral program. Petty's primary area of research focuses on social influence and persuasion. A major theme of this research has been that some attitude change strategies are more effective in some situations than in others, and for some people more than others. It is important to understand the processes by which change occurs because some attitude change strategies produce attitudes that are more persistent over time, resistant to attack, and directive of behavior. His most recent research has emphasized the role of emotional factors in persuasion and how people correct for unwanted biases in their judgments. This research has resulted in 7 books and over 100 journal articles and chapters. In addition to conducting basic research on persuasion processes, Petty is interested in the applicability of this research to important social problems. He has served as a consultant to various agencies such as the National Academy of Sciences on changing attitudes toward diet and health, and the National Institute on Drug Abuse on developing more effective drug abuse prevention efforts.

CHAPTER 6

Attitude Change

Richard E. Petty
Ohio State University

CHAPTER OUTLINE

There is no expedient to which a man will not resort to avoid the real labor of thinking.

—Sir Joshua Reynolds

The man who doesn't make up his mind to cultivate the habit of thinking misses the greatest pleasures in life.

—Thomas A. Edison

INTRODUCTION TO ATTITUDES

Consider the conflicting opinions above. Which best captures your own position? Is thinking difficult and laborious, "the hardest work there is," as Henry

195

Ford once noted, or is thinking fun and pleasant, something to seek out? You probably know some people who are quite reflective and other people who are not. Likewise, you can probably think of factors that encourage thinking on the part of just about everybody and those that discourage thinking. For example, even if you generally hate to think, you probably devoted some thought to selecting a college or graduate school. The theme of this chapter is that in order to understand the underlying processes and consequences of attitude change, it is important to consider the extent to which various situations elicit different amounts and kinds of thinking, and the extent to which people vary in the way they think about persuasive messages.

Attitudes refer to very general evaluations that people hold of themselves, other people, objects, and issues. For example, do you think that you are a good or a bad person? Do you like or dislike ice cream? Do you favor or oppose capital punishment? People's attitudes can be based on (a) *affect* or feelings (such as deciding that you don't like an exotic food because it makes you feel nauseous), (b) *cognitions* or beliefs and knowledge (such as evaluating a food based on its saturated fat content), (c) *behaviors* or actions (such as deciding that you must like *Wendy's* since you eat lunch there every day), or (d) some combination of these elements (Petty & Cacioppo, 1986; Zanna & Rempel, 1988). Just as attitudes can be based on each of these factors, so too can attitudes have an impact on them. Thus, a favorable attitude might cause you to (a) feel happy in the presence of someone you like (affective influence), (b) think of mostly positive characteristics when asked to list the person's traits (cognitive influence), and (c) agree to loan the person lunch money when he forgets his wallet (behavioral influence).

There are, of course, a number of ways to change a person's attitude. Perhaps the most common is by presenting the other person with a message containing information about the attitude object. Attitude change by this strategy is called *persuasion.* Although we will focus on this type of influence because it is the most common means of attempting to bring about attitude change and is the topic of the most research, we will consider other attitude change strategies as well.[1]

People have undoubtedly attempted to influence each other ever since the human race began. Early attempts at influence by both individuals and governments relied largely on force and threatened punishments in order to induce at least behavioral compliance. Today, influence attempts are more often aimed at general attitudes than directly at behavior (e.g., "drugs are bad, so don't use them," "Detergent X works better than the others, so buy it"), and much more sophisticated and subtle techniques are employed. The advantage of attitude change over behavioral compliance is that when people's internalized attitudes are changed, they will presumably choose to engage in consistent behavior even if the person who brought about the attitude change is not present (Kelman, 1958). Attitude change attempts are probably more pervasive today than ever before in history (McGuire, 1985). In fact, it is likely that in the typical week, the average American is confronted with hundreds of persuasion attempts from family, friends, colleagues, billboards, newspapers, magazines, television, radio, door-to-door salespersons, telephone solicitors, and other sources.

Given the importance of attitude change in the twentieth century, it is perhaps not surprising that social psychologists and other behavioral scientists have devoted considerable effort to understanding the factors responsible for attitudinal influence. Over the last 50 to 60 years, it is likely that more research has been conducted and more has been written on the topic of attitude formation and change than on any other single topic in the social sciences. Investigators have studied how various aspects of the message (e.g., how many arguments are presented), the communicator (e.g., how expert the source is), and the setting (e.g., how much distraction is present) determine the extent of influence. Likewise, many different theories of the processes by which attitudes are changed have been proposed (see Eagly & Chaiken, 1993; Petty, Priester, & Wegener, 1994; for recent reviews).

The abundance of variables, studies, and theories has been a mixed blessing, however. The problem is that the accumulated research doesn't always agree on the effect that a particular variable has on persuasion. For example, even for a presumably obvious variable like the credibility of the message source, some studies have found that increasing the perceived credibility of the source increases persuasion, whereas others have found that source credibility has no effect. Still other studies have found that increasing credibility can actually reduce influence. Similarly, different theories have accumulated that attempt to explain these different outcomes by invoking seemingly conflicting psychological processes. Given this state of affairs, it is not surprising that by the 1970s, prominent social psychologists were complaining that it had become very difficult to understand the fundamentals of attitude change processes (see Fishbein & Ajzen, 1972; Himmelfarb & Eagly, 1974; Sherif, 1977). A major cause of this confusion was the implicit assumption that a given variable should only have one effect on attitudes (e.g., credibility should always increase persuasion), and that there was one true process that would bring this about.

In this chapter we take a contemporary look at the phenomena of attitude change in an attempt to understand how even relatively simple variables—such as source credibility—can influence attitudes in rather complex ways. Our review is divided into several parts. First, we examine the underlying bases and structure of attitudes. Second, we examine the specific processes of attitude change. We will see how some of the strategies of attitude change require very little cognitive activity on the part of the target of influence whereas others require considerable cognitive effort. Next, we describe how any one variable, such as source credibility, can lead to attitude change by different processes in different situations. Finally , we examine the consequences of attitudes changed by different processes.

The Bases of Attitudes

To the extent that we understand what the underlying bases of attitudes are and their structure, we can presumably understand how to change attitudes.

Beliefs, Emotions, and Behaviors as Bases of Attitudes

As noted above, beliefs, emotions, and behaviors can all contribute separately to people's attitudes. Early views of attitudes assumed a "tripartite" model in which attitudes were thought to be composed of all three categories of responses (e.g., Rosenberg & Hovland, 1960). More recent research, however, has emphasized the notion that attitudes can be based on just one or two of the components (e.g., Millar & Tesser, 1986b). For example, some attitudes might be based mostly on how the object makes us feel, whereas other attitudes might be based mostly on what the object makes us think. Similarly, although early research tended to emphasize the notion that our thoughts, feelings, and behaviors would tend to be consistent with one another (e.g., Rosenberg, 1960), recent research has begun to emphasize the implications of inconsistency and ambivalence among these bases of attitudes (e.g., see Chaiken, Pomerantz, & Giner-Sorolla, 1995; Millar & Tesser, 1992; Thompson, Zanna, & Griffin, 1995; Wilson, Dunn, Kraft, & Lisle, 1989). That is, we can feel wonderful when we eat ice cream, but also realize that the high fat content of ice cream can produce heart disease. In order to predict whether this ambivalent person will be a high consumer of ice cream, we would need to know whether the affective or the cognitive basis of the attitude was more important.

Functional Bases of Attitudes

Although the tripartite model of attitudes identifies three categories of attributes that can form the basis of an attitude, it is not clear what specific kinds of beliefs, emotions, or behaviors will be the most important. The *functional theorists* (e.g., Katz, 1960; Smith, Bruner, & White, 1956) have addressed this issue in terms of the psychological needs or functions that an attitude can serve for a person. Perhaps the most fundamental purpose of attitudes is to serve a *knowledge function*. That is, virtually all attitudes help a person to understand and make sense of the world. Quickly retrieving an evaluation that tells you whether an object or person you encounter is good (safe) or bad (threatening) makes everyday life easier by minimizing your need to assess and construct an evaluation each and every time the attitude object is encountered (Cacioppo, Petty, & Berntson, 1991; Smith, Bruner, & White, 1956). In fact, if we had to construct an evaluation every time we encountered an object, we would have little time to do much of anything else! Fortunately, a previously formed attitude is usually available (Bargh, Chaiken, Govender, & Pratto, 1992), and this reduces the stress of decision making and daily living (Fazio, 1995; Fazio, Blascovich, & Driscoll, 1992).

In addition to this basic knowledge function, some attitudes are thought to serve more specific motives. For example, some attitudes can protect people from threatening truths about themselves or serve to enhance their self-images (i.e., an *ego-defensive function*). Negative attitudes toward some minority groups (e.g., homosexuals) are thought to serve this function for some people. That is, by derogating the minority group, people can feel superior. Still other attitudes are thought to be based on the extent to which they lead to explicit rewards and/or punishments *(utilitarian function)* or give expression to important values *(value-expressive function)*.

There are two popular approaches to study the functional bases of attitudes. One approach relies on individual differences and suggests that attitudes serve different functions for different kinds of people. For example, Snyder and DeBono (1985) hypothesized that the attitudes of low "self-monitors" (see Snyder, 1979) serve primarily a value-expressive function, whereas the attitudes of high self-monitors serve primarily a social adjustive function. That is, people who score high on the self-monitoring scale are concerned about engaging in actions that provide rewards from other people. Thus, they are influenced more by what other people think is appropriate than by their own internal standards. People who score low on this scale are the opposite. A second approach proposes that many issues and objects serve a common function for a wide variety of people (e.g., Abelson & Prentice, 1989; Shavitt, 1989). For example, attitudes toward air conditioners probably serve a utilitarian function for most people. That is, we like air conditioners for the practical comfort they provide rather than the boost they give to our egos. Of course, exceptions are possible such as a person who dislikes air conditioners because of the negative effect on the earth's ozone layer (i.e., the attitude serves a value-expressive function).

Changing Attitudes with Different Bases

Understanding the bases of attitudes is thought to be important because of the implications for how to change these attitudes. That is, in order to change an attitude, should the person be provided with new arguments and experiences that "match" but counter the basis of the attitude, or would a "mismatching" strategy be more successful? For example, if a person dislikes a new beverage because of how it smells, should you get them to experience how good it tastes (countering negative affect with positive affect), or should you provide them with all sorts of information about the nutritional benefits of the smelly beverage (countering negative affect with favorable cognitions)? Interestingly, in studies examining this question, some investigators have found evidence favoring a matching strategy—especially for attitudes based on affect (Edwards, 1990), whereas others have obtained evidence favoring mismatching (Millar & Millar, 1990). One commonsense resolution of this conflicting evidence would say that you should match if you can effectively undermine the basis of the attitude, but use a mismatching strategy if you cannot (Petty, Gleicher, & Baker, 1991). That is, if your affective strategy is effective in turning initially negative feelings into positive ones, then matching would be successful. However, if you are unable to do this, then your best bet to counter negative affect would be to provide favorable cognitions and convince the person that they should rely less on their feelings and more on their beliefs (i.e., who cares how it smells if it will make you live 20 years longer!).[2]

In contrast to the mixed evidence on the affective and cognitive bases of attitudes, with respect to the functional foundations of attitudes, research has consistently supported the matching principle. In several studies, for example, high and low self-monitors were found to be more susceptible to arguments that matched the presumed functional basis of their attitudes. That is, high self-monitors were more susceptible to arguments based on the image of a consumer product than were low self-monitors (Snyder & DeBono, 1987, 1989; see also DeBono, 1987). Matching arguments to the functions inherent in attitude objects has also been successful (Shavitt, 1990). That is, if people like air conditioners for the comfort they provide (utilitarian function), then in selling a new air conditioner you should emphasize comfort rather than the ego-enhancing benefits of staying cool.

Attitude and Belief Structure

Attitude structure refers to the manner in which attitudes and the associated information are organized in memory. The information we have about an object and our relevant experiences can be very well organized or poorly organized, and if well organized, a number of organizational schemes are possible. For example, consistent with the tripartite model, it is possible that attitudes are organized into affective, cognitive, and behavioral subsystems (e.g., Breckler, 1984). Another possibility is that attitude structures are bipolar with attitude-consistent information clustered together and linked to a separate cluster of attitude-inconsistent information (e.g., Judd & Kulik, 1980; Pratkanis, 1989). Alternatively, the information in memory could be organized in some other fashion such as into the categories of acceptable, objectionable, and noncommittal (Sherif & Hovland, 1961).

A currently popular view of attitude structure relies on an associative network model of memory (e.g., Anderson, 1983) in which an attitude object is linked to an evaluative node as well as to other relevant information and experiences (e.g., Fiske, 1982; Pratkanis & Greenwald, 1989; see Figure 6.1). Although most social psychologists have focused on the structure of individual attitudes (called "intra-attitudinal structure," e.g., Judd & Krosnick, 1989), any one attitude structure can also be linked to other attitude structures that have some basis of similarity such as attitudes that derive from the same basic values (called "inter-attitudinal structure;" see Eagly & Chaiken, 1995). Because of "spreading activation," the activation of one concept spreads to linked nodes in the system. This means that if you ask people about one attitude, they will be able to give you their attitude about a related issue faster than an unrelated issue (Tourangeau, Rasinski, & D'Andrade, 1991). Perhaps the most important implication of viewing attitudes as integrated structures is that if you modify some particular aspect of the attitude structure (e.g., convince someone that Bill is not very friendly; see Figure 6.1), this will likely lead to some change in the overall evaluation of the object (i.e., the attitude) itself, though it might take some time and thought for the change to occur (McGuire, 1981).

In addition to the very general idea that attitudes are contained in organized structures or *schemas*, some theorists have addressed more particular structural notions. For example, attitudes have been conceptualized as the end

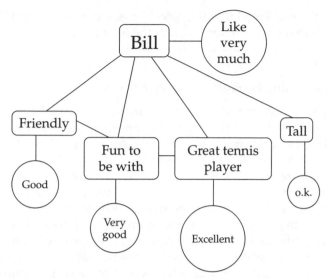

FIGURE 6.1. Attitude structure. In the figure, a person is shown having a favorable attitude toward Bill. This attitude can be retrieved directly from memory or can be constructed based on some subset of the various attributes the person associates with Bill.

result of a syllogistic network of beliefs (e.g., Bem, 1970; McGuire, 1960; Wyer, 1970). That is, at a minimum an attitude can be based on two premises that lead to a conclusion as in the syllogism below.

Premise 1: Bill is intelligent.

Premise 2: I like intelligent people.

Conclusion: I like Bill.

Of course, any conclusion such as the one above can be based on a number of different syllogisms, and each of the premises in the syllogism can itself be based on other syllogisms. Thus, the syllogistic structure for any attitude can become quite complex.

One important issue about attitude structure concerns how a person's specific beliefs about an attitude object combine to form one global evaluation of the object. The most popular approach to this question comes from *expectancy-value theories*. Expectancy-value theorists analyze attitudes by focusing on the extent to which people expect the attitude object to be related to important values or produce positive versus negative consequences (e.g., Peak, 1955). In one influential formulation, Fishbein and Ajzen (1975) contend that the attributes (or consequences) associated with an attitude object are evaluated along both *likelihood* and *desirability* dimensions. Specifically, a person's overall evaluation of some attitude object (e.g., "Bill") is said to be based on the desirability of each attribute [e_i—such as how good it is to be intelligent] associated with the object weighted by the likelihood that the object possesses the attribute [b_i—such as how likely is it that Bill is intelligent], and the quantity is then summed over all attributes. Stated mathematically, the attitude toward the object [A_o] is expressed in the equation below:

Expectancy-Value Formula: $(A_o) = \Sigma \ (b_i{}^*e_i)$

This formula says that attitudes become more favorable as the number of consequences (or attributes) of the object that are likely and desirable increases. Considerable research supports this view (see Ajzen & Fishbein, 1980; Fishbein, 1980; Fishbein & Ajzen, 1975, for reviews).[3]

The major implication of expectancy-value theories for attitude change is that a persuasive message will be effective to the extent that it produces a change in either the likelihood or the desirability component of an attribute that is linked to the attitude object. For example, if a person believes that the probability is moderate ($b_i = .6$) that their friend Bill is intelligent ($e_i = +3$) so that $\Sigma b_i e_i = .6{}^*3 = 1.8$, attitudes toward Bill can be made more favorable either by presenting a message that causes the person to view it as more likely that Bill is intelligent (e.g., moving b_i from .6 to .8 so that $\Sigma b_i e_i$ now $= .8{}^*3 = 2.4$) or by convincing the person that intelligence is a better quality in a friend than previously thought (e.g., moving e_i from +3 to +4 so that $\Sigma b_i e_i$ now $= .6{}^*4 = 2.4$) or by changing both perceptions (i.e., so that $\Sigma b_i e_i$ now $= .8{}^*4 = 3.2$). Although Fishbein and Ajzen's approach has been widely applied to understanding the cognitive bases of attitudes, relatively little work on attitude *change* has been guided explicitly by this framework. Nevertheless, existing research supports the view that messages can influence attitudes by changing either the evaluation or the likelihood component of beliefs (e.g., Lutz, 1975; MacKenzie, 1986).[4]

PROCESSES OF ATTITUDE CHANGE

Now that we have examined the general bases of attitudes and their underlying structure, we can turn to the general theories and strategies that have been proposed for changing attitudes—the focus of this chapter. Research on attitude change has been guided by a general information-processing approach that has been popular in one form or another for a considerable period of time. For example, in a 1922 book on the psychology of selling, Kitson argued that the "mental stream" of influence could be divided into the stages of attention, interest, desire, confidence, decision, and action. The contemporary information-processing approach, however, stems most directly from the Yale Communication Program (Hovland, Janis, & Kelley, 1953). The Yale group proposed that attitude change was most likely if there was attention, comprehension, learning, acceptance, and retention of the message and its conclusion. People were thought to engage in these steps to the extent that the persuasive message or the persuasion context provided incentives for doing so.

Learning and Reception Processes

Over the years, McGuire (1968, 1989) has presented a more formal information-processing model that incorporates and extends the original Yale framework. Although the exact number of steps in McGuire's information-processing model has varied over the years, a consistent theme has been that persuasion was dependent upon various factors related to the reception of message arguments (i.e., receiving, understanding, and learning the arguments) and various factors related to yielding to them (i.e., accepting the arguments). Thus, some variables such as "message comprehensibility" might influence the likelihood of persuasion mostly by determining the extent of message reception. For example, in one study Eagly (1974) compared the persuasiveness of messages that varied in comprehensibility. In the high comprehensibility condition, subjects read a message containing reasonable arguments. In the medium comprehensibility condition, the comprehensible message was reorganized so that the sentences were cut in half and put back together in random order. In this condition, the sentences had the appropriate sentence structure, but made little sense. In the low comprehensibility condition, the words in the message were put together in a random fashion. Not surprisingly, as the messages became less comprehensible, they also became more difficult to understand and learn, and also less persuasive. According to the McGuire model, however, in addition to variables influencing the reception of the message, other variables influence persuasion mostly by determining the extent of message acceptance. For example, holding reception constant, people who are carefully thinking about a message are more likely to yield to it when it presents strong and compelling arguments than weak and specious reasons (Chaiken, 1980; Petty & Cacioppo, 1979b).

Perhaps the most interesting aspect of McGuire's framework is the notion that some variables can have opposite effects on message reception and yielding. For example, as the intelligence of the audience increases, reception might increase (e.g., because greater intelligence should produce greater comprehension and memory) but yielding might decrease (e.g., because an intelligent audience has greater confidence in its initial opinions or can better resist the arguments presented; Eagly & Warren, 1976). For variables having an opposite impact on reception and yielding processes, persuasion should be greatest at a moderate level of the variable (e.g., moderate intelligence; see Figure 6.2).

Although some studies have examined the curvilinear hypothesis from McGuire's model directly (see Rhodes & Wood, 1992), most of the attention devoted to the reception/yielding model has been on attempting to provide evidence for the notion that reception of the message arguments was a necessary step for persuasion. Although it seems obvious that a recipient needs at least to comprehend the *position* taken in a message if change toward that position is to take place, the accumulated research evidence suggests that accurate comprehension or learning of the message arguments is not necessary. As we will see later in the chapter, it is possible for people to be persuaded by a message conclusion even if they didn't receive, understand, or learn the message arguments as long as there is a simple cue in the persuasion context (e.g., an expert source)

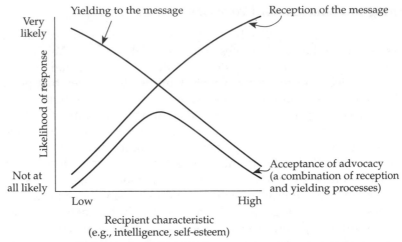

FIGURE 6.2. Reception/yielding model of attitude change. The figure depicts the combined effect of reception and yielding processes on attitude change as a function of an individual difference variable (e.g., intelligence).
Adapted from McGuire, 1969.

that allows a reasonable opinion to be formed in the absence of message scrutiny. Thus, persuasion can occur in the absence of message understanding and learning. That is, message reception is not necessary for attitude change.

Message reception is not sufficient for attitude change either. That is, people can fail to be persuaded even if they completely understand and learn the message. As explained more fully below, when people are actively thinking about the message arguments and evaluating them, their own evaluative thoughts are a more important determinant of attitude change than is their ability to learn and remember the exact information presented (Greenwald, 1968; Petty, Ostrom, & Brock, 1981). When is message learning and retention an important contributor to attitude change? Current research suggests that the recall of the specific information presented in a persuasive message can be an important predictor of attitudes if people are not forming an overall evaluation of the communication at the time it is presented (e.g., Haugtvedt & Petty, 1992; Mackie & Asuncion, 1990; cf., Hastie & Park, 1986). That is, if a person is not thinking about the message at the time it is presented, but is subsequently asked for an opinion, he or she can attempt to retrieve the information in the message and evaluate it at that time. If the arguments are evaluated favorably, then the more arguments recalled, the more persuasion that occurs.[5]

Yielding Processes

As the preceding discussion implies, tracking the mere reception, understanding, and learning of the information in a message is typically inadequate to predict the persuasiveness of the communication. Rather, the processes by which a person reacts to the incoming message must be understood. Our discussion of the processes by which people "yield" to persuasive communications is divided into three parts. First, we discuss the general "cognitive response" idea that it is important to understand an individual's personal reactions to incoming information or an individual's self-generation of information instead of (or in addition to) their reception and learning of the information presented (e.g., Greenwald, 1968; Petty, Ostrom & Brock, 1981). Next we discuss the notion from the elaboration likelihood model (ELM) of persuasion (Petty & Cacioppo, 1981, 1986) that a person's reactions to a message can be based on considerable cognitive effort or on more simplistic analyses (see also the heuristic/systematic model; Chaiken, Liberman, & Eagly, 1989). Then, we discuss various yielding processes that do not rely on careful and effortful scrutiny of the information contained in a persuasive appeal. Finally, we will see how any one variable, such as the credibility of the source, can produce attitude change by invoking different processes in different situations.

Cognitive Response Approach

Cognitive Responses to Messages. Greenwald (1968) proposed that it was not the specific arguments in a message that were associated with the message conclusion (or attitude object) in memory as the Yale approach implied, but rather, a person's unique cognitive responses or reactions to the message arguments were paired with the conclusion, and these cognitive responses determined persuasion or resistance (see also, Brock, 1967). For example, when a political candidate says that she plans to reduce taxes by 15 percent, one person can respond by thinking, "That's terrible, the national debt will increase," but another can think, "That's great, maybe now I can afford a new car!" Even though both people have received and understand the message, only the second person is likely to approve of the candidate. Of course, reception is not irrelevant because individuals can only cognitively *respond* to something that they have received from the message. Nevertheless, the cognitive response approach recognizes that a person's thoughts can concern incorrectly perceived arguments as well as correctly perceived information. In fact, as noted above, a person can generate thoughts about the message conclusion in the absence of receipt of any of the message arguments.

The cognitive response approach is sufficiently general that it includes cognitive responses about the message content (e.g., "That's an ingenious taxation plan"), the message source (e.g., "She seems to know what she is talking about"), or other factors such as the context in which the communication is presented (e.g., "All of these distractions are annoying"). In any case, according to this model, to the extent that a person's cognitive responses are favorable, persuasion is the expected result, but to the extent that the person's thoughts are unfavorable (e.g., counterarguments, source derogations), resistance or even *boomerang* (change in a direction opposite to that advocated) are more likely (Petty, Ostrom, & Brock, 1981). Greenwald (1968) further proposed that persistence of persuasion depends upon the extent to which people can remember their cognitive reactions to the communication rather than their ability to remember the message arguments per se (see Love & Greenwald, 1978). The cognitive response approach has generated a considerable body of evidence consistent with the view that in certain situations people spontaneously produce evaluative thoughts during a message presentation, and that the favorability of these thoughts is a good predictor of postmessage attitudes and beliefs (see reviews by Eagly & Chaiken, 1984; Perloff & Brock, 1980; Petty & Cacioppo, 1986). Although coding cognitive responses into favorable, unfavorable, and neutral categories is the most popular system (see Cacioppo, Harkins, & Petty, 1981), other categorization schemes have proved useful. For example, research demonstrates that thoughts which link the message to the self are better predictors of attitudes than non-self-relevant thoughts (Shavitt & Brock, 1986).

Cognitive Responses in the Absence of a Message. Just as a person's thoughts in response to a persuasive message can determine the extent and direction of attitude change, so too can a person's thoughts in the *absence* of any external message. The powerful effects of getting people to generate their own persuasive messages were shown in early research on "role playing" (e.g., Janis & King, 1954; Watts, 1967). In this research, people were typically asked to act out certain roles (e.g., convince a friend to stop smoking) or generate a message on a certain topic, and the subsequent attitudes of these people were compared to those of control subjects who had either simply witnessed the role playing, passively listened to a communication, or received no message. A consistent result of this research was that active participation in the generation of a message was a successful strategy for producing attitude change, and that these changes tended to persist longer than changes based on passive exposure to the message (e.g., Elms, 1966). Role playing appears to be effective because in order to play the role, people think of arguments that are consistent with their assigned role—ignoring inconsistent arguments. In addition, people find their own arguments to be more original than those that are generated by others, and self-generated arguments are also more memorable (Greenwald & Albert, 1968; Slamecka & Graf, 1978). Presentation of arguments in public rather than in private increases the attitude change obtained from role playing. This might occur, for example, if people tried harder to generate good arguments in public (Tice, 1992).[6]

A person does not have to be asked explicitly to generate a message for self-persuasion to occur. For example, in an extensive series of studies, Tesser (1978) and his colleagues have studied the effects of merely asking someone to think about an issue, object, or person (see Tesser, Martin, & Mendolia, 1995, for a review). For example, in one early study, Sadler and Tesser (1973) introduced subjects to a likable or dislikable partner (via a tape recording). Some of the subjects were instructed to think about the partner, whereas others were distracted from doing so. The thinking manipulation made judgments of the partner more extreme. Specifically, enhanced thinking was associated with more favorable evaluations of the likable partner, but less favorable ratings of the dislikable partner.

Current research indicates that both more extreme (polarization) and less extreme (moderation) attitudes can result from mere thought. The polarization effect requires that subjects have a well-integrated and consistent knowledge structure to guide their thinking, and people must also be motivated to utilize their issue-relevant knowledge (Chaiken & Yates, 1985; Liberman & Chaiken, 1991; Tesser & Leone, 1977). When motivation to think is low or when the issue-relevant information in memory is inconsistent, mere thought is more likely to produce moderation than polarization in attitudes (e.g., Linville, 1982; Millar & Tesser, 1986a).

Two Routes to Persuasion

The cognitive response approach and research on self-generated attitude and belief change have demonstrated quite conclusively that active thought processes are often responsible for attitude change, and that self-generated change can be quite long lasting. Although the cognitive response approach in its broadest framework appears to provide a reasonable account of initial attitude change and its persistence, its focus on the very active and effortful cognitive evaluation of the message (or self-generation of arguments) implies that little attitude change is likely when active thinking about the message is low. Yet, a number of attitude change studies indicate that it might actually be easier to change people's attitudes when they have relatively little interest in or knowledge about the topic of the persuasive message. That is, change is relatively easy when the topic of the message is rather unimportant. If people do not engage in much thinking about messages on unimportant topics, active thinking would not be a requirement for attitude change (see Hovland, 1959; Johnson & Eagly, 1989; Petty & Cacioppo, 1986). How can change occur when thinking is low?

Central and Peripheral Routes to Persuasion. The *elaboration likelihood model* (ELM; Petty & Cacioppo, 1981, 1986) is a theory of persuasion that argues that both effortful and noneffortful processes can produce changes in attitudes (see also subsequent discussion of the heuristic/systematic model; Chaiken, Liberman, & Eagly, 1989). When people carefully and effortfully evaluate all of the information relevant to the merits of the advocated position, they are said to be following the *central route* to persuasion. Consistent with the cognitive response approach, the message recipient under the central route is actively generating favorable and/or unfavorable thoughts in response to the communication. The goal of this cognitive effort is to determine if the position advocated by the source has any merit. Because different people care about different things, and different situations provoke different concerns, what determines whether the arguments have any merit can vary with individual and situational factors. For example, as we noted in discussing the functional theories earlier in this chapter, people whose attitudes serve a social adjustment function are more persuaded by arguments that focus on the social benefits of the advocated position than are people whose attitudes do not serve this function (Snyder &

DeBono, 1987). Similarly, if people view themselves as religious, they are more persuaded by arguments framed in religious than in nonreligious (e.g., legalistic) terms (Cacioppo, Petty, & Sidera, 1982).

Rather than relying on individual differences in the extent to which certain dimensions of judgment are important, some research has demonstrated that different bases of judgment can be primed. Specifically, to examine whether the dimensions along which people evaluate the merits of attitude objects could be manipulated experimentally, college students were asked to evaluate political candidates who had positive attributes on one dimension (e.g., foreign policy) and negative attributes on another (e.g., the economy; see Sherman, Mackie, & Driscoll, 1990). Prior to judging the candidates, the subjects were required to memorize a list of words that were relevant to the foreign policy dimension (e.g., "overseas") or the economic dimension (e.g., "treasury"). This priming manipulation was designed to make one dimension of judgment more salient than the other. The results of this study showed that individuals for whom a particular dimension had been primed were more likely to base their evaluations of the candidates on information relevant to the primed dimension than on the other equally relevant but less accessible dimension. That is, when foreign policy was primed, subjects liked the candidate who had better credentials in foreign policy than economics, but when economics was primed, the reverse occurred.

It has been suggested that the news media can prime various dimensions of judgment by their coverage of news stories. If so, then if the news media play up crime stories during an election, how the candidates stand on the issue of crime will be a more important determinant of candidate evaluations than if the media had emphasized stories on poverty (see Iyengar, Kinder, Peters, & Krosnick, 1984). In any case, the end result of the information processing involved in the central route is typically an attitude that is well thought out and bolstered by supporting information on dimensions seen as central to the merits of the position advocated.

In contrast to the careful and effortful evaluation of information that takes place under the central route, attitudes can also be changed by a *peripheral route* without much thinking about information central to the merits of the attitude issue. The peripheral route recognizes that it is neither adaptive nor possible for people to invest a lot of mental effort thinking about all of the messages and attitude objects to which they are exposed. Much of the information we receive just isn't worth spending our time thinking about. Rather, in order to function in life, we must sometimes act as "lazy organisms" (McGuire, 1969) or "cognitive misers" (Taylor, 1981) and employ much simpler means of evaluation. The peripheral route characterizes attitude change as resulting from the operation of simple cues such as the mere presence of an expert source or the induction of a positive mood. Later in this chapter, some of the specific processes by which simple peripheral cues have their impact will be described, but for now it is sufficient to realize that attitude change via the peripheral route requires relatively little in the way of demanding cognitive effort.

It is best to view the central and the peripheral routes to persuasion as falling along a continuum of attitude change strategies that differ in the amount of effortful message evaluation they require. At one end of the continuum, the person puts virtually no effort into evaluating the message. If any change is produced, it is likely to be the result of very primitive evaluative processes such as those described in the forthcoming section on simple affective mechanisms of attitude change. At the other end of the continuum, people are carefully evaluating all of the information present in the communication context in an attempt to assess the true merits of the position offered. When aspects of the communication, the recipient, and the communication context make the likelihood of effortful evaluation processes high, attitude change is said to occur by the central route. As the likelihood of careful issue-relevant thinking decreases, peripheral route processes become more important determinants of attitudes.

Assessing the Extent of Message Processing. Persuasion researchers have identified a number of ways to assess the extent to which effortful message processing is determining attitude change and thereby determine whether a person is likely to be following the central or the peripheral route to persuasion. One popular procedure has been to vary the quality of the arguments contained in a message and to determine the extent of message processing by the "effect size" of the argument quality manipulation (Petty, Wells, & Brock, 1976; see Johnson & Turco, 1994, for a review).[7] That is, if a variable increases the extent of argument processing, then people's attitudes should be more influenced by the quality of the arguments in the message than if argument processing is low. On the other hand, if a variable decreases the extent of message processing, people's attitudes should be less influenced by the quality of the arguments than if message processing is high. So, if a variable such as distraction decreases thinking about a message, increasing distraction should be good for persuasion (i.e., it will increase attitude change) when the arguments are weak because people, by being distracted from thinking about the arguments, should be less likely to realize the flaws in the message. That is, distraction will disrupt the normal counterarguing of the message thereby increasing its effectiveness. On the other hand, increasing distraction should be bad for persuasion if the arguments are strong because by disrupting thinking about strong arguments, people should be less likely to discover how cogent the arguments are. That is, the normal process of generating favorable thoughts to the message will be disrupted. When researchers first began to test their variables (e.g., external distraction; Petty, Wells, & Brock, 1976) along with a manipulation of argument quality, they began to discover that some variables could either increase or decrease persuasion by influencing the extent of message processing.

In addition to the argument quality procedure, a number of other methods for assessing effortful message processing have been used. For example, investigators have examined the number and profile of thoughts (cognitive responses) generated in response to a message (Petty, Ostrom, & Brock, 1981). As argument processing is increased, people sometimes generate a greater number of message-relevant thoughts (e.g., Burnkrant & Howard, 1984) or thoughts that better reflect the quality of the arguments presented (e.g., Harkins & Petty,

1981). Also, correlations between message-relevant thoughts and postmessage attitudes tend to be greater when argument scrutiny is high (e.g., Chaiken, 1980; Petty & Cacioppo, 1979b).

Motivation versus Ability. According to the ELM, there are many variables (e.g., distraction) capable of affecting the likelihood of thinking about the central merits of an issue (i.e., the elaboration likelihood) and thereby determine the route to persuasion. Some variables affect a person's *motivation* to think about issue-relevant information, whereas others affect their *ability* to do so. Some variables are part of the persuasion *situation*, whereas others are part of the *person*. Some variables affect mostly the *extent* of information-processing activity (i.e., the overall amount of thinking a person does), whereas others tend to influence the *direction* of whatever thinking is taking place (i.e., whether the thoughts elicited are relatively favorable or unfavorable). Table 6.1 illustrates variables falling into each cell of this 2 (motivation vs. ability) × 2 (situation vs. person) × 2 (extent vs. direction of thinking) matrix. We review some of the most important variables falling into each of these categories next.

Motivation to Think. Perhaps the most important variable influencing a person's motivation to think about a message is the perceived personal relevance or importance of the communication (Petty & Cacioppo, 1979b). Personal or self-relevance can stem from a variety of sources such as the attitude object being linked to values, outcomes, groups, possessions, or the people that are important to the message recipient (Boninger, Krosnick, & Berent, in press; Johnson & Eagly, 1989; Petty, Cacioppo, & Haugtvedt, 1992). When the personal importance of an issue is high, people are motivated to scrutinize the information in a message, and attitude change is based largely on the quality of the arguments presented in support of the issue (Leippe & Elkin, 1987; Petty & Cacioppo, 1979b, 1990). That is, increasing self-relevance leads to more persuasion when the message arguments are strong, but less persuasion when the message arguments are weak. Merely changing the pronouns in a message to

TABLE 6.1. Individual and Situational Variables That Motivate or Enable Relatively Objective or Relatively Biased Thinking about a Message

	Motivational Factors		Ability Factors	
	Situational	Individual	Situational	Individual
Extent of processing	Induced personal relevance	Need for cognition	External distraction	General intelligence
Direction of processing	Forewarning of intent to persuade	Open/closed-mindedness	Instructed head movements	Attitude-congruent knowledge

enhance self-relevance (e.g., saying "you will benefit" versus "people will benefit") can produce the same results (Burnkrant & Unnava, 1989) as can enhancing self-awareness by placing message recipients in front of a mirror (Hutton & Baumeister, 1992).

When personal relevance is low, argument scrutiny is reduced and attitudes are affected more by variables serving as peripheral cues such as the status, likability, or attractiveness of the message endorsers. That is, when relevance is low, people might decide to forgo an effortful analysis of the reasons behind the advocacy and agree with someone simply because the source is attractive or expert. For example, in one study undergraduates were told that their university was considering implementing a comprehensive exam that would have to be passed in order for them to graduate (Petty, Cacioppo, & Goldman, 1981). Half of the students were told that the exam was being considered for implementation next year, in which case it would be highly relevant to them. The other half were told that the proposal was for 10 years in the future and therefore would be of no personal importance whatsoever. In addition, half of the students heard strong arguments and half heard weak arguments in favor of the proposal. Finally, half of the students learned that the proposal was endorsed by a high credibility source (a professor of education at Princeton University), whereas half learned that the proposal was endorsed by a low credibility source (a student in a local high school class).

As the results depicted in Figure 6.3 show, when the issue was of high relevance, attitudes were influenced mostly by the quality of the arguments in the message (see top panel of Figure 6.3). When the issue was of low relevance, however, the students devoted relatively little effort to thinking about the message arguments. Instead, their attitudes were based mostly on the expertise of the message source (see bottom panel of Figure 6.3). In sum, when the exam policy would have an impact on the students evaluating the proposal, their attitudes toward it were quite reasonable. That is, the students went along with the exam policy even if it was endorsed only by a high school student, as long as the arguments were compelling. They rejected the policy if the arguments were weak even if it was endorsed by an expert. When the policy was irrelevant to them and would only affect future students, the results were completely different. In this case, the current students thought that the exam policy was a good idea even if the arguments were rather lame, as long as the policy was endorsed by a highly credible source. They rejected the policy if it was endorsed by a high school student even if the arguments were quite good. Such are the dangers of having uninvolved people make decisions via the peripheral route.

Of course, variables other than personal relevance can modify a person's motivation to think carefully about a message. For example, people are more motivated to scrutinize information when they believe that they are individually responsible for evaluating the message (Petty, Harkins, & Williams, 1980) and when they are uniquely accountable (Tetlock, 1983) rather than when they share responsibility with other people. Increasing the number of message sources can enhance information-processing activity (e.g., Harkins & Petty, 1981), especially when the sources are viewed as providing their own indepen-

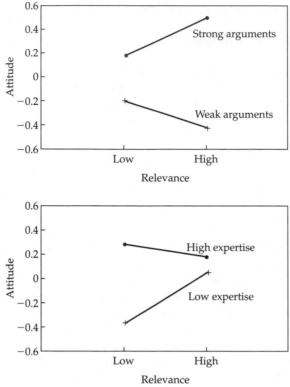

FIGURE 6.3. The effects of involvement, argument quality, and source expertise on attitudes. The top panel shows that high involvement led to greater scrutiny of the arguments than low involvement. The bottom panel shows that low involvement led to greater reliance on source expertise than high involvement.
Figure reprinted by permission from Petty, Cacioppo, & Goldman, 1981.

dent assessments of the issue (Harkins & Petty, 1987). Various incongruities, inconsistencies, and surprises can also increase information-processing activity such as when an expert source presents surprisingly weak arguments (Maheswanan & Chaiken, 1991) or when message recipients learn that a majority of people supports a position that initially seems bad or a minority of people endorses a position that initially seems quite good (Baker & Petty, 1994).

In addition to factors associated with the persuasive message or the persuasion context, there are individual differences in people's motivation to think about persuasive communications. As the quotes at the start of this chapter suggest, some people like to engage in thoughtful cognitive activities, but others do not. The former individuals are described as being high in "need for cognition," whereas the latter are low in this trait (Cacioppo & Petty, 1982). People high in need for cognition tend to form attitudes on the basis of the quality of the arguments in a message, thereby following the central route to persuasion (Cacioppo, Petty, & Morris, 1983). People who do not enjoy thinking are more reliant on simple peripheral cues in the persuasion context such as whether the source is credible or attractive (Axsom, Yates, & Chaiken, 1987; Haugtvedt, Petty, & Cacioppo, 1992).

Another individual difference that is relevant is the "need for closure" (Kruglanski, 1989). People who are high in the need for closure want very quick answers and dislike being without an answer for any length of time. Thus, if these individuals do not have an opinion on an issue, they are likely to accept the first reasonable position offered. On the other hand, if they already have an opinion, they are likely to freeze on this response and change little even in response to cogent persuasive arguments (Krulanski, Webster, & Klem, 1993).

Ability to Think. Just as motivational variables can influence the amount of thinking about a message, so too can variables associated with a person's ability. Among the important variables influencing a person's ability to process issue-relevant arguments is message repetition. Repeating a message a few times gives a person a greater opportunity to think about the arguments (e.g., Cacioppo & Petty, 1989). This will prove beneficial for persuasion as long as the arguments are strong and the arguments are not repeated so often that people get tired of them (e.g., Batra & Ray, 1986; Cacioppo & Petty, 1979). If external distractions are present (e.g., Petty, Wells, & Brock, 1976) or the speaker speaks quite rapidly (Moore, Hausknecht, & Thamodaran, 1986; Smith & Shaffer, 1991), argument elaboration is reduced. As explained previously, reducing thinking about a message is beneficial for persuasion when the message would have been easily counterargued, but is harmful if the message would normally have elicited favorable thoughts. People are also generally better able to process messages that appear in print than messages on radio or TV because people can typically control the pace of written messages (Chaiken & Eagly, 1976; Wright, 1980). On the other hand, placing time pressures on processing (e.g., Kruglanski & Freund, 1983), enhancing physiological arousal via exercise (e.g., Sanbonmatsu & Kardes, 1988), or rendering the message difficult to understand (e.g., Ratneshwar & Chaiken, 1991) reduces ability to process and increases reliance on simple cues.

Just as there are individual differences in motivation to think about messages, there are also individual differences in the ability of people to think about a persuasive communication. For example, as general knowledge about a topic increases, people become more able and perhaps more motivated to think about issue-relevant arguments (Wood, Rhodes, & Biek, 1995).[8] Knowledge is only effective in helping people to process to the extent that it is accessible, however (e.g., Brucks, Armstrong, & Goldberg, 1988). When knowledge is low or inaccessible, people are more reliant on simple cues (e.g., Alba & Hutchinson, 1987; Wood & Kallgren, 1988). For example, in one study (Wood, Kallgren, & Preisler, 1985), people who were knowledgeable about environmental preservation were influenced by the quality of the arguments in an environmental message, but people who had little knowledge about the environment were influenced by the mere length of the arguments (i.e., how wordy they were) without respect to their quality. As we explain further below, the low knowledge individuals, being relatively unable (or unmotivated) to evaluate the quality of the arguments, might have relied instead on a reasonable persuasion rule or heuristic: The longer the arguments, the better they must be (Chaiken, 1987).

Combining Variables. It is important to note that in most communication settings, a combination of factors determines the nature of information-processing activity that takes place rather than just one variable acting in isolation. For example, using a rhetorical question to end an argument (e.g., "Therefore, wouldn't a tax increase help the national debt?") rather than a statement (e.g., "Therefore, a tax increase would help the national debt.") increases thinking about the arguments in the message when people normally would not be motivated to engage in such thinking. That is, asking a question motivates thought that would not normally take place. On the other hand, if people are already motivated to think about the message, then the use of rhetorical questions actually disrupts the normal processing of the message (e.g., see Petty, Cacioppo, & Heesacker, 1981).

Biases in Information Processing. The variables discussed above, such as distraction or need for cognition, tend to influence information-processing activity in a relatively objective manner. That is, all else being equal, distraction tends to disrupt whatever thoughts a person is thinking. If a person is thinking mostly negative thoughts to the message, negative thoughts will be disrupted and persuasion will be increased. If positive thoughts dominate, then positive thoughts are disrupted and persuasion is decreased (Petty, Wells, & Brock, 1976). The distraction does not specifically target one type of thought to disrupt. Similarly, individuals who are high in need for cognition are more motivated to think in general than people low in need for cognition. They are not more motivated to think certain kinds of thoughts (Cacioppo, Petty, & Morris, 1983).

Ability versus Motivation to Be Biased. Consider what happens when a person is asked to evaluate two opposing communications (e.g., one favoring capital punishment and one opposing it). Following analysis of both sides of the issue, people tend to see the message favoring their own position as the more compelling message (Lord, Ross, & Lepper, 1979), and this biased outcome is especially likely when the person's own attitude on the topic is quite strong (Houston & Fazio, 1989). If the messages people receive to process are actually perfectly balanced, why would a biased outcome result?

First, consider the fact that the information in people's heads is not likely to be perfectly balanced. Rather, people tend to have more information in memory that supports their attitudes than information that contradicts it. Because of this, the outcome of message processing might be biased simply because the person's existing knowledge structure enables the person to more easily retrieve information opposing (counterarguing) the message inconsistent with his or her attitude and retrieve information supportive of the attitude-congruent communication. In this case, the biased judgmental outcome results from the relatively unbiased retrieval of information in memory that is biased (Petty & Cacioppo, 1986).

Biased outcomes can also occur primarily for motivational reasons, however. For example, people might be threatened by a message opposing their viewpoint, and thus they might be motivated to marshal all of the evidence and arguments they can retrieve from memory to defend their attitudes. Even if the arguments and facts in their own memories were as balanced as the arguments and facts in the two conflicting messages, people could selectively retrieve information to counterargue the opposing message and bolster the supporting one. Following such motivated biased processing, the supporting message would seem stronger than the opposing one.[9]

A number of general motivations have been linked to biased information processing. Many of these biasing motives stem from some threat to the self such as to self-esteem, to social status, or to the person's freedom to hold certain beliefs and attitudes (i.e., "reactance"; Brehm, 1966). For example, when people are forewarned of a speaker's explicit intent to change their attitudes on a self-relevant topic, they become motivated to *counterargue* the message rather than process it objectively (Petty & Cacioppo, 1979a; see also Liberman & Chaiken, 1992). Perhaps the most studied motive that is postulated to bias information processing is the motive to maintain consistency among one's attitudes, beliefs, emotions, and behaviors, and it is to this motive that we turn next.

Cognitive Dissonance Theory. Of the various theories proposing a motive to maintain cognitive consistency (e.g., Heider, 1958; Kiesler, 1971; Osgood & Tannenbaum, 1955; Rosenberg, 1960), the most prominent is the theory of *cognitive dissonance* (Festinger, 1957, 1964). In Festinger's original formulation of the theory, two elements in a cognitive system (e.g., a belief and an attitude; an attitude and a behavior) were said to be *consonant* if one followed from the other such as "I'm attractive" and "I have many dates." The elements were *dissonant* if one belief implies the opposite of the other such as "I'm attractive" and "I date infrequently." Of course, two elements could also be *irrelevant* to each other such as "I'm attractive" and "The rain in Spain stays mainly on the plain." Festinger proposed that the psychological state of dissonance was aversive and that people would be motivated to reduce it.

Dissonance theorists have proposed a number of ways to reduce dissonance. For example, the person who thinks he is attractive but has few dates could restore consistency by changing one of the dissonant elements. One possibility is for the person to come to believe that he is not really attractive. Although this would certainly reduce the inconsistency, it is unlikely that this would make the person feel any better! Alternatively, the person could redouble his efforts to date. If successful, this would reduce the dissonance. Strategies other than changing the dissonant elements are also possible. For example, the person could try to minimize the importance of one of the cognitions. If dating (or one's attractiveness) comes to be seen as very unimportant, for instance, then the inconsistency would be less bothersome. Alternatively, the person could try to generate cognitions that make the dissonant elements consistent with each other. For example, if the person reasoned, "I'm choosy," this would be consistent with being attractive (since attractive people are expected to be more choosy than unattractive people), and would also be consistent with having few dates.

Researchers have studied a variety of situations in which people's behavior is brought into conflict with an attitude or belief thereby inducing dissonance (see Brehm & Cohen, 1962). For example, one common way of producing dissonance in the laboratory is by inducing a person to write an essay that is inconsistent with the person's attitude under high choice conditions and with little incentive (e.g., Zanna & Cooper, 1974). Because behavior is usually difficult to undo, dissonance can be reduced by changing beliefs and attitudes to bring them into line with the behavior (i.e., "I wouldn't have written this essay unless I believed what I was saying").

In perhaps the most famous dissonance experiment, students at Stanford University were induced to engage in the quite boring task of turning pegs on a board (Festinger & Carlsmith, 1959). Following this, some of the students were told that the experimenter's assistant was absent today, and they were asked to take his place and try to convince a waiting subject that the peg-turning task was actually quite interesting and exciting. Some of these students were informed that they would be paid $1 for assuming this role, and others were told that the pay was $20. After agreeing to serve as the accomplice and talking to the waiting student, all subjects reported to a psychology department secretary who gave them a presumably standard department survey that asked how interesting they found the experimental task to be. As expected by dissonance theory, the subjects who received only $1 rated the task as more interesting than the subjects who received $20. This result was expected because the $1 subjects had insufficient justification for their behavior, whereas the $20 subjects had sufficient justification, and thus no dissonance.

A large number of studies have examined dissonance theory predictions in a wide variety of both laboratory and real-world situations. The results of these studies were quite intriguing because the findings typically were opposite to what people would normally expect. For example, dissonance theorists have discovered that people will come to like a boring group more the more unpleasant the initiation required to get into the group (i.e., "I wouldn't have endured that horribly embarrassing initiation if the group wasn't worthwhile"; Aronson & Mills, 1959). People were found to report liking an exotic food more the more dislikable the person was who induced them to try the food (i.e., "I couldn't have eaten the grasshopper to please this obnoxious person; it must be that I like the taste of grasshoppers"; Zimbardo, Weisenberg, Firestone, & Levy, 1965). Also, it was found that people's evaluations of two objects were greater after a choice between them than before the choice took place. For example, after inducing people to make a decision between two attractive consumer products, people came to like the product they selected more than they did before the choice and came to dislike the product they rejected more than before the choice (i.e., "I wouldn't have selected the toaster over the blender unless it really was better"; Brehm, 1966).

Although it is now clear that many of the situations described by Festinger as inducing dissonance produce the physiological changes and perceptions of "unpleasant tension" expected by the theory (Elkin & Leippe, 1986; Losch & Cacioppo, 1990; see Fazio & Cooper, 1983), it is also clear that the mere performance of an inconsistent action does not always produce dissonance. Thus, the focus of current research has been on understanding the precise cause of the tension that sometimes accompanies inconsistent behavior.

Some theorists have questioned Festinger's view that inconsistency per se produces tension in people, but rather have suggested that it is necessary for people to believe that they have freely chosen to bring about some foreseeable negative consequence for themselves or other people (e.g., Cooper & Fazio, 1984). Thus, if telling a waiting subject that a boring task is interesting (Festinger & Carlsmith, 1959) results in no harmful consequence (e.g., because the waiting subject doesn't believe you), there is no dissonance. But if the harmful consequences are high (e.g., the waiting subject decides to stay and participate in the experiment rather than study for his chemistry final), dissonance occurs and attitude change toward the task results (see Calder, Ross, & Insko, 1973). Other theorists argue that inconsistency is involved, but the inconsistency must concern a critical aspect of oneself or a threat to one's positive self-concept (e.g., Aronson, 1968; Greenwald & Ronis, 1978; Thibodeau & Aronson, 1992).

Interestingly, theorists from both camps have argued that proattitudinal advocacy (making a speech that is consistent with one's attitudes) can also produce dissonance under certain conditions. Advocates of the negative consequences view argue that proattitudinal advocacy can induce dissonance if the proattitudinal advocacy ends up having negative consequences (Scher & Cooper, 1989). Advocates of the self-inconsistency view also argue that proattitudinal advocacy can produce dissonance if as a result of the advocacy people feel hypocritical (which threatens self-esteem). For example, consider a college student who is induced to videotape a speech advocating safe sex. Since the student actually believes in safe sex, there is no inconsistency. However, what if the person is subsequently reminded that he or she often fails to engage in safe sex? In one study (Stone, Aronson, Crain, Winslow, & Fried, 1994), 83 percent of students induced to feel hypocritical about their own safe sex practices in this way purchased condoms when given the opportunity to do so. Only 42 percent of the students in the nonhypocrisy groups (i.e., those who didn't give the speech, were not reminded of past unsafe practices, or both) purchased condoms.

Although research has supported both the negative consequences and the self-inconsistency predictions, disentangling these viewpoints has proved difficult. The reason for this is that each framework generally can accommodate the results generated by the other. The conceptual problem stems from the fact that freely choosing to bring about negative consequences is clearly inconsistent with most people's views of themselves as rational, caring individuals. That is, choosing to bring about negative consequences is inconsistent with one's positive self-view. However, it is also true that when people do something inconsistent with their positive self-views, the resulting feeling of guilt, shame, stupidity, or hypocrisy is an aversive consequence. That is, by choosing to violate one's self-view, one has freely chosen to bring about an aversive outcome.

A third viewpoint on the causes of dissonance is provided by self-affirmation theory (Steele, 1988; see also Baumeister, Chapter 3). According to this framework, dissonance is not produced by inconsistency per se, being responsible for negative consequences, or the distress of self-inconsistency, but rather stems from a violation of self-integrity (see also Tesser & Cornell, 1991). According to this viewpoint, actions produce dissonance only when the behavior threatens one's "moral and adaptive adequacy" (Steele & Spencer, 1991). The self-consistency and self-affirmation points of view have much in common. For example, they agree that if people are given an opportunity to restore or bolster their self-esteem in some manner following a dissonant behavior, dissonance reducing attitude change is less likely. The self-esteem and self-affirmation points of view differ, however, in their predictions of whether high or low self-esteem people should be more susceptible to dissonance effects. In brief, the self-consistency point of view argues that high self-esteem individuals would experience the most dissonance by engaging in esteem threatening behavior because such actions are most inconsistent with their favorable self-conceptions (i.e., good people should do good things, not act like hypocrites). The self-affirmation point of view suggests that low self-esteem individuals should show stronger dissonance effects because high self-esteem individuals can more easily restore self-integrity by thinking about the many positive traits they have. Unfortunately, the research evidence on this question is mixed, with some studies showing greater dissonance effects for low self-esteem individuals (Steele, Spencer, & Lynch, 1993), and other studies showing greater dissonance effects for high self-esteem persons (Gerard, Blevans, & Malcolm, 1964).

In sum, whether dissonance results from the production of aversive consequences, inconsistent self-actions, threats to self-integrity, or some other mechanism, dissonance can result in a reanalysis of the reasons why a person engaged in a certain behavior or made a certain choice, and cause a person to rethink the merits of an attitude object. The end result of this effortful but biased cognitive activity can be a change in attitude toward the object.

Peripheral Route to Attitude Change

In the central route to persuasion, the presumption is that attitude change results from actively considering the merits of the position being advocated. That is, people receive and elaborate arguments, or generate reasons to explain or justify some outcome or behavior. Sometimes this effortful thinking proceeds in a relatively objective manner, but at other times it is clearly biased. In either case, however, the person is engaged in an active processing of all of the issue-relevant information presented.

On the other hand, as we have already noted, attitudes can also be changed as a result of various peripheral cues in the persuasion setting if the motivation or ability to engage in effortful cognitive activity is low. We have not yet explained the mechanisms or processes by which peripheral cues influence attitudes, however. The theories that we discuss next postulate a number of specific peripheral processes. Although many of these peripheral route theories initially proposed that the process involved was quite general, subsequent research has revealed that these peripheral processes tend to operate most strongly when the likelihood of issue-relevant thinking is low. We begin with theories that emphasize relatively simple inference and heuristic processes, and conclude with theories that emphasize relatively simple affective (emotional) processes.

Simple Cognitive Mechanisms: Inferences and Heuristics.

Attribution Approach. As described by Gilbert (Chapter 4), the 1970s brought tremendous interest in examining how people come to understand the causes of their own and other people's behaviors. In his *self-perception theory,* Bem (1972) reasoned that just as people assume that the behavior of other people and the context in which it occurs provides information about the presumed attitudes of these people, so too would a person's own behavior provide information about the person's own attitude. For example, what if you saw Fred come into a room where an experimenter offered him $1000 to smash his tennis racquet? Fred smashes away. Then you see Alice come into the same room, and the experimenter offers her 50¢ to smash her racquet. She complies. Now you are asked to guess which person liked their tennis racquet more. The most reasonable guess that you could make is that Alice liked her racquet less than Fred. After all, Alice destroyed her racquet for a mere 50¢, whereas it took $1000 to get Fred to destroy his racquet. Of course, we can't know what Fred would have done if he had been offered 50¢, but our most reasonable inference based on the evidence at hand is that Alice likes her racquet less than Fred. Now recall the dissonance experiment described previously in which people were induced to say a boring task was interesting for either $1 or $20 (Festinger & Carlsmith, 1959). What if you were an observer to this study? Who would you think really thought the task was more interesting? Just as in the tennis racquet example, it is reasonable to infer that the person paid less agrees with what he or she said more because this person didn't need as much incentive to engage in the behavior. Bem suggested that if you were engaged in the task, you would make the same inference about your own attitude as would a reasonable outside observer.[10]

During much of the 1970s, self-perception theory was thought to provide an alternative account of dissonance effects (Bem, 1972). Subsequent research indicated, however, that both dissonance and self-perception processes operate, but in different domains. In particular, the underlying tension mechanism of dissonance theory operates when a person engages in discrepant actions that are disagreeable or aversive (e.g., advocating a discrepant position in one's latitude of rejection; Fazio, Zanna, & Cooper, 1977; performing self-deprecating behavior; Jones, Rhodewalt, Berglas, & Skelton, 1981), whereas self-perception processes are more likely when a person engages in discrepant actions that are more agreeable (e.g., advocating a discrepant position in one's latitude of acceptance; Fazio, Zanna, & Cooper, 1977; performing a self-enhancing behavior; Jones, Rhodewalt, Berglas, & Skelton, 1981).

Self-perception theory also accounts for some unique attitudinal phenomena. For example, the *overjustification effect* occurs when a person is provided with more than sufficient reward for engaging in an action that is already highly regarded (e.g., Crano, Gorenflo, & Shackelford, 1988; Lepper, Greene, & Nisbett, 1973). Thus, overjustification could occur if a young child was "induced" by the promise of an ice-cream cone to attend a favorite Disney movie. To the extent that the child comes to attribute attending the movie to the ice-cream cone rather than to his or her own intrinsic enjoyment of Disney movies, attitudes toward the movie would be less favorable than for a child who was not overinduced to attend the film (Deci, 1975).

According to the ELM, people should be more likely to rely on the relatively simple self-perception inference process when well-defined attitudes are not very accessible, or the elaboration likelihood is low (see Tybout & Scott, 1983). For example, Wood (1982) examined the power of self-perception processes for people who had relatively high versus low knowledge and experience with the issue of environmental preservation. In this research, students committed themselves to deliver a speech that was consistent with their attitudes after learning that they would receive either $5 or nothing for the task. Following this, they expressed their opinions on the issue. The major result was that an overjustification effect occurred only for subjects with low knowledge and experience. That is, the $5 incentive undermined their positive attitudes (e.g., "I must have made the proenvironmental statements for the money"), but for high knowledge subjects, the incentive had no effect (see also Chaiken & Baldwin, 1981).

The attribution approach has also been useful in understanding how people make inferences about relatively simple cues. For example, Eagly, Chaiken, and Wood (1981) have argued that people often approach a persuasion situation with some expectation regarding the particular position that the communicator will take. According to this model, if the premessage expectation about the position to be taken is confirmed by the communicator's presentation, such as when a bank president says to open a savings account at his bank, little persuasion occurs because the recipient attributes the message to whatever assumptions generated the expectation (e.g., people say things in their self-interest). In such cases, you can't be sure the message is valid, and if you are interested in finding out, you will need to carefully scrutinize the message arguments. However, when the premessage expectation is disconfirmed, such as when a bank president says to open a savings account at another bank, the communicator is seen as being relatively honest and trustworthy, and persuasion is increased without the need to process message arguments (e.g., Eagly, Wood, & Chaiken, 1978). People who don't enjoy thinking (i.e., those low in need for cognition) are especially likely to avoid processing when disconfirmed expectancies lead them to believe that the source is trustworthy (Priester & Petty, in press).

The Heuristic/Systematic Model. Like the attributional framework developed by Eagly and her colleagues, Chaiken's *heuristic/systematic model* of persuasion (HSM) represents an explicit attempt to explain *why* certain peripheral cues such as source expertise or message length have the impact that they do (Chaiken, 1987; Chaiken, Liberman, & Eagly, 1989). In particular, the HSM focuses on heuristics or general persuasion rules that provide a relatively simple way of determining message validity. That is, Chaiken proposes that in contrast to the effortful "systematic" (or central route) processes, many source, message, and other cues are evaluated by means of simple schemas or cognitive heuristics that people have learned on the basis of past experience and observation. To the extent that various persuasion rules of thumb, such as "experts are correct," are available in memory and retrieved, they can help people to evaluate persuasive communications.

According to the HSM, the likelihood of systematic processing increases whenever confidence in one's attitude drops below the level of confidence that is desired (the "sufficiency threshold"). Whenever actual confidence equals or exceeds desired confidence, however, heuristic processing is more likely since there is little motivation to obtain additional information. For example, when motivation or ability to think is low, people could base their acceptance of a message on the mere number of arguments contained in it by invoking the heuristic "the more arguments in favor of something, the more valid it is" (a length implies strength heuristic; Alba & Marmorstein, 1987; Petty & Cacioppo, 1984).

Although some research has varied the accessibility (Roskos-Weoldsen & Fazio, 1992) or vividness (Pallak, 1983) of the heuristic (peripheral) cues in a message, relatively little research has attempted to explicitly test the HSM by determining if peripheral cues work (at least sometimes) by invoking heuristics from memory. Chaiken (1987) reports the most pertinent investigations. In four studies she and her colleagues attempted to make certain decision rules more accessible, and then track their influence on attitudes following message exposure. The general pattern of these studies supported the utility of the heuristic idea. For example, in one study subjects in the experimental condition memorized eight phrases relevant to the length implies strength heuristic (e.g., "the more the merrier"), whereas control subjects memorized eight irrelevant phrases. Subsequently, subjects received a message from a speaker who claimed to have either ten or two reasons in support of mandatory comprehensive exams for seniors. Subjects in the study were also divided into those with high and low need for cognition (Cacioppo & Petty, 1982). The only group to be influenced significantly by the peripheral number cue (i.e., claim of ten versus two reasons) was the low need for cognition subjects who had been primed with the relevant phrases. Thus, it is plausible that some peripheral cues have an impact on attitudes by invoking an appropriate persuasion heuristic.[11]

Simple Affective Mechanisms: Conditioning, Priming, and Mere Exposure. The attribution and heuristic approaches focus on simple cognitive inferences that can modify attitudes. Next, we discuss some approaches that emphasize the role of relatively simple affective processes in attitude change.

Classical Conditioning and Affective Priming. One of the most direct ways of associating "affect" with objects, issues, or people is through classical conditioning. In brief, as in Pavlov's (1927) pioneering research, conditioning occurs when a target stimulus (the conditioned stimulus such as a bell; CS) is associated with another stimulus (the unconditioned stimulus such as food; UCS) that is connected directly or through prior learning to some response (the unconditioned response such as salivation; UCR). By pairing the UCS (food) with the CS (bell), the CS becomes able to elicit a conditioned response (salivation) that is similar to the UCR (see McSweeney & Bierly, 1984).

A large number of studies have shown that people's attitudes can be influenced by pairing some target object with some stimulus about which the person already feels positively or negatively or placing the target object in some context that induces positive or negative feelings. For example, people's evaluations of words, other people, political slogans, consumer products, and persuasive communications have been modified by pairing them with such affect-producing stimuli as unpleasant odors, electric shock, harsh sounds, pleasant pictures, and happy and sad films (e.g., Staats & Staats, 1958; Zanna, Kiesler, & Pilkonis, 1970).

Even relatively simple muscle movements made in the presence of some target stimulus can influence one's attitude toward the stimulus if those movements are associated with agreement/disagreement (cognitive evaluation), pleasantness/unpleasantness (affective evaluation), or approach/avoidance (behavioral evaluation). For example, research shows that people tend to be naturally inclined to nod their heads up and down when they agree with something and from side to side when they dislike something (Darwin, 1872; Eibl-Eibesfeldt, 1972). People smile when they are feeling happiness, but frown when they experience displeasure (Ekman, 1971). People move pleasant stimuli toward them more quickly than unpleasant stimuli, and move unpleasant stimuli away from them more quickly than pleasant stimuli (Solarz, 1960). These findings suggest that these muscle movements might serve as effective conditioning stimuli. Consistent with this notion, research has found that if you get people to make the muscular movements associated with nodding their heads up and down (Wells & Petty, 1980), smiling (Strack, Martin, & Stepper, 1988), or moving objects toward them (Cacioppo, Priester, & Berntson, 1993) during exposure to some target stimulus, they subsequently report agreeing with or liking the stimulus more so than if they had been shaking their heads from side to side, frowning, or flexing the muscles associated with moving the object away from them during exposure to the stimulus.

According to the ELM, people should be especially susceptible to the simple transfer of affect when the likelihood of thinking about the merits of the object is rather low. Consistent with the notion that little or no thinking is needed for affective association to occur, classical conditioning effects have been reduced as the target stimulus becomes easier to think about. For example, in one pertinent experiment, subjects were exposed to initially neutral words (e.g., *chair*) and nonwords (e.g., *raich*) while receiving electric shock either immediately after the words, immediately after the nonwords, or randomly (Cacioppo, Marshall-Goodell, Tassinary, & Petty, 1992). Conditioning was more effective for the items (i.e., nonwords) for which subjects had no preexisting knowledge or associations. That is, conditioning became more effective as the elaboration likelihood was decreased.

In a procedure that bears some similarity to classical conditioning, subjects are presented with some emotion-inducing material just prior to (rather than after or during) receipt of the target stimulus so that positive or negative affect is primed and might therefore influence reactions to any subsequent stimuli. This "backward conditioning" or "affective priming" procedure has also proved successful in modifying attitudes. In one study, for example, subjects were shown a series of nine photos of a target person going about normal daily activities (e.g., getting into a car; Krosnick, Betz, Jussim, & Lynn, 1992). Just prior to each picture of the target person, subjects were exposed to a subliminal photo that was pretested to elicit positive (e.g., a group of smiling friends) or negative (e.g., a bucket of snakes) affect. Subjects exposed to the positive subliminal slides rated the target person more favorably than subjects exposed to the negative slides. It may surprise you to learn that this affective priming procedure works better when the emotional primes are presented outside of conscious awareness (see Murphy & Zajonc, 1993). This is consistent, however, with the notion that simple affective processes work better when the likelihood of thinking about the primes, the targets, and their relationship is low.

Mere Exposure. Another way to modify attitudes through simple affective means is merely to expose a person to a stimulus several times. In a series of studies, Zajonc (1968) demonstrated that presenting the same object to people on multiple occasions (mere exposure) increased liking for the object (Zajonc & Markus, 1982). The most recent work on the mere exposure phenomenon indicates that simple repetition of objects can lead to more positive evaluations even when people do not recognize that they have seen the objects before. In one study, for example, Kunst-Wilson and Zajonc (1980) presented pictures of various shapes to subjects multiple times under conditions where subjects could not consciously recognize the shapes. During a later session, the subjects were shown pairs of shapes under ideal viewing conditions. In each pair, one shape had been seen in the earlier session, but the other was new. Subjects were asked which shape they liked better and which one they had seen before. Even though subjects were unable to recognize beyond chance which of the shapes was new and which was old, they showed a significant preference for the "old" over the new shapes. That is, mere exposure to the shapes increased liking for them.

Mere exposure effects have been shown for other stimuli such as tones, nonsense syllables, Chinese ideograms, photographs of faces, and foreign words (see Bornstein, 1989, for a review). It is interesting to note that all of these stimuli tend to be unfamiliar and thus are relatively unlikely to elicit much thinking. In fact, the simple affective process induced by mere exposure appears to be more successful in influencing attitudes when processing of the repeated stimuli is minimal (Obermiller, 1985) or impossible because the stimuli are presented subliminally (Bornstein & D'Agostino, 1992). When more meaningful stimuli have been repeated such as words or sentences, mere exposure effects have been less common. Instead, when effortful cognitive processing occurs with repetition, the increased exposures enhance the dominant cognitive response to the stimulus. Thus, attitudes toward negative words (e.g., *hate*) and weak message arguments become more unfavorable, but attitudes toward positive words (e.g., *love*) and strong arguments become more favorable, at least until the point of tedium (e.g., Cacioppo & Petty, 1989; Grush, 1976). That is, when the stimulus is meaningful, repetition increases the likelihood of thinking about the merits of the stimulus.

In sum, like studies of classical conditioning, research on mere exposure shows that this simple affective process is most likely to influence attitudes for low knowledge, low relevance, and/or initially meaningless attitude objects or issues. This does not mean, of course, that affect will influence attitudes only when the elaboration likelihood is low. As we will see shortly, affect can modify attitudes when the elaboration likelihood is higher. However, the underlying processes of change are different.

Multiple Roles for Variables in the ELM

Our discussion of central and peripheral processes makes it clear that variables can influence persuasion in a number of ways. That is, we have focused on how some features of a persuasion setting influence either the motivation or the ability to think about the merits of an advocated position. Other features of the persuasion setting impart a motivational or an ability bias to the information-processing activity. Still other features serve as simple cues that encourage attitude change by some peripheral process in the absence of much thinking about any substantive arguments presented. One of the powerful but complex aspects of the elaboration likelihood model is its recognition that any one variable (e.g., the attractiveness of the message source) can serve in multiple roles (Petty & Cacioppo, 1986). That is, a variable can influence attitudes by different processes in different situations. The fact that any one variable can have the same impact on judgments by different processes helps us understand why even simple variables such as source credibility can produce complex outcomes. It also makes it essential that we identify the conditions under which a variable influences attitudes by one process rather than another. Research on this problem is in its early stage, but the existing literature already suggests the general conditions under which variables serve in different roles.

In brief, under conditions of relatively low elaboration likelihood, when people are unmotivated or unable to devote the cognitive effort necessary to scrutinize all of the issue-relevant information presented (such as when personal relevance is low, distraction is high), persuasion-relevant variables such as source attractiveness, to the extent that they have any impact at all, influence attitudes mostly via peripheral route processes. When the elaboration likelihood is low, people know that they do not want to or are not able to evaluate the merits of the arguments presented (or they do not even consider exerting effort to process the message). Thus, if any evaluation is formed at all, it is likely to be the result of a relatively simple association or inference process that can occur without much cognitive effort (e.g., invoking the heuristic "I agree with people I like"; Chaiken, 1987).

When the elaboration likelihood is high, however, people know that they want to evaluate the merits of the arguments presented and that they are able to do so. In these high elaboration situations, persuasion-relevant variables (such as source attractiveness) have relatively little impact by serving as simple cues. Instead the variable can be scrutinized just as are the message arguments and produce attitude change if it provides information relevant to the merits of the attitude object. For example, imagine that an advertisement for a beauty product features an attractive spokesperson. In this instance, scrutiny of the endorser might lead to the thought that "if I use the product, I'll look like that famous model." This "argument" for using the product will be considered along with all other relevant information in assessing the merits of the product. Alternatively, even if the variable is not of central relevance to the merits of the advocacy, it could still influence attitudes under high processing conditions by biasing the ongoing information-processing activity. For example, people might be motivated to generate mostly favorable thoughts about the message if the source is attractive.

Finally, another role for variables, and the one emphasized earlier in this chapter, is that variables can influence the amount of thinking that takes place. When the elaboration likelihood is moderate such as when the message is of uncertain personal relevance, people have moderate knowledge on the issue, and so forth, people might be unsure as to whether or not they should devote effort to processing the message. In these situations, they might examine the persuasion context for guidance as to whether the message is worth thinking about. For example, some people might be more interested in the communication if it comes from an attractive than from an unattractive source (DeBono, 1987). When an attractive source increases thinking about a message, more persuasion is produced in the presence of the attractive source when the arguments are strong, but less persuasion is produced in the presence of the attractive source when the arguments are weak (Puckett, Petty, Cacioppo, & Fisher, 1983).

In order to understand the complex ways in which any one variable can influence attitudes, it is useful to examine the multiple roles for a few variables in some detail. In the next sections we explain the multiple ways in which one internal variable (a person's mood) and one external variable (the credibility of the message source) can influence attitudes.

Multiple Roles for Affect. Although in our previous discussion of affective influence we focused on how affect could influence attitudes by the peripheral route, it is now clear that affective states, such as a person's mood, can influence attitudes in different ways under different elaboration likelihood conditions (see Petty, Gleicher, & Baker, 1991; Schwarz, Bless, & Bohner, 1991). For example consider how being in a more positive mood than normal might influence attitude change. As explained earlier, according to the ELM, a person's mood should serve as a peripheral cue mostly when the likelihood of issue-relevant thinking is low. That is, when thinking is low, positive mood should produce more favorable attitudes than being in a neutral mood. This could occur either because of a relatively simple affect transfer process such as postulated by classical conditioning theory, or because people generate a simple inference based on their mood (e.g., "I feel good, so I must agree with the message").

As the likelihood of thinking increases, however, mood should take on different roles. Specifically, when the elaboration likelihood is more moderate, mood has been shown to have an impact on the amount of thinking a person does about the persuasive message. In general, people in a positive mood have engaged in less thinking about the merits of the advocated position than people in a negative or neutral mood (e.g., Batra & Stayman, 1990; Bless, Bohner, Schwarz, & Strack, 1990; Mackie & Worth, 1989), especially when the message advocates or is expected to advocate something unpleasant (e.g., raising tuition at the students' university). When the message advocates or is expected to advocate something pleasant, positive mood has produced increased message processing over negative mood (Wegener & Petty, in press). This suggests that positive mood influences message processing at least in part due to mood management concerns (Isen & Simmonds, 1978). That is, people in a positive mood tend to avoid message processing when they think it might disrupt their mood (e.g., an unpleasant or counterattitudinal message), but engage in message processing when it will maintain their mood (e.g., a pleasant or proattitudinal message). People in negative moods tend to process regardless of the message. Schwarz and associates (1991) suggest that people in negative moods adopt a problem-solving orientation, and this motivates message processing.

When the elaboration likelihood is high and people are processing the message arguments already, the ELM holds that mood states can influence attitudes by biasing the nature of the thoughts that come to mind. That is, positive mood facilitates the retrieval of positive and/or inhibits the retrieval of negative material from memory (see Blaney, 1986). Under high elaboration conditions, then, mood should influence thoughts which in turn influence attitudes.

Recent research supports the view that mood can influence attitudes in different ways in different situations. In one study, for instance, (Petty, Schumann, Richman, & Strathman, 1993), college students were exposed to a commercial for a new pen in the context of a popular television comedy show (an episode from the *Bill Cosby Show*), or they saw the same commercial in the context of a more neutral informational program. The results of this study revealed that positive mood had an impact on the thoughts and attitudes of subjects who were highly likely to be thinking about the ad (i.e., because the participants were told that they would be asked to select one brand of pen as a take-home gift), but mood influenced attitudes and not thoughts when the elaboration likelihood was low (i.e., when people thought their take-home gift was an alternative product). Furthermore, under high elaboration conditions, statistical analyses were consistent with the idea that mood influenced attitudes because of its biasing influence on thoughts, but in low elaboration conditions, mood had an impact on attitudes despite having no effect on thoughts (see Figure 6.4). That is, under low elaboration conditions, positive mood influenced attitudes by the peripheral route, but under high elaboration conditions, positive mood influenced attitudes by the central route.

Although much recent research has focused on the impact of positive mood states on attitudes, considerable past persuasion research has focused on the effect of associating a persuasive message with negative emotions such as fear. Is it good or bad for persuasion to induce fear in message recipients (e.g., if you don't wear condoms, use seatbelts, stop smoking, you'll DIE)? According to the ELM, fear, like other affects, should be capable of serving in multiple roles. For example, under high processing conditions, fear might bias the interpretation of the information in a message. If a message recipient experiences fear during a message on cigarette smoking, for instance, this could influence the person's perception of the severity of the threat (Schwarz, Servay, & Kumpf, 1985) or the likelihood that the frightening event will actually occur (Wegener, Petty, & Klein, 1994). If motivation or ability to think about the message is low, however, fear would take on a different role. That is, fear might serve as a negative emo-

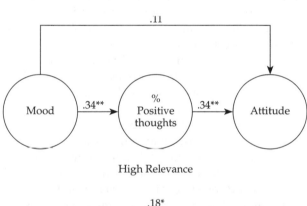

High Relevance

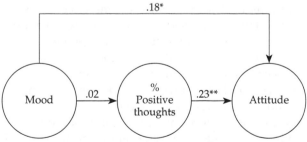

Low Relevance

FIGURE 6.4. Direct and indirect effects of positive mood on attitudes. The top panel shows that when involvement is high, positive mood has an indirect impact on attitudes by influencing thoughts. The bottom panel shows that when involvement is low, positive mood has a direct impact on attitudes without influencing thoughts.
Figure reprinted by permission from Petty, Schumann, Richman, & Strathman, 1993.

tional cue and produce negative feelings toward the message and little persuasion. Also, if fear is too high, it could reduce the overall likelihood of message thinking because people choose to defensively avoid the fearful stimulus (Janis & Feshbach, 1953; Jepson & Chaiken, 1990). Considerable research suggests that fear appeals are most likely to be effective when the message is personally relevant (so that thinking is increased), the fear is moderate (so that defensive avoidance is minimized), and the message presents strong and credible reassurances about the effectiveness of the proposed solution to the threat (see Rogers, 1983, for a review).

Multiple Roles for Source Credibility. As a second example of a variable serving in multiple roles, consider the impact of the seemingly simple variable of source credibility. The most obvious role for source credibility is to serve as a simple cue when people are relatively unmotivated or unable to think about the substantive message arguments provided. In fact, in a study described earlier (Petty, Cacioppo, & Goldman, 1981; see Figure 6.3), source credibility served as a simple cue when the elaboration likelihood was low, but had little effect when the elaboration likelihood was high. Rather, when people were motivated to think about the message, only argument quality influenced attitudes.

According to the ELM, however, source credibility (like other variables) should be capable of serving in other roles as the elaboration likelihood is increased. In one pertinent study, the effect of source credibility was examined at three different levels of elaboration likelihood (Moore, Hausknecht, & Thamodaran, 1986; Experiment 3). In this research, the likelihood of thinking about a message was varied by manipulating how fast the speaker in an advertisement talked. As the speech rate increased, of course, it would become more difficult to process the message. The results of this study showed that source credibility served as a simple cue when the message was presented quite rapidly (i.e., low elaboration likelihood). When the message was presented at the normal pace and was quite easy to process, argument quality had the greatest impact on attitudes and the effect of source credibility was reduced. So far, this study basically replicates prior work on the effects of source credibility under high and low elaboration conditions (e.g., Petty, Cacioppo, & Goldman, 1981; see Figure 6.3). Of greatest interest is what happened when the presentation rate of the message was moderately fast and processing was possible but challenging. In this case, the credibility of the endorser determined how much thinking occurred: The credible source induced more thinking than the nonexpert. Thus, this study clearly identified two roles for source credibility. When the likelihood of thinking was low, source credibility served as a simple cue (the same role served by affect under low elaboration conditions). When the elaboration likelihood was moderate, source credibility determined how much message processing occurred (the same role served by affect under moderate elaboration conditions). Thus, source credibility appears capable of serving as a simple cue and influencing the extent of message scrutiny.

Finally, Chaiken and Maheswaran (1994) have documented that source credibility, like affect, can also serve in a third role—biasing the nature of message processing when the elaboration likelihood is high. In their study, students read a report about a new consumer product. Subjects were told that the report was excerpted from *Consumer Reports* (a high credibility source) or from a Kmart pamphlet (a low credibility source). The report contained either strong arguments about the product, weak arguments, or a mixture of strong and weak arguments (i.e., an ambiguous message). Some students were highly motivated to think about the ad because they were told that the company would use the students' opinions to decide whether to market the product in the students' local area. Other students were not very motivated to think about the ad because they were told that the company was thinking about marketing the product in a distant location and their opinions were relatively unimportant.

The results for the unambiguous messages revealed a pattern that should by now be familiar. That is, under the low importance conditions, attitudes were influenced by source credibility but not argument strength. Under high importance conditions, however, attitudes were influenced by argument strength but not source credibility. This part of the research replicated prior findings (e.g., compare with Figure 6.3). Interestingly, when the evidence in the message was ambiguous (i.e., containing a mixture of strong and weak arguments) rather than being clearly strong or weak, source credibility had an impact on attitudes in both the high and low importance conditions. Consistent with the multiple roles notion, however, ancillary analyses indicated that under high importance conditions, source credibility influenced attitudes in part by biasing the processing of the message. That is, when the source was credible, subjects generated more favorable thoughts about the message content than when the source lacked credibility. Under low importance conditions, source credibility influenced attitudes without having any impact on message-relevant thoughts. That is, when the message was mixed, source credibility served as a simple cue under low processing conditions but biased thinking under high processing conditions. By including both ambiguous (mixed) and unambiguous messages in the same study, Chaiken and Maheswaran (1994) were able to show that source credibility was most likely to serve in the role of biasing message processing when people were motivated to think about the message and the message was ambiguous. When people were not motivated to think or the messages were clearly strong or weak, no biased processing was observed.[12]

Summary of Multiple Roles for Variables. The research reviewed in this section demonstrates that variables that initially seemed quite simple to understand such as a person's mood or the credibility of the message source can actually influence attitudes in rather complicated ways. We have seen that when people are unmotivated or unable to think about a message, their mood and the credibility of the source serve as simple cues. That is, if a person is in a positive mood or the message is endorsed by a credible source, persuasion is increased regardless of the quality of the message arguments. When the likelihood of thinking is high, however, both positive mood and source credibility no longer serve as simple cues but can still influence attitudes by biasing the thoughts that come to mind as the message is processed. This biased processing is most likely if the message arguments are somewhat mixed or ambiguous. Finally, when the elaboration likelihood conditions are moderate, both mood and source credibility determine how much thinking occurs.

CONSEQUENCES OF THE ROUTE TO PERSUASION

We have now reviewed the major processes that have been proposed to determine attitude change. The guiding theme of our review was that sometimes attitudes change because people carefully and effortfully evaluate all of the information in a persuasive communication in order to determine the central merits of the advocacy, but at other times attitudes change because cues in the persuasion environment produce change by much simpler processes. Furthermore, we have seen that any one variable can produce attitude change by either the central or the peripheral route. Does it really matter how one produces attitude change? That is, are not two units of change produced by the central route ultimately the same as two units of change produced by the peripheral route? It turns out that the answer to this question is *no*. In fact, a critical postulate of the ELM is that central route processes tend to produce stronger attitudes than do peripheral route processes (Petty & Cacioppo, 1981, 1986).

Attitude strength refers to the extent to which attitudes possess various qualities. Among the most important characteristics of strong attitudes are that they persist over time, are resistant to countervailing pressures to change, and are predictive of behavior (see Petty & Krosnick, 1995, for a review). Why would attitudes changed by the central route be stronger than attitudes changed by the peripheral route? One reason is that when we do a lot of thinking before changing our attitudes, we are likely to be accessing the attitude and the corresponding knowledge structure quite frequently. This cognitive activity should tend to increase the number of linkages and strengthen the associations among the cognitive elements in the underlying attitude structure. This would tend to make the attitude structure more internally consistent, accessible, and enduring (Crocker, Fiske, & Taylor, 1984; Fazio, Sanbonmatsu, Powell, & Kardes, 1986; McGuire, 1981). In comparison, attitude change that results from a simple inference or heuristic process typically involves accessing the attitude structure only once in order to incorporate the affect or inference associated with a salient persuasion cue (Petty & Cacioppo, 1986; Petty, Haugtvedt, & Smith, 1995). In general, then, these peripheral route attitudes should be weaker. In the sections to follow, we review the primary consequences of changing attitudes by the central versus the peripheral route.

Persistence of Attitude Change

Persistence of persuasion refers to the extent to which an attitude change endures over time. As it turns out, most laboratory studies of attitude change produce quite temporary changes in attitudes (see Cook & Flay, 1978). Thus, it becomes important to understand when attitude changes persist and when they do not. As we noted above, current research is compatible with the view that when attitude changes are based on extensive issue-relevant thinking, they tend to endure (e.g., Mackie, 1987). Many of the early laboratory studies on attitude change used topics that people didn't care very much about such as "admitting Greenland to the world bank!" Because of this, attitude changes were probably based on simple inferences and associations and not careful thinking about the substance of the message. Thus, the changes produced did not last very long. When laboratory persuasion studies began to explicitly include conditions that increased people's motivation and ability to engage in issue-relevant cognitive activity, more enduring attitude changes resulted. For example, research has shown that encouraging self-generation of arguments (e.g., Elms, 1966; Watts, 1967), using interesting or involving communication topics (Ronis, Baumgardner, Leippe, Cacioppo, & Greenwald, 1977), and leading recipients to believe that they might have to explain or justify their attitudes to other people (e.g., Boninger, Brock, Cook, Gruder, & Romer, 1990; Chaiken, 1980) are all associated with increased attitude change persistence. Also, people who characteristically enjoy thinking (high need for cognition) show greater persistence of attitude change than people who do not (Haugtvedt & Petty, 1992; Verplanken, 1991).

Can peripheral route attitude changes ever show high persistence? Interestingly, simple cues can become associated with persistent attitudes if the cues remain salient over time. This can be accomplished by repeatedly pairing the cue and the attitude object so that the cue remains relatively accessible (e.g., Weber, 1972). Alternatively, the attitude object can be associated with multiple cues (e.g., Haugtvedt, Schumann, Schneier, & Warren, 1994), or the cue(s) can be reintroduced at the time of attitude assessment (e.g., Kelman & Hovland, 1953). When a grocery store puts a big picture of a celebrity endorser next to the product, they might be attempting to remind you of a cue that produced only a temporary attitude change when you initially saw the product commercial weeks ago.

The Yale learning group explicitly acknowledged the important role that peripheral cues have in attitude change persistence in their work on the sleeper effect (e.g., Kelman & Hovland, 1953). A *sleeper effect* is said to occur when a message that is accompanied initially by a negative cue (e.g., a low credible source) increases in effectiveness over time (see Cook, Gruder, Hennigan, & Flay, 1979). For example, you might read in a tabloid newspaper that the President had an affair with his secretary. You read the message with interest, but then dismiss it because of the unreliability of the source. Two months later, however, you are having a conversation with a friend and you relay the information about the President's affair quite convincingly. Unfortunately, at this point you have forgotten the source of the information and assume that it is valid.

To account for sleeper effects like this, Kelman and Hovland (1953) proposed that in addition to message arguments, various cues could have an impact on attitude change. These cues were thought to add to (or subtract from) the effects of the persuasive message. Importantly, the cues and message were viewed as *independent* and were postulated to be forgotten at different rates. Thus, a sleeper effect would be produced if a person was exposed to a message with a discounting cue (e.g., an unreliable source) and the following conditions were met: (a) the message alone is strong enough to have an initial positive impact, (b) the discounting is sufficiently negative to suppress the initial positive impact of the message, and (c) the message conclusion becomes dissociated from the discounting cue more quickly than it becomes dissociated from the message content (Cook, Gruber, Hennigan, & Flay, 1979). Thus, at a later point in time, it is possible for the positive residue of the message to outlast the negative effect of the cue, leading to increased agreement with the message conclusion over time.

This formulation suggests that one key to producing a sleeper effect is to construct a situation in which both a strong negative cue *and* strong arguments have some initial impact. One way to do this is to present the discounting cue *after* a strong message is presented (see Pratkanis, Greenwald, Leippe, & Baumgardner, 1988). As we saw earlier, if a discounting cue (low expertise source) is presented before the message, people might ignore the message. At a minimum, if a negative source is presented first, the message recipient should be asked to focus on the message content so that strong arguments are viewed favorably even if the source is not.

In sum, research on attitude change persistence has shown that the more people process the arguments in a persuasive message carefully, the more any change induced by that message is likely to persist (or emerge) over time.

Resistance to Counterpersuasion

Resistance refers to the extent to which an attitude change is capable of surviving an attack from a source with an opposite viewpoint. Although attitude persistence and resistance tend to co-occur, their potential to be independent is shown very clearly in McGuire's (1964) work on cultural truisms. A belief in a truism such as "you should brush your teeth after every meal" tends to last forever if it is not challenged, but it is surprisingly susceptible to influence if it is attacked. As McGuire notes, people have very little practice in defending these beliefs because they have hardly ever been challenged before. These beliefs were likely formed with little issue-relevant thinking at a time during childhood when careful and extensive thinking was relatively unlikely. Instead, the truisms were probably presented repeatedly by powerful, likable, and expert sources. As noted above, the continual pairing of a belief with positive cues can produce a relatively persistent attitude, but these attitudes might not prove resistant when attacked because the person has so little information with which to defend his or her attitude. What can you say when you get a message stating that brushing your teeth will give you gum disease? Retorting with "my mommy said it's good to brush" just won't do the trick!

The resistance of attitudes can be improved by bolstering them with relevant information (e.g., Lewan & Stotland, 1961). In his work on *inoculation theory*, McGuire (1964) demonstrated that two kinds of bolstering can be effective in producing resistance. One form of treatment relies on providing people with a supportive defense of their attitudes or having them self-generate supportive information. For example, in one study, attitudes were made more resistant by getting people to recall times when they engaged in attitude-supportive actions (Ross, McFarland, Conway, & Zanna, 1983). A second type of defense relies on a biological analogy. That is, McGuire suggested that just as people can be made more resistant to a disease by giving them a mild form of the germ (the inoculation) prior to the threatening communication (the disease) and showing them how to refute this information (the antibodies). For example, if you were trying to inoculate voters against upcoming attacks on your favored presidential candidate, you might say that "some people will charge that our candidate wants to raise taxes, but these people don't consider the fact that if taxes are not raised now, we'll all pay much more later to take care of the national debt" (see McGuire & Papageorgis, 1961; Pfau & Burgoon, 1988). Inoculation techniques such as these are part of the popular DARE (Drug Abuse Resistance Education) program administered in schools throughout the country (DeJong, 1987).

Although there is relatively little work on the specific qualities that make attitude changes resistant to attack, the existing data support the view that attitude changes are more resistant to attack when the attitudes result from considerable issue-relevant thinking than when they do not. For example, in one study, individuals who were high or low in need for cognition were presented with an initial message about the safety of an artificial sugar substitute (Haugtvedt & Petty, 1992). The initial message contained strong arguments from an expert source stating that the sweetener was unsafe. This message was followed by an opposite message from another expert source. Although both high and low need for cognition (NC) subjects changed equally to the first message, the newly changed attitudes of the high NC subjects were more resistant to the attacking message. In addition, high NC individuals engaged in greater counterarguing of the attacking message. That is, individuals who formed the stronger initial attitudes showed greater resistance to the subsequent attacking message (see also Wu & Shaffer, 1987).

This finding—that people who process a first message extensively will be more resistant to a second message that takes an opposite point of view than people who change initially because of peripheral cues—has implications for understanding primacy and recency effects in persuasion. In various persuasion settings, people do not receive just one message, but messages on both sides of an issue (e.g., in a jury trial). If you had to choose whether to present your side first or second, which would you select? The ELM and the work on resistance reviewed above suggest that if you expect people to do a lot of thinking about your message, and you have strong arguments to present, you would want to go first. The reason, of course, is that the more successful you are in producing strong, thoughtful attitudes on your side of the issue, the more recipients will be motivated and able to resist the second countering message. That is, they will show a primacy effect—being influenced more by the first than the second communication.

To test this hypothesis, Haugtvedt and Wegener (1994) varied the personal relevance of messages on the topic of instituting comprehensive exams for college seniors. In the high relevance condition, the student subjects were told that their university was considering implementing comprehensive exams next year. In the low relevance conditions, the subjects were informed that a distant university was considering the exams. All subjects received two messages on the exams with one favoring the exams and one opposing the exams. Each message contained five strong arguments in support of its position. The order in which subjects received the messages was varied. That is, half of the subjects received the pro-exam message and then the anti-exam message, and the remaining subjects received the messages in the reverse order.

Figure 6.5 presents the results from the study. When the issue was of high relevance and subjects would therefore be scrutinizing the messages carefully, a primacy effect was observed. That is, subjects were more favorable toward the exam policy when they received the pro-exam message first rather than the anti-exam message first. In addition, supplemental analyses revealed that high relevance subjects engaged in more counterarguing of the second message than low relevance subjects. That is, as expected, high relevance subjects showed greater resistance to the attacking message. Interestingly, the results for the low relevance subjects were exactly the opposite. These individuals showed a recency effect: They went along with whatever position they heard most recently. In addition, the attitudes of low relevance subjects appeared to be determined by the amount of information from the second message that they could recall.

In sum, research on resistance suggests that the more people change as a result of processing the arguments in an initial persuasive message carefully, the more they will resist changing again to a subsequent message taking a contrary point of view.

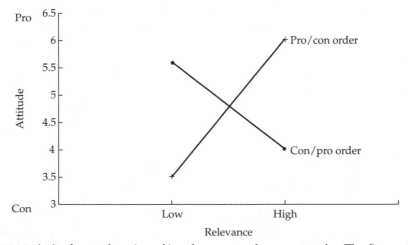

FIGURE 6.5. Attitude as a function of involvement and message order. The figure shows that under high relevance conditions, primacy effects in persuasion are observed. Under low relevance, a recency effect is obtained.
Figure adapted from Haugtvedt & Wegener, 1994.

Attitude-Behavior Consistency

Perhaps the most studied quality of attitudes because of its tremendous practical value is the ability of attitudes to predict and direct people's actions (see Ajzen, 1988, for a review). After all, if you can make a person dislike smoking, or love a certain product, but the person still smokes, and never purchases the product, what good is the attitude change? After a brief period of despair in which social scientists questioned whether attitudes predicted behavior (e.g., Wicker, 1971), it is now clear that attitudes are quite capable of accounting for behavior, at least if you know what you are doing. First, it is important to note that a number of methodological considerations have proved to be important if attitudes are to predict behaviors. In particular, the attitude and behavioral measures should be assessed at the same level of specificity. That is, specific behaviors such as "recycling glass" are predicted better by specific attitudes (i.e., attitude toward recycling glass) rather than the more general attitudes (e.g., attitude toward preserving the environment; see Ajzen & Fishbein, 1977). On the other hand, general attitudes (e.g., toward environmental preservation) are better than specific ones at predicting general behavioral criteria (e.g., an index based on several behavioral opportunities such as circulating environmental petitions, recycling household waste, cleaning up the highways, etc.; see Weigel & Newman, 1976). It is also important to note that behavioral prediction in general can be improved by considering attitudes toward alternative courses of action (e.g., Jaccard, Helbig, Wan, Gutman, & Kritz-Silverstein, 1990; Jaccard, Dittus, Radecki, & Wilson, 1995). That is, I can predict whether or not you will smoke better if I measure both your attitude toward smoking and your attitude toward *not* smoking.

Second, a number of conceptual factors are relevant to understanding when attitudes will predict and guide behaviors. Most importantly, strong attitudes predict behavior better than weak ones. That is, even if two people express the same attitude on a scale, +6 for example, one person's attitude might be more predictive of behavior than the other person's attitude. The key is to understand if the attitude is a strong one or not. If the attitude was formed as a result of considerable issue-relevant thinking (central route), we would expect it to predict behavior better than if it was formed as a result of a peripheral cue process. Consistent with this notion, when attitudes are formed under high personal relevance conditions, they predict behavior and behavioral intentions better than when they are formed under low relevance conditions (Leippe & Elkin, 1987; Petty, Cacioppo, & Schumann, 1983; Sivacek & Crano, 1982). Also, when attitudes are formed as a result of direct personal experience with an attitude object, they predict behavior better than when they are formed as a result of exposure to secondhand information (see Fazio & Zanna, 1981). Increasing personal relevance and experience presumably increase the likelihood that the attitude change is based on issue-relevant thinking rather than peripheral cues.[13]

If we do not know how an attitude was formed, how can we tell if it will predict behavior? First, you could attempt to assess if the person was the type of individual who likely possessed strong attitudes. For example, people who receive a low score on the *self-monitoring scale* show greater consistency of their attitudes with their behaviors (Snyder, 1979). As described in the earlier section on attitude functions, high self-monitors are motivated by situational cues relevant to their image in a group, whereas low self-monitors are motivated by their internal values. Thus, low self-monitors tend to have more stable attitudes that can guide their actions. In addition, people who receive a high score on the *need for cognition* scale would be expected to have stronger attitudes because of their tendency to enjoy thinking about a variety of issues. Consistent with this reasoning, in a study of the 1984 presidential election it was found that the attitudes of high need for cognition individuals toward the candidates allowed greater prediction of voting behavior than did the attitudes of low need for cognition individuals (Cacioppo, Petty, Kao, & Rodgriguez, 1986).

Instead of assessing stable individual differences, you could also attempt to measure the strength of the attitude itself (see Petty & Krosnick, 1995, for a review). For example, you could assess the amount of knowledge a person has about the attitude object (see Wood, Rhodes, & Biek, 1995). The greater the knowledge, the greater the attitude-behavior consistency (e.g., Davidson, Yantis, Norwood, & Montano, 1985; Kallgren & Wood, 1986). You could assess the extent to which the attitude was consistent with underlying beliefs and values (see Chaiken, Pomerantz, & Giner-Sorolla, 1995). The greater the attitude-belief consistency, the greater the attitude-behavior consistency (e.g., Norman, 1975). You could assess the importance or relevance of the attitude object to the person (Boninger, Krosnick, Berent, & Fabrigar, 1995) or how certain the person was about his or her opinion (Gross, Holz, & Miller, 1995). Important attitudes predict behavior better than unimportant ones (e.g., Jaccard & Becker, 1985) as do attitudes about which people express certainty (Davidson, Yantis, Norwood, & Montano, 1985).

One of the most important qualities of an attitude that can be measured in order to determine its strength is how quickly the attitude comes to mind. In a compelling series of studies, Fazio and his colleagues have shown that attitudes that come to mind quickly (i.e., accessible attitudes) are better predictors of behavior than are attitudes that come to mind more slowly (see Fazio, 1995, for a review). For example, in another study of the 1984 presidential election, the accessibility of people's attitudes toward the candidates was determined by how quickly they responded to a survey question. The attitudes of people with accessible attitudes predicted voting behavior better than the attitudes of people with relatively inaccessible attitudes (Fazio & Williams, 1986). One reason that accessible attitudes predict behavior better than inaccessible attitudes is that if an attitude comes to mind quickly, it can bias your perception of the target of evaluation. The more you perceive the object as consistent with your attitude, the more you are likely to behave in an attitude-consistent fashion toward it. The notion that accessibility is a moderator of attitude-behavior relations is an important one and has the potential for integrating a considerable number of research findings. For example, many of the variables found to moderate attitude-behavior consistency might be explained by the accessibility notion. Thus, low self-monitors have more accessible attitudes than high self-monitors (Kardes, Sanbonmatsu, Voss, & Fazio, 1986), and attitudes formed by the central route and via direct experience are more accessible than attitudes formed by the peripheral route (Rennier, 1988), or those that are based only on indirect experience (Fazio & Zanna, 1981). Accessible attitudes are also more persistent over time (Zanna, Fazio, & Ross, in press) and more resistant to change (Bassili & Fletcher, 1991).

Before concluding this section, it is important to note that although attitudes can be important determinants of behavior, attitudes are not the *only* determinants of people's actions. Fishbein and Ajzen's *theory of reasoned action* (Fishbein & Ajzen, 1975) notes that it is sometimes important to consider what other people's attitudes toward some behavior are in addition to one's own. That is, people are sometimes motivated to comply with what important other people want them to do. These normative influences can overpower one's own attitude on occasion. Ajzen's (1991) *theory of planned behavior* suggests that it is also important to consider the extent to which people perceive that they can control their behavior. If people do not have the required skills to carry out their desired actions, attitudes will not predict behavior (see also, Bandura, 1986).

In sum, despite the fact that behavior is determined by multiple forces, the accumulated research suggests quite clearly that attitudes can be powerful determinants of people's behavior when those attitudes are strong (i.e., based on considerable issue-relevant thinking and knowledge).

SUMMARY AND CONCLUSIONS

This chapter opened with the notion that some people enjoy thinking and others do not. We have also seen that in some situations, almost everyone is willing to engage in thought, but in other situations, most people are unlikely to be thinking about the persuasive communication because they are either unmotivated or unable to do so. The goal of this chapter has been to outline the major processes of attitude change, and we have argued that it is useful to separate the theoretical processes responsible for modifying attitudes into those that emphasize effortful thinking about the central merits of the attitude object and those that do not. This framework allows understanding and prediction of what variables affect attitudes and in what general situations. It also permits understanding and prediction of the consequences of attitude change. We have emphasized that all attitudes (whether toward ourselves, other people, objects, or issues) can be based on cognitive, affective, and/or behavioral information, and that any one variable can have an impact on persuasion by invoking different processes under specifiable conditions of elaboration likelihood. Also, we noted that attitudes that appear identical when measured can be quite different in their underlying basis or structure and thus can be quite different in their temporal persistence, resistance, or ability to predict behavior.

Notes

[1]Of course, it is possible to have influence on a person without changing the person's attitude. For example, you might agree to donate money to a charity without coming to believe that the charity is more worthwhile than you did prior to the donation request. Various such "compliance" strategies are discussed by Cialdini (Chapter 7).

[2]The tripartite framework appears to imply that attitudes are based on information and experiences associated with the attitude object during the course of our lives. It is important to note that in addition to these learned associations, attitudes can also have a genetic basis. That is, some people can be predisposed to evaluate certain attributes of objects (e.g., the excitement of roller coasters) favorably for reasons related to genetics (e.g., genetic differences in sensory structures). Such attitudes should be especially difficult to change because it is difficult to change the underlying genetic predisposition contributing to the attitude (see Tesser, 1993).

[3]An alternative formula for integrating the thoughts and beliefs that a person has about an attitude object is provided by Anderson's *information integration theory* (1971). In contrast to Fishbein and Ajzen's additive rule, Anderson suggests that the bits of information about an attitude object are typically combined by an averaging process (see Anderson, 1981). Another difference is that Anderson's formula focuses on the evaluation of each attribute $[s_i]$ along with the *weight* $[w_i]$ of each attribute where the weight is determined by the subjective importance or credibility of the attribute. In most situations, similar outcomes are expected from both additive and averaging formulas (see Anderson, 1981).

[4]In addition to the focus on how the evaluative and likelihood aspects of beliefs combine to form attitudes, some researchers are examining the unique origins of likelihood and evaluation judgments (e.g., see McGuire & McGuire, 1991).

[5]As we will see later, attitudes could also be related to the number of arguments recalled if people make the simple inference "The more arguments in a message, the more valid it must be" (Petty & Cacioppo, 1984). That is, a correlation between the number of arguments recalled and attitude change does not require that attitudes are based on a postmessage evaluation of the arguments (Haugtvedt & Petty, 1992).

[6]In a related stream of experiments, the effects of asking people to generate explanations for some assertion (e.g., Anderson, Lepper, & Ross, 1980) or to imagine the occurrence of some event (e.g., Sherman, Cialdini, Schwartzman, & Reynolds, 1985) have been examined. Consistent with the work on role playing, the work on generating explanations and imagining events has shown consistently that self-generation is a powerful way to change beliefs, and that these beliefs are remarkably resistant to change.

[7]Strong arguments are those that elicit mainly favorable thoughts when people are instructed to think about them, and weak arguments are those that elicit mostly unfavorable thoughts when people are instructed to think about them (see Petty & Cacioppo, 1986, for a complete discussion).

[8]Increasing knowledge might allow people to better understand the information in a message but could also increase their interest in it. Other variables could also influence both motivation and ability to think. For example, placing time pressure on a person might reduce message processing because the person is less able to think in the reduced time allocated, but the time pressure manipulation might also induce a feeling that processing is not worthwhile in this situation—even if enough time really were present.

[9]Biased outcomes can also occur when the information in memory is perfectly balanced if some feature of the persuasion situation is more likely to activate one type of information rather than another. For example, a positive mood can bias retrieval in favor of positive over negative thoughts (Bower, 1981).

[10]Another way in which these inferences might come about is suggested by *inferred value theory* (Freedman, Cunningham, & Krismer, 1992). In this view, people reason that the amount of money associated with a task indicates its value (cf., Leavitt, 1954). That is, people give more money to obtain valuable than valueless objects, but are paid more money to engage in stressful, uninteresting tasks than pleasant ones. Thus, subjects could reason that the experimenter really thinks that the

task is more boring in the $20 than in the $1 condition, and that is why he is offering people more money to induce them to say that it is interesting.

[11]Although the HSM and ELM mostly make the same predictions, there are a number of notable exceptions. For example, the HSM contends that as long as the systematic and heuristic processing modes do not yield conflicting evaluations, as a person's motivation and ability to scrutinize a message increase, heuristic processing *adds to* the impact of systematic processing. The ELM argues that as the elaboration likelihood increases, peripheral processes (such as the invocation of heuristics) are less likely to have a direct impact on attitudes (though they are not necessarily less likely to occur). Rather, as explained in the upcoming section on "multiple roles," a variable that worked by invoking a heuristic under low processing conditions can have an impact under high processing conditions but by a different process. For example, if the variable serving as a cue is now processed as are the arguments, this processing could reveal that the variable is informative as to the central merits of the advocacy. Alternatively, the variable could influence attitudes by biasing the ongoing information-processing activity. That is, just because a variable has a similar impact on attitudes under high and low elaboration conditions, this does not mean that the process by which this impact occurs is the same (see Petty, 1994, for further discussion).

[12]In this study, path analyses using the source credibility manipulation check indicated that perceptions of source credibility also produced a direct effect on attitudes under high importance conditions. This could be because of the co-occurrence of central (systematic) and peripheral (heuristic) processes (see Eagly & Chaiken, 1993), or because source credibility was evaluated along with all other issue-relevant information and judged relevant to the merits of the position advocated (see Petty, 1994), or because the thought-listing measure fails to capture all the variance in elaboration (Baker & Petty, 1994).

[13]Interestingly, if people are asked to think about the basis of their attitudes just prior to attitude measurement, attitude-behavior consistency could be reduced if thinking produces an expressed attitude that is not representative of the true one (Wilson, Dunn, Kraft, & Lisle, 1989). For example, if the central merits of an attitude object are based mostly on affective considerations, but a thinking task makes cognitive rather than affective information salient prior to attitude expression, the attitude expressed after thought will be less predictive of behavior than an attitude expressed without thought—especially if the behavior is affectively based as well (Millar & Tesser, 1986b; see Millar & Tesser, 1992, for a review).

References

ABELSON, R. P., & PRENTICE, D. A. (1989). Beliefs as possessions: A functional perspective. In A. R. Pratkanis, S. J. Breckler, & A. G. Greenwald (Ed.), *Attitude structure and function* (pp. 361–381). Hillsdale, NJ: Erlbaum.

AJZEN, I. (1988). *Attitudes, personality, and behavior*. Chicago, IL: Dorsey.

AJZEN, I. (1991). The theory of planned behavior. *Organizational Behavior and Human Decision Processes, 50*, 179–211.

AJZEN, I., & FISHBEIN, M. (1977). Attitude-behavior relations: A theoretical analysis and review of empirical research. *Psychological Bulletin, 84*, 888–918.

AJZEN, I., & FISHBEIN, M. (1980). *Understanding attitudes and predicting social behavior*. Englewood Cliffs, NJ: Prentice-Hall.

ALBA, J. W., & HUTCHINSON, J. W. (1987). Dimensions of consumer expertise. *Journal of Consumer Research, 13*, 411–454.

ALBA, J. W., & MARMORSTEIN, H. (1987). The effects of frequency of knowledge on consumer decision making. *Journal of Consumer Research, 14*, 14–25.

ANDERSON, C. A., LEPPER, M. R., & ROSS, L. (1980). Perseverance of social theories: The role of explanation in the persistence of discredited information. *Journal of Personality and Social Psychology, 39*, 1037–1049.

ANDERSON, J. R. (1983). *The architecture of cognition*. Cambridge, MA: Harvard University Press.

ANDERSON, N. (1981). Integration theory applied to cognitive responses and attitudes. In R. Petty, T. Ostrom, & T. Brock (Eds.), *Cognitive responses in persuasion* (pp. 361–397). Hillsdale, NJ: Erlbaum.

ANDERSON, N. H. (1971). Integration theory and attitude change. *Psychological Review, 78,* 171–206.

ARONSON, E. (1968). Dissonance theory: Progress and problems. In R. P. Abelson, E. Aronson, W. J. McGuire, T. M. Newcomb, M. J. Rosenberg, & P. H. Tannenbaum (Eds.), *Theories of cognitive consistency: A sourcebook* (pp. 5–27). Chicago: Rand McNally.

ARONSON, E., & MILLS, J. (1959). The effects of severity of initiation on liking for a group. *Journal of Abnormal and Social Psychology, 59,* 177–181.

AXSOM, D., YATES, S. M., & CHAIKEN, S. (1987). Audience response as a heuristic cue in persuasion. *Journal of Personality and Social Psychology, 53,* 30–40.

BAKER, S. M., & PETTY, R. E. (1994). Majority and minority influence: Source-position imbalance as a determinant of message scrutiny. *Journal of Personality and Social Psychology, 67,* 5–19.

BANDURA, A. (1986). *Social foundations of thought and action.* Englewood Cliffs, NJ: Prentice-Hall.

BARGH, J. A., CHAIKEN, S., GOVENDER, R., & PRATTO, F. (1992). The generality of the automatic attitude activation effect. *Journal of Personality and Social Psychology, 62,* 893–912.

BASSILI, J. N., & FLETCHER, J. F. (1991). Response-time measurement in survey research: A method for CATI and a new look at nonattitudes. *Public Opinion Quarterly, 55,* 331–346.

BATRA, R., & RAY, M. L. (1986). Situational effects of advertising repetition: The moderating influence of motivation, ability, and opportunity to respond. *Journal of Consumer Research, 12,* 432–445.

BATRA, R., & STAYMAN, D. M. (1990). The role of mood in advertising effectiveness. *Journal of Consumer Research, 17,* 203–214.

BEM, D. J. (1970). *Beliefs, attitudes, and human affairs.* Belmont, CA: Brooks/Cole.

BEM, D. J. (1972). Self-perception theory. In L. Berkowitz (Ed.), *Advances in experimental social psychology* (Vol. 6, pp. 1–62). New York: Academic Press.

BLANEY, P. H. (1986). Affect and memory: A review. *Psychological Bulletin, 99,* 229–246.

BLESS, H., BOHNER, G., SCHWARZ, B., & STRACK, F. (1990). Mood and persuasion: A cognitive response analysis. *Personality and Social Psychology Bulletin, 16,* 331–345.

BONINGER, D. S., BROCK, T. C., COOK, T. D., GRUDER, C. L., & ROMER, D. (1990). Discovery of reliable attitude change persistence resulting from a transmitter tuning set. *Psychological Science, 1,* 268–171.

BONINGER, D. S., KROSNICK, J. A., BERENT, M., & FABRIGAR, L. (1995). The causes and consequences of attitude importance. In R. E. Petty & J. A. Krosnick (Eds). *Attitude strength: Antecedents and consequences.* Hillsdale, NJ: Erlbaum.

BORNSTEIN, R. F. (1989). Exposure and affect: Overview and meta-analysis of research, 1968–1987. *Psychological Bulletin, 106,* 265–289.

BORNSTEIN, R. F., & D'AGOSTINO, P. R. (1992). Stimulus recognition and the mere exposure effect. *Journal of Personality and Social Psychology, 63,* 545–552.

BOWER, G. H. (1981). Mood and memory. *American Psychologist, 36,* 129–148.

BRECKLER, S. J. (1984). Empirical validation of affect, behavior, and cognition as distinct components of attitude. *Journal of Personality and Social Psychology, 47,* 1191–1205.

BREHM, J. W. (1966). *A theory of psychological reactance.* San Diego, CA: Academic Press.

BREHM, J. W., & COHEN, A. R. (1962). *Explorations in cognitive dissonance.* New York: Wiley.

BROCK, T. C. (1967). Communication discrepancy and intent to persuade as determinants of counterargument production. *Journal of Experimental Social Psychology, 3,* 296–309.

BRUCKS, M., ARMSTRONG, G. M., & GOLDBERG, M. E. (1988). Children's use of cognitive defenses against television advertising: A cognitive response approach. *Journal of Consumer Research, 14,* 471–482.

BURNKRANT, R. E., & HOWARD, D. J. (1984). Effects of the use of introductory rhetorical questions versus statements on information processing. *Journal of Personality and Social Psychology, 47,* 1218–1230.

BURNKRANT, R. E., & UNNAVA, R. (1989). Self-referencing: A strategy for increasing processing of message content. *Personality and Social Psychology Bulletin, 15,* 628–638.

CACIOPPO, J. T., HARKINS, S. G., & PETTY, R. E. (1981). The nature of attitudes and cognitive responses and their relationships to behavior. In R. E. Petty, T. M. Ostrom, & T. C. Brock (Eds.), *Cognitive responses in persuasion* (pp. 31–54). Hillsdale, NJ: Erlbaum.

CACIOPPO, J. T., MARSHALL-GOODELL, B. S., TASSINARY, L. G., & PETTY, R. E. (1992). Rudimentary determinants of attitudes: Classical conditioning is more effective when prior knowledge about the attitude stimulus is low than high. *Journal of Experimental Social Psychology, 28,* 207–233.

CACIOPPO, J. T., & PETTY, R. E. (1979). Effects of message repetition and position on cognitive responses, recall, and persuasion. *Journal of Personality and Social Psychology, 37,* 97–109.

CACIOPPO, J. T., & PETTY, R. E. (1982). The need for cognition. *Journal of Personality and Social Psychology, 42,* 116–131.

CACIOPPO, J. T., & PETTY, R. E. (1989). Effects of message repetition on argument processing, recall, and persuasion. *Basic and Applied Social Psychology, 10,* 3–12.

CACIOPPO, J. T., PETTY, R. E., & BERNTSON, G. G. (1991). Persuasion. In R. Dulbecco (Ed.), *Encyclopedia of human biology* (pp. 799–810). Orlando, FL: Academic Press.

CACIOPPO, J. T., PETTY, R. E., KAO, C. F., & RODRIGUEZ, R. (1986). Central and peripheral routes to persuasion: An individual difference perspective. *Journal of Personality and Social Psychology, 51,* 1032–1043.

CACIOPPO, J. T., PETTY, R. E., & MORRIS, K. J. (1983). Effects of need for cognition on message evaluation, recall, and persuasion. *Journal of Personality and Social Psychology, 45,* 805–818.

CACIOPPO, J. T., PETTY, R. E., & SIDERA, J. (1982). The effects of salient self-schema on the evaluation of proattitudinal editorials: Top-down versus bottom-up message processing. *Journal of Experimental Social Psychology, 18,* 324–338.

CACIOPPO, J. T., PRIESTER, J. R., & BERNTSON, G. G. (1993). Rudimentary determinants of attitudes II: Arm flexion and extension have differential effects on attitudes. *Journal of Personality and Social Psychology, 65,* 5–17.

CALDER, B. J., ROSS, M., & INSKO, C. A. (1973). Attitude change and attitude attribution: Effects of incentive, choice, and consequences. *Journal of Personality and Social Psychology, 25,* 84–99.

CHAIKEN, S. (1980). Heuristic versus systematic information processing in the use of source versus message cues in persuasion. *Journal of Personality and Social Psychology, 39,* 752–766.

CHAIKEN, S. (1987). The heuristic model of persuasion. In M. P. Zanna, J. M. Olson, & C. P. Herman (Eds.), *Social influence: The Ontario symposium* (Vol. 5, pp. 3–39). Hillsdale, NJ: Erlbaum.

CHAIKEN, S., & BALDWIN, M. W. (1981). Affective-cognitive consistency and the effect of salient behavioral information on the self-perception of attitudes. *Journal of Personality and Social Psychology, 41*, 1–12.

CHAIKEN, S., & EAGLY, A. H. (1976). Communication modality as a determinant of message persuasiveness and message comprehensibility. *Journal of Personality and Social Psychology, 34*, 605–614.

CHAIKEN, S., LIBERMAN, A., & EAGLY, A. H. (1989). Heuristic and systematic processing within and beyond the persuasion context. In J. S. Uleman & J. A. Bargh (Ed.), *Unintended thought* (pp. 212–252). New York: Guilford Press.

CHAIKEN, S., & MAHESWARAN, D. (1994). Heuristic processing can bias systematic processing: Effects of source credibility, argument ambiguity, and task importance on attitude judgment. *Journal of Personality and Social Psychology, 66*, 460–473.

CHAIKEN, S., POMERANTZ, E. M., & GINER-SOROLLA, R. (1995). Structural consistency and attitude strength. In R. E. Petty & J. A. Krosnick (Eds.), *Attitude strength: Antecedents and consequences*. Hillsdale, NJ: Erlbaum.

CHAIKEN, S., & YATES, S. M. (1985). Affective-cognitive consistency and thought-induced attitude polarization. *Journal of Personality and Social Psychology, 49*, 1470–1481.

COOK, T. D., & FLAY, B. R. (1978). The persistence of experimentally induced attitude change. In L. Berkowitz (Ed.), *Advances in experimental social psychology* (Vol. 11, pp. 1–57). New York: Academic Press.

COOK, T. D., GRUDER, C. L., HENNIGAN, K. M., & FLAY, B. R. (1979). History of the sleeper effect: Some logical pitfalls in accepting the null hypothesis. *Psychological Bulletin, 86*, 662–679.

COOPER, J., & FAZIO, R. H. (1984). A new look at dissonance theory. In L. Berkowitz (Ed.), *Advances in experimental social psychology* (Vol. 17, pp. 229–266). New York: Academic Press.

CRANO, W. D., GORENFLO, D. W., & SHACKELFORD, S. L. (1988). Overjustification, assumed consensus, and attitude change: Further investigation of the incentive-aroused ambivalence hypothesis. *Journal of Personality and Social Psychology, 55*, 12–22.

CROCKER, J., FISKE, S. T., & TAYLOR, S. E. (1984). Schematic bases of belief change. In R. Eiser (Ed.), *Attitudinal judgment* (pp. 197–226). New York: Springer-Verlag.

DARWIN, C. (1872). *The expression of the emotions in man and animals.* London: Murray.

DAVIDSON, A. (1995). From attitudes to actions to attitude change: The effects of amount and accuracy of information. In R. E. Petty & J. A. Krosnick (Eds.), *Attitude strength: Antecedents and consequences*. Hillsdale, NJ: Erlbaum.

DAVIDSON, A. R., YANTIS, S., NORWOOD, M., & MONTANO, D. E. (1985). Amount of information about the attitude object and attitude-behavior consistency. *Journal of Personality and Social Psychology, 49*, 1184–1198.

DEBONO, K. G. (1987). Investigating the social-adjustive and value-expressive functions of attitudes: Implications for persuasion processes. *Journal of Personality and Social Psychology, 52*, 279–287.

DEJONG, W. (1987). A short term evaluation of project DARE: Preliminary indications of effectiveness. *Journal of Drug Education, 17*, 279–293.

DECI, E. L. (1975). *Intrinsic motivation.* New York: Plenum.

EAGLY, A. H. (1974). Comprehensibility of persuasive arguments as a determinant of opinion change. *Journal of Personality and Social Psychology, 29*, 758–773.

EAGLY, A. H., & CHAIKEN, S. (1984). Cognitive theories of persuasion. In L. Berkowitz (Ed.), *Advances in experimental social psychology*, (Vol. 17, pp. 268–361). New York: Academic Press.

EAGLY, A. H., & CHAIKEN, S. (1993). *The psychology of attitudes*. Fort Worth, TX: Harcourt, Brace, Jovanovich.

EAGLY, A. H., & CHAIKEN, S. (1995). Attitude strength, attitude structure, and resistance to change. In R. E. Petty & J. A. Krosnick (Eds.), *Attitude strength: Antecedents and consequences*. Hillsdale, NJ: Erlbaum.

EAGLY, A. H., CAHIKEN, S., & WOOD, W. (1981). An attribution analysis of persuasion. In J. H. Harvey, W. J. Ickes, & R. F. Kidd (Eds.), *New direction in attribution research* (Vol. 3, pp. 37–62). Hillsdale, NJ: Erlbaum.

EAGLY, A. H., & WARREN, R. (1976). Intelligence, comprehension, and opinion change. *Journal of Personality, 44,* 226–242.

EAGLY, A. H., WOOD, W., & CHAIKEN, S. (1978). Causal inferences about communicators and their effect on opinion change. *Journal of Personality and Social Psychology, 36,* 424–435.

EDWARDS, K. (1990). The interplay of affect and cognition in attitude formation and change. *Journal of Personality and Social Psychology, 59,* 202–216.

EIBL-EIBESFELDT, I. (1972). Similarities and differences between cultures in expressive movement. In R. A. Hinde (Ed.), *Nonverbal communication.* Cambridge: Cambridge University Press.

EKMAN, P. (1971). Universals and cultural differences in facial expressions of emotion. In J. K. Cole (Ed.), *Nebraska symposium on motivation* (Vol. 19). Lincoln: University of Nebraska Press.

ELKIN, R. A., & LEIPPE, M. R. (1986). Physiological arousal, dissonance, and attitude change: Evidence for a dissonance-arousal link and a "Don't remind me" effect. *Journal of Personality and Social Psychology, 51,* 55–65.

ELMS, A. C. (1966). Influence of fantasy ability on attitude change through role-playing. *Journal of Personality and Social Psychology, 4,* 36–43.

FAZIO, R. H. (1995). Attitudes as object-evaluation associations: Determinants, consequences, and correlates of attitude accessibility. In R. E. Petty & J. A. Krosnick (Eds.), *Attitude strength: Antecedents and consequences.* Hillsdale, NJ: Erlbaum.

FAZIO, R. H., BLASCOVICH, J., & DRISCOLL, D. M. (1992). On the functional value of attitudes: The influence of accessible attitudes upon the ease and quality of decision-making. *Personality and Social Psychology Bulletin, 18,* 388–401.

FAZIO, R. H., & COOPER, J., (1983). Arousal in the dissonance process. In J. T. Cacioppo & R. E. Petty (Eds.), *Social psychophysiology: A sourcebook* (pp. 122–152). New York: Guilford Press.

FAZIO, R. H., SANBONMATSU, D. M., POWELL, M. C., & KARDES, F. R. (1986). On the automatic activation of attitudes. *Journal of Personality and Social Psychology, 50,* 229–238.

FAZIO, R. H., & WILLIAMS, C. J. (1986). Attitude accessibility as a moderator of the attitude-perception and attitude-behavior relations: An investigation of the 1984 presidential election. *Journal of Personality and Social Psychology, 51,* 505–514.

FAZIO, R. H., & ZANNA, M. P. (1981). Direct experience and attitude behavior consistency. In L. Berkowitz (Ed.), *Advances in experimental social psychology* (Vol. 14, pp. 161–202). New York: Academic Press.

FAZIO, R. H., ZANNA, M. P., & COOPER, J. (1977). Dissonance and self-perception: An integrative view of each theory's proper domain of application. *Journal of Experimental Social Psychology, 13,* 464–479.

FESTINGER, L. (1957). *A theory of cognitive dissonance.* Evanston, IL: Row, Peterson.

FESTINGER, L. (1964). *Conflict, decision, and dissonance.* Stanford, CA: Stanford University Press.

FESTINGER, L., & CARLSMITH, J. M. (1959). Cognitive consequences of forced compliance. *Journal of Abnormal and Social Psychology, 58,* 203–210.

FISHBEIN, M. (1980). A theory of reasoned action: Some applications and implications. In H. E. Howe, Jr., & M. M. Page (Eds.), *Nebraska symposium on motivation, 1979* (Vol. 27, pp. 65–116). Lincoln: University of Nebraska Press.

FISHBEIN, M., & AJZEN, I. (1972). Attitudes and opinions. *Annual Review of Psychology, 23,* 487–544.

FISHBEIN, M., & AJZEN, I. (1975). *Belief, attitude, intention, and behavior.* Reading, MA: Addison-Wesley.

FISKE, S. T. (1982). Schema triggered affect: Applications to social perception. In M. S. Clark & S. T. Fiske (Eds.), *Affect and cognition: The 17th annual Carnegie Symposium on cognition* (pp. 55–78). Hillsdale, NJ: Erlbaum.

FREEDMAN, J. L., CUNNINGHAM, J. A., & KRISMER, K. (1992). Inferred values and the reverse-incentive effect in induced compliance. *Journal of Personality and Social Psychology, 62,* 357–368.

GERARD, H. B., BLEVANS, S. A., & MALCOLM, T. (1964). Self-evaluation and the evaluation of choice alternatives. *Journal of Personality, 32,* 395–410.

GREENWALD, A. G. (1968). Cognitive learning, cognitive response to persuasion, and attitude change. In A. G. Greenwald, T. C. Brock, & T. M. Ostrom (Ed.), *Psychological foundations of attitudes* (pp. 147–170). New York: Academic Press.

GREENWALD, A. G., & ALBERT, R. D. (1968). Acceptance and recall of improvised arguments. *Journal of Personality and Social Psychology, 8,* 31–34.

GREENWALD, A. G., & RONIS, D. L. (1978). Twenty years of cognitive dissonance: Case study of a theory. *Psychological Review, 85,* 53–57.

GROSS, S. R., HOLZ, R., & MILLER, N. (1995). Attitude certainty. In R. E. Petty & J. A. Krosnick (Eds.), *Attitude strength: Antecedents and consequences.* Hillsdale, NJ: Erlbaum.

GRUSH, J. E. (1976). Attitude formation and mere exposure phenomena: A nonartificial explanation of empirical findings. *Journal of Personality and Social Psychology, 33,* 281–290.

HARKINS, S. G., & PETTY, R. E. (1981). Effects of source magnification of cognitive effort on attitudes: An information processing view. *Journal of Personality and Social Psychology, 40,* 401–413.

HARKINS, S. G., & PETTY, R. E. (1987). Information utility and the multiple source effect. *Journal of Personality and Social psychology, 52,* 260–268.

HASTIE, R., & PARK, B. (1986). The relationship between memory and judgment depends on whether the judgment task is memory-based or on-line. *Psychological Review, 93,* 258–268.

HAUGTVEDT, C. P., & PETTY, R. E. (1992). Personality and persuasion: Need for cognition moderates the persistence and resistance of attitude changes. *Journal of Personality and Social Psychology, 63,* 308–319.

HAUGTVEDT, C. P., PETTY, R. E., & CACIOPPO, J. T. (1992). Need for cognition and advertising: Understanding the role of personality variables in consumer behavior. *Journal of Consumer Psychology, 1,* 239–260.

HAUGTVEDT, C. P., SCHUMANN, D. W., SCHNEIER, W. L., & WARREN, W. L. (1994). Advertising repetition and variation strategies: Implications for understanding attitude strength. *Journal of Consumer Research, 21,* 176–189.

HAUGTVEDT, C. P., & WEGENER, D. T. (1994). Message order effects in persuasion: An attitude strength perspective. *Journal of Consumer Research, 21,* 205–218.

HEIDER, F. (1958). *The psychology of interpersonal relations.* New York: Wiley.

HIMMELFARB, S., & EAGLY, A. H. (1974). Orientations to the study of attitudes and their change. In S. Himmelfarb & A. Eagly (Eds.), *Readings in attitude change* (pp. 2–49). New York: Wiley.

HOUSTON, D. A., & FAZIO, R. H. (1989). Biased processing as a function of attitude accessibility: Making objective judgments subjectively. *Social Cognition, 7*, 51–66.

HOVLAND, C. I. (1959). Reconciling conflicting results derived from experimental and survey studies of attitude change. *American Psychologist, 14*, 8–17.

HOVLAND, C. I., JANIS, I. L., & KELLEY, H. H. (1953). *Communication and persuasion: Psychological studies of opinion change.* New Haven, CT: Yale University Press.

HUTTON, D. G., & BAUMEISTER, R. F. (1992). Self-awareness and attitude-change: Seeing oneself on the central route to persuasion. *Personality and Social Psychology Bulletin, 18*, 68–75.

ISEN, A. M., & SIMMONDS, S. (1978). The effect of feeling good on a helping task that is incompatible with good mood. *Social Psychology Quarterly, 41*, 346–349.

IYENGAR, S., KINDER, D. R., PETERS, M. D., & KROSNICK, J. A. (1984). The evening news and presidential evaluations. *Journal of Personality and Social Psychology, 46*, 778–787.

JACCARD, J., & BECKER, M. A. (1985). Attitudes and behavior: An information integration perspective. *Journal of Experimental Social Psychology, 21*, 440–465.

JACCARD, J., DITTUS, P., RADECKI, C., & WILSON, T. (1995). Methods for identifying consequential beliefs: Implications for understanding attitude strength. In R. E. Petty & J. A. Krosnick (Eds). *Attitude strength: Antecedents and consequences.* Hillsdale, NJ: Erlbaum.

JACCARD, J., HELBIG, D. W., WAN, C. K., GUTMAN, M., & KRITZ-SILVERSTEIN, D. S. (1990). Individual differences in attitude-behavior consistency; The prediction of contraceptive behavior. *Journal of Applied Social Psychology, 20*, 575–617.

JANIS, I. L., & FESHBACH, S. (1953). Effects of fear-arousing communications. *Journal of Abnormal and Social Psychology, 48*, 78–92.

JANIS, I. L., & KING, B. T. (1954). The influence of role playing on opinion change. *Journal of Abnormal and Social Psychology, 49*, 211–218.

JEPSON, C., & CHAIKEN, S. (1990). Chronic issue-specific fear inhibits systematic processing of persuasive communications. *Journal of Social Behavior and Personality, 5*, 61–84.

JOHNSON, B. T., & EAGLY, A. H. (1989). Effects of involvement on persuasion: A meta-analysis. *Psychological Bulletin, 106*, 290–314.

JOHNSON, B. T., & TURCO, R. M. (1994). *Effects of argument quality on persuasion as moderated by outcome- and impression-relevant involvement: A meta-analysis.* Unpublished manuscript, Syracuse University, Syracuse, NY.

JONES, E. E., RHODEWALT, F., BERGLAS, S., & SKELTON, J. A. (1981). Effects of strategic self-presentation on subsequent self-esteem. *Journal of Personality and Social Psychology, 41*, 407–421.

JUDD, C. M., & KROSNICK, J. A. (1989). The structural bases of consistency among political attitudes: Effects of political expertise and attitude importance. In A. R. Pratkanis, S. J. Breckler, & A. G. Greenwald (Eds.), *Attitude structure and function* (pp. 99–128). Hillsdale, NJ: Erlbaum.

JUDD, C. M., & KULIK, J. A. (1980). Schematic effects of social attitudes on information processing and recall. *Journal of Personality and Social Psychology, 38*, 569–578.

KALLGREN, C. A., & WOOD, W. (1986). Access to attitude-relevant information in memory as a determinant of attitude-behavior consistency. *Journal of Experimental Social Psychology, 22*, 328–338.

KARDES, F. R., SANBONMATSU, D. M., VOSS, R. T., & FAZIO, R. H. (1986). Self-monitoring and attitude accessibility. *Personality and Social Psychology Bulletin, 12,* 468–474.

KATZ, D. (1960). The functional approach to the study of attitudes. *Public Opinion Quarterly, 24,* 163–204.

KELMAN, H. C. (1958). Compliance, identification, and internalization: Three processes of attitude change. *Journal of Conflict Resolution, 2,* 51–60.

KELMAN, H. C., & HOVLAND, C. I. (1953). "Reinstatement" of the communicator in delayed measurement of opinion change. *Journal of Abnormal and Social Psychology, 48,* 327–335.

KIESLER, C. A. (1971). *The psychology of commitment: Experiments linking behavior to beliefs.* New York: Academic Press.

KITSON, H. D. (1922). *The mind of the buyer: A psychology of selling.* New York: Macmillan Co.

KROSNICK, J. A., BETZ, A. L., JUSSIM, L. J., & LYNN, A. R. (1992). Subliminal conditioning of attitudes. *Personality and Social Psychology Bulletin, 18,* 152–162.

KROSNICK, J. A., BONINGER, D. S., CHUANG, Y. C., BERENT, M., & CARNOT, C. G. (1993). Attitude strength: One construct or many related constructs? *Journal of Personality and Social Psychology, 65,* 1132–1151.

KRUGLANSKI, A. W. (1989). *Lay epistemics and human knowledge: Cognitive and motivational bases.* New York: Plenum.

KRUGLANSKI, A. W., & FREUND, T. (1983). The freezing and unfreezing of lay-inferences: Effects on impressional primacy, ethnic stereotyping, and numerical anchoring. *Journal of Experimental Social Psychology, 19,* 448–468.

KRUGLANSKI, A. W., WEBSTER, D., & KLEM, A. (1993). Motivated resistance and openness to persuasion in the presence and absence of prior information. *Journal of Personality and Social Psychology, 65,* 861–876.

KUNST-WILSON, W. R., & ZAJONC, R. B. (1980). Affective discrimination of stimuli that cannot be recognized. *Science, 207,* 557–558.

LEAVITT, H. J. (1954). A note on some experimental findings about the meaning of price. *Journal of Business, 27,* 205–210.

LEIPPE, M. R., & ELKIN, R. A. (1987). When motives clash: Issue involvement and response involvement as determinants of persuasion. *Journal of Personality and Social Psychology, 52,* 269–278.

LEPPER, M. R., GREENE, D., & NISBETT, R. E. (1973). Undermining children's intrinsic interest with extrinsic reward: A test of the "overjustification" hypothesis. *Journal of Personality and Social Psychology, 28,* 129–137.

LEWAN, P. C., & STOTLAND, E. (1961). The effects of prior information on susceptibility to an emotional appeal. *Journal of Abnormal and Social Psychology, 62,* 450–453.

LIBERMAN, A., & CHAIKEN, S. (1991). Value conflict and thought-induced attitude change. *Journal of Experimental Social Psychology, 27,* 203–216.

LIBERMAN, A., & CHAIKEN, S. (1992). Defensive processing of personally relevant health messages. *Personality and Social Psychology Bulletin, 18,* 669–679.

LINVILLE, P. W. (1982). The complexity-extremity effect and age-based stereotyping. *Journal of Personality and Social Psychology, 42,* 193–211.

LORD, C. G., ROSS, L., & LEPPER, M. R. (1979). Biased assimilation and attitude polarization: The effects of prior theories on subsequently considered evidence. *Journal of Personality and Social Psychology, 37,* 2098–2109.

LOSCH, M. E., & CACIOPPO, J. T. (1990). Cognitive dissonance may enhance sympathetic tonus, but attitudes are changed to reduce negative affect rather than arousal. *Journal of Experimental Social Psychology, 26,* 289–304.

LOVE, R. E., & GREENWALD, A. G. (1978). Cognitive responses to persuasion as mediators of opinion change. *Journal of Social Psychology, 104*, 231–241.

LUTZ, R. J. (1975). Changing brand attitudes through modification of cognitive structure. *Journal of Consumer Research, 1*, 49–59.

MACKENZIE, S. B. (1986). The role of attention in mediating the effect of advertising on attribute importance. *Journal of Consumer Research, 13*, 174–195.

MACKIE, D. M. (1987). Systematic and nonsystematic processing of majority and minority persuasive communications. *Journal of Personality and Social Psychology, 53*, 41–52.

MACKIE, D. M., & ASUNCION, A. G. (1990). On-line and memory-based modification of attitudes: Determinants of message recall-attitude change correspondence. *Journal of Personality and Social Psychology, 59*, 5–16.

MACKIE, D. M., & WORTH, L. T. (1989). Processing deficits and the mediation of positive affect in persuasion. *Journal of Personality and Social Psychology, 57*, 27–40.

MACKIE, D. M., & WORTH, L. T. (1991). Feeling good, but not thinking straight: The impact of positive mood on persuasion. In J. Forgas (Ed.), *Emotion and social judgment* (pp. 201–219). Oxford, England: Pergamon Press.

MAHESNARAN, D., & CHAIKEN, S. (1991). Promoting systematic processing in low-motivation settings: Effect of incongruent information on processing and judgment. *Journal of Personality and Social Psychology, 61*, 13–33.

MCGUIRE, W. J. (1960). A syllogistic analysis of cognitive relationships. In C. I. Hovland & M. J. Rosenberg (Eds.), *Attitude organization and change: An analysis of consistency among attitude components* (pp. 65–111). New Haven, CT: Yale University Press.

MCGUIRE, W. J. (1964). Inducing resistance to persuasion: Some contemporary approaches. In L. Berkowitz (Ed.), *Advances in experimental social psychology* (Vol. 1, pp. 191–229). New York: Academic.

MCGUIRE, W. J. (1968). Personality and attitude change: An information-processing theory. In A. G. Greenwald, T. C. Brock, & T. M. Ostrom (Eds.), *Psychological foundations of attitudes* (pp. 171–196). New York: Acedemic.

MCGUIRE, W. J. (1969). The nature of attitudes and attitude change. In G. Lindzey & E. Aronson (Eds.), *Handbook of social psychology* (Vol. 3, pp. 136–314). Reading, MA: Addison-Wesley.

MCGUIRE, W. J. (1981). The probabilogical model of cognitive structure and attitude change. In R. E. Petty, T. M. Ostrom, & T. C. Brock (Eds.), *Cognitive responses in persuasion* (pp. 291–307). Hillsdale, NJ: Erlbaum.

MCGUIRE, W. J. (1985). Attitudes and attitude change. In G. Lindzey & E. Aronson (Eds.), *Handbook of social psychology* (Vol. 2, pp. 233–346). New York: Random House.

MCGUIRE, W. J. (1989). Theoretical foundations of campaigns. In R. E. Rice & C. K. Atkin (Eds.), *Public communication campaigns* (pp. 43–66). Newbury Park: Sage.

MCGUIRE, W. J., & MCGUIRE, C. V. (1991). The content, structure, and operation of thought systems. In R. S. Wyer, Jr., & T. Srull (Eds.), *Advances in social cognition* (Vol. 4, pp. 1–78). Hillsdale, NJ: Erlbaum.

MCGUIRE, W. J., & PAPAGEORGIS, D. (1961). The relative efficacy of various types of prior belief-defense in producing immunity against persuasion. *Journal of Abnormal and Social Psychology, 62*, 327–337.

MCSWEENEY, F. K., & BIERLY, C. (1984). Recent developments in classical conditioning. *Journal of Consumer Research, 11*, 619–631.

MILLAR, M. G., & MILLAR, K. U. (1990). Attitude change as a function of attitude type and argument type. *Journal of Personality and Social Psychology, 59*, 217–228.

MILLAR, M. G., & TESSER, A. (1986a). Effects of affective and cognitive focus on the attitude-behavior relation. *Journal of Personality and Social Psychology, 51*, 270–276.

MILLAR, M. G., & TESSER, A. (1986b). Thought-induced attitude change: The effects of schema structure and commitment. *Journal of Personality and Social Psychology, 51,* 259–269.

MILLAR, M. G., & TESSER, A. (1992). The role of beliefs and feelings in guiding behavior: The mis-match model. In L. Martin & A. Tesser (Eds.), *Construction of social judgment* (pp. 277–300). Hillsdale, NJ: Erlbaum.

MOORE, D. L., HAUSKNECHT, D., & THAMODARAN, K. (1986). Time compression, response opportunity, and persuasion. *Journal of Consumer Research, 13,* 85–99.

MURPHY, S. T., & ZAJONC, R. B. (1993). Affect, cognition, and awareness: Affective priming with optimal and suboptimal exposures. *Journal of Personality and Social Psychology, 64,* 723–739.

NORMAN, R. (1975). Affective-cognitive consistency, attitudes, conformity, and behavior. *Journal of Personality and Social Psychology, 32,* 83–91.

OBERMILLER, C. (1985). Varieties of mere exposure: The effects of processing style and repetition on affective response. *Journal of Consumer Research, 12,* 17–30.

OSGOOD, C. E., & TANNENBAUM, P. H. (1955). The principle of congruity in the prediction of attitude change. *Psychological Review, 62,* 42–55.

PALLAK, S. R. (1983). Salience of a communicator's physical attractiveness and persuasion: A heuristic versus systematic processing interpretation. *Social Cognition, 2,* 158–170.

PAVLOV, I. P. (1927). *Conditioned reflexes.* London: Oxford University Press.

PEAK. H. (1955). Attitude and motivation. In M. R. Jones (Ed.), *Nebraska symposium on motivation* (Vol. 3, pp. 149–188). Lincoln: University of Nebraska Press.

PERLOFF, R. M., & BROCK, T. C. (1980). And thinking makes it so: Cognitive responses to persuasion. In M. Roloff & G. Miller (Eds.), *Persuasion: New directions in theory and research* (pp. 67–100). Beverly Hills: Sage.

PETTY, R. E. (1994). Two routes to persuasion: State of the art. In G. d'Ydewalle, P. Eelen, & P. Bertelson (Eds.), *International perspectives on psychological science* (pp. 229–247). Hillsdale, NJ: Erlbaum.

PETTY, R. E., & CACIOPPO, J. T. (1979a). Effects of forewarning of persuasive intent and involvement on cognitive responses and persuasion. *Personality and Social Psychology Bulletin, 5,* 173–176.

PETTY, R. E., & CACIOPPO, J. T. (1979b). Issue-involvement can increase or decrease persuasion by enhancing message-relevant cognitive responses. *Journal of Personality and Social Psychology, 37,* 1915–1926.

PETTY, R. E., & CACIOPPO, J. T. (1981). *Attitudes and persuasion: Classic and contemporary approaches.* Dubuque, IA: Wm. C. Brown.

PETTY, R. E., & CACIOPPO, J. T. (1984). The effects of involvement on responses to argument quantity and quality: Central and peripheral routes to persuasion. *Journal of Personality and Social Psychology, 46,* 69–81.

PETTY, R. E., & CACIOPPO, J. T. (1986). *Communication and persuasion: Central and peripheral routes to attitude change.* New York: Springer-Verlag.

PETTY, R. E., & CACIOPPO, J. T. (1990). Involvement and persuasion: Tradition versus integration. *Psychological Bulletin, 107,* 367–374.

PETTY, R. E., CACIOPPO, J. T., & GOLDMAN, R. (1981). Personal involvement as a determinant of argument-based persuasion. *Journal of Personality and Social Psychology, 41,* 847–855.

PETTY, R. E., CACIOPPO, J. T., & HAUGTVEDT, C. (1992). Involvement and persuasion: An appreciative look at the Sherifs' contribution to the study of self-relevance and attitude change. In D. Granberg & G. Sarup (Eds.), *Social judgment and intergroup relations: Essays in honor of Muzifer Serif* (pp. 147–175). New York: Springer-Verlag.

PETTY, R. E., CACIOPPO, J. T., & HEESACKER, M. (1981). Effects of rhetorical questions on persuasion: A cognitive response analysis. *Journal of Personality and Social Psychology, 40,* 432–440.

PETTY, R. E., CACIOPPO, J. T., & SCHUMANN, D. W. (1983). Central and peripheral routes to advertising effectiveness: The moderating role of involvement. *Journal of Consumer Research, 10,* 135–146.

PETTY, R. E., GLEICHER, F., & BAKER, S. M. (1991). Multiple roles for affect in persuasion. In J. Forgas (Ed.), *Emotion and social judgments* (pp. 181–200). Oxford, England: Pergamon Press.

PETTY, R. E., HARKINS, S. G., & WILLIAMS, K. D. (1980). The effects of group diffusion of cognitive effort on attitudes: An information processing view. *Journal of Personality and Social Psychology, 38,* 81–92.

PETTY, R. E., & HAUGTVEDT, C. P., & SMITH, S. (1995). Elaboration as a determinant of attitude strength: Creating attitudes that are persistent, resistant, and predictive of behavior. In R. E. Petty & J. A. Krosnick (Eds.), *Attitude strength: Antecedents and consequences.* Hillsdale, NJ: Erlbaum.

PETTY, R. E., & KROSNICK, J. A. (1995). *Attitude strength: Antecedents and consequences.* Hillsdale, NJ: Erlbaum.

PETTY, R. E., OSTROM, T. M., & BROCK, T. C. (1981). *Cognitive responses in persuasion.* Hillsdale, NJ: Erlbaum.

PETTY, R. E., PRIESTER, J. R., & WEGENER, D. T. (1994). Cognitive processes in attitude change. In R. S. Wyer & T. K. Srull (Eds.), *Handbook of social cognition* (Vol. 2, pp. 69–142). Hillsdale, NJ: Erlbaum.

PETTY, R. E., SCHUMANN, D. W., RICHMAN, S. A., & STRATHMAN, A. J. (1993). Positive mood and persuasion: Different roles for affect under high- and low-elaboration conditions. *Journal of Personality and Social Psychology, 64,* 5–20.

PETTY, R. E., WELLS, G. L., & BROCK, T. C. (1976). Distraction can enhance or reduce yielding to propaganda: Thought disruption versus effort justification. *Journal of Personality and Social Psychology, 34,* 874–884.

PFAU, M., & BURGOON, M. (1988). Inoculation in political campaign communication. *Human Communication Research, 15,* 91–111.

PRATKANIS, A. R. (1989). The cognitive representation of attitudes. In A. R. Pratkanis, S. J. Breckler, & A. G. Greenwald (Eds.), *Attitude structure and function* (pp. 71–98). Hillsdale, NJ: Erlbaum.

PRATKANIS, A. R., & GREENWALD, A. H. (1989). A sociocognitive model of attitude structure and function. In L. Berkowitz (Ed.), *Advances in experimental social psychology,* (Vol. 22, pp. 245–286). New York: Academic Press.

PRATKANIS, A. R., GREENWALD, A. G., LEIPPE, M. R., & BAUMGARDNER, M. H. (1988). In search of reliable persuasion effects: III. The sleeper effect is dead. Long live the sleeper effect. *Journal of Personality and Social Psychology, 54,* 203–218.

PRIESTER, J. R., & PETTY, R. E. (in press). Source attributions and persuasion: Perceived honesty as a determinant of message scrutiny. *Personality and Social Psychology Bulletin.*

PUCKETT, J. M., PETTY, R. E., CACIOPPO, J. T., & FISHER, D. L. (1983). The relative impact of age and attractiveness stereotypes on persuasion. *Journal of Gerontology, 38,* 340–343.

RADEN, D. (1985). Strength-related attitude dimensions. *Social Psychology Quarterly, 48,* 312–330.

RATNESHWAR, S., & CHAIKEN, S. (1991). Comprehension's role in persuasion: The case of its moderating effect on the persuasive impact of source cues. *Journal of Consumer Psychology, 18,* 52–62.

RENNIER, G. A. (1988). *The strength of the object-evaluation association, the attitude-behavior relationship and the Elaboration Likelihood Model of Persuasion.* Unpublished doctoral dissertation, University of Missouri, Columbia, MO.

RHODES, N., & WOOD, W. (1992). Self-esteem and intelligence affect influenceability: The mediating role of message reception. *Psychological Bulletin, 111,* 156–171.

ROGERS, R. W. (1983). Cognitive and physiological processes in fear appeals and attitude change: A revised theory of protection motivation. In J. T. Cacioppo & R. E. Petty (Eds.), *Social psychophysiology: A sourcebook* (pp. 153–176). New York: Guilford.

RONIS, D. L., BAUMGARDNER, M. H., LEIPPE, M. R., CACIOPPO, J. T., & GREENWALD, A. G. (1977). In search of reliable persuasion effects: I. A computer-controlled procedure for studying persuasion. *Journal of Personality and Social Psychology, 35,* 548–569.

ROSENBERG, M. J. (1960). An analysis of affective-cognitive consistency. In C. I. Hovland & M. J. Rosenberg (Eds.), *Attitude organization and change: An analysis of consistency among attitude components* (pp. 15–64). New Haven, CT: Yale University Press.

ROSENBERG, M. J., & HOVLAND, C. I. (1960). Cognitive, affective, and behavioral components of attitudes. In C. I. Hovland & M. J. Rosenberg (Eds.), *Attitude organization and change: An analysis of consistency among attitude components* (pp. 1–14). New Haven, CT: Yale University Press.

ROSKOS-EWOLDSEN, D. R., & FAZIO, R. H. (1992). The accessibility of source likability as a determinant of persuasion. *Personality and Social Psychology Bulletin, 18,* 19–25.

ROSS, M., MCFARLAND, C., CONWAY, M., & ZANNA, M. P. (1983). Reciprocal relation between attitudes and behavior recall: Committing people to newly formed attitudes. *Journal of Personality and Social Psychology, 45,* 257–267.

SADLER, O., & TESSER, A. (1973). Some effects of salience and time upon interpersonal hostility and attraction. *Sociometry, 36,* 99–112.

SANBONMATSU, D. M., & KARDES, F. R. (1988). The effects of physiological arousal on information processing and persuasion. *Journal of Consumer Research, 15,* 379–385.

SCHER, S. J., & COOPER, J. (1989). Motivational basis of dissonance: The singular role of behavioral consequences. *Journal of Personality and Social Psychology, 56,* 899–906.

SCHWARZ, N., BLESS, H., & BOHNER, G. (1991). Mood and persuasion: Affective states influence the processing of persuasive communications. In M. P. Zanna (Ed.), *Advances in experimental social psychology* (Vol. 24, pp. 161–201). San Diego: Academic Press.

SCHWARZ, N., SERVAY, W., & KUMPF, M. (1985). Attribution of arousal as a mediator of the effectiveness of fear-arousing communications. *Journal of Applied Social Psychology, 15,* 74–84.

SHAVITT, S. (1989). Operationalizing functional theories of attitude. In A. R. Pratkanis, S. J. Breckler, & A. G. Greenwald (Eds.), *Attitude structure and function* (pp. 311–338). Hillsdale, NJ: Erlbaum.

SHAVITT, S. (1990). The role of attitude objects in attitude functions. *Journal of Experimental Social Psychology, 26,* 124–148.

SHAVITT, S., & BROCK, T. C. (1986). Self-relevant responses in commercial persuasion: Field and experimental tests. In J. Olson & K. Sentis (Eds.), *Advertising and consumer psychology* (Vol. 3, pp. 149–171). New York: Praeger.

SHERIF, M. (1977). Crisis in social psychology: Some remarks toward breaking through the crisis. *Personality and Social Psychology Bulletin, 3,* 368–382.

SHERIF, M., & HOVLAND, C. I. (1961). *Social judgment: Assimilation and contrast effects in communication and attitude change.* New Haven, CT: Yale University Press.

SHERMAN, S. J., CIALDINI, R. B., SCHWARTZMAN, D. F., & REYNOLDS, K. D. (1985). Imagining can heighten or lower the perceived likelihood of contracting a disease: The mediating effect of ease of imagery. *Personality and Social Psychology Bulletin, 11*, 118–127.

SHERMAN, S. J., MACKIE, D. M., & DRISCOLL, D. M. (1990) Priming and the differential use of dimensions in evaluation. *Personality and Social Psychology Bulletin, 16*, 405–418.

SIVACEK, J., & CRANO, W. D. (1982). Vested interest as a moderator of attitude-behavior consistency. *Journal of Personality and Social Psychology, 43*, 210–221.

SLAMECKA, N. J., & GRAF, P. (1978). The generation effect: Delineation of a phenomenon. *Journal of Experimental Psychology: Human Learning and Memory, 4*, 592–604.

SMITH, M. B., BRUNER, J. S., & WHITE, R. W. (1956). *Opinions and personality.* New York: Wiley.

SMITH, S. M., & SHAFFER, D. R. (1991). Celerity and cajolery: Rapid speech may promote or inhibit persuasion through its impact on message elaboration. *Personality and Social Psychology Bulletin, 17*, 663–669.

SNYDER, M. (1979). Self-monitoring processes. In L. Berkowitz (Ed.), *Advances in experimental social psychology* (Vol. 12, pp. 85–128). New York: Academic Press.

SNYDER, M., & DEBONO, K. G. (1985). Appeals to images and claims about quality: Understanding the psychology of advertising. *Journal of Personality and Social Psychology, 49*, 586–597.

SNYDER, M., & DEBONO, K. G. (1987). A functional approach to attitudes and persuasion. In M. P. Zanna, J. M. Olson, & C. P. Herman (Eds.), *Social influence: The Ontario symposium* (Vol. 5, pp. 107–125). Hillsdale, NJ: Erlbaum.

SNYDER, M. & DEBONO, K. G. (1989). Understanding the functions of attitudes: Lessons for personality and social behavior. In A. R. Pratkanis, S. J. Breckler, & A. G. Greenwald (Eds.). *Attitude structure and function.* (pp. 339–359). Hillsdale, NJ: Erlbaum.

SOLARZ, A. (1960). Latency of instrumental responses as a function of compatibility with the meaning of eliciting verbal signs. *Journal of Experimental Psychology, 59*, 239–245.

STAATS, A. W., & STAATS, C. K. (1958). Attitudes established by classical conditioning. *Journal of Abnormal and Social Psychology, 57*, 37–40.

STAATS, A. W., STAATS, C. K., & CRAWFORD, H. L. (1962). First-order conditioning of meaning and the parallel conditioning of a GSR. *Journal of General Psychology, 67*, 159–167.

STEELE, C. M. (1988). The psychology of self-affirmation: Sustaining the integrity of the self. In L. Berkowitz (Ed.), *Advances in experimental social psychology* (Vol. 21, pp. 261–302). New York: Academic Press.

STEELE, C. M., & SPENCER, S. J. (1992). The primacy of self-integrity. *Psychological Inquiry, 3*, 345–346.

STEELE, C. M., SPENCER, S. J., & LYNCH, M. (1993). Self-image resilience and dissonance: The role of affirmational resources. *Journal of Personality and Social Psychology, 64*, 885–896.

STONE, J., ARONSON, E., CRAIN, L., WINSLOW, M., & FRIED, C. (1994). Inducing hypocrisy as a means of encouraging young adults to use condoms. *Personality and Social Psychology Bulletin.*

STRACK, F., MARTIN, L., & STEPPER, S. (1988). Inhibiting and facilitating conditions of the human smile: A non-obtrusive test of the facial feedback hypothesis. *Journal of Personality and Social Psychology, 53*, 768–777.

TAYLOR, S. E. (1981). The interface of cognitive and social psychology. In J. H. Harvey (Ed.), *Cognition, social behavior, and the environment* (pp. 189–211). Hillsdale, NJ: Erlbaum.

Tesser, A. (1978). Self-generated attitude change. In L. Berkowitz (Ed.), *Advances in experimental social psychology* (Vol. 11, pp. 289–338). New York: Academic Press.

Tesser, A. (1993). The importance of heritability in psychological research: The case of attitudes. *Psychological Review, 100,* 129–142.

Tesser, A., & Cornell, D. P. (1991). On the confluence of self-processes. *Journal of Experimental Social Psychology, 27,* 501–526.

Tesser, A., & Leone, C. (1977). Cognitive schemas and thought as determinants of attitude change. *Journal of Experimental Social Psychology, 13,* 340–356.

Tesser, A., Martin, L., & Mendolia, M. (1995). The impact of thought on attitude extremity and attitude-behavior consistency. In R. E. Petty & J. A. Krosnick (Eds.), *Attitude strength: Antecedents and consequences.* Hillsdale, NJ: Erlbaum.

Tetlock, P. W. (1983). Accountability and complexity of thought. *Journal of Personality and Social Psychology, 45,* 74–83.

Thibodeau, R., & Aronson, E. (1992). Taking a closer look: Reasserting the role of the self-concept in dissonance theory. *Personality and Social Psychology Bulletin, 18,* 591–602.

Thompson, M. M., Zanna, M. P., & Griffin, D. W. (1995). Let's not be indifferent about (attitudinal) ambivalence. In R. E. Petty & J. A. Krosnick (Eds.), *Attitude strength: Antecedents and consequences.* Hillsdale, NJ: Erlbaum.

Tice, D. M. (1992). Self-concept change and self-presentation: The looking glass self is also a mangifying glass. *Journal of Personality and Social Psychology, 63,* 435–451.

Tourangeau, R., Rasinski, K. A., & D'Andrade, R. (1991). Attitude structure and belief accessibility. *Journal of Experimental Social Psychology, 27,* 48–75.

Tybout, A. M., & Scott, C. A. (1983). Availability of well-defined internal knowledge and the attitude formation process: Information aggregation versus self-perception. *Journal of Personality and Social Psychology, 44,* 474–491.

Verplanken, B. (1991). Persuasive communication of risk information: A test of cue versus message processing effects in a field experiment. *Personality and Social Psychology Bulletin, 17,* 188–193.

Watts, W. A. (1967). Relative persistence of opinion change induced by active compared to passive participation. *Journal of Personality and Social Psychology, 5,* 4–15.

Weber, S. J. (1972). *Opinion change is a function of the associative learning of content and source factors.* Unpublished doctoral dissertation, Northwestern University.

Wegener, D. T., & Petty, R. E. (in press). Effects of mood on persuasion processes: Enhancing, reducing, and biasing scrutiny of attitude-relevant information. In L. L. Martin, & A. Tesser (Eds). *Striving and feeling: Interactions between goals and affect.* Hillsdale, NJ: Erlbaum.

Wegener, D. T., Petty, R. E., & Klein, D. J. (1994). Effects of mood on high elaboration attitude change: The mediating role of likelihood judgments. *European Journal of Social Psychology, 23,* 25–44.

Weigel, R. H., & Newman, L. S. (1976). Increasing attitude-behavior correspondence by broadening the scope of the behavioral measure. *Journal of Personality and Social Psychology, 33,* 793–802.

Wells, G. L., & Petty, R. E. (1980). The effects of overt head movement on persuasion: Compatibility and incompatibility of responses. *Basic and Applied Social Psychology, 1,* 219–230.

Wicker, A. (1971). An examination of the "other variables" explanation of attitude-behavior inconsistency. *Journal of Personality and Social Psychology, 19,* 18–30.

Wilson, T. D., Dunn, D. S., Kraft, D., & Lisle, D. J. (1989). Introspection, attitude change, and attitude-behavior consistency: The disruptive effects of explaining why we feel the way we do. In L. Berkowitz (Ed.), *Advances in experimental social psychology,* (Vol. 22, pp. 287–343). New York: Academic Press.

WOOD, W. (1982). Retrieval of attitude-relevant information from memory: Effects on susceptibility to persuasion and on intrinsic motivation. *Journal of Personality and Social Psychology, 42,* 798–910.

WOOD, W., & KALLGREN, C. A. (1988). Communicator attributes and persuasion: Recipients access to attitude-relevant information in memory. *Personality and Social Psychology Bulletin, 14,* 172–182.

WOOD, W., KALLGREN, C. A., & PREISLER, R. M. (1985). Access to attitude-relevant information in memory as a determinant of persuasion: The role of message attributes. *Journal of Experimental Social Psychology, 21,* 73–85.

WOOD, W., RHODES, N., & BIEK, M. (1995). Working knowledge and attitude strength: An information processing analysis. In R. E. Petty & J. A. Krosnick (Eds.), *Attitude strength: Antecedents and consequences.* Hillsdale, NJ: Erlbaum.

WRIGHT, P. L. (1980). Message-evoked thoughts: Persuasion research using thought verbalizations. *Journal of Consumer Research, 7,* 151–175.

WU, C., & SHAFFER, D. R. (1987). Susceptibility to persuasive appeals as a function of source credibility and prior experience with the attitude object. *Journal of Personality and Social Psychology, 52,* 677–688.

WYER, R. S., Jr. (1970). Quantitative prediction of belief and opinion change: A further test of a subjective probability model. *Journal of Personality and Social Psychology, 16,* 559–570.

ZAJONC, R. B. (1968). Attitudinal effects of mere exposure. *Journal of Personality and Social Psychology Monograph Supplements, 9,* 1–27.

ZAJONC, R. B., & MARKUS, H. (1982). Affective and cognitive factors in preferences. *Journal of Consumer Research, 9,* 123–131.

ZANNA, M. P., & COOPER, J. (1974). Dissonance and the pill: An attribution approach to studying the arousal properties of dissonance. *Journal of Personality and Social Psychology, 29,* 703–709.

ZANNA, M. P., FAZIO, R. H., & ROSS, M. (in press). The persistence of persuasion. In R. C. Schank & E. Langer (Eds.), *Beliefs, reasoning and decision making: Psycho-logic in honor of Bob Abelson.* Hillsdale, NJ: Erlbaum.

ZANNA, M. P., KIESLER, C. A., & PILKONIS, P. A. (1970). Positive and negative attitudinal affect established by classical conditioning. *Journal of Personality and Social Psychology, 14,* 321–328.

ZANNA, M. P., & REMPEL, J. K. (1988). Attitudes: A new look at an old concept. In D. Bar-Tal & A. W. Kruglanski (Eds.), *The social psychology of knowledge* (pp. 315–334). Cambridge, England: Cambridge University Press.

ZIMBARDO, P. G., WEISENBERG, M., FIRESTONE, I., & LEVY, B. (1965). Communicator effectiveness in producing public conformity and private attitude change. *Journal of Personality, 33,* 233–255.

Further Readings

Texts/Monographs

EAGLY, A. H., & CHAIKEN, S. (1993). *The psychology of attitudes.* Fort Worth, TX: Harcourt Brace Jovanovich.

An extraordinarily comprehensive and up-to-date graduate textbook on attitudes. The text provides coverage of all major conceptual positions and empirical findings.

FISHBEIN, M., & AJZEN, I. (1975). *Belief, attitude, intention, and behavior: An introduction to theory and research.* Reading, MA: Addison-Wesley.

The definitive reference for the most popular expectancy-value formulation—the theory of reasoned action.

McGUIRE, W. J. (1985). Attitudes and attitude change. In G. Lindzey & E. Aronson (Eds.), *Handbook of social psychology* (3rd ed., Vol. 2, pp. 233–346). New York: Random House.

An authoritative review of research. This review is particularly valuable because of its treatment of the historical foundations of attitude research and the organization of its review around the major source, message, recipient, and context variables.

PETTY, R. E., & CACIOPPO, J. T. (1981). *Attitudes and persuasion: Classic and contemporary approaches.* Dubuque, IA: Wm. C. Brown.

A text for undergraduates that provides coverage of the major theoretical positions and empirical findings. The book contains many illustrations and real-world examples.

PETTY, R. E., & CACIOPPO, J. T. (1986). *Communication and persuasion: Central and peripheral routes to attitude change.* New York: Springer/Verlag.

This research monograph provides extensive discussion of the elaboration likelihood model of persuasion addressing both conceptual issues and empirical support for the theory.

PRATKANIS, A., & ARONSON, E. (1992). *Age of propaganda: The everyday use and abuse of persuasion.* New York: W. H. Freeman.

This engaging book provides a large number of very short chapters linking a basic persuasion principle to numerous "real world" phenomena such as cult indoctrination.

ZIMBARDO, P. G., & LEIPPE, M. L. (1991). *The psychology of attitude change and social influence.* New York: McGraw-Hill.

An undergraduate text on attitude change with special attention paid to applications of basic research findings to health and legal issues.

Edited Volumes

ABELSON, R. P., ARONSON, E., McGUIRE, W. J., NEWCOMB, T. M., ROSENBERG, M. J., & TANNENBAUM, P. H. (Eds.) (1968). *Theories of cognitive consistency: A sourcebook.*

Produced when consistency theories were at their peak, this large volume contains 84 essays on the importance of consistency notions in a variety of domains.

BROCK, T. C., & SHAVITT, S. (Eds.) (1994). *Persuasion: Psychological insights and perspectives.* Needham Heights, MA: Allyn & Bacon.

A readable volume intended for undergraduates that covers the major conceptual and empirical issues in attitude formation and change. Each chapter is written by a noted expert on the topic of the chapter.

GREENWALD, A. G., BROCK, T. C., & OSTROM, T. M. (1968). New York: Academic Press.

Volume 1 in the Ohio State series on attitudes and persuasion. Contains chapters reviewing the major nonconsistency models of attitudes. Each chapter is written by a prominent attitude theorist.

PETTY, R. E., & KROSNICK, J. A. (Eds.) (1995). *Attitude strength: Antecedents and consequences.* Hillsdale, NJ: Lawrence Erlbaum Associates.

Volume 4 in the Ohio State series on attitudes and persuasion. Contains chapters addressing the major determinants and consequences of having strong attitudes. Each of the major variables linked to strong attitudes is covered in a separate chapter written by a major contributor to the field.

PETTY, R. E., OSTROM, T. M., & BROCK, T. C. (Eds.) (1981). *Cognitive responses in persuasion.* Hillsdale, NJ: Lawrence Erlbaum Associates.

Volume 2 in the Ohio State series on attitudes and persuasion. Contains chapters by noted authors reviewing methodological, empirical, and conceptual issues within the cognitive response approach to attitude change. The book was produced at the peak of interest in this approach.

PRATKANIS, A. R., BRECKLER, S. J., & GREENWALD, A. G. (Eds.) (1989). *Attitude structure and function.* Hillsdale, NJ: Lawrence Erlbaum Associates.

Volume 3 in the Ohio State series on attitudes and persuasion. Contains chapters covering issues related to the structure of attitudes and the functional approach to persuasion. Each chapter is written by an active researcher on the topic.

ZANNA, M. P., OLSON, J. M., & HERMAN, C. P. (Eds.) (1987). *Social Influence.* Hillsdale, NJ: Lawrence Erlbaum Associates.

Volume 5 in the Ontario symposium series on social behavior. Contains chapters by expert authors covering a diversity of contemporary issues in social influence from conformity to persuasion.

Robert B. Cialdini (Ph.D., University of North Carolina—Chapel Hill) is currently Regents' Professor of Psychology at Arizona State University, where he has also been named Graduate College Distinguished Research Professor. His professional interests include the study of social influence, self-presentation, and altruism. He is the author of the book Influence, *which has been published in several editions and seven languages. Cialdini attributes a sensitivity to social influences on human behavior to the fact that he grew up in a wholly Italian family, in a predominantly Polish neighborhood, in a historically German city (Milwaukee), in an otherwise rural state.*

CHAPTER 7

Principles and Techniques of Social Influence

Robert B. Cialdini
Arizona State University

CHAPTER OUTLINE

Blandishing persuasion steals the mind even of the wise.
—HOMER

For well over half a century, social psychologists have been investigating the process of social influence, wherein one person's attitudes, cognitions, or behaviors are changed through the doings of another. Because other authors within this volume have concerned themselves with social influences on attitudes and cognitions, my focus will be on the realm of behavior change and on the factors that cause one individual to comply with another's request for action of some sort. In the process, we will consider a set of six psychological principles that appear to influence behavioral compliance decisions most powerfully. Briefly, these principles involve pressures to comply because of tendencies to (1) return a gift, favor, or service; (2) be consistent with prior commitments; (3) follow the lead of similar others; (4) accommodate the requests of those we know and like; (5) conform to the directives of legitimate authority; and (6) seize opportunities that are scarce or dwindling in availability.

SOCIAL INFLUENCES ON COMPLIANCE

Focusing on Powerful Effects

Within academic social psychology, research into the behavioral compliance process has emphasized two questions: "Which principles and techniques reliably affect compliance?" and "How do these principles and techniques work to affect compliance as they do?" The first of these questions is concerned, of course, with the identification of real effects, while the second is concerned with their theoretical/conceptual mediation. Almost without exception, the vehicle that has been employed to answer these two questions has been the controlled experiment. And this is understandable, as controlled experimentation provides an excellent context for addressing such issues as whether an effect is real (i.e., reliable) and which theoretical/conceptual account best explains its occurrence.

However, a somewhat different approach is called for when one's concern with the compliance process is more than purely academic, as is the case for most of us who find ourselves either interested investigators or interested observers of the interpersonal influence interactions of daily life. We want to know more than whether a particular influence exists and what causes it. We want to know, as well, how powerful it is in the course of naturally occurring behavior, so that we can better decide whether the effect is especially worthy of our attention and study. In referring to the power of an effect on naturally occurring compliance, I mean its ability to change compliance decisions meaningfully over a wide range of everyday situations and circumstances.

Regrettably, when the question of primary interest includes a determination of the power of possible influences on natural compliance behavior, the controlled experiment becomes less suited to the job. The high levels of experimental rigor and precision that allow us to know that an effect is genuine and theoretically interpretable simultaneously decreases our ability to assess the potency of that effect. That is, because the best-designed experiments (1) eliminate or control away all sources of influence except the one under study and (2) possess highly sensitive measurement techniques, they may register whisper-like effects that may be so small as to never make a difference when other (extraneous) factors are allowed to vary naturally, as they typically do in the social environment. What's more, such ecologically trivial effects can be replicated repeatedly in the antiseptic environment of the controlled experiment, giving the mistaken impression of power, when, in reality, all that has been demonstrated is the reliability of the effects.

Thus, rigorous experimentation should not be used as the primary device for deciding which compliance-related influences are powerful enough to be submitted to rigorous experimentation for further study. Some other starting point should be found to identify the most potent influences on the compliance process. Otherwise, valuable time could well be spent seeking to investigate and to apply effects that are merely epiphenomena of the controlled experimental setting.

The Development of Powerful Compliance Inducers

A crucial question thus becomes, "How does one determine which are the most powerful compliance principles and tactics?" One answer involves the systematic observation of the behaviors of commercial compliance professionals.

Who are the commercial compliance professionals, and why should their actions be especially informative as to the identification of powerful influences on everyday compliance decisions? They can be defined as those individuals whose business or financial well-being is dependent on their ability to induce compliance (e.g., salespeople, fund-raisers, advertisers, political lobbyists, cult recruiters, negotiators, con artists). With this definition in place, one can begin to recognize why the regular and widespread practices of these professionals would be noteworthy indicators of the powerful influences on the compliance process: Because the livelihoods of commercial compliance professionals depend on the effectiveness of their procedures, those professionals who use procedures that work well to elicit compliance responses will survive and flourish. Further, they will pass these successful procedures on to succeeding generations (trainees). However, those practitioners who use unsuccessful compliance procedures either will drop them or will quickly go out of business; in either case, the procedures themselves will not be passed on to newer generations.

The upshot of this process is that, over time and over the range of naturally occurring compliance contexts, the strongest and most adaptable procedures for generating compliance will rise, persist, and accumulate. Further, these procedures will point a careful observer toward the major principles that people use to decide when to comply. Several years ago, I resolved to become such an observer. What emerged from this period of systematic observation was a list of six principles on which compliance professionals appeared to base most of their psychological influence attempts: reciprocity, consistency, social validation, friendship/liking, authority, and scarcity. A full account of the origins, workings, and prevalence of these six principles is available elsewhere (Cialdini, 1993). However, the remainder of this chapter offers a summary description of the principles and of the social scientific theory and evidence regarding how each principle functions to motivate compliance.

THE PRINCIPLES

Reciprocation

Pay every debt as if God wrote the bill.
—RALPH WALDO EMERSON

One of the most powerful norms in all human cultures is that for reciprocity (Gouldner, 1960), which obligates individuals to return the form of behavior that they have received from another. Not only does the norm apply to all cultures, but it applies to all behavior within those cultures. For instance, we report liking those who report liking us (Byrne & Rhamey, 1965; Condon & Crano, 1988); we cooperate with cooperators and compete against competitors (Braver, 1975; Rosenbaum, 1980); we self-disclose to those who have self-disclosed to us (Cunningham, Strassberg, & Haan, 1986); we yield to the persuasive appeals of those who have previously yielded to one of our persuasive appeals (Cialdini, Green, & Rusch, 1992); we try to harm those who have tried to harm us (Dengerink, Schnedler, & Covey, 1978); and in negotiations, we make concessions to those who have offered concessions to us (Axelrod, 1984).

A widely shared feeling of future obligation made an enormous difference in human social evolution. For the first time in evolutionary history, one individual could give any of a variety of resources—help, gifts, tools, goods—without actually giving them away. Sophisticated and coordinated systems of gift giving, defense, and trade became possible, bringing immense benefit to the societies that possessed them (Leakey & Lewin, 1978). With such clearly adaptive consequences for the culture, it is not surprising that the norm for reciprocation is so deeply implanted in us by the process of socialization.

A *reciprocation rule* for compliance can be worded as follows: *One should be more willing to comply with a request from someone who has previously provided a favor or concession.* Under this general rule, people will feel obligated to provide gifts, favors, services, and aid to those who have given them such things first (DePaulo, Brittingham, & Kaiser, 1983; Eisenberger, Cotterell, & Marvel, 1987; Tesser, Gatewood, & Driver, 1968), sometimes even returning larger favors than those they have received (Regan, 1971). A number of sales and fund-raising tactics use this factor to advantage. The compliance professional initially gives something to the target person, thereby causing the target to be more likely to give something in return. Often, this "something in return" is the target person's compliance with a substantial request.

The unsolicited gift, accompanied by a request for a donation, is a commonly used technique that employs the norm for reciprocity. One example experienced by many people is the Hare Krishna solicitor who gives the unwary passerby a book or a flower and then asks for a donation. Other organizations send free gifts through the mail; legitimate and less-than-legitimate missionary and disabled veterans organizations often employ this highly effective device. These groups count on the fact that most people will not go to the trouble of returning the gift and will feel uncomfortable about keeping it without reciprocating in some way. For instance, the Disabled American Veterans organization reports that its simple mail appeal for donations produces a response rate of about 18 percent. But when the mailing also includes an unsolicited gift (gummed, individualized address labels), the success rate nearly doubles to 35 percent (Smolowe, 1990).

The socialized sense of discomfort that attends an unpaid debt does not only explain why people will often agree to perform a return favor that is larger than the one they received. It also explains why people frequently refrain from asking for a needed favor if they will not be in a position to repay it (DePaulo, Nadler, & Fisher, 1983; Greenberg & Shapiro, 1971; Riley & Eckenrode, 1986): The saddle of unmet social debt weighs heavily, and we will go to considerable lengths to remove or avoid it.

The features of the rule for reciprocation account nicely for the twin outcomes of a study by Rand Corporation researchers Berry and Kanouse (1987). They found that, by paying physicians first, it was possible to increase the likelihood that the doctors would complete and return a long questionnaire they received in the mail. If a check for $20 accompanied the questionnaire, 78 percent of the physicians filled out the survey and sent it back as requested. But if they learned that the $20 check was to be sent to them after they complied, only 66 percent did so. By giving the check the character of a noncontingent gift rather than of a reward for compliance, the researchers enhanced their success substantially.

The second reciprocation-related finding concerned only the physicians who got the check up front. As indicated, most complied with the questionnaire request, but some did not. Although virtually all (95 percent) of the doctors who had complied cashed their checks, only 26 percent of those who did not comply did so. If they were not in a position to reciprocate the $20 gift, they were not of a mind to accept it, making the "accompanying gift" technique a highly cost effective one for the researchers.

Reciprocal Concessions

A variation of the norm for reciprocation of favors is that for reciprocation of concessions. A reciprocal concessions procedure (or *door-in-the-face technique*) for inducing compliance has been documented repeatedly (e.g., Cialdini, Vincent, Lewis, Catalan, Wheeler, & Darby, 1975; Harari, Mohr, & Hosey, 1980; Reeves, Baker, Boyd, & Cialdini, 1991). A requester uses this procedure by beginning with an extreme request that is nearly always rejected and then retreating to a more moderate favor—the one the requester had in mind from the outset. In doing so, the requester hopes that the retreat from extreme to moderate request will spur the target person to make a reciprocal concession—by moving from initial rejection of the larger favor to acceptance of the smaller one. This reciprocal concessions strategy has been successfully used in fund-raising contexts where, after refusing a larger request for donations, people become substantially more likely than before to give the average contribution (e.g., Reingen, 1978). Cialdini and Ascani (1976) also used this technique in soliciting blood donors. They first requested a person's involvement in a long-term donor program. When that request was refused, the solicitor made a smaller request for a one-time donation. This pattern of a large request (that is refused) followed by a smaller request significantly increased compliance with the smaller request, as compared to a control condition of people who were asked only to perform the smaller one-time favor (50 percent vs. 32 percent compliance rate).

Of special interest to university students is evidence that the door-in-the-face technique can greatly increase a professor's willingness to spend time helping a student (Harari, Mohr, & Hosey, 1980). In that study, only 59 percent of faculty members were willing to spend "15 to 20 minutes" to meet with a student on an issue of interest to the student—when that was the only request the student made. However, significantly more faculty members (78 percent) were willing to agree to that same request if they had first refused the student's request to spend "2 hours a week for the rest of the semester" meeting with the student.

Related to the door-in-the-face technique but somewhat different from it is the *that's-not-all technique* investigated by Burger (1986) and frequently used by sales operators. An important procedural difference between the two techniques is that, in the that's-not-all tactic, the target person does not turn down the first offer before a better second offer is provided. After making the first offer but before the target can respond, the requester betters the deal with an additional item or a price reduction. Burger (1986) found this approach to be useful in selling more goods during a campus bake sale. One reason that this technique works appears to be the target person's desire to reciprocate for the better deal.

Social Validation

If you can keep your head when all around you are losing theirs, you probably haven't grasped the situation.

—JEAN KERR

People frequently use the beliefs, attitudes, and actions of others, particularly similar others, as a standard of comparison against which to evaluate the correctness of their own beliefs, attitudes, and actions. Thus, it is common for individuals to decide on appropriate behaviors for themselves in a given situation by searching for information as to how similar others have behaved or are behaving there (e.g., Festinger, 1954; Latané & Darley, 1970; Schachter & Singer, 1962). This simple principle of behavior accounts for an amazingly varied array of human responses. For instance, research has shown that New Yorkers use it in deciding whether to return a lost wallet (Hornstein, Fisch, & Holmes, 1968), that children with a fear of dogs use it in deciding whether to risk approaching a dog (Bandura & Menlove, 1968), that amusement park visitors use it to decide whether to litter in a public place (Cialdini, Reno, & Kallgren, 1990), that audience members use it in deciding whether a joke is funny (Cupchik & Leventhal, 1974), that pedestrians use it in deciding whether to stop and stare at an empty spot in the sky (Milgram, Bickman, & Berkowitz, 1969), and, on the alarming side, that troubled individuals use it in deciding whether to commit suicide (Phillips & Carstensen, 1988).

Much of this evidence can be understood in terms of Festinger's (1954) *social comparison theory*, which states that (1) people have a constant drive to evaluate themselves (i.e., the appropriateness of their abilities, beliefs, feelings, and behaviors); (2) if available, people will prefer to use objective cues to make these evaluations; (3) if objective evidence is not available, people will rely on social comparison evidence instead; and (4) when seeking social comparison evidence for these self-evaluations, people will look to similar others as the preferred basis for comparison. So, if, while sitting in a seminar, you find yourself feeling the room getting uncomfortably warm, social comparison theory would make some predictions about how you would likely behave. First, you ought to feel a need to assess the appropriateness of your feeling, which should manifest itself as a search for validating information. If, by chance, there is a thermometer on the wall immediately behind your chair, your first inclination would be to glance over to it to get objective verification of your perception. But should no thermometer be present, you would have to resort to social information; so, you might nudge a classmate (a similar other) and whisper something to the effect of "Does it feel warm in here to you?" Only then, and only if the evidence confirmed your perception, would you likely feel justified in taking congruous action (e.g., asking that the thermostat be adjusted or a window be opened).

When the goal is to evaluate the correctness of an opinion or action, research has generally supported Festinger's theory. For example, social comparison is most likely to occur in situations that are objectively unclear (Tesser, Campbell, & Mickler, 1983) and is most likely to be directed at similar others (Goethals & Darley, 1977; Miller, 1984).[1] Thus, when people are unsure, they are most likely to look to and accept the beliefs and behaviors of similar others as valid indicators of what they should believe and do themselves.

The *social validation rule* for compliance can be stated as follows: *One should be more willing to comply with a request for behavior if it is consistent with what similar others are thinking or doing.* Our tendency to assume that an action is more correct if others are doing it is exploited in a variety of settings. Bartenders often "salt" their tip jars with a few dollar bills at the beginning of the evening to simulate tips left by prior customers and, thereby, to give the impression that tipping with folded money is proper barroom behavior. Church ushers sometimes prime collection baskets for the same reason and with the same positive effect on proceeds. Evangelical preachers are known to seed their audiences with "ringers," who are rehearsed to come forward at a specified time to give witness and donations. For example, an Arizona State University research team that infiltrated the Billy Graham organization reported on such advance preparations prior to one of his Crusade visits. "By the time Graham arrives in town and makes his altar call, an army of 6,000 await with instructions on when to come forth at varying intervals to create the impression of spontaneous mass outpouring" (Altheide & Johnson, 1977). Advertisers love to inform us when a product is the "fastest growing" or "largest selling" because they don't have to convince us directly that the product is good; they need only say that many others think so, which seems proof enough. The producers of charity telethons devote inordinate amounts of time to the incessant listing of viewers who have already pledged contributions. The message being communicated to the holdouts is clear: "Look at all the people who have decided to give; it *must* be the correct thing to do."

One tactic that compliance professionals use to engage the principle of social validation has been put to scientific test. Called the *list technique*, it involves asking for a request only after the target person has been shown a list of similar others who have already complied. Reingen (1982) conducted several experiments in which college students or home owners were asked to donate money or blood to a charitable cause. Those individuals who were initially shown a list of similar others who had already complied were significantly more likely to comply themselves. What's more, the longer the list, the greater was the effect.

Consistency

It is easier to resist at the beginning than at the end.
—LEONARDO DA VINCI

Social psychologists have long understood the strength of the consistency principle to direct human action. Prominent early theorists like Leon Festinger (1957), Fritz Heider (1958), and Theodore Newcomb (1953) have viewed the desire for consistency as a prime motivator of our behavior. More recently, other theorists (e.g., Baumeister, 1982; Tedeschi, 1981) have recognized that the desire to *appear* consistent exerts considerable influence over our behavior as well. If we grant that the power of consistency is formidable in directing human action, an important practical question immediately arises: How is that force engaged? Social psychologists think they know the answer—commitment. If I can get you to make a commitment (that is, to take a stand, to go on record), I will have set the stage for your consistency with that earlier commitment. Once a stand is taken, there is a natural tendency to behave in ways that are stubbornly consistent with the stand (Deutsch & Gerard, 1955; Greenwald, Carnot, Beach, & Young, 1987; Howard, 1990; Sherman, 1980).

A *consistency rule* for compliance can be worded as follows: *After committing oneself to a position, one should be more willing to comply with requests for behaviors that are consistent with that position.* Any of a variety of strategies may be used to generate the crucial instigating commitment.

One such strategy is the *foot-in-the-door technique* (Freedman & Fraser, 1966; Schwartzwald, Bizman, & Raz, 1983). A solicitor using this procedure will first ask for a small favor that is virtually certain to be granted. The initial compliance is then followed by a request for a larger, *related* favor. It has been found repeatedly that people who have agreed to the initial small favor are more willing to do the larger one (see Beaman et al., 1983, for a review), seemingly to be consistent with the implication of the initial action. For instance, home owners who had agreed to accept and wear a small lapel pin promoting a local charity were, as a consequence, more likely to contribute money to that charity when canvassed during a subsequent donation drive (Pliner, Hart, Kohl, & Saari, 1974).

Freedman and Fraser (1966) have argued that the foot-in-the-door technique is successful because performance of the initially requested action causes individuals to see themselves as possessing certain traits. For example, in the Pliner and colleagues (1974) study, after taking and wearing the charity pin, subjects would be expected to see themselves as favorable toward charitable causes, especially this particular one. Later, when asked to perform the larger, related favor of contributing to that charity, subjects would be more willing to do so to be consistent with the "charitable" trait they had assigned to themselves. Recent support for this interpretation comes from a study showing that children are not influenced by the foot-in-the-door technique until they are old enough to understand the idea of a stable personality trait (around 6 to 7 years). Once children are old enough to understand the meaning of a stable trait, the foot-in-the-door tactic becomes effective, especially among those children who prefer consistency in behavior (Eisenberg, Cialdini, McCreath, & Shell, 1987).

Other, more unsavory techniques induce a commitment to an item and then remove the inducements that generated the commitment. Remarkably, the commitment frequently remains. For example, the *bait and switch procedure* is used by some retailers who may advertise certain merchandise (e.g., a room of furniture) at a special low price. When the customer arrives to take advantage of the special, he or she finds the merchandise to be of low quality or sold out. However, because customers have by now made an active commitment to getting new furniture at that particular store, they are more willing to agree to examine and, consequently, to buy alternative merchandise there (Joule, Gouilloux, & Weber, 1989).

A similar strategy is employed by car dealers in the *low-ball technique*, which proceeds by obtaining a commitment to an action and *then* increasing the costs of performing the action (Cialdini, Cacioppo, Bassett, & Miller, 1978). The automobile salesperson who "throws the low ball" induces the customer to decide to buy a particular model car by offering a low price on the car or an inflated one on the customer's trade-in. After the decision has been made (and, at times, after the commitment is enhanced by allowing the customer to arrange financing, take the car home overnight, etc.), something happens to remove the reason the customer decided to buy. Perhaps a price calculation error is found, or the used car assessor disallows the inflated trade-in figure. By this time, though, many customers have experienced an internal commitment to that specific automobile and proceed with the purchase. Experimental research has documented the effectiveness of this tactic in settings beyond automobile sales (e.g., Brownstein & Katzev, 1985; Joule, 1987). Additional research indicates that the tactic is effective primarily when used by a single requester (Burger & Petty, 1981) and when the initial commitment is freely made (Cialdini, Cacioppo, Bassett, Miller, 1978).

One thing that these procedures (and others like them) have in common is the establishment of an earlier commitment that is consistent with a later action desired by the compliance professional. The need for consistency then takes over to compel performance of the desired behavior. However, not all types of these earlier commitments are equally effective. There is research evidence suggesting the types of commitments that lead to consistent future responding. The present context does not allow sufficient space for a thorough discussion of that evidence. Nonetheless, I would argue that a fair summary of the research literature is that a commitment is likely to be maximally effective in producing consistent future behavior to the extent that it is active (Bem, 1967), effortful (Aronson & Mills, 1959), public (Deutsch & Gerard, 1955), and viewed as internally motivated (i.e., uncoerced, Freedman, 1965).

Another approach to employing the commitment/consistency principle also has popularity among commercial compliance professionals. Rather than inducing a new commitment to their product or service, many practitioners point out existing commitments within potential customers that are consistent with the product or service being offered. In this way, desirable existing commitments are made more visible to the customer, and the strain for consistency is allowed to direct behavior accordingly. For example, insurance agents are frequently taught to stress to new home owners that the purchase of an expensive house reflects an enormous personal commitment to one's home and the well-being of one's family. Consequently, they argue it would only be consistent with such a commitment to home and family to purchase home and life insurance in amounts that befit the size of this commitment. Research of various kinds indicates that this sort of sensitization to commitments and to consequent inconsistencies can be effective in producing belief, attitude, and behavior change. Ball-Rokeach, Rokeach, & Grube (1984) demonstrated long-term behavioral effects from a television program that focused viewers on their personal commitments to certain deep-seated values (e.g., freedom, equality), on the one hand, and their current beliefs and behaviors, on the other. Not only did uninterrupted viewers of this single program evidence enhanced commitment to these values, but they were significantly more likely to donate money to support causes consistent with the values 2 to 3 months after the program had aired.

A more manipulative tactic than merely focusing people on their existing values is to put them in a situation where to refuse a specific request would be inconsistent with a value that people wish to be known as possessing (Greenwald, Carnot, Beach, & Young, 1987; Sherman, 1980). One such tactic is the *legitimization-of-paltry-favors* (or even-a-penny-would-help) *technique* (Cialdini & Schroeder, 1976). Most people prefer to behave in ways that are consistent with a view of themselves as helpful, charitable individuals. Consequently, a fund-raiser who makes a request that legitimizes a paltry amount of aid ("Could you give a contribution, even a penny would help") makes it difficult for a target to refuse to give at all; to do so risks appearing to be a very unhelpful person. Notice that this procedure does not specifically request a trivial sum; that would probably lead to a profusion of pennies and a small total take. Instead, the request simply makes a minuscule form of aid acceptable, thereby reducing the target's ability to give nothing and still remain consistent with the desirable image of a helpful individual. After all, how could a person remain committed to a helpful image after refusing to contribute when "even a penny would help"?

Experimental research done to validate the effectiveness of the technique has shown it to be successful in increasing the percentage of charity contributors (Brockner, Guzzi, Kane, Levine, & Shaplen, 1984; Cialdini & Schroeder, 1976; Reeves, Macolini, & Martin, 1987; Reingen, 1978; Weyant, 1984). What's more, in each of these studies the even-a-penny procedure proved profitable because subjects didn't actually give a penny but provided the donation amount typically given to charities. Thus, the legitimization-of-paltry-favors approach appears to work by getting more people to agree to give (so as to be consistent with a helpful image); but the decision of how much to give is left unaffected by the mention of a paltry amount. The consequence is increased proceeds.

A last commitment-based tactic deserves mention—one that we might call the "How are you feeling?" technique. Have you noticed that callers asking you to contribute to some cause or another these days seem to begin things by inquiring as to your current health and well-being? "Hello, Mr./Ms. Targetperson?" they say. "How are you feeling this evening?" Or, "How are you doing today?" The caller's intent with this sort of introduction is not merely to seem friendly and caring. It is to get you to respond—as you normally do to such polite, superficial inquiries—with a polite, superficial comment of your own: "Just fine" or "Real good" or "I'm doing great, thanks." Once you have publicly stated that all is well, it becomes much easier for the solicitor to corner you into aiding those for whom all is not well: "I'm glad to hear that, because I'm calling to ask if you'd be willing to make a donation to help out the unfortunate victims of . . ."

The theory behind this tactic is that people who have just asserted that they are doing/feeling fine—even as a routine part of a sociable exchange—will consequently find it awkward to appear stingy in the context of their own admittedly favored circumstances. If all this sounds a bit far-fetched, consider the findings of consumer researcher Daniel Howard (1990), who put the theory to the test. Dallas, Texas, residents were called on the phone and asked if they would agree to allow a representative of the Hunger Relief Committee to come to their homes to sell them cookies, the proceeds from which would be used to supply meals for the needy. When tried alone, that request (labeled the standard solicitation approach) produced only 18 percent agreement. However, if the caller initially asked "How are you feeling this evening?" and waited for a reply before proceeding with the standard approach, several noteworthy things happened. First, of the 120 individuals called, most (108) gave the customary favorable replay ("Good," "Fine," "Real well," etc.). Second, 32 percent of the people who got the how-are-you-feeling-tonight question agreed to receive the cookie seller at their homes, nearly twice the success rate of the standard solicitation approach. Third, true to the consistency principle, almost everyone who agreed to such a visit did in fact make a cookie purchase when contacted at home (89 percent).

Friendship/Liking

The main work of a trial attorney is to make the jury like his client.
—CLARENCE DARROW

A fact of social interaction that each of us can attest to is that people are more favorably inclined toward the needs of those they know and like. Consequently, a *friendship/liking rule* for compliance can be worded as follows: *One should be more willing to comply with the requests of friends or other liked individuals.* Could there be any doubt that this is the case after examining the remarkable success of the Tupperware Corporation and their "home party" demonstration concept (Frenzen & Davis, 1990)? The demonstration party for Tupperware products is hosted by an individual, usually a woman, who invites to her home an array of friends, neighbors, and relatives, all of whom know that their hostess receives a percentage of the profits from every piece sold by the Tupperware representative, who is also there. In this way, the Tupperware Corporation arranges for its customers to buy from and *for* a friend rather than from an unknown salesperson. So favorable has been the effect on proceeds ($2.5 million in sales per day!) that the Tupperware Corporation has wholly abandoned its early retail outlets, and a Tupperware party begins somewhere every 2.7 seconds.

Most influence agents, however, attempt to engage the friendship/liking principle in a different way: Before making a request, they get their targets to like *them*. But how do they do it? It turns out that the tactics that practitioners use to generate liking cluster around certain factors that also have been shown by controlled research to increase liking.

Physical Attractiveness

Although it is generally acknowledged that good-looking people have an advantage in social interaction, research findings indicate that we may have sorely underestimated the size and reach of that advantage. There appears to be a positive reaction to good physical appearance that generalizes to such favorable trait perceptions as a talent, kindness, honesty, and intelligence (See Eagly et al., 1991, for a review). As a consequence, attractive individuals are more persuasive in terms of both changing attitudes (Chaiken, 1979) and getting what they request (Benson, Karabenic, & Lerner, 1976). For instance, a study of the 1974 Canadian Federal elections found that attractive candidates received more than two and a half times the votes of unattractive ones (Efran & Patterson, 1976). Equally impressive results seem to pertain to the judicial system (see reviews by Castellow, Wuensch, & Moore, 1990; and Downs & Lyons, 1991). In a Pennsylvania study, researchers rated the physical attractiveness of 74 separate male defendants at the start of their criminal trials. When much later, the researchers checked the results of these cases via court records, they found that the better-looking men received significantly lighter sentences. In fact, the attractive defendants were twice as likely to avoid incarceration as the unattractive defendants (Stewart, 1980). When viewed in the light of such powerful effects, it is not surprising that extremely attractive models are employed to promote products and services, that sales trainers frequently include appearance and grooming tips in their presentations, or that, commonly, con men are handsome and con women pretty.

Similarity

We like people who are similar to us (Byrne, 1971; Carli, Ganley, & Pierce-Otay, 1991). This fact seems to hold true whether the similarity occurs in the area of opinions, personality traits, background, or lifestyle. Consequently, those who wish to be liked in order to increase our compliance can accomplish that purpose by appearing similar to us in any of a wide variety of ways. For that reason, it would be wise to be careful around salespeople who just *seem* to be just like us. Many sales training programs now urge trainees to "mirror and match" the customer's body posture, mood, and verbal style, as similarities along each of these dimensions have been shown to lead to positive results (LaFrance, 1985; Locke & Horowitz, 1990; Woodside & Davenport, 1974).

Similarity in dress provides still another example. Several studies have demonstrated that we are more likely to help those who dress like us. In one study, done in the early 1970s when young people tended to dress either in "hippie" or "straight" fashion, experimenters donned hippie or straight attire and asked college students on campus for a dime to make a phone call. When the experimenter was dressed in the same way as the student, the request was granted in over two-thirds of the instances; but when the student and requester were dissimilarly dressed, a dime was provided less than half of the time (Emswiller, Deaux, & Willits, 1971). Another experiment shows how automatic our positive response to similar others can be. Marchers in a political demonstration were found not only to be more likely to sign the petition of a similarly dressed requester but to do so without bothering to read it first (Suedfeld, Bochner, & Matas, 1971).

Compliments

Praise and other forms of positive estimation also stimulate liking (e.g., Byrne & Rhamey, 1965). The actor Maclain Stevenson once described how his wife tricked him into marriage: "She said she liked me." Although designed for a laugh, the remark is as much instructive as humorous. The simple information that someone fancies us can be a bewitchingly effective device for producing return liking and willing compliance. Although there are limits to our gullibility—especially when we can be sure that the flatterer's intent is manipulative (Jones & Wortman, 1973)—we tend as a rule to believe praise and to like those who provide it. Evidence for the power of praise on liking comes from a study (Drachman, deCarufel, & Insko, 1978) in which men received personal comments from someone who needed a favor from them. Some of the men got only positive comments, some only negative comments, and some got a mixture of good and bad. There were three interesting findings. First, the evaluator who offered only praise was liked the best. Second, this was so even though the men fully realized that the flatterer stood to gain from their liking of him. Finally, unlike the other types of comments, pure praise did not have to be accurate to work. Compliments produced just as much liking for the flatterer when they were untrue as when they were true.

It is for such reasons that direct salespeople are educated in the art of praise. A potential customer's home, clothes, car, taste, etc., are all frequent targets for compliments.

Cooperation

Cooperation is another factor that has been shown to enhance positive feelings and behavior (e.g., Aronson, Bridgeman, & Geffner, 1978; Bettencourt, Brewer, Croak, & Miller, 1992; Cook, 1990). Those who cooperate toward the achievement of a common goal are more favorable and helpful to each other as a consequence. That is why compliance professionals often strive to be perceived as cooperating partners with a target person (Rafaeli & Sutton, 1991). Automobile sales managers frequently set themselves as "villains" so that the salesperson can "do battle" in the customer's behalf. The cooperative, pulling together kind of relationship that is consequently produced between the salesperson and customer naturally leads to a desirable form of liking that promotes sales.

Scarcity

> *The way to love anything is to realize that it might be lost.*
> —GILBERT KEITH CHESTERTON

Opportunities seem more valuable to us when they are less available (Lynn, 1991). Interestingly, this is often true even when the opportunity holds little attraction for us on its own merits. Take, as evidence, the experience of Florida State University students who, like most undergraduates, rated themselves dissatisfied with the quality of their cafeteria's food. Nine days later, they had changed their minds, rating that food significantly better than they had before. It is instructive that no actual improvement in food service had occurred between the two ratings. Instead, earlier on the day of the second rating students had learned that, because of a fire, they could not eat at the cafeteria for two weeks (West, 1975).

There appear to be two major sources of the power of scarcity. First, because we know that the things that are difficult to possess are typically better than those that are easy to possess, we can often use an item's availability to help us quickly and correctly decide on its quality (Lynn, 1992). Thus, one reason for the potency of scarcity is that, by assessing it, we can get a shortcut indication of an item's value.

In addition, there is a unique, secondary source of power within scarcity: As the things we can have become less available, we lose freedoms; and we *hate* to lose the freedoms we already have. This desire to preserve our established prerogatives is the centerpiece of *psychological reactance theory* (Brehm, 1966; Brehm & Brehm, 1981) developed to explain the human response to diminishing personal control. According to the theory, whenever they are limited or threatened, the need to retain our freedoms makes us want them (as well as the goods and services associated with them) significantly more than previously. So, when increasing scarcity—or anything else—interferes with our prior access to some item, we will *react against* the interference by wanting and trying to possess the item more than before.

One naturally occurring example of the consequences of increased scarcity can be seen in the outcome of a decision by county officials in Miami to ban the use and possession of phosphate detergents. Spurred by the tendency to want what they could no longer have, the majority of Miami consumers came to see phosphate cleaners as better products than before. Compared to Tampa residents, who were not affected by the Miami ordinance, the citizens of Miami rated phosphate detergents as gentler, more effective in cold water, better whiteners and fresheners, more powerful on stains, etc. After passage of the law, they had even come to believe that phosphate detergents poured easier than did the Tampa consumer (Mazis, 1975).

This sort of response is typical of individuals who have lost an established freedom and is crucial to an understanding of how psychological reactance and scarcity work on us. When our freedom to have something is limited, the item becomes less available, and we experience an increased desire for it. However, we rarely recognize that psychological reactance has caused us to want the item more; all we know is that we *want* it. Still, we need to make sense of our desire for the item, so we begin to assign it positive qualities to justify the desire. After all, it is natural to suppose that, if one feels drawn to something, it is because of the merit of the thing. In the case of the Miami antiphosphate law—and in other instances of newly restricted availability—that is a faulty supposition. Phosphate detergents clean, whiten, and pour no better after they are banned than before. We just assume they do because we find that we desire them more.

Other research has suggested that in addition to commodities, limited access to information makes the information more desirable—and more influential (Brock, 1968; Brock & Bannon, 1992). One test of Brock's thinking found good support in a business setting. Wholesale beef buyers who were told of an impending imported beef shortage purchased significantly more beef when they were informed that the shortage information came from certain "exclusive" contacts that the importer had (Knishinsky, 1982). Apparently, the fact that the scarcity news was itself scarce made it more valued and persuasive. Additional evidence—from the literature on censorship—suggests that restricting information can empower that information in unintended ways. Individuals typically respond to censorship by wanting to receive the banned information to a greater extent and by becoming more favorable to it than before the ban (e.g., Worchel & Arnold, 1973; Worchel, 1992). Especially interesting is the finding that people will come to believe in banned information more even though they haven't received it (Worchel, Arnold, & Baker, 1975).

A *scarcity rule* for compliance can be worded as follows: *One should try to secure those opportunities that are scarce or dwindling.* With scarcity operating powerfully on the worth assigned to things, it should not be surprising that compliance professionals have a variety of techniques designed to convert this power to compliance. Probably the most frequently used such technique is the "limited number" tactic in which the customer is informed that membership opportunities, products, or services exist in a limited supply that cannot be guaranteed to last for long.

Related to the limited number tactic is the "deadline" technique in which an official time limit is placed on the customer's opportunity to get what is being offered. Newspaper ads abound with admonitions to the customer regarding the folly of delay: "Last three days." "Limited time offer." "One week only sale." The purest form of a decision deadline—right now—occurs in a variant of the deadline technique in which customers are told that, unless they make an immediate purchase decision, they will have to buy the item at a higher price, or they will not be able to purchase it at all. I found this tactic used in numerous compliance settings. A large child photography company urges parents to buy as many poses and copies as they can afford because "stocking limitations force us to burn the unsold pictures of your children within 24 hours." A prospective health club member or automobile buyer might learn that the deal offered by the salesperson is good for that one time; should the customer leave the premises, the deal is off. One home vacuum cleaner sales company instructed me as a trainee to claim to prospects that "I have so many other people to see that I have the time to visit a family only once. It's company policy that even if you decide later that you want this machine, I can't come back and sell it to you." For anyone who thought about it carefully, this was nonsense; the company and its representatives are in the business of making sales, and any customer who called for another visit would be accommodated gladly. The real purpose of the can't-come-back-again claim was to evoke the possibility of loss that is inherent in the scarcity rule for compliance.

The idea of potential loss plays a large role in human decision making. In fact, people seem to be more motivated by the thought of losing something than by the thought of gaining something of equal value (Tversky & Kahneman, 1981). For instance, home owners told about how much money they could lose from inadequate insulation are more likely to insulate their homes than those told about how much money they could save (Gonzales, Aronson, & Costanzo, 1988). Similar results have been obtained by health researchers (Meyerwitz & Chaiken, 1987; Meyerwitz, Wilson, & Chaiken, 1991): Pamphlets urging young women to check for breast cancer through self-examinations are significantly more successful if they state their case in terms of what stands to be lost (e.g., "You can lose several potential health benefits by failing to spend only 5 minutes each month doing breast self-examination") rather than gained (e.g., "You can gain several potential health benefits by spending only 5 minutes each month doing breast self-examination").

Authority

Follow an expert.
        —Virgil

Legitimately constituted authorities are extremely influential persons (e.g., Aronson, Turner, & Carlsmith, 1963; Blass, 1991; Milgram, 1974). Whether they have acquired their positions through knowledge, talent, or fortune, their positions bespeak of superior information and power. For each of us this has always been the case. Early on, these people (e.g., parents, teachers) knew more than us, and we found that taking their advice proved beneficial—partly because of their greater wisdom and partly because they controlled our rewards and punishments. As adults, the authority figures have changed to employers, judges, police officers, and the like, but the benefits associated with doing as they say have not. For most people, then, conforming to the dictates of authority figures produces genuine practical advantages. Consequently, it makes great sense to comply with the wishes of properly constituted authorities. It makes so much sense, in fact, that people often do so when it makes no sense at all.

Take, for example, the strange case of the "rectal earache" reported by two professors of pharmacy, Michael Cohen and Neil Davis (1981). A physician ordered eardrops to be administered to the right ear of a patient suffering pain and infection there. But instead of writing out completely the location "right ear" on the prescription, the doctor abbreviated it so that the instructions read "place in R ear." Upon receiving the prescription, the duty nurse promptly put the required number of eardrops into the patient's anus. Obviously, rectal treatment of an earache made no sense. Yet, neither the patient nor the nurse questioned it.

Of course, the most dramatic research evidence for the power of legitimate authority comes from the famous Milgram experiment in which 65 percent of the subjects were willing to deliver continued, intense, and dangerous levels of electric shock to a kicking, screeching, pleading other subject simply because an authority figure—in this case a scientist—directed them to do so. Although virtually everyone who has ever taken a psychology course has learned about this experiment, Milgram (1974) conducted a series of variations on his basic procedure that are less well known but equally compelling in making the point about the powerful role that authority played in causing subjects to behave so cruelly. For instance, in one variation, Milgram had the scientist and the victim switch scripts so that the scientist told the subject to stop delivering shock to the victim, while the victim insisted bravely that the subject continue for the good of the experiment. The results couldn't have been clearer: Not a single subject gave even one additional shock when it was a nonauthority who demanded it.

An *authority rule* for compliance can be worded as follows: *One should be more willing to follow the suggestions of someone who is a legitimate authority.* Authorities may be seen as falling into two categories: authorities with regard to the specific situation and more general authorities. Compliance practitioners employ techniques that seek to benefit from the power invested in authority figures of both types. In the case of authority relevant to a specific situation, we can note how often advertisers inform their audiences of the level of expertise of product manufacturers (e.g., "Fashionable men's clothiers since 1841"; "Babies are our business, our only business"). At times, the expertise associated with a product has been more symbolic than substantive, for instance, when actors in television commercials wear physicians' white coats to recommend a product. In one famous Sanka commercial, the actor involved, Robert Young, did not need a white coat, as his prior identity as TV doctor Marcus Welby, M.D., provided the medical connection. It is instructive that the mere symbols of a physician's expertise and authority are enough to trip the mechanism that governs authority influence. One of the most prominent of these symbols, the bare title "Dr.," has been shown to be devastatingly effective as a compliance device among trained hospital personnel. In what may be the most frightening study I know, a group of physicians and nurses conducted an experiment that documented the dangerous degree of blind obedience that hospital nurses accorded to an individual whom they had never met, but who claimed in a phone call to be a doctor (Hofling, Brotzman, Dalrymple, Graves, & Pierce, 1966). Ninety-five percent of those nurses were willing to administer an unsafe level of a drug merely because that caller requested it.

In the case of influence that generalizes outside of relevant expertise, the impact of authority (real and symbolic) appears equally impressive. For instance, researchers have found that, when wearing a security guard's uniform, a requester could produce more compliance with requests (e.g., to pick up a paper bag on the street, to stand on the other side of a Bus Stop sign) that were irrelevant to a security guard's domain of authority (Bickman, 1974; Bushman, 1988). Less blatant in its connotation than a uniform, but nonetheless effective, is another kind of attire that has traditionally bespoken of authority status in our culture—the well-tailored business suit. It also can mediate influence. Take as evidence the results of a study by Lefkowitz, Blake, and Mouton (1955), who found that three and a half times as many people were willing to follow a jay-walker into traffic when he wore a suit and tie versus a work shirt and trousers (but see Mullin, Cooper, & Driskell, 1990).

Con artists frequently make use of the influence inherent in authority attire. For example, a gambit called the bank examiner scheme depends heavily on the automatic deference most people assign to authority figures, or those merely dressed as such. Using the two uniforms of authority we have already mentioned, a business suit and guard's outfit, the con begins when a man dressed in a conservative three-piece suit appears at the home of a likely victim and identifies himself as an official of the victim's bank. The victim is told of suspected irregularities in the transactions handled by one particular teller and is asked to help trap the teller by drawing out all of his or her savings at the teller's window. In this way, the examiner can "catch the teller red-handed" in any wrongdoing. After cooperating, the victim is to give the money to a uniformed bank guard waiting outside, who will then return it to the proper account. Often, the appearance of the "bank examiner" and uniformed "guard" are so impressive that the victim never thinks to check on their authenticity and proceeds with the requested action, never to see the money or those two individuals again.

SUMMARY

At the outset of this chapter it was suggested that an important question for anyone interested in understanding, resisting, or harnessing the process of interpersonal influence is, "Which are the most powerful principles that motivate us to comply with another's request?" It was also suggested that one way to assess such power would be to examine the practices of commercial compliance professionals for their pervasiveness. That is, if compliance practitioners made widespread use of certain principles, this would be evidence for the natural power of these principles to affect everyday compliance. Six psychological principles emerged as the most popular in the repertoires of the compliance pros: reciprocity, social validation, consistency, friendship/liking, scarcity, and authority. Close examination of the principles revealed broad professional usage that could be validated and explained by controlled experimental research. As with most research perspectives, additional work needs to be done before we can have high levels of confidence in the conclusions. However, there is considerable evidence at this juncture to indicate that these six principles engage central features of the human condition in the process of motivating compliance.

Notes

[1]However, when the purpose of social comparison is to make oneself feel better or to motivate oneself to greater accomplishments, people will sometimes compare themselves to others who are not similar but who are below or above them on a relevant dimension (Wood, 1989; Suls & Wills, 1990).

References

ALTHEIDE, D. L., & JOHNSON, J. M. (1977). Counting souls: A study of counseling at evangelical crusades. *Pacific Sociological Review, 20,* 323–348.

ARONSON, E., BRIDGEMAN, D. L., & GEFFNER, R. (1978). The effects of a cooperative classroom structure on students' behavior and attitudes. In D. Bar-Tal & L. Saxe (Eds.), *Social psychology of education: Theory and research.* New York: Halsted Press.

ARONSON, E., & MILLS, J. (1959). The effect of severity of initiation on liking for a group. *Journal of Abnormal and Social Psychology, 59,* 177–181.

ARONSON, E., TURNER, J. A., & CARLSMITH, J. M. (1963). Communicator credibility and communication discrepancy as a determinant of opinion change. *Journal of Abnormal and Social Psychology, 67,* 31–36.

AXELROD, R. (1984). *The evolution of cooperation.* New York: Basic Books.

BALL-ROKEACH, S., ROKEACH, M., & GRUBE, J. W. (1984). *The great American values test.* New York: Free Press.

BANDURA, A., & MENLOVE, F. L. (1968). Factors determining vicarious extinction of avoidance behavior through symbolic modeling. *Journal of Personality and Social Psychology, 8,* 99–108.

BAUMEISTER, R. F. (1982). A self-presentational view of social phenomena. *Psychological Bulletin, 91,* 3–26.

BEAMAN, A. L., COLE, C. M., PRESTON, M., KLENTZ, B., & STEBLAY, N. M. (1983). Fifteen years of foot-in-the-door research: A meta-analysis. *Personality and Social Psychology Bulletin, 9,* 181–196.

BEM, D. J. (1967). Self-perception: An alternative explanation of cognitive dissonance phenomena. *Psychological Review, 74,* 183–200.

BENSON, P. L., KARABENIC, S. A., & LERNER, R. M. (1976). Pretty pleases: The effects of physical attractiveness on race, sex, and receiving help. *Journal of Experimental Social Psychology, 12,* 409–415.

BERRY, S. H., & KANOUSE, D. E. (1987). Physician response to a mailed survey: An experiment in timing of payment. *Public Opinion Quarterly, 51,* 102–114.

BETTENCOURT, B. A., BREWER, M. B., CROAK, M. R., & MILLER, N. (1992). Cooperation and the reduction of intergroup bias. *Journal of Experimental Social Psychology, 28,* 301–319.

BICKMAN, L. (1974). The social power of a uniform. *Journal of Applied Social Psychology, 4,* 47–61.

BLASS, T. (1991). Understanding behavior in the Milgram obedience experiment. *Journal of Personality and Social Psychology, 60,* 398–413.

BRAVER, S. L. (1975). Reciprocity, cohesiveness, and cooperation in two-person games. *Psychological Reports, 36,* 371–378.

BREHM, J. W. (1966). *A theory of psychological reactance.* New York: Academic Press.

BREHM, S. S., & BREHM, J. W. (1981). *Psychological reactance: A theory of freedom and control.* New York: Academic Press.

BROCK, T. C. (1968). Implications of commodity theory for value change. In A. G. Greenwald, T. C. Brock, and T. M. Ostrom (Eds.), *Psychological foundations of attitudes.* New York: Academic Press.

BROCK, T. C., & BANNON, L. A. (1992). Liberalization of commodity theory. *Basic and Applied Social Psychology, 13,* 135–143.

BROCKNER, J., GUZZI, B., KANE, J., LEVINE, E., & SHAPLEN, K. (1984). Organizational fundraising: Further evidence on the effects of legitimizing small donations. *Journal of Consumer Research, 11,* 611–614.

BROWNSTEIN, R., & KATZEV, R. (1985). The relative effectiveness of three compliance techniques in eliciting donations to a cultural organization. *Journal of Applied Social Psychology, 15,* 564–574.

BURGER, J. M. (1986). Increasing compliance by improving the deal: The that's-not-all technique. *Journal of Personality and Social Psychology, 51,* 277–283.

BURGER, J. M., & PETTY, R. E. (1981). The low-ball compliance technique: Task or person commitment? *Journal of Personality and Social Psychology, 40,* 492–500.

BUSHMAN, B. A. (1988). The effects of apparel on compliance. *Personality and Social Psychology Bulletin, 14,* 459–467.

BYRNE, D. (1971). *The attraction paradigm.* New York: Academic Press.

BYRNE, D., & RHAMEY, R. (1965). Magnitude of positive and negative reinforcements as a determinant of attraction. *Journal of Personality and Social Psychology, 2,* 884–889.

CARLI, L. L., GANLEY, R., & PIERCE-OTAY, A. (1991). Similarity and satisfaction in roommate relationships. *Personality and Social Psychology Bulletin, 17,* 419–426.

CASTELLOW, W. A., WUENSCH, K. L., & MOORE, C. H. (1990). Effects of physical attractiveness of the plaintiff and defendant in sexual harassment judgments. *Journal of Social Behavior and Personality, 5,* 547–562.

CHAIKEN, S. (1979). Communicator physical attractiveness and persuasion. *Journal of Personality and Social Psychology, 37,* 1387–1397).

CIALDINI, R. B. (1993). *Influence: Science and practice* (3rd ed.). New York: HarperCollins.

CIALDINI, R. B., & ASCANI, K. (1976). Test of a concession procedure for inducing verbal, behavioral, and further compliance with a request to give blood. *Journal of Applied Psychology, 61,* 295–300.

CIALDINI, R. B., CACIOPPO, J. T., BASSETT, R., & MILLER, J. A. (1978). Low-ball procedure for producing compliance: Commitment then cost. *Journal of Personality and Social Psychology, 36,* 463–476.

CIALDINI, R. B., GREEN, B. L., & RUSCH, A. J. (1992). When tactical pronouncements of change become real change: The case of reciprocal persuasion. *Journal of Personality and Social Psychology, 63,* 30–40.

CIALDINI, R. B., RENO, R. R., & KALLGREN, C. A. (1990). A focus theory of normative conduct: Recycling the concept of norms to educe littering in public places. *Journal of Personality and Social Psychology, 58,* 1015–1026.

CIALDINI, R. B., & SCHROEDER, D. A. (1976). Increasing compliance by legitimizing paltry contributions: When even a penny helps. *Journal of Personality and Social Psychology, 34,* 599–604.

CIALDINI, R. B., VINCENT, J. E., LEWIS, S. K., CATALAN, J., WHEELER, D., & DARBY, B. L. (1975). Reciprocal concessions procedure for inducing compliance: The door-in-the-face technique. *Journal of Personality and Social Psychology, 31,* 206–215.

COHEN, M., & DAVIS, N. (1981). *Medication errors: Causes and prevention.* Philadelphia: G. F. Stickley Co.

CONDON, J. W., & CRANO, W. D. (1988). Inferred evaluation and the relation between attitude similarity and interpersonal attraction. *Journal of Personality and Social Psychology, 54,* 789–797.

COOK, S. W. (1990). Toward a psychology of improving justice. *Journal of Social Issues, 46,* 147–161.

CUNNINGHAM, J. A., STRASSBERG, D. S., & HAAN, B. (1986). Effects of intimacy and sex-role congruency of self-disclosure. *Journal of Social and Clinical Psychology, 4,* 393–401.

CUPCHIK, G. C., & LEVENTHAL, H. (1974). Consistency between evaluative behavior and the evaluation of humorous stimuli. *Journal of Personality and Social Psychology, 30,* 429–442.

DENGERINK, H. A., SCHNEDLER, R. W., & COVEY, M. K. (1978). Role of avoidance in aggressive responses to attack and no attack. *Journal of Personality and Social Psychology, 36,* 1044–1053.

DEPAULO, B. M., BRITTINGHAM, G. L., & KAISER, M. K. (1983). Receiving competence-relevant help. *Journal of Personality and Social Psychology, 45,* 1045–1060.

DEPAULO, B. M., NADLER, A., & FISHER, J. D. (Eds.). (1983). *New directions in helping: Vol. 2. Help seeking.* New York: Academic Press.

DEUTSCH, M., & GERARD, H. B. (1955). A study of normative and informational social influences upon individual judgment. *Journal of Abnormal and Social Psychology, 51,* 629–636.

DOWNS, A. C., & LYONS, P. M. (1991). Natural observations of the links between attractiveness and initial legal judgments. *Personality and Social Psychology Bulletin, 17,* 541–547.

EAGLY, A. H., ASHMORE, R. D., MAKHIJANI, M. G. & LONGO, L. C. (1991). What is beautiful is good but . . . . A meta-analytic review of research on the physical attractiveness stereotype. *Psychological Bulletin, 110,* 109–128.

EFRAN, M. G., & PATTERSON, E. W. J. (1976). *The politics of appearance.* Unpublished manuscript, University of Toronto.

EISENBERG, N. E., CIALDINI, R. B., McCREATH, H., & SHELL, R. (1987). Consistency-based compliance: When and why do children become vulnerable? *Journal of Personality and Social Psychology, 52,* 1174–1181.

EISENBERG, R., COTTERELL, N., & MARVEL, J. (1987). Reciprocation ideology, *Journal of Personality and Social Psychology, 53,* 743–750.

EMSWILLER, T., DEAUX, K., & WILLITS, J. E. (1971). Similarity, sex, and requests for small favors. *Journal of Applied Social Psychology, 1,* 284–291.

FESTINGER, L. (1954). A theory of social comparison processes. *Human Relations, 7,* 117–140.

FESTINGER, L. (1957). *A theory of cognitive dissonance.* Stanford: Stanford University Press.

FREEDMAN, J. L. (1965). Long-term behavioral effects of cognitive dissonance. *Journal of Experimental Social Psychology, 1,* 145–155.

FREEDMAN, J. L., & FRASER, S. C. (1966). Compliance without pressure: The foot-in-the-door technique. *Journal of Personality and Social Psychology, 4,* 195–203.

FRENZEN, J. R., & DAVIS, H. L. (1990). Purchasing behavior in embedded markets. *Journal of Consumer Research, 17,* 1–12.

GOETHALS, G. R., & DARLEY, J. M. (1977). Social comparison theory: An attributional approach. In J. M. Suls & R. L. Miller (Eds.), *Social comparison processes: Theoretical and empirical perspectives.* Washington, D. C.: Hemisphere/Halsted.

GONZALES, M. H., ARONSON, E., & COSTANZO, M. (1988). Increasing the effectiveness of energy auditors: A field experiment. *Journal of Applied Social Psychology, 18,* 1046–1066.

GOULDNER, A. W. (1960). The norm of reciprocity: A preliminary statement. *American Sociological Review, 25,* 161–178.

GREENBERG, M. S., & SHAPIRO, S. P. (1971). Indebtedness: An adverse effect of asking for and receiving help. *Sociometry, 34,* 290–301.

GREENWALD, A. F., CARNOT, C. G., BEACH, R., & YOUNG, B. (1987). Increasing voting behavior by asking people if they expect to vote. *Journal of Applied Psychology, 72,* 315–318.

HARARI, H., MOHR, D., & HOSEY, K. (1980). Faculty helpfulness to students: A comparison of compliance techniques. *Personality and Social Psychology Bulletin, 6,* 373–377.

HEIDER, F. (1958). *The psychology of interpersonal relations.* New York: Wiley.

HOFLING, C. K., BROTZMAN, E., DALRYMPLE, S., GRAVES, N., & PIERCE, C. M. (1966). An experimental study of nurse-physician relationships. *Journal of Nervous and Mental Disease, 143,* 171–180.

HORNSTEIN, H. A., FISCH, E., & HOLMES, M. (1968). Influence of a model's feeling about his behavior and his relevance as a comparison other on observers' helping behavior. *Journal of Personality and Social Psychology, 10,* 222–226.

HOWARD, D. J. (1990). The influence of verbal responses to common greetings on compliance behavior: The foot-in-the-mouth effect. *Journal of Applied Social Psychology, 20,* 1185–1196.

JONES, E. E., & WORTMAN, C. (1973). *Ingratiation: An attributional approach.* Moorestown, NJ: General Learning Corp.

JOULE, R. V. (1987). Tobacco deprivation: The foot-in-the-door technique versus the lowball technique. *European Journal of Social Psychology, 17,* 361–365.

JOULE, R. V., GOUILLOUX, F., & WEBER, F. (1989). The lure: A new compliance procedure. *Journal of Social Psychology, 129,* 741–749.

KNISHINSKY, A. (1982). *The effects of scarcity of material and exclusivity of information on industrial buyer perceived risk in provoking a purchase decision.* Doctoral dissertation, Arizona State University, Tempe.

LAFRANCE, M. (1985). Postural mirroring and intergroup relations. *Personality and Social Psychology Bulletin, 11,* 207–217.

LATANÉ, B., & DANLEY, J. M. (1970). *The unresponsive bystander: Why doesn't he help?* New York: Appleton-Century-Crofts.

LEAKEY, R., & LEWIN, R. (1978). *People of the lake.* New York: Anchor Press.

LEFKOWITZ, M., BLAKE, R. R., & MOUTON, J. S. (1955). Status factors in pedestrian violation of traffic signals. *Journal of Abnormal and Social Psychology, 51,* 704–706.

LOCKE, K. S., & HOROWITZ, L. M. (1990). Satisfaction in interpersonal interactions as a function of similarity in level of dysphoria. *Journal of Personality and Social Psychology, 58,* 823–831.

LYNN, M. (1991). Scarcity effects on value. *Psychology and Marketing, 8,* 43–57.

LYNN, M. (1992). Scarcity's enhancement of desirability. *Basic and Applied Social Psychology, 13,* 67–78.

MAZIS, M. B. (1975). Antipollution measures and psychological reactance theory: A field experiment. *Journal of Personality and Social Psychology, 31,* 654–666.

MEYERWITZ, B. E., & CHAIKEN, S. (1987). The effect of message framing on breast self-examination attitudes, intentions, and behavior. *Journal of Personality and Social Psychology, 52,* 500–510.

MEYERWITZ, B. E., WILSON, D. K., & CHAIKEN, S. (1991). *Loss-framed messages increase breast self-examination for women who perceive risk.* Paper presented at the meeting of the American Psychological Society, Washington, DC.

MILGRAM, S. (1974). *Obedience to authority.* New York: Harper and Row.

MILGRAM, S., BICKMAN, L., & BERKOWITZ, O. (1969). Note on the drawing power of crowds of different size. *Journal of Personality and Social Psychology, 13,* 79–82.

MILLER, C. T. (1984). Self-schemas, gender, and social comparison: A clarification of the related attributes hypothesis. *Journal of Personality and Social Psychology, 46,* 1222–1229.

MULLIN, B., COOPER, C., & DRISKELL, J. E. (1990). Jaywalking as a function of model behavior. *Personality and Social Psychology Bulletin, 16,* 320–330.

NEWCOMB, T. (1953). An approach to the study of communicative acts. *Psychological Review, 60,* 393–404.

PHILLIPS, D. P., & CARSTENSEN, L. L. (1988). The effect of suicide stories on various demographic groups, 1968–1985. *Suicide and Life-Threatening Behavior, 18,* 100–114.

PLINER, P. H., HART, H., KOHL, J., & SAARI, D. (1974). Compliance without pressure: Some further data on the foot-in-the-door technique. *Journal of Experimental Social Psychology, 10,* 17–22.

RAFAELI, A., & SUTTON, R. I. (1991). Emotional contrast strategies as means of social influence. *Academy of Management Journal, 34,* 749–775.

REGAN, D. T. (1971). Effects of a favor and liking on compliance. *Journal of Experimental Social Psychology, 7,* 627–639.

REEVES, R. A., BAKER, G. A., BOYD, J. G., & CIALDINI, R. B. (1991). The door-in-the-face technique: Reciprocal concessions vs. self-presentational explanations. *Journal of Social Behavior and Personality, 6,* 545–558.

REEVES, R. A., MACOLINI, R. M., & MARTIN, R. C. (1987). Legitimizing paltry contributions: On-the-spot vs. mail-in requests. *Journal of Applied Social Psychology, 17,* 731–738.

REINGEN, P. H. (1978). On inducing compliance with requests. *Journal of Consumer Research, 5,* 96–102.

REINGEN, P. H. (1982). Test of a list procedure for inducing compliance with a request to donate money. *Journal of Applied Psychology, 67,* 110–118.

RILEY, D., & ECKENRODE, J. (1986). Social ties: Subgroup differences in costs and benefits. *Journal of Personality and Social Psychology, 51,* 770–778.

ROSENBAUM, M. E. (1980). Cooperation and competition. In P. B. Paulus (Ed.), *The psychology of group influence* (pp. 23–41). Hillsdale, NJ: Erlbaum.

SCHACHTER, S., & SINGER, J. E. (1962). Cognitive, Social, and physiological determinants of emotional state. *Psychological Review, 69,* 379–399.

SCHWARTZWALD, J., BIZMAN, A., & RAZ, M. (1983). The foot-in-the-door paradigm: Effects of request size on donation probability and donation generosity. *Personality and Social Psychology Bulletin, 9,* 443–450.

SHERMAN, S. J. (1980). On the self-erasing nature of errors of prediction. *Journal of Personality and Social Psychology, 39,* 211–221.

SMOLOWE, J. (1990, November 26). Contents require immediate attention. *Time,* p. 64.

STEWART, J. E., II (1980). Defendant's attractiveness as a factor in the outcome of trials. *Journal of Applied Social Psychology, 10,* 348–361.

SUEDFELD, P., BOCHNER, S., & MATAS, C. (1971). Petitioner's attire and petition signing by peace demonstrators: A field experiment. *Journal of Applied Social Psychology, 1,* 278–283.

SULS, J., & WILLS, T. A. (Eds.). (1990). *Social comparison: Contemporary theory and research.* Hillsdale, NJ: Erlbaum.

TEDESCHI, J. T. (Ed.). (1981). *Impression management theory and social psychological research.* New York: Academic Press.

TESSER, A., CAMPBELL, J., & MICKLER, S. (1983). The role of attention to the stimulus, social pressure, and self-doubt in conformity. *European Journal of Social Psychology, 13,* 217–233.

Tesser, A., Gatewood, R., & Driver, M. (1968). Some determinants of gratitude. *Journal of Personality and Social Psychology, 9,* 233–236.

Tversky, A., & Kahneman, D. (1981). The framing of decisions and the psychology of choice. *Science, 211,* 433–458.

West, S. G., (1975). Increasing the attractiveness of college cafeteria food. *Journal of Applied Psychology, 10,* 656–658.

Weyant, J. M. (1984). Applying social psychology to induce charitable donations. *Journal of Applied Social Psychology, 14,* 441–447.

Wood, J. V. (1989). Theory and research concerning social comparisons of personal attributes. *Psychological Bulletin, 106,* 231–248.

Woodside, A. G., & Davenport, J. W. (1974). Effects of salesman similarity and expertise on consumer purchasing behavior. *Journal of Marketing Research, 11,* 198–202.

Worchel, S. (1992). Beyond a commodity theory analysis of censorship: When abundance and personalism enhance scarcity effects. *Basic and Applied Social Psychology, 13,* 79–93.

Worchel, S., & Arnold, S. E. (1973). The effects of censorship and the attractiveness of the censor on attitude change. *Journal of Experimental Social Psychology, 9,* 365–377.

Worchel, S., Arnold, S. E., & Baker, M. (1975). The effect of censorship on attitude change: The influence of censor and communicator characteristics. *Journal of Applied Social Psychology, 5,* 222–239.

Further Readings

Cialdini, R. B. (1993). *Influence: Science and practice* (3rd ed.). New York: HarperCollins.
A more detailed version of the present chapter.

Edwards, J., Tindale, R. S., Heath, L., & Posavac, E. J. (Eds.). (1990). *Social influence processes and prevention.* New York: Plenum Press.
An edited volume of chapters applying social influence principles to a variety of domains such as energy conservation, AIDS prevention, health promotion, and crime reduction.

Fisher, R., & Ury, W. L. (1981). *Getting to YES.* Boston: Houghton Mifflin.
A classic contribution to the psychology of influence in negotiation.

Hassen, Steven (1988). *Combatting cult mind control.* Rochester, VT: Park Street Press.
Examines how powerful social influence practices are used by cults to recruit and retain members.

Jackson, D. W., Jr., Cunningham, W. H., & Cunningham, I. C. M. (1988). *Selling: The personal force in marketing.* New York: Wiley.
A research-based treatment of personal influence in the selling process.

Lifton, R. J. (1989). *Thought reform and the psychology of totalism.* Chapel Hill, NC: University of North Carolina Press.
Examines the psychology of brainwashing as it developed and occurred in China.

Ofshe, R. (1989). Coerced confessions: The logic of seemingly irrational action. *Cultic Studies Journal, 6,* 1–15.
A frightening account of how psychological pressures can be commissioned to induce people to confess to crimes they didn't commit.

Pratkanis, A. R., & Aronson, E. (1992). *Age of propaganda.* New York: W. H. Freeman and Co.

Shows how psychological principles are used in large-scale influence settings such as advertising and political campaigns.

ZIMBARDO, P. G., & LEIPPE, M. R. (1991). *The psychology of attitude change and social influence*. New York: McGraw-Hill, Inc.

An excellent, thoroughgoing analysis of the psychological influences on attitude and behavior change.

Margaret S. Clark (Ph.D., University of Maryland) is currently professor of psychology at Carnegie Mellon University, Pittsburgh. In general, her research interests lie in understanding social relationships. One specific long-term interest has been in distinguishing the norms governing the giving and acceptance of benefits in communal relationships (often exemplified by family relationships, friendships, and romantic relationships) from those governing the giving and acceptance of benefits in exchange relationships (often exemplified by relationships between strangers meeting for the first time, acquaintances, and business associates). More recent interests include (a) understanding how people interpret one another's emotional expressions and how they may, strategically, choose to present their emotional states to others to attain social benefits, and (b) examining why and under what circumstances "opposites" may be attracted to one another.

Sherri Pataki is a Ph.D. candidate at Carnegie Mellon University. She is currently completing her dissertation with the hope of finishing her degree before this text goes into print. Her dissertation focuses on people's emotional reactions to members of stigmatized groups. Her general research interests lie in identifying the factors that promote, or hinder, relationship development and trust.

CHAPTER 8

Interpersonal Processes Influencing Attraction and Relationships

Margaret S. Clark and Sherri P. Pataki
Carnegie Mellon University

CHAPTER OUTLINE

A REINFORCEMENT APPROACH
    The Theory
    Empirical Evidence
    Explaining Established Attraction Phenomena
A SOCIAL NORM APPROACH: DISTINGUISHING BETWEEN
COMMUNAL AND EXCHANGE RELATIONSHIPS
    The Theory
    Empirical Evidence
    Explaining Established Attraction Phenomena
A THEORY OF SELF-EVALUATION MAINTENANCE
    The Theory
    Empirical Evidence
    Explaining Established Attraction Phenomena
A THEORY OF PASSIONATE LOVE
    The Theory
    Empirical Evidence
    Explaining Established Attraction Phenomena
A THEORY OF EXPERIENCING EMOTION IN THE CONTEXT OF
RELATIONSHIPS
    The Theory
    Empirical Evidence

Preparation of this chapter was supported in part by National Science Foundation Grant BNS-9021603 and a James McKeen Cattell sabbatical award to Margaret Clark. Sherri Pataki is now at Seton Hill College.

Where both deliberate the love is slight; whoever loved, that loved not at first sight.

—CHRISTOPHER MARLOWE, 1598

Some things in life should remain unprobed by science's scalpel, and right at the top of the list of those things is the mysterious phenomenon of romantic passion . . . Leave it to poets and mystics, to Irving Berlin, to thousands of high school and college bull sessions, Dear Abby, Ann Landers. . . ."

—WILLIAM PROXMIRE, 1980

Although few would disagree that liking and loving are terribly important phenomena, many people view these phenomena to be mysterious, impossible to understand, certainly not appropriate for scientific study (witness the quote from former Senator Proxmire) and perhaps not even open to analysis by the people involved in the relationship itself (as the quote from Marlowe suggests). Social psychologists, while readily acknowledging that these topics are very complex, disagree. Their research has resulted in a rapidly growing body of scientific literature which suggests that liking, loving, and relationships *can* be studied and understood. A small portion of this research literature, a portion focusing on selected interpersonal processes important to understanding attraction in relationships, is reviewed here—in a way distinct from the way these topics have usually been covered in social psychology texts.

Most textbook chapters on attraction cite certain facts. We are told, for example, that physical proximity, or "propinquity," plays a large role in attraction and relationship formation. We are far more likely to become well acquainted with the person sitting next to us in class or assigned to the room next to us in a dorm than with someone just a few seats or rooms away (Caplow & Forman, 1950). In a classic study it was found that among married couples who had been randomly assigned to apartments, those within 22 feet of one another were much more likely to become friends than were those assigned to apartments 88 or more feet apart (Festinger, Schachter, & Back, 1950).

Another fact often pointed out in chapters on attraction is that we like and make more positive judgments about physically attractive people than about less physically attractive people (Hatfield & Sprecher, 1986). This applies to possible romantic partners (Walster, Aronson, Abrahams & Rottman, 1966), to the positivity of teachers' judgments of students' performances (Clifford & Walster, 1973), to students' judgments regarding other student's essays (Landy & Sigall, 1974), and even to experienced personnel consultants' judgments of job candidates (Cash, Gillen, & Burns, 1977).

Still another fact about attraction and relationships appearing in virtually every social psychology text is that we like others who are similar to us. Numerous studies have shown that similarity of attitudes leads to greater attraction (Byrne, 1971; Griffitt, Nelson, & Littlepage, 1972). There is also abundant evidence that people who are attracted to one another and end up as friends or as romantic partners tend to match on such factors as age, education, religion, and health (Warren, 1966), personality (Boyden, Carroll, & Maier, 1984; Caspi & Harbener, 1990), economic status (Byrne, Clore, & Worchel, 1966), and abilities (Senn, 1971). In sum, the evidence typically cited offers strong support for the veracity of the saying that "birds of a feather flock together." Little evidence is reported supporting the notion that "opposites attract."

Such facts and descriptions are interesting. And *after* citing a particular fact, authors have typically offered a quite plausible theoretical interpretation of it. However, we take a different approach. Rather than starting with such facts and a single possible interpretation, we describe several different researchers' theories about the nature of a variety of *interpersonal processes* in relationships. Then we describe findings regarding attraction and relationships that have arisen from tests of these theories. We will argue that each theory provides us with a different perspective on understanding many different observations about attraction and relationships including why we like those who live near us, those who are physically attractive, and those who have attitudes similar to ours.

We discuss a necessarily selected group of theories of interpersonal processes including (1) reinforcement theory, (2) a distinction between communal and exchange relationships, (3) a theory of self-esteem maintenance in the context of relationships, (4) a theory of passionate love, (5) a theory of the experience of emotion within the context of relationships, (6) an investment model of relationships, and (7) attachment theory (as applied to adults).

In our view, these are not competing theories of relationship processes. They are complementary. Each contributes not only to understanding attraction but also to understanding relationship development, maintenance and change.

A REINFORCEMENT APPROACH

The Theory

An early and simple view of how attraction comes about and relationships form came from reinforcement theorists (Byrne & Clore, 1970; Byrne & Murnen, 1988; Clore & Byrne, 1974; Lott & Lott, 1974; Staats & Staats, 1958). This approach probably has generated more empirical research on attraction than any other. Lott & Lott (1974) summarize the approach succinctly saying, "The basic hypothesis that underlies all our work on the antecedents of interpersonal attraction is that liking for a person will result under those conditions in which an individual experiences *reward in the presence of that person,* regardless of the relationship between the other person and the rewarding event or state of affairs" (pp. 171–172). To put the idea in old-fashioned terms, various stimuli, called unconditioned stimuli (or ones that have become secondary reinforcers through past conditioning), have the ability to make a person feel good. When such stimuli are repeatedly paired with another person over time, that person (the conditioned stimulus) comes to elicit the same sort of positive response— a response that can be called interpersonal attraction.

A person may come to be paired with a stimulus that elicits positive affect in a variety of ways. For example, simply by his or her nature a person may be able to provide pleasure to another. Imagine a person who sings well. Merely listening to the person makes others feel good and causes them to like that other. A person also may come to be associated with positive feelings by directly and intentionally providing positive consequences for the other. An acquaintance may consistently compliment you. If the compliments make you feel good, as compliments generally do, you may come to like the other. Perhaps most interestingly, according to this approach, we may come to like a person merely by that person being associated in time or place with our receiving rewards. This may occur *even though* that other is in no sense responsible for those rewards. Imagine Mr. Smith who loves to watch baseball games and has season tickets. You happen to have season tickets for the seat adjacent to Mr. Smith's seat. Over the course of the season Smith watches lots of games while sitting next to you. Whether the team wins or loses, whether it rains or shines, Smith, being an avid fan, enjoys the games. According to reinforcement theory, Smith should come to like you simply because he will begin to associate you with his enjoyment of the game.

To this point the examples given have all been of another person being associated with something good. Of course the theory also predicts that if the person is associated with the *removal* of a bad thing, that person should also be liked more. The mother who alleviates her young son's fear of the dark by sitting with him each night until he falls asleep should be liked more (although reinforcement theory also suggests that through association of her extreme fatigue with being with him, she may like him less!). Further, if the person is associated with a negative thing or with the removal of a positive thing, that person should be liked less. The professor who gives low grades or picks an exam day immediately following semester break, causing one to feel compelled to cancel a desired vacation, should not be liked much.

Empirical Evidence

What sort of evidence has accumulated to support the reinforcement approach? There actually are a tremendous number of studies providing evidence consistent with it. We describe just two in detail.

One of the earliest supporting studies was reported by Lott and Lott (1960). They predicted children would come to like other children merely as a result of those other children being present when they succeeded at a task. These researchers went to some first and third grade classrooms and determined which children liked which other children using sociometric measures. Then they placed children in three member groups such that each child was placed with two other children about whom that child did not already have strong feelings. Next the child played a "rocket ship" game in the presence of his or her group members. Each child's success or failure on the game had nothing to do with the likelihood of the other children winning or losing. Rather, a randomly chosen half of the children succeeded during each of their four turns. That is, they successfully landed on a planet several times during the game. These fortunate, "successful" children received four plastic cars—each time while in the presence of the other group members. The remaining half of the children failed during each of their four turns. They always had their ship blown up before it could land on a planet. These unfortunate children did not receive any plastic cars. Again this occurred while in the presence of the other group members.

Later the same day, the classroom teacher posed the following question to the children: "Suppose your family suddenly got the chance to spend your next vacation on a nearby star out in space . . . you can invite two children to go on the trip . . . and spend the holiday with you on the star. Which two children in this class would you choose to take with you?" The percentage of choices from within the subjects' group constituted the dependent measure of attraction toward group members. (Keep in mind that none of the group members had been chosen as friends in the sociometric pretests.) What happened *after* the game? The proportion of play group members chosen by rewarded children (23 percent) was significantly greater than the proportion chosen by the children who had failed (6 percent). Whether the other play group members had won or lost *themselves* had no effect. Lott and Lott argued that these results were obtained because successful children experienced positive affect as a result of winning four times, and these good feelings had become classically conditioned to the other children who just happened to be present at the time.

Another study in this tradition was reported by Griffitt (1970). He hypothesized that if one is exposed to information about strangers in an unpleasant environment, one will like the strangers less than if one is exposed to the identical information about the same people in a more pleasant environment. Griffitt recruited subjects for a study of "judgmental processes under altered environmental conditions." For 45 minutes subjects sat in a very hot, humid, unpleasant room *or* in a comfortable room in which the temperature and humidity were normal. During this time they filled out a number of questionnaires. Included in their materials was information about a stranger's responses to an attitude questionnaire. Half the subjects in each environmental condition examined the responses of a stranger who agreed with them on only 25 percent of the issues; the other half received responses which agreed with them on 75 percent of the issues. (The subjects themselves had responded to the same questionnaire earlier in the semester during a pretesting session.) After examining the stranger's responses, subjects indicated how much they liked the stranger.

As you can tell from Figure 8.1, subjects in the pleasant room liked the stranger more than did subjects who were in the unpleasant room. Moreover, the similar stranger was liked more than the dissimilar one. Why? According to Griffitt, the feelings the subjects experienced while in the rooms came to be associated with the stranger. Subjects presumably had more negative feelings when in the hot, humid room than when in the normal room. Also, those feelings presumably were more pleasant when examining the attitudes of another which affirmed their own opinions than when examining attitudes which challenged their own attitudes.

Many, many other studies have been conducted under the rubric of reinforcement theory as well (e.g. Byrne, 1971; Byrne & Clore, 1970; Byrne & Griffitt, 1966; Byrne & Rhamey, 1965). Together they form a large body of evidence consistent with the notion that we like others who are associated with rewards and dislike others who are associated with punishments.

Explaining Established Attraction Phenomena

What would reinforcement theorists say about the three facts regarding attraction cited at the start of our chapter? Think about proximity. For a person to be paired with your positive feelings, that person must be located close in time or space to you. Proximity presumably increases the likelihood of people coming to like one another because it increases the chances for classical conditioning of positive affect to occur. Your college roommate is far more likely to be around you when you receive good grades, are asked out for a date by someone you like, eat a delicious meal, and go to a good concert than is your cousin from another state. Thus, you are likely to like him or her more than that cousin. (Of course, to the extent bad things happen to you, people who are physically close ought to be liked less.)

What about the effects of physical attractiveness? It is presumably pleasant to look at attractive people (and unpleasant to look at less attractive persons). Since people are obviously closely associated with their own looks, the feelings presumably become classically conditioned to all aspects of a person. Finally, what about liking similar people? Griffitt already has answered this question. He argues that we like similar people because their views confirm our own. That makes us feel good, and those feelings become associated with the person.

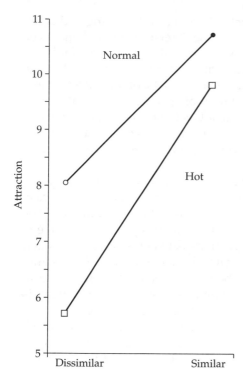

FIGURE 8.1. Attraction to a stranger as a function of room temperature and similarity of the stranger's attitudes to one's own.

This all sounds reasonable, but is reinforcement all there is to attraction and relationships? The answer from other social psychologists is no. Consider a very different approach next.

A SOCIAL NORM APPROACH: DISTINGUISHING BETWEEN COMMUNAL AND EXCHANGE RELATIONSHIPS

The Theory

A very different sort of approach contributing to understanding why people like or dislike each other and how relationships operate over the long run rests on the general assumption that people share social norms. Adherence to agreed upon norms is assumed to promote or maintain attraction and the smooth functioning of relationships. Violation of those norms causes attraction to decrease and relationships to deteriorate. There are, of course, many, many social norms regarding appropriate behavior in relationships. However, social psychologists have been particularly interested in identifying the norms that govern the giving and receiving of benefits in relationships. Clark and Mills' work on a distinction between communal and exchange norms is an example of such work.

Clark and Mills postulate that distinct rules govern the giving and acceptance of benefits in "communal" and in "exchange" relationships—benefits being things that one person intentionally gives to the other. Communal relationships are characterized by feelings of responsibility for the other's well-being. In these relationships, benefits are given in response to the other's needs or simply to please the other. There is no expectation of specific repayment. In contrast, in exchange relationships members do not feel a special responsibility for the other's needs. Rather, they give benefits to repay debts created by the prior receipt of benefits or in anticipation of receiving specific repayment in the future.

Communal relationships are often exemplified by family relationships, romantic relationships, and friendships. Parents, for instance, very often—indeed constantly—provide their young children with benefits without expecting those children to intentionally give them anything in repayment. Exchange relationships are often exemplified by interactions between strangers, acquaintances, and people who do business with one another. Shoppers, for instance, give money to storekeepers expecting to be given specific benefits in return. However, the communal/exchange distinction is not synonymous with a distinction between close and casual relationships. Telling a stranger the time without expectation of repayment is an example of a communal relationship that would not be considered close. Partners who have been in business together for a long time may have an exchange relationship that would not be considered casual (Clark & Mills, 1993).

What lies behind the use of the distinct rules for giving and receiving benefits in communal and in exchange relationships? Consider communal relationships first. Members of communal relationships feel a responsibility for the needs of the other, whereas members of exchange relationships do not. In mutual communal relationships, following communal norms allows members a sense of security regarding having their own needs met regardless of their ability to repay. Having an exchange relationship does not provide this sense of security. A communal relationship also allows each member to nurture the other, which may provide a sense of fulfillment. Recently Clark and Mills have discussed one-sided communal relationships as well (Clark & Mills, 1993; Mills & Clark, 1988), the prototype example being the relationship between a parent and an infant or very young child. Such relationships are essential for human survival, and Mills and Clark have speculated that there may be a biological basis for humans forming communal relationships.

While arguing that communal relationships seem essential for human existence, Clark and Mills simultaneously argue that it is impossible for a person to be responsible for everyone else's needs. It is also not possible or even particularly helpful for everyone to be responsible for all of the person's own needs. Thus another rule must exist allowing for the orderly give-and-take of benefits between a person and others in his or her social world. This other rule is the exchange rule—a rule dictating that benefits should be repaid with comparable benefits.

Finally, Clark and Mills have argued that not only is there a qualitative dis-

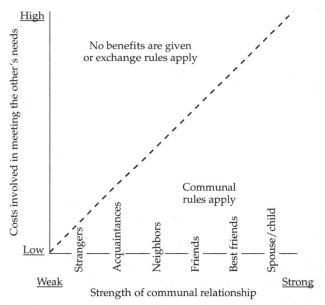

FIGURE 8.2. When the communal norm will be applied as a function of communal relationship strength and cost of the benefit. (The placement of strangers, acquaintances, neighbors, friends, best friends and spouse/child on the communal relationship strength axis is for illustrative purposes only.)

tinction between communal and exchange rules but there is also an important quantitative dimension to communal relationships (Clark & Mills, 1993; Mills & Clark, 1982, 1988). Communal relationships vary in terms of how motivated a person is to meet the other's needs: the more motivation there is, they say, the *stronger* the communal relationship will be. Communal relationships with one's children are, for example, typically stronger than those with friends. The stronger the communal relationship is, the greater the costs a person will incur to meet the other's needs and the more guilt that person will experience if he or she fails to meet the other's needs. Meeting the needs of someone with whom one has a strong communal relationship takes precedence over meeting the needs of someone with whom one has a weaker communal relationship. Figure 8.2 depicts how the combination of relationship strength and the cost of a benefit needed by the other combine to dictate when communal norms will be followed.

Following communal norms (and avoiding the use of exchange norms) in friendships, family relationships, and romantic relationships ought to increase liking and foster the development and maintenance of those relationships. Following exchange norms (and avoiding the use of communal norms) ought to foster liking and the development and maintenance of business relationships and well-functioning acquaintanceships.

Empirical Evidence

A number of studies offer support for the communal/exchange distinction. Many have been experimental in nature. In the communal conditions, desired relationship type has been manipulated by having new college students interact with a physically attractive, friendly other who has expressed an interest in getting to know new people. In the exchange conditions, desired relationship type has been manipulated by having the students interact with the same physically attractive, friendly other, but this time information is included indicating that this person has clearly established ties in the community, is married, and has expressed no particular interest in meeting new people. These manipulations are effective in creating desire for communal and exchange relationships (Clark, 1986; Clark & Waddell, 1985). In other studies the behavior of people in ongoing friendships has been contrasted with that of people who are strangers to one another.

In their first study, Clark and Mills (1979, study 1) predicted that repaying someone for help would enhance attraction in exchange relationships but cause attraction to decrease in communal relationships. To test this hypothesis, Clark and Mills (1979) first induced male subjects to desire either a communal or an exchange relationship with an attractive female confederate in the manner just described. Then the subject and confederate worked simultaneously on a word task involving forming words from letter tiles. The subject finished first, receiving a point toward an extra credit for performing well. Next the experimenter asked if he wished to give some of his extra letter tiles to the other. (All did so.) The other responded by thanking the subject (no repayment condition) *or* by thanking him and repaying him by transferring an extra credit point that she had earned to him—with the experimenter's permission (repayment condition). A bit later the subject had a chance to indicate his liking for the other (supposedly in preparation for a later joint task). The results, shown in Figure 8.3, were clear and they fit the theory. Subjects led to desire an exchange relationship liked the confederate more if she paid him for his help than if she did not. Subjects led to desire a communal relationship liked her better if she did not repay him than if she did.

To get an intuitive feel for how the communal subjects felt about being repaid, imagine giving your best friend some help with his statistics homework and then having that friend offer to pay you. Probably, you would much prefer a simple thank you. To get a feel for how the exchange subjects felt about *not* being repaid, imagine an acquaintance with a child calling and asking you to tutor that child in math. You assume you are being hired for a job, and you accept it. You tutor the child but later all the parent does is say thank you. You are likely to be miffed, feel exploited, and not like that acquaintance much.

In other studies people's tendencies to keep track of the other's needs and of the other's inputs into joint tasks for which there would be a reward were measured (Clark, 1984; Clark, Mills, & Corcoran, 1989; Clark, Mills, & Powell, 1986). First, consider a study on keeping track of individual inputs into a joint project. Clark (1984) predicted that because members of exchange relationships

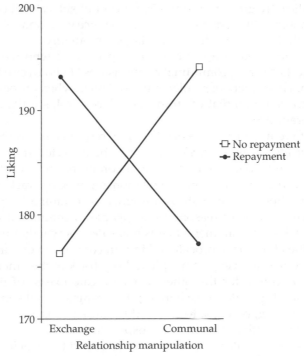

FIGURE 8.3. Liking for another as a function of desired relationship type and receipt of a repayment from the other.

should allocate benefits according to who has contributed what to a relationship, they ought to make efforts to keep track of exactly what each person has contributed to a joint task for which there will be a reward. In contrast, because members of communal relationships should allocate benefits according to needs, they should *not* keep track.

This hypothesis was tested in a study billed as examining perceptual skills. Subjects were led to desire a communal or an exchange relationship with an attractive co-participant. Then partners were given the task of locating and circling number sequences in a large matrix. A reward based on joint performance was to be given. Supposedly the two participants would later divide it among themselves in whatever manner they wished.

The attractive female confederate took a turn first. She circled numbers either with a red or a black pen. The male subject's turn followed. He had both a red and a black pen on his table and could choose either one. Which would he use? Clark reasoned that if he wanted to keep track of how many numbers he found and how many his partner found, he would be motivated to use a different color pen. If he did not wish to keep track, he should not care very much which pen he used. In fact, nearly 90 percent of the exchange subjects chose a different color pen. Only 12.5 percent of the communal subjects did. Ninety percent was significantly greater than the 50 percent of subjects who presumably would have chosen a different color pen if pen choice was random; 12.5 percent was significantly lower than that percentage. Apparently not only do people desiring exchange relationships strive to keep track of who has contributed what, but subjects desiring communal relationships "bend over backwards" to avoid doing so. This pattern of results is also obtained when the behavior of real friends is contrasted with that of strangers (Clark, 1984, studies 2 & 3; Clark, Mills, & Corcoran, 1989).

Quite a different pattern of record keeping, however, is observed for keeping track of *the other person's needs*. As would be expected from the communal/exchange distinction, people desiring a communal relationship are more likely than those desiring an exchange relationship to keep track of the other's needs. In connection with one study designed to examine keeping track of needs, Clark and associates reasoned that people in communal relationships should keep track of one another's needs regardless of whether there is an opportunity for the other to reciprocate in kind. In contrast, in exchange relationships there is no reason to expect people to keep track of the other's needs *unless* a clear opportunity for the other to reciprocate exists. (*If* the other can reciprocate in kind, people in exchange relationships may keep track of the other's needs, hoping, perhaps, to respond to those needs and to obligate the other to repay *them* with something they expect to need.)

To test these ideas college students were recruited to participate in a study on word formation along with an attractive co-participant. Desire for a communal versus an exchange relationship was again manipulated as described above. The two participants were seated in separate rooms. The other had supposedly been assigned to work on a difficult task; the subject to work on an easier one. Both could earn an individual monetary reward if they completed their task within the allotted time. Due to her task being more difficult, the other was allowed to request letters from the subject by passing a note through a slot in the wall, which would fall into a box in the subject's room. The subject, *if* he or she wished, could check the box for notes and help.

At this point, the procedure diverged for subjects assigned to an "opportunity for reciprocation" condition and those assigned to a "no opportunity for reciprocation" condition. Those assigned to the "opportunity" condition were told there would be a second round in which *they* would be assigned the more difficult task and the other would get the easier task. In that round *the subject* could request help. The other could check for requests and help *if* he or she desired.

While each subject worked on the first task, the experimenter, observing through a one-way mirror, counted the number of times the subject checked the (always empty) box for possible notes. In accord with the theory, when there was *no* opportunity for the other to reciprocate, people desiring a communal relationship paid more attention to the other's needs than did those desiring an exchange relationship. Only when there was an opportunity for reciprocation (and thus when the subject had reason to be motivated to indebt the other to him or her) did the exchange subjects check the box as often as did their communal counterparts.

Other studies have supported the communal/exchange distinction as well. It has been found that when exchange (but not when communal) relationships are desired, members of relationships react positively to receiving requests for repayments of benefits received (Clark & Mills, 1979, study 2) and feel exploited when their help is not reciprocated (Clark & Waddell, 1985). On the other hand, members of relationships desired to be communal are more likely than members of relationships desired to be exchange to help one another (Clark, Ouellette, Powell, & Milberg, 1987), to respond positively to the other's emotions (Clark, Ouellete, Powell, & Milberg, 1987; Clark & Taraban, 1991), to feel good after having helped the other (Williamson & Clark, 1989, 1992) and to pay attention to the time another spends selecting something for them (Mehta, Clark, & Mills, 1992).

Explaining Established Attraction Phenomena

What does the communal/exchange distinction have to say about the facts of attraction cited at the beginning of this chapter? It says little about why we like physically attractive people. However, it does suggest a reason, quite different from the one arising from reinforcement theory, for why we may like people with similar attitudes. That is, if we have or desire a communal relationship with another, that other can probably best understand (and meet) our needs and we can best understand (and meet) the other's needs if we share similar attitudes, beliefs, and backgrounds. For example, if both members of a couple believe family ought to come before career, they are likely to meet each other's needs by spending much time at home with each other and the children. If they had different attitudes in this regard, at least one member of the relationship—the more family-oriented one—would be likely to feel unhappy and to resent the other's lack of family involvement.

And what of proximity? One certainly cannot give or accept benefits unless one comes into contact with the other. Therefore one cannot adhere to the norms of *either* a communal or an exchange relationship and one cannot come to be liked as a result of such adherence in either type of relationship unless there is some interaction.

A THEORY OF SELF-EVALUATION MAINTENANCE

The Theory

Still another theory contributing to understanding interpersonal relationships is Tesser's self-evaluation maintenance (SEM) theory—a theory already briefly described by Baumeister in Chapter 3. To review, Tesser begins with the assumption that people strive to behave in ways that maintain or improve their self-esteem. He further assumes that a person's relationships with others can influence that person's self-esteem through two important interpersonal processes—a "reflection" process and a "comparison" process. Each can raise or lower one's self-esteem. However, they do so in very different ways.

The "reflection" process raises self-esteem by allowing one member of a relationship to bask in the other's glory. For instance, the relatives of an actress who has just won the Academy Award may find their self-esteem raised simply by being associated with the prizewinner. The closer the relationship is (in the sense that the two people seem to belong together), the greater the effect will be. The husband of the actress will experience a greater jump in self-esteem than will the actress's second cousin. On the other hand, if a person has the misfortune of being associated with someone with negative attributes or behavior, the reflection process also can cause a person's self-esteem to deteriorate. Consider, for instance, how the new surgeon general, Joycelyn Elders, must have felt when faced with headlines such as the following which appeared in the December 19, 1993, issue of the *St. Louis Post-Dispatch:* "Surgeon General's Son Sought on Drug Charge." In such a case, the theory suggests, self-esteem should drop. Moreover, the theory predicts that the closer a relationship is, the more exaggerated the drop in self-esteem will be. Had the person sought on a drug charge been the surgeon general's nephew rather than her son, the implications for her self-esteem probably would have been less.

The comparison process operates in quite a different way and produces opposite sorts of results. Through this process one's self-esteem may be raised by another person's poor performance by virtue of the fact that the other's poor performance makes one's own performance look better *by comparison.* Imagine receiving an A- on a paper. You expected to do well and are satisfied, but not ecstatic, with your grade. The instructor then hands out the distribution of grades for the entire class. Yours is the top grade in the entire class. The next closest grade is a B. Your self-esteem should take a jump. Again, Tesser predicts this positive effect will be exaggerated the closer the relationship between a person and the person or people with whom the comparison is being made.

Of course, comparison can have the opposite effect as well. If you compare yourself with others and find you have done *worse,* your self-esteem should drop. It should drop more the closer you are to those others.

Since the reflection and comparison processes lead to diametrically opposed predictions regarding the effects of another's good performance on one's own self-esteem as well as the effects of another's bad performance on one's self-esteem, it is important to specify when each process will operate. According to Tesser, the key determinant of which process will apply is the *relevance* of the performance domain to the person in question. When the domain is *not* central to a person's identity, the reflection process predominates. When the domain *is* central to one's self-definition, the comparison process dominates. If musical ability is absolutely irrelevant to me, I should experience great pride and jumps in self-esteem when my sister consistently wins musical competitions. Moreover I should support her efforts in this area and applaud her successes. If, instead, I've always aspired to be a musician and have worked like crazy (but to not much avail) to perform well, her good performance should cause my own to plummet. I should do little to help her, and I may even do things that undermine her performance.

A recent article in a Pittsburgh newspaper provides dramatic illustration of the negative effects of performing less well than a close other in a domain relevant to one's identity. The article reads: "A failing grade on a culinary exam led to tragedy last night in Westwood when a distraught cooking student stabbed to death his girlfriend, who passed the same test he had failed, police said. . . . They both attended the culinary arts institute. They had an exam today. She passed. He flunked. . . . He told us he killed the woman he loved" (*Pittsburgh Post Gazette,* Dec. 4, 1993).

This quote illustrates a dramatic effect that self-esteem maintenance processes may have on a relationship. This sort of an effect is, thankfully, extremely rare. However, we suspect that self-esteem maintenance processes have a great deal to do with the everyday dynamics of forming and maintaining relationships. What specific relationship implications are these processes likely to have? People should like others and prefer relationships with them when such relationships support their self-esteem. They should be reluctant to form, maintain, or strengthen other types of relationships. Moreover, people's behavior within relationships should be such that it promotes the positive (and avoids the negative) consequences of reflection and of social comparison.

Empirical Evidence

Tesser and his colleagues have reported a large number of studies which have consistently lent support for the theory (e.g., Tesser & Campbell, 1980; Tesser & Collins, 1988; Tesser, Millar & Moore, 1988; Tesser & Paulhus, 1983; Tesser, Pilkington & McIntosh, 1989). Here we describe just a few of those studies—the ones with the most obvious relevance to interpersonal relationships.

One straightforward prediction about close relationships that can be made from the theory is that if two individuals choose (or have chosen) *distinct* performance domains as the domains most relevant to their personal identities and as the domains in which they strive to excel, they ought to be more likely to form a close relationship and more able to maintain it easily. In such cases when *each* person succeeds in his or her chosen performance domain, that person will usually be able to benefit by social comparison with the partner while the partner can, simultaneously, benefit from reflection.

Given this, we should be able to observe evidence that complementarity, not similarity, *in chosen performance domains* within close relationships is a good thing, and indeed such evidence exists. Some evidence comes from studies of siblings. Tesser (1980), for example, has found that when subjects reported that their siblings performed better than they did on important dimensions, they also reported decreased identification and increased friction with those siblings. He also found intriguing evidence gleaned from close examinations of the autobiographies of famous scientists that the closeness of the relationships between these scientists and their fathers was a *negative* function of the similarity of their occupations. Finally, Leventhal (1970) reports evidence that, as siblings age, they increasingly tend to specialize in different domains.

Some recent work by Pilkington, Tesser, and Stephens (1991) suggests that complementarity in performance domains may be sought out not only between siblings but also in romantic relationships as well. In one study they report, a large group of male and female undergraduates currently involved in romantic relationships filled out a questionnaire on which they indicated the importance of a large number of performance domains to themselves. They also indicated whether they were better than their partner in the domain or whether the reverse was true. Among the domains important to the respondent, the comparison process appeared to dominate. Respondents perceived themselves to be superior in the clear majority of these areas. In contrast, among domains *unimportant* to the respondent, the reflection process seemed to be more important. The *partner* was judged to be superior in the majority of these identity-irrelevant areas. Further studies reported in the same paper suggest that it's not only what is relevant to your identity but also what you see as relevant to your partner's identity that is related to perceived relative performances in various domains. Respondents were *especially* likely to see their partner as outperforming them in domains with low perceived relevance to them *and simultaneously* high perceived relevance to their partner. They also were especially likely to see themselves as outperforming their partner in domains with high perceived relevance to them *and simultaneously* low perceived relevance to their partners.

Another prediction based on self-evaluation maintenance theory that is quite relevant to understanding relationships is that people will not *always* be more helpful to their friends or to family members than they will be to strangers (in sharp contrast to what the communal norms discussed earlier would suggest). Specifically, Tesser and Smith (1980) predicted that when the relevance of a performance domain for subjects was low, the reflection process would predominate. The closer the other is, the more subjects ought to help the other. In other words, when a task domain is low in relevance to you, the theory suggests you ought to help your friend more than a stranger. *However,* when relevance to you is high, the comparison process should predominate. In this case you ought to be more reluctant to help your friend than to help a stranger. Why? In such circumstances comparison to a friend who does better than you is most likely to make you look bad and to lower your self-esteem.

To test these ideas Tesser and Smith had some subjects perform a task high in relevance to them (it was said to relate to their verbal skills and leadership). Other subjects performed a task low in relevance to them (it was said to relate to very little about them). Then all subjects received feedback indicating they had performed poorly. Still later they had a chance to give easy or difficult clues on the same task to a friend or to a member of a different pair of friends who was a stranger to them. The results are depicted in Figure 8.4. As predicted, when relevance was high, subjects gave more difficult clues to friends than to strangers. In contrast, when relevance was low, subjects gave more difficult clues to strangers than to friends. The implications of these findings for ongoing relationships are intriguing. When close friends, romantic partners, or fam-

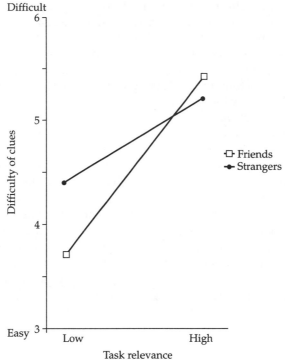

FIGURE 8.4. Difficulty of clues given to another as a function of the closeness of the relationship and relevance of the task to one's own identity.

ily members are striving to perform well in the same domain, they may be quite unlikely to help one another in that domain. While this may protect their self-esteem, at the same time such reluctance to help violates communal norms and may hurt the relationship.

On a more encouraging note, Tesser and Cornell (1991) recently replicated Tesser and Smith's (1980) results but went further as well and provided evidence that if subjects' self-esteem is temporarily bolstered in ways completely separate from the self-evaluation maintenance processes discussed here, the processes appear to be "turned off." The effects predicted on the basis of comparison processes are not obtained. This suggests that people fortunate enough to have friends, romantic partners, or siblings with high self-esteem may find those partners willing to help them even when those partners are simultaneously striving to perform well in the same domain.

Another study supporting the model (and very relevant to relationship dynamics) was reported by Tesser and Campbell (1982). As in the Tesser and Smith study, subjects participated with a friend or with a stranger. All subjects took a test of both social sensitivity and aesthetic judgment (and also rated the relevance of both skills to their own self-definitions). Then each subject received feedback that he or she was right on half the items and wrong on half. Next they guessed how many right their friend and how many right a stranger had gotten on each test. As predicted by the theory, when the task was low in self-relevance, subjects were more likely to guess their friend than a stranger had answered the question correctly. In contrast, when the task was relevant, just the reverse occurred. Subjects were more likely to guess the stranger had answered the question correctly than they were to guess that their friend had done so.

In still another study Pleban and Tesser (1981) showed that the theory could predict how much closeness a person will seek with another when the other outperforms the person on a task. Male subjects first indicated how important various domains of activity were to their self-definition. Then they and another subject, previously unknown to them, answered questions on a topic of relevance to the subject's identity or not of much relevance to the subject's identity. The other did a little better, much better, a little worse, or much worse than the subject. Later how close the subject chose to be to that other was measured. If the domain of task performance was high in relevance to the subject, the greater the margin was by which the other outperformed the subject, the less close the subjects chose to sit to the other, the less desire to work with the other subjects expressed, and the less subjects said the other was "like" them. In contrast, if the domain was low in relevance, the greater the margin was by which the other outperformed the subject, the closer subjects sat to the other, the more desire to work with the other the subjects expressed, and the more subjects said the other was "like" them.

Explaining Established Attraction Phenomena

What does self-evaluation maintenance (SEM) theory have to say about the sorts of established attraction phenomena mentioned at the opening of this chapter? Intriguingly, we think it challenges some of those "facts."

For instance, what of physical proximity? From the perspective of SEM theory, one way of thinking of physical proximity is that it is one factor which causes another person to seem "close." As such, proximity ought to potentiate *both* reflection and comparison processes. If the effects are positive ones, proximity should increase liking and the chances of a relationship forming. Consider this example. I do not aspire to win an Olympic gold medal. Now, imagine that my next-door neighbor has done just that. I may brag that I live next door to him in order to enjoy his reflected glory. My ability to do so may promote my attraction toward him. My pride in him and attraction toward him may, in turn, promote *his* attraction to me (Backman & Secord, 1959; Folkes & Sears, 1977; Sachs, 1976). As a result, a mutually rewarding relationship may develop. It may seem silly but intuitively real (and predicted by the theory) that I cannot enjoy this reflected glory if the medal winner lives four streets away, and without the reflected glory and its consequences, the relationship may never develop. However, the theory also makes it clear that proximity can have negative effects if the outcome of comparison or reflection processes are painful. If my next-door neighbor is a well-known drug dealer, his proximity may activate reflection processes and may cause me pain. This may motivate me to make efforts to dissociate myself from my neighbor. I probably would not feel the same degree of need to disassociate myself from him if he lived four streets away.

And what of the effects of physical attractiveness? Again the theory suggests that whether it helps or hurts attraction and relationships should "depend." If we do not aspire to great attractiveness or do not compete in the same domain of attractiveness (perhaps as a result of being of the opposite sex and/or because there is a significant gap between our own attractiveness and the other's), then we can reflect in an attractive other's glory (cf. Sigall & Landy, 1973), and it should draw us closer to that person. But if the other's attractiveness results in painful social comparison (as it well may if the other is of the same sex) and if we are close enough in attractiveness to make a comparison reasonable (but the other is still more attractive), we may actually like that other *less* as a result of his or her attractiveness. Fitting with this, we recently conducted a longitudinal study of same-sex roommates' participation in joint activities with one another. We found a significant positive correlation between the *discrepancy* in roommates' physical attractiveness and the number of joint activities in which they engage after having spent two semesters together (Clark, Pataki, & Winkler, 1993).[1]

Finally, what of similarity? The theory is pretty much silent when it comes to the effects of similarity of attitudes on attraction (although, as noted earlier, reinforcement theorists have clearly demonstrated similarity of attitudes to be related to attraction). However, as already discussed, self-esteem maintenance theory clearly predicts that if two people aspire to good performance in the same domain, that fact is likely to result in painful comparisons for at least one of them and to less attraction and decreased chances for a good relationship. Indeed, the collection of studies we just described by Leventhal (1970), Tesser (1980), and Pilkington, Tesser, and Stephens (1991) are clearly consistent with the idea that complementarity, not similarity, in performance domains is good for close relationships. Perhaps *both* the saying that "birds of a feather flock together" *and* the saying that "opposites attract" can be true. The former saying may hold true for similarity in attitudes; the latter, for *dis*similarity in relevant performance dimensions.

A THEORY OF PASSIONATE LOVE

The Theory

In the early 1970s Berscheid and Walster (Hatfield) proposed a theory of passionate love (Berscheid & Walster, 1974; Walster & Berscheid, 1971). At the time the reinforcement paradigm described earlier in this chapter was the predominant framework within which to view attraction. However, Walster and Berscheid found it inadequate to explain certain aspects of passionate love. For instance, they found it inadequate to explain such things as the excitement of new romances dying down over time, people often feeling very much in love

with another person who has just dumped them, or the fact that parental interference in love affairs has been observed to be positively associated with intensified romantic feelings between members of a couple (Driscoll, Davis, & Lipitz,
1972). They speculated that a two component theory of love based on
Schachter's theory of emotion (Schachter, 1964) would be more useful for understanding feelings of passion.

Schachter and his colleagues had argued that for a person to experience
emotion, that person must be physiologically aroused and must label or interpret that arousal in emotional terms (Schachter, 1964; Schachter & Singer, 1962).
Berscheid and Walster, building on those ideas, proposed that feelings of passionate love may result from being aroused and labeling that arousal as love felt
for a person (generally) of the opposite sex.

The arousal involved might come from a number of sources. It might be a
direct result of something having to do with the other person. For example, a
person might feel nervous about whether an attractive opposite sex other will
be cordial if approached or will reject any advances. The presence of another
person may elicit feelings of sexual arousal. Alternatively (or in addition), a person may be aroused in another's presence for reasons which have little if anything to do with that other person. For instance, a person may have just exercised, ridden a roller-coaster, watched a horror movie, or argued with a sales
clerk before coming into contact with a person toward whom it is plausible that
person would be attracted. No matter. So long as the arousal is labeled (or *mis*-
labeled as the case may be) as romantic love for another person, it will be experienced as such.

The circumstances under which we will label our arousal as romantic love
are presumably influenced by our culture. Our culture teaches us it is appropriate to be romantically attracted to people of about our own age who are
physically attractive and who come from similar backgrounds. This encourages
us to experience feelings of romantic love in the presence of such people. Our
culture also teaches us it is *in*appropriate to feel certain emotions in those circumstances. This may *dis*courage feelings of love in certain circumstances. For
instance, it may discourage labeling one's arousal as romantic love felt for
someone very much older or very much younger than oneself. Cultural influences may also encourage some *mis*labeling of arousal as romantic love. Both
males and females may experience arousal on a roller-coaster ride, but as a result of cultural norms that males ought not feel fear in such situations, they may
be prone to mislabel their arousal as feelings of romantic love toward the young
woman sitting next to them. Females, feeling it is more permissible to feel
afraid, may be less prone toward mislabeling their arousal as romantic feelings
for the young man sitting next to them and, instead, may readily label it as fear.

Empirical Evidence

A number of studies have lent support to Berscheid and Walster's ideas about
passionate love. Some were conducted by Dutton and Aron (1974). In one of
their studies subjects were young adult males visiting a park in Canada who

were crossing one of two bridges. One bridge was a long, narrow one chosen to be the "experimental" bridge. It was a suspension bridge made of wooden boards attached to cables that ran from one side of a canyon to the other. It was selected for its arousal enhancing qualities, including "(a) a tendency to tilt, sway, and wobble, creating the impression that one is about to fall over the side; (b) very low handrails of wire cable which contribute to this impression; and (c) a 230-foot drop to rocks and shallow rapids below the bridge" (p. 511). The other bridge was definitely *not* an arousal-producing bridge. It was a solid wood bridge only 10 feet above a small, shallow rivulet.

As the male subject crossed the bridge, either a male or female interviewer approached him saying he/she was doing a study on the effects of scenic attractions on creative expression. The subject was then asked to write a brief story and was given the experimenter's phone number along with an offer from the experimenter to explain the study in more detail when she had time. The content of the stories was later scored for sexual imagery, and the number of actual phone calls made to the experimenter was recorded. It was assumed that both sexual imagery and calling the experimenter would be indications of romantic feelings.

The results were in line with the theory. Only when there was reason for subjects to be aroused (i.e., they were on the high, shaky bridge) *coupled* with the presence of a target person who would be an appropriate target for romantic love (i.e., the experimenter was a female) was phone calling common (50 percent of the subjects called) and sexual imagery relatively high (mean = 2.5, on a five-point scale). In contrast, in the control bridge/female experimenter, the experimental bridge/male experimenter, and control bridge/male experimenter conditions the percentage of subjects making phone calls was low: 12.5 percent, 28.5 percent, and 16.7 percent, respectively. The imagery scores also were low: 1.4, .8, and .6, respectively. (Dutton and Aron also followed this study up with two experimental, conceptual replications. Both yielded additional evidence consistent with the theory.)

Considerably later another set of researchers—White, Fishbein and Rutstein (1981)—also conducted a set of studies in an effort both to provide additional support for the Berscheid/Walster theory of passionate love and to extend their ideas to understand feelings of repulsion as well.[2] These researchers argued that not only could arousal be attributed to feelings of love if an appropriate (i.e., attractive) target were available, arousal could also be attributed to feelings of repulsion if an appropriate (i.e., *un*attractive) target for labeling were available.

Here is a description of one study they did to test these ideas. Male subjects volunteered for a study and reported to it individually. The experimenter told each subject that he and supposedly a second participant, a female, were to give their reactions to a variety of stimuli. Later the two would interact with one another on a brief "date." The cover story was that the experimenter was interested in how the similarity of their reactions to the various stimuli predicted how attracted they would be to one another following this "date."

Next, each male subject was exposed to one of three audiotapes (suppos-

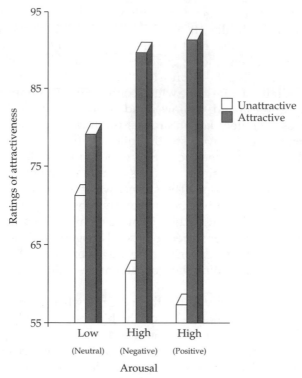

FIGURE 8.5. Romantic attraction as a function of arousal and the other's physical attractiveness.

edly one of the stimuli to which both participants would be responding). Two tapes were designed to elicit arousal, one through exposure to negative stimuli (i.e., "a grisly description of a foreign mob killing and mutilating a missionary while his family watched") and one through exposure to positive stimuli (i.e., a humorous "mix of selections from comedian Steve Martin's album 'A Wild and Crazy Guy' "). The remaining tape was selected so as to be neutral both in terms of affective tone and in its lack of a tendency to elicit arousal (i.e., "a description of the frog circulatory system from a biology text"). Pretests indicated that the two "arousal' tapes *did* heighten subjects' physiological arousal; the control tape did not.

Next, the subject was exposed to a videotape supposedly of his partner/future date. Half the subjects in each arousal condition saw a quite attractive female on the tape; the other half saw a quite *un*attractive female on the tape. Finally, the subject rated his attraction toward that other on a variety of dimensions—how attractive her traits were, how attractive she was in general, how attractive she was romantically. All measures yielded the same pattern. The results on just one, the romantic attraction measure, appear in Figure 8.5.

As expected, when the potential female partner was attractive, arousal, produced *either* by the positive tape *or* by the negative tape, enhanced romantic attraction relative to what it was in the control condition. In contrast, if the potential female partner was unattractive, arousal, again produced *either* by the positive tape *or* by the negative tape, resulted in lowered attraction relative to attraction in the control condition. Apparently Berscheid and Walster's theory of passionate love can be extended to be a theory of repulsion as well.

Explaining Established Attraction Phenomena

How might one relate the Berscheid/Walster theory of passionate love to the "facts" about similarity, physical attractiveness, and proximity noted above. Their theory suggests we may be romantically attracted to physically attractive others and to those who have similar attitudes, a similar religion, a similar educational level, and so forth, because we are *taught* that such people are the most appropriate "targets" for such feelings. Of course, beyond that the theory is silent as to *why* we are taught that such people are more appropriate possible sources for our arousal than are others. As for proximity, people who are close to us should simply be more likely to arouse us or to be near us when we are aroused for other reasons. Thus they are more likely to be seen by us as possible sources for that arousal than are others. If they have positive features, we may label our feelings as attraction or even love. If they have distasteful attributes, we may label our feelings as hate, disgust, or repulsion.

A THEORY OF EXPERIENCING EMOTION IN THE CONTEXT OF RELATIONSHIPS

The Theory

Berscheid has described a theory of emotion in relationships that is clearly an interpersonal process theory (Berscheid, 1982; Kelley et al., 1983, Chapter 4). It concerns certain conditions likely to elicit emotion within the context of relationships, and it is not entirely unrelated to the theory just described as it too involves labeling one's arousal as an emotion (with the label coming from our understanding of the immediate situation).

To understand the theory, one first has to understand Berscheid's conception of a relationship as well as her definition of "closeness" in relationships. Berscheid, along with several others (Kelley et al., 1983), views relationships as existing when changes in the cognitive, physiological, or behavioral state of one person influence the analogous states in another person, and vice versa. In other words, for a relationship to exist, members must have mutual impact on one another. Relationships are close, in these theorists' terms, to the extent to which members have frequent, strong, and diverse impacts on each other over a long period. That is, if people *often* influence each other, influence each other in *diverse* ways (such as influencing the other's social activities, work activities, athletic activities, and sexual life as opposed to influencing, say, just the other's productivity at work), have *strong* influences on one another (for instance, if one person's advice makes the other think about issues for a long time, which, in turn, influences how that other behaves in many situations), and if this goes on for a *long* time, then the relationship clearly is close (Berscheid, Snyder, & Omoto, 1989).

Berscheid argues that an individual's behavior is typically organized into well-practiced action sequences which are often emitted as a unit. These tend to run off in an "automatic" or relatively "unconscious" fashion, and they are very difficult to change once the sequence has been triggered. In the case of close relationships, it is likely that many of a person's organized, automatic action sequences are intimately intertwined with the other's automatic action sequences.

For instance, imagine a husband and a wife coming home from their respective jobs in the evening. Each spouse may have an organized, well-practiced pattern of behavior for weekday evenings. If these routines are quite dependent upon one another, the relationship would be called close. For example, the wife may typically arrive home first. She may prepare some sort of snack and pour each of them a glass of wine. The husband comes in next, picks up his glass of wine and snack, and begins to prepare the main meal (for which he has carefully laid out ingredients early in the day). As he does this, his wife sits down nearby and they discuss their days at work, each soliciting opinions and advice from the other. He finishes fixing dinner and sits down to relax while they continue talking. She automatically gets up, sets the table, and brings the food to the table. They continue talking through dinnertime, at which point the wife clears the table and washes the dishes while the husband begins to do some office work. She prepares coffee, and an hour later they each show up in their den to drink the coffee together and talk some more. They do this every evening, Monday through Friday.

Contrast such closely intertwined routines with two relatively independent ones. The husband may tend to arrive home considerably ahead of the wife, who works late. He fixes his own dinner, eats it in front of the TV set, and then settles down to an evening of paperwork. When the wife comes in, she fixes her own dinner and sits down to her own work. They may continue to work independently throughout the evening.

Now, what does all this have to do with emotion? Relying in part on Mandler's (1975) theory of emotion, Berscheid proposes that interruptions in a person's organized behavior sequences will elicit heightened autonomic system arousal. The arousal, in turn, will cause attention to be focused upon the interrupting stimulus or will elicit a search for the cause of the interruption. The arousal itself forms the basis of emotional responding. If the interruption interferes with completing a desired plan, it is labeled negatively and results in negative emotion. (For example, the wife has prepared the snack, which just happens to be best served hot, and the husband does not return home for an hour, preventing the wife's routine from running off. What will she do with the food? What will she do with the extra hour? She is aroused, and she labels it negatively—she is mad at her husband.) If, however, the interruption *facilitates* a plan and allows a plan to run off more quickly than expected, then it should also produce arousal but that arousal will be labeled positively. Imagine, for example, that the husband has gotten off from work early. He stops at a gourmet shop on the way home, purchases a delicious set of hors d'oeuvres and a special wine, and has it waiting for the wife, who has arrived home at the regular time. She is surprised and experiences a jump in arousal, but this arousal is labeled positively. If the interruption has unexpectedly removed the presence of a stimulus that has previously interrupted a behavioral plan, it too will be labeled positively. In the case of any interruption, arousal will diminish when an original goal has been met, the old plan is reinstated, or a new plan can be substituted.

Berscheid argues that the theory can predict much about emotion within relationships as well as about likely emotion upon the demise of a relationship. How? To predict emotion one must first examine the degree and nature of interdependence within a relationship. If two people's organized behavioral plans are not very intertwined, neither has much power to interrupt the other. As a result, there should be few interruptions, little resulting arousal, and little emotion in that relationship. This applies both during the course of the relationship and to its break up, if that should happen.

In contrast, relationships in which the behavioral plans of the members are highly intertwined have great potential for emotional responding. Berscheid calls these relationships "emotionally invested" because each member has the capability of causing many interruptions in the other's organized behavioral plans. For example, if a child has always successfully relied on his mother to pick him up after his after-school job, she can elicit negative emotion by being late or not showing up at all. On the other hand, if he always walked home after the job, that ability does not exist. Moreover, it seems clear that if a highly intertwined relationship ends (e.g., if the husband or wife of the highly interdependent couple described above dies), the other is very likely to experience a great deal of emotion. But will much emotion be experienced during the *course* of the highly intertwined relationship? Perhaps, but perhaps not. If the participants do not interrupt one another, little emotion will be experienced. However, emotion will be experienced to the extent to which they *do* interrupt one another.

Empirical Work

There has not been a great deal of empirical work done to support this theory. Still, some has been done. Since a central concept of the theory is "closeness," a crucial first empirical step in this case has been the development of a measure of closeness—something which has been done by Berscheid and associates (1989). These authors have argued that how "close" two people are can be tapped by assessing how frequently they interact with one another, how diverse the nature of their interactions are, and the strength of the impact they have on one another. They have developed a scale to tap these things. To pick up on frequency of interaction they ask respondents to indicate the numbers of hours and minutes spent with the other during the morning, afternoon, and evening of each day during the past week. To assess diversity of interactions they developed a long list of varied activities (e.g., watching TV together, working on homework, going to a play, visiting family, engaging in sexual relations) in which two people might engage. Respondents are asked to check off all they have actually jointly engaged in within the last week. Finally, to measure strength they generated an extensive list of items or domains in which the other might influence a person either now or in the future (e.g., financial security, moods, basic values, how one dresses, vacation plans, plans to have children), and respondents are asked to rate the extent to which the other influences them on each. Following some transformations for psychometric purposes scores on each section are added together to yield a measure of closeness.

The question then becomes, Does this measure of closeness serve as a predictor of the sorts of things which Berscheid's theory suggests it should? A study done by Simpson (1987) using an earlier version of the measure suggests the answer is yes. He examined whether the level of closeness in relationships was associated with the level of emotion participants felt upon its breakup. He began by having a large number of undergraduates fill out a measure of closeness with regard to a person whom they were currently dating. Respondents indicated how satisfied they were with that relationship at the time, how long they had been dating, the quality of their best alternative dating partner and best imagined alternative, the ease of finding an alternative and the exclusivity of the current relationship. Approximately 3 months later the participants were recontacted. About one-third were no longer dating the person in question. They were asked a variety of questions designed to assess how much emotional distress they experienced upon breakup. As would be expected from the theory, those who scored higher on the closeness scale and those who had been dating for a longer period of time at the initial point of measurement experienced more emotional distress than did those who scored lower. These are the persons who should have experienced the most disruption of routines at breakup. Also consistent with the theory was the fact that the initially rated ease of finding an alternative partner also predicted less distress following breakup. The easier it is to *substitute* another in one's routine, the less disruption should occur, the less arousal should be experienced, and the less distress should be felt.

Perhaps most interesting, none of the other factors including satisfaction with the relationship at the time of the initial assessment predicted distress upon breakup. While at first blush the fact that satisfaction with the relationship does not predict distress upon breakup is surprising, it is, actually, entirely consistent with the theory. Why? First there ought to be some relationships in which there is little interdependence in the two people's behavior but in which participants are very satisfied. Despite high satisfaction in these relationships there should be very little disruption of ongoing plans on the other's part when the relationship breaks and consequently little arousal and little negative emotion. Second, there may well be many relationships in which interdependence is high and in which there are many well-organized intertwined behavioral sequences yet little emotion—positive or negative. Given the low level of positive emotion, members of such relationships may not think of themselves as highly satisfied. Even so, upon breakup the great disruptions of their activity may cause much distress. Third, it is also the case that members of relationships in which *well-practiced* arguments and conflict regularly take place may actually experience little arousal and little emotion. Yet because of their conflicts members of such couples may describe themselves as dissatisfied. Much to their surprise perhaps, upon breakup they may still be quite distressed (rather than relieved) because their well-practiced low arousal conflicts have now been disrupted.

Explaining Established Attraction Phenomena

Our opinion is that Berscheid's theory of the occurrence of emotion within relationships is silent on the questions of why we ought to be attracted to physically attractive others. Moreover, we are a bit cautious in saying anything about its implications for understanding the effects of similarity and proximity. However, it is interesting to speculate that perhaps proximity simply makes it easier to become close (meaning very interdependent here) with another person thus making it easier for that other person to elicit emotion in you—good or bad. For instance, imagine that you always sit next to the same person in class. Every Monday, Wednesday, and Friday you chat with that person for a few minutes. You even come a few minutes early because you enjoy the conversation. It's become a routine. *Now* the person has at least a bit of power to interrupt your routine and make you feel bad.

With regard to similarity, one can imagine that some similarity might make it easier for one's behavior to become intertwined with that of another. People with similar interests, values, and beliefs may spend more time together—taking the same classes, discussing their work, going to church together, and so forth. Consequently, their routines may become intertwined to a greater extent than will those of people with different interests, and they may be more able to elicit emotion, both positive and negative, in one another. In contrast, having clearly different interests and values might encourage lack of interdependence and less "emotional investment" in the relationship. If I value socializing and my husband does not, we probably will not socialize with others much together. He cannot cause me distress by not showing up at an appointed time for dinner with friends. Neither is he likely to delight me by showing up for such a dinner when I had expected him not to be able to attend.

AN INVESTMENT MODEL OF RELATIONSHIPS

The Theory

Rusbult and her colleagues have been actively developing and testing an investment model of relationships in recent years (Rusbult, 1980a, 1980b, 1983;

Rusbult & Buunk, 1993). Rusbult's work is based in part on Thibaut and Kelley's (1959; Kelley & Thibaut, 1978) original interdependence theory, but it also elaborates on that model.

The model includes a central cognitive construct known as "commitment." Commitment is a psychological state representing one's long-term orientation toward one's relationship with another. It incorporates feeling attached to a partner and wanting to maintain the relationship in the future. It includes beliefs about the relationship and felt emotion about it, and according to Rusbult, it influences a wide range of behavior in relationships. For instance, presumably the more one feels committed to the relationship, the more one will be willing to sacrifice for the benefit of one's partner and the more one will accommodate when one's partner behaves badly in the relationship—as all partners are bound to do sooner or later. Further, the greater the commitment, the more stable the relationship should be.

One might suspect that attraction toward one's partner or liking for him or her would be the major or even the only factor determining commitment. Not so, according to Rusbult. *Many* factors contribute importantly to one's sense of commitment to a relationship. One factor, the one coming closest to attraction, is *satisfaction* with the relationship. An individual's satisfaction is determined by that individual's assessment of his or her outcomes (including both costs and rewards) from the relationship and an evaluation of those outcomes *relative* to the level of outcomes the person feels he or she deserves. That "comparison level" (Thibaut & Kelley, 1959) is determined by such things as experiences in past relationships and observations of relationships that similar others have. People who have experienced terrific relationships in the past are likely to have higher comparison levels than those who have had poor ones. If your outcomes fall above your comparison level, you are satisfied; if they fall below it, you are not.

Satisfaction is just one determinant of commitment, though. *Investments* into the relationship also influence commitment. The more investments there are—including such things as time, emotional effort, self-disclosure (intrinsic investments) and mutual friends, shared memories, or material possessions (extrinsic investments)—the greater the commitment will be. And still another determinant of commitment is the comparison level a person has for alternatives to the relationship (e.g., relationships with others or the option of staying alone). The importance of CL-alt, or the comparison level for alternatives, was first suggested by Thibaut and Kelley (1959), and it refers to the lowest level of outcomes a person will accept given available alternative opportunities. The lower a person's CL-alt, the more likely a person is to stay in a relationship and the more committed to that relationship the person will feel. Variables included in this model are depicted in Figure 8.6.

Based on this model, a number of predictions can be made about relationships. People should be more satisfied with their relationships to the extent that those relationships provide high rewards and low costs and to the extent that the sum of rewards minus costs exceeds the individual's comparison level for

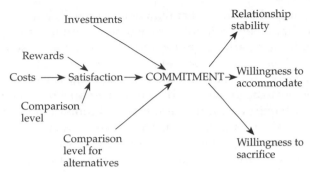

FIGURE 8.6. Some antecedents and consequences of commitment in Rusbult's model.

that relationship. That is straightforward, and it is something with which the reinforcement theorists discussed earlier in the chapter would certainly agree. However, the model further predicts that measures of satisfaction alone often will not be sufficient for the development of commitment to relationships. Thus, the model predicts, somewhat surprisingly, that such measures will not necessarily predict staying in or leaving relationships. If investments are high and there are no good alternatives, the person may stay even if dissatisfied. The model also predicts that people will sometimes leave relationships despite being satisfied. If there are low investments and good alternatives, commitment may well be low. A satisfied person in such a circumstance may find it relatively easy to move on to a different relationship.

Empirical Evidence

To date many, many studies have been completed which support the investment model (e.g., Rusbult, 1980a, 1980b; Rusbult & Farrell, 1983; Rusbult, Johnson, & Morrow, 1986; Rusbult & Martz, 1992; Rusbult, Verette, Whitney, Slovik, & Lipkus, 1991). Here is a description of some of those findings.

In a longitudinal study of heterosexual dating relationships, Rusbult (1983) has found that increases in rewards over time led to corresponding increases in satisfaction. In addition, commitment increased as a joint function of increases in satisfaction, declines in the perceived quality of alternatives, and increased investments. Greater rewards were also associated with increases in commitment to maintain relationships. (The only nonsupporting findings were that increases in costs generally did not reduce commitment or satisfaction.)

Another, more recent study supporting the model, dealt with abusive relationships—specifically romantic relationships in which the man had abused the woman (Rusbult & Martz, 1992). What happens when an abused woman leaves the man who abused her and seeks safety at a woman's shelter? It might seem that the only sensible thing for such a woman to do is to stay away from the relationship. Yet many women do not. They go back. Rusbult and Martz thought the investment model could predict who would go back and who would not. They reasoned that whether or not these women continued to report being at all satisfied with their partners (in the form of having at least some positive feelings toward those partners) would have little to do with whether they returned to those partners or not. Satisfaction among these women should have been generally low to begin with, and according to Rusbult's model such feelings should be just one of several determinants of commitment anyway. Other things such as having joint children, having more than one child (investments), and having enough money to survive on their own (good alternatives) should make important contributions to the return/leave decision. As predicted, but probably contrary to most people's initial intuitions, having positive feelings for their partners (or completely lacking such feelings) did not predict return. Measures of commitment, investments, and the quality of alternatives did.

Other interesting recent results supporting the theory include findings that high subjective commitment is associated with believing one's relationship is superior to others' relationships (Rusbult et al., forthcoming, as reported in Rusbult & Buunk, 1993) and with downplaying an alternative partner's desirability (Johnson & Rusbult, 1989). Rusbult and colleagues (1991) also have found that commitment plays a role in mediating one's willingness to accommodate to a partner's poor behavior (for instance, by reacting positively to your partner even though he or she has reacted negatively to you).

Explaining Established Attraction Phenomena

How would an investment theorist interpret observed effects of similarity, physical attractiveness, and proximity on attraction? These variables can most easily be "fit into" the model in terms of how they influence costs and rewards (and therefore satisfaction) in a relationship. Consider similarity of attitudes, for example. If similar people understand us more quickly, empathize with us more easily, and agree with our opinions thus making us feel good, they are contributing rewards to the relationship. This should enhance satisfaction, which should enhance commitment to the relationship. If dissimilar people make us question our own values or make us nervous just being around them, that contributes costs to the relationship. Costs should decrease satisfaction and consequently commitment as well.

What about proximity? One may be less likely to maintain relationships with people who are not in very close proximity because to do so increases the costs of the relationship. Clearly driving 100 miles to see a friend and paying long-distance phone bills is costly and can deter relationships, but so too might merely having to walk down the steps to another floor in a dorm versus just running into the person in the room next door. Finally, physical attractiveness might be viewed as a reward insofar as it reflects positively on you (as Tesser's model suggests), but so too might it cause costs if it makes you feel ugly in comparison (as Tesser's model also suggests). Perhaps the other's physical attractiveness will count as a reward, in Rusbult's terms, *if* physical attractiveness is not a dimension terribly relevant to your own identity (in Tesser's terms) or if the other does not seem to be a reasonable target for comparison, perhaps because he or she is of the opposite sex. In such cases, attractiveness may promote attraction and relationship development through increasing satisfaction. Otherwise it may create pain through comparison processes, count as a cost, and cause attraction to drop and relationships to flounder.

Further, the investment model makes the important point that the variables of similarity, attractiveness, and proximity should not influence attraction and relationships solely through their impact on satisfaction with our current partner. The concept of comparison level for alternatives alerts us to the fact that the similarity, attractiveness, and proximity of possible *alternative* partners should also influence our commitment to our partner. The more similar (in attitudes, race, background, but perhaps not in performance) such alternatives are, the more attractive they are; and the more proximal they are, the less likely your relationship with your partner will continue.

ATTACHMENT THEORY

The Theory

The final theory we discuss is attachment theory. Attachment theory is unique among the theories discussed in this chapter in providing a developmental perspective on understanding attraction and relationships. The basic premise is that, based on early childhood experiences, people develop general expectations about relationships. Then, once formalized into cognitive structures, these beliefs are resistant to change and have implications for the nature of one's relationships across the life span. Although the theory originates with research on infants by Bowlby (1969, 1973, 1980), its application to adults has been developed by Hazan and Shaver (1987, 1990; Shaver & Hazan, 1992) and later, somewhat differently, by Bartholomew (1990). We begin by briefly summarizing the original formation of attachment theory by Bowlby. Then we discuss its extension to adult romantic relationships.

Bowlby focused on infants' relationships with their primary caregivers, in most cases their mothers. He suggested that this relationship is unique as evidenced by a number of universal responses among infants. First, infants and young children become distressed and tend to protest when separated from their primary caretaker, even when being well cared for by others. Second, as long as their caregiver is nearby, infants show an interest in exploring their environment and interacting with others. Third, when infants experience threat or discomfort, they cease exploration and seek out their caregiver for protection and comfort. From an evolutionary perspective, these responses have adaptive significance through promoting proximity to the caregiver and thereby ensuring the safety of the infant.

The process of forming this relationship with the primary caregiver is known as attachment, and the primary caregiver is often referred to as the attachment figure. According to Bowlby, through repeated interactions with the attachment figure, the child forms generalized expectations about the responsiveness and dependability of others. These beliefs are incorporated into children's working models—mental models—of themselves, of others, and of their relationships with others. In general, if the attachment figure is available and responsive to the child's needs, the child internalizes a general belief that people are responsive and dependable and that he or she is worthy of their attention. In contrast, if the attachment figure is either unavailable or inconsistent in responding to the child, then the child internalizes the general belief that others are *not* responsive or dependable and that he or she is not worthy of their attention. Bowlby suggests these beliefs develop gradually throughout infancy, childhood, and adolescence, and that once incorporated into cognitive models, they tend to persist throughout life.

This original theory led to a vast amount of research with infants and young children, one critical focus being an examination of individual differences in attachment experiences. Based on Bowlby's work, Ainsworth and her colleagues (Ainsworth, Blehar, Waters, & Wall, 1978) developed a procedure for assessing infants' attachment by focusing on children's reactions to separations and reunions with their primary caregiver, known as the "strange situation" methodology. Using this methodology, she delineated three patterns of attachment: secure, anxious/ambivalent, and avoidant.

The secure pattern is the prototype for a well-functioning attachment relationship. It is evidenced by children's distress at separation from the attachment figure, comfort seeking upon reunion, and willingness to explore in the presence of the attachment figure. Primary caregivers of secure infants tend to be sensitive and responsive to their infants' needs. Anxious/ambivalent and avoidant patterns of attachment are believed to reflect less ideal forms of attachment and are often grouped together under the label "insecure." Caregivers of children classified as anxious/ambivalent respond inconsistently to their children's needs. At times, they are unavailable or unresponsive to the child. At other times, they are intrusive or overly demanding of the child's attention. These infants tend to be preoccupied with their caregiver's availability in the strange situation. They are distressed prior to separation and unable to be comforted upon reunion with the caregiver. They are also unwilling to explore in the caregiver's presence. Caregivers of children classified as avoidant tend to avoid close bodily contact with their children and to reject the infants' bids for proximity. These children exhibit little overt distress during separation and little reaction to reunion in the strange situation. They tend to focus their attention on toys or other objects rather than on the caregiver. These reactions, often referred to as detachment, are believed to be active, defensive responses to the mother's unavailability.

Recently researchers have begun to explore the implications of early attachment experiences throughout the life span. Weiss (1986) notes that in order to become an independent, fully functioning adult capable of creating a new family unit, individuals must eventually shift their primary attachment from their parents to a new attachment figure, in most cases, a romantic partner. Interestingly Hazan and Shaver note a number of parallels between adult romantic relationships and infant-caregiver relationships. These include the desire to maintain close physical proximity and reliance on the attachment figure for comfort and security. Hazan and Shaver suggest that "falling in love" can be conceptualized as an attachment process.

As applied to adult relationships, attachment theory suggests there should be some degree of continuity in attachment experiences from infancy into adulthood. People who had a trusting and supportive relationship with an attachment figure as a child should, in adulthood, expect others to respond in a similar trustworthy manner. They should seek out others who meet and confirm these expectations. In contrast, those who did not have a supportive or dependable relationship with an attachment figure during childhood should have lower expectations for others and may even avoid close relationships altogether. They may behave in such a way as to confirm and perpetuate their beliefs about others.

Attachment theory places great emphasis on early relationships based on the assumption that these experiences play a critical role in the development of cognitive models of relationships which, once formalized, are difficult to change. This is not to say, however, that change cannot occur. Rather, people are likely to experience a number of important relationships over time, each of which may confirm or disconfirm features of their mental models and thereby provide an opportunity for revision. Thus, Hazan and Shaver note, continuity between childhood and adult experiences may diminish over time as experiences in new relationships dilute effects of early attachment experiences on one's cognitive representations of relationships.

Subsequent to the initial extension of attachment theorizing to adults, Bartholomew (1990) proposed an expanded model of adult attachment that distinguishes between two forms of adult avoidant attachment, a *dismissing* and a *fearful* style. This model is based on the assumption that there are two underlying dimensions of adult attachment. These two dimensions are represented in the person's internal models of self and others. Bartholomew suggests that the view of self can be dichotomized as either positive or negative (i.e., the self is either worthy or unworthy of love and attention); and the view of others can be similarly dichotomized (i.e., others are trustworthy, caring, and available, or others are rejecting, uncaring, and distant).

Bartholomew proposes that the combination of these two dimensions forms the basis of four attachment categories. (See Figure 8.7.) The secure and preoccupied styles are conceptually similar to Hazan and Shaver's secure and anxious/ambivalent attachment styles. Similarly, the fearful style is similar to the avoidant style described by Hazan and Shaver. The dismissing style, however, is believed to reflect a distinct pattern of avoidant attachment.

To describe the fearful and dismissing style in more detail, fearful attach-

		Internal Models of the Self	
		Negative	Positive
Internal Model of the Other	Negative	Fearful	Dismissing
	Positive	Preoccupied	Secure

FIGURE 8.7. Bartholomew's four attachment styles.

ment is conceptualized as a person who maintains a negative view of both self and others. People who maintain this style of attachment are believed to avoid close relationships in order to protect themselves from anticipated rejection by others. In contrast, the dismissing style is conceptualized as a person who maintains a positive view of the self while holding a negative view of others. People in this category are believed to downplay the importance of close relationships and to emphasize the virtues of self-reliance and independence.

By distinguishing between dismissing and fearful attachment styles, Bartholomew differentiates between those who avoid relationships because of a lack of interest or motivation and those who avoid relationships because of a fear of rejection. Bartholomew and Horowitz (1991) developed a four-item self-report measure as well as an interview to assess an individual's attachment classification based on this model.

Empirical Evidence

Initial empirical evidence in support of attachment theory as applied to adults was reported by Hazan and Shaver (1987). They predicted (a) that adult romantic relationships would be similar to the infant-caregiver relationship in terms of attachment-related behaviors such as proximity seeking and turning to the attachment figure for comfort, (b) that the patterns of attachment identified in infancy would be evident in adult relationships, and (c) that individual differences in adults' relationship orientation would be related to differences in childhood relationships with parents.

To test these predictions, in an initial study, they constructed a "love quiz" and arranged to have it printed in a local newspaper. It asked respondents to answer questions about their most important love relationship and included a three-item measure of adult attachment designed to reflect the three infant attachment styles delineated earlier by Ainsworth (i.e., secure, anxious/ambiva-

TABLE 8.1 Measure of Adult Attachment Types

WHICH OF THE FOLLOWING BEST DESCRIBES YOUR FEELINGS?

Secure: I find it relatively easy to get close to others and am comfortable depending on them and having them depend on me. I don't often worry about being abandoned or about someone getting too close to me.

Avoidant: I am somewhat uncomfortable being close to others; I find it difficult to trust them completely, difficult to allow myself to depend on them. I am nervous when anyone gets too close, and often, love partners want me to be more intimate than I feel comfortable being.

Anxious/ambivalent: I find that others are reluctant to get as close as I would like. I often worry that my partner doesn't really love me or won't want to stay with me. I want to merge completely with another person, and this desire sometimes scares people away.

Source: Hazan & Shaver, 1987. Note that soon after the development of this measure it was revised. The revised version (see Hazan & Shaver, 1990) has been used in much subsequent work.

lent, and avoidant). This measure is shown in Table 8.1. Respondents simply indicated which description best described their feelings.

Hundreds of adults from diverse backgrounds responded. Their responses fit with attachment theory in interesting and meaningful ways. First, the prevalence of the three attachment styles was strikingly similar to that found in studies of infants and young children. That is, 56 percent of the respondents classified themselves as secure, 25 percent as avoidant, and 19 percent as anxious/ambivalent (as compared to approximately 62 percent of American infants classified as secure, 23 percent as avoidant, and 15 percent as anxious/ambivalent). Second, although there appeared to be core features of romantic love common to almost all respondents, respondents who placed themselves in different categories emphasized different things. Secure respondents tended to describe their most important relationship as happy, friendly, and trusting. Avoidant respondents described fear of intimacy, emotional highs and lows, and jealousy in their most important relationship; and anxious/ambivalent respondents described feelings of obsession, extreme sexual attraction, and jealousy. Respondents classifying themselves in the different ways also endorsed different beliefs about romantic relationships in general, beliefs consistent with their attachment classification. Hazan and Shaver believed these reflected the subjects' mental models of relationships. For example, avoidant lovers were most likely to agree with statements such as "It is rare to find a person one can really fall in love with" and "The kind of head-over-heels romantic love depicted in novels and movies does not exist in real life."

In addition to questions about the subjects' most important romantic relationship and beliefs about relationships in general, the questionnaire also included items designed to assess the subjects' attachment history. Secure subjects, in comparison with both avoidant and anxious/ambivalent subjects, reported warmer relationships with both parents as well as warmer relationships between their parents. Insecure subjects, in contrast, recalled less favorable experiences. Avoidant subjects were most likely to describe their mothers as cold and rejecting, and anxious/ambivalent subjects were most likely to describe their fathers as unfair.

Taken together, these results provided preliminary support for attachment theory as applied to adults. Since this initial study, other researchers have reported similar findings based on different populations including populations outside the United States (Feeney & Noller, 1990; Mikulincer, Florian, & Tolmacz, 1990). Researchers have also developed other measures of adult attachment including other self-report measures as well as the adult attachment interview (George, Kaplan, & Main, 1985).

Among the many studies with adults inspired by Hazan and Shaver's extension of attachment theory is a series of studies reported by Collins and Read (1990). They developed a 21-item Adult Attachment Scale based on Hazan and Shaver's 3-item measure, as well as on other characteristics described in the developmental literature on attachment. In addition to developing the scale, Collins and Read (1990, study 3) focused on the importance of experiences with the opposite-sex parent during childhood. They predicted a correspondence between the attachment style dimensions of an individual's romantic partner and the caregiving styles of the parents, especially the opposite-sex parent. This prediction was based on the idea that the opposite-sex parent would be particularly influential as a role model for heterosexual relationships due to the importance of existing mental models of relationships on the nature of new relationships.

To conduct this study, Collins and Read asked both members of dating couples to individually complete a number of measures including their attachment scale and questions about their parents' caregiving styles. In support of their predictions, only descriptions of the opposite-sex parent were related to the attachment style dimensions of the subjects' romantic partners. Specifically, women who perceived their fathers as having been warm and responsive were more likely than women who saw their fathers as cold, distant, or inconsistent to be dating men who felt they could depend on others and who felt comfortable getting close. Men who described their mothers as cold or inconsistent were more likely to be dating women who were anxious. Further, men who described their mothers as cold and distant were somewhat less likely to be dating a woman who felt she could depend on others. Interestingly, these results provide additional evidence that people do seek out others who confirm their expectations about relationships. They also suggest that the opposite-sex parent may play a central role in shaping beliefs and expectations related to heterosexual relationships.

Other researchers have used attachment theory as a basis for understanding specific types of relationships. For example, Tidwell, McCarten, and Shaver (1992) focused on women who choose to stay involved in destructive, punishing heterosexual relationships. They predicted these women would be classified as having an avoidant attachment style and that this classification would be related to their relationship with their father. This prediction was based on their reasoning that avoidant women expect men to be rejecting and that this expectation is incorporated in their working models of relationships. As a result, they are likely to accept male partners who are somewhat rejecting, controlling, or nonnurturant. Tidwell and associates found support for their predictions.

Many other studies of adult romantic relationships based on this theory have also appeared which may be of interest to the reader. For example, researchers have looked at the connection between attachment styles and optimism about future intimate relationships (Carnelley & Janoff-Bulman, 1992), dating couples' reactions to anxiety (Simpson, Rholes, & Nelligan, in press), and strategies used to resolve conflict within romantic relationships (Pistole, 1989).

Explaining Established Attraction Phenomena

How might attachment theory relate to the "facts" of interpersonal attraction and relationships? Our view is that it has little to say about the effects of either proximity or of physical attractiveness. However, we can speculate that proximity should be important in relationship formation for secure people given that the ideal function of the attachment system is to promote security. Attachment theory indicates that we seek close relationships with others who can provide us with a sense of comfort and security. According to the theory, this sense is maintained through contact with the attachment figure (whether this is a caregiver during childhood or a romantic partner during adulthood). On this basis, people may be more likely to establish a close relationship when proximity is feasible. This suggests a person will be less likely to fall in love with someone who is relatively inaccessible (for example, someone who lives in another city or state) than someone who is nearby. For those who have an anxious-ambivalent style, perhaps maintaining proximity is even *more* important than it is for others for they may be especially fearful of losing the other. For avoidant people, perhaps a long-distance relationship is fine. From their perspective, they do not really need the other person anyway!

With respect to similarity in relationships, the theory suggests to us that people should seek out and form relationships with others who have a similar attachment style—i.e., people who share the same sort of mental models of relationships as they do. Thus, it is not surprising to us that a number of studies have been conducted to determine whether people do indeed choose others with similar attachment styles for close relationships. Somewhat surprisingly the results of these studies are mixed. For example, Collins and Read (1990) found small but significant correlations indicating that secure people tend to form relationships with other secure people. However, other studies have failed to find this effect (Davis & Kirkpatrick, 1994; Simpson, 1990). Taken together, there is little evidence of matching on attachment styles.

SOME CONCLUDING COMMENTS

Comments About Our Coverage of Attachment and Relationship Work

We have now reviewed a variety of social psychological theories relevant to understanding attraction and relationships: reinforcement theory, a distinction between communal and exchange relationships, a theory of passionate love, a theory of when people will experience positive and negative emotion in their relationships, a theory of self-evaluation maintenance, an investment model of relationships, and a theory of attachment styles. We have been selective. We have mentioned just seven theories. There are many others to which any student in this area ought to attend. Some—such as Heider's balance theory (1958), Festinger's cognitive dissonance theory (1957), Altman and Taylor's (1973) social penetration theory, Walster and Berscheid's (1978) equity theory, and Thibaut and Kelley's (1959) exchange theory—are classic works which have been and remain very relevant resources for understanding attraction and relationships.

Other, more recent social psychological work of importance for any student of attraction and relationships include Reis and Shaver's (1988) model of intimacy processes and empirical support for that model supplied by Lin (1992), Holmes' recent work on trust (1991; Holmes & Rempel, 1989), and some of Kelley's and Thibaut's own extensions of their earlier theory (1978; Kelley, 1979). There are also other large bodies of research often from different disciplines which are relevant to relationships. For example, there are many descriptive studies by social psychologists, epidemiologists, anthropologists, communications researchers, and sociologists which tell us a great deal about relationships. There is work by clinicians interested in identifying what distinguishes distressed from nondistressed marriages; work by developmentalists interested in how children's relationships evolve; work by epidemiologists, social psychologists, and sociologists on the nature of social support and how it relates to health. Unfortunately, it is simply beyond the scope of the present chapter to tackle all that is relevant. Still, students of attraction and relationships ought to know that it exists and ought to become well acquainted with it.

Fitting Work on Interpersonal Processes in Relationships Together

Before concluding let's consider an important question. How do the various programs of work we have chosen to cover relate to one another? Work on the seven theories discussed in this chapter has proceeded almost entirely independently. The same can be said about work on most other social psychological theories relevant to attraction and relationships. What tends to happen in this area is that a psychologist will propose some theoretical processes. Then that psychologist and his or her students and sometimes a few others work on documenting the validity and implications of these ideas. It takes years to do this. As they work, others are working on their own theories, separately. This happens even though researchers in the attraction/relationship area are generally well aware of each other's work. The result is a very segmented picture of different relationship processes.

Does it all fit together? If so, how? Does it form a coherent picture of attraction and relationships? Researchers in this area have not worried too much about integration, so we cannot say too much about fitting their work with that of others. However, we would like to make a few comments and to speculate a bit in this regard.

First, we think it important not to think of the lack of integration as too serious a problem. The approaches discussed are largely complementary rather than competing or contradictory. The communal/exchange work deals with reactions to following vs. violating rules governing the giving and receiving of benefits, the Berscheid/Walster theory of passionate love deals with labeling feelings of arousal, the self-evaluation maintenance theory deals with reactions to our own and other's performances, and so forth. To a great extent they deal with different relationship phenomena. Thus, one reasonable way to think of these programs of research is as pieces of a large puzzle. There are many such pieces. We have identified and described quite a few. There are more pieces to identify, but we *have* made considerable progress.

How can we make more progress? One way is to identify and describe more pieces of the puzzle. Another way is to be more explicit about boundary conditions within which the processes we have discussed are most likely to operate. Some boundary conditions are included in the statements of the theories. For example, Clark and Mills say their theory deals with the giving and receiving of benefits that one person can intentionally give to the other. Tesser says his theory deals with reactions to our own and others' performances, etc. However, there are undoubtedly other boundary conditions, not inherent in the theories themselves as stated but which might be identified. Tesser and Cornell (1991), for instance, have recently suggested that the entire SEM set of processes might well be "turned off" when a person is experiencing high self-esteem for whatever reason. Or, to take another example, it seems to us that the impact of classical conditioning on attraction might well be most potent when the person to whom feelings are being conditioned starts off as a relatively neutral stimulus—that is, when we have no history of positive or negative feelings toward that person. We suspect it would be very hard to "move around" attraction toward a person with whom one has an established relationship through classical conditioning (cf. Cacioppo, Marshall-Goodell, Tassinary, & Petty, 1992). To give a third example, we suspect the sort of labeling of arousal as romantic is more prominent among U.S. adolescents who *expect* to fall in love and is less prominent among elderly people who believe they have "gotten over" such things. The general point here is that by identifying boundary conditions we will better understand where in the puzzle to place the pieces we have identified.

Also, despite what we have just said, we need to recognize the puzzle analogy is, in fact, not an altogether good one. That is, we are sure it is *not* true that there are a set number of *independent* puzzle pieces which, when placed together, will fit neatly, each filling its own boundary lines. The truth is that more than one theory often is applicable to understanding any given relationship phenomenon. Indeed, we have been trying to emphasize that throughout this chapter by speculating on what the six different theories we have covered might have to "say" about the impact of physical attractiveness, similarity, and proximity on attraction and relationships. And any number of other relationship phenomena might have been used as examples in the same manner. Moreover, it may be the case that the theories can be combined to make predictions that could not be made on the basis of one theory alone. In any case, we do need to think about how the theoretical processes discussed here may interact or combine with one another and about what the result will be.

In some cases the effects will probably be additive. For instance, what happens when someone with whom we desire a communal relationship gives us a gift—no strings attached? Classical conditioning says we ought to feel good and like the other more. Since the other is attending to our needs, based on the communal norm we also ought to like the person more. The effects of both processes may simply add together. In other cases, some processes may increase liking; others may decrease liking, and levels of attraction may simply result from the effect of the processes which increase attraction minus the effects of those which detract from attraction. For example, imagine that you are a student of computer science. As you have all semester, you are struggling with a programming assignment. Your friend, also a computer science student, stops by and tells you how to solve your problem. You solve it. Your heart rate jumps. Your assignment is finally complete. There are some theoretical reasons to expect to like your friend more. He has behaved in a manner appropriate for a communal relationship. He has interrupted your routine of working for three nights on each assigned programming problem, you are aroused as a result, and you may label it as felt gratitude toward him. On the other hand, your self-esteem may be hurt through the process of social comparison. A close friend of similar ability clearly is better at this task than you are. Perhaps the sum of these theoretical effects will be a fairly small jump in attraction toward your friend.

Still another possibility is that one process will simply take precedence over (override) another. If, for example, you are the student in the situation, you are a senior with good but not outstanding grades, and you are anxiously awaiting responses to your applications to computer science graduate schools, the negative effect of the social comparison process may simply override any possible positive effects of other processes. The negative implications of your inability to quickly solve the problem when others can easily do so may engulf your thoughts—leaving no room to even consider the positive implications of your friend's behavior for the "communalness" of your relationship nor room to label your arousal as gratitude toward your friend.

Note, however, that one need not assume that the processes form some sort of hierarchy in which those higher in the hierarchy will always override those lower in the hierarchy. Indeed, we suspect thinking of how the theories may relate in that way is likely to be quite *un*productive. Rather, which process will dominate will probably vary considerably by situation. In a situation in which performance concerns are utmost in one's mind, such as that just described, self-evaluation maintenance processes are likely to predominate. In a different situation, another process might predominate. For example, if you were a brand-new, lonely freshman anxious to form and to solidify new friendships and the same basic scenario occurred, the effects of the other having followed a communal norm might be far more important and might override the effects of the self-evaluation maintenance processes.

Not only may the situation make a difference, but so too, the personalities of the people involved may have an impact. A person with chronically high self-esteem may be less likely to engage in self-evaluation maintenance processes than a person chronically low or medium in self-esteem. An avoidant person may be far less prone to experience romantic love as a result of labeling arousal in that way than will an anxious-avoidant person.

This last example actually brings us to a third way of thinking about how the processes described by different theorists may fit together. That is, the various processes we have discussed may sometimes *interact* with one another. In this regard we can offer another example involving how the processes Berscheid and Hatfield have discussed and how those discussed by attachment theorists might fit together.

Recall not only the Berscheid/Walster ideas about the possibility of arousal being labeled as romantic attraction toward another but also White and colleagues' extension of those ideas to the possibility of arousal being labeled as a repulsion from another. Also note Berscheid's ideas about interruptions in routines causing arousal. Keeping all that *and* attachment theory in mind, imagine what might happen to a married man whose evening routine has long been very enmeshed with that of his wife. She hardly ever breaks her routine of being home at six and greeting her husband, who then tells her about his day. However, on a given night she is late. The husband's routine is interrupted, and he experiences a jump in arousal. How will he label it? Will it increase his attraction toward his wife or decrease it? The answers to these questions may depend upon his attachment history. If he was and is securely attached, he may believe that his wife's intentions would never be to hurt him. Thus he may interpret his arousal in terms of his worry for her welfare and his love for her. Feelings of love may jump as a result. If, however, he is an anxious/ambivalent type, he might interpret her absence as an indication of her lack of consideration and caring for him. He may label his arousal as anger toward her or jealousy that she may be out with another man. Feelings of love may drop.

Conclusion

Clearly we have a long way to go in coming to fully understand attraction and relationships. There are more processes to identify and much integration work to be done. However, we personally are optimistic about research in this area.

Research in the attraction/relationship field is expanding at a very rapid rate. There are new areas to be explored and many opportunities for integration of existing bodies of research. Clearly our bias is toward theoretical work aimed at elucidating the interpersonal processes that operate in relationships and the outcomes of such processes. We see this approach as offering our best hope for an integrated understanding of relationships as well as for, simultaneously, yielding a scientific base for practical applications to important fields such as marriage and family counseling and social skills training (Clark & Bennett, 1992).

Notes

[1]This increase in activities with increasing discrepancies in attractiveness did tend to fall off at the highest levels of discrepancies. Perhaps when an extremely attractive person is paired with an extremely unattractive person, they simply do not have enough in common to make the relationship work.

[2]Note that, although we will not go into it here, between the appearance of Dutton and Aron's (1974) work and White and associates (1981) work, a reinterpretation of Dutton and Aron's work in terms of reinforcement theory had appeared (Kenrick & Cialdini, 1977). In large part, White and his colleagues' work was a response to this challenge.

References

AINSWORTH, M. D. S., BLEHAR, M. C., WATERS, E., & WALL, S. (1978). *Patterns of attachment: Assessed in the strange situation and at home.* Hillsdale, NJ: Lawrence Erlbaum Associates.

ALTMAN, I., & TAYLOR, D. A. (1973). *Social penetration: The development of interpersonal relationships.* New York: Holt, Rinehart & Winston.

ANONYMOUS (1993). Surgeon general's son sought on drug charge. *St. Louis Post-Dispatch* (Dec. 19), p. 3A.

BACKMAN, C. W., & SECORD, P. F. (1959). The effect of perceived liking on interpersonal attraction. *Human Relations, 12,* 379–384.

BARTHOLOMEW, K. (1990). Avoidance of intimacy: An attachment perspective. *Journal of Social and Personal Relationships, 7,* 147–178.

BARTHOLOMEW, K., & HOROWITZ, L. (1991). Attachment styles among young adults: A test of a four-category model. *Journal of Personality and Social Psychology, 61,* 226–244.

BERSCHEID, E. (1982). Attraction and emotion in interpersonal relations. In M. S. Clark & S. T. Fiske (Eds)., *Affect and cognition: The seventeenth annual Carnegie symposium on cognition.* Hillsdale, NJ: Lawrence Erlbaum Associates.

BERSCHEID, E., SNYDER, M., & OMOTO, A. M. (1989). The relationship closeness inventory: Assessing the closeness of interpersonal relationships. *Journal of Personality and Social Psychology, 57,* 792–807.

BERSCHEID, E., & WALSTER, E. (1974). A little bit about love. *Foundations of interpersonal attraction.* New York: Academic Press.

BOWLBY, J. (1969/1982). *Attachment and loss. Vol. I, Attachment.* New York: Basic Books.

BOWLBY, J. (1973). *Attachment and loss, Vol. II, Separation: Anxiety and anger.* New York: Basic Books.

BOWLBY, J. (1980). *Attachment and loss, Vol. III, Loss: Sadness and depression.* New York: Basic Books.

BOYDEN, T., CARROLL, J. S., & MAIER, R. A. (1984). Similarity and attraction in homosexual males: The effects of age and masculinity-femininity. *Sex Roles, 10,* 939–948.

BYRNE, D. (1971). *The attraction paradigm.* New York: Academic Press.

BYRNE, D., & CLORE, G. L. (1970). A reinforcement model of evaluative responses. *Personality: An International Journal, 1,* 103–128.

BYRNE, D., & GRIFFITT, W. (1966). Developmental investigation of the law of attraction. *Journal of Personality and Social Psychology, 4,* 699–702.

BYRNE, D., & RHAMEY, R. (1965). Magnitude of positive and negative reinforcements as determinants of attraction. *Journal of Personality and Social Psychology, 2,* 884–889.

BYRNE, D., CLORE, G., & WORCHEL, P. (1966). The effect of economic similarity-dissimilarity on interpersonal attraction. *Journal of Personality and Social Psychology, 4,* 220–224.

BYRNE, D., & MURNEN, S. K. (1988). Maintaining loving relationships. In R. J. Sternberg & M. L. Barnes (Eds.), *The psychology of love* (pp. 293–310). New Haven, CT: Yale University Press.

CACIOPPO, J. T., MARSHALL-GOODELL, B. S., TASSINARY, L. G., & PETTY, R. E. (1992). Rudimentary determinants of attitudes: Classical conditioning is more effective when prior knowledge about the attitude stimulus is low than high. *Journal of Experimental Social Psychology, 28,* 207–233.

CAMPBELL, J. (1980). Complementarity and attraction: A reconceptualization in terms of dyadic behavior. *Representative Research in Social Psychology, 11,* 74–95.

CAPLOW, T., & FORMAN, R. (1950). Neighborhood interaction in a homogenous community. *American Sociological Review, 15,* 357–366.

CARNELLEY, K. B., & JANOFF-BULMAN, R. (1992). Optimism about love relationships: General vs. specific lessons from one's personal experiences. *Journal of Social and Personal Relationships, 9,* 5–20.

CASH, T. F., GILLEN, B., & BURNS, D. S. (1977). Sexism and 'beautyism' in personnel consultant decision making. *Journal of Applied Psychology, 62,* 301–310.

CASPI, A., & HARBENER, E. S. (1990). Continuity and change: Assortive marriage and the consistency of personality in adulthood. *Journal of Personality and Social Psychology, 58,* 250–258.

CLARK, M. S. (1984). A distinction between two types of relationships and its implications for development. In J. C. Masters & K. Yarkin-Levin (Eds.), *Boundary areas in social and developmental psychology.* New York: Academic Press, Inc.

CLARK, M. S. (1986). Evidence for the effectiveness of manipulations of communal and exchange relationships. *Personality and Social Psychology Bulletin, 12,* 414–425.

CLARK, M. S., & BENNETT, M. E. (1992). Research on relationships: Implications for mental health. In D. N. Ruble, P. R. Costanzo, & M. E. Oliveri (Eds.), *The social psychology of mental health: Basic mechanisms and applications.* New York: The Guilford Press.

CLARK, M. S., & MILLS, J. (1979). Interpersonal attraction in exchange and communal relationships. *Journal of Personality and Social Psychology, 37,* 12–24.

CLARK, M. S., & MILLS, J. (1993). The difference between communal and exchange relationships: What it is and is not. *Personality and Social Psychology Bulletin, 19,* 684–691.

CLARK, M. S., MILLS, J., & CORCORAN, D. (1989). Keeping track of needs and inputs of friends and strangers. *Personality and Social Psychology Bulletin, 15,* 533–542.

CLARK, M. S., MILLS, J., & POWELL, M. C. (1986). Keeping track of needs in communal and exchange relationships. *Journal of Personality and Social Psychology, 51,* 333–338.

CLARK, M. S., PATAKI, S., & WINKLER, C. (1993). Discrepancies in physical attractiveness and companionship. Unpublished manuscript, Carnegie Mellon University.

CLARK, M. S., OUELLETTE, R., POWELL, M. C., & MILBERG, S. (1987). Recipient's mood, relationship type and helping. *Journal of Personality and Social Psychology, 53,* 94–103.

CLARK, M. S., & TARABAN, C. B. (1991). Reactions to and willingness to express emotion in communal and exchange relationships. *Journal of Experimental Social Psychology, 27,* 324–336.

CLARK, M. S., & WADDELL, B. (1985). Perception of exploitation in communal and exchange relationships. *Journal of Social and Personal Relationships, 2,* 403–413.

CLIFFORD, M., & WALSTER, E. (1973). The effect of physical attractiveness on teacher expectation. *Sociology of Education, 46,* 248.

CLORE, G. L., & BYRNE, D. (1974). A reinforcement-affect model of attraction. In T. Huston (Ed.)., *Foundations of interpersonal attraction.* New York: Academic Press.

COLLINS, N. L., & READ, S. J. (1990). Adult attachment, working models, and relationship quality in dating couples. *Journal of Personality and Social Psychology, 58,* 644–663.

DAVIS, K. E., & KIRKPATRICK, L. A. (1994). Attachment style, gender, and relationship stability: A longitudinal analysis. *Journal of Personality and Social Psychology, 66,* 502–512.

DRISCOLL, R., DAVIS, K. E., & LIPITZ, M. S. (1972). Parental interference and romantic love: The Romeo and Juliet effect. *Journal of Personality and Social Psychology, 24,* 1–10.

DUTTON, D. G., & ARON, A. P. (1974). Some evidence for heightened sexual attraction under conditions of high anxiety. *Journal of Personality and Social Psychology, 30,* 510–517.

FEENEY, J., & NOLLER, P. (1990). Attachment style as a predictor of adult romantic relationships. *Journal of Personality and Social Psychology, 58,* 281–291.

FESTINGER, L. (1957). *A theory of cognitive dissonance.* Stanford, CA: Stanford University Press.

FESTINGER, L., SCHACHTER, S., & BACK, K. (1950). *Social pressures in informal groups: A study of a housing community.* New York: Harper.

FOLKES, V. S., & SEARS, D. O. (1977). Does everybody like a liker? *Journal of Experimental Social Psychology, 13,* 505–519.

GEORGE, C., KAPLAN, N., & MAIN, M. (1985). The Berkeley adult attachment interview. Unpublished protocol, Department of Psychology, University of California, Berkeley.

GRIFFITT, W. (1970). Environmental effects of interpersonal affective behavior: Ambient effective temperature and attraction. *Journal of Personality and Social Psychology, 15,* 240–244.

GRIFFITT, W., NELSON, J., & LITTLEPAGE, G. (1972). Old age and response to agreement-disagreement. *Journal of Gerontology, 27,* 269–274.

HATFIELD, E., & SPRECHER, S. (1986). *Mirror, mirror . . . The importance of looks in everyday life.* Albany, NY: State University of New York Press.

HAZAN, C., & SHAVER, P. R. (1987). Romantic love conceptualized as an attachment process. *Journal of Personality and Social Psychology, 52,* 511–524.

HAZAN, C., & SHAVER, P. R. (1990). Love and work: An attachment-theoretical perspective. *Journal of Personality and Social Psychology, 59,* 270–280.

HEIDER, F. (1958). *The psychology of interpersonal relations.* New York: Wiley.

HOLMES, J. G. (1991). Trust and the appraisal process in close relationships. In W. H. Jones & D. Perlman (Eds.), *Advances in personal relationships* (pp. 57–107). London: Jessica Kingsley Publishers.

HOLMES, J. G., & REMPEL, J. K. (1989). Trust in close relationships. In C. Hendrick (Ed.), *Review of personality and social psychology* (pp. 187–220). Beverly Hills, CA: Sage.

JOHNSON, D. J., & RUSBULT, C. E. (1989). Resisting temptation: Devaluation of alternative partners as a means of maintaining commitment in close relationships. *Journal of Personality and Social Psychology, 57,* 967–980.

KELLEY, H. H. (1979). *Personal relationships: Their structures and processes.* Hillsdale, NJ: Lawrence Erlbaum Associates.

KELLEY, H. H., BERSCHEID, E., CHRISTENSEN, A., HARVEY, J. H., HUSTON, T. L., LEVINGER, G., McCLINTOCK, E., PEPLAU, L. A., & PETERSON, D. R. (1983). *Close relationships.* New York: Freeman.

KELLEY, H. H., & THIBAUT, J. W. (1978). *Interpersonal relationships: A theory of interdependence.* New York: Wiley.

KENRICK, D. T., & CIALDINI, R. B. (1977). Romantic attraction: Misattribution versus reinforcement explanations. *Journal of Personality and Social Psychology, 35,* 381–391.

LANDY, D., & SIGALL, H. (1974). Beauty is talent: Task evaluation as a function of the performer's physical attractiveness. *Journal of Personality and Social Psychology, 29,* 299–304.

LEVENTHAL, G. S. (1970). Influence of brothers and sisters on sex-role behavior. *Journal of Personality and Social Psychology, 16,* 452–465.

LIN, Y. (1992). The construction of the sense of intimacy from everyday social interaction. Unpublished dissertation, University of Rochester, Rochester, NY.

LOTT, B. E., & LOTT, A. J. (1960). The formation of positive attitudes toward group members. *Journal of Abnormal and Social Psychology, 61,* 297–300.

LOTT, A. J., & LOTT, B. E. (1974). The role of reward in the formation of positive interpersonal attitudes. In T. Huston (Ed.), *Foundations of interpersonal attraction.* New York: Academic Press.

MANDLER, G. (1975). *Mind and emotion.* New York: Wiley.

MEHTA, P., CLARK, M. S., & MILLS, J. (1992). Interest in time another spends making a selection for oneself: The impact of relationship type. Unpublished manuscript, Carnegie Mellon University.

MIKULINCER, M., FLORIAN, V., & TOLMACZ, R. (1990). Attachment styles and fear of personal death: A case study of affect regulation. *Journal of Personality and Social Psychology, 58,* 273–280.

MILLS, J., & CLARK, M. S. (1982). Communal and exchange relationships: In L. Wheeler, (Ed.), *Review of personality and social psychology,* Beverly Hills: Sage.

MILLS, J., & CLARK, M. S. (1988, July). Communal and exchange relationships: New research and old controversies. Invited address at the biannual meeting of the International Society for the Study of Personal Relationships, Vancouver, BC.

NEWCOMBE, T. M. (1961). *The acquaintance process.* New York: Holt, Rinehart and Winston.

PLEBAN, R., & TESSER, A. (1981). The effects of relevance and quality of another's performance on interpersonal closeness. *Social Psychology Quarterly, 44,* 278–285.

PILKINGTON, C. J., TESSER, A., & STEPHENS, D. (1991). Complementarity in romantic relationships: A self-evaluation maintenance perspective. *Journal of Social and Personal Relationships, 8,* 481–504.

PISTOLE, C. (1989). Attachment in adult romantic relationships: Style of conflict resolution and relationship satisfaction. *Journal of Social and Personal Relationships, 6,* 505–510.

PROXMIRE, W. (1980). *The Fleecing of America.* Boston: Houghton-Miflin.

REIS, H. T., & SHAVER, P. R. (1988). Intimacy as an interpersonal process. In S. W. Duck (Ed.), *Handbook of Personal Relationships*. New York: John Wiley & Sons.

RUSBULT, C. E. (1980a). Commitment and satisfaction in romantic associations: A test of the investment model. *Journal of Experimental Social Psychology, 16,* 172–186.

RUSBULT, C. E. (1980b). Satisfaction and commitment in friendships. *Representative Research in Social Psychology, 11,* 96–105.

RUSBULT, C. E. (1983). A longitudinal test of the investment model: The development (and deterioration) of satisfaction and commitment in heterosexual involvements. *Journal of Personality and Social Psychology, 45,* 101–117.

RUSBULT, C. E., & BUUNK, B. P. (1993). Commitment processes in close relationships: An interdependence analysis. *Journal of Social and Personal Relationships, 10,* 175–204.

RUSBULT, C. E., & FARRELL, D. (1983). A longitudinal test of the investment model: The impact of job satisfaction, job commitment, and turnover of variations in rewards, costs, alternatives, and investments. *Journal of Applied Psychology, 68,* 429–438.

RUSBULT, C. E., & MARTZ, J. (1992). The decision to remain in an abusive relationship: An investment model analysis. Unpublished manuscript, University of North Carolina at Chapel Hill.

RUSBULT, C. E., VERETTE, J., WHITNEY, G. A., SLOVIK, L. F., & LIPKUS, I. (1991). Accommodation processes in close relationships: Theory and preliminary evidence. *Journal of Personality and Social Psychology, 60,* 53–78.

RUSBULT, C. E., JOHNSON, D. J., & MORROW, G. D. (1986). Predicting satisfaction and commitment in adult romantic involvements: An assessment of the generalizability of the investment model. *Social Psychology Quarterly, 49,* 81–89.

RUSBULT, C. E., VAN LANGE, P. A. M., & VERETTE, J. (forthcoming). *Perceived superiority of one's relationship as a relationship maintenance mechanism.* Manuscript in preparation, University of North Carolina at Chapel Hill.

SACHS, D. H. (1976). The effects of similarity, evaluation, and self-esteem on interpersonal attraction. *Representative Research in Social Psychology, 7,* 44–50.

SCHACHTER, S. (1964). The interaction of cognitive and physiological determinants of emotional state. In L. Berkowitz (Ed.), *Advances in experimental social psychology.* New York: Academic Press.

SCHACHTER, S., & SINGER, J. F. (1962). Cognitive, social and physiological determinants of emotional state. *Psychological Review, 69,* 379–399.

SCHACKNER, B. (Dec. 4, 1993). Student who failed chef's exam held in knife death of girlfriend. *Pittsburgh Post-Gazette,* p. D-7.

SENN, D. (1971). Attraction as a function of similarity-dissimilarity in task performance. *Journal of Personality and Social Psychology, 18,* 120–123.

SHAVER, P. R., & HAZAN, C. (1992). Adult romantic attachment: Theory and evidence. In D. Perlman & W. Jones (Eds.), *Advances in personal relationships, Vol. 4.* Greenwich, CT: JAI.

SHAVER, P., HAZAN, C., BRADSHAW, D. (1988). Love and attachment: The integration of three behavioral systems. In R. J. Sternberg & M. Banners (Eds.), *The psychology of love.* New Haven, CT: Yale University Press.

SIGALL, H., & LANDY, D. (1973). Radiating beauty: Effects of having an attractive partner on person perception. *Journal of Personality and Social Psychology, 28,* 218–224.

SIMPSON, J. A. (1987). The dissolution of romantic relationships: Factors involved in relationship stability and emotional distress. *Journal of Personality and Social Psychology, 39,* 683–692.

SIMPSON, J. A. (1990). The influence of attachment styles on romantic relationships. *Journal of Personality and Social Psychology, 59,* 971–980.

SIMPSON, J. A., RHOLES, W. S., & NELLIGAN, J. S. (in press). Support-seeking and support giving within couple members in an anxiety-provoking situation: The role of attachment styles. *Journal of Personality and Social Psychology.*

STAATS, A. W., & STAATS, C. K. (1958). Attitudes established by classical conditioning. *Journal of Abnormal and Social Psychology, 57,* 37–40.

TESSER, A. (1980). Self-esteem maintenance in family dynamics. *Journal of Personality and Social Psychology, 39,* 77–91.

TESSER, A., & CAMPBELL, J. (1980). Self-definition: The impact of the relative performance and similarity of others. *Social Psychology Quarterly, 43,* 341–347.

TESSER, A., & CAMPBELL, J. (1982). Self-evaluation maintenance and the perception of friends and strangers. *Journal of Personality, 59,* 261–279.

TESSER, A., & COLLINS, J. E. (1988). Emotion in social reflection and comparison situations: Intuitive, systematic and exploratory approaches. *Journal of Personality and Social Psychology, 55,* 695–709.

TESSER, A., & CORNELL, D. P. (1991). On the confluences of self-processes. *Journal of Experimental Social Psychology, 27,* 501–526.

TESSER, A., MILLAR, M., & MOORE, J. (1988). Some affective consequences of social comparison and reflection processes: The pain and pleasure of being close. *Journal of Personality and Social Psychology, 54,* 49–61.

TESSER, A., & PAULHUS, D. (1983). The definition of self: Private and public self-evaluation management strategies. *Journal of Personality and Social Psychology, 44,* 672–682.

TESSER, A., PILKINGTON, C. J., & MCINTOSH, W. D. (1989). Self-evaluation maintenance and the mediational role of emotion: The perception of friends and strangers. *Journal of Personality and Social Psychology, 57,* 442–456.

TESSER, A., & SMITH, J. (1980). Some effects of friendship and task relevance on helping: You don't always help the one you like. *Journal of Experimental Social Psychology, 16,* 582–590.

THIBAUT, J. W., & KELLEY, H. H. (1959). *The social psychology of groups.* New York: Wiley.

TIDWELL, M., MCCARTEN, K., & SHAVER, P. R. (1992). Avoidant females' relationships with parents and destructive romantic partners. Paper presented at the meetings of the Eastern Psychological Association.

WALSTER, E., ARONSON, V., ABRAHAMS, D., & ROTTMAN, L. (1966). The importance of physical attractiveness in dating behavior. *Journal of Personality and Social Psychology, 4,* 508–516.

WALSTER, E., & BERSCHEID, E. (1971). Adrenaline makes the heart grow fonder. *Psychology Today, 5,* 47–62.

WALSTER, E., WALSTER, G. W., & BERSCHEID, E. (1978). *Equity: Theory and research,* Boston: Allyn & Bacon, Inc.

WALSTER, E., WALSTER, G. W., & TRAUPMANN, J. (1987). Equity and premarital sex. *Journal of Personality and Social Psychology, 37,* 82–92.

WARREN, B. L. (1966). A multiple variable approach to the assortive mating phenomenon. *Eugenics Quarterly, 13,* 285–298.

WEISS, R. S. (1986). Continuities and transformations in the social provisions of relationships from childhood to adulthood. In W. Hartup & Z. Rubin (Eds.), *Relationships and development.* Hillsdale, NJ: Lawrence Erlbaum Associates.

WHITE, G. L., FISHBEIN, S., & RUTSTEIN, J. (1981). Passionate love and the misattribution of arousal. *Journal of Personality and Social Psychology, 41,* 56–62.

WILLIAMSON, G. M., & CLARK, M. S. (1989). Providing help and desired relationship type as determinants of changes in moods and self-evaluations. *Journal of Personality and Social Psychology, 56,* 722–734.

WILLIAMSON, G. M., & CLARK, M. S. (1992). Impact of desired relationship type on affective reactions to choosing and being required to help. *Personality and Social Psychology Bulletin, 18,* 10–18.

Annotated Bibliography

BARTHOLOMEW, K., & HOROWITZ, L. (1991). Attachment styles among young adults: A test of a four-category model. *Journal of Personality and Social Psychology, 61,* 226–244.

A discussion of the theoretical reasons behind Bartholomew's expanded model of attachment. This article also provides empirical support for four different attachment styles.

BERSCHEID, E. (in press). Interpersonal relationships. In M. R. Rosensweig & L. W. Porter (Eds.), *Annual Review of Psychology.* Palo Alto, CA: Annual Reviews, Inc.

The most recent annual review article on attraction and relationships written by one of the researchers who launched the field. Particular emphasis is placed on the role of cognition in relationships.

BERSCHEID, E., SNYDER, M., & OMOTO, A. M. (1989). Issues in studying close relationships: Conceptualizing and measuring closeness. In C. Hendrick (Ed.), *Close Relationships.* Newbury Park: Sage.

These authors address important questions about closeness in relationships. What is a close relationship? In what different ways might closeness be defined? How can closeness be measured?

BREHM, S. S. (1992). *Intimate relationships, 2d Ed.* New York: McGraw-Hill.

A recent text focusing on intimate relationships. It reviews much research that could not be covered in the present chapter.

BYRNE, D. (1971). *The attraction paradigm.* New York: Academic Press.

Byrne has conducted more studies on the relationship of attitude similarity to attraction than anyone. This book serves as a reference for many of these studies and a theoretical statement of the reinforcement approach to understanding attraction which dominated the attraction area in its early years.

COLLINS, N., & READ, S. (in press). Cognitive representations of attachment: The content and function of working models. In D. Perlman & K. Bartholomew (Eds.), *Advances in personal relationships, Vol. 5: Adult attachment relationships.* London: Jessica Kingsley Publishers.

Collins and Read provide an in-depth analysis of the cognitive representations (or working models) of attachment.

HATFIELD, E., & SPRECHER, S. (1986). *Mirror, mirror . . . the importance of looks in everyday life.* Albany: State University of New York Press.

An extensive discussion of the effects of physical attractiveness in interpersonal relationships.

HOLMES, J. G., & REMPEL, J. K. (1989). Trust in close relationships. In C. Hendrick (Ed.), *Close relationships.* Newbury Park: Sage. (pp. 187–220).

Holmes and Rempel discuss the development and impact of trust within the context of close relationships. Some original empirical work on trust is included as well as a discussion of the impact of a breakdown in trust.

KELLEY, H. H. (1979). *Personal relationships: Their structures and process.* Hillsdale, NJ: Lawrence Erlbaum.

KELLEY, H. H., & THIBAUT, J. W. (1978). *Interpersonal relationships: A theory of interdependence.* New York: John Wiley.
Both books discuss the nature of interdependence in relationships in depth.

REIS, H. T., & SHAVER, P. R. (1988). Intimacy as an interpersonal process. In S. W. Duck (Ed.), *Handbook of personal relationships.* New York: John Wiley.
A theoretical discussion of the processes contributing to a sense of intimacy in close relationships. Empirical research based on this relatively new theory is just appearing in the literature now.

SHAVER, P., & HAZAN, C. (1994). Adult romantic attachment: Theory and evidence. In D. Perlman & W. Jones (Eds.), *Advances in personal relationships, Vol. 4.* London: Jessica Kingsley Publishers.
The authors discuss their original formulation of attachment theory as applied to adults. They also review ongoing research and questions generated by attachment theory.

Dan Batson (Ph.D., Princeton University) is currently professor of psychology at the University of Kansas. He studies motives for prosocial and antisocial behavior, focusing on vicarious emotions (such as empathy) and personal values (such as religion) as sources of these motives. Over the past few years, his research on prosocial motivation has attempted to answer the altruism question: When we help others, is our ultimate goal to benefit them, or is it always, somehow, to benefit ourselves? In the present chapter, he addresses that question but also seeks to move beyond it to consider a wider range of possible prosocial motives. Dan is the author of The Altruism Question: Toward a Social-Psychological Answer *and co-author of* The Religious Experience *and* Religion and the Individual, *as well as a number of chapters and research articles. When not teaching or fretting about research, he is apt to be riding his bike, scratching or walking the dogs, reading philosophy, sipping something while staring at the lake, or watching a* Mary Tyler Moore Show *or* M.A.S.H. *rerun.*

CHAPTER 9

Prosocial Motivation: Why Do We Help Others?

C. Daniel Batson
University of Kansas

CHAPTER OUTLINE

Preparation of this chapter was supported in part by National Science Foundation Grant BNS-8906723, C. Daniel Batson, Principal Investigator, and by the University Center for Human Values, Princeton University.

Bitzer: I am sure you know that the whole social system is a question of self-interest. What you must always appeal to is a person's self-interest. It's your only hold. We are so constituted.

Mr. Sleary: There is a love in the world, not all self-interest after all, but something very different.

—BOTH FROM *HARD TIMES* BY CHARLES DICKENS

Not only are we humans social animals, but we are *pro*social animals—at least some of the time. Much of our effort and energy is directed toward benefiting others. We show small kindnesses every day—answering questions, holding doors, sharing food, smiling, and saying thanks. We show large kindnesses too. We stay up all night to comfort a friend who has just suffered a broken relationship. We send money to rescue famine victims halfway around the world, or to save whales, or to support public TV. We stop on a busy highway to help a stranded motorist change a flat, or spend an hour in the cold to push a friend's—even a stranger's—car out of a snowdrift.

It has been estimated that currently in the United States charitable contributions exceed $50 billion annually. And over 80 million people serve as volunteers, giving on the average 5 hours per week to help either in institutional settings such as hospitals, nursing homes, AIDS hospices, fire departments, rescue squads, shelters, halfway houses, peer counseling programs, church programs, and the like, or informally caring for friends and neighbors (Wuthnow, 1991). That is over 20 billion hours of volunteer help per year!

At times, what people do for others can be truly spectacular. Soldiers have been known to throw themselves on live grenades to protect their comrades. Lenny Skutnik risked his life diving into the icy waters of the Potomac to save an airline crash victim, while in the same tragedy Arland Williams, the "sixth man," lost his life after continually giving up his place in the rescue helicopter. Mother Teresa dedicated her life to the dying of Calcutta, the poorest of the poor, and brought care and comfort to thousands. Rescuers of Jews in Nazi Europe, like Miep Gies (1987) who helped hide Anne Frank and her parents, risked their own lives—and often the lives of their loved ones—day after day for months, even years. Not only was this helping dangerous, but it was also quite costly in terms of scarce food supplies shared, inconvenience of living arrangements, and time spent ministering to the needs of one or more "invisible" members of the household.

THE QUESTION OF MOTIVES:
WHY DO WE ACT TO BENEFIT OTHERS?

Such examples are heartwarming, even inspiring. For the social psychologist, they are also a puzzle. They raise the question of motives. Clearly, we humans can and do act to benefit others. But why? Why do we spend so much of our time, money, and energy on others? How are we to explain the Mother Teresas, Miep Gieses, Lenny Skutniks, thousands of volunteers, and billions of charity dollars?

As we shall see, by far the dominant answer in social psychology is that we benefit other people because doing so benefits us, that our ultimate goal in all we do is some self-interest. Yet is it really true that we help others only to help ourselves? Are we never, in any degree, capable of seeking another person's welfare for their sake and not simply our own? Can we not act for the collective good or to uphold some moral principle? Was Gheslin really right when he said: "Scratch an 'altruist' and watch a 'hypocrite' bleed" (1974, p. 247)?

Answers to such questions may seem locked within an impregnable fortress. Even to approach the ramparts brings a rain of sharply barbed prior questions like: How can we ever know someone's true motives, especially in a value-laden area like helping? What about all the subtle self-benefits of bene-fiting someone else: The self-benefit of imagined praise and glory? Of knowing I have done a good thing? Of avoiding guilt? Of, if we believe in heaven, in-creasing our chances of going there—rather than someplace else?

Under this onslaught, it is tempting to flee to the safety of a nonmotiva-tional stance, justifying our retreat with the retort: What difference does it make why people help others, as long as they do? This retreat is a coward's response. It keeps us safe from some thorny questions, but it also keeps us in the dark. Think about it—at three levels.

First, at a pragmatic level, who does not wish for a more caring, more hu-mane society? Yet, as the saying goes, wishes are not horses, or beggars would ride. If we would like there to be more prosocial action in the world—more con-cern and care for the homeless, for the victims of AIDS, for battered children, for the displaced and starving, for the environment—then we need to know the motives that produce such action. Only then can we consider ways to develop and stimulate these motives. Without this knowledge, our efforts to encourage more care and concern will be shots in the dark, quite likely a waste of time, or worse. If we humans are capable of caring for others for their sakes, of caring for society, or of caring about moral principles, then we should spend time stim-ulating these capacities. But if our concern for others, society, and morality is limited to those situations in which the concern serves our own interests, then we had best know and accept this, lest idealistic rhetoric and dreams seduce us into counterproductive sentimentality and doomed efforts at social reform.

Second, at a theoretical level, progress toward understanding the nature of prosocial motivation may provide us with valuable information about the na-ture and function of human motivation more generally. In the past quarter-century—with the fervor and zeal of psychology's cognitive revolution—issues of motivation have been sadly, and at times willfully, neglected. Most of our current ideas about motivation date from the 1950s or earlier, to a time when motives were thought of as need-based drives or states of diffuse arousal im-pelling action, any action. Whatever we can learn about prosocial motives may help stimulate a general reexamination of human motivation. Because prosocial motives are subtle and complex, they invite an analysis that takes advantage of the contemporary cognitive *zeitgeist* yet does not simply turn motivation into a qualifier on or a form of cognition.

Third and even more far-ranging, progress toward understanding prosocial motivation may tell us something rather fundamental about human nature. Is our capacity to care limited to ourselves? Is it really true that other people, however dear, are simply complex objects in our environment—important sources of stimulation and gratification, of facilitation and inhibition—as we each pursue self-interest? Or can we care for others too? If so, for whom—for our immediate family, friends, nation, species? Can we care about moral ideals? Answers to these questions should tell us something about how interconnected humans really are, about how truly social we are—or are capable of becoming.

A Little History

Long before psychology was born as a separate discipline, philosophers puzzled over prosocial motivation and its implications for human nature, often with insight and wit. The debate has raged for centuries—from Plato and Aristotle, to St. Thomas Aquinas, Thomas Hobbes, the Duke de la Rochefoucauld, Bernard Mandeville, David Hume, Adam Smith, Jeremy Bentham, John Stuart Mill, and Friedrich Nietzsche. Among these philosophers, the majority view—but by no means the unanimous view—is that everything we humans do, including everything we do for others, is always, ultimately, done to benefit ourselves; we are unremitting egoists.

La Rochefoucauld put it prosaically: "The most disinterested love is, after all, but a kind of bargain, in which the dear love of our own selves always proposes to be the gainer some way or other" (1691, Maxim 82). Or in the words of the Roman Greek Epictetus, writing early in the second century:

> Did you never see little dogs caressing and playing with one another, so that you might say there is nothing more friendly? But that you may know what friendship is, throw a bit of flesh among them, and you will learn. Throw between yourself and your son a little estate, and you will know how soon he will wish to bury you and how soon you wish your son to die. . . . For universally, be not deceived, every animal is attached to nothing so much as to its own interest. Whatever then appears to it an impediment to this interest, whether this be a brother, or a father, or a child, or beloved, or lover, it hates, spurns, curses: For its nature is to love nothing so much as its own interest; this is father, and brother and kinsman, and country, and God. . . . For this reason if a man put in the same place his interest, sanctity, goodness, and country, and parents, and friends, all these are secured; but if he puts in one place his interest, in another his friends, and his country and his kinsmen and justice itself, all these give way being borne down by the weight of interest. For where the I and the Mine are placed, to that place of necessity the animal inclines (1877, pp. 177–178).

This majority view in Western philosophy has reigned within psychology as well. The founding father of experimental psychology in America, William James, is, as usual, worth quoting:

> Each mind, to begin with, must have a certain minimum of selfishness in the shape of instincts of bodily self-seeking in order to exist. This minimum must

be there as a basis for all further conscious acts, whether of self-negation or of a selfishness more subtle still. . . .

And similarly with the images of their person in the minds of others. I should not be existent now had I not become sensitive to looks of approval or disapproval on the faces among which my life is cast. Looks of contempt cast on other persons need affect me in no such peculiar way. Were my mental life dependent exclusively on some other person's welfare, either directly or in an indirect way, then natural selection would unquestionably have brought it about that I should be as sensitive to the social vicissitudes of that other person as I now am to my own. Instead of being egoistic I should be spontaneously altruistic (1890, Chapter 10, Section 5, paragraphs 2, 12, and 13).

Equally strong assumptions of universal egoism may be found in the psychoanalytic and behaviorist traditions. In his 1975 Presidential Address to the American Psychological Association, Donald Campbell summarized the situation: "Psychology and psychiatry . . . not only describe man as selfishly motivated, but implicitly or explicitly teach that he ought to be so" (1975, p. 1104). Universal egoism is still the majority view in psychology (Wallach & Wallach, 1983); it is the majority view in economics and political science as well (Mansbridge, 1990).

A Question for the 1960s and 1970s: Why Don't People Help?

Given this historical context, it is no surprise that when social psychologists became interested in helping behavior in the late 1960s, they were not trying to answer the question of the nature of prosocial motivation. That question was assumed either already clearly answered or clearly unanswerable. They were instead trying to understand why people fail to help when we think they should. Specifically, they were trying to understand why the 38 witnesses to the brutal stabbing and eventual murder of Kitty Genovese in the Kew Gardens neighborhood of Queens, New York, on the night of March 13, 1964, did nothing to help her—not even call the police.

John Darley and Bibb Latané (1968; Latané & Darley, 1970) came up with an ingenious answer to this question. They suggested that once we notice a possible need situation, we must make a number of decisions in sequence before we help. First, we must decide that a need exists; second, we must decide that it is our personal responsibility to act; and third, we must decide that there is something we can do to help. Only if we decide that there is a need, that we are responsible for helping, and that there is something we can do will we try to help. Latané and Darley (1970) pointed out that the presence of other bystanders can influence this decision sequence at each step, tipping the scales toward inaction.

What's the Problem? Deciding That No Real Need Exists

Emergencies are unusual, unexpected, and ambiguous events. Are screams in the night a woman being attacked, or two lovers having a quarrel? Uncertain, we may turn to others present, seeking cues to help us decide. No one wishes to appear foolishly excited over an event that may not be an emergency after all, so we react initially with a calm outward demeanor, while looking at others' reactions. But the others are doing the same. No one appears upset; a state of *pluralistic ignorance* (Miller & McFarland, 1987) develops, in which everyone decides that because no one else is upset, the event must not be an emergency. And so no one helps.

As this analysis predicts, researchers have found that helping is more likely when an emergency is not ambiguous (Clark & Word, 1972). As this analysis also predicts, in ambiguous need situations people are strongly influenced by the reactions of other bystanders. Latané and Darley (1968) found that students were more likely to respond to smoke pouring into their testing room when they were alone than when they were with two experimental confederates who did not react to the smoke. More important for Latané and Darley's (1970) analysis, when three students—none confederates—were in the room, they were again less likely to respond. Apparently, cues from the others led each to interpret the smoke as benign. Extending this process to a helping situation, Latané and Rodin (1969) found that the presence of one or more strangers reduced the likelihood of individuals responding to a crash and cries of pain from a woman in an adjoining room.

Subsequent research has confirmed that it is not the mere presence of another bystander that affects responses; it is the cue value of the other bystander. Ross and Braband (1973) found that if bystanders thought that another bystander (a confederate) was blind, then his failure to react to odorless smoke did not affect their response. If, however, the emergency was one that a blind person could notice—a woman's scream—then the confederate's failure to respond did decrease responses. Darley, Teger, and Lewis (1973) found that if two people were seated in a face-to-face position, the presence of the other person did not reduce response to a crash and sounds of someone possibly hurt in a fall. People were as likely to respond as if they were single bystanders. If the two people were sitting back-to-back, however, they were less likely to respond. Darley, Teger, and Lewis reasoned that people able to see one another's initial startle responses were led to define the situation as an emergency, whereas those not able to see this response were not.

Is It My Responsibility? Deciding That Someone Else Should Help

The presence of other bystanders may also affect whether or not we accept personal responsibility for helping. If others are available, each individual may feel less personal obligation to come forward and help. One call to the police is as helpful, if not more helpful, than 20 calls. No doubt others also heard the screams, and someone else has probably called already. In Darley and Latané's (1968) terms, there is a *diffusion of responsibility* among all the bystanders present, making it less likely that any one bystander will help.

To test this possibility, Darley and Latané (1968) had research participants overhear another participant down the hall (actually a confederate) apparently having a seizure. At the time of the seizure, some participants believed that only they knew it was happening; others believed that they and one other participant knew; still others, that they and four others knew. As expected, the greater the number of bystanders, the less likely participants were to help. This effect has been replicated many times (Latané & Nida, 1981).

As the principle of diffusion of responsibility would suggest, the knowledge that there are other bystanders does *not* reduce helping if the others cannot help. If, for example, the others are not in the same building as the person in need, but I am, then I still shoulder the full responsibility for helping (Bickman, 1972).

What Can I Do? Deciding That I Lack the Skill to Help

A major factor affecting the decision about whether we can help is our sense of competence. In some situations, we may feel that we lack the necessary skill; we may not have the strength to swim out and save someone caught in a strong undertow, or we may not know what to do if someone has a heart attack or epileptic seizure. In other situations we may feel only relatively incompetent; we may feel that we could do something, but that others present could do better. For example, we are likely to defer to the medically trained if someone seems sick (Piliavin, Piliavin, & Rodin, 1975; Schwartz & Clausen, 1970). In still other situations we may feel a general sense of incompetence, which can affect our readiness to attempt any difficult task, including helping. The most obvious source of a general sense of incompetence is having just failed at some task, and predictably, people who have just failed are less likely to try to help someone in need (Isen, 1970). Our ability to help may also be restricted by prior commitments and lack of time (Batson, Cochran, Biederman, Blosser, Ryan, & Vogt, 1978; Darley & Batson, 1973).

As the research mentioned indicates, Latané and Darley's (1970) answer to the question of why none of the 38 witnesses to the murder of Kitty Genovese helped has stood up remarkably well to experimental test. But neither Darley and Latané's answer, nor the large mountain of subsequent work during the 1970s on situational factors affecting the likelihood of helping, addressed the question of why anyone would *help* Kitty Genovese. The presence of others can lead a bystander to misinterpret the situation or to diffuse responsibility, failing to help when he or she otherwise might (bystanders alone in these emergency studies are very likely to help), but the question of what motivates helping when it does occur—and whether helping might ever be motivated by concerns for the other rather than by self-concern—was ruled out of bounds. Darley and Latané said of this question: It is "a general one, of enormous social interest and importance, and of a semiphilosophic nature. It probably will never be completely answered by reference to data" (1970, p. 84). They quickly let it drop.

Back to the Question of Motives

As difficult as an assault on understanding the nature of prosocial motivation may be, in the past decade, a number of social psychologists have begun a serious attempt to answer this question—by reference to data. These quixotic social psychologists have drawn heavily on general theories of motivation, especially those stemming from the work of Sigmund Freud, Clark Hull, and various social learning theorists (e.g., Dollard & Miller; Bandura). But they have been most importantly influenced by the motivational theories of Kurt Lewin.

Lewin (1935, 1951) did not think of motives as blind pushes from within, impelling any action, as did the drive theorists of his day. Lewin thought of motives as goal-directed forces. Thus, his analysis included complex cognitive processes of the sort that have become central in psychology as a result of the cognitive revolution. Yet Lewin did not simply substitute a cognitive analysis for a motivational one; he incorporated complex cognitive processes into an analysis that remained fundamentally motivational. Like Edward Tolman (1932), who spoke of cognitive maps, Lewin believed that our behavior is purposeful; we live in a psychological reality or *life space* that includes not only those parts of our physical and social environment that are important to us but also imagined states that do not currently exist.

Reflecting our values or preferences, various regions of our life space have positive or negative valences because they are desired or not desired. These valences induce goals, which in turn produce force fields that draw us toward or impel us away from the valenced region, not unlike the way the poles of one magnet draw or repel another magnet. These force fields are motives. Thus, Lewin thought of motives as goal-directed forces within the life space of the individual. And this is how motives have typically been conceived by the social psychologists seeking to answer the question of the nature of prosocial motivation.

Thinking of motives as goal-directed forces allows us to make some key distinctions, the distinctions among instrumental goals, ultimate goals, and unintended consequences. An *instrumental goal* is sought as a means to reach some other goal. An *ultimate goal* is sought as an end in itself. An *unintended consequence* is a result of acting to reach a goal but is not itself sought as a goal. Employing these distinctions, it becomes clear that the debate over the nature of prosocial motivation is a debate over whether benefiting others is an instrumental goal on the way to some self-interested ultimate goal or an ultimate goal in its own right with the self-benefits being unintended consequences.

In the pages that follow, I wish to consider four possible ultimate goals of acting to benefit someone else: Self-benefit *(egoism)*, benefiting another individual *(altruism)*, benefiting a group *(collectivism)*, and upholding a moral principle *(principlism)*. These goals are not mutually exclusive; any or all might be ultimate goals of acting to benefit someone. Before considering these possible goals, however, let us first consider an important contemporary answer to the question of why we help others, one that has nothing to do with goal-directed motivation, the sociobiological answer.

THE SOCIOBIOLOGICAL ANSWER:
BENEFITING ANOTHER TO BENEFIT OUR GENES

Maybe we act in ways that help or harm others without being motivated at all. Johnny's answer to his teacher's stern question about why he bumped Julie and knocked her down may be: "I'm not to blame; it was Jack; he pushed me." Similarly, the sociobiologist's answer to why we benefit others is: We aren't to blame; it's our genes; they push us.

Why would our genes push us to expend effort to benefit someone else, especially if—as in the case of Lenny Skutnik, Arland Williams, or Miep Gies—doing so threatened our own survival? Is that not contrary to the theory of natural selection?

Think about it. Any attribute that diminishes the reproductive potential of an organism relative to its competitors will decrease the likelihood of the genes carried by that organism appearing in the next generation. Risking one's own life to save a friend who is drowning is certainly such an attribute, and when played out over enough generations, so is even relatively minor expenditure of energy to help others. Now, if such an attribute is caused by a particular genetic alternative or *allele*, then over generations this allele should decrease in the population, and so should the attribute. Thus, a genetically based inclination to help seems contrary to the theory of natural selection.

For humans, we can easily get around this potential contradiction by arguing that helping is not a product of genetic evolution; it is a product of cultural evolution (Campbell, 1975; Freud, 1930). Society may use its powerful carrots and sticks—praise and censure, glory and guilt—to override the genetic call to look out only for Number One. But what about for other species? How can we explain self-sacrificial helping among them?

Self-Sacrificial Helping in Other Species

There are many examples of animals other than humans risking danger, expending effort, giving up food, even their life, to benefit others. Consider the following:

1. As we all know, bees, wasps, and other social insects rush to the attack when their hive is threatened. Not only does flying forth to face the foe benefit the other members of the hive while incurring risk to the attacking bee or wasp, but in the case of bees, the act of stinging the attacker is almost always fatal for the bee. Its entrails remain attached to the embedded sting as the bee flies away (Hamilton, 1964; Wilson, 1975).

2. Certain fish called cleaner fish, such as wrasse, will swim into the mouth of large fish, such as grouper, which could easily eat them, to clean away ectoparasites. This behavior provides food for the wrasse and a beneficial cleaning for the grouper, but the grouper forgoes the additional benefit of eating the wrasse after the job is done (Trivers, 1971).

3. Robins, thrushes, and titmice have been observed emitting cries to warn other birds of the approach of a hawk, cries that call attention to their own presence. Mother grouse will risk capture by feigning a broken wing and attracting attention to lead a predator away from her chicks in the nest (Wilson, 1975).

4. An elephant injured by a falling tree, weapon, or in a fight may be aided by other elephants, who cluster around and use their foreheads, trunks, and

tusks to help it rise. Once on its feet, the injured elephant may be supported by others walking or running alongside (Sikes, 1971).

5. African wild dogs return from hunting and regurgitate pieces of meat to feed both the young pups and the adults who stayed behind to care for the litter (van Lawick & van Lawick-Goodall, 1971). Domestic dogs can be highly protective of the children in their human family, including children who do not feed or pet them (Hebb & Thompson, 1968). Here is a newspaper story I read several years ago:

> Mr. and Mrs. Bruce R. Morris of Harvester, Missouri, left their two-year-old daughter, Margaret, asleep in the car while they visited a dealer's showroom to look for a new car. Red, a stray Irish setter which the Morrises had adopted three weeks earlier, was also left in the car. The old car suddenly burst into flames, apparently as a result of faulty wiring. Red quickly jumped through the window to safety. Margaret, awakened by the smoke, stood up in the back seat, swinging her arms in fright. Mr. Morris, who witnessed the incident from the showroom reported, "As soon as Red hit the ground, he jumped up, put his paws on the side of the car and reached his head through the smoke coming out the window." Red grabbed Margaret's coat collar with his teeth and dragged the little girl out of the window, then pushed her away from the car. Flames quickly engulfed the car. Margaret was taken to a hospital where she was treated for minor burns and released. Red suffered singed hair and a slight cut on his nose.

6. Porpoises have been seen risking their lives to support a harpooned porpoise on the surface so that it can breathe. There are also reports of porpoises rescuing drowning men in the same way (Dawkins, 1976; McIntyre, 1974).

7. Chimpanzees share food with lower status chimps who beg. Orphaned infant chimps may be adopted and reared by their adult brothers or sisters and, more rarely, even by nonkin. Chimps in captivity have been observed pulling other chimps' hands back as they reach toward potential danger (Goodall, 1990).

Evolutionary Explanations

How are we to account for these behaviors? Just flukes? Sociobiologists say no. They have set themselves the task of explaining how these and similar acts that diminish the reproductive potential of the actor, and so seem to violate the theory of natural selection, really do not. Edward Wilson (1975), Richard Dawkins (1976), and other sociobiologists point out that, although reproduction occurs at the level of the individual organism, natural selection occurs at the level of the gene, and under certain circumstances, genes can enhance their own survival by leading the individual carrying them to risk his or her own survival to benefit another. Note that there need be no goal-directed motivation involved, any more than there is when we breathe. The individual acts *as if* motivated to benefit the other—indeed, as if motivated to benefit the other in order to benefit the individual's own genes. But although goal-directed motives might sometimes be involved, they need not be and often clearly are not. The behavior may be relatively hardwired and automatic—or instinctive—as in the case of stinging by wasps and bees.

Helping Kin

Think, for example, of a circumstance in which the benefactor and the benefited share the same genes, and as a result of the benefactor's help, the benefited has a greater chance of placing these genes in the next generation. In this case, it may be to the shared genes' advantage to have the benefactor pay attention to survival of the benefited as well as to survival of self. William Hamilton (1964, 1971) used this logic of *inclusive fitness* to explain the self-sacrificial behavior of the sterile worker castes among the social insects, including social bees and wasps. It can also explain care of offspring by mammalian parents and the helping of other close kin.

Inclusive fitness is the sum of an individual's own fitness to place his or her genes in the next generation plus the sum of the effects of his or her behavior on the related fitness of all other individuals carrying the same genes, that is, all kin. To illustrate the principle of inclusive fitness, if an individual helps a brother, even at some cost to his or her own personal fitness, this act may increase rather than decrease the probability that the genes he or she is carrying will survive. On the average, half of the genes of siblings are identical by descent. So, an act that more than doubles a brother's fitness relative to the amount that it decreases the benefactor's fitness should increase the individual's genes inclusive fitness, even if the act costs the benefactor his or her life. Similarly, an act that more than quadruples a nephew's fitness relative to the amount that it decreases the benefactor's fitness will do the same. The general formula for when benefiting kin would enhance the gene's survival is

$$k > \frac{1}{r}$$

where k is the ratio of gain in the benefited's fitness relative to the loss in the benefactor's fitness, and r is the average coefficient of relationship, which is .5 in the case of brothers and sisters, .25 in the case of nephews and nieces, and so on.

In the worker caste among the social insects, the situation is even more extreme. A worker is sterile; it has no chance of passing its genes directly into the next generation. Therefore, loss in the benefactor's fitness is zero, so k becomes infinite. Moreover, the sterile worker shares not .5 but .75 of her genes with her sister workers. Self-sacrifice to protect the fertile queen and other workers is not in the best survival interest of the individual bee that does the stinging; it dies. But it is clearly in the best survival interest of that bee's genes.

Reciprocal Benefit

What about acts that benefit nonkin, even members of other species such as the wrasse and grouper? Robert Trivers (1971) points out that such behavior can still be genetically based and consistent with the theory of natural selection if it is a case of *reciprocal benefit* (which Trivers inaccurately calls "reciprocal altruism"; the terms *egoism* and *altruism* refer to motives, not to behavior, and behavior is all that Trivers means). The idea is that helping another survive could be in the best interest of the benefactor's genes if the benefited is likely to return the favor, either to the benefactor or to another organism carrying the same genes. As Trivers (1971) says: "Reciprocal altruism can also be viewed as a symbiosis, each partner helping the other while he helps himself. The symbiosis has a time lag, however; one partner helps the other and must then wait a period of time before he is helped in turn" (p. 39).

The time lag introduces the possibility of *cheaters*, individuals who gladly accept the assistance of others when needed but then do not reciprocate, either at all or as much. In order for an allele promoting reciprocal benefit to prosper, cheating must not pay; it must have adverse effects on the reproductive potential of the cheater that outweigh the benefits of not reciprocating. One way to discourage cheating is for other individuals in the society of potential benefactors to refuse all future benefit to the individual who does not reciprocate. Or there could be active punishment of cheating in the form of moral aggression or retribution. In general, for reciprocal benefit to be advantageous to the genes of organisms in a society, (a) need situations must arise fairly frequently (increasing the probability that an opportunity to receive benefit will occur), (b) proximity of other organisms who can help must be high, and (c) cheating must not be worthwhile.

Trivers (1971) notes that the conditions for reciprocal benefit are essentially those that exist in what game theorists call the *Prisoner's Dilemma* (Luce & Raiffa, 1957). In a Prisoner's Dilemma game, two players each must choose between two behavioral options: cooperation, which is beneficial to the other player, and defection, which is not. The payoff each player receives depends on not only what that player chooses but also what the other player chooses, but neither player knows the other's choice until both have chosen. Payoffs are structured so that, whatever the other player does, choosing to defect (or cheat) always produces the highest payoff to the chooser; yet, if both players defect, they each get less than if both cooperate. Hence, the dilemma.

A standard payoff matrix for the Prisoner's Dilemma is presented in Table 9.1. C_1 and C_2 represent the cooperating choices by Players 1 and 2, respectively; D_1 and D_2 represent the defecting choices. The game is structured so that among the different possible payoffs, $T > R > P > S$. In Table 9.1, standard payoff values are used: $T = 5$, $R = 3$, $P = 1$, and $S = 0$. The initials for the different payoffs provide a mnemonic that links the Prisoner's Dilemma to reciprocal benefit. R stands for the *reward* each individual gets from an exchange in which each benefits the other and neither cheats; T stands for the *temptation to cheat* (which, in the short term, produces the maximum reward); S stands for the *sucker's payoff* received by an individual who benefits the other and is then cheated; and P stands for the *punishment* that both individuals get if both try to cheat and not act beneficially (adapted from Rapoport & Chammah, 1965; Trivers, 1971).

TABLE 9.1. Payoff Matrix for Prisoner's Dilemma Game

Choices of Player 1	Choices of Player 2	
	C_2	D_2
C_1	R,R (3,3)	S,T (0,5)
D_1	T,S (5,0)	P,P (1,1)

Note: The first letter in each cell is the payoff for Player 1; the second letter is the payoff of Player 2. (R = reward; T = temptation; S = sucker's payoff; P = punishment.) Typical numeric values of payoffs are in parentheses.

A simple Prisoner's Dilemma game has only one trial. An iterated Prisoner's Dilemma game has repeated trials, with both players learning what the other did on each trial at the end of that trial. Iteration adds the time lag that is crucial for reciprocal benefit to occur. It allows each individual to respond on one trial to what the other individual did on the preceding trial.

One way to learn whether reciprocal benefit as Trivers conceived it can, in fact, compete successfully with other genetic strategies in such an environment is to pit players using different strategies against each other in iterated Prisoner's Dilemma games and see who wins. When Axelrod and Hamilton (1981) did this, using computer simulation to play 200 moves with the payoff matrix in Table 9.1, the strategy that proved best of the 14 often quite elaborate strategies proposed by game theorists in economics, sociology, political science, and mathematics was *tit for tat*. This strategy is quite simple; it involves cooperating on the first trial and then doing whatever the other player did on the preceding trial. Tit for tat is one version of reciprocal benefit described above: Benefit others as long as they benefit you, but do not benefit cheaters.

Implications of and Problems with Evolutionary Explanations

So, what has sociobiology's appeal to evolutionary theory revealed about why we benefit others? It has shown that benefiting another need not contradict the theory of natural selection, and it has suggested some possible circumstances under which natural selection might promote certain forms of genetically based benefit. These are important and useful contributions. Still, it remains unclear what evolutionary explanations can tell us about why humans benefit one another. There are two problems.

First, in most sociobiological arguments theoretical possibility is substituted for empirical reality. The question asked by sociobiologists is whether under the specified conditions an allele to benefit would tend to increase in a population relative to an allele not to benefit. But logical—even mathematical— demonstration that an allele would increase is not the same as demonstrating that this allele exists. Not every potentially successful allele actually exists;

moreover, an allele that exists in one species may not exist in other species for which it would be adaptive.

Second, sociobiologists seek general explanations that apply across the phylogenetic spectrum, regardless of the nature of the underlying motivation or, indeed, regardless of the presence of any motivation at all. The self-sacrificial behavior of social insects and the symbiotic relationship between cleaner fish and their hosts seem quite amenable to an evolutionary explanation because these behaviors are almost certainly genetically hardwired. As one moves up the phylogenetic scale, however, and associative areas of the brain become more dominant relative to the sensory areas (Hebb, 1949), behavior is much less likely to be a product of a direct, hardwired, genetic push and much more likely to be a product of flexible mediating mechanisms that can adapt to changing and diverse environmental circumstances. These mediating mechanisms include learning, thought, emotion, and motivation. Before an evolutionary explanation is applied to human behavior, including human helping behavior, attention must be given to how the proposed genetic impulse—whether an impulse toward inclusive fitness, reciprocal benefit, or some other impulse—might be mediated.

Unfortunately, sociobiologists tend to wax fanciful about mediation. They appear content once again with appeals to possibility rather than reality. A more serious attempt to identify specific mechanisms that are themselves genetically based and, in turn, encourage us to benefit one another has been made by developmental psychologist Martin Hoffman (1981a). Hoffman reasoned that among humans: "What therefore must have been acquired through natural selection is a predisposition or motive to help that, although biologically based, is nevertheless amenable to control by perceptual or cognitive processes" (p. 128). Hoffman named two candidates: (a) a mechanism for internalizing social norms and (b) empathic emotion.

Herbert Simon (1990) has pursued the first of these options, suggesting that "docility—receptiveness to social influence" (p. 1665)—might fill the bill as a genetically based mediator of helping behavior because docility would make individuals susceptible to societal prescriptions regarding helping (Campbell, 1975). At the same time, their docility would permit these individuals to benefit from cultural wisdom and the experience of others rather than learning only from their own hard knocks. Thus, individuals carrying a "docility allele" would incur the costs of helping, but these costs would be outweighed by the more general benefits derived from access to the cultural wisdom.

Hoffman (1981a) himself preferred the second option: mediation through empathic feelings evoked by seeing another individual in need. Perhaps, Hoffman suggested, a mother is genetically predisposed to feel distress or sympathy when she sees her child in distress, and this emotion evokes motivation to see the child's distress reduced, either as an end in itself or as a means to reduce the mother's distress. Either of these motives could lead the mother to rush to relieve the child's distress. Buck and Ginsburg (1991) recently suggested a similar but more elaborate emotional mediator. They proposed that genetically based spontaneous communication of emotion by facial expression, tone of voice, and body posture (e.g., the wince, gasp, and stiffening when in pain) serve to create emotional attachment or bonding, which in turn evokes prosocial motivation when the person to whom one is attached is in need.

Once we begin to consider mediators like these, the most fruitful level of analysis shifts. We are back to the question of the nature of the prosocial motives—not blind genetically based pushes but goal-directed motives—a question that is best addressed to psychology, not biology. So what can psychology tell us?

FOUR PSYCHOLOGICAL ANSWERS

Egoism: Benefiting Another as a Means to Self-Benefit

You probably do not need to be convinced that we humans are capable of benefiting others as a means to benefit ourselves. When our ultimate goal is self-benefit, our motivation is egoistic. This is true no matter how beneficial to others or how noble our behavior may be.

The list of possible self-benefits that can motivate us to benefit others is long. Limiting myself to those for which there is reasonable empirical evidence, I came up with the list in Table 9.2, and I am sure it is not complete. As you can see, I have organized the list into three general categories, reflecting three fundamental forms of egoistic prosocial motivation: (a) motives to benefit others as a means to gain material, social, or self-rewards (the entries are organized in

TABLE 9.2. Possible Self-Benefits from Benefiting Another

1. Material, Social, and Self-Rewards Received	
Payment	Praise
Gifts	Honor
Reciprocity credit	Enhanced self-image
Thanks	Mood enhancement (maintenance)
Esteem	Empathic joy
Heaven	

2. Material, Social, and Self-punishments Avoided	
Fines/imprisonment	Sanctions for norm violation
Attack	Shame
Censure	Guilt
Recrimination	Empathy costs
Hell	

3. Aversive-Arousal Reduction
Escape distressing situation
Escape discrepant situation
Escape unjust situation

rough order of material, then social, then self-rewards); (b) motives to benefit others as a means to avoid material, social, and self-punishments (again, in rough order); and (c) motives to reduce aversive arousal evoked by seeing another in need. In each case, benefiting the other is an instrumental goal that is sought as a means to reach the ultimate goal specified.

Gaining Rewards

Among the rewards that a helper may be seeking, perhaps the only three that need any explanation are reciprocity credit, mood enhancement (maintenance), and empathic joy.

Reciprocity Credit. Reciprocity credit is the self-benefit of knowing that the person you have benefited owes you one. Sociologist Alvin Gouldner (1960) identified what he called the "universal norm of reciprocity"—the norm that for a benefit received an equivalent benefit ought eventually to be returned. After reviewing the evidence, Gouldner concluded that "a norm of reciprocity is, I suspect, no less universal and important an element of culture than the incest taboo" (1960, p. 171). This norm prescribes the same behavior as Trivers' genetic principle of reciprocal benefit (no surprise because Gouldner's work was an important source for Trivers), but Gouldner assumed that the norm is instilled through socialization. He thought that it need not be genetically based, although it might be.

Reciprocity credit can lead us to look for an opportunity to help someone from whom we want some reward in the future, as occurs with ingratiation (Jones, 1964). It may also lead at least some of us to help others whom we know cannot reciprocate; we may help them because of belief in *generalized reciprocity,* a feeling that we get in equal measure to what we give to the world in general.

Some people strongly believe in a "just world" (Lerner, 1980)—that people get what they deserve in life and deserve what they get. Perhaps you are such a person. If you are, think what you might do if someone asked for help shortly before you were to take an important exam. You might reason that if you did something good by helping, you would ensure something good in return, namely, a good grade on the exam. This logic may sound purely superstitious, but at least some of us seem to think this way. Zuckerman (1975) found that shortly before the midterm exam in their psychology course, students who scored high on a measure of belief in a just world helped others more than did those who scored low. After the exam was over, however, there was no difference. Zuckerman (1975) concluded that those who had a strong belief in a just world helped more before the exam to make themselves more deserving of a good grade. These results suggest that a motive to establish reciprocity credit has a wide range of applicability. In this study reciprocity was not operating between two individuals; it was operating between an individual and that individual's perception of the world at large.

Mood Enhancement (Maintenance). Mood enhancement can also be a reason for helping. Cialdini, Darby, and Vincent (1973) proposed that we are more likely to help someone when we feel bad because we know that we can give ourselves a pat on the back when we do something nice like helping, and this will make us feel better. Consistent with this *negative-state relief model*, Cialdini and his colleagues found that people who felt bad (i.e., were in a negative state) because they had accidentally harmed someone—or had seen another person harm someone—were more likely to volunteer to make phone calls for a worthy cause than were people who did not feel bad. But when people who felt bad had their negative state relieved by receiving praise or a dollar before being given the chance to volunteer, they did *not* help more. Presumably, they did not help more because once their negative state had been relieved by the praise or the dollar, they no longer needed the self-reward that comes from helping.

If this negative-state relief logic is correct, then think about what would happen if people who felt bad believed that their negative state could not be improved by helping. These people should not help. In a clever experiment to test this prediction, Manucia, Baumann, and Cialdini (1984) led some students to believe that their negative state (induced by thinking about a sad experience) was unalterable for the next 30 minutes, due to a mood-fixing drug they had taken. Consistent with the negative-state relief prediction, these students did not help more than students not induced to feel bad. Apparently, when they could no longer anticipate the self-rewards that come from helping, the fixed-mood students were less motivated to help.

Not only does helping have reward value for a person feeling bad, but it also seems to be rewarding for persons who feel good. Indeed, the effect seems even stronger when people are in a good mood. Alice Isen and her associates have used a number of ingenious techniques to enhance people's moods—having them succeed at a task, giving them a cookie while they studied in the library, having them find a coin in the return slot of a phone booth. She found that each of these experiences increased the likelihood of a person giving help to good causes (Isen, 1970; Isen & Levin, 1972). Weyant (1978) found that undergraduates who were in a good mood because they just learned that they did well on an aptitude test helped more than undergraduates in a neutral mood, regardless of the worthiness of the cause or the cost of helping.

What accounts for this pervasive reward value of helping for people in a good mood? One possibility is desire for good-mood maintenance. Seeing another person in need can throw a wet blanket on our good mood, so we help in order to shed this blanket and maintain our mood (Isen & Levin, 1972; Levin & Isen, 1975). Isen (1987; Isen, Shalker, Clark, & Karp, 1978) has also suggested a second possibility: Being in a good mood may bias our memories about the positive and negative aspects of various activities, including helping. She suggested that when we are in a good mood, we are more likely to recall and attend to positive rather than negative aspects of our lives. Applied to helping, this makes us more likely to remember and attend to the positive, rewarding features and less likely to attend to the negative features, such as the costs involved (also see Berkowitz, 1987; Clark & Waddell, 1983; Cunningham, Shaffer, Barbee, Wolff, & Kelley, 1990).

Empathic Joy. Empathic joy is the vicarious feeling of pleasure one has at seeing the person in need experience relief. As Hoffman (1981a) described it, "When the victim shows visible signs of relief or joy after being helped, the helper may actually feel empathic joy. Having experienced empathic joy, he or she may subsequently be motivated to help in order to experience it again" (p. 135). At the time Hoffman wrote, there was no empirical evidence for the existence of such a motive; now there is (Batson, Batson, Slingsby, Harrell, Peekna, & Todd, 1991). Interestingly, this evidence suggests that seeking empathic joy is a motive among individuals feeling little empathic concern for the person in need but not among individuals feeling considerable empathic concern.

Avoiding Punishments

Probably the only punishments listed in Table 9.2 that need explanation are fines/imprisonment, sanctions for norm violation, and empathy costs.

Fines/Imprisonment. In some countries, especially in Europe, there are Good Samaritan laws. If you fail to offer aid when (a) someone's life is in danger, (b) there is no serious risk for you, and (c) no one better qualified is available, then you are liable for a fine or a jail sentence. The reason for these laws is, of course, to motivate people to help in order to avoid these penalties.

Sanctions for Norm Violation. A number of social norms apply to helping. They tell us that we should help people in need—at least some people under some circumstances—lest we suffer socially administered or self-administered sanctions. One norm already mentioned is the *norm of reciprocity*. In addition to leading us to expect repayment when we help, this norm dictates that we should help those who help us. Although Gouldner (1960) believed that the norm of reciprocity is universal, he also believed that the pressure on us to help in return depends on the circumstances under which we received help: (a) how badly we needed help, (b) our perception of how much the other person gave us relative to his or her total resources, (c) our perception of the other person's motives for helping (for example, was it a bribe?), and (d) whether the other person helped voluntarily or was pressured into it.

There is much research evidence that people are motivated to comply with the norm of reciprocity. For example, Wilke and Lanzetta (1970, 1982) found a direct relationship between the amount of help received and the amount of help reciprocated; the more help people are given, the more they give in return. Consistent with one of the qualifications suggested by Gouldner, Pruitt (1968) found that the amount of help people reciprocate depends not on the absolute amount they are given but on their judgment of how much of the other person's total resources has been given to them. This kind of effect has been found in Japan and Sweden as well as the United States, lending some support to Gouldner's contention that the norm of reciprocity is universal (cf., Gergen, Ellsworth, Maslach, & Seipel, 1975).

A second norm that psychologists have suggested motivates helping is the *norm of social responsibility*. This norm tells us that we should help a person in need who is dependent upon us—that is, when others are not available to help and so the person is counting specifically on us. Although such a norm does seem to exist, its effect has been surprisingly difficult to demonstrate. In fact, after over a decade of research trying, Berkowitz (1972) concluded, "The findings do not provide any clear-cut support for the normative analysis of help-giving. . . . The potency of the conjectured 'social responsibility norm' was greatly exaggerated" (pp. 68, 77).

Why has evidence that the norm of social responsibility leads to helping been so hard to find? Darley and Latané (1970) suggested that this norm may be at once too general and too specific. The norm may be too general in that everyone in our society adheres to it. If this is true, then it cannot account for why one person helps and another does not. On the other hand, the norm may be too specific in that along with it comes a complex pattern of exceptions, situations in which an individual may feel exempt from acting in accordance with the norm. To take an extreme example, if someone is dependent upon you for help with what you believe to be an immoral act—such as performing a robbery—you will likely feel no normative pressure to help. Thus, the norm of social responsibility seems to be characterized not simply by a rule that says "If someone is dependent on you for help, then help" but by a more complex rule that says "If someone is dependent on you for help, then help, *except when . . .*" The exceptions will vary for different individuals and different social situations.

Other researchers have suggested that the problem with social norms may lie in our focus of attention. Only when our attention is focused on a particular norm as a standard for our behavior is concern about violating it likely to affect our behavior (Cialdini, Kallgren, & Reno, 1991). Consistent with this suggestion, Gibbons and Wicklund (1982) found that if standards of helpfulness or a sense that one ought to help were salient and so a focus of attention, then also focusing on oneself increased helping. Presumably, being self-focused when the norm was salient highlighted the threat of sanctions for failing to act in line with personal standards. But in the absence of salient standards for helpfulness, Gibbons and Wicklund (1982) found that people who were self-focused were *less* helpful than people who were not self-focused. Presumably, in this case self-focus inhibited attention to others' needs.

Becuase general social norms like the norm of social responsibility have limited ability to predict whether a person will help, Shalom Schwartz (1977) suggested that we change the focus of our thinking about norms. Rather than thinking about general social norms, Schwartz suggested that we think of more specific, personal norms. By *personal norms* he meant internalized rules of conduct that are learned from social interaction, rules that vary between individuals within the same society and that function to direct behavior in particular situations.

Applied to helping, a personal norm involves a sense of obligation to perform a *particular* helping act. For example, people may say, either publicly or to themselves, "I ought to give a pint of blood in the blood drive." Such statements appear to be far more predictive of whether a person will give blood than are statements of agreement with more general social norms like the norm of social responsibility. Specific statements like this are particularly powerful as predictors when one also takes into account extenuating circumstances such as whether the person was in town during the blood drive, had no major scheduling conflicts, and was physically fit to give blood (Zuckerman & Reis, 1978). Of course, at this level of specificity, it is not clear whether the statement about giving blood reflects a sense of personal obligation stemming from an internalized rule of conduct—a personal norm—or simply an intention to act in a particular way.

Empathy Costs. Empathy costs are the discomfort and distress you anticipate feeling because of the empathy you will feel for the person in need as he or she continues to suffer. Piliavin, Dovidio, Gaertner, and Clark (1981) have suggested that desire to avoid these costs is one source of motivation to help.

Reducing Aversive Arousal

The three self-benefits under aversive-arousal reduction in Table 9.2 may be less familiar to you than the self-benefits under rewards and punishments. The general idea of aversive-arousal reduction is that it is upsetting to see someone else suffer, and we prefer not to be upset. To eliminate this aversive arousal, one option is to relieve the other person's suffering because it is the stimulus causing our suffering. Once again, the prosocial aspect of this motivation is instrumental, not ultimate; the ultimate goal is the self-benefit of having our discomfort go away.

Why should the suffering of others cause us to suffer? Answers vary. One is that we have learned over the years that when others are suffering, there is a greater chance that we will soon suffer too (St. Thomas Aquinas, among others, suggested this). Another answer is that we have a genetic predisposition to be distressed by the distress of others (Sagi & Hoffman, 1976). Whatever the source, our aversion to television news footage showing the mangled body of a victim of terrorism or the hollow stares of starving refugees suggests that we often find the suffering of others aversive. Sometimes this aversion leads us only to look away and cover our ears or to seek distraction, but at other times it may lead us to help.

Each of the three self-benefits under aversive arousal in Table 9.2 is based on the assumption that witnessing another in distress is aversive; yet each specifies a different form of aversive arousal.

Escaping One's Own Distress. Most straightforward is the possibility suggested by Piliavin and colleagues (1981); Hoffman (1981b); Dovidio, Piliavin, Gaertner, Schroeder, and Clark (1991), among others. They propose that the witness's vicarious distress has much the same character as the victim's distress; both are aversive, and the witness is motivated to escape his or her own distress. One way to escape is to help, because helping terminates the stimulus causing the distress. Of course, running away may enable the witness to escape just as well and at less cost, as long as "out of sight, out of mind" works.

Escaping Discrepancy. Janusz Reykowski (1982) has proposed a quite different source of prosocial motivation, but still one that involves reduction of an aversive tension state: "The sheer discrepancy between information about the real or possible state of an object and standards of its normal or desirable state will evoke motivation" (p. 361). Reykowski applies this general psychological principle—which is closely akin to cognitive dissonance (Festinger, 1957)—to prosocial motivation as follows: If a person perceives a discrepancy between the current state and the expected or ideal state of another person (i.e., perceives the other to be in need), then this will produce cognitive inconsistency and motivation to reduce this uncomfortable inconsistency. Relieving the other's need by helping is one way to remove the inconsistency and escape the discrepant situation. Another, less prosocial way is to change one's perception and decide that the other's suffering is acceptable, even desirable. This has been called *blaming the victim* (Ryan, 1971).

Escaping Injustice. Melvin Lerner's (1980) *just-world hypothesis* led him to a similar but more specific view. If we believe in a just world—a world in which people get what they deserve and deserve what they get—then witnessing an innocent victim suffer should be upsetting because it violates this belief. In order to reduce the discomfort produced by this threat, we may help the victim. Once again, however, there is an alternative way to escape the aversive arousal. We may instead derogate or blame the victim; if the victim is less deserving, then his or her suffering is more just and less upsetting. Consistent with Lerner's analysis, research suggests that if people can easily help in order to relieve the suffering of an innocent victim, they are likely to do so, but if they cannot easily help, they are likely to derogate the victim (Lerner & Simmons, 1966; Mills & Egger, 1972).

Conclusion

Reviewing the evidence that people help others in order to gain one or more from the long list of self-benefits summarized in Table 9.2, Hatfield, Walster, and Piliavin (1978) concluded:

> The majority of scientists—[us] included—are fairly cynical. They interpret apparent altruism in cost-benefit terms, assuming that individuals, altruists included, learn to perform those acts that are rewarded . . . and to avoid those acts that are not. Either self-congratulation or external reward, then, must support apparently altruistic behavior. . . . Most often scientists attribute apparent altruism to more selfish motives (pp. 128–129).

This seems a fair and accurate description of the majority view, not only in 1978 when Hatfield and her colleagues wrote but throughout the history of psychology. In the past decade or so, however, this description has been seriously challenged.

Altruism: Benefiting Another as an End in Itself

Both for philosophers through the ages and for behavioral and social scientists today, the most intriguing and the most controversial question raised by human helping behavior is whether it provides evidence for altruistic motivation. Is it possible for one person to have another person's welfare as an ultimate goal rather than simply as an instrumental means of reaching the ultimate goal of one or another form of self-benefit? Many, including me, have gone to the mat over the answer to this question.

One rejoinder to the possibility of altruism that we need to lay to rest at the outset goes like this: Even if it were possible for a person to be motivated to increase another's welfare, such a person would be pleased by attaining this desired goal, so even this apparent altruism would actually be a product of egoism. This argument, based on the general principle of *psychological hedonism,* is in the words of Edward Tolman's (1923) well-turned epithet "more brilliant than cogent" (p. 203). It has been shown to be flawed by philosophers who have pointed out that it involves a confusion between two different forms of hedonism. The strong form of psychological hedonism asserts that attainment of personal pleasure is always the goal of human action; the weak form asserts only that goal attainment always brings pleasure. The weak form is not inconsistent with the possibility that the ultimate goal of some action is to benefit another rather than to benefit oneself; the pleasure obtained can be a consequence of reaching the goal without being the goal itself. The strong form of psychological hedonism is inconsistent with the possibility of altruism, but to affirm this form of hedonism is simply to assert that altruism does not exist; it is an empirical assertion that may or may not be true. (See MacIntyre, 1967; Milo, 1973; Nagel, 1970, for discussion of these philosophical arguments.)

Advocates of universal egoism, like Hatfield and her colleagues (1978) quoted above, argue for the strong form of psychological hedonism. They assert that some self-benefit is always the ultimate goal of helping; benefiting the other is simply an instrumental goal on the way to one or another ultimately self-serving end. They remind us of all the self-benefits of helping, like those listed in Table 9.2. Advocates of altruism argue back that simply to show that self-benefits follow from benefiting someone does not prove that the self-benefits were the helper's ultimate goal. It is at least logically possible that the self-benefits were unintended consequences of reaching the ultimate goal of benefiting the other. If so, then the motivation was altruistic, not egoistic.

Advocates of altruism claim more than logical possibility, of course. They claim that altruistic motivation is an empirical reality, that at least some people under some circumstances act with the ultimate goal of increasing another person's welfare. They claim that people can want another person to be happy and free of distress, not because it is upsetting to them if he or she is not—although it quite likely *is* upsetting—but because they care about the other's welfare as an end in itself.

Who is right? To arrive at an answer, we must disentangle the confounding of the two possible ultimate goals: benefit to self and benefit to the other. This is difficult because benefiting the other seems inevitably to bring self-benefits (like those in Table 9.2). Yet disentangling these goals no longer seems impossible.

Where to Look for Altruism

Where might we expect to find evidence of altruistic motivation, if it exists? One might think that the most natural strategy would be to seek out those paragons of helpfulness celebrated by our society—the Mother Teresas, Albert Schweitzers, Mahatma Gandhis, the rescuers of Jews from the Nazis, the heroes who risk their lives helping in emergencies. After all, if anyone is altruistic, is it not people like these?

A little reflection reveals that this strategy is flawed, for two reasons. First, it focuses on behavior, not motivation. Paragons of goodness are clearly outstanding for their helpfulness. But the question of the existence of altruism is not about helpfulness; it is about the nature of the motivation for helping. We cannot assume any necessary relationship between the amount of helping an individual displays and the nature of his or her motivation. The amount may reveal something about the quantity of underlying motivation, but it does not reveal the quality.

Second, seeking out paragons of helpfulness blurs an important distinction between a psychological and a moral perspective on altruism. From a moral perspective, one may decide that a Mother Teresa or an Albert Schweitzer is a better person than the rest of us, a saint perhaps. But the psychologist's concern is not with assessment of moral goodness; it is with understanding human motives and potential. The psychologist wants to know whether, when people help, the goal is ever to benefit the other as an end in itself, or whether the goal is always, ultimately, some form of self-benefit.

From a moral perspective, one may assert that altruism, if it exists, is morally good (e.g., Blum, 1980), although not everyone would agree (e.g., Nietzsche, 1888/1927; Rand, 1964). It is far less clear that this assertion can be reversed. Moral goodness need not be altruistic. Feeding the hungry, housing the homeless, and comforting the sick are likely to be seen as morally good, regardless of the underlying motive. Such goodness certainly attracts the psychologist's attention because the motivation *might* be altruistic, but we cannot simply assume that it is.

Where, then, should we look? Both in classic philosophy and in contemporary psychology, the most commonly proposed source of altruistic motivation is empathic emotion. By *empathy* I mean other-oriented feelings congruent with the perceived welfare of another person. If the other is perceived to be in need, empathy includes feelings of sympathy, compassion, tenderness, and the like. Empathy is usually considered to be a product not only of perceiving the other as in need but also of adopting the perspective of the other, which means imagining how the other is affected by his or her situation (Stotland, 1969). It is for this reason that empathic feelings are called other-oriented. Such feelings have been named as a source—if not *the* source—of altruism by Thomas Aquinas, David Hume, Adam Smith, Charles Darwin, Herbert Spencer, William McDougall, and in contemporary psychology by Martin Hoffman (1976),

Dennis Krebs (1975), and myself (Batson, 1987, 1991). I shall call the proposal that feeling empathy for a person in need evokes altruistic motivation to relieve that need the *empathy-altruism hypothesis.*

Empathic Emotion as a Source of Altruistic Motivation: The Empathy-Altruism Hypothesis and Its Egoistic Alternatives

There is considerable evidence that feeling empathy for a person in need leads to increased helping of that person (Batson, Duncan, Ackerman, Buckley, & Birch, 1981; Coke, Batson, & McDavis, 1978; Dovidio, Allen, & Schroeder, 1990; Fultz, Batson, Fortenbach, McCarthy, & Varney, 1986; Krebs, 1975; Toi & Batson, 1982; see Eisenberg & Miller, 1987, for an extensive review). To observe an empathy-helping relationship, however, tells us nothing about the nature of the motivation that underlies this relationship. It could be egoistic rather than altruistic.

To ascertain the nature of the prosocial motivation evoked by empathy, researchers have turned to the experimental methods that have become the trademark of social psychology in the last 50 years. They have sought, first, to identify plausible self-benefits of the helping evoked by empathy and, second, to conduct experiments that manipulate the viability of helping as a means to reach these self-benefits. Typically in these experiments, some participants are given a chance to help a person in need when helping is the best means to reach the self-benefit in question, while other participants are given this chance when helping is not the best means. If less helping is observed in the latter condition than in the former, then there is evidence that the self-benefit in question was the ultimate goal. If as much helping is observed in the latter condition as in the former, then there is evidence that this self-benefit was not the goal (assuming there is also evidence that the experimental manipulation was effective and the helping measure was sensitive). Then what was the ultimate goal? It may have been some other self-benefit, which must be checked until all plausible possibilities have been examined, or it may have been to benefit the person in need. If the latter, the motivation was altruistic.

The first step in testing the empathy-altruism hypothesis is, then, to identify plausible self-benefits of empathy-induced helping. Scholars and researchers have had no difficulty doing this. Proposed egoistic alternatives to the empathy-altruism hypothesis have been based on each of the three general categories of self-benefits listed in Table 9.2. Some scholars have suggested that the ultimate goal of the helping evoked by empathy is to gain empathy-specific rewards; others, that it is to avoid empathy-specific punishments; and still others, that it is to reduce empathy-based aversive arousal. In the past decade or so, experiments have been conducted to test each of these egoistic alternatives against the empathy-altruism hypothesis. Because the issue of the existence of altruistic motivation is so controversial and because research strategies used to test the empathy-altruism hypothesis provide a model for testing the existence of other nonegoistic prosocial motives, I shall go into the logic of this research in some detail. Let me consider the egoistic alternatives in reverse order because that is how they have come to the fore.

Aversive-Arousal Reduction. The most frequently proposed egoistic explanation of the empathy-helping relationship has long been aversive-arousal reduction. Martin Hoffman (1981b) put it in a nutshell: "Empathic distress is unpleasant and helping the victim is usually the best way to get rid of the source" (p. 52). According to this explanation, empathically aroused individuals help in order to benefit themselves by eliminating their empathic feelings, much as we noted in the previous section is true for individuals experiencing upset or distress as a result of seeing another person suffer. Benefiting the victim is simply a means to this self-serving end.

To test this aversive-arousal reduction explanation against the empathy-altruism hypothesis, experiments have been conducted varying the ease of escaping further exposure to a suffering victim without helping. Because empathic arousal is a result of witnessing the victim's suffering, either terminating this suffering by helping or terminating exposure to it by escaping should serve to reduce the aversive arousal. Escape is not, however, a viable means of reaching the altruistic goal of relieving the victim's distress; it does nothing to promote that end.

The difference in viability of escape as a means to these two goals produces competing predictions in an escape (easy vs. difficult) × empathy (low vs. high) experimental design. Among individuals experiencing low empathy for the person in need, both the aversive-arousal reduction explanation and the empathy-altruism hypothesis predict more helping when escape is difficult than when it is easy. This is because both assume that the motivation of individuals feeling low empathy is egoistic. Among individuals feeling high empathy, the aversive-arousal reduction explanation predicts a similar (perhaps even greater) difference; it assumes that empathically induced motivation is also egoistic. In contrast, the empathy-altruism hypothesis predicts high helping even when escape is easy among individuals feeling high empathy. Across the four cells of an escape × empathy design, then, the aversive-arousal reduction explanation predicts less helping under easy escape in each empathy condition; the empathy-altruism hypothesis predicts a 1-versus-3 pattern: relatively low helping in the easy-escape/low-empathy cell and high helping in the other three cells. These competing predictions are summarized in Table 9.3.

Note that to test these competing predictions, the pattern of helping across all four cells of the escape × empathy design is important. If one were to compare helping under easy- and difficult-escape conditions only for high-empathy individuals, then the empathy-altruism hypothesis would predict no difference. Such a result could occur simply because the escape manipulation was too weak, or the measure of helping was insensitive. If, however, the escape manipulation has a significant effect on the helping of low- but not high-empathy individuals, then the lack of difference for high-empathy individuals cannot be attributed to a weak escape manipulation or an insensitive measure.

Over half a dozen experiments have now been run using this escape × empathy design (see Batson, 1987, 1991, for reviews). In a typical procedure, participants observe a "worker" who they believe is reacting badly to a series of uncomfortable electric shocks; they are then given a chance to help the worker

TABLE 9.3. Predictions for Rate of Helping in Escape × Empathy Design

Aversive-Arousal Reduction Explanation		
	Low Empathy	High Empathy
Easy escape	Low	Low
Difficult escape	High	High/very high

Empathy-Altruism Hypothesis		
	Low Empathy	High Empathy
Easy escape	Low	High
Difficult escape	High	High

by taking the shocks themselves. To manipulate ease of escape, some participants are informed that if they do not help, they will continue observing the worker take the shocks (difficult escape); others are informed that they will observe no more (easy escape). Empathy has been manipulated by similarity information, by an emotion-specific misattribution technique, and by perspective-taking instructions adopted when learning of the other's need. (Low-empathy perspective-taking instructions ask participants to remain objective; high-empathy instructions ask participants to imagine the other's feelings.) Empathy has also been measured by self-reports of feelings of sympathy, compassion, softheartedness, tenderness, and the like.

Results of these experiments have consistently conformed to the pattern predicted by the empathy-altruism hypothesis (bottom half of Table 9.3), not to the pattern predicted by the aversive-arousal reduction explanation (top half of Table 9.3). Only among individuals experiencing a predominance of personal distress rather than empathy (i.e., feeling relatively anxious, upset, distressed, and the like) does the chance for easy escape reduce helping. This is precisely what we would expect if feelings of personal distress evoke egoistic motivation to have this aversive arousal reduced, but feelings of empathy do not. In spite of the popularity of the aversive-arousal reduction explanation of the empathy-helping relationship, this explanation appears to be wrong.

Empathy-Specific Punishment. The second egoistic explanation of the empathy-helping relationship claims that we have learned through socialization that an additional obligation to help, and so additional shame and guilt for failure to help, is attendant on feeling empathy for someone in need. As a result, when we feel empathy, we are faced with impending social or self-censure above and beyond any general punishment associated with not helping. We say to ourselves, "What will others think—or what will I think of myself—if I don't help when I feel like this?" and we help out of an egoistic desire to avoid these empathy-specific punishments.

Several different techniques have been used to test this empathy-specific punishment explanation against the empathy-altruism hypothesis. The most frequently used technique has been to provide justification for not helping. If a person is helping to avoid social or self-punishment, then receiving information that increases the justification for not helping should lower the rate of helping. But if a person is helping out of an altruistic desire to reduce the other's suffering, then even with increased justification, the rate of helping should remain high. Therefore, the empathy-specific punishment explanation and the empathy-altruism hypothesis predict a different pattern of helping across the four cells of a justification for not helping (low vs. high) × empathy (low vs. high) experimental design. These different predictions appear in Table 9.4.

Batson, Dyck, Brandt, Batson, Powell, McMaster, & Griffitt (1988) conducted three studies employing different versions of this justification x empathy design. In the first, justification was provided by *information about the inaction of other potential helpers*. Batson and colleagues (1988) reasoned that if most people asked have said no to a request for help, then one should feel more justified in saying no as well. Individuals induced by a perspective-taking manipulation to feel either low or high empathy for a young woman in need were given an opportunity to pledge time to help her. Information on the pledge form about the responses of previously asked peers indicated that either five of seven had pledged (low justification for not helping) or two of seven had pledged (high justification). The young woman's plight was such that others' responses did not affect her need for help. As depicted in Table 9.4, the empathy-specific punishment explanation predicted more helping in the low-justification condition than in the high by individuals feeling high empathy. In contrast, the empathy-altruism hypothesis predicted high helping by these individuals in both justification conditions. The latter pattern was found. Only among individuals feeling low empathy were those in the high-justification condition less likely to help than those in the low-justification condition.

In the second study, justification was provided by *attributional ambiguity*.

TABLE 9.4. **Predictions for Rate of Helping in Justification × Empathy Design**

	EMPATHY-SPECIFIC PUNISHMENT EXPLANATION	
	Low Empathy	High Empathy
Low justification	Moderate	High
High justification	Low	Low
	EMPATHY-ALTRUISM HYPOTHESIS	
	Low Empathy	High Empathy
Low justification	Moderate	High
High justification	Low	High

Batson and associates (1988) reasoned that if individuals can attribute a decision not to help to helping-irrelevant features of the decision, then they should be less likely to anticipate social or self-punishment. Accordingly, individuals feeling either low or high empathy for a peer they thought was about to receive electric shocks were given a chance to work on either or both of two task options. For each correct response on option A, they would receive one raffle ticket for a $30 prize for themselves; for each correct response on option B, they would reduce by one the shocks the peer was to receive. Information about helping-irrelevant attributes of the two task options indicated either that the two tasks were quite similar and neither was preferred (low justification for not helping) or that one task involved numbers, the other letters, and most people preferred to work on the numbers (letters), whichever was paired with the nonhelpful option A (high justification). Once again, competing predictions for helping (i.e., working on option B) were those in Table 9.4, and once again, results patterned as predicted by the empathy-altruism hypothesis, not the empathy-specific punishment explanation.

In the third study, justification for not helping was provided by *information about difficulty of the performance standard on a qualifying task*. Batson and colleagues (1988) reasoned that were potential helpers to believe that even if they volunteered they would only be allowed to help if they met the performance standard on a qualifying task, then performance on the qualifying task would provide a behavioral measure of motivation to reduce the victim's suffering (which required qualifying) or to avoid social and self-punishment (which did not). This should be true, however, only if poor performance could be justified, which it could if the performance standard on the qualifying task was so difficult that most people fail. If the standard was this difficult, a person could not be blamed for not qualifying—either by self or others. In this case, individuals motivated to avoid self-punishment should either (a) decline to help because of the low probability of qualifying or (b) offer to help but not try very hard on the qualifying task, ensuring that they do not qualify. Bluntly put, they should take a dive.

In the study, individuals feeling either low or high empathy for a peer who they believed was reacting badly to a series of uncomfortable electric shocks were given a chance to help the peer by taking the remaining shocks themselves. But even if they volunteered, they had to meet the performance standard on the qualifying task to be eligible to help. Information about the difficulty of the standard indicated either that most college students qualify (low justification for not helping) or that most do not (high justification).

Once more, results supported the empathy-altruism hypothesis. Helping again patterned as predicted in the bottom half of Table 9.4. The performance measure also patterned as predicted by the empathy-altruism hypothesis: Performance of low-empathy individuals was lower when the qualifying standard was difficult than when it was easy; performance of high-empathy individuals was higher when the qualifying standard was difficult. This interaction pattern suggested that the motivation of low-empathy individuals was at least in part directed toward avoiding self-punishment; whereas, contrary to the empathy-specific punishment explanation, the motivation of high-empathy individuals was not. The motivation of high-empathy individuals appeared to be directed toward the altruistic goal of relieving the other's suffering.

In all three studies, then, results conformed to the pattern predicted by the empathy-altruism hypothesis (bottom half of Table 9.4), not to the pattern predicted by the empathy-specific punishment explanation (top half of Table 9.4). Results from other studies using different techniques to test the empathy-specific punishment explanation have patterned similarly (see Batson, 1991, for a review). In no study has support for this explanation of the empathy-helping relationship been found. Apparently, this second egoistic alternative to the empathy-altruism hypothesis is also wrong.

Empathy-Specific Reward. The final major egoistic alternative to the empathy-altruism hypothesis claims that we learn through socialization that special rewards in the form of praise, honor, and pride are attendant on helping a person for whom we feel empathy. As a result, when we feel empathy, we think of these rewards and help out of an egoistic desire to gain them.

Two versions of this empathy-specific reward explanation have been proposed. The first claims that we learn through prior reinforcement that after helping those for whom we feel empathy we can expect a special mood-enhancing pat on the back—either from others in the form of praise, or from ourselves in the form of enhanced self-image. When we feel empathy, we think of this good feeling and are egoistically motivated to obtain it. The second version claims that it is not the social or self-reward that is empathy specific; instead, it is the *need* for this reward. Feeling empathy for a person who is suffering involves a state of temporary sadness, which can be relieved by any mood-enhancing experience, including obtaining the social and self-rewards that accompany helping. According to this second version, the egoistic desire for negative-state relief accounts for the increased helping of empathically aroused individuals.

Social and Self-Rewards Associated with the Empathy-Helping Relationship. Batson and associates (1988) reported two studies designed to test the first version of the empathy-specific reward explanation. Let me describe just one, in which they assessed the effect on mood of depriving high-empathy individuals of the opportunity to help. Because social and self-rewards for helping are given only to the helper, the empathy-specific reward explanation predicts that empathically aroused individuals will feel worse if deprived of an anticipated opportunity to help (assuming that helping is low-cost and effective). In contrast, the empathy-altruism hypothesis predicts that empathically aroused individuals will feel as good when the victim's need is relieved by other means as when it is relieved by their own action.

The empathy-altruism hypothesis also predicts that when empathically aroused individuals are deprived of the opportunity to help, they will feel better when the victim's need is relieved by other means than when it is not relieved. The empathy-specific reward explanation predicts no difference in mood across these two conditions, because neither relief of the need nor lack of relief per se is relevant to the egoistic goal of obtaining mood-enhancing rewards for helping.

To test these predictions, Batson and colleagues (1988) led individuals reporting either low or high empathy for a person about to receive electric shocks to believe that they would have a no-cost, no-risk opportunity to help the person avoid the shocks. Later, half of the individuals learned that by chance they would not have the opportunity to help after all. Among both the individuals who would have the opportunity to help and those who would not, half learned that the person was still scheduled to receive the shocks, and half learned that by chance this threat had been removed. These variations produced an empathy (low vs. high) × prior relief of victim's need (no prior relief vs. prior relief) × perform helping task (perform vs. not perform) design. The major dependent measure was change in self-reported mood after participants were or were not allowed to help.

Results for individuals reporting high empathy revealed the pattern of mood change that was predicted by the empathy-altruism hypothesis, not the pattern predicted by the empathy-specific reward explanation. There was more positive mood change in the three cells in which the victim's need was relieved than in the one in which it was not; prior relief of the victim's need did not lead to the negative mood change predicted by the empathy-specific reward explanation. Moreover, this pattern was specific to high-empathy individuals; it did not approach statistical reliability among low-empathy individuals. Results from the other experiment (Batson et al., 1988, study 5) also supported the empathy-altruism hypothesis, not the first version of the empathy-specific reward explanation.

A Variant on Version 1 of the Empathy-Specific Reward Explanation: Empathic Joy. Smith, Keating, and Stotland (1989) suggested an interesting variant on the first version of the empathy-specific reward explanation. They proposed that, rather than helping to gain the rewards of seeing oneself or being seen by others as a helpful person, empathically aroused individuals help in order to gain the good feeling of sharing vicariously in the joy of the needy individual's relief: "It is proposed that the prospect of empathic, joy, conveyed by feedback from the help recipient, is essential to the special tendency of empathic witnesses to help. . . . The empathically concerned witness to the distress of others helps in order to be happy" (Smith, Keating, & Stotland, 1989, p. 641).

Unlike other forms of version 1 of the empathy-specific reward explanation, the rewards at issue here are contingent on the victim's need being relieved, not on the empathically aroused individual being the agent of this relief. The agent might be another person, or time (which, it is said, heals all wounds), or chance, and the empathic joy would be as sweet. Because of this difference, the prior evidence against version 1 did not rule out the possibility that the ultimate goal of empathically aroused helpers is to get the egoistic self-benefit of empathic joy. All the prior evidence dealt with rewards from helping, not from seeing the victim's need relieved.

To test their empathic-joy hypothesis, Smith and associates (1989) conducted an experiment in which they manipulated the expectation of feedback concerning the effect of one's helping efforts. They reasoned that if the empathic-joy hypothesis is correct, then the empathy-helping relationship should be found only when prospective helpers anticipate receiving feedback on the effect of their helping efforts. If the empathy-altruism hypothesis is correct, then the empathy-helping relationship should be found even under no-feedback conditions; helping can still relieve the victim's need.

In a feedback (anticipated vs. not) × empathy (low vs. high) design, Smith and colleagues (1989) found an empathy-helping relationship in both the anticipated-feedback and no-feedback conditions. This was the pattern predicted by the empathy-altruism hypothesis, not the empathic-joy hypothesis. But a failed manipulation check led Smith and associates (1989) to disregard these results and focus instead on an internal analysis in which low- and high-empathy conditions were created by a median split on a measure of self-reported empathy minus self-reported distress. In this internal analysis, there was a positive relationship between relative empathy and helping in the anticipated-feedback condition but no relationship between relative empathy and helping in the no-feedback condition, which was the pattern predicted by the empathic-joy hypothesis. Smith and his collegues concluded that their empathic-joy hypothesis was correct.

I have doubts, for several reasons. First, there are reasons to doubt the validity of a measure of self-reported empathy minus distress in the particular research procedure used by Smith and associates (see Batson, 1991). Even more telling, three subsequent experiments—one using a feedback × empathy design like Smith and colleagues' in which the empathy manipulation was clearly successful and two using a different procedure—all failed to provide support for the empathic-joy hypothesis (Batson et al., 1991). Results of each of these experiments, like the results in the Smith and associates experimental design, patterned as predicted by the empathy-altruism hypothesis.

Given these results, it does not appear that empathically aroused individuals are motivated simply to gain the pleasure of sharing vicariously in the needy person's relief. The empathic-joy hypothesis, like the earlier form of the first version of the empathy-specific reward explanation, seems unable to account for the empathy-helping relationship.

Negative-State Relief and the Empathy-Helping Relationship. Turning to the second version of the empathy-specific reward explanation, Cialdini and his colleagues (Cialdini, Schaller, Houlihan, Arps, Fultz, & Beaman, 1987; Schaller & Cialdini, 1988) have argued that it is the need for the rewards of helping, not the rewards themselves, that is empathy specific. They claim that individuals who experience empathy when witnessing another person's suffering are in a negative affective state—one of temporary sadness or sorrow—and these individuals help in order to relieve this negative state: "Because helping contains a rewarding component for most normally socialized adults . . . , it can be used instrumentally to restore mood" (Cialdini, Schaller, Houlihan, Arps, Fultz, & Beaman, 1987, p. 750).

Once again, there has been some disagreement about the truth of this explanation of the empathy-helping relationship. Cialdini and his colleagues have claimed support (Cialdini, Schaller, Houlihan, Arps, Fultz, & Beaman, 1987; Schaller & Cialdini, 1988); Schroeder and his colleagues (Schroeder, Dovidio, Sibicky, Matthews, & Allen, 1988) claimed lack of support. Part of the disagreement seems to be due to the inadvertent presence of a distraction confound in the original Cialdini and associates (1987) experiments.

In order to avoid this confound, the technique that seems best suited to testing the negative-state relief explanation is to confront individuals with an opportunity to help after leading some of them to believe that even if they do not help, they can anticipate a cost-free mood-enhancing experience. The negative-state relief explanation predicts that anticipating such an experience will eliminate the empathy-helping relationship; the empathy-altruism hypothesis predicts that it will not. These competing predictions across the four cells of an anticipated mood enhancement (no vs. yes) × empathy (low vs. high) design are presented in Table 9.5.

Schaller and Cialdini (1988) conducted an experiment with an anticipated mood enhancement x empathy design and claimed support for the negative-state relief explanation. They admitted, however, that the evidence was weak. On a scaled measure of helping (amount of help offered), their results were more consistent with the negative-state relief explanation than with the empathy-altruism hypothesis, but these results were not statistically reliable except using an uncorrected post hoc analysis including time of semester as a variable. On a dichotomous measure (proportion of participants helping), their results were at least as consistent with the empathy-altruism hypothesis as with the negative-state relief explanation.

In an independent effort to assess the relative merits of the negative-state relief explanation and the empathy-altruism hypothesis, Batson and colleagues (1989) conducted two studies using an anticipated mood enhancement × empathy design much like the one used by Schaller and Cialdini (1988). In the first, participants were given an opportunity to help a same-sex peer by taking elec-

TABLE 9.5. Predictions for Rate of Helping in Anticipated Mood Enhancement × Empathy Design

NEGATIVE-STATE RELIEF EXPLANATION		
	Low Empathy	High Empathy
No anticipated mood enhancement	Low	High
Anticipated mood enhancement	Low	Low

EMPATHY-ALTRUISM HYPOTHESIS		
	Low Empathy	High Empathy
No anticipated mood enhancement	Low	High
Anticipated mood enhancement	Low	High

tric shocks in his or her stead; in the second, participants could volunteer to spend time helping a young woman struggling to support her younger brother and sister after the tragic death of her parents. Results of these two studies both conformed to the pattern predicted by the empathy-altruism hypothesis (bottom half of Table 9.5), not the pattern predicted by the negative-state relief explanation (top half of Table 9.5).

In sum, Cialdini and his colleagues have claimed support for the negative-state relief version of the empathy-specific reward explanation, although they have noted ambiguities and inconsistencies in their evidence. Other researchers using procedures less subject to interpretational ambiguity have found support for the empathy-altruism hypothesis, not the negative-state relief explanation. Considering the evidence as a whole, it does not appear that this second version of the empathy-specific reward explanation can account for the motivation to help evoked by empathy.

A Tentative Conclusion. In the words of Sherlock Holmes, "When you have eliminated the impossible, whatever remains, *however improbable,* must be the truth." It seems impossible for any of the three major egoistic explanations of the empathy-helping relationship to account for the research evidence that has been produced by the over 25 experiments to date designed to test the empathy-altruism hypothesis against the egoistic alternatives. Instead, with remarkable consistency, the evidence has patterned as predicted by the empathy-altruism hypothesis. Only it remains. So, pending new evidence or a plausible new egoistic explanation of the existing evidence, if we follow Holmes' dictum, then it appears that we must accept the empathy-altruism hypothesis, however improbable, as true. Apparently, in spite of the strong majority in philosophy, psychology, and the other behavioral and social sciences who have assumed that egoism is the only form of prosocial motivation, Adam Smith's bold assertion at the opening of *The Theory of Moral Sentiments* (1759/1853) was empirically—if not politically—correct:

> How selfish soever man may be supposed, there are evidently some principles in his nature, which interest him in the fortune of others, and render their happiness necessary to him, though he derives nothing from it except the pleasure of seeing it. Of this kind is pity or compassion, the emotion which we feel for the misery of others, when we either see it, or are made to conceive it in a very lively manner (I. i. 1. 1).

Twenty years ago, this statement appeared quite naive and archaic; today, it seems remarkably insightful and up to date.

Other Possible Sources of Altruistic Motivation

If empathic feelings are a source of altruistic motivation, might there be other sources as well? Several have been proposed, including an "altruistic personality" (Oliner & Oliner, 1988), principled moral reasoning (Kohlberg, 1976), and internalized prosocial values (Eisenberg, 1991a; Staub, 1974). Although there is some evidence that each of these potential sources is associated with increased prosocial motivation, there is, as yet, no clear evidence that this motivation is altruistic. Instead, what little evidence exists suggests that helping associated with these sources is an instrumental means to the egoistic ultimate goals of (a) maintaining one's positive self-concept or (b) avoiding guilt (Batson, 1991; Batson, Bolen, Cross, & Neuringer-Benefiel, 1986; but also see Eisenberg et al., 1989). More and better research exploring these possibilities is badly needed.

Thinking even more broadly, beyond the egoism-altruism debate that has been a focus of attention and contention for the past decade, might there be other forms of prosocial motivation, forms in which the ultimate goal is neither to benefit self nor to benefit another individual? Two seem especially worthy of consideration.

Collectivism: Benefiting Another to Benefit a Group

One is collectivism. Collectivism involves motivation to benefit others as a means to benefit some group as a whole. Our ultimate goal is not our own welfare; it is not the welfare of the specific others who are benefited; our ultimate goal is the group's welfare. Benefiting the specific others within the group is an instrumental goal on the way to this ultimate goal. Robyn Dawes and his colleagues put it succinctly: Our concern is "not me or thee but we" (Dawes, van de Kragt, & Orbell, 1988).

It does appear that, in addition to caring about ourselves and other people as individuals, we can care about collectives or groups. The group may be large or small, from 2 to over 2 billion. It may be a marriage or a partnership; it may be a sports team, a university, a community, a nation; it may be all humanity; it may even be all living things. The group may be one's race, religion, sex, political party, or social class.

If the group's welfare is threatened or can be enhanced in some way, then collectivist motivation may be aroused, promoting action to benefit the group. At times, we can act in a way that benefits the group as a whole; more often, we can benefit only some members, perhaps only a single person. Still, if enhancing the group's welfare is the ultimate goal, then the motive for benefiting this person is collectivism, not altruism. The ultimate goal, not the number of people benefited, determines the nature of the prosocial motive.

To illustrate, the person who supports and comforts a spouse, not out of concern for the spouse per se or for the self-benefits imagined but strictly "for the sake of the marriage," is displaying collectivist prosocial motivation. So is the rescuer of a Jewish family in Nazi Europe whose ultimate goal is to benefit humanity in whatever way possible. Such is the sentiment expressed by the motto on the Yad Vashem medal for recognized rescuers: "Whosoever saves one life, he has saved all of humanity."

Problems and Promise of Collectivism

Collectivist prosocial motives are not problem free. Typically, we care about collectives of which we are members, an *us*. Identifying with a group or collective in this way usually involves recognition of an out-group; an *us* implies a *them* who is not us. Indeed, a them-us comparison is often used to define a collective, as Henri Tajfel (1981) and John Turner (1987) have pointed out. When this occurs, harming *them* may be one way to enhance the comparative welfare of *us*. We rejoice at their difficulties and defeats, even if we do not directly benefit as a result (Tajfel & Turner, 1986). We scapegoat. As Dawes, van de Kragt, and Orbell (1990) remind us, Rudolph Hoess, the commandant at Auschwitz, systematically murdered 2.9 million members of an out-group to benefit his National Socialist in-group.

It is also possible to care about collectives of which we are not ourselves members. A right-to-life advocate may be motivated to protect "unborn children"; Mother Teresa may be motivated to care for the "poorest of the poor"; a well-to-do do-gooder may be motivated to help the homeless. Each of these motives is likely to lead to action to benefit individuals in these groups, not for the sake of the individuals themselves but for the sake of the group. There is an extra danger when one is not a member of the collective; one is more likely to misjudge what is in the members' best interest.

In addition to these very real dangers, collectivist prosocial motivation has some virtues that neither egoism nor altruism has. Egoism is directed toward our own self-interest. Altruism, especially empathy-induced altruism, is directed toward the interest of specific other individuals. It seems unlikely that we can feel empathy for an abstract social category like *humanity, the poor,* or *AIDS victims,* although empathic feelings for specific individuals may be generalized to groups of similar others (Dovidio, Schroeder, Allen, & Matthews, 1986). To paraphrase Stalin, one person suffering is a tragedy; a million suffering is a statistic. Further, the likelihood that the needs of different individuals will evoke empathic feelings is not equal. These feelings are more likely to be felt for those (a) who are friends, kin, or similar to us in some way; (b) to whom we are emotionally attached; (c) for whom we feel responsible; or (d) whose perspective we adopt (Batson, 1991; Krebs, 1975; Stotland, 1969). As a result, many of our most pressing social problems are not likely to evoke empathy. The people in need are too remote, or the problem too abstract.

Think, for example, of mass starvation in Africa, of suffering refugees in Cambodia, of poverty and illiteracy in Central America, of pollution, global warming, overpopulation, energy conservation, endangered species; the list goes on and on. These problems are particularly difficult to address because they are *social dilemmas.* A social dilemma, of which the Prisoner's Dilemma considered earlier can be an example, arises when (a) individuals in a group or collective have a choice about how to allocate personally held scarce resources (e.g., money, time, energy), and (b) allocation to the group provides more benefit for the group as a whole than does allocation to any single individual (e.g., oneself), but allocation to a single individual provides that individual with more benefit than does allocation to the group as a whole (Dawes, 1980).

In a social dilemma, the action that is best for each individual—whether for me or for thee—is to allocate resources to meet that individual's needs, ignoring the needs of other members of the group and the group as a whole. But if everyone tries thus to maximize their own welfare or the welfare of those others for whom they feel special concern, the attempt will backfire. Everyone, including the person or persons they were seeking to benefit, is worse off. As in the Prisoner's Dilemma game, unilateral pursuit of what is best for each individual creates a situation in which everyone suffers more. If we rely on straightforward egoistic or altruistic prosocial motivation to address the pressing social dilemmas we face, the prognosis looks bleak. Like lemmings heading for the sea, we seem to be racing pell-mell toward destruction.

But the situation is not really this grim. There is considerable evidence that when faced with a social dilemma, whether in a research laboratory or in real life, many people do not attend only to their own welfare or to the welfare of those for whom they feel special concern. Under certain conditions, people also attend to the group welfare and act to benefit the group as a whole (Alfano & Marwell, 1980; Brewer & Kramer, 1986; Dawes, McTavish, & Shaklee, 1977; Kramer & Brewer, 1984; Orbell, van de Kragt, & Dawes, 1988; Yamagishi & Sato, 1986). The conditions that seem most effective in evoking attention to group welfare are those that promote *group identity*. As a result, the most common current explanation for this attention to group welfare is in terms of collectivist prosocial motivation (Dawes, van de Kragt, & Orbell, 1990).

Does Collectivism Exist?

As has been done for altruism, it is important to consider the possibility that what looks like collectivism is actually a subtle form of egoism. Perhaps attention to group welfare in a social dilemma is simply an expression of enlightened self-interest. After all, if one recognizes that headlong pursuit of self-benefit will only lead to less self-benefit in the end, one may decide to benefit the group as a means to reach the ultimate goal of maximizing overall self-benefit. Certainly, appeals to enlightened self-interest are commonly used persuasive strategies by politicians and social activists trying to encourage prosocial responses to social dilemmas: They warn us of the long-term consequences for ourselves and our children of pollution or of squandering natural resources; they remind us that if the plight of the poor becomes too severe, we may face revolution. Such appeals seem to assume that collectivism is not a third form of prosocial motivation independent of egoism and altruism; it is simply a special case of egoism.

The most direct evidence that collectivism is independent of egoism comes from research by Dawes and his colleagues (Dawes, van de Kragt, & Orbell, 1990; Orbell, van de Kragt, & Dawes, 1988). Their research examined the responses of individuals who were given a choice between allocating resources (money—$5 or $6) to themselves or to a group, when allocation to self maximized individual but not group profit, whereas allocation to the collective maximized group but not individual profit.

Dawes and his colleagues found that if individuals are placed in such a social dilemma after having discussed the dilemma with other members of the group, they give more to the group than if they have had no prior discussion. Moreover, this effect is specific to the in-group with whom the discussion occurred; allocation to an out-group is not enhanced by discussion. Based on this research, Dawes and colleagues (1990) draw a sweeping conclusion:

Our experiments have led us to conclude that cooperation rates can be radically affected by one factor in particular, which is independent of the consequences for the choosing individual. That factor is group identity. Such identity—or solidarity—can be established and consequently enhance cooperative responding in the absence of any expectation of future reciprocity, current reward or punishment, or even reputational consequences among other group members. Moreover, this identity operates independently of the dictates of conscience. In other words, our experiments indicate that group solidarity increases cooperation independently of the side payments—either external or internal—often associated with such identity (p. 99).

In sum, Dawes and associates claim evidence for collectivist prosocial motivation independent of egoism.

I must confess that I am not yet convinced. As Dawes and his colleagues point out, there are two major egoistic explanations for an individual choosing to benefit the group in a social dilemma: (a) enlightened self-interest and (b) socially instilled conscience. The former may find expression in some form of social contract or in anticipated reciprocity; the latter rests on anticipated social or self-censure for failure to act normatively and on related feelings of shame and guilt. Each appeals to *side payments*, to nonmaterial self-benefits that make cooperation preferable to keeping the money oneself as a means of enhancing one's own welfare.

Dawes and his associates claim to have eliminated all side payments from their experiments by making participants' choices anonymous and by providing some participants with the choice between allocating to themselves or to the in-group, whereas others are provided with the choice between allocating to themselves or to an out-group. They claim that a socially instilled norm to cooperate would dictate allocation to the out-group just as much as to the in-group. Yet this seems doubtful. The research on norms reviewed earlier suggests that norms can be more refined than Dawes and his co-workers allow. We may have a norm that says "share with your buddies" rather than a norm that says "share." Underscoring this possibility, Dawes and his colleagues found that during the discussion period in their experiments participants often made (and elicited from others) promises to cooperate. Promises were, of course, made only to members of the in-group with whom participants discussed, not to members of the out-group. Reneging on a promise in order to gain a few dollars may be no small side cost for most people. Even if others do not know that you reneged, you know.

Further complicating matters, in an earlier experiment by Dawes and colleagues some groups faced with a social dilemma had prior discussion but were not allowed to discuss the dilemma and possible strategies. In these groups, discussion did not increase cooperative responses (Dawes, McTavish, & Shaklee, 1977). This lack of increase seems hard to explain if, as Dawes and his associates (1990) claim, the personalizing contact of discussion evokes group identity and collectivist prosocial motivation. Instead, this result seems to suggest that the motivation of participants who discuss is enlightened egoism: If possible, they use the discussion to create a social contract to protect their self-interest; if not, they pursue self-interest directly.

To discount these interpretative problems, Dawes and his co-workers (1990) turned to research participants' self-reports of why they cooperated. When there was no prior discussion, most cooperators cited "doing the right thing" as their major motive; when there was discussion, most cited "group welfare." These self-reports are certainly of interest and are suggestive, but I do not believe they are enough to justify the conclusion that collectivist prosocial motivation is not reducible to egoism. More and better evidence is needed. Perhaps some of the research procedures used to test egoistic alternatives to the empathy-altruism hypothesis could be used to provide clearer evidence.

Principlism: Benefiting Another to Uphold a Moral Principle

Principlism is motivation with the ultimate goal of upholding some moral principle, such as justice or the greatest good for the greatest number. It is probably not surprising that most moral philosophers have argued for the importance of a prosocial motive other than egoism. But most moral philosophers since Kant (1724–1804) have argued for a prosocial motive other than altruism and collectivism as well. These philosophers reject appeals to feelings of empathy, sympathy, and compassion as a source of prosocial motivation because they find these emotions too fickle and too circumscribed. We do not feel empathy for everyone in need, at least not to the same degree. They reject appeals to collectivist prosocial motivation because this motivation is bounded by the limits of the collective. Group identity not only permits but may even encourage doing harm to those not included. Given these problems with altruism and collectivism, moral philosophers have typically called for prosocial motivation with an ultimate goal of upholding some universal and impartial moral principle.

Universal and Impartial Moral Principles

Kant, for example, argued that the Judeo-Christian commandment to love one's neighbor as oneself should be understood as a moral principle to be upheld rather than as an expression of personal compassion or social identity (1785/1889, Section 1, paragraph 13). Tolstoy echoed Kant's view, calling the law of love "the highest principle of life" and asserting that laws should be "free from anything personal, from the smallest drop of personal bias towards its object. And such love can only be felt for one's enemy, for those who hate and offend" (1908/1987, p. 230). Similarly, the utilitarian principle of the greatest good for the greatest number is universal and impartial; it affirms that one should give no more weight to what is good for oneself than to what is good for someone else (Mill, 1861).

More recently, John Rawls (1971) has argued for a principle of justice based on the allocation of goods to the members of society from an initial position behind the Veil of Ignorance, where no one knows his or her place in society— prince or pauper, laborer or lawyer, male or female, black or white. Why does Rawls require such a stance? Because it eliminates partiality and seduction by special interest. A universal, impartial principle of justice much like Rawls' is the basis for Lawrence Kohlberg's (1976) postconventional or principled moral reasoning, the highest level in his stage model of moral development.

Universalist, impartial views of morality have not gone unchallenged. Writers like Lawrence Blum (1980), Carol Gilligan (1982), Thomas Nagel (1991), Nel Noddings (1984), Joan Tronto (1987), and Bernard Williams (1981) call for recognition of forms of morality that allow for special interest in the welfare of certain others or certain relationships. In opposition to an ethic based on justice and fairness, these writers propose an ethic of care. Sometimes, it seems that these writers are proposing care as an alternative principle to justice, either as a substitute for justice or in dynamic tension with it; at other times, it seems that they are proposing care as an alternative to principled morality altogether. If care is an alternative principle, then it too might be an expression of principlism; one might act to benefit others as a means to uphold the principle of care. If, however, care is a special feeling—(a) for another individual, (b) for oneself, or (c) for a relationship—that inclines one to act, and it has at times been presented as each, then care would seem to be a form of altruism, egoism, or collectivism, respectively.

Does Principlism Exist?

Is acting with an ultimate goal of upholding some moral principle really possible? When Kant briefly shifted his focus from analysis of what ought to be to what is, he was ready to admit that even when the concern we show for others appears to be prompted by duty to principle, it may actually be prompted by self-love (1785/1889, Section 2, paragraph 2). The goal of upholding a moral principle may, then, only be an instrumental goal, a means to reach the ultimate goal of self-benefit. If so, the principle-based prosocial motivation is actually egoistic.

When one begins to look for possible self-benefits attained by upholding a moral principle, one finds many: One gains the social and self-rewards of being seen and seeing oneself as a good person; even more plausible perhaps, one avoids the social and self-punishments of shame and guilt for failing to do the right thing. Any or all of these self-benefits could be the ultimate goal of wanting to uphold a moral principle. As Freud suggested in *Civilization and Its Discontents* (1930), society may inculcate such principles in the young in order to bridle our antisocial impulses by making it in our best personal interest to act morally (also see Campbell, 1975).

The issue here is much the same as it was for altruism and for collectivism. Once again, we need to know the nature of a prosocial motive: Is the desire to love one's neighbor, to uphold justice, to respect and preserve human life, etc., an instrumental goal on the way to the ultimate goal of self-benefit? If so, then principled morality is a subtle and sophisticated form of egoism. Alternatively, is this desire the ultimate goal, with the ensuing self-benefits unintended consequences? If so, then principlism is a fourth form of prosocial motivation, independent of egoism, altruism, and collectivism.

At this point, I do not think anyone knows the answers to these questions. We have empirical evidence, limited and weak, that adherence to at least some moral principles, such as Kohlberg's (1976) principle of universal justice, can lead to increased prosocial behavior (Eisenberg, 1991b; Emler, Renwick, & Malone, 1983; Erkut, Jaquette, & Staub, 1981; Sparks & Durkin, 1987;

Underwood & Moore, 1982). But to the best of my knowledge, there is no empirical evidence that justice or any other moral principle is or can be upheld as an ultimate goal. Nor is there empirical evidence that rules this possibility out.

To ascertain the ultimate goal of the motivation to uphold a moral principle, we need to follow the same steps used to test for the existence of altruistic motivation. First, we need to think carefully to come up with plausible egoistic explanations of the principle-helping relationship. Then, self-benefit by self-benefit, we need to conduct experiments to vary conditions, leading individuals to believe that acting in a principled way either is necessary to gain a given self-benefit or is not necessary. If the principle-helping relationship disappears when the upholding of the principle is not necessary in order to gain the self-benefit, then we have evidence that obtaining this self-benefit was the ultimate goal; if it does not disappear, then we have evidence to the contrary. In this way, we may be able to determine whether acting out of a sense of pure duty to principle, as Kant advocated, is only a prescriptive ideal or is an empirical possibility.

Prosocial Implications of Moral Principles

If individuals act on principle only to gain rewards or avoid punishment, then we may expect antipathy to develop between the spirit of the principle and the inclination of the individual, just as antipathy is likely to develop in a child who studies to get rewards (Lepper, Greene, & Nisbett, 1973). Moral principles will be experienced as a drag, something we wish to be free from—although we may wish them to bind other people. As a result, our adherence to these principles will likely be selective and limited, reminiscent of the behavior of Trivers' cheaters. If we can gain the rewards and avoid the punishments without incurring the cost of acting on the principle, then we should jump at the chance. And often we can.

Most of us are quite adept at rationalization, at justifying to ourselves—if not to others—why a situation that benefits us or those we care about does not violate our moral principles. Why, in Jonathan Kozol's (1991) apt phrase, the "savage inequalities" between the public school systems of rich and poor communities in the United States are not really unjust. Why storing our nuclear waste in someone else's backyard or our using a disproportionate amount of the earth's natural resources is fair. Why terrorist attacks by our side are regrettable but necessary evils, whereas terrorist attacks by the other side are atrocities. The abstractness of most moral principles makes such rationalization especially easy.

Our skill in dodging the thrust of the moral principles we espouse may explain the disappointingly weak empirical relation between principled morality and prosocial action (Eisenberg, 1991b). It is at least possible that moral principles are used more to censure or extol others' actions than to motivate our own.

To the extent that moral principles are adhered to as a means to the end of gaining rewards or avoiding punishments, much of the potential that has attracted philosophers to rationally derived universal and impartial moral principles is lost. If principlism is only a special case of egoism, then it seems at least as fragile and fickle a source of prosocial action as altruism or collectivism. On the other hand, if upholding moral principles can serve as an ultimate goal, defining a form of prosocial motivation independent of egoism, then perhaps these principles can provide a rational basis for caring for others that transcends reliance on self-interest or on vested interest in and feeling for the welfare of certain other individuals or groups. At this point, we do not know which possibility is true; it seems well worth conducting research to find out.

SUMMARY AND CONCLUSION

Why do we act prosocially, benefiting others even at considerable cost to ourselves? What does this behavior tell us about our capacity to care, about the degree of interconnectedness among us, about how social an animal we humans really are? These classic philosophical questions have resurfaced in the behavioral and social sciences in the past decade or so. Sociobiologists have suggested ways in which benefiting others can be predicted from the theory of natural selection, but they have not addressed the question of motives. Social psychologists have begun to address the question of the nature of prosocial motivation by drawing on (a) Kurt Lewin's ideas about goal-directed motivation and the resulting distinctions among instrumental goals, ultimate goals, and unintended consequences, and (b) the experimental research methods that have become their trademark over the past 50 years.

Specifically, social-psychological research has, first, added to and documented a long list of self-benefits that may serve as the ultimate goal of egoistic prosocial motives. This list includes material, social, and self-rewards to be obtained; material, social, and self-punishments to be avoided; and three forms of aversive arousal to be reduced.

Social-psychological research has also been used to test the claim that altruistic prosocial motives—motives with the ultimate goal of increasing another's welfare—exist that are independent of and irreducible to egoistic motives. Results of the over 25 experiments designed to test the empathy-altruism hypothesis against egoistic alternatives have proved remarkably supportive of this hypothesis, leading to the tentative conclusion that feeling empathy for a person in need evokes altruistic motivation to help that person. Sources of altruistic motivation other than empathy have also been proposed, but as yet, we lack compelling research evidence to support these proposals.

Thinking beyond the egoism-altruism debate, two additional forms of prosocial motivation seem especially worthy of consideration: collectivism and principlism. Collectivism—motivation with the ultimate goal of benefiting some group or collective as a whole—has been claimed to result from group identity and to account for prosocial responses to social dilemmas. Principlism—motivation with the ultimate goal of upholding some moral principle—has long been advocated by religious teachers and moral philosophers. Whether either is a separate form of prosocial motivation, independent of and irreducible to egoism, is not yet clear. The research done to test the independent status of empathy-induced altruism from egoism may serve as a useful model for future research assessing the independent status of collectivism and principlism.

We know more now than a few years ago about why we act to benefit others. As a result, we know more about human motivation in general and even about human nature. These are substantial gains. Still, many questions remain about prosocial motivation and the motivational resources we can tap in trying to build a more caring, humane society. Fortunately, our legacy from Lewin—both his rich conceptual framework for understanding motivation and his use of laboratory experiments to isolate and identify complex social motives—places social psychologists in an ideal situation to provide further answers. A lot may rest on our ability to marshal these resources and deliver.

References

ALFANO, G., & MARWELL, G. (1980). Experiments on the provision of public goods by groups III: Non-divisibility and free riding in "real" groups. *Social Psychology Quarterly, 43,* 300–309.

AXELROD, R., & HAMILTON, W. D. (1981). The evolution of cooperation. *Science, 211,* 1390–1396.

BATSON, C. D. (1987). Prosocial motivation: Is it ever truly altruistic? In L. Berkowitz (Ed.), *Advances in experimental social psychology* (Vol. 20, pp. 65–122). New York: Academic Press.

BATSON, C. D. (1991). *The altruism question: Toward a social-psychological answer.* Hillsdale, NJ: Erlbaum Associates.

BATSON, C. D., BATSON, J. G., GRIFFITT, C. A., BARRIENTOS, S., BRANDT, J. R., SPRENGELMEYER, P., & BAYLY, M. J. (1989). Negative-state relief and the empathy-altruism hypothesis. *Journal of Personality and Social Psychology, 56,* 922–933.

BATSON, C. D., BATSON, J. G., SLINGSBY, J. K., HARRELL, K. L., PEEKNA, H. M., & TODD, R. M. (1991). Empathic joy and the empathy-altruism hypothesis. *Journal of Personality and Social Psychology, 61,* 413–426.

BATSON, C. D., BOLEN, M. H., CROSS, J. A., & NEURINGER-BENEFIEL, H. E. (1986). Where is the altruism in the altruistic personality? *Journal of Personality and Social Psychology, 50,* 212–220.

BATSON, C. D., COCHRAN, P. J., BIEDERMAN, M. F., BLOSSER, J. L., RYAN, M. J., & VOGT, B. (1978). Failure to help when in a hurry: Callousness or conflict? *Personality and Social Psychology Bulletin, 4,* 97–101.

BATSON, C. D., DUNCAN, B., ACKERMAN, P., BUCKLEY, T., & BIRCH, K. (1981). Is empathic emotion a source of altruistic motivation? *Journal of Personality and Social Psychology, 40,* 290–302.

BATSON, C. D., DYCK, J. L., BRANDT, J. R., BATSON, J. G., POWELL, A. L., MCMASTER, M. R., & GRIFFITT, C. (1988). Five studies testing two new egoistic alternatives to the empathy-altruism hypothesis. *Journal of Personality and Social Psychology, 55,* 52–77.

BENTHAM, J. (1876). *An introduction to the principles of morals and legislation.* Oxford: The Clarendon Press. (Original work published in 1789.)

BERKOWITZ, L. (1972). Social norms, feelings, and other factors affecting helping and altruism. In L. Berkowitz (Ed.), *Advances in experimental social psychology* (Vol. 6, pp. 63–108). New York: Academic Press.

BERKOWITZ, L. (1987). Mood, self-awareness, and willingness to help. *Journal of Personality and Social Psychology, 52,* 721–729.

BICKMAN, L. (1972). Social influence and diffusion of responsibility in an emergency. *Journal of Experimental Social Psychology, 8,* 438–445.

BLUM, L. A. (1980). *Friendship, altruism, and morality.* London: Routledge & Kegan Paul.

BREWER, M. B., & KRAMER, R. M. (1986). Choice behavior in social dilemmas: Effects of social identity, group size, and decision framing. *Journal of Personality and Social Psychology, 50,* 543–549.

BUCK, R., & GINSBURG, B. (1991). Spontaneous communication and altruism: The communicative gene hypothesis. In M. S. Clark (Ed.), *Prosocial behavior* (pp. 149–175). Newbury Park, CA: Sage.

CAMPBELL, D. T. (1975). On the conflicts between biological and social evolution and between psychology and moral tradition. *American Psychologist, 30,* 1103–1126.

CIALDINI, R. B., DARBY, B. L., & VINCENT, J. E. (1973). Transgression and altruism: A case for hedonism. *Journal of Experimental Social Psychology, 9,* 502–516.

CIALDINI, R. B., KALLGREN, C. A., & RENO, R. R. (1991). A focus theory of normative conduct: A theoretical refinement and reevaluation of the role of norms in human behavior. In M. P. Zanna (Ed.), *Advances in experimental social psychology* (Vol. 24, pp. 201–234). Orlando, FL: Academic Press.

CIALDINI, R. B., SCHALLER, M., HOULIHAN, D., ARPS, K., FULTZ, J., & BEAMAN, A. L. (1987). Empathy-based helping: Is it selflessly or selfishly motivated? *Journal of Personality and Social Psychology, 52,* 749–758.

CLARK, M. S., & WADDELL, B. A. (1983). Effect of moods on thoughts about helping, attraction, and information acquisition. *Social Psychology Quarterly, 46,* 31–35.

CLARK, R. D., & WORD, L. E. (1972). Why don't bystanders help? Because of ambiguity? *Journal of Personality and Social Psychology, 24,* 392–401.

COKE, J. S., BATSON, C. D., & MCDAVIS, K. (1978). Empathic mediation of helping: A two-stage model. *Journal of Personality and Social Psychology, 36,* 752–766.

CUNNINGHAM, M. R., SHAFFER, D. R., BARBEE, A. P., WOLFF, P. L., & KELLEY, D. J. (1990). Separate processes in the relation of elation and depression to helping: Social versus personal concerns. *Journal of Experimental Social Psychology, 26,* 13–33.

DARLEY, J. M., & BATSON, C. D. (1973). From Jerusalem to Jericho: A study of situational and dispositional variables in helping behavior. *Journal of Personality and Social Psychology, 27,* 100–108.

DARLEY, J. M., & LATANÉ, B. (1968). Bystander intervention in emergencies: Diffusion of responsibility. *Journal of Personality and Social Psychology, 10,* 202–214.

DARLEY, J. M., & LATANÉ, B. (1970). Norms and normative behavior: Field studies of social interdependence. In J. Macaulay & L. Berkowitz (Eds.), *Altruism and helping behavior* (pp. 83–101). New York: Academic Press.

DARLEY, J. M., TEGER, A., & LEWIS, L. (1973). Do groups always inhibit individuals' responses to potential emergencies? *Journal of Personality and Social Psychology, 26,* 395–399.

DAWES, R. M. (1980). Social dilemmas. *Annual Review of Psychology, 31,* 169–193.

DAWES, R. M., MCTAVISH, J., & SHAKLEE, H. (1977). Behavior, communication, and assumptions about other people's behavior in a commons dilemma situation. *Journal of Personality and Social Psychology, 35,* 1–11.

DAWES, R., VAN DE KRAGT, A. J. C., & ORBELL, J. M. (1988). Not me or thee but we: The importance of group identity in eliciting cooperation in dilemma situations: Experimental manipulations. *Acta Psychologica, 68,* 83–97.

DAWES, R., VAN DE KRAGT, A. J. C., & ORBELL, J. M. (1990). Cooperation for the benefit of us—not me, or my conscience. In J. J. Mansbridge (Ed.), *Beyond self-interest* (pp. 97–110). Chicago: University of Chicago Press.

DAWKINS, R. (1976). *The selfish gene.* New York: Oxford University Press.

DOVIDIO, J. F., ALLEN, J. L., & SCHROEDER, D. A. (1990). The specificity of empathy-induced helping: Evidence for altruistic motivation. *Journal of Personality and Social Psychology, 59,* 249–260.

DOVIDIO, J. F., SCHROEDER, D. A., ALLEN, J. L., & MATTHEWS, L. L. (1986, March). Altruistic versus egoistic motivations for helping. Paper presented at the annual meeting of the Southeastern Psychological Association, Orlando, FL.

DOVIDIO, J. F., PILIAVIN, J. A., GAERTNER, S. L., SCHROEDER, D. A., & CLARK, R. D., III (1991). The arousal:cost-reward model and the process of intervention: A review of the evidence. In M. S. Clark (Ed.), *Prosocial behavior* (pp. 86–118). Newbury Park, CA: Sage.

EISENBERG, N. (1991a). Values, sympathy, and individual differences: Toward a pluralism of factors influencing altruism and empathy. *Psychological Inquiry, 2,* 128–131.

EISENBERG, N. (1991b). Meta-analytic contributions to the literature on prosocial behavior. *Personality and Social Psychology Bulletin, 17,* 273–282.

EISENBERG, N., & MILLER, P. (1987). Empathy and prosocial behavior. *Psychological Bulletin, 101,* 91–119.

EISENBERG, N., MILLER, P. A., SCHALLER, M., FABES, R. A., FULTZ, J., SHELL, R., & SHEA, C. L. (1989). The role of sympathy and altruistic personality traits in helping: A re-examination. *Journal of Personality, 57,* 41–67.

EMLER, N., RENWICK, S., & MALONE, B. (1983). The relationship between moral reasoning and political orientation. *Journal of Personality and Social Psychology, 45,* 1073–1080.

EPICTETUS. (1877). *The discourses of Epictetus: With the Encheiridion and fragments* (G. Long, Trans.). London: George Bell & Sons.

ERKUT, S., JAQUETTE, D. S., & STAUB, E. (1981). Moral judgment-situation interaction as a basis for predicting prosocial behavior. *Journal of Personality, 49,* 1–14.

FESTINGER, L. (1957). *A theory of cognitive dissonance.* Stanford, CA: Stanford University Press.

FREUD, S. (1930). *Civilization and its discontents* (J. Riviere, Trans.). London: Hogarth.

FULTZ, J., BATSON, C. D., FORTENBACH, V. A., MCCARTHY, P. M., & VARNEY, L. L. (1986). Social evaluation and the empathy-altruism hypothesis. *Journal of Personality and Social Psychology, 50,* 761–769.

GERGEN, K. J., ELLSWORTH, P., MASLACH, C., & SEIPEL, M. (1975). Obligation, donor resources, and reactions to aid in 3 cultures. *Journal of Personality and Social Psychology, 31,* 390–400.

GHESLIN, M. T. (1974). *The economy of nature and the evolution of sex.* Berkeley: University of California Press.

GIBBONS, F. X., & WICKLUND, R. A. (1982). Self-focused attention and helping behavior. *Journal of Personality and Social Psychology, 43,* 462–474.

GIES, M. (1987). *Anne Frank remembered: The story of the woman who helped to hide the Frank family.* New York: Simon & Schuster.

GILLIGAN, C. (1982). *In a different voice: Psychological theory and women's development.* Cambridge, MA: Harvard University Press.

GOODALL, J. (1990). *Through a window: My thirty years with the chimpanzees of Gombe.* Boston: Houghton Mifflin.

GOULDNER, A. W. (1960). The norm of reciprocity: A preliminary statement. *American Sociological Review, 25,* 161–179.

HAMILTON, W. D. (1964). The genetical theory of social behavior (I, II). *Journal of Theoretical Biology, 7,* 1–52.

HAMILTON, W. D. (1971). Selection of selfish and altruistic behavior in some extreme models. In J. F. Eisenberg & W. S. Dillon (Eds.), *Man and beast: Comparative social behavior.* Washington, D. C.: Smithsonian Institution Press.

HATFIELD, E., WALSTER, G. W., & PILIAVIN, J. A. (1978). Equity theory and helping relationships. In L. Wispé (Ed.), *Altruism, sympathy, and helping: Psychological and sociological principles* (pp. 115–139). New York: Academic Press.

HEBB, D. O. (1949). *The organization of behavior: A neuropsychological theory.* New York: Wiley.

HEBB, D. O., & THOMPSON, R. (1968). The social significance of animal studies. In G. Lindzey & E. Aronson (Eds.), *The handbook of social psychology* (2nd ed., Vol. 2). Reading, MA: Addison-Wesley.

HOFFMAN, M. L. (1976). Empathy, role-taking, guilt, and development of altruistic motives. In T. Lickona (Ed.), *Moral development and behavior: Theory, research, and social issues* (pp. 124–143). New York: Holt, Rinehart & Winston.

HOFFMAN, M. L. (1981a). Is altruism part of human nature? *Journal of Personality and Social Psychology, 40,* 121–137.

HOFFMAN, M. L. (1981b). The development of empathy. In J. P. Rushton & R. M. Sorrentino (Eds.), *Altruism and helping behavior: Social, personality, and developmental perspectives* (pp. 41–63). Hillsdale, NJ: Erlbaum.

HUME, D. (1896). *A treatise of human nature* (L. A. Selby-Bigge, Ed.). Oxford: Oxford University Press. (Original work published in 1740.)

ISEN, A. M. (1970). Success, failure, attention and reaction to others: The warm glow of success. *Journal of Personality and Social Psychology, 15,* 294–301.

ISEN, A. M. (1987). Positive affect, cognitive organization, and social behavior. In L. Berkowitz (Ed.), *Advances in experimental social psychology* (Vol. 20). New York: Academic Press.

ISEN, A. M., & LEVIN, P. F. (1972). Effect of feeling good on helping: Cookies and kindness. *Journal of Personality and Social Psychology, 21,* 344–348.

ISEN, A. M., SHALKER, T. E., CLARK, M., & KARP, L. (1978). Affect, accessibility of material in memory, and behavior: A cognitive loop? *Journal of Personality and Social Psychology, 36,* 1–13.

JAMES, W. (1890). *Principles of psychology* (Vol. 1). New York: Henry Holt.

JONES, E. E. (1964). *Ingratiation.* New York: Appleton-Century-Crofts.

KANT, I. (1889). *Kant's Critique of Practical Reason and other works on the theory of ethics* (4th ed.) (T. K. Abbott, Trans.). New York: Longmans, Green & Co. (Original work published in 1785.)

KOHLBERG, L. (1976). Moral stages and moralization: The cognitive-developmental approach. In T. Lickona (Ed.), *Moral development and behavior: Theory, research, and social issues* (pp. 31–53). New York: Holt, Rinehart & Winston.

KOZOL, J. (1991). *Savage inequalities: Children in America's schools.* New York: Crown.

KRAMER, R. M., & BREWER, M. B. (1984). Effects of group identity on resource use in a simulated commons dilemma. *Journal of Personality and Social Psychology, 46,* 1044–1057.

KREBS, D. L. (1975). Empathy and altruism. *Journal of Personality and Social Psychology, 32,* 1134–1146.

LA ROCHEFOUCAULD, F., DUKE DE (1691). *Moral maxims and reflections, in four parts.* London: Gillyflower, Sare, & Everyingham.

LATANÉ, B., & DARLEY, J. M. (1968). Group inhibition of bystander intervention. *Journal of Personality and Social Psychology, 10,* 215–221.

LATANÉ, B., & DARLEY, J. M. (1970). *The unresponsive bystander: Why doesn't he help?* New York: Appleton-Century-Crofts.

LATANÉ, B., & NIDA, S. A. (1981). Ten years of research on group size and helping. *Psychological Bulletin, 89,* 308–324.

LATANÉ, B., & RODIN, J. A. (1969). A lady in distress: Inhibiting effects of friends and strangers on bystander intervention. *Journal of Experimental Social Psychology, 5,* 189–202.

LAWICK, H. VAN, & LAWICK-GOODALL, J. VAN (1971). *Innocent killers.* Boston: Houghton Mifflin.

LEPPER, M. R., GREENE, D., & NISBETT, R. E. (1973). Undermining children's intrinsic interest with extrinsic reward: A test of the "overjustification" hypothesis. *Journal of Personality and Social Psychology, 28,* 129–137.

LERNER, M. J. (1980). *The belief in a just world: A fundamental delusion.* New York: Plenum.

LERNER, M. J., & SIMMONS, C. H. (1966). Observer's reaction to the "innocent victim": Compassion or rejection? *Journal of Personality and Social Psychology, 4,* 203–210.

LEVIN, P. F., & ISEN, A. M. (1975). Further studies on the effect of feeling good on helping. *Sociometry, 38,* 141–147.

LEWIN, K. (1935). *Dynamic theory of personality.* New York: McGraw-Hill.

LEWIN, K. (1951). *Field theory in social science.* New York: Harper.

LUCE, R. D., & RAIFFA, H. (1957). *Games and decisions: Introduction and critical survey.* New York: Wiley.

McDOUGALL, W. (1908). *Introduction to social psychology.* London: Methuen.

MacINTYRE, A. (1967). Egoism and altruism. In P. Edwards (Ed.), *The encyclopedia of philosophy* (Vol. 2, pp. 462–466). New York: Macmillan.

MacINTYRE, J. (1974). *Mind in the waters.* New York: Scribners.

MANSBRIDGE, J. J. (Ed.) (1990). *Beyond self-interest.* Chicago: University of Chicago Press.

MANUCIA, G. K., BAUMANN, D. J., & CIALDINI, R. B. (1984). Mood influences on helping: Direct effects or side effects? *Journal of Personality and Social Psychology, 46,* 357–364.

MILL, J. S. (1861). *Utilitarianism.* London: Parker, Son, & Bourn.

MILLER, D. T., & McFARLAND, C. (1987). Pluralistic ignorance: When similarity is interpreted as dissimilarity. *Journal of Personality and Social Psychology, 53,* 298–305.

MILLS, J., & EGGER, R. (1972). Effect on derogation of a victim of choosing to reduce his stress. *Journal of Personality and Social Psychology, 23,* 405–408.

MILO, R. D. (Ed.). (1973). *Egoism and altruism.* Belmont, CA: Wadsworth.

NAGEL, T. (1970). *The possibility of altruism.* Princeton, NJ: Princeton University Press.

NAGEL, T. (1991). *Equality and partiality.* New York: Oxford University Press.

NIETZSCHE, F. (1927). Ecce homo. In *The philosophy of Nietzsche* (C. P. Fadiman, Trans.). New York: Random House. (Original work published in 1888.)

NODDINGS, N. (1984). *Caring: A feminine approach to ethics and moral education.* Berkeley: University of California Press.

OLINER, S. P., & OLINER, P. M. (1988). *The altruistic personality: Rescuers of Jews in Nazi Europe.* New York: The Free Press.

ORBELL, J. M., VAN DE KRAGT, A. J., & DAWES, R. M. (1988). Explaining discussion-induced cooperation. *Journal of Personality and Social Psychology, 54,* 811–819.

PILIAVIN, I. M., PILIAVIN, J. A., & RODIN, J. (1975). Costs, diffusion, and the stigmatized victim. *Journal of Personality and Social Psychology, 32,* 429–438.

PILIAVIN, J. A., DOVIDIO, J. F., GAERTNER, S. L., & CLARK, R. D., III (1981). *Emergency intervention,.* New York: Academic Press.

PRUITT, D. G. (1968). Reciprocity and credit building in a laboratory dyad. *Journal of Personality and Social Psychology, 8,* 143–147.

RAND, A. (1964). *The virtue of selfishness: A new concept of egoism.* New York: New American Library.

RAPOPORT, A., & CHAMMAH, A. M. (1965). *Prisoner's dilemma.* Ann Arbor: University of Michigan Press.

RAWLS, J. (1971). *A theory of justice.* Cambridge, MA: Harvard University Press.

REYKOWSKI, J. (1982). Motivation of prosocial behavior. In V. J. Derlega & J. Grzelak (Eds.), *Cooperation and helping behavior: Theories and research* (pp. 352–375). New York: Academic Press.

ROSS, A. S., & BRABAND, J. (1973). Effect of increased responsibility on bystander intervention II: The cue value of a blind person. *Journal of Personality and Social Psychology, 25,* 254–258.

RYAN, W. (1971). *Blaming the victim.* New York: Random House.

SAGI, A., & HOFFMAN, M. L. (1976). Empathic distress in newborns. *Developmental Psychology, 12,* 175–176.

SCHALLER, M., & CIALDINI, R. B. (1988). The economics of empathic helping: Support for a mood-management motive. *Journal of Experimental Social Psychology, 24,* 163–181.

SCHROEDER, D. A., DOVIDIO, J. F., SIBICKY, M. E., MATTHEWS, L. L., & ALLEN, J. L. (1988). Empathy and helping behavior: Egoism or altruism? *Journal of Experimental Social Psychology, 24,* 333–353.

SCHWARTZ, S. H. (1977). Normative influences on altruism. In L. Berkowitz (Ed.), *Advances in experimental social psychology* (Vol. 10). New York: Academic Press.

SCHWARTZ, S. H., & CLAUSEN, G. T. (1970). Responsibility, norms, and helping in an emergency. *Journal of Personality and Social Psychology, 16,* 299–310.

SIKES, S. K. (1971). *The natural history of the African elephant.* New York: American Elsevier Publications.

SIMON, H. (1990). A mechanism for social selection and successful altruism. *Science, 250,* 1665–1668.

SMITH, A. (1853). *The theory of moral sentiments.* London: Henry G. Bohn. (Original work published in 1759.)

SMITH, K. D., KEATING, J. P., & STOTLAND, E. (1989). Altruism reconsidered: The effect of denying feedback on a victim's status to empathic witnesses. *Journal of Personality and Social Psychology, 57,* 641–650.

SPARKS, P., & DURKIN, K. (1987). Moral reasoning and political orientation: The context sensitivity of individual rights and democratic principles. *Journal of Personality and Social Psychology, 52,* 931–936.

STAUB, E. (1974). Helping a distressed person: Social, personality, and stimulus determinants. In L. Berkowitz (Ed.), *Advances in experimental social psychology* (Vol. 7, pp. 293–341). New York: Academic Press.

STOTLAND, E. (1969). Exploratory studies of empathy. In L. Berkowitz (Ed.), *Advances in experimental social psychology* (Vol. 4, pp. 271–313). New York: Academic Press.

TAJFEL, H. (1981). *Human groups and social categories: Studies in social psychology.* Cambridge: Cambridge University Press.

TAJFEL, H., & TURNER, J. C. (1986). The social identity theory of intergroup behavior. In S. Worchel & W. Austin (Eds.), *Psychology of intergroup relations* (pp. 7–24). Chicago: Nelson-Hall.

TOI, M., & BATSON, C. D. (1982). More evidence that empathy is a source of altruistic motivation. *Journal of Personality and Social Psychology, 43,* 281–292.

TOLMAN, E. C. (1923). The nature of instinct. *Psychological Bulletin, 20,* 200–218.

TOLMAN, E. C. (1932). *Purposive behavior in animals and men.* New York: Century.

TOLSTOY, L. (1987). The law of love and the law of violence. In *A confession and other religious writings* (J. Kentish, Trans.). London: Penguin Books. (Original work published in 1908.)

TRIVERS, R. L. (1971). The evolution of reciprocal altruism. *Quarterly Review of Biology, 46,* 35–57.

TRONTO, J. (1987). Beyond gender differences to a theory of care. *Signs, 12,* 644–663.

TURNER, J. C. (1987). *Rediscovering the social group: A self-categorization theory.* London: Basil Blackwell.

UNDERWOOD, B., & MOORE, B. (1982). Perspective-taking and altruism. *Psychological Bulletin, 91,* 143–173.

WALLACH, M. A., & WALLACH, L. (1983). *Psychology's sanction for selfishness: The error of egoism in theory and therapy.* San Francisco: W. H. Freeman.

WEYANT, J. M. (1978). Effects of mood states, costs, and benefits on helping. *Journal of Personality and Social Psychology, 36,* 1169–1176.

WILKE, H., & LANZETTA, J. T. (1970). The obligation to help: The effects of amount of prior help on subsequent helping behavior. *Journal of Experimental Social Psychology, 6,* 483–493.

WILKE, H., & LANZETTA, J. T. (1982). The obligation to help: Factors affecting response to help received. *European Journal of Social Psychology, 12,* 315–319.

WILLIAMS, B. (1981). Persons, character, and morality. In B. Williams, *Moral luck: Philosophical papers 1973–1980* (pp. 1–19). Cambridge: Cambridge University Press.

WILSON, E. O. (1975). *Sociobiology: The new synthesis.* Cambridge, MA: Belkap Press of Harvard University Press.

WUTHNOW, R. (1991). *Acts of compassion: Caring for others and helping ourselves.* Princeton, NJ: Princeton University Press.

YAMAGISHI, T., & SATO, K. (1986). Motivational bases of the public goods problem. *Journal of Personality and Social Psychology, 50,* 67–73.

ZUCKERMAN, M. (1975). Belief in a just world and altruistic behavior. *Journal of Personality and Social Psychology, 31,* 972–976.

ZUCKERMAN, M., & REIS, H. T. (1978). Comparison of three models for predicting altruistic behavior. *Journal of Personality and Social Psychology, 36,* 498–510.

Further Readings

BATSON, C. D. (1991). *The altruism question: Toward a social-psychological answer.* Hillsdale, NJ: Erlbaum Associates.

Reviews arguments and empirical evidence for the existence of altruism, especially the recent social-psychological research on the empathy-altruism hypothesis.

CLARK, M. S. (Ed.). (1991). *Prosocial behavior.* Newbury Park, CA: Sage Publications.

Presents a sampler of recent social-psychological theory and research on helping behavior.

DAWKINS, R. (1976). *The selfish gene.* New York: Oxford University Press.

A delightfully written introduction to sociobiological thinking about altruism.

EISENBERG, N. (Ed.). (1982). *The development of prosocial behavior.* New York: Academic Press.

Presents chapters by major developmental psychologists who have contributed to theory and research on helping behavior.

FREUD, S. (1930). *Civilization and its discontents* (J. Riviere, Trans.). London: Hogarth.

A provocative classic, outlining why and how society cajoles us into moral action.

GILLIGAN, C. (1982). *In a different voice: Psychological theory and women's development.* Cambridge, MA: Harvard University Press.

Proposes a morality of care and mutual responsibility as an alternative to Kohlberg's morality of justice.

LATANÉ, B., & DARLEY, J. M. (1970). *The unresponsible bystander: Why doesn't he help?* New York: Appleton-Century-Crofts.

A social-psychological classic summarizing theory and research on bystander intervention.

LEWIN, K. (1951). *Field theory in social science.* New York: Harper.

Collection of papers by Lewin presenting his ideas on the nature of science, on motives as goal-directed forces in the life space, and on group process.

MANSBRIDGE, J. J. (Ed.). (1990). *Beyond self-interest.* Chicago: University of Chicago Press.

A useful collection of recent challenges to the assumption of self-interest by sociologists, political theorists, and economists, including articles by Amartya Sen, Christopher Jenks, Robert Frank, Robyn Dawes and colleagues, Howard Margolis, and Stephen Holmes.

MESSICK, D. M., & BREWER, M. B. (1983). Solving social dilemmas: A review. In L. Wheeler & P. Shaver (Eds.), *Review of personality and social psychology* (Vol. 4, pp. 11–44). Beverly Hills, CA: Sage Publications.

Overview of theory and research on social dilemmas.

OLINER, S. P., & OLINER, P. M. (1988). *The altruistic personality: Rescuers of Jews in Nazi Europe.* New York: The Free Press.

Reports results of major research project involving interviews with rescuers of Jews in Nazi Europe.

RAWLS, J. (1971). *A theory of justice.* Cambridge, MA: Harvard University Press.

Major contemporary proposal for a morality based on universal and impartial adherence to a principle of justice.

SMITH, A. (1853). *The theory of moral sentiments.* London: Henry G. Bohn. (Original work published in 1759.)

Beautifully written discourse on emotional response to the plight of others and on the implications of these emotions for moral action and judgment.

WALLACH, M. A., & WALLACH, L. (1983). *Psychology's sanction for selfishness: The error of egoism in theory and therapy.* San Francisco: W. H. Freeman.

Critical analysis of the impact of the assumption of universal egoism on psychological theory, research, and clinical practice.

Russell G. Geen (Ph.D. University of Wisconsin, 1967) is Curator's Professor of Psychology at the University of Missouri at Columbia. He is the author of Personality: The Skein of Behavior *(1976),* Human Aggression *(1990), and* Human Motivation: A Social Psychological Approach *(1995); co-author of* Human Motivation: Physiological, Social, and Behavioral Approaches *(1984); and co-editor of* Perspectives on Aggression *(1976) and* Aggression: Theoretical and Empirical Reviews *(1983). From 1977 to 1988 he was editor of the* Journal of Research in Personality *and since 1991 has been editor of the* Journal of Personality and Social Psychology: Personality Processes and Individual Differences. *He and his wife live in Columbia in the house built by the first chairman of the psychology department, Max Meyer.*

CHAPTER 10

Human Aggression

Russell G. Geen
University of Missouri

CHAPTER OUTLINE

Aggression is part of the basic equipment of man, but it is also culturally formed, exacerbated, and can be, at least in part, redirected. Our culture is not simply a given, but is also us.

—ROLLO MAY, *POWER AND INNOCENCE*

Human aggression is explained in many ways by psychologists, with any given explanation depending on the particular orientation of the individual. Even within the subspeciality of social psychology, variation in viewpoints can be found, with some stressing cognitive factors, others pinpointing emotional and affective determinants, and still others dealing with aggression as a part of broader social interaction systems. On one matter, however, virtually all social psychologists agree Aggression is a *response to specific conditions in the environment.* What those conditions are, how their effects interact with characteristics of the person, and what psychological processes are set off by this interaction are the subjects of this chapter.

Aggression is a proper topic for social psychology because it always presupposes at least two people: an aggressor and a victim Definitions of aggression vary widely, because the term is taken from everyday speech and is used to refer to behaviors ranging from first-degree murder to verbal insults and social snubs. A precise scientific definition that is universally accepted has yet to be devised. However, a formulation that serves as a good working definition is offered by Baron and Richardson (1994): "Aggression is any form of behavior directed toward the goal of harming or injuring another living being who is motivated to avoid such treatment." This definition makes several important points: (1) It defines aggression as an act of harm doing against another person, (2) it stipulates that the harm doing is intentional, (3) it notes that the victim must regard the harm doing as aversive and unwanted, and (4) it leaves open the question of the means used by the harm doer, emphasizing instead the intent to harm.

What conditions in the environment provoke aggression? Again, no simple and universally accepted answer can be given. The eliciting conditions for aggression are often, but not always, social in nature, involving some provocation that comes from other persons. Explicit provocations—such as interpersonal conflict, frustrations, and attacks—are the ones most commonly studied. Aggression, however, may be a reaction to such stimuli as irritants in the environment which, although ultimately the handiwork of human beings, are neither direct nor, usually, intentional. We will note on a subsequent section of this chapter that the differences among the various aggression-eliciting conditions is probably not as important as what they have in common: the fact that they are all aversive.

INSTIGATORS OF AGGRESSION

Is Aggression Innate?

The study of aggression as a psychological phenomenon is of relatively recent origin. One question that has characterized this study from the beginning is, To what extent is aggressive behavior related to innate processes that are acquired through biological inheritance? The theory of aggression that prevailed in early American psychology treated aggressive behavior as something that flows from innate characteristics of the person, usually referred to as *instincts.* William James, for example, believed that aggression is so much a part of innate human nature that it can be controlled only through substitute activity whereby people drain off their instinctual aggressive drive into prosocial behavior. "Our ancestors have bred pugnacity into our bone and marrow," wrote James, "and thousands of years of peace won't breed it out of us" (James, 1910/1987, p. 1283). Earlier, William McDougall (1908) traced the innate aggressiveness of humans to a central affective-emotional arousal that is elicited by situational conditions, such as an attack or other provocation. Although the conditions that elicit this state and the behaviors that the state engenders are subject to modification through learning, the central state (which McDougall called the *instinct of pugnacity*) does not change in the person's lifetime. It is fixed and "wired into" the person, waiting only to be set off by some adequate condition.

In the second decade of the twentieth century, Freudian psychoanalysis began to receive serious attention in the United States. At that time, Freud's theorizing on the nature of aggression was based on the relation of the self to objects around it and whether those objects evoke pleasure or pain. "When the object becomes a source of pleasurable feelings," Freud wrote, ". . . we speak of the 'attraction' exercised by the pleasure-giving object, and say that we 'love' that object. Conversely, when the object is the source of painful feelings, . . . we feel a 'repulsion' from the object and hate it; this hate can then be intensified to the point of an aggressive tendency towards the object, with the intention of destroying it" (Freud, 1915/1963, p. 100). Later, however, Freud (1920/1959) revised his approach by linking aggression to his newly proposed construct of the *death wish*. The death wish leads ultimately to self-destructive action. However, if the person expresses anger and aggression toward other people, the consequences of the death wish may be turned away from the self and the person will survive. This idea had serious effects on Freud's overall view of life. For example, he believed that war is inevitable because the "destructive instinct" that motivates war is really a form of self-preservation: We kill each other in order to avoid turning our destructive wishes against ourselves (Freud 1932/1963).

An early attempt to develop a unified theory of aggression is found in the *frustration-aggression hypothesis* of Dollard and his colleagues (Dollard, Doob, Miller, Mowrer, & Sears, 1939). This work was important because it approached the study of aggression with a set of concepts derived from contemporary research in learning and motivation based on the then-dominant behavioral theory of Clark Hull. At the same time it retained several constructs from Freudian psychoanalysis redefined in more behavioral terms. Briefly stated, the frustration-aggression hypothesis is that frustration (i.e., the blocking of goal-directed behavior) evokes a state of instigation to aggress, which is a drive state that motivates behavior in the same way as primary drives like hunger and thirst. Just as hunger motivates food seeking, aggressive drive engendered by frustration motivates aggression. Once aggression has occurred, drive reduction follows in much the same way as it does after primary appetitive behavior. Dollard and his associates called this drive reduction catharsis, the term Freud had used to describe a similar process in 1894. What is probably most important about the frustration-aggression hypothesis, however, is its assertion that the inner state of *aggressive drive* that is elicited by frustration always leads to aggression unless it is inhibited by fear, moral revulsion, or some other counter-aggressive motive. This drive state therefore has the same *functional* status as an instinct but is considered to be a response to situational conditions. The frustration-aggression hypothesis therefore retained the essential motivational features of instinct theory while being expressed in the conceptual language of behaviorism.

From the publication of the frustration-aggression hypothesis until now, the major emphasis in the social psychology of aggression, at least within American psychology, has been on the situational conditions that elicit the instigation to aggression and the intervening psychological processes that are set in motion thereafter. Relatively little attention has been paid to the possibility of innate and instinctual causes of aggression. During the 1960s and 1970s, the situationist approach was epitomized by the *social learning theory* of Bandura and his associates (e.g., Bandura, 1973). This theory describes the interrelated processes through which aggressive behavior is acquired, instigated, and maintained. Major features of the theory are its descriptions of how novel aggressive behaviors are learned through observation and imitation of aggressive models and how aggressive behaviors are maintained through social reinforcement.

Even though mainstream North American social psychology placed little emphasis on genetic factors in aggression during the heyday of social learning theory, arguments for such factors were being advanced elsewhere. Physiological psychologists were identifying certain sites within the central nervous system that appeared to be involved in various kinds of aggressive behavior. Most of this work involved the use of animal subjects, but certain extensions to humans were also proposed. Research along these lines led Moyer (1976) to build a sophisticated model that linked several kinds of aggressive behavior to activity in specific brain centers. Moyer pointed out that this activity must be elicited by stimuli in the environment that are appropriate to the specific centers. For example, what he called *irritable aggression* is controlled by activity in the hypothalamus and reticular formation after a provoking event (such as frustration, deprivation, or pain) has occurred. As we will note below, the viewpoint that aggression involves both a predisposing state of the person (which could include the potential level of activity in brain centers) and an external stimulus is one with which most social psychologists today would agree.

On a somewhat different level, other theorists were using animal models as the basis for advocating more broadly based theories of human aggression. One was *ethology:* the study of how specific environmental stimuli elicit fixed action patterns that are "wired into" members of a species (e.g., Lorenz, 1966). It had long been known, for example, that among certain species of fish, fighting among males is evoked by the appearance of colored spots on the body. On the basis of such findings, some ethologists speculated that human beings also react to sign-stimuli with stereotyped patterns of aggressive activity (e.g., Eibl-Eibesfeldt, 1977). Another theory of innate aggression that was advanced in the 1970s was *sociobiology* (e.g., Barash, 1977), which is based on the idea that aggression is one act by which animals try to protect their kinship group (i.e., others that share their genes) against outsiders. Aggressive competition with non-related competitors helps to ensure survival of the kinship group by securing adequate food, shelter, and mating partners.

Although the prospects of a human ethology and human sociobiology are intriguing, direct evidence for such possibilities has not been produced. In recent years, however, the proposition that human aggression may be in part due to hereditary factors has been gaining some support from another quarter: the emerging field of *behavior genetics*. The method most commonly used in this field for studying the hereditary basis of aggressiveness is one in which co-variance in the trait between identical (monozygotic: MZ) twins is compared with co-variance between nonidentical (dizygotic:DZ) ones. If it is assumed that environmental effects on MZ and DZ pairs are approximately equal, then a finding of larger co-variation between members of MZ pairs than among members of DZ pairs is taken as evidence of a hereditary influence. Using this method, Rushton and his associates (1986) found evidence that aggressiveness is partly determined by heredity in humans. More than 500 pairs of adult MZ and DZ twins responded to questionnaires that assessed five personality variables: altruism, empathy, nurturance, assertiveness, and aggressiveness. Higher co-variations were found among MZ pairs than among DZ pairs in the case of all five variables. These findings indicate some genetic determination of two self-reported traits that are related to aggression (aggressiveness and assertiveness) and three that are usually considered to be antithetical to aggression (nurturance, altruism, and empathy).

Additional evidence for heritability has been reported by Ghodsian-Carpey and Baker (1987), who measured aggressive behavior in MZ and DZ twin pairs between the ages of 4 and 7. A wide range of aggressive actions (e.g., destructiveness, physical attack, verbal threats) was assessed through both ratings made by the mothers of the children and observation of the children in their homes. Both types of measures yielded significantly higher co-variance in total aggression scores among pairs of MZ twins than among DZ pairs.

We must be careful in interpreting evidence for heritability of aggressiveness. Modern behavior geneticists do not propose that aggressive behavior is determined or driven by some innate fixed tendency in the same way that the earlier instinct theorists did. Instead, they define behavioral heritability largely in terms of inherited temperaments, or dispositions to respond to environmental stimulation (Buss & Plomin, 1984). The temperament that a person inherits from his or her parents—which is a function of neural, endocrine, and other aspects of one's biological makeup—gives each person a certain potential or *capacity* for aggression. For aggression actually to occur, some condition of the environment must elicit it. The form that the aggression takes, as well as its intensity, is determined by an interaction between the characteristics of the situation and certain characteristics of the person (Endler & Hunt, 1968), some of which reflect hereditary influence.

A Model for Aggression

This chapter is addressed to an analysis of some of the main eliciting causes of human aggression and the intervening psychological mechanisms by which they work. It is organized around the simple conceptual model shown in Figure 10.1. The steps in this model will be explained and elaborated upon in the text of the chapter, and research will be cited to support the model's assumptions. A subsequent section will use the premises of the model as a basis for a discussion of some ways in which human aggression may be controlled. Two lines of

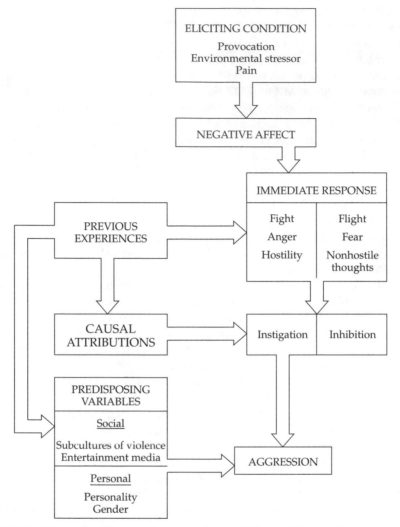

FIGURE 10.1. Schematic diagram of some major variables and intervening constructs in human aggression (see text for explanation).

theory and research have been addressed to the question of how situational conditions elicit aggressive behavior in humans. One describes an immediate and short-term reaction to provocation that precedes higher level cognitive processing and is driven entirely by negative affect. The other describes processes that involve higher cognitive activity by means of which people construct meanings of the events that provoke them and respond accordingly. These processes are described in the model as *sequential* events, with the immediate affective reaction preceding and leading up to cognitive appraisal and subsequent action.

The model specifies that aggression can be traced back to an eliciting condition. Three such conditions (provocation, environmental stress, and pain) have been listed as examples in Figure 10.1 because they arise later in the chapter and are discussed in their appropriate contexts. The immediate effect of any eliciting condition is an increase in negative affect, which, for reasons to be discussed at length later, evokes an immediate reaction to the situation. This response is either an active approach response by which the person confronts the situation or an avoidance response by which he or she avoids confrontation. Each of these reactions has behavioral, affective, and cognitive components: fight vs. flight at the behavioral level, anger vs. fear at the affective, and hostility vs. nonhostility at the cognitive. Which of these two broad classes of response will occur is determined party by the situation and partly by the person's previous history.

This immediate fight or flight response to conditions in the environment takes place before information processing begins. It is followed by cognitive processing of information, involving largely the judgments that the person makes about the eliciting condition. Depending on those judgments, and the person's attributions of what caused the negative affect, the initial fight/flight reaction leads to either an instigation to aggress in response to the eliciting condition or a tendency to inhibit aggression. At this point, the instigation/inhibition tendency is moderated by certain variables that predispose a person to be relatively aggressive or nonaggressive. Some of these are social in nature. For example, people who live in a culture that places a high value on aggressive behavior will aggress more intensely when instigated to aggress than people who come from a less violent culture. In addition, people who are exposed to heavy doses of violence in the entertainment media will often react to being provoked with greater aggression than people who have had less exposure. Both of these matters are discussed at length below. Other predisposing moderator variables relate to characteristics of the person, such as gender and personality. We have already noted that individual personality differences related to aggressiveness may also be partially determined by heredity.

Immediate Affect and Aggression

Reactions to Negative Affect

Berkowitz (1988) has proposed that the *immediate* response to aversive stimulation is entirely affective and not under cognitive control. This affective state evokes certain related states through a process that Berkowitz labels *cognitive neoassociationism*. The underlying basis for this theory is to be found in the concept of associative networks in memory. The starting point in the theory is that a person's immediate response to an aversive condition is the experience of negative affect. Following the suggestion of certain cognitive theorists (e.g., Bower, 1980), Berkowitz considers negative affective states to be encoded in hypothetical central connecting points, called *nodes*, in memory. Linked to affect in these nodes are related thoughts, emotions, and expressive motor patterns, so that activation of an affective condition in turn activates these other processes

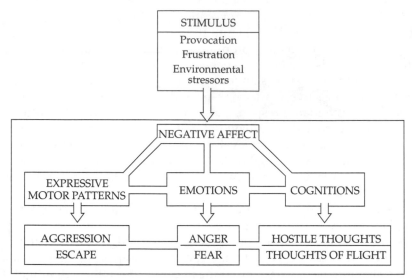

FIGURE 10.2. Schematic diagram of processes described in Berkowitz' (1989) cognitive-neoassociationist approach to human aggression (see text for explanation).

along directional pathways. The immediate affective reaction to aversive stimulation sets in motion a complex of emotions and thoughts related to either aggression or to escape from the aversive situation along with what may appear to be related reflexive behaviors usually described as *"fight or flight."* The system is described schematically in Figure 10.2.

The theory predicts that any stimulus can elicit aggression if it generates sufficient negative affect. Traditionally, the conditions that have been most often studied are those involving interpersonal provocations. The roles played in aggression by physical attack (Dengerink & Bertilson, 1974), intent to harm (Taylor & Epstein, 1967), verbal insult (Geen, 1981), and frustration (Geen, 1968) have been extensively documented. According to Berkowitz' formulation, however, a number of other conditions not directly connected to interpersonal provocation may also elicit negative affect and, as a result, activate associative networks that include aggressive motor patterns. One such condition is physical pain. In an experiment illustrating this point, Berkowitz, Cochran, and Embree (1981) found that subjects who held their nondominant hands in icewater as they delivered bursts of aversive noise to another person (supposedly as punishment for poor performance by that person) gave a greater number of such bursts than subjects who held their hands in comfortably warm water. Because the other person was in no way responsible for the subject's discomfort, this tendency to aggress on the part of subjects undergoing cold stress was attributed to the negative affect that they were experiencing. Furthermore, if negative affect is the immediate antecedent of reactive aggression, it may also explain the reported links between aggression and certain conditions of the environment such as noise (Geen, 1978), air pollution (Rotton & Frey, 1985), population density (Hutt & Vaizey, 1966), and high ambient temperatures (Anderson, 1989). Emotional states associated with negative affect, such as depression, may also be antecedents of aggression (Hynan & Grush, 1986; Julian & McKenry, 1993).

One interesting aspect of the model devised by Berkowitz (1989) and shown in Figure 10.2 is that because cognitions, emotions, and expressive motor patterns are linked within an associative network, each functions relatively independently of the others. Any of the three can therefore initiate activity in the others. One implication of this general principle is that the emotion of anger can be activated by either (1) an increase in negative affect arising from some condition in the environment, (2) the initiation of thoughts about aggression and hostility, or (3) the enactment of aggressive behavior. In a series of experiments, Berkowitz and Heimer (1989) instructed subjects to hold a hand in either ice water or water that was more tepid while thinking of either punishment or some less punitive matter. They found that both thinking about punishment and suffering from the cold stress led subjects to administer a greater number of bursts of aversive noise to another person and also to report stronger feelings of anger than did subjects in the appropriate control conditions. The most important finding of the studies was that pain and thoughts about punishment contributed to punitiveness independently of each other. Even when no stimulus for negative affect is present, thinking about aggression may trigger anger and/or aggressive motor tendencies. This process of activating a node by stimulating a node that is linked to it is referred to as *priming* the associative network.

The phenomenon of priming within the context of hostility and aggression has been shown in several ways. Srull and Wyer (1979) found that subjects attributed greater hostility to another person if the ratings of the other person were made after the subject had completed a verbal task containing words denoting hostility. In a subsequent and related study, Wann and Branscombe (1990) found a similar effect on ratings of hostility after subjects had been exposed to the names of violent sports such as hockey and prizefighting. In both of these studies, words linked to hostility and aggression caused a semantic priming of nodes within an associative network, eliciting thoughts related to aggression.

Effects of Previous Experience

Whether tendencies to fight or tendencies to escape are evoked by negative affect depends to some extent upon the person's past experiences in settings that have aroused such affect. Past experiences are encoded within the associative network. Thus, a provocation that elicits thoughts of aggression, hostility, and fighting tendencies in one person may, because of prior learning, elicit withdrawal in another. The influence of past experience is expressed to a large degree in the person's history of reward and punishment. Apropos of this, Seymour Feshbach (1964) made a valuable distinction when he pointed out that young children are capable of manifesting highly agitated activity when they are frustrated or otherwise involved in interpersonal conflict. They may scream, yell, kick, and make all manner of high intensity responses. In the process they may even hit another child or an adult, but at no time does any of this really qualify as aggression until the child learns to do it with intent. Eventually, of course, this happens. On some of the occasions that the infant strikes out and hits someone, the consequence of that act may be pleasing. Perhaps it will result in another child's relinquishing a desired toy, or it may cause an antagonist to stop doing something that displeases the child. In such instances, we would say that the *hitting* behavior is rewarded. Of course, on other occasions it may lead to undesirable consequences and hence be punished. Experiencing desired outcomes following aggression teaches the child that the emotionally driven hitting response can be used deliberately to hurt other people, and it is at this point, where hitting becomes *hurting*, that aggression is born.

At approximately the same time as Feshbach was analyzing hitting vs. hurting behavior, Bandura and his associates were demonstrating that children may learn aggressive responses simply by observing the actions of another person behaving aggressively (e.g., Bandura, Ross, & Ross, 1963). However, the study of social learning has shown that even though aggression may be learned through observation and modeling, it is *maintained* by reinforcement. A person with a long history of attaining valuable ends through aggressing in certain situations comes to believe that continued aggression in the same settings will continue to deliver worthwhile rewards. As a result, aggression will have a high degree of utility and will likely be repeated when appropriate situational cues are present (Kornadt, 1984; Perry, Perry, & Rasmussen, 1986).

We may summarize what we have reviewed in this section as follows: The immediate eliciting condition for aggression is something that causes increased negative affect in the individual. Negative affect elicits associated emotions, cognitions, and expressive motor behavior patterns in long-term memory. It is also possible that each of the associated elements in the network—emotions, affective states, cognitions, or behaviors—can prime any of the others. The person's network of associations also includes other elements learned through previous experience that determine whether the initial reaction to the negative affect will be aggression, anger, and hostility, or flight, fear, and escape-related cognitions.

Cognitive Processes in Aggression

Interaction of Affect and Cognition

The cognitive-neoassociationist theory of aggression treats the emotional, cognitive, and behavioral consequences of negative affect as parallel processes. None *necessarily* elicits either of the others, even though they may manifest considerable influence on each other. One consequence of this independence is that the theory does not treat the emotion of anger as a necessary condition for aggression. The experience of anger is an involuntary state that is usually elicited along with the instigation to attack but does not play any causal role in the latter. Situations may occur in which anger becomes dissociated from aggression;

we can think, for example, of cases in which a person is pushed or shoved by another person and shoves back immediately, without experiencing any clear feeling of anger toward the other. At this point the dominant feeling of the person who has been shoved is rather one of undifferentiated negative affect.

Other theories make anger a necessary hypothetical construct that mediates the relationship of provocation to aggression. One example of such a theory is that of Zillmann (1988), who defines anger as a conscious experience that is generated by an increase in *physiological arousal* arising from "social or environmental conditions that pose a threat to welfare and well-being" (Zillmann, 1988, p. 52) and information from the environment by which this arousal state is explained. Subsequent reappraisals of the environment may either support and sustain the perception of endangerment or indicate that the danger is minimal. In either case, intensity of anger and level of aggression go hand in hand, and both are a function of the level of physiological excitation. Defining anger in this way, Zillmann has further proposed that arousal elicited by events other than provocations may under some conditions become mistakenly associated with the latter. This phenomenon, called *excitation transfer,* pertains to situations in which two arousing conditions occur in sequence. Autonomic arousal does not dissipate immediately upon termination of the condition that elicits it. Therefore, if two arousing events are separated by a short amount of time, some of the arousal caused by one may be transferred to the other and, as a result, increase the intensity of emotion experienced in response to that setting.

The two events involved can be qualitatively different from each other. Two experiments illustrate this. In one study, Zillmann (1971) first arranged for male subjects to be provoked to anger by another person and then showed these subjects one of three short sequences from commercial movies. One group saw an affectively neutral film involving travel, another saw a violent scene from a prizefight, and still others saw an erotic but nonviolent scenario. It had been established beforehand that the erotic film was more arousing than the violent film, which was in turn more arousing than the neutral one. After the film had been shown, each subject was given a chance to retaliate against the person who had provoked him by delivering a variable number of electric shocks. The aggressiveness of the retaliation was directly related to the arousal value of the film that had been seen: The most intense shocks were given by subjects who had seen the erotic film, followed by those who had seen the violent one. This was apparently because residual arousal from the film was labeled as anger at the time of retaliation.

Similar results following a different induction of arousal were found in a study by Zillmann, Katcher, and Milavsky (1972). Some subjects were provoked by another person, after which they engaged in vigorous physical exercise on a stationary bicycle. Other subjects took part in a sedentary activity after having been provoked. When the subjects were later allowed to retaliate against the person who had provoked them, those who had taken the strenuous exercise were more aggressive than those who had done the physically less demanding task. Zillmann and his associates reasoned that arousal elicited by the exercise was still operative at the time of retaliation and was mistakenly labeled as anger.

The different roles assigned to the experience of anger by Berkowitz and Zillmann reflect the underlying natures of the respective theories. As we have already noted, the cognitive-neoassociationist process is *precognitive* in that it involves reactions that are driven by negative affect and involve only associative activity. Zillmann describes processes that come into play after the initial associative reaction, at which time the person begins to engage in higher level cognitive processing. The anger that is initially evoked by increased negative affect is only "rudimentary" (Berkowitz, 1993), and it may or may not form the basis for a more elaborated state of anger, depending on the outcome of the cognitive processing that follows (cf. Figure 10.1). If we recall the first premise of the definition of aggression with which this chapter began—the administration of an aversive stimulus with the intent to harm—it is obvious that cognitive activity is necessary if we wish to explain the phenomenon completely. Much of this cognitive activity consists of assigning meaning to the provoking event, and this in turn involves the invocation of certain beliefs and values shared by most people within a culture. Certain norms and social customs govern the expression of aggression. The person who experiences hostility and anger and is thereby prepared to behave aggressively will do so only to the extent that aggression is considered to be acceptable within normative limits. Judgments of the acceptability of aggression, in turn, vary with the meaning that the person attributes to the originally eliciting event. A blow deliberately delivered, for example, is more likely to evoke an aggressive reaction than an accidental jolt. We must therefore consider the instigation to aggression in the context of the *causal attributions* that the person makes.

Effects of Causal Attributions

The general subject of causal attribution is discussed elsewhere in this book (see Chapter 4). In this section we will highlight the application of attributional principles to the analysis of provocation and aggression. Provocations, as noted above, must usually be regarded as intentional and malicious in intent before they lead to aggression. They must also be considered a violation of normal social behavior in the situation. They must, in addition, lead to outcomes that are regarded as alternatives to other outcomes; i.e., they must be considered avoidable. These are a few of the attributes of a provocative act—intent, counter normality, avoidability—that cause the provocation to invite aggression in return. An extensive analysis of the attributional process in aggression has been made by Ferguson and Rule (1983). It is based on the answers to three questions that a person asks after having been harmed by someone. These are:

1. What was the act of harm that was done?
2. What ought to have been done under the circumstances?
3. Does any discrepancy exist between what was done and what ought to have been done?

Evaluation of Harm doing. The first question raises the issue of whether or not the other person acted intentionally. If intent to hurt is attributed to the other person, a second judgment is made of whether the intention was malevolent. If the act is judged to have been unintentional, a further determination is made of whether or not the harm doer could foresee the result of the act. An act of harm doing may therefore be classified as representing one of four types: intentional and malevolent, intentional but not malevolent, not intended but foreseeable, and unintentional and unforeseeable. The last type represents truly accidental harm doing. Table 10.1 shows the four types of attribution, along with an example of each.

Deliberate and premediated murder, for example, is the most extreme case of intentional malevolence. An example of intentional but nonmalevolent harm doing would be coming to the aid of a mugging victim by hitting the mugger, not to harm him but to drive him away. Unintentional but foreseeable harm doing is exemplified by the person who drives an automobile after drinking, knowing that such driving is unsafe, and hitting another person. Unintentional and unforeseeable harm doing would be perceived if the driver hit the other person because of unexpected brake failure.

Judging What Should Have Happened. Each of the four types of harm doing can be compared to a norm that prescribes activity in the situation in question. These norms reflect the basic values of the persons involved and are determined by the culture. Most cultures have a norm that condemns the infliction of intentional malevolent harm on another person. Most also have a norm that excuses or justifies the occasional infliction of intentional but non-malevolent harm. The pain caused by a police officer in the line of duty falls into this category. Society prescribes that the police should use only as much violence as is necessary in carrying out their responsibilities and should not inflict such violence out of malicious intent. Use of excessive force or use of force out of malice toward the victim is labeled "police brutality" and is considered anti-normative behavior. Another widely shared norm states that it is wrong to do nothing to prevent a foreseeable act of harm to another person. The person who commits harm that is willfully malevolent is judged to be more culpable than someone who commits harm that is not malicious, and unintentional but foreseeable harm doing is judged more blameworthy than that which is unintentional and unforeseeable (Rule & Nesdale, 1976). It would appear, therefore, that the two types of harm doing for which a person is held most responsible

TABLE 10.1. Examples of Harm Doing Along Dimensions of Intent, Motive, and Foreseeability

Intention	Motive	Example
Intentional	Malicious	Premeditated murder
Intentional	Not malicious	Restraint of mugger
Unintentional	Foreseeable	Injury due to driving while drunk
Unintentional	Not foreseeable	Injury due to unknown mechanical failure

are the intentional-malicious and unintentional foreseeable, with the former more so than the latter.

Aggression as a Reaction to Antinormative Behavior. The attributional approach to aggression may be summarized as follows: provocations elicit judgments of culpability depending on the meaning that is attached to them and the extent to which they deviate from normative judgments of what should have happened in the situation. Counternormative provocation increases anger toward the harm doer; i.e., the unpleasant state of affect engendered by the provocation will, quite logically, be labeled anger (cf. Zillmann, 1979). Aggression is a normal reaction to the emotion of anger and is directed toward the person seen to be the cause of that anger. Such aggression is in fact usually called *angry* or *affective* aggression and is sharply differentiated form aggression that is carried out primarily for practical ends. The latter, called *instrumental* aggression, may or may not include a component of anger; it is, at any rate, not motivated by anger but by the pursuit of some goal (Geen, 1990). We will return to this distinction later in the chapter.

Summary

At different times in the past, human aggression has been studied as a manifestation of innate characteristics of the person and as the outcome of situational conditions. At the present time we recognize that both of these factors are involved: The human being inherits a capacity for aggressive behavior that interacts with situational elicitors to shape the nature of the aggressive response. In this section we have considered how environmental conditions instigate aggressive responses. The first effect of these conditions is negative affect, which in turn activates thoughts, emotions, and expressive motor patterns associated with this affective state along directional pathways. Because the latter are parallel processes, none is a necessary mediator of any of the others; all are simultaneously activated by negative affect. At this stage, therefore, anger is not a mediator of aggression. The processes that are activated by negative affect constitute either an approach-aggressive response or an avoidance-flight reaction. This initial response is followed by cognitive activity by means of which the person interprets an understands the situation. This activity consists largely of judging the instigating event and assigning some level of blame to the instigator. The outcome is an experience of anger that mediates subsequent aggressive behavior.

BACKGROUND OR PREDISPOSING VARIABLES

Several contemporary approaches to social psychology have emphasized the importance of *interactions* between the person and the environment in the determination of behavior. To this point we have been concerned mainly with the environment in the form of conditions that arise in the immediate situation and which provoke the individual and elicit anger, hostility, and aggressive behavior. A more complete understanding of aggression must also take into account individual variables that enter into the process. These may be thought of as background variables that *predispose* persons to become aggressive under the appropriate conditions (Geen, 1990). We will first consider two social variables that play important roles in disposing people to be more or less aggressive. One is the "culture of violence" in which some people live and which sets certain expectancies of aggression on the part of individuals. The second is the wide dissemination of symbols of violence in the mass media of entertainment.

The Culture of Violence

Most societies sanction aggression to some degree. Historically, some nations have been identified as warrior states; whereas others, though relatively more pacific, have still maintained that some violence is necessary to preserve the social order and to guard the society against its external enemies. The espousal of violence within the norms and values of a society provides a predisposing variable that makes aggression more or less probable under suitably provoking conditions. An insult to a citizen of a peaceful society will probably invite less retaliation than one to a person from a culture in which violent behavior is normal.

We have evidence showing that aggressive values play an important part in the overall national value system of the United States (Mulvihill & Tumin, 1969). In this large survey study, for example, 78 percent of all respondents agreed with the statement "Some people don't understand anything but force," and 70 percent agreed with the item "When a boy is growing up, it is important for him to have a few fist fights." Sixty-five percent believed that police use no more force than is necessary to carry out their duties, and 56 percent accepted the statement "Any man who insults a policeman has no complaint if he gets roughed up in return." Such opinions, moreover, generalized to beliefs about international conflict; 62 percent, for example, believed that in "dealing with other countries in the world we are frequently justified in using military force."

With beliefs such as these being widely held in American society, it is not surprising that aggressive attitudes enter into everyday social interactions. After reviewing the case histories of several individuals who manifested high levels of violence in their lives, Toch (1969) concluded that much of the behavior he had studied was guided by "violence-prone premises." Social encounters that might for some people lead to innocuous outcomes often erupt into aggression among violent people. Toch has observed that "persons who tend to interpret situations as threatening, or goading, or challenging, or overpowering can turn harmless encounters into duels, purges, struggles for survival, or violent escapes" (1969, p. 189). From where do these violence-prone ways of interpreting situations come? Toch suggests that in certain segments of American society such premises are widely accepted, and are therefore available for adoption as beliefs by individuals.

Some recent studies have indicated also the existence of regional cultural differences in aggression *within* the United States (Nisbett, 1993; Rotton, 1986). Nisbett and his colleagues have found, for example, that homicide rates among white non-Hispanic offenders living in rural or small town environments in the southern part of the country are higher than corresponding rates in similar settings in other regions. Regional differences in homicide rates among residents of large cities are smaller. In addition, Nisbett has presented evidence of differences between the South and other regions in attitudes toward violence and in beliefs in the proper way to react to insults. White Southern men are more likely than white males living elsewhere in the country to believe that aggression is justified in defense of human life and property and to think that aggression in response to an insult is justified and proper. Attitudes favoring punitive discipline of children also tend to be more strongly held in the South than elsewhere. Furthermore, white male homicide rates are higher in those parts of the rural south in which the herding and tending of animals is the main basis for agriculture than in those regions characterized by farming.

What does all of this mean? On the basis of his studies, Nisbett (1993) has ruled out some of the possible theoretical explanations, such as high ambient temperature and poverty, for these regional differences in aggressive attitudes and behavior. He has concluded that the relatively high valuation placed on aggression in the rural South is the result of the cultural history of the region. In particular, he proposes that economies based on herding are historically more likely than farming or urban economies to value aggression because such action has traditionally been required to guard the herd. The demands for aggressive protection of grazing livestock give rise to a cultural valuation of strong and forceful manhood, motivated by a code of honor and self-esteem. These concepts have helped to shape the dominant values of that culture to this day.

The idea that certain "subcultures of violence" exist within the larger culture was first proposed by Wolfgang and Ferracuti (1967) on the basis of their findings that some groups are more likely than others to use violence in solving their problems. This phenomenon is not restricted to any one society or nation. The origins of the particular subcultures of violence depend on the history and circumstances of the society, but regardless of origins, the subculture mandates the values, beliefs, and practices of the members. In various societies we can observe the vendetta, the blood feud, and the stereotyped toughness of the *machismo* syndrome. In the United States this pattern is often manifested in violent juvenile gangs.

To a certain extent the violence of gangs reflects the society's prevailing standards of aggression. In addition, gang violence has been shown to have more precise origins in the rapid social change found in societies in transition, like that of the inner-city neighborhood (Klein, 1969). Such changes produce a breakdown in traditional norms and a consequent loss of communal control over the aggression of individuals and small groups. In such a setting, aggression eventually becomes a part of the new normative structure that emerges to replace the old one. The gang serves as a focus for young people in that it provides a means of instant gratification, a powerful peer group, social status, and an opportunity to assert masculinity and toughness. In turn, the gang legitimizes aggression. It also promotes aggressive behavior through a "shared understanding" (Klein, 1969): Each member of the gang assumes that the norms of the peer group demand more aggression than the individual would ordinarily prefer to undertake. In this way the gang implicitly compels a certain level of violence from each of its members.

Aggression in the Communications Media

The question of whether observation of violence in the mass entertainment media is related to aggression among viewers is one that has aroused concern within both the scientific community and society at large. Much of this concern is associated with violence shown on television. Does the observation of violence cause increased aggression? Evidence pertaining to this question comes from two sources: research conducted in experimental laboratories under controlled conditions and studies of aggression in natural settings.

Laboratory Studies

A large amount of the research evidence on the effects of media violence has been gathered in studies carried out in laboratories under controlled experimental conditions. Before considering the findings of that research, it will be instructive to review briefly the basic methodology that has been used. Two treatments are common to virtually every study that has been reported: One person (the subject) (1) is ostensibly provoked to aggress by the actions of another person and then (2) is shown a passage from a motion picture or television program portraying a moderate-to-high level of violent action. Of course, each treatment is coupled with an appropriate control condition in which the manipulations (i.e., provocation and/or exposure to violence) are not implemented. The subject is typically provoked by something that the other person does in the course of the experiment. Sometimes the other person is an assistant of the experimenter, carrying out a prescribed role. At other times the subject is only led to believe that there is another person present, as the experimenter surreptitiously carries out the provocation. Provocations sometimes involve the direct administration of noxious stimuli such as electric shocks or loud noise and at other times take the form of insults, verbal abuse, or frustration.

Several variations on this simple two-treatment paradigm have been used. Sometimes several films or video segments are shown, so that the amount of violent content shown to the subjects can be varied. For example, Bushman and Geen (1990) showed five videotapes to five groups of subjects; four of these five tapes had been judged beforehand to manifest four gradations in violent content, and the fifth showed a nonviolent control scene. Another variation on the basic design involves instructions to the subject telling her or him that the violence being shown is either real of fictitious (e.g., Berkowitz & Alioto, 1973).

Once the person has been provoked and exposed to the violent movie or video, he or she is given an opportunity to retaliate by doing something aversive to the provoker. Several experimental paradigms have been used. In one, often used by Berkowitz and his colleagues, the subject is given a chance to deliver a variable number of shocks or bursts of noise to the target person; aggression is operationally defined as the number and/or duration of stimuli thus administered. In another commonly used paradigm, first developed by Buss (1961), the subject chooses the intensity of a retaliatory stimulus by pressing one of ten buttons on a control panel. Each button is labeled to indicate the relative intensity of the stimulus that it governs. Another methodology calls for the subject's retaliating against the provocateur by expressing verbal dislike for that person, or by having the opportunity to disparage that person's performance (e.g., Geen, 1981). This latter methodology has become relatively common in recent years as rules and procedures for ethical treatment of human subjects have prohibited the use of electric shocks and other physically aversive stimuli. It should be noted that the methods described here for provoking the subject and for the subject's aggressing in return are typical for most laboratory experiments on aggression, and not just those involving media violence.

The literature from laboratory research has been reviewed many times (e.g., Geen, 1990; Geen & Thomas, 1986; Hearold, 1986; Roberts & Maccoby, 1985). This literature is extensive, and a detailed examination of its findings is beyond the scope of this chapter. A few conclusions are cited here. When violence shown on television is said to be real, it evokes more aggression in viewers than when it is described as fictitious (Berkowitz & Alioto, 1973). Violence that is perceived as morally justified by the situation is more likely to elicit aggression than that which is less justified (Geen, 1981). Judgments of the motives of the observed aggressor may also influence the ways in which media violence affects aggression. Of the many imaginable motives for aggression, revenge or retaliation would probably be considered at least somewhat justified by most people (e.g., Carpenter & Darley, 1978). Several experiments have shown that when violence is described as revenge, it elicits more aggression in subjects who have previously been angered than the same acts attributed to other motives (e.g., Geen & Stonner, 1973). These studies suggest that the observation of violence may involve a social comparison process. The person who has been made angry by some interpersonal conflict or provocation and is motivated to aggress against the person responsible may compare his or her situation with that of the person seeking revenge in the media presentation. The sight of the other person aggressing may send the message that aggression is permissible, or even socially desirable, under such conditions. The social comparison hypothesis is further supported by studies showing that when subjects are instructed to identify with perpetrators of successful violence in the media, their level of aggression is enhanced (Perry & Perry, 1976; Turner & Berkowitz, 1972).

The studies cited above all show that the context of observed aggression gives meaning to the actions of the aggressors and that this meaning influences subsequent behavior in the viewer. In addition, experimental studies have shown that the social setting in which the observation takes place can also have effects. For example, Eisenberg (1980) found that children who witnessed an adult making approving statements about violence being seen on television were later more aggressive than children who had observed a disapproving adult. Other studies have shown that aggression seen on television is more likely to be imitated by a child when another child in the same situation imitates the aggressive action (e.g., O'Neal, McDonald, Cloninger, & Levine, 1979). Taken together, these studies suggest that social support for aggression after observation of televised violence may facilitate enactment of such actions by observers.

Naturalistic Studies

Critics of laboratory research on effects of media violence base their arguments on the allegation that the behavior seen in such contrived situations is not representative of behavior in real life. Partly because of such arguments, interest in laboratory experiments on the subject began to want in the 1970s and to be replaced by research based on naturalistic studies. Although some commentators have criticized even these studies and claimed that they lack internal validity (e.g., Freedman, 1984), others have concluded that they have strengths as well as some weaknesses (see Friedrich-Cofer & Huston, 1986, for a detailed discussion of these issues). A recently reported meta-analysis reviewed 28 field experiments conducted between 1956 and 1988 in which children engaged in unconstrained interaction with strangers, classmates, and friends (Wood, Wong, & Chachere, 1991). The conclusion of the analysis was that observation of media violence enhances aggression in such settings because of both short-term changes in affect and longer-term processes of imitation.

One major longitudinal investigation was a project by Eron and his associates that began in the late 1950s and spanned a period of more than 20 years. This research began with the study of third-grade students in a rural county in upstate new York (Eron, Walder, & Lefkowitz, 1971). Each child's level of aggressiveness was passed through ratings by parents, peers, and the children themselves. In addition, each child's preference for violent television programs was measured. These same variables were then assessed at intervals of 10 and 22 years in many of the children from the original sample.

The results of the 10-year followup (Lefkowitz, Eron, Walder, & Huesmann, 1977) revealed that among boys the amount of televised violence watched during third grade was positively correlated with aggressiveness 10 years later, whereas the correlation between the aggressiveness in grade three and the amount of violent television watched a decade later was essentially zero. Eron and his associates inferred from these findings a causal relation between the amount of time spent watching violent television and subsequent aggressiveness. No such relationship was found among girls, however. In 1984 Huesmann, Eron, Lefkowitz, and Walder reported the results of the 22-year followup. A positive relationship between childhood television viewing and aggressiveness later in life was again suggested: The seriousness of crimes for which males were convicted by age 30 was significantly correlated with the amount of television the men had watched and their preference for violent programs as 8-year-olds.

The same general conclusion of a connection between observation of violent television and aggressiveness was reached by Singer and Singer (1981) on the basis of a 1-year study of nursery school children. At four times during the year, 2-week intervals were designated as probe periods during which parents kept logs of their children's television viewing. At the same time, observers recorded instances of aggressive behavior by the children during school hours. When data were combined across all four probes, aggressive behavior was found to be correlated with the total amount of time spent in watching "action-adventure" programs, all of which manifested high levels of violence. This effect was found among both boys and girls.

In the early phases of the study (i.e., across the first three probes), the direction of the effect was clear: Observation of violence led to aggressiveness in behavior. By the last probe, however, another effect had emerged: Aggressiveness was still being elicited by the viewing of violence, but in addition, aggressive children were now watching more "action-adventure" programs than they had previously. The Singers' finding that aggressive people may have a greater liking for violent programs than less aggressive people had been reported previously (Diener & DuFour, 1978; Fenigstein, 1979), and it provides another possible explanation for why observation of violence is related to aggressive behavior.

One of the most comprehensive field studies on the effects of television violence was carried out during the 1980s by a team of investigators working in five countries under the general direction of Huesmann and Eron (1986a). In one of the studies, involving two groups of American children in grades one through five, Huesmann and Eron (1986b) found that frequency of viewing televised violence was positively correlated with contemporary peer ratings of aggression. The effect was found among both boys and girls. In addition, aggression by boys was related to the degree to which the boys identified with aggressive characters seen on television. Findings that were generally similar to those obtained from the American sample characterized the investigations carried out in the other countries: Finland, Poland, Australia, and Israel. In each of these countries, a positive relationship was found between frequency of watching violent television and peer-related aggression. The only exception was that in Israel the effect was found among children living in cities but not among those living in rural collective farms (Bachrach, 1986). Aggression was also found to be moderated by identification with violent television characters in these countries, as it was in the United States.

Personality Variables in Aggression

Subcultures of violence and portrayals of aggression in the media are social conditions that can create differential levels of disposition to aggress in the person. A third source of individual variation in tendencies to aggress is personality. Everyday experience suggests that individual differences in personality play an important role in aggression. For example, the "aggressive personality" that is usually thought to be fairly typical among violent criminals is a well-known category. People who advocate harsh and punitive treatment of such criminals are often motivated by the conviction that little can be done about such "personalities" and that nothing is to be gained by attempts at rehabilitation or changing the persons' environments. We do have grounds for assuming the reality of aggressive personalities, but it is probably correct to think of these personalities as moderators of situational influences rather than as causes of aggression in and of themselves. Following the approach taken in this chapter, we treat aggressiveness as a disposing variable that helps determine the level of aggression following provocation.

Stability of Aggressiveness

Some psychologists do not believe that human behavior manifests much stability across time and situations, so that the whole concept of personality is to be questioned. Applying this belief to the study of aggressive behavior, such investigators have concluded that aggression shows little consistency and is best accounted for in terms of situation causes (e.g., Campbell, Bibel, & Muncer, 1985). Others (e.g., Deluty, 1985) have reported high levels of consistency in aggressive behaviors across a wide range of naturally occurring activities. Perhaps the strongest case for a stable aggressive personality has been made by Olweus (1979), who reviewed a large number of longitudinal studies of aggressive behavior and reaction patterns in children, noting in each case the coefficient of stability in aggressive behavior from one measurement period to another (i.e., the magnitude of correlation across instances of aggression). The lengths of time intervening between measurements varied from study to study, as did the ages of the children at the outset of each study. Measures of aggressiveness included direct observation, teacher ratings, clinical ratings, and judgments made by other children.

Considerable evidence for stability of aggressive behavior was found. For example, clear individual differences in level of aggressiveness emerged as early as the age of 3, with such stability lasting for as long as 12 to 18 months. Children aged 8 to 9 showed aggressive behavior patterns that were correlated with aggressiveness as long as 10 to 14 years later. In some instances, the magnitude of correlation was sufficient to account for 25 percent of the variance at the later age. Aggressive behavior at ages 12 to 13 also showed a high degree of stability for periods of 1 to 5 years, with between 50 and 90 percent of the variance accounted for. Such findings indicate that aggressive behavior is to some degree a function of generalized aggressiveness.

Such stability in aggressiveness cannot easily be explained in terms of social learning theory. In fact, as Olweus points out, children who show aggressiveness early in life are probably punished for it, and this, according to social learning principles, should inhibit subsequent aggression. In addition, aggressive children are probably also the objects of attempts by teachers and others to reduce their aggressiveness. Olweus (1979) has therefore concluded that aggressive behavior "is often maintained irrespective of considerable environmental variation and in opposition to forces acting to change this same behavior" (p. 871).

Personality and Cognitive Functioning

Findings such as the ones reported here do not necessarily indicate that people have a trait of aggressiveness, i.e., a stable tendency to behave aggressively most of the time and in most places. Instead, Olweus (1979) suggests that individual differences contribute to aggression in concert with cognitive appraisals of events, emotional reactions, and personal tendencies toward inhibition of aggression. Huesmann and Eron (1984) have explained stable and persistent aggressive behavior in terms of the internal cognitive representations, or *schemata*, that people form of their environments. The person who, as a child, uses aggression as an approach to interpersonal conflicts exposes himself or herself to a large number of aggressive events, or *scenarios*, by virtue of this behavior. These scenarios become encoded in memory and maintained through rehearsal. In addition, the child may elaborate upon these scenarios and, as a result, develop more abstract and generalized aggressive strategies or *scripts* (Abelson, 1976) for dealing with conflicts. The end result is a high probability that the child will retrieve an *aggressive script* when conflicts arise. Aggressive behavior is guided by such a script. This aggression, in turn, adds other scenarios to the cognitive structure, and the process is repeated. In this way aggression can become self-perpetuating in ongoing cycles.

Individual differences in intellectual functioning, manifested in such skills as reading comprehension or mathematical ability, can affect aggressiveness and also be affected by it. Poor intellectual functioning produces frustration and arousal in normal problem-solving settings such as those encountered by children in school. This can have several consequences. The child may react to frustration with aggression but, because of his or her intellectual deficit, not be as able as other children to understand the inappropriateness of aggression or to formulate alternative responses to it. The child's behavior also results in a low rate of reinforcement for nonaggressive responses. The child therefore encodes an aggressive strategy for such situations.

Once an aggressive strategy has been encoded, it tends to persist and, in turn, to exert a reciprocating effect on intellectual processes. Aggressiveness, by hindering good relationships between children and their teachers and peers, interferes with opportunities for intellectual enrichment. This leads to poor achievement in school, which perpetuates the low level of intellectual functioning. Whereas the child's low intellectual level originally led to aggression, aggression now becomes a source of continuing intellectual deficits. To support this conclusion, Huesmann and Eron (1984) reported findings from their 22-year longitudinal study cited earlier in the chapter which showed that aggressiveness in children at age 8 was highly correlated with both antisocial behavior and intellectual deficit in those children when they reached adulthood. Aggressiveness at age 8 was a better predictor of intellectual functioning at age 30 than intellectual functioning at age 8 was of adult aggressiveness.

Personality and Attributions of Hostility

It was noted earlier in the chapter that aggression following provocation is influenced by the intention attributed to the provoker. If the latter is perceived as someone who acted out of malice, retaliation is more likely than if such an attribution is not made (Dodge, Murphy, & Buchsbaum, 1984). Perceptions of hostility and malice are in turn affected to some extent by personality. In a study reported by Dodge (1980), boys who had previously been classified by teachers and peers as being customarily either aggressive or nonaggressive were prevented from completing a puzzle by the intrusion of another boy. For some subjects the intruder acted out of clearly hostile intent, whereas for others his interference was an accidental blunder. For still other subjects the intentions of the other boy were vague and ambiguous. All subjects were then given a chance to retaliate against the other by destroying a puzzle on which he was working. As was expected, the hostile boy invited more retribution than the benign or ambiguous one. In addition, subjects who had been classified as aggressive were more aggressive toward the other boy than were nonaggressive subjects only when the other boy's motives were ambiguous. When the motives of an attacker are clearly understood, people retaliate or do not retaliate on the basis of those motives. When an attacker's motives are not clear, individual differences in aggressiveness predict the victim's behavior.

The tendency of aggressive boys to attribute hostile intent to another even when the latter's actions are ambiguous has been called the *hostile attribution bias* (Nasby, Hayden, & DePaulo, 1979). It is a result of a generally aggressive disposition. The concept has been further refined by Dodge and Coie (1987), who propose that people show individual differences in tendencies to commit both affective and instrumental aggression. The personality variables related to these types of aggression are designated, respectively, as *reactive* and *proactive* aggressiveness. The former is typified by such behaviors as striking back when provoked and responding angrily to minor annoyances. The latter is manifested in actions calculated to dominate and bully others. Dodge and Coie (1987) have developed scales to measure each of these personality variables. In one study involving the use of the scales, Dodge and Coie (1987) found that children who scored high in reactive aggressiveness showed the hostile attribution bias more than low scorers, but that individual differences in proactive aggressiveness were unrelated to commission of the bias.

Gender as a Predisposing Variable in Aggression

Folk wisdom in most cultures holds that men are typically more physically aggressive than women. Statistics tend to support this generalization. Men are more likely than women to commit crimes like murder, armed robbery, and aggravated assault and also more likely to react aggressively to a wide range of interpersonal conflicts (Reinisch & Sanders, 1986). Such gender differences are also found in cultures other than our own (Whiting & Edwards, 1973). Although most psychologists would probably agree that men are generally more aggressive than women, certain differences of opinion can be found concerning the reasons for this phenomenon, the various conditions under which it occurs, and the role played by the particular type of aggression being studied. In fact, some recent reviews of the subject (Eagly & Steffen, 1986; Hyde, 1984) have shown that gender differences in aggression are not as great as is usually imagined.

Although some psychologists argue that some of the differences between the sexes where aggression is concerned are determined by biological factors (e.g., Maccoby & Jacklin, 1980), this conclusion has been challenged by others (e.g., White, 1983). All parties agree that social and cultural factors play an important, if not exclusive, role in gender differences. Several social and cultural variables are involved. Men and women differ in the type of aggression that each is most likely to practice, with physical violence being more typical of men than of women (Shope, Hedrick, & Geen, 1978). Some differences have also been found in the types of provocation that anger women and men. Whereas men tend to be angered most by overt aggression from other men and by condescending treatment from women, what angers women most is being treated in a condescending way by both men and other women (Frodi, Macaulay, & Thome, 1977). Other studies show that women may be more inhibited about aggressing than men and experience more anxiety, fear, and guilt after aggressing (Eagly & Steffen, 1986). All of these differences can be accounted for in terms of differential socialization of boys and girls.

Violence against Women

A number of the variables described above are involved in the study of domestic violence in general and of violence against women in particular. The number of women battered each year by their male partners in the United States is estimated at close to 2 million (Straus & Gelles, 1986). Situational, social, and personal variables all play a role in mediating such acts. In this section a few of these variables will be identified.

Violence committed by men against women is widely recognized as a response to the stresses and strains of everyday life. It has also been observed that violent behavior under stressful conditions is tolerated by our society when it is carried out in the context of the family (Gelles & Straus, 1979). However, stress alone does not account for the widespread practice of spouse abuse. Such abuse is more likely to occur when relationships are of poor quality and marked by discord than when they are relatively satisfactory (Julian & McKenry, 1993). In addition, the overall social network in which the relationship is embedded has an effect on the probability that stress will evoke aggression. A woman who lacks a strong base of social support is more vulnerable to being attacked by a potentially abusive male partner than one who has close friends to whom she can turn for assistance. The woman most at risk of being battered is one living with an abusive partner who enjoys strong social support while she stands alone (Baumgartner, 1993).

Personality variables also influence spouse abuse. Depressed males have been found to be more violent toward their partners than nondepressed ones (Julian & McKenry, 1993). Bersani and colleagues (1992) also found that males convicted for spouse battering differed from nonabusive men in several respects. Batterers were more socially active, outgoing, and assertive, but they were also more nervous, depressed, hostile, impulsive, and indifferent. The authors concluded that the findings reveal "a profile of men who are highly social, but lack the internal dynamics or balance to achieve positive social interaction" (Bersani, Chen, Pendleton, & Denton, 1992, p. 131). Possibly batterers' high levels of sociability are a factor in their enjoying strong social support, while other facets of their personalities incline them to be aggressive and abusive toward their mates.

Rape is a particular type of violence against women that is especially prevalent in our society (Kloss, Gidycz, & Wisniewski, 1987). Whereas rape was once considered to be forcible sexual assault on a woman by a stranger, it is now defined in terms of absence of the woman's consent regardless of her relationship to the male. Several variables have been shown to be involved in acquaintance rape, especially that which occurs in the context of a date. In a study of self-reported incidents of sexual aggression, Muehlenhard and Linton (1987) isolated several "risk factors" for date rape: the man's initiating the date, paying all the expenses, and doing the driving; miscommunication about sexual intentions; heavy alcohol or drug use; and male attitudes that tended to place women in the role of adversaries of men. Date rape was also related to men's beliefs that women enjoy being sexually dominated by men, the so-called rape myth. Other investigators (e.g., Quackenbush, 1989) have shown that males who embrace the traditional male role are more likely to hold beliefs conducive to rape, such as acceptance of the rape myth, than are males who are more androgynous in their sex roles.

A question that has generated considerable controversy is whether *pornography,* the depiction of sexual violence against women, contributes to male aggression against female victims. Some of the evidence from controlled laboratory studies indicates that pornography may have this effect. Donnerstein (1980) found that males who watched a videotape of a violent rape scene subsequently gave more intense electric shocks to a female victim than did men who had seen a control tape that was neither violent nor sexual. Males who watched a tape that was highly erotic but not violent gave shocks of no greater intensity than those given by men who saw the control tape. This was true, moreover, even when the female victim had done nothing to deserve the attack.

In a related experiment, Donnerstein and Berkowitz (1981) found that when they showed a tape describing a sexual assault on a woman during which the woman appears to become sexually aroused—thereby fostering the rape myth—male subjects were more aggressive against a female victim than when no such imputations of enjoyment were made. Furthermore, the tendency of males to believe the rape myth is facilitated by exposure to pornography. Malamuth and Check (1981) conducted a large-scale experiment in a natural setting in which more than 200 men and women watched either two violent pornographic movies or two neutral ones. All persons later filled out two attitude scales; one measured acceptance of violence against women, and the other assessed belief in the rape myth. Among male viewers, those who had witnessed pornography expressed higher acceptance of violence against women and greater belief in the rape myth than those who saw the neutral films. Women showed the opposite effects on both measures, with exposure to pornography further depressing already low scores on both scales.

Summary

In this section we have examined some of the variables that dispose a person to respond more or less aggressively to some of the eliciting conditions reviewed in the previous section. One such variable is the cultural background of the person. Certain cultures and subcultures place a high value on aggressive behavior by their members. These values may translate into aggressive beliefs and attitudes as well as tendencies toward violent behavior. Another contributor to the person's disposition to aggress is the ambience of the symbols of violence, such as weapons and depictions of aggression in the media. Both laboratory and naturalistic studies have shown violence in the media to be positively associated with aggressive behavior in the observer, at least under certain conditions. Individual differences in personality and gender differences also dispose individuals to differing levels of aggressive behavior. We see many of these predisposing factors in aggression come together in the social problem of male violence against women.

ADDITIONAL TOPICS IN AGGRESSION

Aggression as Goal-Seeking Behavior

Given sufficient provocation and enough of a predisposition to aggress, the ordinary person will probably commit some sort of aggressive act. We must now inquire as to the goal or purpose of aggression. True, we have already observed that aggression is motivated by an intention to hurt another person, but this does not really explain the behavior. Why does the aggressor wish to hurt the victim? We must dig more deeply to find the more basic causes. When we do, we come up against a still unresolved issue: To what extent is aggression a unitary phenomenon?

This is a difficult question to answer, because of the great complexity of aggression. Still, some observers have sought to answer it by postulating at least two different kinds of aggression. The first, usually called angry or *affective aggression*, is characterized by anger or some other negative emotion; whereas the other, called *instrumental aggression*, is carried out in a less affectively charged way for purposes having nothing to do with feelings for the victim. The first type is characteristic of a crime of passion in which one person kills another out of hatred or fury. The second type is exemplified by a professional killing conducted for a fee. This distinction has been commonly drawn (e.g., Bandura, 1973; Geen, 1990) and has some utility, but it may oversimplify or even distort the nature of aggression and the goals that aggression serves.

For one thing, there is less reason to make a sharp distinction between instrumentality and affect in aggression than we might suppose. Most acts of aggression are characterized by both. The aggression visited on a victim by an emotionally aroused perpetrator is not, except perhaps in cases of temporary insanity, without instrumental value. A person who has been insulted or humiliated by another may feel angry and try to hurt the other in order to restore a sense of self-esteem (Felson, 1984; Kernis, Grannemann, & Mathis 1991). One who has been frustrated in her attempts to reach a goal by the meddling of a friend may aggress angrily, but also, in part at least, to cause a cessation of the meddling. Even urban riots, which appear on the surface to be random and pointless, may reflect a feeling on the part of the rioters that the distribution of goods in society is unfair and that equity can be restored if the "have-nots" destroy some of the property of the "haves." Nor is instrumental aggression completely separable from affect. Generation of negative affect may, for example, facilitate the carrying out of aggression that is motivated mainly by instrumental concerns. For example, it is common during wartime for governments to encourage hatred toward the people against whom the war is being fought, even though most people on both sides have no real reason to hate their adversaries.

By diminishing the traditional distinction between affective and instrumental aggression, we are in a better position to understand aggression as a more or less normative part of human interaction rather than as a pathological behavioral aberration (DaGloria, 1984; Felson & Tedeschi, 1993). In most instances aggression is not an isolated act. It arises in the context of an ongoing relationship in which all parties have certain expectations regarding normal behavior. Some writers have argued that the norm that is implicit in such settings prescribes that each person will cause only as much discomfort to others as it necessary for attaining his or her goals. Should any people exceed the normative level, their behavior will be considered by the others to be excessive and motivated by intent to hurt. It will, in other words, be regarded as a malicious act of aggression.

Such acts are commonly observed in sporting events. If, for example, an ice hockey player goes beyond the normal rough contact of that sport by hitting an adversary over the head with his stick, he will be condemned for excessive violence. Likewise, a baseball pitcher who throws pitches near a batter to keep him loose is called a good competitor; one who deliberately throws at a batter's head is branded as a "dirty player." The initial response to such judgments of intent and malice is, as we have already seen above, anger and a desire to retaliate. If the retaliation is exact and in kind, the normative state that existed before the malicious transgression will be restored (Mummendey & Mummendey, 1983). Thus, according to this viewpoint, the major provocation for aggression is violation of a behavioral norm (DaGloria & DeRidder, 1977, 1979; Ohbuchi, 1982).

Can Aggression Be Controlled?

Whether one believes that aggression is a part of normal social life or that it is a manifestation o behavioral pathology, most people would probably agree that society would be well served if the level of social aggression and violence could be controlled. Nobody has a quick and certain answer to the question of how society may control human violence. Nevertheless, social psychologists who study the causes of aggression are well situated to make at least some suggestions regarding control on the basis of their evidence. In this final section, therefore, a few suggestions will be offered concerning possible means of controlling aggressive behavior in society.

Attempts to control aggression are usually made on two levels. The first is individualistic. The assumption behind this approach is that control is best manifested at the personal level. Thus, for example, it may be possible for society to reduce the level of violence through a change in socialization and child-rearing practices. If children can be taught to use constructive and nonviolent methods to resolve interpersonal conflict, they may be less likely to retrieve aggressive scripts from memory in such settings. In addition, nonreinforcement of aggressive behavior may in time shape a less violent nature in the child.

Parents may also help control aggression in their children by reducing the amount of exposure that children have to the symbols and artifacts of violence, such as weapons and the portrayal of aggression in the media, and by making them more discriminating viewers of such materials. Eron (1986) has reviewed research in which attempts have been made to educate children to become more critical viewers of television and to formulate cognitive scripts that are incompatible with aggression, such as those calling for socially cooperative and helpful behavior. This research gives some encouraging signs that such practices may help reduce aggression in children.

 Human aggression will not be controlled entirely through efforts at the level of the individual, however. Many of the causes of aggression are inherent in society and must be approached at the social level. Measures calling for gun control, for example, could have a dual effect of reducing the availability of the weapons of violence while at the same time reducing the prevalence of a stimulus for possible aggressive reactions (Berkowitz & LePage, 1967). Possibly the subculture of violence that is so widespread in our cities could be reduced by the recruitment of potential aggressors, such as members of adolescent gangs, for constructive activity in rebuilding and policing neighborhoods. Such activity might provide something akin to what William James once called "the moral equivalent of war" (the channeling of potentially destructive urges into socially useful activity).

Finally, many social scientists agree that a major attack on aggressive behavior must include an effort at ending social and economic injustice and inequity. When gross inequalities between the very rich and the very poor become characteristic of society, and particularly when large segments of the population decide that their situation is hopeless and that they have nothing to lose, violence may be regarded as the only means of restoring a norm of fairness.

CHAPTER SUMMARY

Aggression is the product of an interaction between characteristics of the person and environmental conditions that aggravate the person and induce negative affect. The initial and immediate reaction to such situations is associative, in that negative affect activates thoughts, emotions, and action tendencies related to aggression. This immediate reaction comprises a tendency either to aggress or to avoid the situation. It is followed by cognitive processing of information about the situation whereby the person interprets the source of provocation and attributes causes to it. The outcome of the attribution process may be increased anger toward the agent of the provocation along with a perception that a social norm has been violated by that person's action. Both of these states may then lead to aggressive behavior.

Characteristics of the person create a disposition to respond with varying levels of aggression to suitably aggravating situations. These characteristics are the result of both genetic inheritance and experience. Personality and gender differences in aggression may be linked to both genetic and experiential factors. Social and cultural conditions also contribute to the person's disposition to aggress, by providing value systems that support and encourage aggressive behavior and by supplying symbols of violence such as those observed in the mass media of communication. Both personality and cultural factors enter into the antecedent conditions of male violence against women.

Aggression, once it has come under the control of cognitive processes, is goal-directed behavior. The goal may be restoration of self-esteem or revenge motivated by anger, or it may be some reward largely unrelated to the aggression itself. We have typically referred to these types of aggression as affective and instrumental, respectively. Some theorists argue that what has been called affective aggression should be considered instead as normal human interactive behavior, with a basis in social customs, and with the goal being restoration of a normative state following the violation of the norm by the provoking party.

The control of aggression and violence is a major challenge faced by society. To some extent violence may be controllable at the individual level through changing patterns of child rearing, the inculcation of values that are incompatible with aggression, and the control of violent symbols in the environment. However, control of violence will also require social changes aimed at promoting social justice and enhancing the significance and worth of all members of society.

References

ABELSON, R. P. (1976). Script processing in attitude formation and decision making. In J. S. Carroll & J. W. Payne (Eds.), *Cognition and social behavior* (pp. 33–46). Hillsdale, NJ: Erlbaum.

ANDERSON, C. A. (1989). Temperature and aggression: The ubiquitous effects of heat on the occurrence of human violence. *Psychological Bulletin, 106,* 74–96.

BACHRACH, R. S. (1986). The differential effects of observation of violence on kibbutz and city children in Israel. In L. R. Huesmann & L. D. Eron (Eds.), *Television and the aggressive child: A cross-national comparison* (pp. 201–238). Hillsdale, NJ: Erlbaum.

BANDURA, A. (1973). *Aggression: A social learning analysis.* Englewood Cliffs, NJ: Prentice-Hall.

BANDURA, A., ROSS, D., & ROSS, S. A. (1963). Imitation of film-mediated aggressive models. *Journal of Abnormal and Social Psychology, 66,* 3–11.

BARASH, D. P. (1977). *Sociobiology and behavior.* Amsterdam: Elsevier.

BARON, R. A., & RICHARDSON, D. (1994). *Human aggression.* New York: Plenum.

BAUMGARTNER, M. P. (1993). Violent networks: The origins and management of domestic conflict. In R. B. Felson & J. T. Tedeschi (Eds.), *Aggression and violence: Social interactionist perspectives* (pp. 209–231). Washington, DC: American Psychological Association.

BERKOWITZ, L. (1988). Frustrations, appraisals, and aversively stimulated aggression. *Aggressive Behavior, 14,* 3–11.

BERKOWITZ, L. (1989). The frustration-aggression hypothesis: An examination and reformulation. *Psychological Bulletin, 106,* 59–73.

BERKOWITZ, L. B. (1993). *Aggression: Its causes, consequences, and control.* New York: McGraw-Hill.

BERKOWITZ, L., & ALIOTO, J. (1973). The meaning of an observed event as a determinant of its aggressive consequences. *Journal of Personality and Social Psychology, 28,* 206–217.

BERKOWITZ, L., COCHRAN, S. T., & EMBREE, M. (1981). Physical pain and the goal of aversively stimulated aggression. *Journal of Personality and Social Psychology, 40,* 687–700.

BERKOWITZ, L., & HEIMER, K. (1989). On the construction of the anger experience: Aversive events and negative priming in the formation of feelings. In L. Berkowitz (Ed.), *Advances in experimental social psychology* (Vol. 22, pp. 1–37). New York: Academic Press.

BERKOWITZ, L., & LEPAGE, A. (1967). Weapons as aggression-eliciting stimuli. *Journal of Personality and Social Psychology, 7,* 202–207.

BERSANI, A., CHEN, H. T., PENDLETON, B. F., & DENTON, R. (1992). Personality traits of convicted male batterers. *Journal of Family Violence, 7,* 123–134.

BOWER, G. (1980). Mood and memory. *American Psychologist, 36,* 129–148.

BUSHMAN, B. J., & GEEN, R. G. (1990). Role of cognitive-emotional mediators and individual differences in the effects of media violence on aggression. *Journal of Personality and Social Psychology, 58,* 156–163.

BUSS, A. H. (1961). *The psychology of aggression.* New York: Wiley.

BUSS, A. H. (1963). Physical aggression in relation to different frustrations. *Journal of Abnormal and Social Psychology, 63,* 1–7.

BUSS, A. H., & PLOMIN, R. (1984). *Temperament: Early developing personality traits.* Hillsdale, NJ: Erlbaum.

CAMPBELL, A., BIBEL, D., & MUNCER, S. (1985). Predicting our own aggression: Person, subculture, or situation? *British Journal of Social Psychology, 24,* 168–180.

CARPENTER, B., & DARLEY, J. M. (1978). A naive psychological analysis of counteraggression. *Personality and Social Psychology Bulletin, 4,* 68–72.

DAGLORIA, J. (1984). Frustration, aggression, and the sense of justice. In A. Mummendey (Ed.), *Social psychology of aggression: From individual behavior to social interaction* (pp. 127–141). New York: Springer-Verlag.

DAGLORIA, J., & DERIDDER, R. (1977). Aggression in dyadic interaction. *European Journal of Social Psychology, 7,* 189–219.

DAGLORIA, J., & DERIDDER, R. (1979). Sex differences in aggression: Are current notions misleading? *European Journal of Social Psychology, 9,* 49–66.

DELUTY, R. H. (1985). Consistency of assertive, aggressive, and submissive behavior for children. *Journal of Personality and Social Psychology, 49,* 1054–1065.

DENGERINK, H. A., & BERTILSON, H. S. (1974). The reduction of attack-instigated aggression. *Journal of Research in Personality, 8,* 254–262.

DIENER, E., & DUFOUR, D. (1978). Does television violence enhance program popularity? *Journal of Personality and Social Psychology, 36,* 333–341.

DODGE, K. A. (1980). Social cognition and children's aggressive behavior. *Child Development, 51*, 162–170.

DODGE, K. A., & COIE, J. D. (1987). Social-information-processing factors in reactive and proactive aggression in children's peer groups. *Journal of Personality and Social Psychology, 53*, 1146–1158.

DODGE, K. A., MURPHY, R. R., & BUCHSBAUM, K. (1984). The assessment of intention-cue detection skills in children: Implications for developmental psychopathology. *Child Development, 55*, 163–173.

DOLLARD, J., DOOB, L. W., MILLER, N. E., MOWRER, O. H., & SEARS, R. R. (1939). *Frustration and aggression.* New Haven, CT: Yale University Press.

DONNERSTEIN, E. (1980). Aggressive erotica and violence against women. *Journal of Personality and Social Psychology, 39*, 269–277.

DONNERSTEIN, E., & BERKOWITZ, L. (1981). Victim reactions in aggressive erotic films as a factor in violence against women. *Journal of Personality and Social Psychology, 41*, 710–724.

EAGLY, A. H., & STEFFEN, F. J. (1986). Gender and aggressive behavior: A meta-analytic review of the social psychological literature. *Psychological Bulletin, 100*, 309–330.

EIBL-EIBESFELDT, I. (1977). Phylogenetic adaptation as determinants of aggressive behavior in man. In W. Hartup & J. DeWit (Eds.), *Origins of aggression* (pp. 27–55). The Hague: Mouton.

EISENBERG, G. J. (1980). Children and aggression after observed film aggression with sanctioning adults. *Annals of the New York Academy of Science, 347*, 304–318.

ENDLER, N. S., & HUNT, J. McV. (1968). S-R inventories of hostility and comparisons of the proportions of variance from persons, responses, and situations for hostility and anxiousness. *Journal of Personality and Social Psychology, 9*, 309–316.

ERON, L. D. (1986). Interventions to mitigate the psychological effects of media violence on aggressive behavior. *Journal of Social Issues, 42*, 155–169.

ERON, L. D., WALDER, L. O., & LEFKOWITZ, M. M. (1971). *Learning of aggression in children.* Boston: Little, Brown.

FELSON, R. B. (1984). Patterns of aggressive social interaction. In A. Mummendey (Ed.), *Social psychology of aggression: From individual behavior to social interaction.* (pp. 107–126). New York: Springer-Verlag.

FELSON, R. B., & TEDESCHI, J. T. (Eds.). (1993). *Aggression and violence: Social interactionist perspectives.* Washington, DC: American Psychological Association.

FENIGSTEIN, A. (1979). Does aggression cause a preference for viewing media violence? *Journal of Personality and Social Psychology, 37*, 2307–2317.

FERGUSON, T. J., & RULE, B. G. (1983). An attributional perspective on anger and aggression. In R. G. Geen & E. Donnerstein (Eds.), *Aggression: Theoretical and empirical reviews (Vol. 1: Theoretical and methodological issues*, pp. 41–74). New York: Academic Press.

FESHBACH, S. (1964). The function of aggression and the regulation of aggressive drive. *Psychological Review, 71*, 257–272.

FREEDMAN, J. L. (1984). Effect of television violence on aggressiveness. *Psychological Bulletin, 96*, 227–246.

FREUD, S. (1915/1963). Instincts and their vicissitudes. In P. Rieff (Ed.), *Freud: General psychological theory.* New York: Collier Books.

FREUD, S. (1920/1959). *Beyond the pleasure principle.* New York: Bantam Books.

FREUD, S. (1932/1963). Why war? In P. Rieff (Ed.), *Freud: Character and culture* (pp. 134–147). New York: Collier Books.

FRIEDRICH-COFER, L., & HUSTON, A. C. (1986). Television violence and aggression: The debate continues. *Psychological Bulletin, 100*, 364–371.

FRODI, A., MACAULAY, J., & THOME, P. R. (1977). Are women always less aggressive than men? A review of the experimental literature. *Psychological Bulletin, 84,* 634–660.

GEEN, R. G. (1968). Effects of frustration, attack, and prior training in aggressiveness upon aggressive behavior. *Journal of Personality and Social Psychology, 9,* 316–321.

GEEN, R. G. (1978). Effects of attack and uncontrollable noise on aggression. *Journal of Research in Personality, 12,* 15–29.

GEEN, R. G. (1981). Behavioral and physiological reactions to observed violence: Effects of prior exposure to aggressive stimuli. *Journal of Personality and Social Psychology, 40,* 868–875.

GEEN, R. G. (1990). *Human Aggression.* Pacific Grove, CA: Brooks-Cole.

GEEN, R. G., & STONNER, D. M. (1973). Context effects in observed violence. *Journal of Personality and Social Psychology, 25,* 145–150.

GEEN, R. G., & THOMAS, S. L. (1986). The immediate effects of media violence on behavior. *Journal of Social Issues, 42,* 7–27.

GELLES, R., & STRAUS, M. (1979). Determinants of violence in the family: Toward a theoretical integration. In W. Burr, R. Hill, F. Nye, & I. Riess (Eds.), *Contemporary theories about the family* (pp. 549–581). New York: Free Press.

GHODSIAN-CARPEY, J., & BAKER, L. A. (1987). Genetic and environmental influences on aggression in 4- to 7-year-old twins. *Aggressive Behavior, 13,* 173–186.

HEAROLD, S. (1986). A synthesis of 1043 effects of television on social behavior. In G. Comstock (Ed.), *Public communication and behavior* (Vol. 1, pp. 65–133). New York: Academic Press.

HUESMANN, L. R., & ERON, L. D. (1984). Cognitive processes and the persistence of aggressive behavior. *Aggressive Behavior, 10,* 243–251.

HUESMANN, L. R., & ERON, L. D. (Eds.). (1986a). *Television and the aggressive child: A cross-national comparison.* Hillsdale, NJ: Erlbaum.

HUESMANN, L. R., & ERON, L. D. (1986b). The development of aggression in American children as a consequence of television violence viewing. In L. R. Huesmann & L. D. Eron (Eds.), *Television and the aggressive child: A cross-national comparison* (pp. 45–80). Hillsdale, NJ: Erlbaum.

HUESMANN, L. R., ERON, L. D., LEFKOWITZ, M. M., & WALDER, L. O. (1984). Stability of aggression over time and generations. *Developmental Psychology, 20,* 1120–1134.

HUTT, C., & VAIZEY, M. J. (1966). Differential effects of group density on social behavior. *Nature, 209,* 1371–1372.

HYDE, J. S. (1984). How large are gender differences in aggression? A developmental meta-analysis. *Developmental Psychology, 20,* 722–736.

HYNAN, D. J. & GRUSH, J. E. (1986). Effects of impulsivity, depression, provocation, and time on aggressive behavior. *Journal of Research in Personality, 20,* 158–171.

JAMES, W. (1910/1987). The moral equivalent of war. *William James: Writings 1902–1910* (pp. 1281–1293). New York: Library of America.

JULIAN, T. W. & MCKENRY, P. C. (1993). Mediators of male violence toward female intimates. *Journal of Family Violence, 8,* 39–56.

KERNIS, M. H., GRANNEMANN, B. D., & MATHIS, L. C. (1991). Stability of self-esteem as a moderator of the relation between level of self-esteem and depression. *Journal of Personality and Social Psychology, 61,* 80–84.

KLEIN, M. W. (1969). Violence in American juvenile gangs. In D. J. Mulvihill & M. M. Tumin (Eds.), *Crimes of violence: A staff report submitted to the National Commission on the Causes and Prevention of Violence, Vol. 13* (pp. 1427–1460). Washington, DC: United States Government Printing Office.

KORNADT, H.-J. (1984). Development of aggressiveness: A motivation theory perspective. In R. M. Kaplan, V. J. Konecni, & R. W. Novaco (Eds.), *Aggression in children and youth* (pp. 73–87). The Hague: Nijhoff.

Koss, M. P., Gidycz, C. A., & Wisniewski, N. (1987). The scope of rape: Incidence and prevalence of sexual aggression and victimization in a national sample of higher education students. *Journal of Consulting and Clinical Psychology, 55,* 162–170.

Lefkowitz, M. M., Eron, L. D., Walder, L. O., & Huesmann, L. R. (1977). *Growing up to be violent.* New York: Pergamon.

Lorenz, K. (1966). *On Aggression.* New York: Harcourt Brace.

Maccoby, E. E., & Jacklin, C. N. (1980). Sex differences in aggression: A rejoinder and reprise. *Child Development, 51,* 964–980.

Malamuth, N., & Check, J. (1981). The effects of violent sexual movies: A field experiment. *Journal of Research in Personality, 15,* 436–446.

May, R. (1972). *Power and innocence.* New York: Norton.

McDougall, W. (1908). *An introduction to social psychology.* London: Methuen.

Moyer, K. E. (1976). *The psychobiology of aggression.* New York: Harper & Row.

Muehlenhard, C. L., & Linton, M. A. (1987). Date rape and sexual aggression in dating situations: Incidence and risk factors. *Journal of Counseling Psychology, 34,* 186–196.

Mulvihill, D. J., & Tumin, M. M. (Eds.). (1969). *Crimes of violence: A staff report submitted to the National Commission on the Causes and Prevention of Violence, Vol. 13.* Washington, DC: United States Government Printing Office.

Mummendey, A., & Mummendey, H. D. (1983). Aggressive behavior of soccer players as social interaction. In J. H. Goldstein (Ed.), *Sports violence* (pp. 111–128). New York: Springer-Verlag.

Nasby, W., Hayden, B., & DePaulo, B. M. (1979). Attributional bias among aggressive boys to interpret unambiguous social stimuli as displays of hostility. *Journal of Abnormal Psychology, 89,* 459–468.

Nisbett, R. E. (1993). Violence and U.S. regional culture. *American Psychologist, 48,* 441–449.

Ohbuchi, K. (1982). On the cognitive integration mediating reactions to attack patterns. *Social Psychology Quarterly, 45,* 213–218.

Olweus, D. (1979). Stability of aggressive reaction patterns in males: A review. *Psychological Bulletin, 86,* 852–875.

O'Neal, E. C., McDonald, P. J., Cloninger, C., & Levine, D. (1979). Coactor's behavior and imitative aggression. *Motivation and Emotion, 3,* 373–379.

Perry, D. G., & Perry, L. C. (1976). Identification with film characters, covert aggressive verbalization, and reactions to film violence. *Journal of Research in Personality, 10,* 399–409.

Perry, D. G., Perry, L. C., & Rasmussen, P. (1986). Cognitive social learning mediators of aggression. *Child Development, 57,* 700–711.

Quackenbush, R. L. (1989). A comparison of androgynous, masculine sex-typed, and undifferentiated males on dimensions of attitudes toward rape. *Journal of Research in Personality, 23,* 318–342.

Reinisch, J. M., & Sanders, S. A. (1986). A test of sex differences in aggressive response to hypothetical conflict situations. *Journal of Personality and Social Psychology, 50,* 1045–1049.

Roberts, D. F., & Maccoby, N. (1985). Effects of mass communication. In G. Lindzey & E. Aronson (Eds.), *Handbook of social psychology* (Vol. 2, pp. 539–598). New York: Random House.

Rotton, J. (1986). Determinism *redux:* Climate and cultural correlates of violence. *Environment and Behavior, 18,* 346–368.

Rotton, J., & Frey, J. (1985). Air pollution, weather, and violent crimes: Concomitant time-series analysis of archival data. *Journal of Personality and Social Psychology, 49,* 1207–1220.

RULE, B. G. & NESDALE, A. R. (1976). Emotional arousal and aggressive behavior. *Psychological Bulletin, 83,* 851–863.

RUSHTON, J. P., FULKER, D. W., NEALE, M. C., NIAS, D. K. B., & EYSENCK, H. J. (1986). Altruism and aggression: The heritability of individual differences. *Journal of Personality and Social Psychology, 50,* 1192–1198.

SHOPE, G. L., HEDRICK, T. E., & GEEN, R. G. (1978). Physical/verbal aggression: Sex differences in style. *Journal of Personality, 46,* 23–42.

SINGER, J. L., & SINGER, D. G. (1981). *Television, imagination, and aggression: A study of preschoolers.* Hillsdale, NJ: Erlbaum.

SRULL, T. K., & WYER, R. S. (1979). The role of category accessibility in the interpretation of information about persons: Some determinants and implications. *Journal of Personality and Social Psychology, 37,* 1660–1672.

STRAUS, M., & GELLES, R. (1986). Societal change in family violence from 1975 to 1985 as revealed in two national surveys. *Journal of Marriage and the Family, 48,* 785–793.

TAYLOR, S. P., & EPSTEIN, S. (1967). Aggression as a function of the interaction of the sex of the aggressor and the sex of the victim. *Journal of Personality, 35,* 474–486.

TOCH, H. (1969). *Violent men: An inquiry into the psychology of violence.* Chicago: Aldine.

TURNER, C. W., & BERKOWITZ, L. (1972). Identification with film aggressor (covert role taking) and reactions to film violence. *Journal of Personality and Social Psychology, 21,* 256–264.

WANN, D. L., & BRANSCOMBE, N. R. (1990). Person perception when aggressive or nonaggressive sports are primed. *Aggressive Behavior, 16,* 27–32.

WHITE, J. W. (1983). Sex and gender issues in aggression research. In R. G. Geen & E. Donnerstein (Eds.), *Aggression: Theoretical and empirical reviews, Vol. 2: Issues in research* (pp. 1–26). New York: Academic Press.

WHITING, B., & EDWARDS, C. P. (1973). A cross-cultural analysis of sex differences in the behavior of children aged 3 through 11. *Journal of Social Psychology, 91,* 171–188.

WOLFGANG, M., & FERRACUTI, F. (1967). *The subculture of violence: Toward an integrated theory of criminality.* London: Tavistock.

WOOD, W., WONG, F., & CHACHERE, J. (1991). Effects of media violence on viewers' aggression in unconstrained social interaction. *Psychological Bulletin, 109,* 371–383.

ZILLMANN, D. (1971). Excitation transfer in communication-mediated aggressive behavior. *Journal of Experimental Social Psychology, 7,* 419–434.

ZILLMAN, D. (1979). *Hostility and aggression.* Hillsdale, NJ: Erlbaum.

ZILLMANN, D. (1988). Cognition-excitation interdependencies in aggressive behavior. *Aggressive Behavior, 14,* 51–64.

ZILLMANN, D., KATCHER, A. H., & MILAVSKY, B. (1972). Excitation transfer from physical exercise to subsequent aggressive behavior. *Journal of Experimental Social Psychology, 8,* 247–259.

Further Readings

BARON, R. A., & RICHARDSON, D. (1994). *Human aggression.* New York: Plenum.

A comprehensive introduction to the psychology of aggression organized around contemporary theories and research, and organized along lines of the major areas of investigation.

BERKOWITZ, L. B. (1993). *Aggression: Its causes, consequences, and control.* New York: McGraw-Hill.

An advanced treatment of the psychology of aggression that includes a thorough discussion of the cognitive-neoassociationist position. The book also provides excellent reviews on family and domestic violence.

FELSON, R. B., & TEDESCHI, J. T. (Eds.). (1993). *Aggression and violence: Social interactionist perspectives*. Washington, DC: American Psychological Association.

A collection of papers setting forth the view that aggressive behavior is a part of normal human social interaction and is to be studied in that context.

FRIEDRICH-COFER, L., & HUSTON, A. C. (1986). Television violence and aggression: The debate continues. *Psychological Bulletin, 100,* 364–371.

A review of studies on the relationship of televised violence to aggression, emphasizing the results of naturalistic studies and focusing on current theoretical controversies.

HUESMANN, L. R. (1988). An information-processing model for the development of aggression. *Aggressive Behavior, 14,* 13–24.

A concise overview of the theory of the role of aggressive scripts in the social learning of aggression.

ZILLMANN, D. (1988). Cognition-excitation interdependencies in aggressive behavior. *Aggressive Behavior, 14,* 51–64.

A concise and informative theoretical review of the interaction of affect and cognition in the construction of anger and aggression, along with a discussion of relevant evidence.

Left: John Levine (Ph.D., University of Wisconsin) is currently a professor in the psychology department and a senior scientist in the Learning Research and Development Center at the University of Pittsburgh. He has published theoretical and empirical papers on several topics, including group socialization, social comparison, and majority/minority influence. This work has benefitted greatly from his long collaboration with Richard Moreland. Dr. Levine's current research focuses on cognition in social contexts, specifically the impact of anticipated and actual interaction on thinking and the determinants of information sharing and use in groups working under stress. In line with this interest, he has recently co-edited a volume entitled Perspectives on Socially Shared Cognition *with L. Resnick and S. Teasley. Dr. Levine is editor of the* Journal of Experimental Social Psychology *and a member of the Social and Group Processes Review Committee of the National Institute of Mental Health. For additional fun, he swims, plays squash, and reads history books.*

Right: Richard Moreland (Ph.D., University of Michigan) is currently a professor in the psychology department at the University of Pittsburgh. He has published numerous chapters and articles on small groups, focusing on such neglected topics as group formation and development, group composition effects, and group socialization. Much of this work was completed with the help of his colleague and friend, John Levine. In his spare time (which seems to decrease every year), Richard enjoys eating, reading, and listening to music. He pursues all three activities with lots of enthusiasm but little refinement.

CHAPTER 11

Group Processes

John M. Levine and Richard L. Moreland
University of Pittsburgh

CHAPTER OUTLINE

*Preparation of this chapter was supported by funds from the Office of Educational Research and Improvement, Department of Education, and from the Office of Naval Research.

. . . to our left rear, we saw a Marine stretcher team bringing a casualty back through the rain. . . . As the stretcher team approached the cover of some trees, Japanese riflemen to our left front opened up on them . . . we watched helplessly as the four stretcher bearers struggled across the muddy field with bullets falling all round them. It was one of those terribly pathetic, heartrending sights that seemed to rule in combat: men struggling to save a wounded comrade, the enemy firing at them as fast as they could, and the rest of us utterly powerless to give any aid. . . . To our dismay, the two carriers in the rear got hit by a burst of fire. Each loosened his grip on the stretcher. Their knees buckled, and they fell over backwards onto the muddy ground. The stretcher pitched onto the deck. . . . The two Marines at the other end of the stretcher threw it down, spun around, and grabbed the stretcher casualty between them. Then each supported a wounded carrier with his other arm. As we cheered, all five assisted one another and limped and hobbled into the cover of the bushes, bullets still kicking up mud all around them.

—E. B. SLEDGE, *With the old breed, at Peleliu and Okinawa*. New York: Oxford University Press, 1990, pp. 215–216 (first published by Presidio Press, Novato, CA, 1981)

Q: How many people did you round up?

A: Well, there was about 40–45 people that we gathered in the center of the village. And we placed them in there, and it was like a little island, right there in the center of the village, I'd say . . . . And . . .

Q: What kind of people—men, women, children?

A: Men, women, children.

Q: Babies?

A: Babies. And we all huddled them up. We made them squat down, and Lieutenant Calley came over and said, "You know what to do with them, don't you?" And I said yes. So I took it for granted that he just wanted us to watch them. And he left, and came back about 10 or 15 minutes later and said, "How come you ain't killed them yet?" And I told him I didn't think you wanted us to kill them, that you just wanted us to guard them. He said, "No, I want them dead." So—

.

.

.

Q: And you killed how many? At that time?

A: Well, I fired them automatic, so you can't—you just spray the area on them and so you can't know how many you killed 'cause they were going fast. So I might have killed ten or fifteen of them.

Q: Men, women, and children?

A: Men, women, and children.

Q: And babies?

A: And babies.

Interview with Paul Meadlo, participant in the My Lai massacre. *New York Times*,
November 25, 1969.

GROUPS: GOOD OR BAD?

These two examples of behavior by military personnel, one involving heroic sacrifice on behalf of in-group members and the other involving savage brutality against out-group members, raise an old question about the role that groups play in human affairs. Some social philosophers argue that people are intrinsically good (e.g., Rogers, 1980). According to this view, positive behaviors spring from our benign natures, whereas negative behaviors are produced by social forces. Selfish and aggressive acts thus stem from the pernicious impact of groups on weak, though basically virtuous, individuals. If only group constraints on individual behavior were weakened, the argument goes, civilization would flower. Other social philosophers take just the opposite position, namely, that people are inherently bad (e.g., Freud, 1930/1961). According to this view, negative behaviors spring from our malignant natures, whereas positive behaviors are produced by social forces. Selfish and aggressive acts thus stem from the failure of groups to control the antisocial impulses of individuals. If only group constraints on individual behavior were strengthened, the argument goes, civilization would flower.

Which position is correct? Are groups fundamentally good or bad? The answer to this question, like the answers to so many questions involving right and wrong, is not as simple as we might wish. Instead, the answer depends on what aspect of group behavior we are considering and what evaluative criteria we are using. A careful examination of any group would probably reveal some processes and outcomes that were praiseworthy and others that were not. In addition, different observers (e.g., allies versus enemies) might offer different evaluations of a particular group process (e.g., authoritarian leadership) or outcome (e.g., the emergence of factions). Thus, we are forced to conclude that participation in groups can have *both* positive and negative consequences and that the value of any consequence is determined by the judgment (and biases) of the observer.

So far, our discussion has focused on how outsiders, or nonmembers, evaluate the consequences of group activity. It is also important to consider how insiders, or members, evaluate their group experiences. Why do people join groups in the first place, why do they remain members after they join, and why do groups persist for long periods of time? The ubiquity of groups in human (and many animal) societies is due to their ability to fulfill members' basic needs (cf. Forsyth, 1990; Mackie & Goethals, 1987; Moreland, 1987; Shaver & Buhrmester, 1983). Several such needs can be identified. Groups satisfy members' survival needs by facilitating their ability to conceive and rear children, acquire food and shelter, and defend themselves against enemies. Groups satisfy members' psychological needs by allowing them to affiliate with others, avoid loneliness, and exercise power. Groups satisfy members' informational needs by clarifying the rewards and costs of particular behaviors and allowing members to evaluate themselves through comparison with others. And groups satisfy members' identity needs by providing a social basis for their self-definitions. Although group membership does not always produce need fulfillment, the rewards of group membership are usually great enough to ensure that most people, from the very young to the very old, belong to groups of some kind.

DEFINITIONAL CONSIDERATIONS

We have argued that, from the perspective of outsiders, groups have both positive and negative consequences and, from the perspective of insiders, that groups often facilitate need satisfaction. It is time to be more specific about what we mean by the term *group*. Textbooks are littered with definitions of groups, and a few examples should be sufficient to indicate their general flavor. For Cartwright and Zander (1968), a group is "a collection of individuals who have relations to one another that make them interdependent to some significant degree" (p. 46). For Shaw (1981), a group is "two or more persons who are interacting with one another in such a manner that each person influences and is influenced by each other person" (p. 8). And for Turner (1987), a psychological group is "one that is psychologically significant for the members, to which they relate themselves subjectively for social comparison and the acquisition of norms and values . . . , that they privately accept membership in, and which influences their attitudes and behaviour" (pp. 1–2).

These definitions imply that it is both possible and profitable to make a clear-cut distinction between groups and nongroups. However, McGrath (1984) has argued that we should abandon this goal and instead view "groupness" as a continuum. He has suggested that different types of social aggregates (e.g., crowds, organizations, friendship groups, families) possess different degrees of groupness. According to McGrath, three criteria determine the degree to which an aggregate is a group. These criteria are size, interdependence, and temporal pattern. McGrath suggests that a social aggregate is a group to the extent that (a) the number of members is low, (b) members interact freely on a wide range of activities, and (c) members have a long history together and anticipate a long future. On the basis of these criteria, friendship groups and families are "groupier" than crowds and organizations. In the discussion that follows, we will restrict our attention primarily to "groupy" social aggregates, as defined by McGrath.

Although we will focus on small groups, we disagree with McGrath about how two-person aggregates, or *dyads*, should be treated. His size criterion implies that, all other things being equal, dyads are groupier than aggregates with three or more members. We think it is better to consider dyads separately (see, for example, Chapter 8 by Clark and Pataki on attraction and intimate relationships) and to reserve the term *group* for aggregates containing three or more members. This is because dyads differ from larger aggregates in several important ways (Simmel, 1950). For example, unlike aggregates of three or more people, dyads are destroyed by the loss of a single member. And certain kinds of processes that are common in larger aggregates—such as mediation of conflicts, coalition formation, and majority and minority influence—cannot occur in dyads. These differences have important implications, suggesting that it is useful to distinguish dyads from groups. This does not mean, of course, that certain processes (e.g., interpersonal attraction) cannot operate similarly in the two cases.

THE ECOLOGY OF SMALL GROUPS

When we think about a small group, we often focus on what happens inside the group, such as the distribution of power among members, the ways that members interact with one another, the group's success at achieving its goals, and so on. However, it is important to recognize that small groups do not exist in a vacuum, isolated from their surroundings. All groups are embedded in particular environments, and these environments profoundly influence the ways that members behave toward one another and the rewards and costs they experience. Three aspects of a group's environment are especially important—*physical, social,* and *temporal.*

Physical Environments

Perhaps the most obvious group environment is the physical setting in which the group operates. We should not be surprised to learn, for example, that groups forced to work in dangerous and confining physical environments—such as beneath the ground (e.g., coal miners), under water (e.g., submariners), or in outer space (e.g., astronauts)—develop particular forms of interaction adapted to the harsh conditions they face (George, 1981; Harrison & Connors, 1984; Kanas, 1985). Evidence indicates that groups in these environments (at least successful groups) tend to be characterized by strong leadership, high cohesiveness, and substantial conformity pressure. These characteristics, which increase the group's ability to take coordinated action and reduce conflicts among members, are quite adaptive to the demands of harsh and unforgiving environments.

In a study of how coal miners adapt to the stresses of working below ground under dangerous conditions, Vaught and Smith (1980) discuss several mechanisms by which work groups elicit cohesion and conformity in their members. One such mechanism involves ritualized ceremonies for initiating

new members into the group. For example, Vaught and Smith describe a cere-
mony in which a newcomer is bound from head to foot with electrical tape, a
length of wire is tied to his genitals and stretched tightly to a roof bolt overhead,
and other group members toss small rocks at the wire, eliciting expressions of
discomfort from the newcomer each time a rock hits the wire. Rituals such as
these serve several functions, including convincing newcomers that their safety
depends on the goodwill of fellow miners, helping old-timers estimate how
newcomers will respond to the rigors of coal mining, illustrating the group's
power to punish nonconformity in old as well as new members, and promoting
a sense of solidarity within the group.

Of course, physical environments need not be dangerous in order to influence the groups that operate in them. Research indicates that various physical
aspects of factories and offices—such as lighting, temperature, floor space, and
noise—can affect worker performance and satisfaction (Oldham & Rotchford,
1983; Sundstrom, 1986). Such influence can operate at the individual level, as
when the lighting is so low that each member of a work team has difficulty operating his or her machine, or it can operate at the group level, as when the noise
is so high that team members cannot communicate information needed to co-
ordinate their actions. In either case, environmental factors can substantially influence group productivity and member morale.

It is important to note that workers' evaluations of many environmental
stimuli are not determined solely by the physical characteristics of the stimuli
(e.g., the decibel level of a whistle). Frequently, social influence is important.
For example, older workers may provide explicit interpretations of the physical environment for newer workers. Social comparison also may occur when
workers try to figure out the "correct" response to a physical stimulus by comparing their own reactions to those of their co-workers (cf. Festinger, 1954;
Salancik & Pfeffer, 1978). For example, new workers in dangerous occupations
(e.g., police officers, submariners) often learn to control their anxiety by observing the seemingly relaxed actions of veteran workers. Haas (1974, 1977) reported that apprentice high-steel ironworkers, who must walk on beams many
stories above the ground, learn to control their fear of falling by watching old-
timers' apparent nonchalance as they move quickly and confidently from beam
to beam.

The increasing use of computers in factories and offices is producing much
interest in how technology affects work groups (DeSanctis & Gallupe, 1987;
Kiesler, Siegel, & McGuire, 1984). Electronic communication is receiving particular attention, because it is becoming such a commonplace way for group members to share information. Research suggests that electronic communication affects groups in several ways, including reducing the level of overall
communication in the group, equalizing participation rates among members,
and weakening the power of status systems (Hiltz, Johnson, & Turoff, 1986;
McGuire, Kiesler, & Siegel, 1987; Siegel, Dubrovsky, Kiesler, & McGuire, 1986).
Computer-mediated communication also seems to reduce group members' inhibitions against violating conventional norms of social interaction. For example, Siegel and her associates (1986) created three-person groups and asked

them to reach consensus on problems involving alternatives with varying degrees of risk. The groups engaged in face-to-face communication on some problems and in computer-mediated communication on other problems. Siegel and her colleagues found that groups communicating via computer were much less inhibited. That is, they were more likely to swear, insult each other, and engage in name calling than were the same groups communicating face to face. This kind of uninhibited verbal behavior, or "flaming," in computer groups has become a problem in some business and educational institutions where large numbers of people communicate using computers.

Social Environments

Groups are also embedded in social environments composed of other groups and individuals, and the presence of these social actors can substantially influence group processes and outcomes. There are several ways in which the social environment can be conceptualized. One common approach, which has dominated thinking on intergroup relations in social psychology, assumes that only two groups are involved, that they are completely separate from one another (e.g., do not share any members), and that their relationship is characterized by friendly competition at best or murderous hostility at worst (cf. Messick & Mackie, 1989; Stephan, 1985; Devine, Chapter 12 in this volume). Given that intergroup relations of this sort are all too common and lie at the heart of humanity's bloodiest and most intractable conflicts, such as those now occurring in Africa and the Balkans, it is easy to understand why social psychologists have devoted so much attention to them. But the relations between groups and their social environments can take other forms as well.

For example, intergroup relations are often cooperative and friendly rather than competitive and hostile. In some cases, this cooperation is rather indirect, as when one group seeks to improve its productivity by imitating the successful procedures of another group (cf. Galaskiewicz & Wasserman, 1989) or evaluates the adequacy of its outcomes by comparing them to the outcomes of some similar group (e.g., Levine & Moreland, 1987). In other cases, this cooperation is more direct, as when groups exchange information or other valuable resources (e.g., Gatewood, 1984), form alliances to attain mutually desirable outcomes (e.g., Moore, Vigil, & Garcia, 1983), or even surrender their distinctive identities by merging into new groups (e.g., Gaertner, Mann, Murrell, & Dovidio, 1989).

Many small groups are also embedded in large organizations, such as business corporations (Alderfer & Smith, 1982; Ancona, 1987) and social movements (Fine & Stoecker, 1985; Lofland & Jamison, 1984). Organizations often provide supportive environments that allow groups to flourish (Fontana, 1985; Tichy, 1981), but unsuccessful organizations can weaken the groups embedded within them (Greenhalgh, 1983; Krantz, 1985). Embedded groups are by no means powerless, however. Ancona (1987; Ancona & Caldwell, 1988) argues that work groups in organizations seek to control their fate by engaging in such activities as bargaining for resources, acquiring information, impressing others, and defending themselves against outside interference. In order to ensure the success of these activities, such groups develop specialized roles for their members. These roles include the "scout" (who imports information and resources that the group needs), the "ambassador" (who exports information and resources to outsiders), the "sentry" (who controls information and resources that outsiders want to send into the group), and the "guard" (who controls information and resources that the group sends to outsiders).

So far we have implicitly assumed that a person belongs to only one group and therefore different groups have different (i.e., nonoverlapping) memberships. However, this is not always the case. Shared members are an important way in which groups are influenced by their social environments. When a person belongs to multiple groups, these groups become interdependent because the person's experiences in one group can affect his or her behavior in the others. For example, a child's physical, intellectual, and social development, which is strongly influenced by experiences within the family, is also affected by other groups to which family members belong, such as schools, churches, and business corporations (Bronfenbrenner, 1986). In some cases, two groups overlap so much in membership that the boundaries between them become blurred, and people have difficulty separating their roles in one group from their roles in the other. This often happens, for example, when family members are also business associates. Davis and Stern (1980) suggest several techniques that are helpful in separating "family" relationships from "business" relationships. These include developing broadly accepted rules about the transition of power across generations and dividing business responsibilities along lines of conflict within the family.

Finally, the social environments of small groups often contain people who are not actually group members, but who can still influence the group. These people include prospective members and ex-members (Levine & Moreland, 1985), friends and relatives (Stark & Bainbridge, 1980), customers and clients (Greer, 1983), and enemies (Reitzes & Diver, 1982). In some cases, outsiders exert unintentional influence, as when the mere presence of an enemy causes group members to close ranks. In other cases, outsiders exert intentional influence, as when valued customers put pressure on a business to fire an employee whom they dislike. Another example of how intentional influence from outsiders can affect a group is the "home field advantage" in athletic competition. Sports fans, even though they are not members of the teams competing on the field, can influence athletic contests by cheering the home team and booing the visiting team. For example, Greer (1983) found that spectator booing at college basketball games produced a home field advantage, which was due primarily to reduced performance by the visiting team rather than enhanced performance by the home team. It is important to note, however, that athletic teams cannot always count on a human field advantage. Baumeister and Steinhilber (1984) discovered a home field *disadvantage* during championship games, presumably because the home team's desire to look good to its fans causes it to become too self-attentive, which in turn disrupts its performance.

Temporal Environments

Groups vary tremendously in longevity. Some groups exist for only minutes, such as several strangers who cooperate briefly to help an accident victim. Other groups exist for centuries, such as families that can trace their ancestors back to the Mayflower. Between these two extremes are groups with life spans ranging from hours to years.

When groups exist long enough for membership turnover to occur, the temporal environment influences group processes and outcomes in two important ways. First, as time passes, changes occur in the group as a whole. We will refer to these changes as *group development.* Group development can be viewed as analogous to the changes that individuals undergo as they mature. Second, temporal changes also occur in the relationship between the group and each of its members. We will refer to these changes as *group socialization.* Although group development and group socialization are different, they can influence one another in complex ways.

Probably the best-known theory of group development was offered by Tuckman (1965; Tuckman & Jensen, 1977), who argued that groups move through five stages. In the *forming* stage, members seek to orient themselves to the group. They are anxious and uncertain about how they will fit in, and they engage in polite interactions designed to learn about other members and the group task. In the *storming* stage, members try to alter the group to satisfy their personal needs. They become more assertive about how the group should operate, and politeness gives way to conflict and hostility. In the *norming* stage, members endeavor to resolve the disagreements and tensions that threaten group success. They establish norms and roles for carrying out the group task and feel a greater sense of cohesiveness as a result. In the *performing* stage, members attempt to maximize group performance and productivity. Through role taking and joint problem solving, they work together to achieve group goals. Finally, in the *adjourning* stage, members disengage from the group both emotionally and behaviorally. They withdraw from social relationships with other members and reduce their task-related activities.

Tuckman's theory of group development is widely accepted, especially for certain kinds of groups (e.g., therapy, training, self-help). It is not without problems, however. For example, the psychological mechanisms that underlie shifts from one developmental stage to the next are not well specified, and little is said about the factors that determine a group's rate of movement through the five stages (Moreland & Levine, 1988). In addition, research indicates that the pattern of shifts specified by Tuckman's model is not universal (Gersick, 1988; Seeger, 1983). In a study of naturally occurring project teams, Gersick (1988) found that, rather than progressing through a discrete series of stages, the teams showed a pattern of "punctuated equilibrium." By the end of their first meeting, the groups had adopted a problem-solving strategy that they used until half of their calendar time had elapsed. At this point, the groups abruptly shifted to a different strategy, which they retained for the remainder of their meetings. An analogous example of punctuated equilibrium in individual development is the well-known "midlife" crisis, during which people reassess their career goals and their relationships with others.

As we suggested, a distinction can be made between group development (temporal changes in the group as a whole) and group socialization (temporal changes in the relationship between the group and each of its members). Group socialization can be analyzed in terms of three psychological processes—*evaluation, commitment,* and *role transition* (Levine & Moreland, 1985, in press; Moreland & Levine, 1982, 1984, 1989). Evaluation involves judgments by the group and the individual about the rewardingness of their own and alternative relationships. These judgments influence how much commitment the two parties feel toward one another. Whenever mutual commitment rises or falls to a previously established level, called a "decision criterion," a role transition occurs and the relationship between the group and the individual changes. Evaluation proceeds, often along different dimensions, producing further changes in commitment and subsequent role transitions. In this way, the individual passes through five stages of group membership, separated by four role transitions (see Figure 11.1).

The relationship between a person and a group begins with a period of *investigation*. During investigation, the person engages in reconnaissance, looking for groups that can contribute to the satisfaction of personal needs, while the group engages in recruitment, looking for people who can contribute to the achievement of group goals. A college freshman, for example, might attend several fraternity rush parties, looking for the group that he would most like to join. And at those same parties, active members of the fraternity are looking for the freshmen that they would most like to pledge. If the commitment levels of both parties rise to their respective entrance criteria (EC), then the role transition of *entry* occurs and the person becomes a new member. Entry is often marked by an induction ritual, such as a welcoming party.

The second phase of group membership is *socialization*. During socialization, the person tries to change the group so that it can better satisfy his or her personal needs, while the group tries to change the person so that he or she can contribute more to the achievement of group goals. A new pledge, for example, might suggest that the rooms in his fraternity house be redecorated, while the active members in the fraternity advise him to spend less time in his room and more time participating in group activities. When these and other socialization attempts are successful, the group experiences accommodation and the person experiences assimilation. If the commitment levels of both parties rise to their respective acceptance criteria (AC), then the role transition of *acceptance* occurs and the person becomes a full group member. Acceptance is often marked by access to various secrets that are only known to full members of the group.

During *maintenance*, there is considerable negotiation between the person and the group as they try to find a specialized role that maximizes both satisfaction of the person's needs and achievement of the group's goals. A fraternity brother, for example, might be asked by the group to become its next president

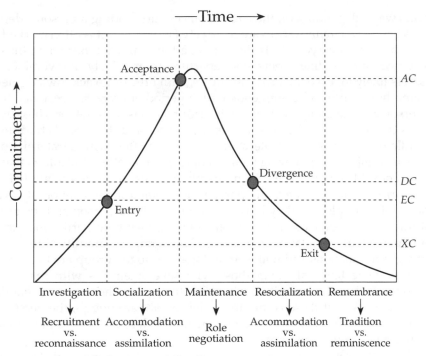

FIGURE 11.1. A model of group socialization.

because of his popularity and leadership skills. He might agree to take the job, but only if someone else in the group carried out the onerous duty (usually performed by the president) of representing the fraternity at student government meetings. If role negotiations such as these succeed, then the commitment levels of both parties remain high. But if role negotiation fails and the commitment levels of both parties fall to their respective divergence criteria (DC), then the role transition of *divergence* occurs and the person becomes a marginal member. Divergence, like acceptance, is often marked in some way, such as giving the person the cold shoulder and excluding him from activities in which full members normally participate.

The fourth phase of group membership is *resocialization*. Once again, the person tries to produce accommodation in the group, while the group tries to produce assimilation in the person. A fraternity brother who has fallen behind in his dues, for example, might suggest that everyone's dues be lowered, while other members advise him to spend less money on compact discs and designer jeans. If the commitment levels of both parties rise again to their respective divergence criteria, then a special role transition (convergence) occurs and the person regains full membership in the group. But if the commitment levels of both parties fall to their respective exit criteria (XC), then the role transition of *exit* occurs and the person becomes an ex-member of the group. (This second and more common outcome is shown in the diagram.) Exit can be marked in various ways, depending on the circumstances surrounding a person's departure. When these circumstances are relatively favorable, exit is often marked by a party at which everyone bids the person a fond farewell. But when the circumstances surrounding a person's departure are relatively unfavorable, the person is likely to leave the group abruptly, with little or no acknowledgment.

Finally, group membership ends with a period of *remembrance,* when both the person and the group evaluate their prior relationship together. These evaluations become part of the person's reminiscences and the group's traditions. At a college reunion, for example, a man might recall the exciting fraternity parties he once enjoyed, comparing them favorably to the rather dull affairs that he now attends. Meanwhile, the current members of that fraternity might tell colorful stories about the same man's party antics, comparing him favorably to the rather dull set of pledges they have just admitted. If the person and the group continue to have some contact with one another, then both parties may try to evaluate their current relationship as well. For example, fraternity alumni who attend group functions and make large donations to the group are likely to be evaluated more favorably than those who sever their ties with the group. Eventually, feelings of commitment between the person and the group stabilize at some low level. If these commitment levels fall far enough, the person no longer thinks about the group to which he once belonged, and that group forgets that he was once a member.

Although group development and group socialization are distinct phenomena, there are several ways in which they might influence one another (Moreland & Levine, 1988). Regarding the impact of development on socialization, some kinds of socialization activities rarely, if ever, occur in certain stages of development. For example, the socialization activities of maintenance, resocialization, and remembrance are unlikely during the forming stage of development, because group norms (which guide these socialization activities) have not yet evolved. Socialization activities that do occur in more than one developmental stage also may operate differently in those stages. For example, groups may demand less assimilation and exhibit more accommodation during the adjourning than the performing stage of development. Regarding the impact of group socialization on group development, the need to engage in certain socialization activities (e.g., resocialization of marginal members) may inhibit group development by deflecting members from tasks that would otherwise move the group forward (Goodman, 1981; Yalom, 1970). The complex interplay between group development and group socialization has not yet been studied seriously.

THE COMPOSITION OF SMALL GROUPS

In order to predict and understand behavior in a small group, it is essential to know the group's composition, that is, the number of people who belong to the group and their personal characteristics (e.g., age, sex, personality, ability).

Group composition can be viewed from three analytical perspectives (Moreland & Levine, 1992).

Composition as a Consequence

Composition can be treated as a *consequence* of various social and psychological processes. Here, the question is why particular groups have particular compositions. For example, why do natural groups tend to be small? Most groups contain fewer than 20 members, and many contain only 2 or 3 (e.g., Burgess, 1984; McPherson, 1983). And why do members of such groups tend to be similar, or homogeneous? The members of most groups are homogeneous with regard to age and sex (McPherson & Smith-Lovin, 1987), beliefs and opinions (Levine & Moreland, 1991), and personalities (Magaro & Ashbrook, 1985).

Several explanations have been offered for the small size of natural groups. One possibility is that small groups are easier to form and maintain than large ones, because the number of potential relationships between members is lower in small groups. A second possibility is that small groups are more satisfying than large ones, because members of small groups tend to have greater control over the group's activities and resources. A third (and related) possibility is that evolutionary pressures have caused people to prefer small groups, because of their advantages in satisfying such elemental needs as child rearing and food gathering.

Group homogeneity has been explained in two major ways. One explanation assumes that members are similar *before* they join the group. According to this view, people belong to fairly homogeneous social networks (e.g., co-workers who are similar in age, sex, and socioeconomic status), and groups tend to form and recruit new members among people who share the same network affiliation (McPherson, 1990). Another explanation assumes that members become similar *after* they join the group. According to this view, efforts to socialize new members (Moreland & Levine, 1989; Van Maanen & Schein, 1979) and to resocialize marginal members (Levine, 1989) cause the people in a group to become more similar over time. Clearly, both processes probably operate to produce homogeneity in most natural groups.

Composition as a Context

Composition can also be treated as a *context* that shapes or moderates various social psychological phenomena, rather than causing them directly. For example, group cohesion affects group performance differently depending on the group's dominant work norms (e.g., Schachter, Ellertson, McBride, & Gregory, 1951; Seashore, 1954). When these norms are positive, cohesion increases productivity, but when these norms are negative, cohesion decreases productivity.

Another contextual effect of group composition involves behavior in mixed-sex work groups where males often outnumber females. As the proportions of men and women in a group diverge, conventional sex roles often become more salient, which in turn strengthens members' tendencies to adopt these roles. Thus, the sex composition of the group moderates the impact of each person's sex on his or her behavior. This process produces special problems for *token* members of work groups (e.g., women in predominantly male groups). According to Kanter (1977), the presence of token women in work groups has certain perceptual and behavioral consequences. First, because of their rarity, token women are highly visible, which increases pressure on them to match or exceed the performance of their male co-workers. Second, because the presence of token women causes group members to focus on differences rather than similarities between men and women, the social boundaries between the two sexes are strengthened. Finally, token women are often viewed by men in stereotypical ways, which increases the likelihood that they will be trapped in stereotypical roles (e.g., "mother," "cheerleader," "mascot"). According to Kanter, the problems that token women experience are not due to their sex per se, but rather to a contextual factor, namely, the imbalanced sex compositions of the groups in which they participate. Women should thus experience fewer problems in work groups where sex ratios are more balanced.

Indirect evidence for Kanter's (1977) claims can be found in studies of social perception in small groups. For example, compared to nontokens, token men and women do attract more attention from other group members (Lord & Saenz, 1985; Taylor, Fiske, Etcoff, & Ruderman, 1978) and often are more aware of their sex (Cota & Dion, 1986; McGuire & Padawer-Singer, 1976). And this visibility can be distracting for tokens and lead to lower task performance (Saenz & Lord, 1989). Finally, studies indicate that group members who are unusual in some respect are often viewed in prototypical and perhaps stereotypical ways (cf. Mullen, 1991).

More direct evidence regarding Kanter's (1977) claims can be found in studies of work groups containing token men and women. Although some of these studies seem to confirm her claims (e.g., Izraeli, 1983; Yoder, Adams, & Prince, 1983), other studies do not (e.g., Higgins & King, 1981; South, Bonjean, Markham, & Corder, 1982). Among the latter studies, several interesting trends can be discerned. For example, token men do not seem to have the same problems as token women (Crocker & McGraw, 1984; Wharton & Baron, 1987), and high-status token women have fewer problems than low-status tokens (Alexander & Thoits, 1985; Eagly & Johnson, 1990). The problems of tokenism also can be reduced when women behave in certain ways. For example, token women fare better when they emphasize their concern about group welfare (Ridgeway, 1982), display task competence (Bradley, 1980; Ridgeway, 1982), or attribute their successful performance to external rather than internal factors (Taps & Martin, 1990). These findings have led several reviewers to conclude that Kanter's analysis is too simplistic (Fairhurst & Snavely, 1983; Martin, 1985; Yoder, 1991). Apparently, the problems experienced by token women are not due merely to the imbalanced sexual composition of their work groups, but are also affected by such variables as cultural stereotypes about the sexes, status differences between men and women, relative levels of task competence, and the fact that token women are often unwelcome newcomers in formerly all-male groups.

Composition as a Cause

Finally, composition can be viewed as a *cause* that influences other aspects of group life. As an example, let us consider how the abilities of members affect group performance (Bass, 1980; Jackson, 1992; Shaw, 1981). This issue has great practical importance, because work groups and sports teams often spend considerable time and money identifying individual abilities that influence group success, recruiting members who already possess or seem likely to acquire these abilities, and improving the abilities of new and old members through training.

In many cases, the abilities of individual members combine additively to determine a group's performance. The more high-ability people there are in the group, the better the group's performance is likely to be. For example, Laughlin and his colleagues found that group performance on a difficult cognitive task was proportional to the number of members who demonstrated high ability when working on the task alone (see Laughlin, 1978). And there is evidence that member abilities of other types—such as brainstorming ability, athletic skills, and conceptual complexity—affect group performance in an additive fashion (Graham & Dillon, 1974; Jones, 1974; Kennedy, 1971; Tuckman, 1964).

Even though additive effects are often found, they are not the whole story. For example, even in studies that find a positive relationship between members' abilities and group performance, this performance is often lower than would be expected if individual abilities were simply added (Egerbladh, 1976; Hill, 1982), and on some kinds of tasks the group can succeed if only one or two members know the correct answer (Hastie, 1986; Laughlin & Ellis, 1986). In addition, member ability does not always have a strong effect on group performance. O'Brien and Owens (1969), for example, found that when different subtasks were allocated to different members, group performance was affected by both the average ability of members and the ability of the dullest member. In contrast, when members cooperated on all aspects of the task, neither of the two ability variables influenced group performance.

The additive model clearly needs to be supplemented. One refinement is the notion of *assembly effects* (Rosenberg, Erlick, & Berkowitz, 1955). These interactive effects, which occur when certain combinations of member abilities produce unexpected levels of group performance, arise because members make different contributions to group performance depending on who else is in the group (Hill, 1982). For example, Laughlin, Branch, and Johnson (1969) found that the presence vs. absence of high-ability members influenced the relative contribution that medium-ability members made on a cognitive task. And Tziner and Eden (1985) found both additive and interactive effects in a study of tank crew performance. Three-man crews were assembled to represent all possible distributions of members' abilities (e.g., three low-ability members, two high-ability members and one low-ability member). Crew performance was assessed by unit commanders following 2 months of military exercises. Tziner and Eden found that group performance varied positively with the number of high-ability crew members, indicating the occurrence of additive effects. In addition, they found the uniformly high-ability crews performed much better, and uniformly low-ability crews performed much worse, than predicted by the sum of their individual abilities, indicating the occurrence of interactive effects.

The existence of assembly effects has sparked interest in whether group performance is facilitated by homogeneity (similarity) or heterogeneity (dissimilarity) in members' abilities. Steiner (1972) offered a useful analysis of this issue, arguing that the impact of homogeneity/heterogeneity depends on the type of task a group faces. For example, he suggested that heterogeneity in members' abilities can increase the group's potential productivity on *disjunctive tasks*, which can be completed by one member (e.g., determining the correct answer to a math problem). On these tasks, the best member's contribution determines group performance, and the more heterogeneous the group, the more likely it is to contain at least one member who possesses the skill necessary to achieve the group goal. In contrast, heterogeneity in members' abilities can decrease potential productivity on *conjunctive tasks*, which have to be completed by all members (e.g., winning a relay race against another team). On these tasks, the worst member's contribution determines group performance, and the more heterogeneous the group, the more likely it is to contain at least one member who lacks the skill necessary to achieve the group goal.

THE STRUCTURE OF SMALL GROUPS

The physical, social, and temporal environments in which a group is embedded, and the number and characteristics of its members, establish important constraints on group processes and outcomes. But these environmental and compositional factors are by no means sufficient to explain how a group operates. In addition, the group's *structure,* or the pattern of relationships among its members, must be taken into account. Three critical aspects of group structure are *norms, roles,* and *status systems.*

Norms

Norms are shared expectations about how group members ought to behave. Norms involve aspects of behavior that are important and problematical for group survival and success, including how members should share the rewards and costs of group participation, how conflicts between members should be controlled, how the group's core values should be expressed, and how contacts with outsiders should be regulated. Even though all norms are similar in that they specify how group members ought to act, they also differ in several ways. For example, norms vary regarding (a) the number and type of people to whom they apply (everyone in the group or particular role occupants), (b) their level of acceptance among members (universal or partial), (c) the range of permissible behavior they allow (small or large), and (d) the sanctions that occur when they are violated (weak or strong).

There are several theories about how norms develop in groups. One approach suggests that norms solidify from initial patterns of behavior that later prove adaptive in dealing with group problems (cf. Opp, 1982). Other approaches suggest that norms can be negotiated among group members, mandated by group leaders or powerful cliques, and imported from outside the group (cf. Feldman, 1984). Finally, it has been argued that some norms arise as a consequence of basic cognitive processes. Bettenhausen and Murnighan (1985), for example, suggest that people entering a group already possess cognitive scripts specifying correct behavior in different situations, and these scripts are activated whenever a new situation is classified as similar to an old one. Therefore, the speed with which norms evolve in a group and the amount of negotiation they require depend on the degree to which group members share initial scripts and classify new situations in the same way.

The major goal and consequence of norms is to regulate behavior on the part of group members. One common norm in small groups is that members should hold similar views on important issues. A substantial amount of research indicates that individuals who violate this norm are rejected by their fellow group members. In a classic study by Schachter (1951), for example, subjects were assigned to groups that were either high or low in cohesiveness and then asked to discuss an opinion topic that was either relevant or irrelevant to the group's purpose. Each group contained five to seven naive subjects and three confederates of the experimenter (mode, slider, and deviate). The mode agreed with the subjects throughout the discussion; the slider started out disagreeing, but gradually came to agree; and the deviate disagreed with the subjects throughout the discussion. During the discussion, communication to the mode remained uniform over time, communication to the slider decreased, and communication to the deviate tended to increase in all conditions but one. In this condition (high cohesive-relevant), communication to the deviate showed a final decrease, suggesting that subjects gave up trying to persuade the deviate and psychologically excluded him from the group. Following the discussion, subjects evaluated all three confederates. In general, the deviate was rejected more than the slider or the mode, who were liked about equally. There was also some evidence that the deviate was rejected more when cohesiveness and relevance were high rather than low.

Subsequent research indicates that the level of rejection an opinion deviate elicits is influenced by a number of factors. These include the extremity, content, and consistency of the deviate's position; the deviate's interference with group goal attainment; and the deviate's status (Levine, 1989). Compared to low-status deviates, for example, high-status deviates are severely punished when they cause major interference with group goal attainment, are only mildly punished when they cause minor interference, and are highly rewarded when they facilitate goal attainment (e.g., Suchner & Jackson, 1976; Wiggins, Dill, & Schwartz, 1965).

Roles

Roles are positions in a group that are associated with certain expected behaviors. Even when an individual knows that he or she is involved in a simulated situation, being assigned to a particular role can elicit dramatic changes in behavior (Messé, Kerr, & Sattler, 1992). In a well-known demonstration of this phenomenon, Haney, Banks, and Zimbardo (1973) created a simulated prison and randomly assigned college students to the role of guard or prisoner. This role assignment had major behavioral consequences: Prisoners became passive and withdrawn, whereas guards became domineering and brutal. In fact, these role-induced behaviors were so strong and pervasive that the investigators decided to terminate the 2-week study after just a few days. Role playing also can influence a person's self-perceptions. Evidence indicates that being assigned to a role often causes a person to internalize this role and to believe that he or she possesses the attributes normally associated with it (Rosenberg, 1981; Stryker & Statham, 1985). Thus, in an important sense, our social identities are derived from the roles we play (see the discussion in Chapter 3 by Baumeister on social identities). Finally, role playing can affect how the role occupant is perceived by others. For example, Humphrey (1985) demonstrated that people who play managerial work roles are evaluated more favorably on a variety of role-related behaviors (e.g., leadership, assertiveness, supportiveness, talkativeness) than are people who play subordinate work roles, regardless of whether the evaluator is a manager or a subordinate (see also Ross, Amabile, & Steinmetz, 1977). These results suggest that errors in the cognitive processing of information (e.g., overattributions to dispositions, sample bias) may distort people's perceptions of role occupants' behaviors.

Although roles are quite useful in enhancing the predictability and controllability of social interactions, they are also problematic in various ways (Heiss, 1981). For example, problems arise when role occupants lack sufficient knowledge to play their roles effectively (*role ambiguity*). This might occur because a person is asked to play a role that has never existed in the group before (e.g., affirmative action officer in a company that has traditionally ignored this issue). Other problems arise when members of complementary roles disagree about how their own and/or the other person's role should be played (*role dissensus*). A common example is disagreement between a teacher and a student about how knowledge should be assessed in a course (essay vs. multiple-choice tests). Finally, problems arise when role occupants have trouble meeting the expectations of roles they accept (*role strain*) due to incompatibilities within or between roles. Simultaneously fulfilling the roles of parent and corporate executive, for example, may pose serious challenges. These kinds of problems can have negative consequences for groups as well as individuals. Studies in work groups indicate that role ambiguity, dissensus, and strain can lead to increased tension and propensity to leave the group and decreased job satisfaction, organizational commitment, and productivity (Fisher & Gitelson, 1983; Jackson & Schuler, 1985).

In addition to the difficulties associated with playing specific roles, *transi-*

tions between roles can also produce problems (Allen & van de Vliert, 1984). For example, role transitions within and between work groups are often quite stressful (Brett, 1980; Louis, 1980). These transitions are particularly difficult when role occupants are forced to give up the rewards of one group with no guarantee that they can obtain similar rewards in other groups. Examples of these kinds of transitions include dismissals, layoffs, plant closings, and mergers (Brockner, 1988; Dooley & Catalano, 1988; Greenhalgh, 1983; Marks & Mirvis, 1986). Role transitions can also produce interpersonal conflicts between group members. These conflicts stem from disagreements about whether a particular role transition should occur and, if so, exactly when it should happen and how it should be handled (Moreland & Levine, 1984).

Status Systems

Not all group members are equal. Or, to paraphrase George Orwell, some group members are more equal than others. The *status system* of a group reflects the distribution of power and prestige among its members. Status systems are usually hierarchical, with some members having more power and prestige than others. Members who possess higher status behave differently than those who possess lower status. For example, higher-status people tend to stand up straighter, maintain more eye contact, and speak in a firmer voice (e.g., Harper, 1985). They also speak more often; are more likely to criticize, command, and interrupt others; and receive more communications from others (e.g., Skvoretz, 1988; Weisfeld & Weisfeld, 1984). And these behaviors have consequences. Compared to people with lower status, those with higher status exert more influence over group activities, are evaluated more positively by others, and have more self-esteem (see Levine & Moreland, 1990).

Although the responsibilities of leadership are often burdensome and high-status deviates may be punished severely when they harm the group (Levine, 1989), most people would prefer to occupy high-status rather than low-status positions. Therefore, the acquisition and maintenance of status are important activities in most groups. It has traditionally been assumed that status is a reward that people earn for contributing to group welfare (e.g., by working on group tasks and conforming to group norms). But this explanation for status acquisition is called into question by two sources of evidence. First, people often seem to have more or less status than they deserve on the basis of their contributions to the group (Strodtbeck & Lipinski, 1985). Second, some status systems develop quickly, often within minutes after a group is formed (Barchas & Fisek, 1984). Because it is unlikely that members could earn status via contributions to group welfare in so short a time, other mechanisms for status formation that require little or no interaction among members have been proposed.

Expectation states theorists (Berger, Rosenholtz, & Zelditch, 1980) suggest that group members develop expectations about one another's likely contributions to group goal attainment soon after they meet. These expectations are based on personal characteristics that are assumed to predict one's contributions. People whose characteristics elicit higher expectations are assigned higher status within the group. This mechanism for status acquisition has two negative features. First, personal characteristics that have no direct bearing on task performance (e.g., sex, race) are sometimes perceived as relevant, and this causes some people to have lower (or higher) initial status than they deserve. Second, although these status assignments can be modified by making higher (or lower) contributions to group goal attainment than were expected, people whose initial status assignments are unfairly low often find it difficult to prove their worth and thus are locked into low-status positions (Ridgeway, 1982).

Ethological theorists (Mazur, 1985) suggest that, soon after meeting, group members use appearance and demeanor cues (e.g., size, musculature, facial expression) to assess one another's strength. People who seem particularly weak or strong are immediately assigned low or high status, respectively. All others engage in brief dominance contests (e.g., staring until one person looks away or interrupting); the winners and losers of these contests are assigned status commensurate with the strength they demonstrate. The initial status hierarchy can be modified if new information suggests that people are stronger or weaker than they seemed at first.

Support has been obtained for both expectation states theory (Berger & Zelditch, 1985) and ethological theory (Dovidio & Ellyson, 1985). Although debate continues between advocates of the two approaches, a recent effort to integrate the two theories (Ridgeway, 1984, 1987) suggests that both provide useful perspectives on status acquisition. Ridgeway argues that status allocation is generally a cooperative process, based on performance expectations that reflect a person's perceived capacity to contribute to the group task. However, competitive challenges, or dominance contests, occasionally occur when a group member claims a higher status than he or she appears to deserve on the basis of performance expectations. The success of these challenges depends on several factors, including the type of nonverbal dominance behavior that the challenger uses and the amount of coalitional support that he or she receives from others in the group.

CONFLICTS WITHIN SMALL GROUPS

Conflict, defined as group members' belief that their personal goals cannot be achieved simultaneously (Pruitt & Rubin, 1986), is a common aspect of group life. Conflict can arise over many issues, including access to information, distribution of physical resources, and power to influence group decisions. Certain types of conflict can enhance group welfare, for example, by stimulating innovation (Levine & Moreland, 1985; Moscovici, 1985; Nemeth & Staw, 1989). However, conflict often has just the opposite effect, producing interpersonal hostility, impaired performance, and (in extreme cases) dissolution of the group. Because the potential costs of conflict are so great, group members expend considerable energy trying to control the type and intensity of conflict that occurs.

Social Dilemmas

Substantial research attention has been devoted to *social dilemma* conflicts (Messick & Brewer, 1983; Orbell & Dawes, 1981; Stroebe & Frey, 1982; Wilke, Messick, & Rutte, 1986). Social dilemmas pit short-term individual welfare against long-term group welfare, with the group often losing out. A social dilemma occurs when "(1) each person has an individually rational choice that, when made by all members of the group, (2) provides a poorer outcome than that which the members would have received if no members made the rational choice" (Messick & Brewer, 1983, p. 15).

Two types of social dilemmas can be identified. In *"collective traps,"* behaviors that are rewarding for individuals produce negative group (and individual) outcomes when exhibited by enough people. An example is "the tragedy of the commons" (Hardin, 1968), which involves a parable about herdsmen who graze their animals on a common pasture. Each herdsman finds it profitable to increase the size of his herd, because his potential profits go up with the number of animals he owns, whereas his grazing costs are shared. Unfortunately, however, these rational individual decisions have negative consequences for all the herdsmen, because their large herds eventually destroy the common pasture and all the animals that graze there. Other collective traps occur when people deplete water reservoirs by using lawn sprinklers during droughts and cause brownouts by using air conditioners during heat waves.

In *"collective fences,"* behaviors that are costly for individuals produce negative group (and individual) outcomes when avoided by enough people. An example is the problem of public goods (Olson, 1965), which occurs when more people benefit from a public good than are needed to provide it. In the case of public television, for example, it is rational for individuals not to donate to the station, because they can watch programs without contributing. However, if too many people in the community fail to contribute, the station must reduce its programming or go off the air, and then everyone who watches the station will suffer.

Several research paradigms have been used to study how group members behave in social dilemmas (Messick & Brewer, 1983). One of the most popular paradigms involves a laboratory simulation of the tragedy of the commons. Several people are brought together and given the opportunity to withdraw as many tokens (worth money) as they wish from a common pool of tokens. The pool regenerates itself at a predetermined rate, such that slow withdrawal allows the pool to maintain a reasonable supply of tokens for subsequent use, whereas fast withdrawal exhausts the pool. Many studies indicate that group members often act selfishly when exposed to this kind of replenishable resource trap, withdrawing so many tokens so fast that the pool dries up.

Several variables have been found to affect how people respond to social dilemmas. Some of these are individual characteristics, such as social values and cultural background (e.g., Liebrand, 1986; Sattler & Kerr, 1991). For example, Kramer, McClintock, and Messick (1986) found that subjects previously classified as cooperators exhibited more self-restraint when a shared resource was threatened than did subjects classified as noncooperators. And Yamagishi (1988) found that when there was no system for punishing people who behaved selfishly in a social dilemma, Japanese subjects cooperated less than did American subjects. This presumably occurred because social control is enforced more externally in Japanese than in American society, which in turn causes Japanese to be less trusting of their fellow group members when mutual monitoring and sanctioning do not exist.

Another factor that affects behavior in social dilemmas is the opportunity for communication among group members. Evidence indicates that such communication often increases cooperation (e.g., Bornstein & Rapoport, 1988; Dawes, McTavish, & Shaklee, 1977; Jorgenson & Papciak, 1981). Why is discussion effective? Orbell, van de Kragt, and Dawes (1988) suggest two reasons. First, discussion may enhance cooperation because it promotes a feeling of group identity, which causes individuals to become concerned about group welfare rather than personal welfare (cf. Kramer & Brewer, 1986). Second, discussion may enhance cooperation because it provides an opportunity for members to make promises to one another that they will cooperate.

Cooperation in social dilemmas can also be increased by "structural" solutions involving coordinated group actions designed to alter the incentive structure of the dilemma. These structural solutions include converting commonly owned resources into privately owned resources, electing powerful leaders who can mandate cooperation, and developing punishment systems for people who refuse to cooperate. Evidence suggests that such structural solutions are most likely to be implemented under certain conditions, namely, when the group fails to deal with the common resource efficiently and free access to the resource causes large inequities in members' outcomes (e.g., Samuelson & Messick, 1986; Samuelson, Messick, Wilke, & Rutte, 1986).

Coalition Formation

Conflict can often be resolved through *coalition formation*, which involves two or more group members agreeing to cooperate in order to achieve a mutually desired outcome. Coalitions typically contain people who disagree on other issues ("strange bedfellows") but who decide to put their differences aside, at least temporarily, to strive for a goal that they all want but cannot attain by themselves (Murnighan, 1978). Because people typically select coalition partners on the basis of their perceived utility for obtaining a particular goal rather than their personal attractiveness, coalitions tend to be rather fragile. Coalition members are often quite willing to abandon their current partners if they believe they can get a better deal in another coalition or on their own.

Although coalitions can help to resolve conflicts between group members, they do not transform competitive group environments into purely cooperative ones. For example, coalition formation necessarily involves including some people and excluding others. Those who are excluded may become angry and react in a hostile manner to those who rejected them, perhaps by forming coalitions of their own. In addition, relations between coalitions are usually quite competitive, with each coalition seeking to enhance its outcomes at the expense of other coalitions (Thibaut & Kelley, 1959). Finally, relations within coalitions are often competitive as well, with coalition members jockeying to get a bigger piece of the pie than their partners and keeping an eye peeled for better alternatives outside.

Coalition formation has been studied by social psychologists, mathematical game theorists, sociologists, and political scientists, using a variety of methodologies (see Kahan & Rapoport, 1984; Komorita, 1984; Murnighan & Vollrath, 1984; Wilke, 1985). Much of the work on coalitions has involved *simple games,* in which all coalitions are defined as either winning or losing, and all winning coalitions are worth one value and all losing coalitions are worth a smaller value. For example, imagine a situation in which four stockholders (A, B, C, and D) control blocks of stock in a company, but no single stockholder owns a majority of the shares (A has 800,000; and B, C, and D each have 300,000). In order to gain control of the company and decide how its profits are to be divided, stockholders must agree to pool their shares (i.e., form a coalition). In this case, there are four *minimal winning coalitions* (i.e., winning coalitions that become losing coalitions if one person is deleted). These are AB, AC, AD, and BCD, each of which can vote a majority of the 1,700,000 outstanding shares. The number of shares owned by the stockholders are *resource weights,* which reflect the potential size of each member's contribution to a winning coalition. These resource weights can affect the number and sizes of minimal winning coalitions. In addition, they can affect the division of rewards within winning coalitions by providing a frame of reference for defining a "just" or "fair" distribution. For example, someone who contributed more votes might claim a bigger share of the profits.

The research on coalition behavior in simple games can be summarized in terms of several propositions (Komorita & Kravitz, 1983). Three of these are sufficient to give the flavor of the research. First, the probability of a coalition varies inversely with its size (i.e., small coalitions are more likely than large coalitions). This occurs because whatever prize the coalition wins must be shared among its members, and the fewer members there are, the larger their shares. Also, it is generally harder to build and maintain larger coalitions than smaller ones. Second, a member's share of the coalition prize is directly related to the number of alternative minimum winning coalitions (MWCs) that include the member, relative to the number that include other coalition members. This occurs because the better a member's options outside a coalition, the more tempted the person is to defect, and therefore the more the person can demand to remain in the coalition. A third finding, which probably occurs for the same reason, is that a member's share of the coalition prize is inversely related to the mean size of the member's MWCs, relative to the sizes of the other members' MWCs.

As these propositions suggest, much has been learned about coalition behavior by studying simple games in laboratory settings. But coalitions also occur in more complex social environments, such as organizations, which differ from laboratory settings in important ways. These differences include the presence of earned (as opposed to assigned) resource weights, restrictions on information and communication, and the fact that ideological factors make some coalitions more attractive than others (Miller & Komorita, 1986). Families and work groups are two contexts in which coalitions often occur. For example, evidence indicates that family coalitions serve to maintain existing status relations between parents and their children (Bonacich, Grusky, & Peyrot, 1985). During disputes, fathers and mothers give much more support to one another than they give to their children. In addition, the behavior of work group leaders affects the formation of "revolutionary coalitions" among their subordinates (Lawler, 1983). Co-optation tactics on the part of leaders (e.g., offers of promotion) are more effective in preventing revolts among subordinates than are threat tactics (e.g., threats of demotion).

Majority and Minority Influence

In many groups, individuals belong to factions that disagree about some issue. Often there are two such factions that differ in size (i.e., a larger faction, or majority, and a smaller faction, or minority) and attempt to influence one another. These influence efforts reduce conflict on some occasions (e.g., when a minority succumbs to majority pressure to change its position) but exacerbate it on other occasions (e.g., when a minority holds out against majority pressure).

Systematic research on *majority influence,* or *conformity,* began with Asch's (1951, 1955, 1956) classic studies. Asch brought groups of seven to nine people into the laboratory to participate in a study ostensibly dealing with visual perception. Their task, matching the length of a standard line against three comparison lines, was quite easy. Each group contained only one real subject. The remaining group members were confederates who had been instructed to give unanimously incorrect responses on some trials. Asch also included a control condition in which subjects made judgments privately, without any majority pressure. The results of the experiment were quite dramatic. Control subjects made errors less than 5 percent of the time. In contrast, subjects exposed to majority pressure conformed about 33 percent of the time, and 75 percent of these subjects conformed at least once.

In subsequent studies, Asch investigated how conformity was influenced by the size and unanimity of the majority. Size refers to the number of people in the majority faction; unanimity refers to the degree of consensus among majority members regarding the issue under consideration. Both of these variables elicited a good deal of research attention in the years following Asch's groundbreaking experiments (see Levine & Russo, 1987).

Research on how one-person minorities react to disagreement from different size majorities initially produced a rather confusing picture. Asch (1951) found that conformity increased until the majority reached three persons and then leveled off. Although some later studies reported similar effects (e.g., Rosenberg, 1961; Stang, 1976), others did not (e.g., Gerard, Wilhelmy, & Conolley, 1968; Kidd, 1958). Wilder (1977, 1978) resolved this issue by arguing that the impact of majority size on conformity depends on the subject's interpretation of why majority members agree with one another. His data suggested that conformity increases with majority size if majority members are perceived as having arrived independently at their common position, but not if they are seen as having influenced one another.

Asch also stimulated interest in the impact of majority unanimity. To test the importance of unanimity, Asch (1951) had one of his confederates dissent from the erroneous majority on the line judgment task by giving the correct answer. The presence of this *social supporter* reduced conformity dramatically, compared to a unanimous condition. Next Asch (1955) tested the impact of a different kind of dissenter, one who gave an even more incorrect response than the erroneous majority. The presence of this *extreme dissenter* reduced conformity almost as much as a social supporter. Asch concluded that the social supporter's effectiveness was due to breaking group unanimity, rather than agreeing with the subject. Later research revealed that Asch's conclusion is correct for simple perceptual stimuli, but not for opinion stimuli, where a dissenter must agree with the subject in order to reduce conformity (Allen & Levine, 1968, 1969).

Two major explanations have been offered for the effectiveness of social support (Levine & Russo, 1987). One explanation is that the partner reduces the subject's fear of majority punishment. The subject may believe, for example, that the majority will divide its hostility among all the dissenters present, and therefore the supporter will absorb some of the punishment that otherwise would be directed solely at the subject (Allen, 1975). A second explanation is that the partner reduces the subject's concern about giving an incorrect response by providing verification of the subject's answer (Allen & Levine, 1971; Morris, Miller, & Sprangenberg, 1977). Of course, in many majority pressure situations, a social supporter may fulfill both functions—reducing the subject's fear of punishment while simultaneously bolstering the subject's confidence in the correctness of his or her answer.

These two interpretations of social support are closely tied to Deutsch and Gerard's (1955) influential analysis of why people conform to majority opinion. These researchers argued that two mechanisms underlie conformity: *normative influence* and *informational influence.* Normative influence occurs because people desire rewards that others control and assume that others are more likely to reward agreement than disagreement. Consistent with this explanation of conformity, people are more likely to yield to majority opinion when other group members can see their responses and when they are dependent on these others for rewards (see Allen, 1965). A social supporter who reduces a subject's fear of majority punishment, then, reduces the majority's ability to elicit normative influence. Informational influence occurs because people desire to have an accurate view of reality and assume that others are more likely to be accurate than they are. Consistent with this explanation of conformity, people are more likely to yield to majority opinion when they are confronted with a difficult or ambiguous task and are unsure about the validity of their responses (see Allen, 1965). A social supporter who verifies a subject's perception of reality, then, reduces the majority's ability to elicit informational influence.

Interest in majority influence continues, but since the early 1970s social psychologists have become more intrigued with the other side of the coin, namely, *minority influence,* or *innovation* (Levine, 1989; Moscovici, 1985; Mugny & Perez, 1991; Nemeth, 1986). The primary impetus for this work was provided by Moscovici, who argued that too little attention has been paid to how minorities produce social change by provoking conflict with majorities. Moscovici and his colleagues have conducted a number of studies that reveal the power of minorities to change majorities (see Moscovici, 1976, 1980, 1985). Moscovici argues that minority and majority influence are fundamentally different processes, with minorities producing private agreement (*conversion*) and majorities producing public agreement (*compliance*). He also believes that the primary determinant of successful minority influence is *behavioral style,* particularly the minority's consistency in espousing its position.

Recently, Nemeth (1986) has offered a somewhat different perspective on minority influence. She argues that disagreement from majorities and minorities has different effects on attention, thought, and problem solving. According to Nemeth, majorities produce a narrow attentional focus on their own position, whereas minorities elicit a broader focus on alternative positions and new information. As a result, exposure to a majority tends to produce convergent thinking and uncreative problem solving, whereas exposure to a minority tends to produce divergent thinking and creative problem solving (cf. Maass, West, & Cialdini, 1987). Nemeth and her colleagues have demonstrated these differences in several experiments. For example, Nemeth and Kwan (1987) had subjects name words embedded in letter strings (e.g., *tDOGe*) and told them that either a majority or a minority of other group members had adopted a nonobvious, or dissenting, strategy (reading the letters backward). When subjects were subsequently asked to form all the words they could from letter strings, subjects who had been exposed to minority dissent employed more strategies of all sorts (forward, backward, mixed) and therefore detected more words than did subjects who had been exposed to majority dissent. This study suggests that minorities sometimes stimulate better problem solutions than they themselves exhibit.

THE PERFORMANCE OF SMALL GROUPS

In the previous section, we emphasized the competitive aspects of group dynamics and the strategies that members use to reconcile divergent interests. Of course, group dynamics also involve cooperation among members who have common motives and interests, who work together to produce a group product, and who share the rewards that the product brings. Group performance, defined as the process and outcome of members' joint efforts to achieve a collective goal, is intimately linked with conflict, because a group's failure to resolve conflict can severely limit its performance. In this section, we explore the mechanisms that groups use to facilitate cooperative effort and the problems that arise when these mechanisms fail to produce the motivation and coordination necessary for group success.

Leadership

In order to succeed, a group must ensure that certain functions are carried out. These functions (e.g., obtaining the resources needed to produce the group product, motivating members to do their best, coordinating members' contributions) are typically assigned to certain individuals, or leaders, who are empowered to organize and direct group activities. Leaders, then, are the members who have the most power and influence in a group (Hollander, 1985).

One explanation of leadership focuses on specific traits that distinguish leaders from their followers. This approach is an old one, and many studies have sought to identify the special traits that characterize leaders. The *trait approach* was dealt a serious blow by Stogdill (1948), whose review of the literature indicated that personality characteristics are generally poor predictors of leadership. This is not to say, of course, that individual characteristics have no impact on who becomes a leader. There is evidence, for example, that leaders tend to be intelligent (Mann, 1959), talkative (Bavelas, Hastorf, Gross, & Kite, 1965), dominant (Nyquist & Spence, 1986), success- and affiliation-oriented (Sorrentino & Field, 1986), and perhaps adaptive and flexible (Kenny & Zaccaro, 1983).

There is also evidence of a relationship between sex and leadership. Although common stereotypes assert that men are more likely than women to become leaders (Hollander, 1985), a recent meta-analysis of sex differences in emergent leadership suggests a more complex picture. In this analysis, Eagly and Karau (1991) found that men were more likely to emerge as leaders on measures of general and task leadership, whereas women were more likely to emerge on measures of social leadership. These findings can be explained by a gender role analysis that assumes men specialize in "agentic" (task-related) aspects of group process while women specialize in "communal" (interpersonal) aspects (cf. Eagly, 1987).

Although personal characteristics can influence who becomes a leader, it is not the case that all leaders share exactly the same characteristics or that certain critical characteristics determine leadership in all situations. How then can we explain leadership effectiveness? Several answers to this question have been offered (Chemers, 1983, 1987).

According to *contingency* theory, leadership effectiveness depends on the fit, or compatibility, between the leader's characteristics and the demands of the situation in which the leader is working. Several contingency theories have been developed (e.g., House, 1971; Vroom & Yetton, 1973), but the best-known is probably Fiedler's (1967, 1978) theory. According to Fiedler, leaders differ in their preferred leadership style. Some leaders are task-oriented, emphasizing successful group performance rather than harmony among group members. Other leaders are relationship-oriented, emphasizing harmony among group members rather than successful group performance. Fiedler argues that the effectiveness of these two kinds of leaders depends on their level of situational control, which is determined by the quality of the leader's relations with other members, the clarity of the group's task, and the leader's power over other members. Fiedler's theory suggests that relationship-oriented leaders are most effective when the situation provides them with moderate control, whereas task-oriented leaders are most effective when the situation provides them with either high control or low control. Fiedler's theory has been supported by many, but by no means all, of the studies that have been done to test it (Chemers, 1987; Peters, Hartke, & Pohlmann, 1985; Rice & Kastenbaum, 1983; Strube & Garcia, 1981).

If Fiedler is right, we might expect leaders who work in "unfavorable" situations (e.g., relationship-oriented leaders in low-control situations) to experience more stress than those who work in "favorable" situations (e.g., relationship-oriented leaders in moderate-control situations). Recent evidence suggests that mismatches between leadership style and situational control do in fact induce stress and physical health symptoms (Chemers, Hays, Rhodewalt, & Wysocki, 1985). To the extent that a leader's preferred style reflects an enduring personality characteristic, efforts to change leader behaviors are likely to fail. Instead, it might be more productive to train leaders to modify their situations to fit their personal motivational styles. A training program (*Leader Match*) based on this idea has proved to be quite effective (Fiedler, 1978).

Other theories of leadership effectiveness emphasize the role of followers. According to *transactional* theory, leadership depends on the development and maintenance of leader-follower relations through the exchange of rewards (e.g., the leader makes good decisions for the group, and the followers agree to obey the leader's orders). Perhaps the best-known transactional theory is vertical dyad linkage theory, developed by Graen and his colleagues (Dansereau, Graen, & Haga, 1975). This theory assumes that leaders develop different exchange relationships with different subordinates or subgroups of subordinates and that the quality of these exchanges affects subordinates' motivation, satisfaction, and organizational commitment (see Chemers, 1983, 1987; Vecchio & Gobdel, 1984). According to *cognitive* theory, leadership effectiveness is determined by leaders' and followers' thoughts about one another. For example, Green and Mitchell (1979) have argued that leaders make attributions about their followers' behavior, which in turn affect how they evaluate and treat their followers (see Ashkanasy, 1989). And evidence suggests that followers possess shared beliefs about leaders' behaviors and traits, which influence how they encode leader information, form perceptions of leaders, and recall relevant information (e.g., Lord, 1985; Rush & Russell, 1988).

Transactional theories generally assume that leaders must earn *legitimacy* in order to exert influence over their followers. Several factors can affect this legitimacy, including the leader's conformity to group norms, the leader's competence on the group task, and the source of the leader's authority (Hollander & Julian, 1970). It has been found, for example, that a high-competence person who deviates from group norms after initially conforming is more influential than a person who deviates without initially conforming (Hollander, 1958, 1960; but see Levine, 1989). Other research is consistent with the idea that a person's competence on the group task, as well as commitment to group goals, affects the likelihood that he or she will gain legitimacy as a leader (e.g., Hollander & Julian, 1970; Ridgeway, 1981). Finally, studies show that legitimacy gained through election versus appointment has different effects on leader-follower relations (Ben-Yoav, Hollander, & Carnevale, 1983; Hollander, 1985). For example, elected leaders are more likely to be deposed after failure than are appointed leaders.

Productivity

Many theories of group productivity stress the importance of members' interactions as they carry out joint tasks. For example, in analyzing the effectiveness of work groups in organizations, Hackman (1987) argued that the group interaction process can have either negative or positive consequences for group performance. In the former case, group interaction produces performance that is inferior to what would be predicted by knowing the abilities of individual members ("process loss"). In the latter case, group interaction produces performance that is superior to what would be predicted by knowing the abilities of individual members ("process gain").

Steiner (1972) suggested two causes for process loss. First, *coordination loss* occurs when group members do not combine their individual responses in the optimal way, for example, when several people on a tug-of-war team pull on the rope at different times. Second, *motivation loss* occurs when group members do not exert maximal effort on the group task. An example of motivation loss is *social loafing*, which occurs when individual responses are "pooled" in a way that obscures the efforts of individual group members (Harkins & Szymanski, 1987).

In an early social loafing experiment (Latané, Williams, & Harkins, 1979, Experiment 2), students were asked to shout as loudly as they could. Subjects performed either alone, in dyads, or in six-person groups. Care was taken to ensure that subjects could not tell how hard other group members were working and could not interfere with each other's performance. Results indicated that sound pressure per person decreased as group size increased, indicating more loafing in larger than in smaller groups. The social loafing effect has been replicated many times, using cognitive as well as physical tasks (e.g., Harkins & Petty, 1982; Kerr & Bruun, 1981). But research indicates that loafing is not inevitable. It can be reduced or eliminated, for example, by increasing the identifiability and uniqueness of individual task contributions (e.g., Harkins & Petty, 1982; Kerr & Bruun, 1981), the ease of evaluating these contributions (e.g., Harkins & Szymanski, 1987), members' task involvement and accountability (e.g., Brickner, Harkins, & Ostrom, 1986; Weldon & Gargano, 1988), and task attractiveness (e.g., Zaccaro, 1984).

Steiner's analysis of process loss is also applicable to process gain. Just as response coordination and member motivation can inhibit group performance under some circumstances, so they can facilitate this performance under other circumstances. For example, response coordination might be improved by a division of labor that allows members to specialize on certain subtasks and by training procedures designed to help members interact smoothly and efficiently. Member motivation might be improved by intragroup competition, in which members compete with one another for individual goals (e.g., bonuses), and by manipulations that lead members to feel that they have special responsibility for the group product. In regard to the latter technique, recent work on "social compensation" indicates that under certain conditions (e.g., when coworkers are not trusted to perform well and the group product is important), individuals will exert *more* effort when working collectively than when working alone (Williams, Karau, & Bourgeois, 1993).

Because group productivity is often reduced by motivation loss (e.g., social loafing) and coordination loss, a number of techniques have been developed to improve group effectiveness. Three rather popular techniques require work groups to make substantial changes in how they function. *Team building* is designed to increase group members' interpersonal and task skills by creating a strong sense of interdependence through problem identification, role analysis, and sensitivity training activities (e.g., Buller, 1986; Dyer, 1987). *Quality circles*, popularized by Japanese businesses, involve regular meetings in which members of work groups identify production problems and offer solutions to these problems (e.g., Greene & Matherly, 1988; Marks, Mirvis, Hackett, & Grady, 1986). *Autonomous work groups* allow members who work on interdependent tasks to control how these tasks are managed and executed (e.g., Goodman, Devadas, & Hughson, 1988; Pearce & Ravlin, 1987). Although none of these techniques works in every case, each appears to be useful in some situations.

Decision Making

One of the most important activities that groups perform is making joint decisions. These decisions, which can have important implications for the welfare of the group and/or outsiders, frequently involve debate and argument between members holding different views. There is a general belief that groups make better decisions than do individuals. This belief is based on the assumptions that (a) groups are more likely than individuals to possess the requisite expertise to analyze a problem and develop solutions for it and (b) the process of group discussion reduces the impact of personal biases and increases the likelihood that good solutions will be adopted. In addition, it is widely assumed that decisions made collectively have more group support and hence are easier to implement than are those "imposed" on a group. Because of these assumptions, virtually all organizations (e.g., business, educational, military, governmental) entrust their important decisions to small groups rather than to single individuals. But as we shall see below, this trust in group decision making is sometimes misplaced.

In order to understand the strengths and weaknesses of group decision making, it is first necessary to understand the process by which groups make decisions. In an analysis of how organizations make unstructured, strategic decisions, Mintzberg, Raisinghani, and Theoret (1976) identified three phases of decision making that are applicable to small groups as well as organizations. The first phase is identification, during which the group assesses problems and opportunities, decides that a decision is necessary, and obtains information needed to formulate a decision. The second phase is development, during which the group attempts to find ready-made solutions to its problem or (if this is not successful) creates custom-made solutions. The third phase is selection, during which the group chooses the "best" solution from among those it has found or created.

It is interesting that social psychological research on group decision making has all but ignored the first two phases identified by Mintzberg and associates (1976). Instead, subjects in group decision-making studies are typically told that a problem exists, given ready-made solutions to that problem, and asked to choose one of those solutions. For example, in jury decision-making studies, subjects are told that a defendant is charged with a crime, that the person is either guilty or not guilty, and that their job is to reach consensus on one of these options. Unless all group members initially favor the same solution, the decision-making process thus involves transforming initial disagreement into final agreement. Researchers have demonstrated that some simple rules, called *social decision schemes,* are quite useful in predicting a group's final decision from the distribution of members' initial positions (see Laughlin & Ellis, 1986; Stasser, Kerr, & Davis, 1989). For example, the *majority wins* rule, which stipulates that the group will select the position that has majority support, is most often used on judgmental tasks without demonstrable correct answers (e.g., whether a criminal defendant is guilty or innocent). The *truth wins* rule, which stipulates that the group will select the correct position if only one person supports it, is most applicable on verbal intellective tasks with obvious demonstrable correct answers (e.g., "Eureka" or insight problems). And the *truth-supported wins* rule, which stipulates that the group will select the correct position if two people support it, is most accurate on verbal intellectual tasks with nonobvious demonstrable correct answers (e.g., vocabulary, analogy, and world knowledge problems). In addition to predicting the final distribution of members' positions (Davis, 1973), analyses based on social decision schemes also shed light on how groups move through stages of agreement/disagreement en route to final consensus (Kerr, 1981) and how members' decision preferences and certainty levels change over time (Stasser & Davis, 1981).

Groups do not always make good decisions. One reason is that group members often fail to exchange all the information they have. Stasser and his colleagues have investigated information exchange in decision-making groups by distributing both shared information (which all members receive) and unshared information (which only one individual receives) and then assessing how much of each type of information is discussed (Stasser, 1992; Stasser, Taylor, & Hanna, 1989). The results of these studies indicate that group members spend most of their time discussing information that they already share and that supports their existing preferences. Clearly, if groups need unshared information to reach sound decisions (e.g., because reliance on only shared information would lead to a poor decision), the failure to exchange unshared information can severely compromise group performance.

The costs of failing to exchange information have been documented by Janis (1982) in his work on *groupthink*. According to Janis, several factors—such as situational threats, directive leaders, and high group cohesiveness—produce symptoms of groupthink. These symptoms include pressure on dissenters, feelings of invulnerability, and tendencies to ignore information suggesting that the group is wrong. Groupthink, in turn, has negative consequences for decision making, including restricted consideration of alternative solutions and biased information processing. Janis analyzed several historical cases of poor group decision making (e.g., the lack of readiness at Pearl Harbor, the abortive Bay of Pigs invasion) that seemed consistent with his position. Although the groupthink idea has been quite influential, critics have pointed out problems with Janis' theory and suggested that it oversimplifies group decision making in several ways (e.g., Longley & Pruitt, 1980; McCauley, 1989; Tetlock, Peterson, McGuire, Chang, & Feld, 1992). For example, in an examination of several historical cases of political decision making, Tetlock and colleagues (1992) found that, contrary to Janis' theory, group cohesiveness and situational threats were not independent predictors of symptoms of groupthink.

One alleged outcome of groupthink is the tendency for groups to endorse (unduly) risky courses of action. The question of when and why groups make risky decisions has intrigued researchers for some time. Beginning with Stoner (1961), many investigators found that groups make riskier decisions than do individuals on choice dilemma problems. This tendency was labeled the *risky shift*. Later evidence, however, suggested that groups sometimes shift toward caution rather than risk and even show opinion shifts on issues where risk and caution are irrelevant. These findings led investigators to recognize that the risky shift is really a special case of *group polarization*, defined as the tendency for group discussion to make individuals more extreme in whatever direction they are initially leaning (Moscovici & Zavalloni, 1969; Myers & Lamm, 1976). In one demonstration of group polarization, Myers and Bishop (1970) created groups of relatively prejudiced and unprejudiced high school students, measured their opinions on racial issues, had them discuss these issues, and then assessed their opinions a second time. The results showed that group discussion caused high-prejudice subjects to give *more* prejudiced responses and low-prejudice subjects to give *less* prejudiced responses.

Many explanations of group polarization have been offered, but the two most popular are *persuasive arguments* and *social comparison* (Isenberg, 1986). The former is based on informational influence, whereas the latter is based on normative influence (Deutsch & Gerard, 1955). According to persuasive arguments theory, group polarization occurs because group members are exposed during discussion to novel and persuasive arguments that favor their initial position, which causes them to shift further in the direction they are already leaning (e.g., Burnstein & Sentis, 1981; Hinsz & Davis, 1984). Consistent with this explanation, evidence shows that polarization can be influenced by varying the proportion of pro and con arguments that subjects hear. According to social comparison theory, polarization occurs because group members discover during discussion that the group norm is more extreme than they thought, which causes them to adopt a more extreme position in order to conform to this norm or to move beyond it and thereby positively differentiate themselves from other members (e.g., Baron & Roper, 1976; Myers, 1978). Consistent with this explanation, evidence shows that polarization can be produced by mere knowledge of others' positions, in the absence of supporting arguments. Both of these explanations, as well as newer ones such as self-categorization theory (e.g., Mackie, 1986; Turner, 1991), shed light on the mechanisms underlying group polarization.

Because group decision making can go awry for so many reasons, techniques have been developed to help groups make better decisions. Some of these are simply computational schemes for combining members' preferences to enhance group accuracy (e.g., Shapley & Grofman, 1984). Others involve some type of intervention in the group's activities. Perhaps the best-known intervention technique is *brainstorming*, in which group members are encouraged to come up with novel ideas in a tolerant and criticism-free environment. Unfortunately, however, brainstorming doesn't work: "Nominal groups" (i.e., sets of people working alone) generally perform better than real groups (Diehl & Stroebe, 1987; Mullen, Johnson, & Salas, 1991). Although brainstorming groups are not effective, people who participate in such groups *believe* that they are productive (Paulus, Dzindolet, Poletes, & Camacho, 1993), which may partially explain the popularity of this procedure. Other intervention techniques for improving group decision making have also been suggested (e.g., Bartunek & Murnighan, 1984; Erffmeyer & Lane, 1984), but the boundary conditions for their effectiveness have not been established. Therefore, although social psychologists have done a good job in identifying the problems that arise in decision-making groups, they have been less successful in developing a "sure cure" for these problems.

CONCLUSION

The study of small groups has a long and distinguished history in social psychology. As the research reviewed in this chapter suggests, much has been learned about the ecology, composition, and structure of groups, as well as about how groups handle conflict and strive to attain members' collective goals. One of the hallmarks of this work is its focus on practical issues, such as improving group productivity. Much of the world's work is done by small groups, including juries, work units, army squads, and athletic teams. Therefore, people in all walks of life care deeply about group performance, and their concern is shared by many researchers who study groups.

In recent years, this practical orientation has influenced both the theories developed to explain group processes and the methods used to test these theories. Rather than developing theories to account for simple behavior in laboratory groups, investigators are building models to explain complex behavior in natural groups. And rather than relying primarily on experimental methods, researchers are conducting more field studies (e.g., observations of work groups in organizations) and archival studies (e.g., analyses of historical records of the deliberations of governmental policy groups). These theoretical and methodological trends, as well as the interest in small groups by researchers from several disciplines (e.g., social and organizational psychology, sociology, communications, political science), bode well for the future of the field.

References

ALDERFER, C. P., & SMITH, K. K. (1982). Studying intergroup relations embedded in organizations. *Administrative Science Quarterly, 27*, 35–65.

ALEXANDER, V. D., & THOITS, P. A. (1985). Token achievement: An examination of proportional representation and performance outcome. *Social Forces, 64*, 332–340.

ALLEN, V. L. (1965). Situational factors in conformity. In L. Berkowitz (Ed.), *Advances in experimental social psychology* (Vol. 2, pp. 133–175). New York: Academic Press.

ALLEN, V. L. (1975). Social support for nonconformity. In L. Berkowitz (Ed.), *Advances in experimental social psychology* (Vol. 8, pp. 1–43). New York: Academic Press.

ALLEN, V. L., & LEVINE, J. M. (1968). Social support, dissent, and conformity. *Sociometry, 31*, 138–149.

ALLEN, V. L., & LEVINE, J. M. (1969). Consensus and conformity. *Journal of Experimental Social Psychology, 5*, 389–399.

ALLEN, V. L., & LEVINE, J. M. (1971). Social support and conformity: The role of independent assessment of reality. *Journal of Experimental Social Psychology, 7*, 48–58.

ALLEN, V. L., & VAN DE VLIERT, E. (Eds.). (1984). *Role transitions: Explorations and explanations.* New York: Plenum.

ANCONA, D. G. (1987). Groups in organizations: Extending laboratory models. In C. Hendrick (Ed.), *Review of personality and social psychology* (Vol. 9, pp. 207–230). Newbury Park, CA: Sage.

ANCONA, D. G., & CALDWELL, D. F. (1988). Beyond task and maintenance: Defining external functions in groups. *Group and Organization Studies, 13*, 468–494.

ASCH, S. E. (1951). Effects of group pressure upon the modification and distortion of judgments. In H. Guetzkow (Ed.), *Groups, leadership, and men* (pp. 177–190). Pittsburgh, PA: Carnegie Press.

ASCH, S. E. (1955). Opinions and social pressure. *Scientific American, 193*, 31–35.

ASCH, S. E. (1956). Studies of independence and submission to group pressure: I. A minority of one against a unanimous majority. *Psychological Monographs, 70* (Whole No. 417).

ASHKANASY, N. M. (1989). Causal attribution and supervisors' response to subordinate performance: The Green and Mitchell model revisited. *Journal of Applied Social Psychology, 19*, 309–330.

BARCHAS, P. R., & FISEK, M. H. (1984). Hierarchical differentiation in newly formed groups of rhesus and humans. In P. R. Barchas (Ed.), *Essays toward a sociophysiological perspective* (pp. 23–33). Westport: Greenwood Press.

BARON, R. S., & ROPER, G. (1976). Reaffirmation of social comparison views of choice shifts: Averaging and extremity effects in an autokinetic situation. *Journal of Personality and Social Psychology, 33*, 521–530.

BARTUNEK, J. M., & MURNIGHAN, J. K. (1984). The nominal group technique: Expanding the basic procedure and underlying assumptions. *Group and Organization Studies, 9,* 417–432.

BASS, B. M. (1980). Team productivity and individual member competence. *Small Group Behavior, 11,* 431–504.

BAUMEISTER, R. F., & STEINHILBER, A. (1984). Paradoxical effects of supportive audiences on performance under pressure: The home field disadvantage in sports championships. *Journal of Personality and Social Psychology, 47,* 85–93.

BAVELAS, A., HASTORF, A. H., GROSS, A. E., & KITE, W. R. (1965). Experiments on the alteration of group structure. *Journal of Experimental Social Psychology, 1,* 55–70.

BEN-YOAV, O., HOLLANDER, E. P., & CARNEVALE, P. J. D. (1983). Leader legitimacy, leader-follower interaction, and followers' ratings of the leader. *Journal of Social Psychology, 121,* 111–115.

BERGER, J., ROSENHOLTZ, S. J., & ZELDITCH, M. (1980). Status organizing processes. *Annual Review of Sociology, 6,* 479–508.

BERGER, J., & ZELDITCH, M. (Eds.). (1985). *Status, rewards, and influence.* San Francisco: Jossey-Bass.

BETTENHAUSEN, K., & MURNIGHAN, J. K. (1985). The emergence of norms in competitive decision-making groups. *Administrative Science Quarterly, 30,* 350–372.

BONACICH, P., GRUSKY, O., & PEYROT, M. (1985). Family coalitions: A new approach and method. *Social Psychology Quarterly, 48,* 42–50.

BORNSTEIN, G., & RAPOPORT, A. (1988). Intergroup competition for the provision of step-level public goods: Effects of preplay communication. *European Journal of Social Psychology, 18,* 125–142.

BRADLEY, D. H. (1980). Sex, competence, and opinion deviation: An expectation states approach. *Communication Monographs, 47,* 101–110.

BRETT, J. M. (1980). The effect of job transfers on employees and their families. In C. L. Cooper & R. Payne (Eds.), *Current concerns in occupational stress* (pp. 99–136). New York: Wiley.

BRICKNER, M. A., HARKINS, S. G., & OSTROM, T. M. (1986). Effects of personal involvement: Thought-provoking implications for social loafing. *Journal of Personality and Social Psychology, 51,* 763–769.

BROCKNER, J. (1988). The effects of work layoffs on survivors: Research, theory, and practice. In B. M. Staw & L. L. Cummings (Eds.), *Research in organizational behavior* (Vol. 10, pp. 213–255). Greenwich, CT: JAI Press.

BRONFENBRENNER, U. (1986). Ecology of the family as a context for human development: Research perspectives. *Developmental Psychology, 22,* 737–742.

BULLER, P. F. (1986). The team building–task performance relation: Some conceptual and methodological refinements. *Group and Organization Studies, 11,* 147–168.

BURGESS, J. W. (1984). Do humans show a "species-typical" group size? Age, sex, and environmental differences in the size and composition of naturally-occurring causal groups. *Ethology and Sociobiology, 5,* 51–57.

BURNSTEIN, E., & SENTIS, K. (1981). Attitude polarization in groups. In R. E. Petty, T. M. Ostrom, & T. C. Brock (Eds.), *Cognitive responses in persuasion* (pp. 197–216). Hillsdale, NJ: Erlbaum.

CARTWRIGHT, D., & ZANDER, A. (1968). *Group dynamics: Research and theory* (3rd ed.). New York: Harper & Row.

CHEMERS, M. M. (1983). Leadership theory and research: A systems-process integration. In P. B. Paulus (Ed.), *Basic group processes* (pp. 9–39). New York: Springer-Verlag.

CHEMERS, M. M. (1987). Leadership processes: Intrapersonal, interpersonal, and societal influences. In C. Hendrick (Ed.), *Review of personality and social psychology* (Vol. 8, pp. 252–277). Newbury Park, CA: Sage.

CHEMERS, M. M., HAYS, R. B., RHODEWALT, F., & WYSOCKI, J. (1985). A person-environment analysis of job stress: A contingency model explanation. *Journal of Personality and Social Psychology, 49,* 628–635.

COTA, A. A., & DION, K. L. (1986). Salience of gender and sex composition of ad hoc groups: An experimental test of distinctiveness theory. *Journal of Personality and Social Psychology, 50,* 770–776.

CROCKER, J., & McGRAW, K. M. (1984). What's good for the goose is not good for the gander: Solo status as an obstacle to occupational achievement for males and females. *American Behavioral Scientist, 27,* 357–369.

DANSEREAU, F., GRAEN, G., & HAGA, W. J. (1975). A vertical dyad linkage approach to leadership within formal organizations: A longitudinal investigation of the role making process. *Organizational Behavior, 13,* 46–78.

DAVIS, J. H. (1973). Group decision and social interaction: A theory of social decision schemes. *Psychological Review, 80,* 97–125.

DAVIS, P., & STERN, D. (1980). Adaptation, survival, and the growth of the family business: An integrated systems perspective. *Human Relations, 34,* 207–224.

DAWES, R. M., McTAVISH, J., & SHAKLEE, H. (1977). Behavior, communication, and assumptions about other people's behavior in a commons dilemma situation. *Journal of Personality and Social Psychology, 35,* 1–11.

DeSANCTIS, G., & GALLUPE, B. (1987). A foundation for the study of group decision support systems. *Management Science, 33,* 589–609.

DEUTSCH, M., & GERARD, H. B. (1955). A study of normative and informational social influences upon individual judgment. *Journal of Abnormal and Social Psychology, 51,* 629–633.

DIEHL, M., & STROEBE, W. (1987). Productivity loss in brainstorming groups: Toward the solution of a riddle. *Journal of Personality and Social Psychology, 53,* 497–509.

DOOLEY, D., & CATALANO, R. (Eds.). (1988). Psychological effects of unemployment. *Journal of Social Issues, 44* (Whole No. 4).

DOVIDIO, J. F., & ELLYSON, S. L. (1985). Patterns of visual dominance behavior in humans. In S. L. Ellyson & J. F. Dovidio (Eds.), *Power, dominance, and nonverbal behavior* (pp. 129–149). New York: Springer-Verlag.

DYER, W. G. (1987). *Team building: Issues and alternatives* (2nd ed.). Reading, MA: Addison-Wesley.

EAGLY, A. H. (1987). *Sex differences in social behavior: A social-role interpretation.* Hillsdale, NJ: Erlbaum.

EAGLY, A. H., & JOHNSON, B. T. (1990). Gender and leadership style: A meta-analysis. *Psychological Bulletin, 108,* 233–256.

EAGLY, A. H., & KARAU, S. J. (1991). Gender and the emergence of leaders: A meta-analysis. *Journal of Personality and Social Psychology, 60,* 685–710.

EGERBLADH, T. (1976). The function of group size and ability level on solving a multidimensional complementary task. *Journal of Personality and Social Psychology, 34,* 805–808.

ERFFMEYER, R. C., & LANE, I. M. (1984). Quality and acceptance of an evaluative task: The effects of four group decision-making formats. *Group and Organization Studies, 9,* 509–529.

FAIRHURST, G., & SNAVELY, B. K. (1983). Majority and token minority group relationships: Power acquisition and communication. *Academy of Management Review, 8,* 292–300.

FELDMAN, D. C. (1984). The development and enforcement of group norms. *Academy of Management Review, 9,* 47–53.

FESTINGER, L. (1954). A theory of social comparison processes. *Human Relations, 7,* 117–140.

FIEDLER, F. (1967). *A theory of leadership effectiveness.* New York: McGraw-Hill.

FIEDLER, F. (1978). The contingency model and the dynamics of the leadership process. In L. Berkowitz (Ed.), *Advances in experimental social psychology* (Vol. 11, pp. 59–112). New York: Academic Press.

FINE, G. A., & STOECKER, R. (1985). Can the circle be unbroken? Small groups and social movements. In E. J. Lawler (Ed.), *Advances in group processes* (Vol. 2, pp. 1–28). Greenwich, CT: JAI Press.

FISHER, C. D., & GITELSON, R. (1983). A meta-analysis of the correlates of role conflict and ambiguity. *Journal of Applied Psychology, 68,* 320–333.

FONTANA, L. (1985). Clique formation in a regional health planning agency. *Human Relations, 38,* 895–910.

FORSYTH, D. R. (1990). *Group dynamics* (2nd ed.). Pacific Grove, CA: Brooks/Cole Publishing Company.

FREUD, S. (1951). *Civilization and its discontents* (J. Strachey, Trans.). New York: Norton. (Original work published in 1930.)

GAERTNER, S. L., MANN, J., MURRELL, A., & DOVIDIO, J. F. (1989). Reduction of intergroup bias: The benefits of recategorization. *Journal of Personality and Social Psychology, 57,* 239–249.

GALASKIEWICZ, J., & WASSERMAN, S. (1989). Mimetic processes within an interorganizational field: An empirical test. *Administrative Science Quarterly, 34,* 454–479.

GATEWOOD, J. B. (1984). Cooperation, competition, and synergy: Information-sharing groups among Southeast Alaskan salmon seiners. *American Ethnologist, 11,* 350–370.

GEORGE, A. L. (1981). Primary groups, organization, and military performance. In R. W. Little (Ed.), *Handbook of military institutions* (pp. 293–318). Beverly Hills, CA: Sage.

GERARD, H. B., WILHELMY, R. A., & CONOLLEY, E. S. (1968). Conformity and group size. *Journal of Personality and Social Psychology, 8,* 79–82.

GERSICK, C. J. G. (1988). Time and transition in work teams: Toward a new model of group development. *Academy of Management Journal, 31,* 9–41.

GOODMAN, M. (1981). Group phases and induced countertransference. *Psychotherapy: Theory, Research, and Practice, 18,* 478–486.

GOODMAN, P. S., DEVADAS, R., & HUGHSON, T. L. G. (1988). Groups and productivity: An analysis of self-managing teams. In J. P. Campbell (Ed.), *Productivity in organizations* (pp. 295–327). San Francisco: Jossey-Bass.

GRAHAM, W. K., & DILLON, P. C. (1974). Creative supergroups: Group performance as a function of individual performance on brainstorming tasks. *Journal of Social Psychology, 93,* 101–105.

GREEN, S. G., & MITCHELL, T. R. (1979). Attributional processes of leaders in leader-member interactions. *Organizational Behavior, 23,* 429–458.

GREENE, C. N., & MATHERLY, T. A. (1988). Quality circles: A need for caution and evaluation of alternatives. In R. S. Schuler, S. A. Youngblood, & V. L. Huber (Eds.), *Readings in personnel and human resource management* (pp. 509–517) (3rd ed.). St. Paul: West Publishing Company.

GREENHALGH, L. (1983). Organizational decline. In S. B. Bacharach (Ed.), *Research in the sociology of organizations* (Vol. 22, pp. 231–276). Greenwich, CT: JAI Press.

GREER, D. L. (1983). Spectator booing and the home advantage: A study of social influence in the basketball arena. *Social Psychology Quarterly, 46,* 252–261.

HAAS, J. (1974). The stages of the high-steel ironworker apprentice career. *The Sociological Quarterly, 15,* 93–108.

HAAS, J. (1977). Learning real feelings: A study of high steel ironworkers' reactions to fear and danger. *Sociology of Work and Occupations, 4,* 147–170.

HACKMAN, J. R. (1987). The design of work teams. In J. Lorsch (Ed.), *Handbook of organizational behavior* (pp. 315–342). Englewood Cliffs, NJ: Prentice-Hall.

HANEY, C., BANKS, C., & ZIMBARDO, P. (1973). Interpersonal dynamics in a simulated prison. *International Journal of Criminology and Penology, 1,* 69–97.

HARDIN, G. (1968). The tragedy of the commons. *Science, 162,* 1243–1248.

HARKINS, S. G., & PETTY, R. E. (1982). Effects of task difficulty and task uniqueness on social loafing. *Journal of Personality and Social Psychology, 43,* 1214–1229.

HARKINS, S. G., & SZYMANSKI, K. (1987). Social loafing and social facilitation: New wine in old bottles. In C. Hendrick (Ed.), *Review of personality and social psychology* (Vol. 9, pp. 167–188). Newbury Park, CA: Sage.

HARPER, R. G. (1985). Power, dominance, and nonverbal behavior: An overview. In S. L. Ellyson & J. F. Dovidio (Eds.), *Power, dominance, and nonverbal behavior* (pp. 29–48). New York: Springer-Verlag.

HARRISON, A. A., & CONNORS, M. M. (1984). Groups in exotic environments. In L. Berkowitz (Ed.), *Advances in experimental social psychology* (Vol. 18, pp. 49–87). Orlando, FL: Academic Press.

HASTIE, R. (1986). Review essay: Experimental evidence on group accuracy. In G. Owen & B. Grofman (Eds.), *Information pooling and group decision making* (pp. 129–157). Westport, CT: JAI Press.

HEISS, J. (1981). Social roles. In M. Rosenberg & R. H. Turner (Eds.), *Social psychology* (pp. 94–129). New York: Basic Books.

HIGGINS, E. T., & KING, G. (1981). Accessibility of social constructs: Information processing consequences of individual and context variability. In N. Cantor & J. F. Kihlstrom (Eds.), *Cognition, social interaction, and personality* (pp. 69–121). Hillsdale, NJ: Erlbaum.

HILL, G. W. (1982). Group versus individual performance: Are $N + 1$ heads better than one? *Psychological Bulletin, 91,* 517–539.

HILTZ, S. R., JOHNSON, K., & TUROFF, M. (1986). Experiments in group decision making: Communication process and outcome in face-to-face versus computerized conferences. *Human Communication Research, 13,* 225–252.

HINSZ, V. B., & DAVIS, J. H. (1984). Persuasive arguments theory, group polarization, and choice shifts. *Personality and Social Psychology Bulletin, 10,* 260–268.

HOLLANDER, E. P. (1958). Conformity, status, and idiosyncrasy credit. *Psychological Review, 65,* 117–127.

HOLLANDER, E. P. (1960). Competence and conformity in the acceptance of influence. *Journal of Abnormal and Social Psychology, 61,* 365–369.

HOLLANDER, E. P. (1985). Leadership and power. In G. Lindzey & E. Aronson (Eds.), *The handbook of social psychology* (Vol. 2, pp. 485–537). New York: Random House.

HOLLANDER, E. P., & JULIAN, J. W. (1970). Studies in leader legitimacy, influence and innovation. In L. Berkowitz (Ed.), *Advances in experimental social psychology* (Vol. 5, pp. 34–69). New York: Academic Press.

HOUSE, R. J. (1971). A path-goal theory of leader effectiveness. *Administrative Science Quarterly, 16,* 321–338.

HUMPHREY, R. (1985). How work roles influence perception: Structural-cognitive processes and organizational behavior. *American Sociological Review, 50,* 242–252.

ISENBERG, D. J. (1986). Group polarization: A critical review and meta-analysis. *Journal of Personality and Social Psychology, 50,* 1141–1151.

IZRAELI, D. N. (1983). Sex effects or structural effects? An empirical test of Kanter's theory of proportions. *Social Forces, 62,* 153–165.

JACKSON, S. E. (1992). Team composition in organizational settings: Issues in managing an increasingly diverse work force. In S. Worchel, W. Wood, & J. A. Simpson (Eds.), *Group process and productivity* (pp. 138–173). Newbury Park, CA: Sage.

JACKSON, S. E., & SCHULER, R. S. (1985). A meta-analysis and conceptual critique of research on role ambiguity and role conflict in work settings. *Organizational Behavior, 36,* 16–78.

JANIS, I. L. (1982). *Groupthink* (2nd ed.). Boston: Houghton Mifflin.

JONES, M. B. (1974). Regressing group on individual effectiveness. *Organizational Behavior and Human Performance, 11,* 426–451.

JORGENSON, D. O., & PAPCIAK, A. S. (1981). The effects of communication, resource feedback, and identifiability on behavior in a simulated commons. *Journal of Experimental Social Psychology, 17,* 373–385.

KAHAN, J. P., & RAPOPORT, A. (1984). *Theories of coalition formation.* Hillsdale, NJ: Erlbaum.

KANAS, N. (1985). Psychosocial factors affecting simulated and actual space missions. *Aviation, Space, and Environmental Medicine, 56,* 806–811.

KANTER, R. M. (1977). Some effects of proportions on group life: Skewed sex ratios and responses to token women. *American Journal of Sociology, 82,* 965–990.

KENNEDY, J. L. (1971). The system approach: A preliminary exploratory study of the relation between team composition and financial performance in business games. *Journal of Applied Psychology, 55,* 46–49.

KENNY, D. A., & ZACCARO, S. L. (1983). An estimate of variance due to traits in leadership. *Journal of Applied Psychology, 68,* 678–685.

KERR, N. L. (1981). Social transition schemes: Charting the group's road to agreement. *Journal of Personality and Social Psychology, 41,* 684–702.

KERR, N. L., & BRUUN, S. E. (1981). Ringelmann revisited: Alternative explanations for the social loafing effect. *Personality and Social Psychology Bulletin, 7,* 224–231.

KIDD, J. S. (1958). Social influence phenomena in a task-oriented group situation. *Journal of Abnormal and Social Psychology, 56,* 13–17.

KIESLER, S., SIEGEL, J., & McGUIRE, T. W. (1984). Social psychological aspects of computer-mediated communication. *American Psychologist, 39,* 1123–1134.

KOMORITA, S. S. (1984). Coalition bargaining. In L. Berkowitz (Ed.), *Advances in experimental social psychology* (Vol. 18, pp. 183–245). Orlando, FL: Academic Press.

KOMORITA, S. S., & KRAVITZ, D. A. (1983). Coalition formation: A social psychological approach. In P. B. Paulus (Ed.), *Basic group processes* (pp. 179–203). New York: Springer-Verlag.

KRAMER, R. M., & BREWER, M. B. (1986). Social group identity and the emergence of cooperation in resource conservation dilemmas. In H. A. M. Wilke, D. M. Messick, & C. G. Rutte (Eds.), *Experimental social dilemmas* (pp. 205–234). Frankfurt am Main: Verlag Peter Lang.

KRAMER, R. M., McCLINTOCK, C. G., & MESSICK, D. M. (1986). Social values and cooperative response to a simulated resource conservation crisis. *Journal of Personality, 54,* 576–592.

KRANTZ, J. (1985). Group process under conditions of organizational decline. *Journal of Applied Behavioral Science, 21,* 1–17.

LATANÉ, B., WILLIAMS, K., & HARKINS, S. (1979). Many hands make light the work: The causes and consequences of social loafing. *Journal of Personality and Social Psychology, 37,* 823–832.

Laughlin, P. R. (1978). Ability and group problem solving. *Journal of Research and Development in Education, 12,* 114–120.

Laughlin, P. R., Branch, L. G., & Johnson, H. H. (1969). Individual versus triadic performance on a unidimensional complementary task as a function of initial ability level. *Journal of Personality and Social Psychology, 12,* 144–150.

Laughlin, P. R., & Ellis, A. L. (1986). Demonstrability and social combination processes on mathematical intellectual tasks. *Journal of Experimental Social Psychology, 22,* 177–189.

Lawler, E. J. (1983). Cooptation and threats as "divide and rule" tactics. *Social Psychology Quarterly, 46,* 89–98.

Levine, J. M. (1989). Reaction to opinion deviance in small groups. In P. B. Paulus (Ed.), *Psychology of group influence* (2nd ed., pp. 187–231). Hillsdale, NJ: Erlbaum.

Levine, J. M., & Moreland, R. L. (in press). Group socialization: Theory and research. In W. Stroebe & M. Hewstone (Eds.), *The European review of social psychology* (Vol. 5). Chichester: John Wiley & Sons.

Levine, J. M., & Moreland, R. L. (1985). Innovation and socialization in small groups. In S. Moscovici, G. Mugny, & E. Van Avermaet (Eds.), *Perspectives on minority influence* (pp. 143–169). Cambridge: Cambridge University Press.

Levine, J. M., & Moreland, R. L. (1987). Social comparison and outcome evaluation in group contexts. In J. C. Masters & W. P. Smith (Eds.), *Social comparison, social justice, and relative deprivation: Theoretical, empirical, and policy perspectives* (pp. 105–127). Hillsdale, NJ: Erlbaum.

Levine, J. M., & Moreland, R. L. (1990). Progress in small group research. *Annual Review of Psychology, 41,* 585–634.

Levine, J. M., & Moreland, R. L. (1991). Culture and socialization in work groups. In L. B. Resnick, J. M. Levine, & S. D. Teasley (Eds.), *Perspectives on socially shared cognition* (pp. 257–279). Washington, DC: American Psychological Association.

Levine, J. M., & Russo, E. M. (1987). Majority and minority influence. In C. Hendrick (Ed.), *Review of personality and social psychology.* (Vol. 8, pp. 13–54). Newbury Park, CA: Sage.

Liebrand, W. B. G. (1986). The ubiquity of social values in social dilemmas. In H. A. M. Wilke, D. M. Messick, & C. G. Rutte (Eds.), *Experimental social dilemmas* (pp. 113–133). Frankfurt am Main: Verlag Peter Lang.

Lofland, J., & Jamison, M. (1984). Social movement locals: Modal member structures. *Sociological Analysis, 45,* 115–129.

Longley, J., & Pruitt, D. G. (1980). Groupthink: A critique of Janis' theory. In L. Wheeler (Ed.), *Review of personality and social psychology* (pp. 74–93). Beverly Hills, CA: Sage.

Lord, R. G. (1985). An information processing approach to social perceptions, leadership and behavioral measurement in organizations. In L. L. Cummings & B. M. Staw (Eds.), *Research in organizational behavior* (Vol. 7, pp. 87–128). Greenwich, CT: JAI Press.

Lord, R. G., & Saenz, D. S. (1985). Memory deficits and memory surfeits: Differential cognitive consequences of tokenism for tokens and observers. *Journal of Personality and Social Psychology, 49,* 918–926.

Louis, M. R. (1980). Surprise and sense making: What newcomers experience in entering unfamiliar organizational settings. *Administrative Science Quarterly, 25,* 226–251.

Maass, A., West, S. G., & Cialdini, R. B. (1987). Minority influence and conversion. In C.

Hendrick (Ed.), *Review of personality and social psychology,* (Vol. 8, pp. 55–79). Newbury Park, CA: Sage.

MACKIE, D. M. (1986). Social identification effects in group polarization. *Journal of Personality and Social Psychology, 50,* 720–728.

MACKIE, D. M., & GOETHALS, G. R. (1987). Individual and groups goals. In C. Hendrick (Ed.), *Review of personality and social psychology* (pp. 144–166). Newbury Park, CA: Sage.

MAGARO, P. A., & ASHBROOK, R. M. (1985). The personality of societal groups. *Journal of Personality and Social Psychology, 48,* 1479–1489.

MANN, R. D. (1959). A review of the relationships between personality and performance in small groups. *Psychological Bulletin, 56,* 241–270.

MARKS, M. L., & MIRVIS, P. H. (October, 1986). The merger syndrome. *Psychology Today,* pp. 36–42.

MARKS, M. L., MIRVIS, P. H., HACKETT, E. J., & GRADY, J. F. (1986). Employee participation in a Quality Circle program: Impact on quality of work life, productivity, and absenteeism. *Journal of Applied Psychology, 71,* 61–69.

MARTIN, P. Y. (1985). Group sex composition in work organizations: A structural-normative model. In S. B. Bacharach & S. M. Mitchell (Eds.), *Research in the sociology of organizations* (Vol. 4, pp. 311–349). Greenwich, CT: JAI Press.

MAZUR, A. (1985). A biosocial model of status in face-to-face groups. *Social Forces, 64,* 377–402.

McCAULEY, C. (1989). The nature of social influence in groupthink: Compliance and internalization. *Journal of Personality and Social Psychology, 57,* 250–260.

McGrath, J. E. (1984). *Groups: Interaction and performance.* Englewood Cliffs, NJ: Prentice-Hall.

McGUIRE, T. W., KIESLER, S., & SIEGEL, J. (1987). Group and computer-mediated discussion effects in risk decision making. *Journal of Personality and Social Psychology, 52,* 917–930.

McGUIRE, W. J., & PADAWER-SINGER, A. (1976). Trait salience in the spontaneous self-concept. *Journal of Personality and Social Psychology, 33,* 743–754.

McPHERSON, J. M. (1983). The size of voluntary associations. *Social Forces, 61,* 1044–1064.

McPHERSON, J. M. (1990). Evolution in communities of voluntary associations. In J. Singh (Ed.), *Organizational evolution* (pp. 224–245). New York: Sage.

McPHERSON, J. M., & SMITH-LOVIN, L. (1987). Homophily in voluntary organizations: Status distance and the composition of face-to-face groups. *American Sociological Review, 52,* 370–379.

MESSÉ, L. A., KERR, N. L., & SATTLER, D. N. (1992). "But some animals are more equal than others": The supervisor as a privileged status in group contexts. In S. Worchel, W. Wood, & J. A. Simpson (Eds.), *Group process and productivity* (pp. 203–223). Newbury Park, CA: Sage.

MESSICK, D. M., & BREWER, M. B. (1983). Solving social dilemmas: A review. In L. Wheeler & P. Shaver (Eds.), *Review of personality and social psychology* (Vol. 4, pp. 11–44). Beverly Hills, CA: Sage.

MESSICK, D. M., & MACKIE, D. M. (1989). Intergroup relations. *Annual Review of Psychology, 40,* 45–81.

MILLER, C. E., & KOMORITA, S. S. (1986). Coalition formation in organizations: What laboratory studies do and do not tell us. In R. J. Lewicki, B. H. Sheppard, & M. H. Bazerman, (Eds.), *Research on negotiation in organizations* (Vol. 1, pp. 117–137). Greenwich, CT: JAI Press.

Mintzberg, H., Raisinghani, D., & Theoret, A. (1976). The structure of "unstructured" decision processes. *Administrative Science Quarterly, 21*, 246–275.

Moore, J., Vigil, D., & Garcia, R. (1983). Residence and territoriality in Chicano groups. *Social Problems, 31*, 182–194.

Moreland, R. L. (1987). The formation of small groups. In C. Hendrick (Ed.), *Review of personality and social psychology* (Vol. 8, pp. 80–109). Newbury Park, CA: Sage.

Moreland, R. L., & Levine, J. M. (1982). Socialization in small groups: Temporal changes in individual-group relations. In L. Berkowitz (Ed.), *Advances in experimental social psychology* (Vol. 15, pp. 137–192). New York: Academic Press.

Moreland, R. L., & Levine, J. M. (1984). Role transitions in small groups. In V. L. Allen & E. van de Vliert (Eds.), *Role transitions: Explorations and explanations* (pp. 181–195). New York: Plenum.

Moreland, R. L., & Levine, J. M. (1988). Group dynamics over time: Development and socialization in small groups. In J. E. McGrath (Ed.), *The social psychology of time: New perspectives* (pp. 151–181). Newbury Park, CA: Sage.

Moreland, R. L., & Levine, J. M. (1989). Newcomers and oldtimers in small groups. In P. B. Paulus (Ed.), *Psychology of group influence* (2nd ed., pp. 143–186). Hillsdale, NJ: Erlbaum.

Moreland, R. L., & Levine, J. M. (1992). The composition of small groups. In E. J. Lawler, B. Markovsky, C. Ridgeway, & H. A. Walker (Eds.), *Advances in group processes* (Vol. 9, pp. 237–280). Greenwich, CT: JAI Press.

Morris, W. N., Miller, R. S., & Sprangenberg, S. (1977). The effects of dissenter position and task difficulty on conformity and response conflict. *Journal of Personality, 45*, 251–266.

Moscovici, S. (1976). *Social influence and social change.* New York: Academic Press.

Moscovici, S. (1980). Toward a theory of conversion behavior. In L. Berkowitz (Ed.), *Advances in experimental social psychology* (Vol. 13, pp. 209–239). New York: Academic Press.

Moscovici, S. (1985). Social influence and conformity. In G. Lindzey & E. Aronson (Eds.), *The handbook of social psychology* (Vol. 2, pp. 347–412). New York: Random House.

Moscovici, S., & Zavalloni, M. (1969). The group as a polarizer of attitudes. *Journal of Personality and Social Psychology, 12*, 124–135.

Mugny, G., & Perez, J. A. (1991). *The social psychology of minority influence.* Cambridge: Cambridge University Press.

Mullen, B. (1991). Group composition, salience, and cognitive representations: The phenomenology of being in a group. *Journal of Experimental Social Psychology, 27*, 297–323.

Mullen, B., Johnson, C., & Salas, E. (1991). Productivity loss in brainstorming groups: A meta-analytic integration. *Basic and Applied Social Psychology, 12*, 3–23.

Murnighan, J. K. (1978). Models of coalition behavior: Game theoretic, social psychological, and political perspectives. *Psychological Bulletin, 85*, 1130–1153.

Murnighan, J. K., & Vollrath, D. A. (1984). Hierarchies, coalitions and organizations. In S. B. Bacharach & E. J. Lawler (Eds.), *Research in the sociology of organizations* (Vol. 3, pp. 157–187). Greenwich, CT: JAI Press.

Myers, D. G. (1978). Polarizing effects of social comparison. *Journal of Experimental Social Psychology, 14*, 554–563.

Myers, D. G., & Bishop, G. D. (1970). Discussion effects on racial attitudes. *Science, 169*, 778–779.

Myers, D. G., & Lamm, H. (1976). The group polarization phenomenon. *Psychological Bulletin, 63*, 602–627.

NEMETH, C. J. (1986). Differential contributions of majority and minority influence. *Psychological Review, 93,* 23–32.

NEMETH, C. J., & KWAN, J. L. (1987). Minority influence, divergent thinking and detection of correct solutions. *Journal of Applied Social Psychology, 17,* 788–799.

NEMETH, C. J., & STAW, B. M. (1989). The tradeoffs of social control and innovation in groups and organizations. In L. Berkowitz (Ed.), *Advances in experimental social psychology* (Vol. 22, pp. 175–210). San Diego, CA: Academic Press.

NYQUIST, L. V., & SPENCE, J. T. (1986). Effects of dispositional dominance and sex role expectations on leadership behaviors. *Journal of Personality and Social Psychology, 50,* 87–93.

O'BRIEN, G. E., & OWENS, A. G. (1969). Effects of organizational structure on correlations between members' abilities and group productivity. *Journal of Applied Psychology, 53,* 525–530.

OLDHAM, G., & ROTCHFORD, N. L. (1983). Relationships between office characteristics and employee reactions: A study of the physical environment. *Administrative Science Quarterly, 28,* 542–556.

OLSON, M. (1965). *The logic of collective action.* Cambridge, MA: Harvard University Press.

OPP, K. D. (1982). The evolutionary emergence of norms. *British Journal of Social Psychology, 21,* 139–149.

ORBELL, J. M., & DAWES, R. (1981). Social dilemmas. In G. M. Stephenson & J. H. Davis (Eds.), *Progress in applied social psychology* (Vol. 1, pp. 37–65). Chichester: Wiley.

ORBELL, J. M., VAN DE KRAGT, A. J. C., & DAWES, R. M. (1988). Explaining discussion-induced cooperation. *Journal of Personality and Social Psychology, 54,* 811–819.

PAULUS, P. B., DZINDOLET, M. T., POLETES, G., & CAMACHO, L. M. (1993). Perception of performance in group brainstorming: The illusion of group productivity. *Personality and Social Psychology Bulletin, 19,* 78–89.

PEARCE, J. A., II., & RAVLIN, E. C. (1987). The design and activation of self-regulating work groups. *Human Relations, 40,* 751–782.

PETERS, L. H., HARTKE, D. D., & POHLMANN, J. T. (1985). Fiedler's contingency theory of leadership: An application of the meta-analysis procedures of Schmidt and Hunger. *Psychological Bulletin, 97,* 274–285.

PRUITT, D. G., & RUBIN, J. Z. (1986). *Social conflict: Escalation, stalemate, and settlement.* New York: Random House.

REITZES, D. C., & DIVER, J. K. (1982). Gay bars as deviant community organizations: The management of interactions with outsiders. *Deviant Behavior, 4,* 1–18.

RICE, R. W., & KASTENBAUM, D. R. (1983). The contingency model of leadership: Some current issues. *Basic and Applied Social Psychology, 4,* 373–392.

RIDGEWAY, C. L. (1981). Nonconformity, competence, and influence in groups: A test of two theories. *American Sociological Review, 46,* 333–347.

RIDGEWAY, C. L. (1982). Status in groups: The importance of motivation. *American Sociological Review, 47,* 76–88.

RIDGEWAY, C. L. (1984). Dominance, performance, and status in groups. In E. J. Lawler (Ed.), *Advances in group processes* (Vol. 1, pp. 59–93). Greenwich, CT: JAI Press.

RIDGEWAY, C. L. (1987). Nonverbal behavior, dominance, and the basis of status in task groups. *American Sociological Review, 52,* 683–694.

ROGERS, C. R. (1980). *A way of being.* Boston: Houghton Mifflin.

ROSENBERG, L. A. (1961). Group size, prior experience, and conformity. *Journal of Abnormal and Social Psychology, 63,* 436–437.

ROSENBERG, M. (1981). The self-concept: Social product and social force. In M. Rosenberg

& R. H. Turner (Eds.), *Social psychology: Sociological perspectives* (pp. 593–624). New York: Basic Books.

Rosenberg, S., Erlick, D. E., & Berkowitz, L. (1955). Some effects of varying combinations of group members on group performance measures and leadership behaviors. *Journal of Abnormal and Social Psychology, 51,* 195–203.

Ross, L. D., Amabile, T. M., & Steinmetz, J. L. (1977). Social roles, social control, and biases in social-perception processes. *Journal of Personality and Social Psychology, 35,* 485–494.

Rush, M. C., & Russell, J. E. A. (1988). Leader prototypes and prototype-contingent consensus in leader behavior descriptions. *Journal of Experimental Social Psychology, 24,* 88–104.

Saenz, D. S., & Lord, C. G. (1989). Reversing roles: A cognitive strategy for undoing memory deficits associated with token status. *Journal of Personality and Social Psychology, 56,* 698–708.

Salancik, G., & Pfeffer, J. (1978). A social information processing approach to job attitudes and task design. *Administrative Science Quarterly, 23,* 224–253.

Samuelson, C. D., & Messick, D. M. (1986). Inequities in access to and use of shared resources in social dilemmas. *Journal of Personality and Social Psychology, 51,* 960–967.

Samuelson, C. D., Messick, D. M., Wilke, H. A. M., & Rutte, C. G. (1986). Individual restraint and structural change as solutions to social dilemmas. In H. A. M. Wilke, D. M. Messick, & C. G. Rutte (Eds.), *Experimental social dilemmas* (pp. 29–53). Frankfurt am Main: Verlag Peter Lang.

Sattler, D. N., & Kerr, N. L. (1991). Might versus morality explored: Motivational and cognitive bases for social motives. *Journal of Personality and Social Psychology, 60,* 756–765.

Schachter, S. (1951). Deviation, rejection, and communication. *Journal of Abnormal and Social Psychology, 46,* 190–207.

Schachter, S., Ellertson, N., McBride, D., & Gregory, D. (1951). An experimental study of cohesiveness and productivity. *Human Relations, 4,* 229–238.

Seashore, S. E. (1954). *Group cohesiveness in the industrial work group.* Ann Arbor, MI: Institute for Social Research.

Seeger, J. A. (1983). No innate phases in group problem solving. *Academy of Management Review, 8,* 683–689.

Shapley, L., & Grofman, B. (1984). Optimizing group judgmental accuracy in the presence of interdependencies. *Public Choice, 43,* 329–343.

Shaver, P., & Buhrmester, D. (1983). Loneliness, sex-role orientation, and group life: A social needs perspective. In P. B. Paulus (Ed.), *Basic group processes* (pp. 259–288). New York: Springer-Verlag.

Shaw, M. E. (1981). *Group dynamics: The psychology of small group behavior* (3rd ed.). New York: McGraw-Hill.

Siegel, J. Dubrovsky, V., Kiesler, S., & McGuire, T. (1986). Group processes in computer-mediated communication. *Organizational Behavior, 37,* 157–187.

Simmel, G. (1950). *The sociology of Georg Simmel.* Glencoe, IL: Free Press.

Skvoretz, J. (1988). Models of participation in status-differentiated groups. *Social Psychology Quarterly, 51,* 43–57.

Sorrentino, R. M., & Field, N. (1986). Emergent leadership over time: The functional value of positive motivation. *Journal of Personality and Social Psychology, 50,* 1091–1099.

South, S. J., Bonjean, C. M., Markham, W. T., & Corder, J. (1982). Social structure and intergroup interaction: Men and women of the federal bureaucracy. *American Sociological Review, 47,* 587–599.

STANG, D. J. (1976). Group size effects on conformity. *Journal of Social Psychology, 98,* 175–181.

STARK, R., & BAINBRIDGE, W. S. (1980). Networks of faith: Interpersonal bonds and recruitment to cults and sects. *American Journal of Sociology, 85,* 1376–1395.

STASSER, G. (1992). Pooling of unshared information during group discussions. In S. Worchel, W. Wood, & J. A. Simpson (Eds.), *Group process and productivity* (pp. 48–67). Newbury Park, CA: Sage.

STASSER, G., & DAVIS, J. H. (1981). Group decision making and social influence: A social interaction sequence model. *Psychological Review, 88,* 523–551.

STASSER, G., KERR, N. L., & DAVIS, J. H. (1989). Influence processes and consensus models in decision-making groups. In P. B. Paulus (Ed.), *Psychology of group influence* (2nd ed., pp. 279–326). Hillsdale, NJ: Erlbaum.

STASSER, G., TAYLOR, L. A., & HANNA, C. (1989). Information sampling in structured and unstructured discussions of three- and six-person groups. *Journal of Personality and Social Psychology, 57,* 67–78.

STEINER, I. D. (1972). *Group process and productivity.* New York: Academic Press.

STEPHAN, W. G. (1985). Intergroup relations. In G. Lindzey & E. Aronson (Eds.), *Handbook of social psychology* (Vol. 2, pp. 599–658). New York: Random House.

STOGDILL, R. M. (1948). Personal factors associated with leadership: A survey of the literature. *Journal of Psychology, 25,* 35–71.

STONER, J. A. F. (1961). *A comparison of individual and group decisions involving risk.* Unpublished master's thesis, Massachusetts Institute of Technology, Cambridge.

STRODTBECK, F. L., & LIPINSKI, R. M. (1985). Becoming first among equals: Moral considerations in jury foreman selection. *Journal of Personality and Social Psychology, 49,* 927–936.

STROEBE, W., & FREY, B. S. (1982). Self-interest and collective action: The economics and psychology of public goods. *British Journal of Social Psychology, 21,* 121–137.

STRUBE, M. J., & GARCIA, J. E. (1981). A meta-analytic investigation of Fiedler's contingency model of leadership effectiveness. *Psychological Bulletin, 90,* 307–321.

STRYKER, S., & STATHAM, A. (1985). Symbolic interaction and role theory. In G. Lindzey & E. Aronson (Eds.), *Handbook of social psychology* (Vol. 1, pp. 311–378). New York: Random House.

SUCHNER, R. W., & JACKSON, D. (1976). Responsibility and status: A causal or only a spurious relationship? *Sociometry, 39,* 243–256.

SUNDSTROM, E. (1986). *Workplaces: The psychology of the physical environment in offices and factories.* Cambridge: Cambridge University Press.

TAPS, J., & MARTIN, P. Y. (1990). Gender composition, attributional accounts, and women's influence and likability in task groups. *Small Group Research, 21,* 471–491.

TAYLOR, S. E., FISKE, S. T., ETCOFF, N. L., & RUDERMAN, A. J. (1978). Categorical and contextual bases of person memory and stereotyping. *Journal of Personality and Social Psychology, 36,* 778–793.

TETLOCK, P. E., PETERSON, R. S., MCGUIRE, C., CHANG, S., & FELD, P. (1992). Assessing political group dynamics: A test of the groupthink model. *Journal of Personality and Social Psychology, 63,* 403–425.

THIBAUT, J. W., & KELLEY, H. H. (1959). *The social psychology of groups.* New York: Wiley.

TICHY, N. M. (1981). Networks in organizations. In P. C. Nystrom & W. H. Starbuck (Eds.), *Handbook of organizational design* (Vol. 2, pp. 225–249). New York: Oxford University Press.

TUCKMAN, B. W. (1964). Personality structure, group composition, and group functioning. *Sociometry, 27,* 469–487.

TUCKMAN, B. W. (1965). Developmental sequence in small groups. *Psychological Bulletin, 63,* 384–399.

TUCKMAN, B. W., & JENSEN, M. A. C. (1977). Stages of small-group development revisited. *Group and Organization Studies, 2,* 419–427.

TURNER, J. C. (1987). *Rediscovering the social group: A self-categorization theory.* Oxford: Basil Blackwell.

TURNER, J. C. (1991). *Social influence.* Pacific Grove, CA: Brooks/Cole Publishing Company.

TZINER, A., & EDEN, D. (1985). Effects of crew composition on crew performance: Does the whole equal the sum of its parts? *Journal of Applied Psychology, 70,* 85–93.

VAN MAANEN, J., & SCHEIN, E. H. (1979). Toward a theory of organizational socialization. In B. M. Staw (Ed.), *Research in organizational behavior: An annual series of analytical essays and critical reviews* (Vol. 1, pp. 209–264). Greenwich, CT: JAI Press.

VAUGHT, C., & SMITH, D. L. (1980). Incorporation and mechanical solidarity in an underground coal mine. *Sociology of Work and Occupations, 7,* 159–187.

VECCHIO, R. P., & GOBDEL, B. C. (1984). The vertical dyad linkage model of leadership: Problems and prospects. *Organizational Behavior, 34,* 5–20.

VROOM, V. H., & YETTON, P. W. (1973). *Leadership and decision-making.* Pittsburgh, PA: University of Pittsburgh Press.

WEISFELD, G. E., & WEISFELD, C. C. (1984). An observational study of social evaluation: An application of the dominance hierarchy model. *Journal of Genetic Psychology, 145,* 89–99.

WELDON, E., & GARGANO, G. M. (1988). Cognitive loafing: The effects of accountability and shared responsibility on cognitive effort. *Personality and Social Psychology Bulletin, 14,* 159–171.

WHARTON, A. S., & BARON, J. N. (1987). So happy together? The impact of gender segregation on men at work. *American Sociological Review, 52,* 574–587.

WIGGINS, J. A., DILL, F., & SCHWARTZ, R. D. (1965). On "status liability." *Sociometry, 28,* 197–209.

WILDER, D. A. (1977). Perception of groups, size of opposition, and social influence. *Journal of Experimental Social Psychology, 13,* 253–268.

WILDER, D. A. (1978). Homogeneity of jurors: The majority's influence depends upon their perceived independence. *Law and Human Behavior, 2,* 363–376.

WILKE, H. A. M. (Ed.). (1985). *Coalition formation.* Amsterdam: Elsevier.

WILKE, H. A. M., MESSICK, D. M., & RUTTE, C. G. (Eds.). (1986). *Experimental social dilemmas.* Frankfurt am Main: Verlag Peter Lang.

WILLIAMS, K., KARAU, S., & BOURGEOIS, M. (1993). Working on collective tasks: Social loafing and social compensation. In M. A. Hogg & D. Abrams (Eds.), *Group motivation: Social psychological perspectives* (pp. 130–148). New York: Harvester Wheatsheaf.

YALOM, I. D. (1970). *The theory and practice of group psychotherapy.* New York: Basic Books.

YAMAGISHI, T. (1988). The provision of a sanctioning system in the United States and Japan. *Social Psychology Quarterly, 51,* 265–271.

YODER, J. D. (1991). Rethinking tokenism: Looking beyond numbers. *Gender and society, 5,* 178–192.

YODER, J. D., ADAMS, J., & PRINCE, H. T. (1983). The price of a token. *Journal of Political and Military Sociology, 11,* 325–337.

ZACCARO, S. J. (1984). Social loafing: The role of task attractiveness. *Personality and Social Psychology Bulletin, 10,* 99–106.

Further Readings

FORSYTH, D. R. (1990). *Group dynamics* (2nd ed.). Pacific Grove, CA: Brooks/Cole Publishing Company.
This textbook provides a comprehensive and very readable overview of research on group dynamics.

HENDRICK, C. (Ed.). (1987). *Review of personality and social psychology* (Vols. 8 and 9). Newbury Park, CA: Sage.
These two volumes review current research and theory on a range of topics, including majority and minority influence, group formation, group performance, and intergroup relations.

HOGG, M. A., & ABRAMS, D. (1993). *Group motivation: Social psychological perspectives.* New York: Harvester Wheatsheaf.
This volume includes chapters on several facets of motivation in group contexts, including the role of distinctiveness in social identity and group behavior, the impact of group membership on self-esteem, the role of commitment in group socialization, and social loafing and social compensation.

LEVINE, J. M., & MORELAND, R. L. (1990). Progress in small group research. *Annual Review of Psychology, 41,* 585–634.
This chapter summarizes research on small groups published between 1980 and 1990.

MCGRATH, J. E. (1984). *Groups: Interaction and performance.* Englewood Cliffs, NJ: Prentice-Hall.
This scholarly book provides a useful framework for understanding and integrating work on small group processes.

PAULUS, P. B. (Ed.). (1983). *Basic group processes.* New York: Springer-Verlag.
This volume contains chapters on several aspects of group dynamics, including leadership, minority influence, coalition formation, and bargaining.

PAULUS, P. B. (Ed.). (1989). *Psychology of group influence.* (2nd ed.). Hillsdale, NJ: Erlbaum.
This book summarizes theory and research on social influence in group contexts. Representative chapters deal with social facilitation, deindividuation and self-regulation, newcomers and old-timers, and group decision making.

WORCHEL, S., WOOD, W., & SIMPSON, J. A. (1992). *Group process and productivity.* Newbury Park, CA: Sage.
This volume focuses on group productivity, with chapters on such topics as problem identification by groups, pooling of unshared information during group discussion, minority dissent as a stimulant to group performance, and team composition in organizational settings.

*Patricia G. Devine (Ph.D., Ohio State University) is currently Vilas Associate Professor of Psychology at the University of Wisconsin–Madison. Her primary research area focuses on the nature of prejudice and intergroup tension. She has also done research on eyewitness identification, impression formation, social hypothesis testing, and dissonance theory. Devine edited a book with David Hamilton and Thomas Ostrom (*Social Cognition: Impact on Social Psychology*) and is currently working on a book with James Jones on prejudice and intergroup relations. Although too often found in her office, she enjoys a variety of outdoor winter and summer activities and loves music.*

CHAPTER 12

Prejudice and Out-Group Perception

Patricia G. Devine
University of Wisconsin–Madison

CHAPTER OUTLINE

INTRODUCTION
CONSEQUENCES OF CATEGORIZATION FOR OUT-GROUP
PERCEPTION
PREJUDICE
CONCLUSIONS AND NEW CHALLENGES

INTRODUCTION

Without knowledge of the roots of hostility we cannot hope to employ our intelligence effectively in controlling its destructiveness.
—ALLPORT (1954, P. XVII)

*Preparation of this chapter was supported by a Vilas Associate Award, Vilas Trustees, University of Wisconsin–Madison. I would like to thank Terri Conley whose assistance was invaluable throughout the preparation of the chapter. I also would like to thank Sophie Evett, David Myers, Abraham Tesser, Julie Zuwerink, and several anonymous reviewers for comments on a draft of this chapter.

467

No one is immune to or unaffected by prejudice. All of us have experienced it at one level or another—as victim, as oppressor, or as observer. At times its effects are so heinous that they defy comprehension (e.g., the holocaust, lynchings, recent efforts at "racial cleansing" in Bosnia), and at other times its effects are so commonplace as to go almost unnoticed (e.g., stereotypic portrayals of minorities and women in the media). As a phenomenon with wide-ranging effects, it draws our attention and begs for explanation. What are the origins of prejudice and intergroup hostilities? What are the effects of prejudice for its victims and perpetrators? Can prejudice be reduced and intergroup harmony be promoted? How?

In the preface to his classic volume *The Nature of Prejudice,* Allport (1954) warned us that the story of intergroup prejudice would not easily be told. This was hardly an understatement. Allport noted that "it required years of labor and billions of dollars to uncover the secret of the atom. It will take still a greater investment to gain the secrets of man's irrational nature. It is easier, someone has said, to smash an atom than a prejudice" (p. xvii). Despite the daunting nature of the challenge to understand the secret of prejudice and the difficulty in reducing it, social psychologists have made great strides in identifying at least some of the important pieces in the puzzle of intergroup prejudice. Tajfel (1982) observed, however, that despite a substantial accumulation of research and some important theoretical advances, the study of prejudice, discrimination, and intergroup relations still presents "one of the most difficult and complex knots of problems which we confront in our times" (p. 1). In this chapter we will piece together some of the puzzle in hopes of improving our understanding of the nature and consequences of intergroup prejudice.

The first part of the chapter examines the implications of the categorization of others into groups for intergroup bias or conflict. Indeed, any form of intergroup bias takes as its starting point the perception of differences between groups. We begin by considering relatively meaningless groups and then examine the consequences of categorization when the groups are real and meaningful. By examining in detail the consequences of categorization for out-group perception, we will try to glean insights about how to reduce intergroup conflict and improve intergroup relations. In the second part of the chapter, our goal is to define prejudice, examine various theories about the origins of prejudice, both classic and contemporary, and discuss strategies for prejudice reduction. Finally, we consider possible new directions for research on intergroup conflict and tension.

CONSEQUENCES OF CATEGORIZATION FOR OUT-GROUP PERCEPTION

The human mind must think with aid of categories. Once formed, categories are the basis for normal prejudgment. We cannot possibly avoid the process. Orderly living depends on it (Allport, 1954, p. 20).

Like heuristics, where do you draw the line b/w "adaptive functioning + stereotyping with a negative connotation

Long ago, Gordon Allport (1954) suggested that the *categorization* of people into groups was necessary for adaptive functioning. That is, just as it is necessary to categorize objects according to function or similarity in appearance in order to reduce the complexity of the physical world, it is also necessary to use social categorization strategies in order to reduce the complexity of the social world. Responding to all persons as individuals would quickly overload social perceivers' cognitive processing and storage capacities (Hamilton, 1981; Hamilton & Trolier, 1986; see Fiske, Chapter 5). Categorizing others into groups by identifying some common attributes or characteristics serves to reduce the amount of information to be dealt with and thereby reduces the complexity of the social world.

Although such categorization may be adaptive and facilitate information processing, it is important to recognize that other consequences also follow from this simplification strategy, consequences that may be involved in creating and maintaining (perceived) differences between members of different groups. Hamilton and Trolier (1986) point out that, in part, categorization of persons into groups involves recognizing real similarities and differences between groups and their members. After all, there are ways in which men and women or blacks and whites differ, and when categorization reflects those real similarities and differences, it represents a sensible and useful strategy for reducing the complexity of the social world. However, categorization also leads to consequences that often do not appear to be based on real similarities and differences, consequences that some have suggested create the basis for *ethnocentrism,* which is belief that one's own group is superior to other groups. For example, the mere categorization of people into *in-groups* (i.e., the group to which the individual belongs) and *out-groups* (i.e., any group other than the in-group) leads social perceivers to differentiate between members of the in-group and members of the out-group in ways that most often favor the in-group.

The Minimal Group and Intergroup bias

A large body of social psychological literature suggests that even when categorization into groups is arbitrary and unrelated to psychologically meaningful characteristics, minimal conditions necessary for intergroup bias favoring the in-group are established (Brewer, 1979; Messick & Mackie, 1989). That is, the *mere* categorization of people into groups is sufficient to increase attraction to in-group members and may at times lead to a devaluation of out-group members (Brewer, 1979; Rosenbaum & Holtz, 1985).

Pioneered by Henri Tajfel, the *minimal group paradigm* has provided social psychologists with a useful tool for examining the effects of such mere categorization into in-group and out-group. In a typical minimal group study, subjects are led to believe that they are assigned to groups on a rather arbitrary basis (i.e., performance on an initial task such as estimating the number of dots on a series of slides or their preference for one artist over another). Thus, groups are created, but they are not groups in any meaningful sense. In reality, the assignment of subjects to in-groups and out-groups in these studies is random.

The significance of classifying individuals into functionally meaningless groups is demonstrated by effects on a broad array of dependent variables. In the minimal group paradigm, in-group members typically allocate greater rewards to in-group than out-group members (e.g., Tajfel, Flament, Billig, & Bundy, 1971), evaluate in-group members more favorably (e.g., Ferguson & Kelley, 1964; Rabbie, 1982; Rabbie & Horowitz, 1969), and associate more desirable personal and physical attributes to in-group than out-group members (e.g., Doise, Csepeli, Dann, Gouge, Larsen, & Ostell, 1972). In-group members have also been observed to behave in more prosocial ways toward in-group than toward out-group members (Hornstein, 1976; Piliavin, Dovidio, Gaertner, & Clark, 1981) and to be more cooperative (e.g., to exercise more restraint in the use of limited common resources) when interacting with in-group members than with out-group members (Kramer & Brewer, 1984). In addition, assignment to such minimal groups also leads in-group members to overestimate the similarities within groups and the dissimilarities between groups (e.g., Allen & Wilder, 1979; Brown & Abrams, 1986; Doise, 1978; Hogg & Abrams, 1988; McGarty & Penny, 1988; Stein, Hardyck, & Smith, 1965; Tajfel, Flament, Billig, & Bundy, 1971; Tajfel & Wilkes, 1963; Wilder, 1978).

These biases are striking because in the typical minimal group situation, there is neither conflict of interest nor previously existing hostility between the groups. Furthermore, no social interaction takes place, and there is no rational link between economic self-interest and the strategy of in-group favoritism, a link that is often assumed to be at the heart of intergroup tension in real group situations. Even when the assignment to groups is obviously arbitrary (e.g., assignment by flip of a coin) and clearly socially meaningless (e.g., the blue group), biases that favor in-group members are obtained (Allen & Wilder, 1975; Billig & Tajfel, 1973; Locksley, Ortiz, & Hepburn, 1980; Rabbie, 1982).

These perceived similarities and differences generalize beyond the presumed basis for assignment to groups. For example, Allen & Wilder (1979) found that subjects assumed that an in-group member would express beliefs similar to their own on issues unrelated to the dimension that was the presumed basis for assignment to groups (e.g., art preferences). It is important to note that such biases are exaggerated by manipulations that increase the salience of intergroup boundaries. For example, discussing possible conflicts with other groups leads individual in-group members to perceive other in-group members as more similar to the self particularly on dimensions that are central to group membership (Brewer & Miller, 1984; Hogg & Turner, 1987). The importance of the salience of intergroup boundaries is a theme to which we will return in our analysis of strategies designed to reduce intergroup hostilities.

Linguistic Influences on Intergroup Bias

In a recent set of provocative studies, Dovidio, Gaertner, and their colleagues suggest that even the language we use to refer to in-group and out-group status may conspire to create and perpetuate intergroup biases (Dovidio, Tobriner, Rioux, & Gaertner, 1991; Perdue, Dovidio, Gurtman, & Tyler, 1990). For example, in one experiment (Perdue, Dovidio, Gurtman, & Tyler, 1990, experiment 1), in-group and out-group pronouns (e.g., *we* and *they*, respectively) were systematically paired with nonsense syllables (e.g., *xhe*) in the context of a lexical decision task (i.e., deciding if a string of letters is a word). The goal of the experiment was to determine if, through classical conditioning, in-group and out-group designators could establish evaluative responses to novel unfamiliar stimuli (see also Staats & Staats, 1958). Subjects were presented with trials pairing in-group designators with a nonsense syllable, trails pairing out-group designators with a nonsense syllable and control trials in which the nonsense syllable was presented without an associated pronoun. Following the lexical decision task, subjects rated the pleasantness of the nonsense syllables. As displayed in Figure 12.1, Perdue and co-workers found that nonsense syllables paired with in-group pronouns were rated more favorably than either the nonsense syllables paired with out-group pronouns or those not paired with pronouns. (The ratings in the latter two conditions did not differ from one another.)

Another study (Perdue, Dovidio, Gurtman, & Tyler, 1990, experiment 2) revealed that in-group and out-group pronouns influence the relative accessibility of positive and negative constructs. For example, subjects respond more quickly to evaluatively positive words (e.g., sunshine) following in-group pronouns (we) than out-group pronouns (they). Interestingly, in these studies subjects did not report awareness of the effect of the pronouns. These findings led Dovidio and Gaertner (1993) to argue that words designating in-group and out-group status may automatically introduce evaluative intergroup biases, biases once again favoring the in-group.

In a particularly interesting extension of this work, Dovidio, Tobriner,

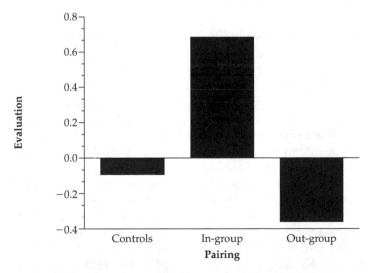

Standardized ratings of target syllables as a function of pronoun pairing. (Higher standardized ratings indicate more positive [pleasant] evaluations: the control evaluations consist of the mean standardized evaluation for the four syllables paired with non-group-designating pronouns.)

FIGURE 12.1. Evaluation of nonsense syllables when paired with in-group labels, out-group labels, or control words.
From Perdue et al. (1990).

Rioux, and Gaertner (1991) demonstrated that expectations for the pleasantness of an impending social interaction are affected by the in-group or out-group pronouns used to describe their prospective interaction partners. Specifically, subjects had more positive expectations when interaction partners were described by in-group than out-group pronouns. Why would this be important? If out-group pronouns lead to negative expectations for intergroup interactions, it is possible that in-group members convey (perhaps unconsciously) these negative feelings to the out-group member. These circumstances could easily lead to a self-fulfilling prophecy: The out-group member recognizes the in-group member's negative expectations and responds accordingly, further impeding intergroup relations.

Several studies further suggest that the mere categorization of people into in-groups and out-groups leads social perceivers to process information about in-group and out-group members in ways that will perpetuate intergroup differentiation and may cause such differences to appear legitimate and justified (Hamilton & Trolier, 1986). For example, Howard and Rothbart (1980), using the minimal group paradigm, presented subjects with a mix of positive and negative information about alleged in-group and out-group members. They found that subjects generated more favorable expectations about in-group than out-group members and that these differential expectancies affected subjects' retention of information about in-group and out-group members. Specifically, subjects manifested better recall for negative out-group behavior than for negative in-group behavior. Wilder (1981) found that subjects showed better memory for the ways in which in-group members are similar to and out-group members are dissimilar to themselves.

Reasons for Intergroup Bias in the Minimal Group Paradigm

Efforts to understand the origin of intergroup biases in the minimal group paradigm have led to a discussion of both cognitive and motivational processes that promote or encourage differentiation of in-group and out-group members. For example, the research on linguistic and memory biases lends support to the notion that general biases in cognitive processing contribute to intergroup biases. Some of these effects are subtle (e.g., the "we" and "'they" studies) and are not likely to be intentional or motivated in any formal sense. However, other findings are not easily explained in terms of purely cognitive processes. These findings suggest that motivational forces are also likely to contribute to positive in-group biases. For example, the categorization of objects always accentuates intercategory differences. However, in the case of social categorization, these differences are accentuated only when they are favorable to the in-group. In fact, these differences tend to be minimized if they are favorable to the out-group (Brewer & Kramer, 1985; Tajfel, 1981; Turner, 1981). A partial explanation for such in-group favoritism is provided by *social identity theory* (Tajfel, 1982; Tajfel & Turner, 1986; Turner, 1987), which suggests that social categorization initiates basic motivational processes in individuals that induce intergroup competition (for reviews, see Brewer & Kramer, 1985; Messick & Mackie, 1989).

A key assumption of social identity theory is that people are motivated to establish and maintain their self-esteem and that their various group memberships have esteem implications. To enhance self-esteem, one can (1) affiliate with social groups that already are considered attractive and successful and/or (2) try to view one's social category memberships as positively as possible. Tajfel and Turner suggest that social identity motivations underlie the preferential treatment and perceptions of in-group relative to out-group members in the minimal group paradigm.

According to Tajfel and Turner, when group boundaries are made salient, people will engage in a motivated search for intercategory differences that are favorable to the group to which they belong or with which they identify. That is, the need for a positive social identity creates a competitive intergroup orientation. This competitive orientation leads to perceptual biases and discriminatory behavioral strategies, which are attempts to differentiate between the in-group and the out-group in a manner favoring the in-group. As a result, differences favorable to the in-group will be exaggerated and emphasized, whereas differences favoring the out-group may be minimized or ignored.

A number of studies have investigated the relationship between self-esteem and intergroup bias in minimal group situations. For example, two studies have shown that if subjects who are categorized into minimal groups (e.g., based on artistic preferences) are given the opportunity to show in-group favoritism in a reward allocation task (i.e., by discriminating against the out-group member), they show increases in self-esteem (Lemyre & Smith, 1985; Oakes & Turner, 1980). Correspondingly, social identity theory would also suggest that a threat to one's self-esteem should heighten one's need for in-group favoritism. The findings with regard to this assumption, however, are decidedly mixed. Although people with low self-esteem appear to be the most negative toward out-groups, they are also negative about the in-group (Wills, 1981). Experimental studies designed to test the assumption that ego threatened people are the most hostile to out groups have also produced mixed results (Crocker, Thompson, McGraw, & Ingerman, 1987; Meindl & Lerner, 1984). Although the research has not uniformly supported social identity theory, the theory provides a provocative integration of cognitive and motivational principles to help explain the origin of intergroup biases. Because of these strengths, social identity theory is likely to continue to stimulate intriguing research in the area of intergroup relations.

Real Groups and Intergroup Bias

Up to this point, we have been discussing minimal groups. But what about real groups? Certainly, the relationship between in-groups and out-groups is infinitely more complex for groups that exist outside of the laboratory. Real groups differ from minimal groups in a variety of ways that are likely to make intergroup boundaries and the distinction between "we" and "they" more salient. In the context of real intergroup situations, an individual usually possesses a great deal of knowledge about both the in-group and the out-group and may have enduring and intense feelings of identification with the in-group.

Furthermore, in contrast to minimal groups, real groups may have a history of highly emotional interactions and, in some cases, conflict (e.g., blacks and whites, men and women). In addition, real groups typically have salient cues for social categorization (e.g., race, sex, age). Real groups may also be segregated in space (i.e., live in different sections of town) and may possess different cultural norms that may contribute to the perception of differences between the groups. Add to these issues the learned biases and stereotypes that are acquired through socialization into a particular culture and it becomes clear that intergroup biases are likely to be significantly stronger and more difficult to eradicate in real intergroup situations. There is, in fact, concrete evidence available to support these concerns. In this section, we examine the implications of real group status for in-group and out-group perception and how stereotypes can produce a number of information-processing biases that help to maintain the stereotypes over time.

Out-group Homogeneity

Out-group members are perceived to be more homogeneous in their characteristics, opinions, and behaviors than are in-group members. Whereas people tend to see and appreciate the diversity of the in-group, their attitude toward the out-group can be summed up by the common cliché "They're all alike" (Linville, Salovey, & Fischer, 1986; Quattrone, 1986). This *out-group homogeneity* effect suggests that out-group members are not only seen as being different from the in-group but also seen as being more similar to each other and more interchangeable with each other (Mullen & Hu, 1989). One implication of this process is that people tend to perceive a member of an out-group as just another anonymous group member rather than perceiving him or her as an individual. This bias has been observed in the mutual perceptions of men and women (Park & Rothbart, 1982), political conservatives and liberals (Quattrone & Jones, 1980), blacks and whites (Linville & Jones, 1980), young and elderly people (Brewer & Lui, 1984; Linville, 1982), and members of different clubs on campus (Jones, Wood, & Quattrone, 1981).

What accounts for the perception of less variability on the part of in-group members when thinking about the out-group? A number of possibilities have been suggested. One possibility focuses on the opportunity for *learning* about the diversity of out-group members, whereas a second possibility focuses on *memory* and retrieval processes that may favor the perception of more diversity among in-group than out-group members.

Quattrone (1986), for example, argues that out-groups are perceived to be homogenous because of limited contact with out-group members (i.e., people simply have more opportunities to witness the diversity of in-group members' behavior). For example, people often interact with only a limited sample of all possible out-group members. In addition, the nature of the contact with out-group members may be qualitatively different than the contact with in-group members. For example, groups tend to interact with each other only under limited situations that often constrain the nature of group members' behaviors. For instance, when fans of rival university football teams come together for the purpose of cheering their team on to victory, group members are likely to display a uniform set of behaviors relevant to the specific context. If that is the only set of circumstances in which people have contact with out-group members, it is unlikely that the full diversity of out-group members' characteristics will be appreciated.

Memory processes may also contribute to the out-group homogeneity effect (Judd & Park, 1988; Park & Rothbart, 1982). Judd and Park (1988) suggested that whereas people think about specific representatives of in-groups, they think more abstractly about out-groups. As a result, it may be easier to retrieve memories of specific individuals when thinking about the in-group than the out-group. A failure to retrieve specific examples of out-group members may contribute to the in-group members' perception that out-group members are homogeneous.

[handwritten: (2) I think the opposite. People can have 1 neg encounter w/ outgroup + generalize to all people of that group w/out ?]

Biased Explanations for Positive and Negative Behaviors

The attributions used by in-group members when evaluating out-group members' behaviors may encourage the perception that in-groups are more favorable than out-groups. For example, in-group positive behaviors are more likely to be attributed to internal, stable causes than in-group negative behaviors; the opposite is observed for out-group members' behavior (Taylor & Jaggi, 1974). In addition, social perceivers generate different explanations for in-group and out-group success and failure experiences (Deaux, 1976; Hewstonne, Jaspers, & Lalljee, 1982). Wang and McKillip (1978) found that in making attributions of responsibility for an automobile accident, subjects assigned greater responsibility for the accident to out-group than in-group members and more favorably evaluated in-group members on a series of personality characteristics. Thus, overall, the subjects were more charitable in their attributions for in-group members' negative behavior.

Such asymmetries in in-group members' explanations of positive and negative behaviors of an out-group have been termed the *ultimate attribution error* (Pettigrew, 1979). Pettigrew notes that, for out-group members, the valence of the behavior seems to determine the nature of the attribution (i.e., to dispositional or situational factors). Negative out-group behaviors are readily accepted and attributed to enduring personality characteristics of the out-group members. Such behaviors are congruent with in-group members' expectations, and situational explanations for such behaviors are ignored. In contrast, positive behaviors of out-group members, which are not consistent with in-group members' expectations, are not accepted and are most typically explained away. For example, one strategy for explaining positive out-group behavior is to assume that it reflects luck or unfair advantage. Note that this strategy does not *deny* the positive outcome, but it does not give the out-group member credit for *producing* that outcome. Alternative strategies involve simply viewing the positive outcome as anomalous and nonrepresentative of typical out-group performance or attributing the positive outcome to an extraordinarily high level of motivation and effort implying that out-group members lack the necessary talent or ability to succeed.

Maass, Salvi, Arcuri, and Semin (1989) recently demonstrated that these bi-ases can be understood in terms of the language used to encode positive and negative out-group behaviors. Behaviors (e.g., hit someone with a fist) can be encoded in relatively abstract (e.g., aggressive) or concrete (e.g., punch) terms. Behaviors encoded at an abstract level are relatively resistant to disconfirma-tion and imply stability over time (e.g., personality traits), whereas behaviors encoded at a concrete level are much more amenable to situational explana-tions. Consistent with Pettigrew's analysis, Maass and colleagues found that negative out-group behaviors were typically encoded in abstract terms and positive out-group behaviors were typically encoded in concrete terms. Maass and associates suggest that such attributional asymmetries can create a self-per-petuating cycle in which biased language use maintains or even aggravates ini-tial intergroup biases.

Perhaps the most significant way minimal and real groups differ is that stereotypes are commonly associated with real groups. Social stereotypes often set up preconceptions which influence in-group members' evaluation of out-group members. The role that stereotypes play in intergroup biases is the focus of the next section of the chapter.

Social Categories and Social Stereotypes

Hamilton and Trolier (1986) suggested that social categories involve much more than the mere categorization of people into different groups because we very often come to associate specific characteristics (e.g., personality or behav-ioral characteristics) with these categories. That is, *stereotypes* come to be asso-ciated with meaningful social categories such as men, women, blacks, elderly, Latinos, gays, librarians, waitresses, etc. When asked to do so, people can eas-ily generate the characteristics commonly associated with social groups (e.g., Brewer, Dull, & Lui, 1981; Devine, 1989; Devine & Elliot, in press; Katz & Braly, 1933), and there appears to be a fair amount of consensus about characteristics commonly associated with the major meaningful social categories. The term *stereotype* first acquired its modern meaning in the writings of Walter Lippman (1922). Lippman argued that rather than deal with the complexity of the real world around us, we create cognitive simplifications—stereotypes—to guide how we perceive others and how we process social information.

An ever burgeoning literature, one too large to be completely reviewed here, testifies to the fact that stereotypes shape our memory and evaluation of others (see also Fiske, Chapter 5). Specifically, many theorists believe that stereotypes supply general expectations about social groups and serve to sim-plify the task of perceiving and evaluating individual group members. These simplifications, however, often work to the disadvantage of out-groups and mi-nority groups. In this section of the chapter, we consider some representative findings to illustrate the powerful effect of social stereotypes on how we process, organize, store, and use social information about group members. Many of these findings suggest that we respond to others as members of their group rather than as individuals.

First, consider that the prevailing models of impression formation (e.g.,

Brewer, 1988; Fiske & Neuberg, 1990) posit that social perceivers first respond to others as group members and then as individuals only if there is sufficient motivation to do so. According to these models, salient social categories are so frequently activated in the context of social discourse that they are highly accessible and are, thus, habitually used in social perception. That is, social categories (i.e., group memberships) appear to be spontaneously attended to even in the absence of explicit intentions to attend to them (e.g., Banaji & Greenwald, in press; Devine, 1989; Gilbert & Hixon, 1991). Such implicit or unintended stereotype effects may be particularly difficult to recognize let alone overcome (see Greenwald & Banaji, 1993, for a review).

Second, several studies suggest that new information learned about group members tends to be stored and organized in terms of the group members' salient social categories rather than in terms of the individual stimulus persons encountered (Park & Rothbart, 1982; Taylor, 1981; Taylor & Falcone, 1982; Taylor, Fiske, Etcoff, & Rudderman, 1978). After listening to a taped discussion between several men and women, people's memory for who said what reveals the organization of information around the salient social categories. That is, although people are likely to remember whether a man or woman made a comment (i.e., they are unlikely to make between-group errors), they are much less accurate in their memory for exactly which man or which woman made the comment (i.e., they are likely to make within-group errors). In an important recent development in this literature, Stangor, Lynch, Duan, and Glass (1992) found that attitudes can affect the likelihood of using salient social categories to organize newly learned social information. For example, racially prejudiced subjects were more likely to use race cues (i.e., make more within- than between-race errors) than were nonprejudiced subjects.

Third, stereotypes lead to several information-processing biases (e.g., encoding, interpretation, memory) that are likely to make stereotypes tenacious and resistant to change. For example, stereotypes have been shown to affect what people attend to and remember about members of the stereotyped group. In general, information that fits with stereotypic expectations is better remembered than information that fits less well with those expectations (Bodenhausen & Wyer, 1985; Cohen, 1981; Hamilton & Rose, 1980; Rothbart, Evans, & Fulero, 1979; Snyder & Uranowitz, 1978). It has further been demonstrated that expectancies based on stereotypes may be perceived as being confirmed, even when confirming evidence is absent (Bodenhausen & Wyer, 1985; Rothbart, Evans, & Fulero, 1979).

Stereotypes can affect how information about others is encoded and interpreted such that the exact same behavioral cues are interpreted differently depending on the social category of the person who performed them (Darley & Gross, 1983; Duncan, 1976; Sager & Schofield, 1980). In Darley and Gross (1983), for example, subjects evaluated the academic performance of a fourth grade student. The student's performance was neither uniformly positive nor uniformly negative (i.e., she got some easy items right and some wrong; the same was true for difficult items). All subjects watched the exact same videotaped performance. However, some of the subjects were led to believe that the student was from a high socioeconomic status (SES) family, whereas the other subjects were led to believe that she was from a low SES family. Darley and Gross suggested that people stereotypically associate better academic performance with students from high SES families. This manipulation clearly affected which aspects of the student's performance the subjects attended to and remembered. Subjects who believed the student to be of a low SES selectively attended to and showed better memory for her failure on easy items; the subjects who thought the student was of a high SES attended to and remembered her success on difficult items and appeared to minimize her failure on easy items. That is, the stereotype also seemed to affect subjects' attributions for expectancy incongruent behavior.

Darley and Gross (1983) suggested a two-stage process through which stereotypes can exert their influence on the perception and interpretation of evidence. Specifically, they argued that stereotypes set up hypotheses (i.e., expectancies) that are then tested in a biased fashion. When subjects were provided with the SES information, but were not given any evidence regarding the student's performance (i.e., did not watch the videotape), their judgments of the student were not biased. Subjects in both SES conditions expected that she would perform at her grade level. These data suggest that a stereotype confirming bias only emerges when the opportunity for testing the hypothesis is provided. Thus, the stereotype provides the lens through which ambiguous behaviors are observed. This lens produces distortions which lead to stereotype confirmation.

Finally, research on *self-fulfilling prophecies* suggests that the effect of stereotypes is not limited to our perceptions of others. In fact, there is considerable evidence to suggest that our own behaviors in interpersonal interactions with outgroup members can lead to behavioral confirmation of our stereotypes (e.g., Snyder, Tanke, & Berscheid, 1977; Word, Zanna, & Cooper, 1974). In other words, our expectations about others may influence our strategies for interacting with them, and these strategies may draw out behaviors from the out-group member that will confirm our initial expectancy. For example, if we expect someone to be hostile, we may interact with them in a cold or distant fashion. This person may respond in kind—also behaving in a rather hostile fashion—thus confirming the original expectation. The person need not be dispositionally hostile for this prophecy to be fulfilled (Snyder & Swann, 1978). It is only necessary that others *expect* the person to be hostile.

Implications

The research in both the minimal group and the real group literatures converge to suggest that the perception of group boundaries produces a broad array of intergroup information processing and judgment biases. These biases often lead to negative outcomes for out-group members that are not related to the out-group members' personal or individual characteristics. Moreover, there is a fair amount of agreement in the literature that the factors that increase the salience of intergroup boundaries and heighten the perception of "we" and "they" are likely to facilitate intergroup bias (Brewer, 1979; Gaertner, Mann, Dovidio, Murrell, & Pomare, 1990; Wilder, 1978; Worchel, 1986). For example, biases favoring the in-group over the out-group are especially pronounced when social categories are made particularly salient by factors such as competition, in-group cohesion, and the belief that the out-group is dissimilar to the in-group (Billig & Tajfel, 1973; Doise, 1978; Ferguson & Kelley, 1964; Wilder & Shapiro, 1991). In addition, increasing the accessibility or salience of the out-group facilitates the processing of stereotypic traits (Dovidio, Evans, & Tyler, 1986; Perdue & Gurtman, 1990; Smith & Branscombe, 1986) and of prototypic physical characteristics (Klatsky, Martin, & Kane, 1982).

Considering such evidence, many theorists have speculated that the root of the problem of intergroup bias is that perceivers respond to people outside their group as "group members" rather than as individuals. That is, when dealing with out-group members, perceivers engage in *intergroup responding* rather than *interpersonal responding* (Brewer & Miller, 1984, 1986; Brown & Turner, 1981; Gaertner, Dovidio, Anastasio, Bachman, & Rust, 1993; Worchel, 1986). This appears to be true for both "minimal" and "real" groups. A key implication of this process is that out-group members become depersonalized, undifferentiated, and interchangeable with one another (Linville, Salovey, & Fischer, 1986; Mullen & Hu, 1989; Park & Rothbart, 1982). *what about collectivistic societies?*

Reducing Intergroup Bias

If group boundaries maintain and perpetuate intergroup biases, a reasonable strategy for reducing such biases would be to decrease the salience or importance of group boundaries. The overarching goal is to decrease the reliance on category-based, or "we" versus "they," processing. Several different strategies for disrupting category-based responding, or decategorizing the out-group, have been shown to be effective in reducing intergroup bias. For example, revealing diversity in the opinion of out-group members or encouraging in-group members to respond to out-group members as individuals rather than as a group leads to reductions in intergroup bias (Caspi, 1984; Katz, 1973; Katz & Zalk, 1978; Langer, Bashner, & Chanowitz, 1985; Wilder, 1978, 1981). Several studies have shown that after in-group/out-group identities have been established, if new subgroups are formed that are composed of both former in-group and out-group members, the initial basis for categorization becomes less salient and intergroup bias is correspondingly reduced (Brewer, Ho, Lee, & Miller, 1987; Deschamps & Doise, 1978). *Like on reality shows when they change up the teams — move people around. Have to rethink their group.*

Creating a superordinate identity for in-group and out-group members also has the effect of reducing intergroup biases (Aronson, Blaney, Stephan, Sikes, & Snapp, 1978; Sherif, Harvey, White, Hood, & Sherif, 1954; Turner, 1981; Worchel, 1979, 1986). This has commonly been achieved by placing in-group and out-group members in a situation in which they must cooperate in order to achieve a common, mutually rewarding goal. Brewer and Miller (1984) argue that such *cooperative interdependence* among in-group and out-group members lessens intergroup bias because such conditions encourage more personalized interactions with out-group members. Brewer and Miller suggest that category boundaries suppress interpersonal differentiation and set the stage for intergroup bias (see Figure 12.2). Miller and Brewer's empirical work (e.g., Miller & Brewer, 1986; Miller, Brewer, & Edwards, 1985) supports the contention that interactions that encourage interpersonal orientations do lead to reductions in intergroup bias.

As an alternative to personalized responding as a strategy for reducing intergroup bias, Gaertner and his colleagues have argued that various forms of recategorizing group members are effective in reducing intergroup bias (Gaertner, Mann, Dovidio, Murrell, & Pomare, 1990; Gaertner, Mann, Murrell, & Dovidio, 1989). Gaertner and associates examined the implications of recategorizing out-group members (1) as separate individuals (similar to personalized responding) or (2) as new in-group members (i.e., drawing former out-group members into one's own group).

Gaertner and his colleagues' (1989) empirical strategy was to create two groups in the first phase of their experiment. Each group was clearly identified with name badges signifying group membership, and the members of each group worked closely together on a problem-solving task. During phase 2, three conditions were created. In the "two groups" condition, subjects were induced to retain the original two-group category structure. These subjects kept their phase 1 group name badges and were seated in a segregated fashion (i.e., groups seated at separate tables). In the "one group" condition, subjects were induced to replace the former intergroup boundary with an inclusive superordinate boundary. These subjects jointly selected a new single group name, wore name badges sporting the new group name, and were seated in an integrated fashion (i.e., alternate seating). In the "separate individuals" condition, intergroup boundaries were completely eliminated. In this condition, subjects created personalized nicknames, replaced the former group badge with their new nickname badges, and were seated individually.

Subjects made a number of evaluative judgments about each of the original in-group and out-group members (i.e., they rated how much they liked each participant, each person's honesty and cooperativeness, the value of each person's contributions to the task). These judgments provided the key measure of intergroup bias. Gaertner and associates found that both the one-group and the separate individual strategies produced a reduction in intergroup bias (i.e., smaller difference in the ratings of in-group and out-group members) in comparison to the two-group representation.

The pattern of mean evaluation scores in Table 12.1 suggests that although both *recategorization strategies* reduced intergroup bias, they did so in different ways. It appears that when former out-group members are recategorized into a single inclusive category, they receive the benefits of the positive biases previously extended only to in-group members. That is, ratings of former out-group members become more positive, whereas the ratings of former in-group members do not differ from the ratings in the two-group condition. In contrast, the separate individuals representation, which attacks the integrity of both in-group and out-group boundaries, reduces the in-group/out-group bias

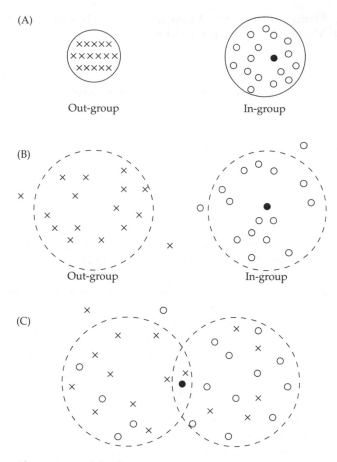

Alternative models of intergroup contact: (A) category-based, (B) differentiated, (C) personalized. (From Brewer & Miller, 1984.)

FIGURE 12.2. Brewer and Miller's (1984) continuum of category-based to personalized responding. Brewer & Miller (1984) describe a continuum of responses to out-group members that range from category-based responding on one end to personalized responding on the other end. Category-based (or intergroup) responding involves unelaborated processing of out-group members as members of "that group." It is efficient and likely to maintain or perpetuate intergroup biases. With differentiated responding, out-group members are no longer seen as interchangeable units, but the basic distinction between in-group and out-group is preserved. That is, despite the fact that out-group members are distinct individuals, the basic perceived similarity of out-group members to oneself and to other in-group members is preserved. Once again, category membership is likely to play a strong role in the perception and evaluation of out-group members. Personalized (or interpersonal) responding involves responding to another person as a unique individual who is complex and possesses diverse characteristics. The hallmark of personalized responding is that one attends to personal information about the individual that is not correlated with category membership. Thus, individual characteristics replace category or group identity as the basis for perception, evaluation, or interaction strategies with the person.

TABLE 12.1. Effects of Cognitive Representation of In-Group and Out-Group Members on Intergroup Bias

	Type of Representation		
	One Group	Two Groups	Separate Individuals
Average evaluation*			
Former in-group	5.71	5.80	5.39
Former out-group	5.54	5.31	5.12
Difference	.17	.49	.27

*Average of ratings of like, honesty, cooperative, and valuable. All ratings were made on seven-point Likert-type scales. Adapted from Gaertner et al. (1989).

through a different route: It causes former in-group members to be evaluated less positively than in the two-group condition and does not affect the ratings of the former out-group members.

Which strategy of reducing intergroup bias is better? Gaertner and his co-workers (1989) clearly favor the strategy of drawing former out-group members into a single, inclusive superordinate category. They argue, for example, that although the separate individuals strategy may lead to changes in the perceived homogeneity of out-group members, this strategy changes the salient self-identity from "we" to "me." Therefore, ratings of former in-group members suffer as a result, and ratings of former out-group members are not improved. In contrast, according to Gaertner and his colleagues, the benefits of recategorizing former out-group members into one's own group are many. First, ratings of former out-group members are improved, while ratings of in-group members do not suffer. Recategorizing out-group members into a single superordinate category draws these former out-group members closer to the self (i.e., "they" become "we"). Second, such recategorization does not assume that initial reductions of intergroup bias require that out-group members first be perceived as individuals rather than as group members (cf. Brewer & Miller, 1984). Indeed, Gaertner and his associates (1989) suggest that this strategy capitalizes on the proclivity of social perceivers to categorize. They argue that such recategorization has the potential to harness some of the cognitive and motivational processes that contribute to the development of intergroup bias and redirect those processes to help establish more positive intergroup relations. They further argue that creating a common group identity sets the stage for later, more personalized individuating interactions. Therefore, the creation of a superordinate group identity may provide the opportunity for the benefits of personalized interactions (i.e., learning about the diversity of group members) to be realized.

Gaertner and his colleagues (1990) argued that recategorization processes may be responsible for the positive effects of cooperative interdependence between in-group and out-group members in reducing intergroup bias (Allport, 1954; Aronson, Blaney, Stephan, Sikes, & Snapp, 1978; Cook, 1985; Sherif, Harvey, White, Hood, & Sherif, 1954; Slavin, 1985; Slavin & Madden, 1979; see also the section on the contact hypothesis later in the chapter). For example, in the now famous "Robbers Cave" experiment, Sherif and associates created hostilities between two groups of summer campers by creating competition between the groups (e.g., athletic competitions) and encouraging the group members to strongly identify with their group (e.g., campers named their groups, had group colors, wore group identifying T-shirts). In efforts to reduce the hostilities, Sherif and colleagues introduced several superordinate goals which could be accomplished only through cooperation between the groups (e.g., the camp truck broke down and needed to be towed up a steep hill). This cooperation experience required that the groups interact with each other, work toward a common goal, and experience a sense of shared fate regarding the outcome of the joint venture. In this experiment, cooperation proved to be quite effective in reducing intergroup hostilities. In their analysis of the positive effects of cooperation in the Robbers Cave experiment, Gaertner and associates (1990) suggest that cooperation may have been efficacious because it reduced the salience of intergroup boundaries and created a superordinate, inclusive identity for the campers (i.e., replacing the "us" and "them" representations with the more inclusive "we" representation).

Gaertner and co-workers (1990), based on their own empirical work, concluded that the causal relation between cooperation and reduced intergroup bias is mediated by transformations in group members' cognitive representations of the in-group and out-group members into an inclusive superordinate category. Cooperation, according to Gaertner and colleagues, "degraded the two-groups representation and induced the members to recategorize themselves primarily as one larger group" (p. 700). Once recategorized, former out-group members were evaluated more positively producing the decrease in intergroup bias.

To date, the direct benefits of recategorization have been demonstrated only with minimal groups (i.e., groups established for the purpose of the study that have no history of prior interaction or conflict). It remains an empirical question whether cooperative interdependence instigates similar processes with real groups who may have as a starting point a long history of conflict and mistrust (as is the case between blacks and whites in the United States). Indeed, Worchel (1979, 1986) noted that it is often difficult to encourage cooperation among conflicting groups. However, the strength of the analysis developed by Gaertner and his colleagues is that they have tried to identify the theoretical mechanisms by which cooperation, a strategy long looked on with favor in efforts to reduce intergroup hostilities, has its beneficial effects. Only when such mechanisms are clearly understood can we use the empirical literature effectively in applied settings.

Color-blind or Multicultural Society: Which Should We Strive For?

In his famous "I have a dream" speech, Martin Luther King Jr. made a plea for all people to be judged by the content of their character and not by the color of their skin. According to King, the criterion for evaluating each person should be individual merit rather than group membership. The implication of King's plea is that people should be responded to individually, not categorically. Such a goal is laudable and clearly consistent with the central principles underlying the United States Constitution. However, the realities of social thinking and information processing introduce many difficulties that may prevent the achievement of this goal, some of which may not be rooted in motivated discrimination.

There are some who have argued that differences between racial groups should be ignored and that we should strive to have a *color-blind society* in which color and ethnic heritage play no role in how people are treated (Rist, 1974). This argument is consistent with the view of America as "The Great Melting Pot," in which bits and pieces of all different cultures are mixed together to become a unified whole. However, others have argued that the color-blind approach to intergroup relations is neither possible (i.e., skin color is perceptually salient) nor desirable. Worchel (1986), for example, suggested that there are real differences between groups and that such differences may (1) be important to the identity of the group (e.g., history, cultural heritage), (2) be important to group members' self-concepts (e.g., group pride, self-esteem), and (3) enrich the interaction between groups (e.g., through diversity of experience, background, and opinion). Worchel suggests that "rather than reduce or make light of these differences, group members should be taught to recognize and appreciate these distinctions" (p. 300).

Consistent with Worchel's suggestions, various political groups have recently made appeals for a more *multicultural society* and have presented a challenge to the "melting pot" conceptualization of America. Proponents of multiculturalism argue that we must learn to recognize and celebrate diversity in our society. Only the celebration of differences, they argue, can lead to mutual respect between all groups of people. Many factions in society (e.g., media, educational institutions) have accepted these pleas and have taken actions that are in accordance with the tenets of multiculturalism. For example, within the past few years, the media have introduced more racially and ethnically diverse television programs and commercial advertisements; popular magazines are featuring more articles that address the needs of racial and ethnic minorities. Many colleges and universities have introduced multicultural curricula and have implemented major campuswide campaigns to encourage the celebration of differences.

Although proponents of multiculturalism label such changes as progress, others argue that the emphasis on multiculturalism and celebration of differences has created a new form of separatism (e.g., separate dorms, student unions, sororities, and fraternities). These critics argue that separatism has highlighted the perception of differences between groups and made intergroup boundaries salient by establishing concrete differences between "we" and "they." To the extent that intergroup boundaries are made salient, without also finding some common ground between groups, this voluntary separatism may harm intergroup relations and escalate intergroup hostilities (e.g., Raspberry, 1993; Schlesinger, 1992; Steele, 1990).

In summary, we seem to be faced with two contradictory goals: (1) Reduce the use of categories for intergroup perception because they lead to biased inferences (i.e., the United States should be a "color-blind" society), and (2) encourage a multicultural society and celebrate diversity. Decisions about which would be the best path to take challenge theorists and practitioners alike. Based on our consideration of the out-group perception literature, a cautionary note is in order. Encouraging the celebration of differences, even with the best of intentions, can have the effect of heightening or sharpening the perception of difference between groups (i.e., by making intergroup boundaries more salient). The social psychology literature on intergroup perception identifies some of the potential dangers of encouraging the perception of differences. If this alone is done, it could heighten or intensify intergroup biases. This is not to say that action should not be taken, only that it should be taken from an informed perspective. Before we encourage the celebration of differences, we may need to find the dimensions of commonality or inclusion that supersede these differences.

PREJUDICE

Up to this point, we have focused on the consequences of social categorization for the creation and perpetuation of intergroup biases. At this point, we turn our attention to another factor often implicated in hostilities between real groups—prejudice. Prejudice is not limited to one time or place. It is not limited to one group of people. And it is not limited to one level of analysis (e.g., sociocultural, individual) (see Duckitt, 1992a,b). It is a topic for the historian, anthropologist, sociologist, psychologist, and layperson. Each has been interested in trying to identify the origins and consequences of intergroup prejudice as well as finding strategies to reduce prejudice and hostilities. In this section of the chapter, we first examine various definitions of prejudice found in the social psychological literature. Then, we consider a brief review of the causes of prejudice, as well as recent theorizing about prejudice in our contemporary society. Finally, we examine some of the strategies developed to try to reduce intergroup prejudice.

Before proceeding, it is important to point out that our analysis focuses primarily on racial prejudice, specifically between whites and blacks. There are several reasons for this focus. First, racial prejudice is an important problem. Second, most of the theories concerning the origins and nature of prejudice, both historically and contemporarily, were developed in the context of efforts to understand racial prejudice. Third, efforts to improve intergroup relations and reduce prejudice have similarly focused on racial prejudice. The emphasis on racial prejudice, however, is not meant to imply that prejudice directed toward other groups (e.g., women, Latinos, Jews, gays) is not important or worthy of study. Indeed, we would like to challenge the reader to consider the adequacy and relevance of the various theories of the origins of racial prejudice and the attempts to reduce racial prejudice for understanding these other prejudices.

Defining Prejudice

Prejudice, which everyone seems to understand intuitively, has proved to be difficult to adequately define. Prejudice is commonly defined as negative feelings toward persons based solely on their group memberships. It is most commonly measured in the form of attitude surveys. However, it is frequently argued that prejudice is multifaceted and that it has cognitive and behavioral components as well. In line with the tripartite model of attitudes, some theorists define prejudice as having three interrelated components: affect (prejudice), cognition (negative stereotypes), and behavior (discrimination). According to this conceptualization of prejudice, negative stereotypes provide the rationalization for negative or prejudiced feelings. Discrimination involves expressing one's negative thoughts and feelings in terms of negative behaviors. One of the major concerns among those interested in intergroup prejudice is that discrimination will follow from negative attitudes. Indeed, the tripartite model suggests that there should be consistency among the affective, cognitive, and behavioral components of prejudice.

Although intuitively appealing, the tripartite conceptualization of prejudice runs into difficulty. The three components of attitudes are not always consistent. For example, some nonprejudiced people also possess knowledge of negative stereotypes about various groups (Devine, 1989). Moreover, discrimination does not always follow from negative attitudes (e.g., LaPiere, 1934; Wicker, 1969; see Petty, Chapter 6). Several theorists, unsatisfied with the tripartite conceptualization of prejudice, have offered their own definitions of prejudice. Because there is no single best definition of prejudice, Table 12.2 presents a number of definitions offered in the literature. Each definition emphasizes different aspects of the phenomenon that can contribute to intergroup hostilities. As you review the definitions in Table 12.2, try to identify the common elements in the definitions so that you can begin to develop a working definition of prejudice.

Ashmore (1970) abstracted four basic points of agreement in the various definitions of prejudice. Specifically, Ashmore argued that prejudice is (1) an intergroup phenomenon (i.e., between social groups), (2) a negative orientation toward the target of prejudice (i.e., aggression or avoidance), (3) bad (i.e., unfair and overgeneralized), and (4) an attitude (i.e., negative evaluation). Integrating these elements, Ashmore suggested that "prejudice is a negative attitude toward a socially defined group and toward any person perceived to be a member of that group" (p. 253). Although not wholly satisfying, Ashmore's definition captures many of the essential elements that people typically think of when they think of prejudice. Therefore, this will serve as our working definition of prejudice.

Theories of the Origins of Prejudice

For the social scientist, prejudice is a phenomenon that is simultaneously fascinating and frustrating. The source of both the fascination and the frustration is

TABLE 12.2. Some Definitions of Prejudice

"Prejudice is a pattern of hostility in interpersonal relations which is directed against an entire group or against its individual members; it fulfills a specific irrational function for its bearer." (Ackerman & Jahoda, 1954, p. 3–4)

"Ethnic prejudice is an antipathy based upon a faulty and inflexible generalization. It may be felt or expressed. It may be directed toward a group as a whole or toward an individual because he is a member of that group." (Allport, 1954, p. 9)

"Prejudice is defined as hostility or aggression toward individuals on the basis of their group membership." (Buss, 1961, p. 245)

"Literally, *prejudice* means prejudgment, a judgment before knowledge. By group prejudice, then, we should mean both (1) a judgment, an evaluation of an ethnic or other group and its individual members, and (2) an incomplete or otherwise inadequate factual base to this evaluation." (Peterson, 1958, p. 342)

"Prejudice is a set of attitudes which causes, supports, or justifies discrimination." (Rose, 1951, p. 5)

"We shall define prejudice as an emotional rigid attitude (a *pre*disposition to respond to a certain stimulus in a certain way) toward a group of people." (Simpson & Yinger, 1965, p. 10)

the complexity of the phenomenon. Most theorists agree that prejudice is determined by many factors. Indeed, this complexity is reflected in the fact that there is no all-encompassing theory of prejudice. Instead there are a number of overlapping theories about the determinants of prejudice and "as a rule most 'theories' are advanced by their authors to call attention to some important causal factor, without implying that no other factors are operating" (Allport, 1954, p. 207).

For example, even if we narrow our focus to a psychological analysis of prejudice (i.e., an analysis at the individual level), various cognitive, motivational, social, cultural, and historical factors come into play and can operate simultaneously. That is, these factors are not independent, and they can have dynamic and reciprocal effects. To the extent that we focus our analysis on one set of factors, we may be minimizing the impact of the others. According to Allport (1954), "this is the inevitable defect in any analytical treatment of the subject. The problem as a whole is multi-faceted" (p. 17). Allport warned us that while examining one facet, it is important to keep in mind the simultaneous existence of many other facets. A failure to do so, will inevitably lead to an incomplete analysis of prejudice.

The study of prejudice has not yielded straightforward and conclusive statements about the origins of prejudice. A historical review of the research trends in this literature reveals decade-by-decade shifts in theoretical analyses and questions of interest about the origins of prejudice most popular during those periods. John Duckitt (1992a), in a comprehensive review of the historical developments in the study of prejudice, suggests that research in this area is shaped as much by historical events and social circumstances as by the ordinary evolution of knowledge. This progression has led to many and varied theoretical and empirical approaches to the study of the origins of intergroup prejudice. Duckitt's review suggests that many research questions were abandoned when social circumstances drew attention to new, equally important issues. Table 12.3 provides a review of the questions and theoretical approaches that took center stage in the study of prejudice during the past seven decades.

The table outlines the social and historical circumstances that led to the scientific question of concern to social scientists, the image of prejudice during the decade, and the theoretical orientation and the research orientation preferred during the period. The dominant theoretical perspective during a given time period reflects the different explanatory goals and research objectives of that era. The shifts do not necessarily reflect the systematic replacement of theories and approaches that have been refuted or shown to be inadequate by better or more powerful theories. To the extent that these research objectives and theoretical foci emerged from fundamentally different questions about the nature of prejudice, Duckitt (1992a) points out that "the resulting perspectives would each make partial, but essential and complementary contributions to the understanding of prejudice" (p. 47). In what follows, we attempt to identify some of the central theoretical perspectives concerning the origins of prejudice. The perspectives describe basic perceptual, cognitive, or motivational processes that could account for the pervasiveness of prejudice as a feature of human social behavior.

Inherent Human Potential for Prejudice

As the review of research on the minimal group paradigm earlier in this chapter suggests, there may be fundamental, universal psychological processes that contribute to intergroup bias and prejudice. Indeed, some have suggested that such processes lead to an inherent human potential for prejudice. The work reviewed earlier on social categorization and social identification and their implications for in-group favoritism illustrate the widespread impact of these processes. Similarly, Rokeach, Smith and Evans (1960) suggested a universal tendency for people to dislike groups with dissimilar values and beliefs; this dislike can escalate into prejudice. Locating the origins of prejudice and intergroup bias in ordinary cognitive and motivational processes would help to explain why prejudice and discrimination are such ubiquitous and almost universal phenomena. However, this perspective cannot, by itself, explain all aspects of prejudice.

Intergroup Dynamics

Not all out-groups are disliked equally. In addition, the patterns of negative intergroup attitudes tend to be socially shared. Social and intergroup dynamics can determine the target for prejudice in any given society. For example, *realistic conflict theory* holds that direct competition for valuable but limited resources is responsible for the development of prejudice (Levine & Campbell, 1972). Group conflicts, which create differences in group status or power, help deter-

TABLE 12.3. Historical Evolution of the Psychological Understanding of Prejudice

Social and Historical Problem	Social Scientific Question	Image of Prejudice	Theoretical Orientation	Research Orientation
Up to the 1920s: White domination and colonial rule of "backward peoples"	Identifying the deficiencies of "backward peoples"	A natural response to "inferior peoples"	"Race theories"	Comparative studies of the abilities of different races
The 1920s and 1930s: The legitimacy of White domination challenged	Explaining the stigmatization of minorities	Prejudice as irrational and unjustified	Conceptualizing prejudice as a social problem	Measurement and descriptive studies
The 1930s and 1940s: The ubiquity of White racism in the United States	Identifying universal processes underlying prejudice	Prejudice as unconscious defense	Psychodynamic theory: Defensive processes	Experimental
The 1950s: Nazi racial ideology and the holocaust	Identifying the prejudice-prone personality	Prejudice as an expression of a pathological need	Individual differences	Correlational
The 1960s: The problem of prejudice in the American South	How social norms and influences determine prejudice	Prejudice as a social norm	Sociocultural: Social transmission of prejudice	Observational and correlational
The 1970s: The persistence of U.S. racism and discrimination	How prejudice is rooted in social structure and intergroup relations	Prejudice as an expression of group interests	Sociocultural: Intergroup dynamics of prejudice	Sociological and historical research
The 1980s: The inevitability and universality of prejudice and intergroup conflict	What universal psychological processes underlie intergroup conflict and prejudice	Prejudice as an inevitable outcome of social categorization	Cognitive perspective	Experimental

Note: From The social psychology of prejudice by J. Duckitt, 1992, New York: Praeger. Copyright 1992 by John Duckitt. Adapted by permission of the Greenwood Publishing Group, Inc. Westport, CT.

mine which groups are the disliked groups (Blauner, 1972; Bonacich, 1972; Cox, 1948; Sherif & Sherif, 1953; van den Berghe, 1967). Thus, the nature of contact between groups can direct prejudice toward specific target groups and can lead to consensual agreement among the members of a group about which out-groups are targeted for prejudice.

The realities of group competition (e.g., struggle for land, jobs, power), then, seem to contribute to a great deal of prejudice in the world (Olzak & Nagel, 1986). However, the realistic conflict analysis cannot be applied to all situations, and this analysis sometimes falls short in its ability to account for intergroup attitudes and hostilities. For example, realistic conflict theory would predict that those who believe that the quality of their life is being threatened by members of another group would be the most prejudiced people. The research evidence does not support this hypothesis. In a study of white Americans, parents living in school districts where children were bused to distant desegregated schools were not more prejudiced against blacks than adults who were not parents or parents whose children were not affected by busing (Kinder & Sears, 1981; Sears & Kinder, 1985). Additional work is needed to determine the specific conditions under which realistic group conflict produces intergroup hostilities.

Individual Differences

Historically, an important approach to the study of prejudice was to search for individual differences that were responsible for the development of prejudiced attitudes. Following the massive genocide of Jews perpetrated by the Nazis in World War II, the conception of prejudice as a universal and essentially normal process that was characteristic of all people became threatening and unacceptable. Hence, the search began for the disturbed personality structure (i.e., the prejudice-prone personality or bigot) that could be held responsible for such heinous acts. This search resulted in the famous research program of Adorno, Frenkel-Brunswick, Levinson, and Sanford (1950) on the authoritarian personality. This perspective conceptualized prejudice as a personality disorder characterized by rigid adherence to and fear of punishment for deviating from conventional values, an exaggerated need to submit to and identify with strong authority, generalized hostility, and intolerance for groups that differed from one's own. The *authoritarian personality* was thought to develop as a result of the child-rearing techniques of status-anxious parents who used a great deal of physical discipline and few, if any, open displays of affection toward their children. These children experienced feelings of inadequacy, the theory posits, and considerable hostility toward their parents. However, because their parents were punitive and powerful, children could not express their anger toward their parents directly. Consequently, the children repressed their anger and feelings of inadequacy. The theory suggests that, in order to relieve their repressed hostilities and anxieties, people reared under these conditions take advantage of various defense mechanisms, such as displacing their aggression toward safe targets (i.e., minority groups) rather than the true targets (i.e., parents).

In sum, the theory suggests that high authoritarians would be more pre-

TABLE 12.4. Sample Items from the F Scale*

Obedience and respect for authority are the most important virtues children should learn.

A person who has bad habits, manners, and breeding can hardly expect to get along with decent people.

Some people are born with the urge to jump from high places.

Young people sometimes get rebellious ideas, but as they grow up, they ought to get over them and settle down.

Sex crimes, such as rape and attacks on children, deserve more than mere imprisonment; such criminals ought to be publicly whipped, or worse.

Nowadays, more and more people are prying into matters that should remain personal and private.

The wild sex life of the old Greeks and Romans is tame compared to some of the goings-on in this country, even where people might least expect it.

Most people don't realize how much of our lives are controlled by plots hatched in secret places.

*Subjects are instructed to indicate their amount of agreement with each item on the scale ranging from +3 (strong support, agreement) to -3 (strong opposition, disagreement). The scale has no zero point.

disposed to develop prejudices toward members of groups that differed from their own than their low authoritarian counterparts. Research into the authoritarian personality has provided, at best, mixed support. In the decades following the 1950s, interest in the authoritarian personality subsided. Several factors contributed to the decrease of interest in this approach. First, the assessment of authoritarianism was plagued with measurement problems. For example, the questions on the F scale, the key measure of authoritarianism, were all phrased such that affirmative answers reflected high authoritarian responses (see Table 12.4). Thus, it was not clear whether the respondents' answers reflected authoritarianism or a general *acquiescence bias* (i.e., a tendency to respond yes to all questions). This criticism also applies to the E scale (a measure of ethnocentrism) and the A-S scale (a measure of anti-Semitism). Because of these problems, a great deal of research focused on these methodological issues and less research focused on the theoretical implications of authoritarianism. In addition to problems with acquiescence bias, the items on the F scale revealed very low internal consistency, another critical methodological shortcoming of the scale. Second, Adorno and colleagues (1950) provided no direct evidence that related scores on the F scale to fascist or authoritarian tendencies. A consequence of these unresolved theoretical and methodological issues is that interest in individual differences in prejudice waned and progress toward understanding the authoritarian personality was stalled.

However, in recent years there has been a resurgence of interest in authoritarianism. Altemeyer (1981, 1988), for example, developed a new measure of authoritarianism, the *right wing authoritarianism* (RWA) scale, which does not suffer from the psychometric problems of the original F scale. The RWA scale has proved to have adequate reliability and validity and may permit researchers to move beyond the unresolved methodological controversies and inconclusive findings that plagued the study of authoritarianism. The availability of a reliable and valid scale may facilitate research about the nature of authoritarian personalities.

Each of the theoretical perspectives briefly reviewed above has received a great deal of research attention, and each has received at least some support in the empirical literature. However, it should be noted that none of the perspectives alone is able to account for the complex pattern of findings in the literature on the origins of intergroup prejudice (see Duckitt, 1992a,b). One significant problem with this literature, as we saw in the case of the authoritarian personality, is that because of methodological shortcomings and failures to rule out alternative explanations, many intriguing theoretical propositions have not been adequately tested. A second problem is that because research in this area appears to be shaped as much by historical events as it is by the evolution of knowledge, many research questions were abandoned when social circumstances drew attention to new issues. For example, the advent of the civil rights movement in the 1950s and 1960s and increasing racial tensions steered social scientists away from individual-psychological factors that determine prejudice to broader social and cultural factors. In sum, there are many avenues of inquiry concerning the origins of intergroup prejudice that are only partially explored. Exploring the links between the various theoretical perspectives may provide fruitful directions for research on issues related to the origins of intergroup prejudice.

Contemporary Models of Prejudice

In this section, we examine several of the contemporary theoretical models of prejudice, which were not included in Duckitt's review. As with many other trends in the prejudice literature, the development of some of these theoretical models was prompted by important changes in the social climate in the United States with regard to race relations. These theories focus less on the origins of prejudice than on reasons for the complex, often contradictory, nature of contemporary racial attitudes. As such, the contemporary theories are not to be considered alternatives to the theories reviewed in the previous section. To provide you with the context for appreciating these models, we first provide some background on the historical circumstances that encouraged the development of the contemporary models.

Social scientists, legislators, and laypeople alike have long been concerned with the paradox of racism in a nation founded on the fundamental value of human equality (see Gaertner & Dovidio, 1986; Jones, 1972; Katz, Wackenhut, & Hass 1986; McConahay, 1986; Myrdal, 1944). The government responded with the landmark legal decisions of the 1950s and 1960s which made overt discrimination based on race illegal and functionally made admitting to prejudices socially taboo (e.g., Supreme Court ruling on school segregation and the Civil

TABLE 12.5. Changes in Whites' Racial Attitudes over Time

General Principles	Approximate Date of Surveys		
	1963	1980	Change
Percentage who oppose laws against intermarriage	39	66	+27
Percentage who favor desegregation	27	35	+ 8
Percentage who agree that white and black children should attend the same schools	65	90	+35
Percentage who would vote for a well-qualified black candidate	45	81	+36
Percentage who disagree that whites should be able to keep blacks out of their neighborhood	39	71	+32

Adapted from Schuman, Steeh, & Bobo (1985), Table 3.1. The dates were selected to portray the changes in attitudes between the mid-1960s to the early 1980s.

Rights Laws). In the wake of these changes at the societal level, social scientists have also been interested in the extent to which there have been changes at the individual level.

Certainly at the societal level, the changes have been dramatic. In many ways, we have been successful at eliminating overt discriminatory treatment of others based on race. For example, no longer in this country are there separate water fountains, lunch counters, or rest rooms for blacks and whites. Nor are blacks required by law to sit in the back of a bus. Changes at the individual level also appear to have occurred. Survey studies of racial and ethnic attitudes and beliefs suggest that racial prejudice is declining in the United States (Greeley & Sheatsley, 1971; Hochschild & Herk, 1990; Hyman & Sheatsley, 1956, 1964; Schuman, Steeh, & Bobo, 1985; Taylor, Sheatsley, & Greeley, 1978). Whereas a majority of whites expressed overt racism in the 1950s (which was legally sanctioned), only a minority do today. As can be seen in Table 12.5, over time white Americans have become more positive in attitudes toward integration of schools, housing, and jobs. Stereotypes about blacks have become more favorable over time, and fewer people endorse negative characteristics about blacks (e.g., that they are lazy, superstitious, stupid) (see Devine & Elliot, in press; Dovidio & Gaertner, 1986). Self-reported attitudes toward blacks have become more favorable. In the political arena, a smaller percentage of whites say that they would not vote for a well-qualified black presidential candidate. There also appears to be a decrease in racial stereotyping in the mass media (e.g., television programs, movies, advertisements) (see Dovidio & Gaertner, 1986, for a review). In sum, overt, direct forms of prejudice (often labeled "old-fashioned" forms of prejudice) have declined.

Despite the abandonment of old-fashioned attitudes evident in survey studies, support for specific governmental policies that would promote racial equality (e.g., affirmative action, busing for integration, spending for programs that would benefit blacks) has remained weak over time. In addition, in a number of experimental studies, subtle indicators (e.g., unobtrusive measures, nonverbal responses) continue to reveal negative treatment toward blacks even among those who claim to have renounced prejudice (see Crosby, Bromley, & Saxe, 1980, for a review). How should these paradoxical reactions be understood? Any model developed to understand this paradox must address why negative (prejudiced) responses persist in the face of changes in attitudes or beliefs. Several contemporary models have taken on this challenge. Although each of the contemporary models of prejudice acknowledges the persistence of negative responses despite changes in self-reported attitudes, the models make different assumptions about (1) the process that gives rise to the conflicting reactions and (2) the prospects for promoting further change (i.e., eliminating subtle prejudiced tendencies). The prospects for further change will be reviewed in the section on prejudice reduction.

Impression Management: Illusory Change. One interpretation of the paradoxical reactions is that prejudice has not truly been reduced at the individual level. Rather, claims of being nonprejudiced merely reflect compliance with (as opposed to internalization of) society's nonprejudiced values (Crosby, Bromley, & Saxe, 1980; Dovidio & Fazio, 1992; Gaertner & Dovidio, 1986; Jones & Sigall, 1971). According to this analysis, prejudice has not truly been reduced, but rather overt expressions of prejudice have simply been replaced with more covert, subtle forms of prejudice. For example, to assess racial attitudes, Crosby and colleagues (1980) clearly favored nonthoughtful, spontaneous responses, arguing that the strength of such measures is that they do not involve careful, deliberate, and intentional thought (see also Dovidio & Fazio, 1992). Thus, their analysis centered on the assumption that the less controllable nonconscious responses were inherently more trustworthy than the more controllable verbal responses. This type of analysis seems to assume that change has truly occurred only if all of one's responses are consistent with one's overtly expressed nonprejudiced beliefs.

The *impression management perspective* suggests that change is more superficial than real. Thus, researchers who endorse this perspective have attempted to develop increasingly subtle measures of bias that are believed to reveal people's true attitudes (Dovidio & Fazio, 1992; Gaertner & Dovidio, 1986). In contrast, each of the models reviewed below was developed with the explicit goal of understanding the conflicting reactions whites have toward blacks. That is, each model begins with the task of explaining the paradox. Unlike the impression management perspective, these models do not consider people's verbal reports of their attitudes to be necessarily untrustworthy. Thus, each of the models focuses on people who have changed rather than those who remain overtly racist. As you read about the models, evaluate them in terms of their implications for future change and progress in overcoming prejudice at the individual level.

Modern or Symbolic Racism. Several theorists have argued that *old-fashioned racism* is no longer very widespread and that it has been replaced with a new, more modern, or "symbolic" form of racism (Kinder & Sears, 1981; McConahay, 1986; McConahay & Hough, 1976; Sears & McConahay, 1973). *Modern racists* reject traditionally racist beliefs (e.g., the belief that black people are not as smart as white people) and embrace abstract principles of justice and fair treatment. However, they are considered ambivalent in their reactions to blacks because negative feelings toward blacks that were learned early in socialization persist into adulthood. Kinder and Sears (1981) suggest that racism, though not overt, remains in a disguised form and is linked in complex ways to traditional American values. They write that *symbolic racism* is "a blend of anti-black affect and the kind of traditional American moral values embodied in the Protestant work ethic. . . . Symbolic racism represents a form of resistance to change in the racial status quo based on moral feelings that Blacks violate traditional American values such as individualism and self-reliance, the work ethic, obedience, and discipline" (p. 416).

According to McConahay (1986) and others, modern racists' disaffection for blacks is expressed indirectly and symbolically, in terms of opposition to busing or affirmative action and other policies designed to promote racial equality, instead of overtly, as in support for segregation. Thus, to cope with their ambivalence, modern racists rationalize their negative feelings in terms of abstract political and social issues. Modern or symbolic racists tend to endorse items such as "Blacks have gotten more economically than they deserve" and "Blacks should not push themselves where they are not wanted." It is relatively easy to generate nonracial explanations for agreeing with such statements. Modern racists' reactions to blacks, expressed in terms of abstract ideological symbols, reflect their feelings that blacks are violating cherished values and are making illegitimate demands for change in the racial status quo.

Ambivalence: Conflicting Value and Attitude Structures. According to Katz and his colleagues' theory of ambivalence-induced behavior amplification (e.g., Katz, 1981; Katz & Hass, 1988; Katz, Wackenhut, & Hass, 1986), many white Americans simultaneously hold two sets of conflicting values which have direct implications for their reactions to blacks. One of these core value orientations is egalitarianism, which supports democratic and humanitarian principles. The other value orientation is individualism, which is grounded in principles associated with the Protestant ethic, such as personal freedom, self-reliance, devotion to work, and achievement. According to Katz, each of these value orientations encourages the development of more specific attitudes. Egalitarian values, for example, give rise to genuine pro-black sentiments, including sympathy for and favorable stereotypes about the target group (e.g., whites recognize that blacks have been unfairly disadvantaged historically). Commitment to principles of individualism, however, gives rise to antiblack sentiments, including beliefs that negative outcomes—such as unemployment, drug addiction, and criminal behavior—are rooted in personal weakness such as lack of ambition rather than in situational factors. This "attitude-duality" creates *ambivalence*. Katz and Hass (1988) provided empirical support for the existence of these value-attitude structures in regard to whites' reactions toward blacks.

The simultaneous existence of largely independent negative and positive cognitive structures has implications for people's responses toward the target group. Specifically, Katz and his colleagues maintain that ambivalent attitudes give rise to psychological discomfort and behavioral instability (Hass, Katz, Rizzo, Bailey, & Moore, 1992; Katz, 1981; Katz, Wackenhut, & Hass, 1986). Responses are either positive or negative, depending on which component of the ambivalent attitude is activated in a given situation. Furthermore, both positive and negative responses can threaten the ambivalent person's self-esteem because either response would discredit the opposing component of the ambivalent disposition. In order to reduce this threat, either the positive or the negative response is amplified (Katz, Glass, & Cohen, 1973; Katz, Glass, Lucido, & Farber, 1979). That is, "the ambivalent subject's extreme evaluations of the black are viewed theoretically as an attempt to disavow the contradicted attitude and thereby restore positive self-regard" (Katz, Wackenhut, & Hass, 1986, p. 54).

In sum, the work of Katz and his colleagues suggests that two core value orientations commonly held by Americans are associatively linked in memory with the attitude toward blacks. The egalitarian value is linked to a pro-black attitude, and the individualistic value is linked to an antiblack attitude. Such ambivalence helps to explain the persistence of prejudiced responses among people who sometimes appear to be low in prejudice. Despite the existence of genuine pro-black sentiments, situations that activate the unfavorable attitude structure will give rise to negative responses. Further, considering motivational factors (i.e., efforts to protect one's self-esteem), as well as cognitive factors, helps to explain the amplification of positive or negative behaviors (although the link between amplification and self-esteem has not yet been empirically explored).

Aversive Racism: Conflict between Egalitarian Values and Prejudiced Beliefs and Feelings. According to Gaertner and Dovidio (1986), most Americans are strongly committed to egalitarian values. They, therefore, desire to maintain an image of the self as fair, just, and nonprejudiced, causing them to report nonprejudiced, nondiscriminatory attitudes. However, according to Gaertner and Dovidio, aversive racists also possess negative feelings and beliefs toward blacks, which result from being born into a historically racist culture coupled with cognitive and motivational biases that promote in-group favoritism (such as those reviewed early in this chapter).

Gaertner and Dovidio (1986; see also Kovel, 1970) maintain that *aversive racists* will alternate between positive and negative behaviors toward members of the racial group. Which type of response will be generated is thought to depend on the normative structure in a given situation and the potential for generating a nonracial justification for a prejudiced response. If the situation clearly calls for a nonprejudiced response or if a justification or rationalization for engaging in a prejudiced response cannot be generated, the response will be positive. When normative prescriptions are weaker or more ambiguous, or when a justification is readily available, aversive racists' negative tendencies will be manifested. Their biased responses go unacknowledged by the self, however, so that their egalitarian self-image will not be threatened. Thus, although aversive racists' prejudiced feelings and beliefs are in conflict with their egalitarian values, the conflict supposedly is not consciously recognized.

Based on the aversive racism framework, prejudiced tendencies among people who often appear to be nonprejudiced can be explained in terms of coexisting egalitarian values and unacknowledged prejudiced feelings and beliefs. Because people are motivated to protect their egalitarian self-image, they will respond in accord with their egalitarian values in a limited set of circumstances, most notably when the situation clearly calls for a nonprejudiced response. However, in many other more ambiguous situations, responses will be subtly biased, largely because of normal cognitive processes that presumably operate spontaneously.

Dissociation Model: Conflict between Stereotype-Based Responses and Personal Beliefs. A final model that explains the persistence of prejudiced responses among people who espouse nonprejudiced attitudes is the dissociation model developed by Devine (1989). Devine argued that to understand the nature of contemporary forms of prejudice, one must distinguish between two types of stored information: (1) stereotypes and (2) personal beliefs (or attitudes) about group members. In the *dissociation model*, a stereotype is defined as *knowledge* of the attributes that are stereotypically associated with a particular group. Prejudiced personal beliefs are defined as the endorsement or acceptance of the content of a negative cultural stereotype. Importantly, being knowledgeable about the stereotype does not necessarily entail endorsement of the stereotype, so that the content of the stereotype would not be a part of the low prejudiced individual's personal beliefs about the target group (see Devine & Elliot, in press).

Conceptualizing stereotypes and beliefs as distinct cognitive structures differs from the long-standing tradition of essentially equating the two. That is, a stereotype is often defined as "a set of beliefs about the personal attributes of a group of people" (Stroebe & Insko, 1989, p. 5; see also Ashmore & Del Boca, 1981; Brigham, 1971). Yet Devine argued that the distinction is important because the activation of stereotypes and personal beliefs is governed by different cognitive processes: automatic and controlled processes, respectively (Posner & Snyder, 1977; Schneider & Shiffrin, 1977; Shiffrin & Schneider, 1977).

One implication of this analysis is that the two cognitive structures should provide the basis for responses under different circumstances. To understand this suggestion, it is important to understand the distinction between automatic and controlled processes. *Automatic processes* involve the unintentional (sponta-neous) activation of previously developed associations in memory that have been established through a history of repeated activation. Thus, these processes can be initiated by the presence of relevant environmental cues without requir-ing conscious attention, and they are difficult to bypass (Neely, 1977; Shiffrin & Dumais, 1981). In contrast, *controlled processes* involve the intentional activation of information stored in memory. They are more flexible than automatic processes, but they can be initiated only with active attention and not under conditions in which one's cognitive capacity is limited. Importantly, automati-cally activated responses can be inhibited by controlled processes only if there is enough time and cognitive capacity for a conscious expectancy to develop and inhibit the more spontaneous, automatic response (Neely, 1977).

Because stereotypes typically have a long socialization history and have been frequently activated, Devine (1989) argued that they can be automatically activated, providing a "default" basis for responding in the presence of mem-bers of the stereotyped group or their symbolic equivalent (see also Brewer, 1988; Fiske & Neuberg, 1990; Klinger & Beall, 1992). Thus, low prejudiced peo-ple (who renounce prejudice) and high prejudiced people (who do not) are equally susceptible to the automatic activation and use of stereotypes because they are equally knowledgeable about the cultural stereotype (Brigham, 1972; Devine, 1989, Devine & Elliot, in press; Katz, 1976). In contrast to stereotypes, personal beliefs about a target group are often developed after the initial, early learning of the stereotype (see Allport, 1954; Katz, 1976; Proshansky, 1966). As a result, they are less accessible cognitive structures than stereotypes and rely on controlled processing for their activation. The important implication of this analysis is that the default response, even among low prejudiced people, is a stereotype-based response (Banaji & Greenwald, in press; Klinger & Beall, 1992; Jamieson & Zanna, 1989; Sherman & Gorkin, 1980; but see Gilbert & Hixon, 1991). That is, low prejudiced people can inhibit stereotype-based responses only if they have the time and the cognitive capacity to initiate controlled processes so as to bring their personal beliefs to mind.

Klinger and Beall (1992) compared the effects of automatic vs. controlled stereotype activation on the likelihood that low and high prejudiced people would make stereotype-based responses about a target person. The experiment was conducted in two phases. During phase 1, low and high sexist subjects were presented with words (primes) that would activate the stereotype (e.g., fe-male, woman, girl) or control words that were unrelated to the stereotype (e.g., fender, wham, gild). The key manipulation was that for half the subjects the primes were presented subliminally (i.e., below subjects' threshold for con-scious recognition), whereas for the other half of the subjects primes were pre-sented supraliminally (i.e., well above subjects' threshold for conscious recog-nition). In phase 2, subjects read a paragraph describing the narrator's day at work and evaluated the job-related success of the narrator. The paragraph was ambiguous with regard to job-related success. Klinger and Beall argued that rating the narrator as less successful in the stereotype priming condition compared with the control prime condition would provide evidence of stereotype-based processing. If Devine's analysis is correct, both low and high sexist subjects should show stereotype-based processing in the subliminal priming conditions, but only high sexist subjects should show such processing in the supraliminal priming conditions. That is, only when the primes were presented supraliminally would low sexist subjects have the opportunity to use controlled processes to override stereotype-based effects and make judgments based on their personal beliefs.

Klinger and Beall's findings strongly supported Devine's (1989) analysis. They found that both low and high sexist subjects in the subliminal stereotype priming condition rated the narrator as less successful than their control prime counterparts. In the visible priming condition, a different pattern of results was obtained. Whereas, the type of priming (stereotype vs. control) did not affect the success judgments of high sexist subjects, it clearly affected the responses of low sexist subjects. Specifically, low sexist subjects who were exposed to the stereotype-related primes supraliminally used their controlled processes to override stereotype-based effects and rated the narrator as more successful than did their control prime counterparts.

In summary, Devine's (1989) analysis suggests that many low prejudiced people appear to be prone to a conflict between their nonprejudiced beliefs and their actual prejudiced responses that arise due to automatic stereotype activation. Moreover, many people appear to be aware of this conflict. That is, they recognize and are willing to admit that in a variety of situations their responses are more prejudiced than their personal beliefs indicate is appropriate (Devine, Monteith, Zuwerink, & Elliot, 1991; Monteith, Devine, & Zuwerink, 1993; Pressly & Devine, 1992; Zuwerink, Monteith, Devine, & Cook, 1994). The goal for these low prejudiced people, then, becomes learning how to inhibit well-learned stereotype-based responses and replace them with belief-based responses, which likely takes considerable attention and time (see Devine & Monteith, 1993). This analysis suggests that subtle, contemporary forms of prejudice exist in part because many low prejudiced people have not progressed far enough in the prejudice reduction process in order to be efficient and effective at generating nonprejudiced responses that are consistent with their nonprejudiced beliefs.

Reducing Prejudice

As research into the causes of prejudice proceeded, many social scientists were simultaneously consumed with the possibility of developing strategies to reduce prejudice and intergroup conflict. Interest in both the origin and reduction of intergroup prejudice stemmed from a social problem perspective. According to this perspective, prejudice was regarded as a problem with detrimental consequences. Therefore, social scientists felt justified in conducting value-oriented research because prejudice needed to be eliminated in order to improve society.

At the heart of the strategies to reduce prejudice was the assumption that majority group members' *negative attitudes* toward minority group members were the key obstacle to harmonious intergroup relations. Thus, the main goal for each of the strategies proposed at the time was to change the negative attitudes of majority group members. Only then, it was thought, could the stage be set for less antagonistic and more harmonious intergroup relations. Several of the strategies attempted to change the negative attitudes directly (e.g., education, propaganda, sensitivity training), whereas strategies stemming from the contact hypothesis attempted to modify negative attitudes indirectly, through contact with minority group members.

In considering the various prejudice reduction strategies that have been explored, keep in mind that the tactics for promoting change often were chosen in an atheoretical manner. This fact is demonstrated in the major reviews of the prejudice literature (Harding, Kunter, Proshansky, & Chein, 1954; Stephan, 1985; see also Monteith, Zuwerink, & Devine, 1994). Researchers have been forced to organize their research around "the various change-producing experiences that have been investigated rather than around the various psychological processes that were presumably at work" (Harding, Kunter, Proshansky, & Chein, 1954, p. 1046). It is of interest to note that even though several theoretical explanations have been advanced concerning the processes involved in the acquisition of prejudice, there has been a paucity of research that uses these theories in order to identify the processes involved in the reduction of prejudice. As a consequence of this nearly complete divorce between theories and strategies for change, prejudice-reduction techniques seemed to have a "hit-or-miss" quality about them; the processes responsible for the technique's successes and failures often were—and remain—unknown.

Changing Negative Attitudes Directly

Attempts to change prejudiced attitudes through *propaganda* in the form of oral presentations, written materials, and movies have met with variable success (see Harding, Kunter, Proshansky, & Chein, 1954; Simpson & Yinger, 1965; Stephan, 1985; Williams, 1947). Propaganda is most effective when dealing with a poorly informed public, when the propaganda has a monopoly in the field of communication (as in the case of censorship), and when the social and political values of the public are diffuse or poorly structured, or the message maps on to already well-structured value of the public. For the most part, propaganda reaches those who already agree with it. Such selective exposure effects are likely to limit the effectiveness of any propaganda strategy for reducing prejudiced attitudes. Cooper and Jahoda (1947) found that, even when exposed to antiprejudice propaganda, prejudiced people developed highly effective mechanisms to evade the message (e.g., distortion, rationalization). Flowerman (1947) argued that for propaganda to have any influence, the following conditions must be met: (1) The propaganda must be received under favorable conditions so that it will be processed; (2) it must attract the person's attention; (3) it must be enjoyable and not cause psychological discomfort; and (4) it must be understood, not evaded by misunderstanding. None of these conditions are easily met.

Education has long been targeted as a tool that can be used to improve intergroup attitudes by increasing people's knowledge and understanding of other groups. However, the notion that specific school courses and, more generally, college education will have liberalizing effects upon students' intergroup attitudes has been supported in as many studies as it has been refuted (see Harding, Kunter, Proshansky, & Chein, 1954; Simpson & Yinger, 1965; Stephan, 1985). However, identifying reasons for the variable success of education as a change strategy may be difficult because of inherent differences between studies or methodological shortcomings of particular studies. Most studies did not use appropriate control groups and failed to measure long-term outcomes of such educational programs. Moreover, although these studies often measured attitude change, rarely were measures of behavioral change obtained. Thus, the link between attitudes and behavior in these studies is unknown. This issue is particularly important because, as was made clear in Chapter 6, attitudes only sometimes predict behavior. In addition, many of the studies may have been tainted by demand characteristics for positive changes in attitudes. However, the greatest impediment to understanding why the techniques were successful only some of the time is the failure to identify theoretically relevant processes that either facilitated or hindered attitude change.

The same problem is found in prejudice-reduction approaches that are based on therapeutic and group interaction techniques (see Simpson & Yinger, 1965; Stephan, 1985). For example, client-centered counseling, sensitivity training, therapeutic techniques, and systematic desensitization have proved somewhat successful in reducing prejudiced attitudes. However, the atheoretical nature of this research leaves us unsure about what types of people at which stages of prejudice reduction are most likely to benefit from the techniques (Stephan, 1985). Furthermore, the potential risks of inappropriately applying the techniques are great. For example, Myers and Bishop (1970) found that prejudice-reduction discussion groups actually increased prejudice among people holding highly prejudiced attitudes.

The final strategy for changing highly prejudiced attitudes that we will consider in this section is Rokeach's (1973) *self-confrontation technique*. An influential impetus for Rokeach's work was Gunner Myrdal's (1944) characterization of the *American dilemma*. According to Myrdal, many white Americans who are committed to the general egalitarian tenets of the "American Creed" but simultaneously have specific prejudiced tendencies experience an internal moral conflict. Rokeach reasoned that self-dissatisfaction should arise when people are encouraged to realize that their egalitarian self-conception (i.e., their view of themselves as fair-minded, tolerant, compassionate) is inconsistent with their prejudiced values, attitudes, and/or behaviors. This self-dissatisfaction should then motivate individuals to change the prejudiced aspects of their belief system and bring their behaviors more in line with their egalitarian self-image.

To explore the efficacy of this prejudice reduction strategy, Rokeach (1973) designed a feedback procedure in which subjects (1) rank ordered their values including the key values of freedom and equality, (2) indicated their attitudes toward blacks and civil rights, and (3) were provided with an explicit opportunity to reflect on the extent to which their values and attitudes were consistent or inconsistent with their egalitarian self-conceptions. At a later point in time, subjects again rank ordered their values and reported their attitudes toward blacks.

In several experiments, Rokeach (1973) found evidence to support his analysis that making subjects aware of their prejudice-related inconsistencies heightened feelings of self-dissatisfaction, which then motivated change to reduce the inconsistencies. For example, Rokeach found that subjects who initially ascribed little personal importance to the values of "equality" and "freedom" came to view equality and freedom as very important after they were confronted with the inconsistency between their low rankings of the values and their views of themselves as fair, tolerant, democratic, etc. These increases in the rankings of equality and freedom were associated with the levels of self-reported dissatisfaction that were elicited in response to subjects' initial rankings of these values. Moreover, these value changes were eventually followed by attitude change, such that subjects revised their antiblack attitudes to be consistent with their egalitarian values. Several behavioral measures (e.g., joining the NAACP) also provided evidence for positive change as a consequence of the self-confrontation technique. In addition to these encouraging findings, Rokeach's program of research is impressive because it underscores the theoretical processes involved in changing prejudiced attitudes. In this respect, the work is unique among the prejudice reduction strategies that have attempted to change negative attitudes directly.

Changing Negative Attitudes Indirectly through Intergroup Contact

> Prejudice (unless deeply rooted in the character structure of the individual) may be reduced by equal status contact between majority and minority group members in the pursuit of common goals. The effect is greatly enhanced if this contact is sanctioned by institutional supports (i.e., by law, custom, or local atmosphere), and provided it is the sort that leads to the perception of common humanity between members of the two groups (Allport, 1954, p. 281).

> Attitude change favorable to a disliked group will result from equal status contact with stereotype disconfirming persons from that group, provided that the contact is cooperative and of such a nature as to reveal the individual characteristics of the person contacted and that it takes place in a situation characterized by norms favoring equality and equalitarian association among the participating groups (Cook, 1978, pp. 97–98).

Perhaps the most extensively investigated strategy for reducing intergroup hostilities derives from the *contact hypothesis.* In the era following World War II, many social scientists suggested that negative attitudes toward minority groups stem at least partially from ignorance of other groups, which was created and maintained by pervasive racial segregation (e.g., in schools, housing, jobs). One way to improve intergroup relations, it was suggested, was to reduce ignorance by creating opportunities for contact between members of different groups. Creating the opportunity for interracial contact was expected to reduce ignorance of the other group, break down stereotypes, and ultimately reduce whites' racial prejudice.

Although intuitively appealing, it quickly became clear that contact alone was not sufficient to reduce intergroup hostilities. The most succinct and accurate summary of research on the contact hypothesis is that contact *sometimes* produces positive effects in the form of reducing negative attitudes and intergroup hostilities. The early evidence relevant to the contact hypothesis came from studies of naturally occurring interracial contact situations. For example, in the decades following World War II, many of America's major institutions became less racially segregated than in the decades preceding the war. Changes in the military, education, and professional sports provided an opportunity to study the effects of contact. In the Army, surveys indicated that most military personnel were opposed to desegregating military units. However, after desegregating the units, opposition diminished, and there was a great deal of support for desegregation among the white soldiers who had the closest contact with black soldiers (Stouffer, Suchman, DeVinney, Star, & Williams, 1949). Contact in integrated housing projects were associated with less prejudiced attitudes among those tenants than for tenants living in segregated housing units (Deutch & Collins, 1951). Hamilton, Carpenter, and Bishop (1984) found that although white suburban residents initially reacted negatively to blacks moving into their neighborhoods, the negative reactions dissipated during the first year, and having black neighbors had a positive effect on the white residents' racial attitudes. Taken together, these findings were seen as encouraging, suggesting that intergroup contact had potentially beneficial effects. In contrast, however, Amir (1969, 1976) found that intergroup contact produced no decrease in prejudiced attitudes, nor did it increase these attitudes.

The school setting was one area in which there was great hope for contact to produce positive effects on intergroup relations following the 1954 Supreme Court ruling that racially separate schools were inherently unequal. However, the research on contact in desegregated schools led to pessimism about the benefits of intergroup contact. In a review of this literature, Stephan (1987) concluded that more often than not desegregation produced *increases* rather than *decreases* in white prejudice toward blacks. In addition, contact rarely had positive effects on the black students. Careful evaluation of the conditions under which contact most often took place in school settings suggested that it is the type of interracial contact, rather than contact itself, that is responsible for outcomes of contact. A review of the literature on the contact hypothesis suggests that a large number of conditions must be met before contact is likely to ameliorate intergroup tension. These conditions are listed in Table 12.6 (see Allport, 1954; Amir, 1969; Cook, 1978; Stephan, 1985, 1987).

The first four conditions listed in Table 12.6 are viewed as minimal conditions necessary for contact to have ameliorative effects. Specifically, members of each group should be of equal status and should engage in cooperative activities in which they join together to achieve superordinate goals (see Sherif and colleagues' Robbers Cave experiment described earlier in the chapter). According to research on intergroup contact, the contact situation should allow

TABLE 12.6. Necessary Conditions for Contact to Reduce Intergroup Conflict

1. Equal status among participants both within and outside the contact situation
2. Cooperative rather than competitive interaction
3. Institutional support for the contact (e.g., the authorities should support contact)
4. Contact should involve relatively high levels of intimacy (e.g., one-on-one interactions among individual members of the two groups)
5. The outcomes of contact should be positive
6. Interaction with similar competence other
7. Interaction with nonstereotypic other
8. Similarity in beliefs and values
9. Contact with a variety of group members in a variety of situations

for intimate interactions, which provide the best chance for disconfirming stereotypes and reducing ignorance. Furthermore, there should be strong institutional support for contact. Without strong support on the part of relevant authorities (e.g., if teachers and parents resist contact), it will be difficult for contact to have beneficial effects.

However, even meeting these conditions does not ensure that contact will produce positive effects. Indeed, there are a number of interdependencies among the factors listed in Table 12.6, which lead to the conclusion that contact is likely to have beneficial effects only under a highly specialized (or, perhaps, idealized) set of circumstances. For example, cooperative interdependence works, but only if cooperation leads to a successful outcome. When cooperative endeavors end in failure, conflict can be intensified (Worchel, 1986; Worchel & Norvell, 1980). Failures amplify negative evaluations of out-group members in cooperative groups (Burnstein & McRae, 1962; Gibbons, Stephan, Stephenson, & Petty, 1981). For example, whites interacting with a black confederate liked him less when the group failed than when it succeeded (Burnstein & McRae, 1962). When things go badly, it is too easy to blame the minority group member for the failure (e.g., the ultimate attribution error operating). Competence of group members is also important. For example, in a cooperative task, incompetent blacks were liked less than competent blacks, especially when the group failed (Blanchard, Weigel, & Cook, 1975). It has been further suggested that contact will be most beneficial when the contact occurs with a variety of nonstereotypic minority group members in a variety of situations. Prospects for positive outcomes are increased when majority and minority group members have similar beliefs and values. The list in Table 12.6, although long, is certainly not exhaustive. For example, it has also been suggested that contact will be more likely to have positive effects when it is voluntary and involves equal numbers of majority and minority group members (Stephan, 1985).

This list represents a very specific set of conditions that are not representative of the most frequent intergroup contact situations (either historically or contemporarily). Consider, for example, the extent to which the conditions listed in Table 12.6 were likely to be met in the newly desegregated schools in which black children were bused into predominately white schools. As you think about this issue, keep in mind the research discussed earlier on the negative consequences of heightening the salience of intergroup boundaries. It is quite likely that intergroup differences were made salient in the desegregated classroom. First, the desegregation of schools was met with a fair amount of resistance. In some circumstances, the resistance escalated into overt hostility and violence. Second, Cohen (1980) noted that white children in the typical desegregated classroom came from more affluent families and were better prepared academically than their black classmates. Preexisting differences between groups are likely to carry over into the school setting and, thus, set the stage for unequal status contact. In efforts to bring black students up to the academic level of their white classmates, remedial assistance was very often provided to black students. This type of "tracking" perpetuated the perception of differences and further underscored the differences in "academic status" between the black and white students. Although it was laudable to provide remedial assistance when needed, the unintended outcome was further separation between students of different racial groups (Epstein, 1985; Schofield, 1982). Third, the traditional classroom encouraged a competitive rather than a cooperative orientation among students (e.g., students compete for grades, the teacher's attention). Finally, the traditional classroom situation does not foster close and sustained contact over time (i.e., children return to their segregated surroundings after school).

In practice, then, desegregation of schools through busing typically has not created the conditions necessary for positive intergroup contact. This situation is further complicated by the fact that there is a great deal of *resegregation* after the school bus arrives. That is, on the playground and at the lunch table students tend to gravitate to members of their own racial group (Epstein, 1985). Close intimate contact between members of different groups occurs infrequently even in desegregated schools. There is no guarantee that desegregation of schools will lead to the type of contact necessary to dispel stereotypes and create positive interactions between members of different groups. Similar concerns have been expressed about occupational settings in which minority group members are the beneficiaries of affirmative action policies (Pettigrew & Martin, 1987).

To address some of the limitations in the traditional classroom, Elliot Aronson and his colleagues (Aronson, Blaney, Stephan, Sikes, & Snapp, 1978; Aronson & Osherow, 1980) developed the *jigsaw classroom* technique. The jigsaw technique is a cooperative learning method that builds on the central tenets of the contact hypothesis. Specifically, children work together in multiethnic groups on standard course material. The jigsaw technique creates interdependence by employing peer teaching; each student is responsible for learning a subset of the assigned material and must teach that material to the other students in his or her group. For example, if students are to learn about John F. Kennedy's life, the material is subdivided into as many segments as there are students in each group (e.g., childhood, college, navy service, senator, president). Each student then learns one piece of the puzzle and then shares the material with the other students in the group. Although students are graded independently, the only way to complete the full puzzle (i.e., succeed) is to cooperate and learn from the other students. Thus, with the jigsaw method, students are engaged in a cooperative interdependent activity. Moreover, the task requires close and intimate contact among group members, and it is clearly sanctioned by the teacher (who serves as a facilitator but does not directly teach any material). Perhaps most important, because each student is put into the role of expert, students are of equal status in the learning situation.

Overall, the findings from the jigsaw classrooms are impressive and encouraging (Aronson, Blaney, Stephan, Sikes, & Snapp, 1978). Compared to students in traditional classrooms, students participating in the jigsaw classroom showed increases in peer liking across racial and ethnic groups, liked school more, and increased in self-esteem. Moreover, while the academic performance of minority group students improved, the academic performance of the majority group students was not adversely affected by the teaching method. The jigsaw technique is not likely to be a panacea for reducing intergroup hostilities, however. First, the technique is not likely to work well with all material (i.e., some material may be difficult to master without direct instruction). Second, it is not clear how much class time should be devoted to cooperative learning. Third, the jigsaw technique does not guarantee that the outcome of the cooperative learning task will be success. Low-competence group members can prohibit other group members from learning a segment of the material, and as noted previously, cooperative failure can escalate conflict and hostilities. Rosenfield, Stephan, and Lucker (1981) found that the jigsaw technique was not sufficient to eliminate negative evaluations of low-competence minority group members. These researchers suggested that low-competence minority group members were blamed for hindering the learning process of more competent students. A potentially dangerous outcome of this scenario is that the poor performance of minority group members may confirm negative stereotypes and expectancies. Such outcomes could feed into existing biases rather than eliminate them.

The literature on the contact hypothesis is large and complex. One limitation in this literature is that the beneficial effects of contact rarely generalize beyond the contact situation (i.e., contact has rarely produced changes in general prejudice) (Brewer & Miller, 1984; Stephan, 1985, 1987). The issue of how to promote the generalization of favorable changes beyond the specific contact situation has received scant attention. Furthermore, the complexity of the literature makes it difficult to draw firm conclusions about which aspects of cooperative intergroup contact promote favorable intergroup relations (Stephan, 1985, 1987). A second limitation of this literature is that although a long list of necessary conditions has been identified, until recently little attention has been devoted to examining the theoretical mechanisms that underlie the beneficial effects of cooperative interdependent contact (Brewer & Miller, 1984; Gaertner, Mann, Dovidio, Murrell, & Pomare, 1990). As the reader has probably noted, these issues are inextricably intertwined with the research on social categorization reviewed earlier in this chapter. For example, Gaertner and colleagues

(1990) suggested that the key process underlying the beneficial effects of cooperation involved recategorization of former out-group members as in-group members. We believe that focusing on such theoretical mechanisms will enable social psychologists to make further progress toward *understanding* how and why contact has its effects.

Contemporary Models of Prejudice and Prospects for Future Change

The contemporary models of prejudice take as their starting point that there has already been some change in racial attitudes. What do each of these models suggest about the possibility for further reductions in prejudice? The impression management perspective is rather pessimistic in its implications for future progress in reducing prejudice. In a sense, because overt, public expressions of low prejudiced beliefs are by definition untrustworthy, the impression management approach does not really allow for questioning of "old" beliefs and the development of new beliefs. In other words, it does not really allow for change.

Prospects for future change are also dim from the modern racism and aversive racism perspectives. Neither modern nor aversive racists see themselves as racist and, thus, have no need to change. In addition, modern and aversive racists are not consciously aware of their conflicted reactions. Change would require, at minimum, first becoming aware of their subtle negative biases. From the perspective of the ambivalence-amplification model, future change might be brought about by strengthening the egalitarian values to make the positive aspect of the attitudinal structure highly accessible (and more accessible than the negative aspect of their attitudinal structure). The most direct and encouraging prospects for further reductions in prejudice are found in the work following from Devine's (1989) dissociation model.

Devine and her colleagues have conceptualized the process of reducing prejudice as analogous to the process involved in breaking a bad habit. The undesirable response is the default response, and it must be inhibited and replaced with more desirable responses. As with breaking any habit, people are likely to meet with mixed success. Figure 12.3 depicts the processes involved in the prejudice reduction process (Devine & Monteith, 1993). Before examining the model in detail, note that (1) these processes are relevant to those who have renounced prejudice and are committed to responding to members of stereotyped groups in fair and nonprejudiced ways and that (2) reducing prejudice is not easily accomplished; it is a process that happens over time and with learning. Despite the difficult nature of the task, the empirical evidence suggests that with effort and practice people can learn to respond consistently with their nonprejudiced personal standards.

The entry point for the model is the establishment and internalization of nonprejudiced standards. However, establishing and internalizing nonprejudiced personal standards (i.e., defining oneself as low prejudiced) does not imply that change is complete. During the early phases of the prejudice reduction process, people are expected to follow the path indicated by the solid lines in Figure 12.3 (cf. Devine, 1989). That is, contact with members of a stereotyped

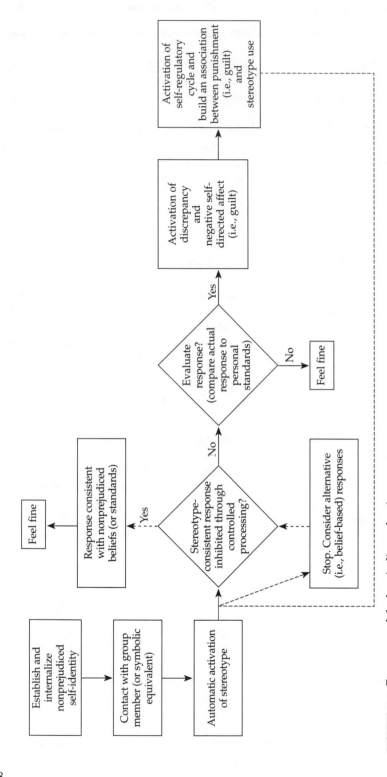

FIGURE 12.3 Process model of prejudice reduction.
From Devine & Monteith (1993).

group will lead to the automatic activation of the stereotype and its associated negative affect. Moreover, during these early phases of the prejudice reduction process, low prejudiced people are not expected to be particularly effective or efficient at using controlled processes to inhibit this activation. As a consequence, low prejudiced people are likely to experience discrepancies between their nonprejudiced standards and their actual responses. If they evaluate their actual responses and recognize them as being more prejudiced than their personal standards permit, they will experience a threat to their nonprejudiced self-identity. Such failure experiences are associated with feelings of negative self-directed affect such as guilt and self-criticism (Devine, Monteith, Zuwerink & Elliot, 1991; Monteith, Devine, & Zuwerink, 1993; Pressly & Devine, 1992; Zuwerink, Monteith, Devine, & Cook, 1994). If, however, low prejudiced people do not evaluate their actual prejudiced responses in light of their personal standards, they will exit the process and will not experience any negative affect.

The model indicates that discrepancies from well-internalized standards combined with negative self-directed affect instigate self-regulatory mechanisms (Monteith, 1993). These mechanisms appear to include self-focused attention that specifically concerns the prejudice-related discrepancy and enhanced attention to discrepancy relevant information (e.g., trying to assess what factors led to the discrepant response). The operation of these mechanisms enables low prejudiced individuals to build associations between (1) cues present when the discrepancy occurred, (2) the discrepant response, and (3) the negative self-directed affect. The consequence of building these associations is that on future occasions, the dashed lines shown in Figure 12.3 should be followed (see Devine & Monteith, 1993). Following stereotype activation, people should stop and consider belief-based alternative responses before actually generating a response. Thus, in the later phases of the change process, this additional event should enable individuals to avoid discrepancies and to generate responses that are, instead, consistent with their nonprejudiced beliefs and standards. The encouraging aspect of this model is that it suggests that people can benefit from their failure experiences and can make progress in learning to respond consistently with their nonprejudiced standards. Indeed, Monteith's (1993) research showed that discrepancies that were followed by guilt and self-regulatory processes actually enabled low prejudiced subjects to avoid a discrepant response on a future occasion. Although it is not easy and clearly requires effort, time, and practice, prejudice appears to be a habit that can be broken.

Despite the encouraging possibilities highlighted from this prejudice reduction model, the model focuses on the processes involved in overcoming prejudice among those who have already renounced prejudice and who have internalized nonprejudiced values. As such, it does not directly address the experiences of high prejudiced people. Although there is evidence that both society and individuals have made some progress in overcoming prejudice, the enduring challenge to prejudice theorists remains the same—to devise effective strategies for encouraging high prejudiced people to renounce prejudice and to take on the challenges associated with the prejudice reduction process.

CONCLUSIONS AND NEW CHALLENGES

The literature on prejudice and out-group perception is voluminous, and true to Allport's warning, the story of intergroup prejudice is not easily told. This somewhat selective sampling of the literature was geared toward identifying some of the pieces of the puzzle of intergroup prejudice, but the puzzle is far from complete. The literature does not yield simple and conclusive theoretical statements. The clearest conclusion that can be drawn from this literature is that the problem of intergroup prejudice is multifaceted, and as such, its solutions will have to be multifaceted as well. The complete puzzle of intergroup prejudice will require simultaneous consideration of individual psychological processes and the social and cultural systems in which individuals function.

Implicit in all the work on the origins of prejudice is the assumption that if we understood its origin, we could figure out how to reduce it and improve intergroup relations. Concern over improving intergroup relations is explicit in the work on prejudice reduction strategies. Before concluding the chapter, it is important to point out some limitations of the conceptualizations of prejudice and prejudice reduction reviewed in this chapter, particularly for addressing the issues of intergroup conflict and tension. Social psychologists have generally conceived of the problem of intergroup conflict and prejudice in terms of majority group members' negative attitudes toward minority group members. The key assumption in the literature is that if majority group members' attitudes became more positive, then positive interpersonal relations between majority and minority group members would follow. We believe that this analysis of intergroup prejudice is too global and incomplete to address the complex dynamics associated with intergroup conflict (see Devine, Evett, & Vasquez-Suson, in press, for a complete discussion).

First, although majority group members' negative attitudes clearly contribute to the problem of intergroup conflict, they are only part of the problem. As discussed in the previous section, even those with low prejudiced attitudes do not always behave in accord with those attitudes, responding instead with rather spontaneous negative responses. In addition, Evett and Devine (1993) recently found that some low prejudiced people who intend to respond consistently with their standards are anxious about their ability to do so. Specifically, their anxiety undermines their ability to positively interact with minority group members. These concerns are qualitatively distinct from the concerns high prejudiced people have about intergroup interaction (e.g., hostility, avoidance). Second, any analysis of intergroup conflict must consider the perspectives of both majority and minority group members and the reciprocal dynamics between these individuals when they come together in intergroup settings. The contact hypothesis, for example, offers little insight regarding either the perspective of minority group members or the nature of the interpersonal dynamics of contact situations (the direct attitude change strategies are equally deficient with regard to these issues). Indeed, surprisingly few studies in social psychology have afforded the opportunity to study the interpersonal dynamics of interactions between majority and minority group members, and the nature of the tensions that arise in intergroup contact situations (Stephan, 1987). This should be a high priority for future research.

We would also like to encourage greater attention to the perspective of minority group members in research on intergroup conflict. Historically, social psychological research on minority group members has focused on the long-term effects on self-esteem and adjustment as a consequence of being in a disadvantaged or otherwise stigmatized group. The literature has virtually ignored the role played by minority group members in interpersonal intergroup contact situations (see Ickes, 1984, for an exception). One theme that does consistently emerge in the literature, however, is that minority group members are generally mistrusting and suspicious of majority group members' intentions and motives (Crocker & Major, 1989; Crocker, Voekl, Testa, & Major, 1991; Duke & Morin, 1992; Feagin, 1989; Major & Crocker, 1993; Pettigrew & Martin, 1987). In an important program of research on minority group members' expectations for how they are likely to be treated by majority group members, Crocker, Major, and their colleagues (Crocker, Voekl, Testa, & Major, 1991) have shown that minority group members attribute both positive and negative performance feedback to prejudice when their minority group status is known by the majority group evaluators. Positive feedback was interpreted as an attempt to "appear" nonprejudiced despite actual prejudiced attitudes; negative feedback was interpreted to reflect prejudice directly (i.e., the majority group members' negative behaviors were consistent with their prejudiced attitudes). Anticipating negative reactions from majority group members and suspicion about majority group members' intentions or motives is likely to be a source of tension and potential miscommunication in intergroup contact settings (Devine, Evett, & Vasquez-Suson, in press).

This type of *attributional ambiguity* is likely to lead minority group members to experience a fair amount of stress and uncertainty about how to handle interpersonal encounters with majority group members. Are their suspicions valid (and how can they tell)? Should they act in accordance with their suspicions? What if they are wrong? The suspicions and uncertainties of minority group members are quite understandable in the context of a history of prejudice and discriminatory treatment. However, they could have adverse effects on the interpersonal aspects of intergroup contact (i.e., they may be ready to "see bias" when it is not present or intended). A failure to attend to such issues in our future explorations into the nature of intergroup conflict will leave us ill-equipped to explore the reciprocal dynamics of interpersonal, intergroup interaction and to develop strategies that will promote harmonious intergroup relations at the interpersonal level.

In summary, the problem of intergroup conflict and tension is much more than a majority group problem. We believe that the nature of intergroup tensions in interpersonal relations must be understood before intervention strategies to alleviate such tensions can be developed. To the extent that such tensions are not understood and addressed, there is the potential for them to escalate, and thus further impede the development of positive intergroup relations. The escalation of intergroup tensions and hostility is likely to be stressful for both minority and majority group members. In addition, the tension is likely to hinder people's functioning in many domains involving intergroup contact (e.g., educational, occupational). Such negative effects at the individual level will have cumulative, adverse effects for society as a whole. We believe that the research reviewed in this chapter helps us to unravel the complex knot Tajfel (1982) referred to in describing the nature of prejudice. We are confident that with continued work on the origins of intergroup prejudice and strategies for reducing it, we may be able to use our intelligence effectively to produce more harmonious intergroup relations.

List of Terms

ambivalence-amplification model   Theory of contemporary racial attitudes that holds that whites simultaneously possess conflicting positive and negative attitudes that derive from commitment to values of egalitarianism and individualism, respectively.

authoritarian personality   Personality trait characterized by rigidity, submissiveness to authority, and rejection of those who are different.

automatic processes   Cognitive processes that involve the unintentional activation of information in memory; they are initiated by the presence of environmental cues and are difficult to bypass.

aversive racism model   Theory of contemporary racial attitudes that holds that whites sincerely embrace egalitarian values, but also harbor unacknowledged negative beliefs and feelings giving rise to ambivalent reactions to blacks.

categorization   The process by which we perceive stimuli in groups rather than perceiving each individual stimulus in isolation from others. In social categorization, the stimuli of interest are people (e.g., blacks, women, lawyers, etc.).

contact hypothesis   The hypothesis that prejudice against a social group can be reduced by appropriate kinds of contact with members of that group (e.g., equal status contact, cooperative contact).

controlled processes   Cognitive processes that involve the intentional activation of information stored in memory; they require active attention and are limited by capacity.

decategorization   Removing group boundaries and labels so that no group structure exists and only individuals remain.

discrimination   The behavioral component of intergroup prejudice.

dissociation model   Contemporary theory of racial attitudes which argues that stereotypes are activated automatically for both low and high prejudiced persons and that activation of personal beliefs requires controlled processes.

ethnocentrism   The belief that the in-group is the center of the social world and superior to out-groups.

in-group   A group to which an individual belongs.

in-group favoritism   The tendency to give greater rewards or more positive evaluations to in-group than out-group members.

jigsaw classroom   A cooperative learning method used to reduce intergroup prejudice through interaction in group efforts.

old-fashioned racism   Old-fashioned stereotypes of white racial supremacy, segregation, and opposition to racial equality.

out-group   Any group other than the in-group.

prejudice   A negative intergroup attitude toward a socially defined group and toward any person perceived to be a member of that group.

minimal group paradigm   A research paradigm developed by Tajfel to examine intergroup bias, most specifically in-group favoritism. Subjects are arbitrarily assigned to groups and then allowed to allocate rewards to in-group and out-group members.

modern racism model   Theory of contemporary racial attitudes that holds that whites' disaffection for blacks is expressed indirectly and symbolically, in terms of opposition to policies designed to promote racial equality. It is specifically contrasted with old-fashioned (overt) forms of racism.

out-group homogeneity effect   The perception that out-group members are more similar to each other than in-group members are to each other.

realistic group conflict theory   A theory which argues that antagonism and hostilities between groups arises from real conflicts of interest, such as competition for resources.

recategorization   A strategy for altering existing group structures so that perceptions of group boundaries are modified. For example, an initial two-group representation can be recategorized to form one single, all-inclusive group.

social identity theory   The theory that people favor in-groups over out-groups in order to maintain or enhance their self-esteem.

stereotypes   Characteristics commonly associated with members of a social group.

superordinate goals   Shared goals that can only be achieved through cooperation.

symbolic racism   Antagonism toward a group based on symbols or values rather than self-interest.

ultimate attribution error   An attributional bias in which minority group members' negative behaviors and outcomes are seen as caused by dispositional qualities, whereas minority group positive behaviors are seen as caused by situational or transient factors.

References

ACKERMAN, N. W., & JAHODA, M. (1950). *Antisemitism and emotional disorder: A psychoanalytic interpretation.* New York: Harper.

ADORNO, T. W., FRENKEL-BRUNSWICK, E., LEVINSON, D. J., & SANFORD, R. N. (1950). *The authoritarian personality.* New York: Harper & Row.

ALLEN, V. L., & WILDER, D. A. (1975). Categorization, belief similarity, and intergroup discrimination. *Journal of Personality and Social Psychology, 32,* 971–977.

ALLEN, V. L., & WILDER, D. A. (1979). Group categorization and attitude belief of similarity. *Small Group Behavior, 10,* 73–80.

ALLPORT, G. W. (1954). *The nature of prejudice.* Reading, MA: Addison-Wesley.

ALTEMEYER, B. (1981). *Right-wing authoritarianism.* Winnipeg: University of Manitoba Press.

ALTEMEYER, B. (1988). *Enemies of freedom: Understanding right-wing authoritarianism.* San Francisco: Jossey-Bass.

AMIR, Y. (1969). Contact hypothesis in ethnic relations. *Psychological Bulletin, 71,* 319–342.

AMIR, Y. (1976). The role of intergroup contact in changes of prejudice and ethnic relations. In P. A. Katz (Ed.), *Towards the elimination of racism* (pp. 345–408). New York: Pergamon.

ARONSON, E., BLANEY, N., STEPHAN, C., SIKES, J., & SNAPP, M.(1978). *The jigsaw classroom.* Beverly Hills, CA: Sage.

ARONSON, E., & OSHEROW, N. (1980). Cooperation, prosocial behavior and academic performance: Experiments in the desegregated classroom. In L. Bickman (Ed.), *Applied social psychology annual*. Beverly Hills, CA: Sage.

ASHMORE, R. (1970). The problem of intergroup prejudice. In B. E. Collins (Ed.), *Social psychology* (pp. 245–296). Reading, MA: Addison-Wesley.

ASHMORE, R. D., & DEL BOCA, F. K. (1976). Psychological approaches to understanding intergroup conflict. In P. Katz (Ed.), *Towards the elimination of racism* (pp. 73–123). New York: Pergamon.

ASHMORE, R. D., & DEL BOCA, F. K. (1981). Conceptual approaches to stereotypes and stereotyping. In D. L. Hamilton (Ed.), *Cognitive processes in stereotyping and intergroup behavior* (pp. 1–35). Hillsdale, NJ: Erlbaum.

BANAJI, M. R., & GREENWALD, A. G. (1994). Implicit stereotyping and unconscious prejudice. In M. P. Zanna & J. M. Olson (Eds.), *The psychology of prejudice: The Ontario Symposium* (Vol. 7, pp. 55–76). Hillsdale, NJ: Erlbaum.

BILLIG, M., & TAJFEL, H. (1973). Social categorization and similarity in intergroup behavior. *European Journal of Social Psychology, 3,* 27–52.

BLANCHARD, F. A., WEIGEL, R. H., & COOK, S. W. (1975). The effect of relative competence of group members upon interpersonal attraction in cooperating interracial groups. *Journal of Personality and Social Psychology, 32,* 519–530.

BLAUNER, R. (1972). *Racial oppression in America.* New York: Harper & Row.

BODENHAUSEN, G. V., & WYER, R. S., JR. (1985). Effects of stereotypes on decision-making and information-processing strategies. *Journal of Personality and Social Psychology, 48,* 267–282.

BONACICH, E. (1972). A theory of ethnic antagonism: The split labor market. *American Sociological Review, 37,* 447–559.

BREWER, M. B. (1979). In-group bias in the minimal intergroup situation: A cognitive-motivational analysis. *Psychological Bulletin, 86,* 307–324.

BREWER, M. B. (1988). A dual process model of impression formation. In T. K. Srull & R. S. Wyer, Jr. (Eds.), *Advances in social cognition: Vol. 1. A dual process model of impression formation* (pp. 1–36). Hillsdale, NJ: Erlbaum.

BREWER, M. B., DULL, V., & LUI, L. (1981). Perceptions of the elderly: Stereotypes as prototypes. *Journal of Personality and Social Psychology, 41,* 656–670.

BREWER, M. B., HO, H., LEE, J., & MILLER, N. (1987). Social identity and social distance among Hong Kong school children. *Personality and Social Psychology Bulletin, 13,* 156–165.

BREWER, M. B., & KRAMER, R. M. (1985). The psychology of intergroup attitudes and behavior. *Annual Review of Psychology, 36,* 219–243.

BREWER, M. B., & LUI, L. (1984). Categorization of the elderly by the elderly: Effects of perceiver's category membership. *Personality and Social Psychology Bulletin, 10,* 585–595.

BREWER, M. B., & MILLER, N. (1984). Beyond the contact hypothesis: Theoretical perspectives on desegregation. In N. Miller & M. B. Brewer (Eds.), *Groups in contact: The psychology of desegregation* (pp. 281–302). Orlando: Academic Press.

BRIGHAM, J. C. (1971). Ethnic stereotypes. *Psychological Bulletin, 76,* 15–38.

BRIGHAM, J. C. (1972). Racial stereotypes: Measurement variables and the stereotypes-attitude relationship. *Journal of Applied Social Psychology, 2,* 63–76.

BROWN, R. J., & ABRAMS, D. (1986). The effects of intergroup similarity and goal interdependence on intergroup attitudes and task performance. *Journal of Experimental Social Psychology, 22,* 78–92.

BROWN, R. J., & TURNER, J. C. (1981). Interpersonal and intergroup behavior. In J. C.

Turner & H. Giles (Eds.), *Intergroup behavior* (pp. 33–65). Chicago: University of Chicago Press.

BURNSTEIN, E., & McRAE, A. V. (1962). Some effects of shared threat and prejudice in racially mixed groups. *Journal of Abnormal and Social Psychology, 64,* 257–263.

BUSS, A. H. (1961). *The psychology of aggression.* New York: Wiley.

CASPI, A. (1984). Contact hypothesis and inter-age attitudes: A field study of cross-age contact. *Social Psychology Quarterly, 47,* 74–80.

COHEN, C. E. (1981). Person categories and social perception: Testing some boundaries of the processing effects of prior knowledge. *Journal of Personality and Social Psychology, 40,* 441–452.

COHEN, E. (1980). Design and redesign of the desegregated school: Problems of status, power, and conflict. In W. G. Stephan & J. Feagin (Eds.), *School desegregation* (pp. 251–280). New York: Plenum.

COOK, S. W. (1978). Interpersonal and attitudinal outcomes operating in interracial groups. *Journal of Research in Development and Education, 12,* 97–113.

COOK, S. W. (1985). Experimenting on social issues: The case of school desegregation. *American Psychologist, 40,* 452–460.

COOPER, E., & JAHODA, M. (1947). The evasion of propaganda: How prejudiced people respond to antiprejudice propaganda. *Journal of Psychology, 23,* 15–25.

COX, O. (1948). *Caste, class and race: A study in social dynamics.* New York: Doubleday.

CROCKER, J., HANNAH, D. B., & WEBER, R. (1983). Person memory and causal attributions. *Journal of Personality and Social Psychology, 40,* 441–452.

CROCKER, J., & MAJOR, B. (1989). Social stigma and self-esteem: The self-protective properties of stigma. *Psychological Review, 96,* 608–630.

CROCKER, J., THOMPSON, L. L., McGRAW, K. M., & INGERMAN, C. (1987). Downward comparison, prejudice, and evaluation of others: Effects of self-esteem and threat. *Journal of Personality and Social Psychology, 52,* 907–916.

CROCKER, J., VOEKL, K., TESTA, M., & MAJOR, B. (1991). Social stigma: The affective consequences of attributional ambiguity. *Journal of Personality and Social Psychology, 60,* 218–228.

CROSBY, F., BROMLEY, S., & SAXE, L. (1980). Recent unobtrusive studies of black and white discrimination and prejudice: A literature review. *Psychological Bulletin, 87,* 546–563.

DARLEY, J. M., & GROSS, P. H. (1983). A hypothesis-confirming bias in labeling effects. *Journal of Personality and Social Psychology, 44,* 20–33.

DEAUX, K. (1976). Sex: A perspective on the attribution process. In J. H. Harvey & R. F. Kidd (Eds.), *New directions in attribution research* (Vol. 1, pp. 335–352). Hillsdale, NJ: Erlbaum.

DESCHAMPS, J. C., & DOISE, W. (1978). Crossed-category membership in intergroup relations. In H. Tajfel (Ed.), *Differentiation between social groups* (pp. 141–158). London: Academic Press.

DEUTSCH, M., & COLLINS, M. E. (1951). *Interracial housing: A psychological evaluation of a social experiment.* Minneapolis: University of Minnesota Press.

DEVINE, P. G. (1989). Stereotypes and prejudice: Their automatic and controlled components. *Journal of Personality and Social Psychology, 56,* 5–18.

DEVINE, P. G., & ELLIOT, A. J. (in press). Are racial stereotypes *really* fading? The Princeton trilogy revisited. *Personality and Social Psychology Bulletin.*

DEVINE, P. G., EVETT, S. R., & VASQUEZ-SUSON, K. (in press). Exploring the interpersonal dynamics of intergroup contact. In R. Sorrentino & E. T. Higgins (Eds.), *Handbook of motivation and cognition: The interpersonal context* (Vol. 3). New York: Gullford.

Devine, P. G., Monteith, M. J., Zuwerink, J. R., & Elliot, A. J. (1991). Prejudice with and without compunction. *Journal of Personality and Social Psychology, 60,* 817–830.

Devine P. G., & Monteith, M. J. (1993). The role of discrepancy-associated affect in prejudice reduction. In D. M. Mackie & D. L. Hamilton (Eds.), *Affect, cognition, and stereotyping: Interactive processes in intergroup perception* (pp. 317–344). San Diego: Academic Press.

Doise, W. (1978). *Groups and individuals: Explanations in social psychology.* Cambridge: Cambridge University Press.

Doise, W., Csepeli, G., Dann, H. Gouge, C., Larsen, K., & Ostell, A. (1972). An experimental investigation into the formation of intergroup relations. *European Journal of Social Psychology, 2,* 202–204.

Dovidio, J. F., Evans, N., & Tyler, R. B. (1986). Racial stereotypes: The contents of their cognitive representations. *Journal of Experimental Social Psychology, 22,* 22–37.

Dovidio, J. F., & Fazio, R. H. (1992). New technoligies for the direct and indirect assessment of attitudes. In J. M. Tanur (Ed.), *Questions about questions: Inquiries into the cognitive bases of surveys* (pp. 204–237). New York: Russell Sage Foundation.

Dovidio, J. F., & Gaertner, S. L. (1986). Prejudice, discrimination, and racism: Historical trends and contemporary approaches. In J. F. Dovidio & S. L. Gaertner (Eds.), *Prejudice, discrimination, and racism* (pp. 1–34). San Diego: Academic Press.

Dovidio, J. F., & Gaertner, S. L. (1993). Stereotypes and evaluative intergroup bias. In D. M. Mackie & D. L. Hamilton (Eds.), *Affect, cognition, and stereotyping: Interactive processes in intergroup perception* (pp. 167–193). San Diego: Academic Press.

Dovidio, J. F., Tobriner, M., Rioux, S., & Gaertner, S. L. (1991). Say "we": Priming interpersonal expectations. Unpublished manuscript. Department of Psychology, Colgate University, Hamilton, NY.

Duckitt, J. (1992a). *The social psychology of prejudice.* New York: Praeger.

Duckitt, J. (1992b). Psychology and prejudice: A historical analysis and integrative framework. *American Psychologist, 47,* 1182–1193.

Duke, L., & Morin, R. (1992, March 8). Focusing on race: Candid dialogue, elusive answers. *Washington Post.*

Duncan, S. L. (1976). Differential social perception and attribution of intergroup violence: Testing the lower limits of the stereotyping of Blacks. *Journal of Personality and Social Psychology, 34,* 590–598.

Epstein, J. L. (1985). After the bus arrives: Resegregation in desegregated schools. *Journal of Social Issues, 41,* 23–43.

Evett, S. R., & Devine, P. G. (1993). *Prejudice and the nature of intergroup tension.* Paper presented at the 65th annual meeting of the Midwestern Psychological Association, Chicago.

Feagin, J. R. (1989). The continuing significance of race: Antiblack discrimination in public places. *American Sociological Review, 56,* 101–116.

Ferguson, C. K., & Kelley, H. H. (1964). Significant factors in overvaluation of own group's products. *Journal of Abnormal and Social Psychology, 69,* 223–228.

Fiske, S. T., & Neuberg, S. L. (1990). A continuum of impression formation, from category-based to individuating processes: Influences of information and motivation on attention and interpretation. In M. P. Zanna (Ed.), *Advances in experimental social psychology* (Vol. 23, pp. 1–63). San Diego: Academic Press.

Flowerman, S. H. (1947). Mass propaganda in the war against bigotry. *Journal of Abnormal and Social Psychology, 47,* 429–439.

Gaertner, S. L., & Dovidio, J. F. (1986). The aversive form of racism. In J. F. Dovidio & S. L. Gaertner (Eds.), *Prejudice, discrimination, and racism* (pp. 61–89). San Diego: Academic Press.

GAERTNER, S. L., DOVIDIO, J. F., ANASTASIO, P. A., BACHMAN, B. A., & RUST, M. C. (1993). The common intergroup identity model: Recategorization and the reduction of intergroup bias. In W. Stroebe & M. Hewstone (Eds.), *European review of social psychology* (Vol. 4, pp. 1–26). New York: John Wiley.

GAERTNER, S. L., MANN, J., DOVIDIO, J. F., MURRELL, A., & POMARE, M. (1990). How does cooperation reduce intergroup bias? *Journal of Personality and Social Psychology, 59,* 692–704.

GAERTNER, S. L., MANN, J., MURRELL, A., & DOVIDIO, J. F. (1989). Reducing intergroup bias: The benefits of recategorization. *Journal of Personality and Social Psychology, 57,* 239–249.

GIBBONS, F. X., STEPHAN, W. G., STEPHENSON, B., & PETTY, C. R. (1981). Contact relevance and reactions to stigmatized others: Response amplification vs. sympathy. *Journal of Experimental Social Psychology, 16,* 591–605.

GILBERT, D. T., & HIXON, J. G. (1991). The trouble with thinking: Activation and application of stereotypic beliefs. *Journal of Personality and Social Psychology, 60,* 509–517.

GREELEY, A., & SHEATSLEY, P. (1971). Attitudes toward racial integration. *Scientific American, 222,* 13–19.

GREENWALD, A. G., & BANAJI, M. R. (in press). Implicit social cognition: Attitudes, self-esteem, and stereotypes. *Psychological Review.*

HAMIL, R., WILSON, T. D., & NISBETT, R. E. (1980). Insensitivity to sample bias: Generalizing from atypical cases. *Journal of Personality and Social Psychology, 39,* 578–589.

HAMILTON, D. L. (1981). *Cognitive processes in stereotyping and intergroup behavior.* Hillsdale, NJ: Erlbaum.

HAMILTON, D. L., CARPENTER, S., & BISHOP, G. D. (1984). Desegregation in suburban neighborhoods. In N. Miller & M. B. Brewer (Eds.), *Groups in contact: The psychology of desegregation* (pp. 97–121). Orlando: Academic Press.

HAMILTON, D. L., & ROSE, T. L. (1980). Illusory correlation and the maintenance of stereotypic beliefs. *Journal of Personality and Social Psychology, 46,* 44–56.

HAMILTON, D. L., & TROLIER, T. K. (1986). Stereotypes and stereotyping: An overview of the cognitive approach. In J. F. Dovidio & S. L. Gaertner (Eds.), *Prejudice, discrimination, and racism.* Orlando: Academic Press.

HARDING, J., KUNTER, B., PROSHANSKY, H., & CHEIN, I. (1954). Prejudice and ethnic relations. In G. Lindzey (Ed.), *The handbook of social psychology* (Vol. II, pp. 1021–1061). Cambridge, MA: Addison-Wesley.

HASS, R. G., KATZ, I., RIZZO, N., BAILEY, J., AND MOORE, L. (1992). When racial ambivalence evokes negative affect, using a disguised measure of mood. *Personality and Social Psychology Bulletin, 18,* 786–797.

HEWSTONE, M., JASPARS, J., & LALLJEE, M. (1982). Social representations, social attribution and social identity: The intergroup images of "public" and "comprehensive" schoolboys. *European Journal of Social Psychology, 12,* 241–269.

HOCHSCHILD, J. L., & HERK, M. (1990). "Yes, but . . .": Principles and caveats in American racial attitudes. In J. W. Chapman & A. W. Wertheimer (Eds.), *Majorities and minorities* (pp. 308–335). New York: New York University Press.

HOGG, M. A., & ABRAMS, D. (1988). *Social identifications: A social psychology of intergroup relations and intergroup processes.* New York: Rutledge.

HOGG, M. A., & TURNER, J. C. (1987). Intergroup behaviour, self-stereotyping and the salience of social categories. *British Journal of Social Psychology, 26,* 325–340.

HORNSTEIN, H. A. (1976). *Cruelty and kindness: A new look at aggression and altruism.* Englewood Cliffs, NJ: Prentice-Hall.

HOWARD, J. M., & ROTHBART, M. (1980). Social categorization and memory for in-group and out-group behavior. *Journal of Personality and Social Psychology, 38,* 301–310.

HYMAN, H. H., & SHEATSLEY, P. B. (1956). Attitudes toward desegregation. *Scientific American, 195,* 35–39.

HYMAN, H. H., & SHEATSLEY, P. B. (1964). Attitudes toward desegregation. *Scientific American, 211,* 16–23.

ICKES, W. (1984). Compositions in black and white: Determinants of interaction in inter-racial dyads. *Journal of Personality and Social Psychology, 47,* 330–341.

JAMIESON, D. W., & ZANNA, M. P. (1989). Need for structure in attitude formation and ex-pression. In A. R. Pratkanis, S. J. Breckler, & A. G. Greenwald (Eds.), *Attitude struc-ture and function* (pp. 383–406). Hillsdale, NJ: Erlbaum.

JONES, E. E., & SIGALL, H. (1971). The bogus pipeline: A new paradigm for measuring af-fect and attitude. *Psychological Bulletin, 76,* 349–364.

JONES, E. E., WOOD, G. C., & QUATTRONE, G. A. (1981). Perceived variability of personal characteristics in in-groups and out-groups: The role of knowledge and evaluation. *Personality and Social Psychology Bulletin, 7,* 523–528.

JONES, J. M. (1972). *Prejudice and racism.* Reading, MA: Addison-Wesley.

JUDD, C. M., & PARK, B. (1988). Out-group homogeneity: Judgments of variability at the individual and group levels. *Journal of Personality and Social Psychology, 54,* 778–788.

KATZ, D., & BRALY, K. (1933). Racial stereotypes in 100 college students. *Journal of Abnormal and Social Psychology, 28,* 280–290.

KATZ, I. (1981). *Stigma: A social psychological analysis.* Hillsdale, NJ: Erlbaum.

KATZ, I., GLASS, D. C., & COHEN, S. (1973). Ambivalence, guilt, and the scapegoating of minority group victims. *Journal of Experimental Social Psychology, 9,* 423–436.

KATZ, I., GLASS, D. C., LUCIDO, D. J., & FARBER, J. (1979). Harm-doing and victim's racial or orthopedic stigma as determinants of helping behavior. *Journal of Personality, 47,* 430–434.

KATZ, I., & HASS, R. G. (1988). Racial ambivalence and American value conflict: Correlational and priming studies of dual cognitive structures. *Journal of Personality and Social Psychology, 55,* 893–905.

KATZ, I., WACKENHUT, J., & HASS, R. G. (1986). Racial ambivalence, value duality, and be-havior. In J. F. Dovidio & S. L. Gaertner (Eds.), *Prejudice, discrimination, and racism* (pp. 35–60). San Diego: Academic Press.

KATZ, P. A. (1973). Stimulus differentiation and modification of children's racial atti-tudes. *Child Development 44,* 232–237.

KATZ, P. A. (1976). The acquisition of racial attitudes in children. In P. A. Katz (Ed.), *Towards the elimination of racism* (pp. 125–164). New York: Pergamon Press.

KATZ, P. A., & ZALK, S. R. (1978). Modification of children's racial attitudes. *Developmental Psychology, 14,* 447–461.

KINDER, D. R., & SEARS, D.O. (1981). Prejudice and politics: Symbolic racism versus racial threats to the good life. *Journal of Personality and Social Psychology, 40,* 414–431.

KLATZKY, R. L., MARTIN, G. L., & KANE, R. A. (1982). Increase in social category activation on processing of visual information. *Social Cognition, 1,* 95–109.

KLINGER, M., & BEALL, P. (1992). *Conscious and unconscious effects of stereotype activation.* Paper presented at the 64th annual meeting of the Midwestern Psychological Association, Chicago.

KOVEL, J. (1970). *White racism: A psychohistory.* New York: Pantheon.

KRAMER, R. M., & BREWER, M. B. (1984). Effects of group identity on resource use in a sim-ulated commons dilemma. *Journal of Personality and Social Psychology, 46,* 1044–1056.

LANGER, E. J., BASHNER, R. S., CHANOWITZ, B. (1985). Decreasing prejudice by increasing discrimination. *Journal of Personality and Social Psychology, 49,* 113–120.

LaPIERE, R. T. (1934). Attitude vs. actions. *Social Forces, 13,* 230–237.

LEMYRE, L., & SMITH, P. M. (1985). Intergroup discrimination and self-esteem in the minimal group paradigm. *Journal of Personality and Social Psychology, 49,* 660–670.

LEVINE, R. A., & CAMPBELL, D. T. (1972). *Ethnocentrism: Theories of conflict, ethnic attitudes and group behavior.* New York: Wiley.

LINVILLE, P. W. (1982). The complexity-extremity effect and age-based stereotyping. *Journal of Personality and Social Psychology, 42,* 192–211.

LINVILLE, P. W., & JONES, E. E. (1980). Polarized appraisals of outgroup members. *Journal of Personality and Social Psychology, 38,* 689–703.

LINVILLE, P. W., SALOVEY, P., & FISCHER, G. W. (1986). Stereotyping and perceived distributions of social characteristics: An application to ingroup-outgroup perception. In J. F. Dovidio & S. L. Gaertner (Eds.), *Prejudice, discrimination, and racism* (pp. 165–208). San Diego: Academic Press.

LIPPMAN, W. (1922). *Public opinion.* New York: Harcourt Brace Jovanovich.

LOCKSLEY, A., ORTIZ, V., & HEPBURN, C. (1980). Social categorization and discriminatory behavior: Extinguishing the minimal intergroup discriminatory effect. *Journal of Personality and Social Psychology, 39,* 773–783.

MAASS, A., SALVI, D., ARCURI, L., & SEMIN, G. (1989). Language use in intergroup contexts: The linguistic intergroup bias. *Journal of Personality and Social Psychology, 57,* 981–993.

MAJOR, B., & CROCKER, J. (1993). Social stigma: The consequences of attributional ambiguity. In D. M. Mackie & D. L. Hamilton (Eds.), *Affect, cognition, and stereotyping: Interactive processes in intergroup perception* (pp. 345–370). San Diego: Academic Press.

McCONAHAY, J. B. (1986). Modern racism, ambivalence, and the Modern Racism Scale. In J. F. Dovidio & S. L. Gaertner (Eds.), *Prejudice, discrimination, and racism* (pp. 91–125). San Diego: Academic Press.

McCONAHAY, J. B., & HOUGH, J. C., JR. (1976). Symbolic racism. *Journal of Social Issues, 32,* 23–45.

McGARTY, C., & PENNY, R. (1988). Categorization, accentuation, and social judgment. *British Journal of Social Psychology, 27,* 147–157.

MEINDL, J. R., & LERNER, M. J. (1984). Exacerbation of extreme responses to an outgroup. *Journal of Personality and Social Psychology, 47,* 71–84.

MESSICK, D. M., & MACKIE, D. M. (1989). Intergroup relations. *Annual Review of Psychology, 40,* 51–81.

MILLER, N., & BREWER, M. B. (1986). Categorization effects on ingroup and outgroup perception. In J. F. Dovidio & S. L. Gaertner (Eds.), *Prejudice, discrimination, and racism* (pp. 209–230). San Diego: Academic Press.

MILLER, N., BREWER, M. B., & EDWARDS, K. (1985). Cooperative interaction in desegregated settings: A laboratory analogue. *Journal of Social Issues, 41,* 63–75.

MONTEITH, M. J. (1993). Self-regulation of prejudiced responses: Implications for progress in prejudice reduction. *Journal of Personality and Social Psychology, 65,* 469–485.

MONTEITH, M. J., DEVINE, P. G., & ZUWERINK, J. R. (1993). Self-directed vs. other-directed affect as a consequence of prejudice-related discrepancies. *Journal of Personality and Social Psychology, 64,* 198–210.

MONTEITH, M. J., ZUWERINK, J. R., & DEVINE, P. G. (1994). Prejudice reduction: Classic challenges, contemporary approaches. In P. G. Devine, D. L. Hamilton, & T. M. Ostrom (Eds.), *Social cognition: Impact on social psychology* (pp. 323–346). San Diego: Academic Press.

MULLEN, B., & HU, L. T. (1989). Perceptions of ingroup and outgroup variability: A meta-analytic integration. *Basic and Applied Social Psychology, 10,* 233–252.

MYERS, D. G., & BISHOP, G. D. (1970). Discussion effects on racial attitudes. *Science, 169,* 778–789.

MYRDAL, G. (1944). *An American dilemma.* New York: Harper & Row.

NEELY, J. H. (1977). Semantic priming and retrieval from lexical memory: Roles of inhibitionless spreading activation and limited-capacity attention. *Journal of Experimental Psychology, 106,* 226–254.

OAKES, P. J., & TURNER, J. C. (1980). Social categorization and intergroup behavior: Does the minimal intergroup situation make social identity more positive? *European Journal of Social Psychology, 10,* 295–301.

OLZAK, S., & NAGEL, J. (1986). *Competitive ethnic relations.* New York: Academic Press.

PARK, B., & ROTHBART, M. (1982). Perception of outgroup homogeneity and levels of social categorization: Memory for the subordinate attributes of ingroup and outgroup members. *Journal of Personality and Social Psychology, 42,* 1050–1060.

PERDUE, C. W., DOVIDIO, J. F., GURTMAN, M. B., & TYLER, R. B. (1990). "Us" and "Them": Social categorization and the process of intergroup bias. *Journal of Personality and Social Psychology, 59,* 475–486.

PERDUE, C. W., & GURTMAN, M. B. (1990). Evidence for the automaticity of ageism. *Journal of Experimental Social Psychology, 26,* 199–216.

PETERSON, W. (1958). Prejudice in American society: A critique of some recent formulations. *Commentary, 26,* 342–348.

PETTIGREW, T. F. (1979). The ultimate attribution error: Extending Allport's cognitive analysis of prejudice. *Personality and Social Psychology Bulletin, 5,* 461–476.

PETTIGREW, T. F., & MARTIN, J. (1987). Shaping the organizational context for Black American inclusion. *Journal of Social Issues, 43,* 41–78.

PILIAVIN, J. A., DOVIDIO, J. F., GAERTNER, S. L., & CLARK, R. D., III (1981). *Emergency intervention.* New York: Academic Press.

POSNER, M. I., & SNYDER, C. R. R. (1977). Attention and cognitive control. In R. L. Solso (Ed.), *Information processing and cognition: The Loyola symposium* (pp. 55–85). Hillsdale, NJ: Erlbaum.

PRESSLY, S. L., & DEVINE, P. G. (1992). *Sex, sexism, and compunction: Group membership or internalization of standards?* Paper presented at the 64th annual meeting of the Midwestern Psychological Association, Chicago.

PROSHANSKY, H. M. (1966). The development of intergroup attitudes. In L. W. Hoffman & M. L. Hoffman (Eds.), *Review of child development research* (pp. 311–371). New York: Russell Sage.

QUATTRONE, G. A. (1986). On the perception of a group's variability. In S. Worchel & W. G. Austin (Eds.), *Psychology of intergroup relations* (2nd ed.). Chicago, IL: Nelson-Hall.

QUATTRONE, G. A., & JONES, E. E. (1980). The perception of variability within ingroups and outgroups: Implications for the law of small numbers. *Journal of Personality and Social Psychology, 38,* 141–152.

RABBIE, J. M. (1982). The effects of intergroup competition and cooperation on intragroup and intergroup relationships. In V. J. Derlega & J. Grezlak (Eds.), *Cooperation and helping behavior: Theories and research* (pp. 123–149). New York: Academic Press.

RABBIE, J. M., & HOROWITZ, M. (1969). Arousal of ingroup-outgroup bias by a chance win or loss. *Journal of Personality and Social Psychology, 13,* 269–277.

RASPBERRY, W. (1993, April 15). The "us-them" college culture. *The Washington Post,* p. 29.

RIST, C. (1974). Race, policy, and schooling. *Society, 12,* 59–63.

ROKEACH, M. (1973). *The nature of human values.* New York: Free Press.

ROKEACH, M., SMITH, P., & EVANS, R. (1960). Two kinds of prejudice or one? In M. Rokeach (Ed.), *The open and the closed mind* (pp. 132–168). New York: Basic Books.

ROSE, A. M. (1951). *The roots of prejudice*. Paris: UNESCO.

ROSENBAUM, M. E., & HOLTZ, R. (1985). *The minimal intergroup discrimination effect: Outgroup derogation, not ingroup favoritism*. Paper presented at the 93rd Annual Convention of the American Psychological Association, Los Angeles.

ROSENFIELD, D., STEPHAN, W. G., & LUCKER, G. W. (1981). Attraction to competent and incompetent members of cooperative and competitive groups. *Journal of Applied Social Psychology, 11,* 416–433.

ROTHBART, M., EVANS, M., & FULERO, S. (1979). Recall for confirming events: Memory processes and the maintenance of social stereotypes. *Journal of Experimental Social Psychology, 15,* 343–355.

ROTHBART, M., & JOHN, O. (1985). Social categorization and behavior episodes: A cognitive analysis of the effects of intergroup contact. *Journal of Social Issues, 41,* 81–104.

SAGAR, H. A., & SCHOFIELD, J. W. (1980). Racial and behavioral cues in black and white children's perceptions of ambiguously aggressive acts. *Journal of Personality and Social Psychology, 39,* 590–598.

SCHLESINGER, A. M. (1992). *The disuniting of America*. New York: Norton.

SCHNEIDER, W., & SHIFFRIN, R. M. (1977). Controlled and automatic human information processing: I. Detection, search and attention. *Psychological Review, 84,* 1–66.

SCHOFIELD, J. W. (1982). *Black and white in school: Trust, tension, or tolerance?* New York: Praeger.

SCHUMAN, H., STEEH, C., & BOBO, L. (1985). *Racial attitudes in America: Trends and interpretation*. Cambridge, MA: Harvard University Press.

SEARS, D. O., & KINDER, D. R. (1985). Whites' opposition to busing: On conceptualizing and operationalizing group conflict. *Journal of Personality and Social Psychology, 48,* 1141–1147.

SEARS, D. O., & MCCONAHAY, J. B. (1973). *The politics of violence: The new urban blacks and the Watts riot*. Boston: Houghton Mifflin. Reprinted by University Press of America, 1981.

SHERIF, M., HARVEY, O. J., WHITE, B. J., HOOD, W. R., & SHERIF, C. (1954). *Experimental study of positive and negative intergroup attitudes between experimentally produced groups: Robbers Cave experiment*. Norman, OK: University of Oklahoma.

SHERIF, M., & SHERIF, C. W. (1953). *Groups in harmony and tension*. New York: Harper.

SHERMAN, S. J., & GORKIN, L. (1980). Attitude bolstering when behavior is inconsistent with central attitudes. *Journal of Experimental Social Psychology, 16,* 388–403.

SHIFFRIN, R. M., & DUMAIS, S. T. (1981). The development of automatism. In J. R. Anderson (Ed.), *Cognitive skills and their acquisition* (pp. 111–140). Hillsdale, NJ: Erlbaum.

SHIFFRIN, R. M., & SCHNEIDER, W. (1977). Controlled and automatic human information processing: II. Perceptual learning, automatic attending, and a general theory. *Psychological Review, 84,* 127–190.

SIMPSON, G. E., & YINGER, J. M. (1965). *Racial and cultural minorities*. New York: Plenum Press.

SIMPSON, G. E., & YINGER, J. M. (1985). *Racial and cultural minorities* (5th ed). New York: Plenum Press.

SLAVIN, R. E. (1985). Cooperative learning: Applying contact theory in desegregated schools. *Journal of Social Issues, 41,* 45–62.

SLAVIN, R. E., & MADDEN, N. A. (1979). School practices that improve social relations. *American Education Research Journal, 16,* 169–180.

SMITH, E. R., & BRANSCOMBE, N. R. (1986). *Stereotypes can be processed automatically.* Unpublished manuscript, Purdue University, Lafayette, Indiana.

SNYDER, M., & SWANN, W. B., JR. (1978). Hypothesis-testing processes in social interaction. *Journal of Personality and Social Psychology, 36,* 1202–1212.

SNYDER, M., TANKE, E. D., & BERSCHEID, E. (1977). Social perception and interpersonal behavior: On the self-fulfilling nature of social stereotypes. *Journal of Personality and Social Psychology, 35,* 656–666.

SNYDER, M., & URANOWITZ, S. W. (1978). Reconstructing the past: Some cognitive consequences of person perception. *Journal of Personality and Social Psychology, 36,* 941–950.

STAATS, C. K., & STAATS, A. W. (1958). Attitudes established by conditioning. *Journal of Abnormal and Social Psychology, 57,* 74–80.

STANGOR, C., LYNCH, L., DUAN, C., & GLASS, B. (1992). Categorization of individuals on the basis of multiple social categories. *Journal of Personality and Social Psychology, 62,* 207–218.

STEELE, S. (1990). *The content of our character: A new vision of race in America.* New York: Harper Collins.

STEIN, D. D., HARDYCK, J. A., & SMITH, M. B. (1965). Race *and* belief: An open and shut case. *Journal of Personality and Social Psychology, 1,* 281–299.

STEPHAN, W. G. (1985). Intergroup relations. In G. Lindzey & E. Aronson (Eds.), *The handbook of social psychology* (3rd ed., Vol. 2, pp. 599–658). New York: Random House.

STEPHAN, W. G. (1987). The contact hypothesis in intergroup relations. In C. Hendrick (Ed.), *Group processes in intergroup relations: Review of personality and social psychology* (Vol. 9, pp. 13–40). Newbury Park, CA: Sage.

STEPHAN, W. G., & STEPHAN, C. W. (1985). Intergroup anxiety. *Journal of Social Issues, 41,* 157–175.

STOUFFER, S. A., SUCHMAN, E. A., DEVINNEY, L. C., STAR, S. A., & WILLIAMS, R. M., JR. (1949). *The American soldier: Adjustment during army life.* New York: Wiley.

STROEBE, W., & INSKO, C. A. (1989). Stereotype, prejudice, and discrimination: Changing conceptions in theory and research. In D. Bar-Tal, C. F. Graumann, A. W. Kruglanski, & W. Stroebe (Eds.), *Stereotyping and prejudice: Changing conceptions* (pp. 3–34). Berlin: Springer.

TAJFEL, H. (1981). *Human groups as social categories.* Cambridge: Cambridge University Press.

TAJFEL, H. (1982). Social psychology of intergroup attitudes. *Annual Review of Psychology, 33,* 1–39.

TAJFEL, H., FLAMENT, C., BILLIG, M. G., & BUNDY, R. F. (1971). Social categorization: An intergroup phenomenon. *European Journal of Social Psychology, 1,* 149–177.

TAJFEL, H., & TURNER, J. C. (1979). An integrative theory of intergroup conflict. In W. Austin & S. Worchel (Eds.), *The social psychology of intergroup relations* (pp. 33–47). Monterey, California: Brooks/Cole.

TAJFEL, H., & TURNER, J. C. (1986). The social identity theory of intergroup behavior. In S. Worschel & W. G. Austin (Eds.), *Psychology of intergroup relations* (2nd ed., pp. 7–24). Chicago: Nelson-Hall.

TAJFEL, H., & WILKES, A. (1963). Classification and quantitative judgment. *British Journal of Psychology, 54,* 101–114.

TAYLOR, D. G., SHEATSLEY, P. B., & GREELEY, A. M. (1978). Attitudes toward racial integration. *Scientific American, 238,* 42–49.

TAYLOR, D. M., & JAGGI, V. (1974). Ethnocentrism and causal attribution in a South Indian context. *Journal of Cross-Cultural Psychology, 5,* 162–171.

TAYLOR, S. E. (1981). A categorization approach to stereotyping. In D. L. Hamilton (Ed.),

Cognitive processes in stereotyping and intergroup behavior (pp. 83–114). Hillsdale, NJ: Erlbaum.

TAYLOR, S. E., & FALCONE, H. (1982). Cognitive bases of stereotyping: The relationship between categorization and prejudice. *Personality and Social Psychology Bulletin, 8,* 426–432.

TAYLOR, S. E., FISKE, S. T., ETCOFF, N. L., & RUDDERMAN A. J. (1978). Categorical bases of person memory and stereotyping. *Journal of Personality and Social Psychology, 26,* 778–793.

TURNER, J. C. (1981). The experimental social psychology of intergroup behavior. In J. C. Turner & H. Giles (Eds.), *Intergroup behavior* (pp. 1–32). Chicago: University of Chicago Press.

TURNER, J. C. (1987). *Rediscovering the social group: A self-categorization theory.* Oxford, UK: Basil Blackwell.

VAN DEN BERGHE, P. L. (1967). Race attitudes in Durban, South Africa. *Journal of Social Psychology, 57,* 55–72.

WANG, H., & MCKILLIP, J. (1978). Ethnic identification and judgments of an accident. *Personality and Social Psychology Bulletin, 4,* 296–299.

WICKER, A. (1969). Attitudes vs. actions: The relationship of verbal and overt behavioral responses to attitude objects. *Journal of Social Issues, 25,* 41–78.

WILDER, D. A. (1978). Reduction of intergroup discrimination through individuation of the outgroup. *Journal of Personality and Social Psychology, 36,* 1361–1374.

WILDER, D. A. (1981). Perceiving persons as groups: Categorization and intergroup relations. In D. L. Hamilton (Ed.), *Cognitive processes in stereotyping and intergroup behavior* (pp. 213–257). Hillsdale, NJ: Erlbaum.

WILDER, D. A., & SHAPIRO, P. (1991). Facilitation of outgroup stereotype by enhanced ingroup identity. *Journal of Experimental Social Psychology, 27,* 431–452.

WILLIAMS, R. M., JR. (1947). *The reduction of intergroup tensions: A survey on research problems of ethnic, racial, and religious group relations.* New York: Plenum Press.

WILLS, T. A. (1981). Downward social comparison and principles in social psychology. *Psychological Bulletin, 90,* 245–271.

WORCHEL, S. (1979). Cooperation and the reduction of intergroup conflict: Some determining factors. In W. G. Austin & S. Worchel (Eds.), *The social psychology of intergroup relations.* Monterey, CA: Brooks/Cole.

WORCHEL, S. (1986). The role of cooperation in reducing intergroup conflict. In S. Worchel & W. G. Austin (Eds.), *Psychology of intergroup relations* (2nd ed., pp. 288–304). Chicago: Nelson-Hall.

WORCHEL, S., & NORVELL, N. (1980). Effect of perceived environmental conditions during cooperation on intergroup attraction. *Journal of Personality and Social Psychology, 38,* 764–772.

WORD, C. O., ZANNA, M. P., & COOPER, J. (1974). The nonverbal mediation of self-fulfilling prophecies in interracial interaction. *Journal of Experimental Social Psychology, 10,* 109–120.

ZUWERINK, J. R., MONTEITH, M. J., DEVINE, P. G., & COOK, D. (1994). *Prejudice toward Blacks: With and without compunction?* Unpublished manuscript, University of Wisconsin, Madison, WI.

Further Readings

ALLPORT, G. W. (1954). *The nature of prejudice.* Reading, MA: Addison Wesley.
    Allport's book is a "must read" for students of prejudice and intergroup relations.

It is a classic, but is also remarkably contemporary. It is a rich source of good ideas and hypotheses about the nature and consequences of prejudice.

DOVIDIO, J. F., & GAERTNER, S. L. (Eds.). (1986). *Prejudice, discrimination, and racism.* San Diego: Academic Press.

Dovidio and Gaertner's book summarizes the research programs of a number of influential theorists in contemporary prejudice research. It provides analysis of both majority and minority group perspectives and a discussion of the color-blind society notion.

DUCKITT, J. (1992). *The social psychology of prejudice.* New York: Praeger.

Duckitt's volume is a fairly comprehensive summary of theory and research on the origins of prejudice. It provides a clear analysis of the current state of research on classic issues in the literature on prejudice and suggests important new directions for research.

JONES, J. M. (1972). *Prejudice and racism.* New York: Random House.

Jones provides a thoughtful analysis of the historical factors that contribute to the development and maintenance of prejudice in our society. It is a highly readable and thought-provoking summary of the relevance of social psychological research for understanding prejudice.

MACKIE, D. M., & HAMILTON, D. L. (Eds.). (1993). *Affect, cognition, and stereotyping: Interactive processes in intergroup perception.* San Diego: Academic Press.

Mackie and Hamilton's volume provides readers with a summary of the most recent research on a variety of stereotype-related phenomena and their relevance to intergroup perception. The chapters, written by experts in the field, set an agenda for future research in the study of intergroup processes.

MILLER, N., & BREWER, M. B. (Eds.). (1984). *Groups in contact: The psychology of desegregation.* San Diego: Academic Press.

Miller and Brewer's volume provides a comprehensive collection of articles on the contact hypothesis. It is a "must read" for those who wish to study the effects of intergroup contact on the nature of intergroup relations.

SCHUMAN, H., STEEH, C., & BOBO, L. (1985). *Racial attitudes in America: Trends and interpretation.* Cambridge, MA: Harvard University Press.

Schuman, Steeh, and Bobo provide a comprehensive summary of the changes in white Americans' racial attitudes in the post-World War II era.

SHERIF, M., HARVEY, O. J., WHITE, B. J., HOOD, W. R., & SHERIF, C. W. (1961). *Intergroup conflict and cooperation: The robbers cave experiment.* Norman: University of Oklahoma Press.

This book provides a comprehensive summary of one of social psychology's classic experiments. It's a good example of how to do good field research and the power of experimental research to address important theoretical and applied issues.

TAJFEL, H. (1982). *Social identity theory and intergroup relations.* Cambridge: Cambridge University Press.

Tajfel's volume represents a clear summary of theory and research on social identity theory.

WORCHEL, S., & AUSTIN, W. G. (Eds.). (1986). *Psychology of intergroup relations* (2nd ed.). Chicago: Nelson-Hall.

Worchel and Austin's book contains a collection of chapters summarizing major topics of research on the social psychology of intergroup relations.

Subject Index

*The n. after a page number refers to a note; the t. to a table.

Name Index

*The f. after a page number refers to a figure; the n. to a note; and the t. to a table.